MUḤAMMAD B. M
AL-ʿAYYĀSH

Tafsīr al-ʿAyyāshī

A Fourth/Tenth Century
Shīʿī Commentary on the Qurʾan

تفسير العياشي

Translated by
NAZMINA DHANJI

Edited by
WAHID M. AMIN

Introduction by
MEIR M. BAR-ASHER

VOLUME II

AMI PRESS

AMI Press
60 Weoley Park Road, Selly Oak
Birmingham, B29 6RB
United Kingdom

First published 2020

A catalogue record for this book is available from the British Library

Vol. 1 ISBN 978-1-8380320-7-4
Vol. 2 ISBN 978-1-8380320-8-1
Vol. 3 ISBN 978-1-8380320-9-8
Set ISBN 978-1-8380320-6-7

Designed and typeset by Titus Nemeth, assisted by Doris Lang

تفسير العياشي

Contents

Volume 1

Preface
Introduction *i*
1. Al-ʿAyyāshī's Life and Work *i*
    1.1 Work *v*
        1.1.1 Al-ʿAyyāshī's Commentary on the Qur'an *vi*
        1.1.2 Manuscripts and Printed Editions of Tafsīr al-ʿAyyāshī *viii*
        1.1.3 Tafsīr al-ʿAyyāshī as a prominent representation of the pre-Buwayhid Imāmī Shīʿī school of Exegesis *viii*
2. The question of the integrity of the Qur'an *xi*
3. The Qur'an as a multilayered and polyvalent text *xvii*
4. The Imam as the primary authority for Qur'an interpretation *xix*
5. Concluding Remarks *xxvi*

Prelude 2
On the Virtues of the Qur'an 2
Casting aside reports (*riwāyāt*) that contradict the Qur'an 22
The Content of what has been revealed in the Qur'an 26
The meaning of the terms 'abrograting' (*al-nāsikh*), 'abrogated' (*al-mansūkh*), 'the apparent' (*al-ẓāhir*), 'the hidden' (*al-bāṭin*), 'the ambiguous' (*al-muḥkam*) and 'the unambiguous' (*al-mutashābih*) 30
The Interpretation of the Seven Revealed Recitations of the Qur'an having various aspects 36
References to the Imams in the Qur'an 36

The Imams and their Knowledge of the Qur'an's Interpretation (*ta'wīl*) *40*
On Those Who Interpret The Qur'an According To Their Own Opinion *50*
On the Reprehensibility of Using the Qur'an for the Purpose of Disputation *54*

1. The Opening *58*
2. The Cow *74*
3. The Family of 'Imrān *406*
4. Women *536*

Volume 2

5. The Feast *2*
6. Livestock *154*
7. The Heights *236*
8. The Battle Gains *320*
9. The Impunity *378*
10. Yūnus *492*
11. Hūd *542*
12. Yūsuf *604*

Volume 3

13. The Thunder *2*
14. Ibrāhīm *52*
15. Ḥijr *94*
16. The Bee *124*
17. The Children of Israel *174*
18. The Cave *278*
19. Mary *352*
20. Ṭā-hā *356*
21. The Prophets *360*
22. The Pilgrimage *366*
23. The Believers *374*
24. Light *380*
25. The Criterion *384*
26. The Poets *388*
27. The Ants *392*
28. The Story *398*
29. The Spider *404*
31. Luqmān *408*
35. The Creator *412*
36. Yā-Sīn *416*
37. Ranged in Rows *424*
38. Ṣād *434*
39. The Throngs *440*
42. Consultation *446*
43. Ornaments of Gold *450*
48. Triumph *456*
52. The Mountain *462*
54. The Moon *466*
55. The All-Compassionate Lord *470*

56. The Imminent Event *476*
57. Iron *480*
58. The Dispute *486*
61. Solid Lines *490*
65. Divorce *494*
66. The Prohibition *500*
67. Sovereignty *504*
68. The Pen *508*
74. Wrapped in his Cloak *512*
75. The Resurrection *516*
76. Man *520*
78. The Announcement *530*
80. He Frowned *534*
81. Shrouded in Darkness *538*
83. Those Who Give Short Measure *542*
84. The Ripping Apart *546*
85. The Towering Constellations *550*
87. The Most High *554*
90. The City *558*
92. The Night *562*
93. The Morning Brightness *566*
94. Relief *570*
97. The Night of Ordainment *574*
102. Rivalry for More *578*
104. The Slanderer *582*
105. The Elephants *586*
106. Quraysh *590*
107. Common Kindness *594*
114. People *598*

Bibliography *601*
Index of Groups, Sects and Tribes *607*
Index of Names *611*
Index of Places *627*
Index of Subjects *629*

The Feast

5. The Feast

1. From Zurāra b. A'yan, from Abū Ja'far عليه السلام who said, "Alī b. Abī Ṭālib, may God's blessings be upon him, said that the Chapter of the Feast (*sūrat al-mā'ida*) was revealed two or three months before the Prophet صلى الله عليه وآله passed away.'

   There is also another narration from Zurāra from Abū Ja'far عليه السلام to that effect.

2. From 'Īsā b. 'Abd Allāh, on his father's authority, on his grandfather's authority, from 'Alī عليه السلام who said, 'Certain parts of the Qur'an would abrogate other parts based on the Prophet's command of what the latest of it [to be revealed] was. The last thing to be revealed to him was the Chapter of the Feast (*sūrat al-mā'ida*), which abrogated what came before it and was not itself abrogated by anything else. It was revealed to him whilst he was mounted on a grey mule, and the revelation was so weighty upon him that it made the mule stop and slump to the ground until its belly was touching the earth and causing the Messenger of God صلى الله عليه وآله to faint, such that he had to rest his arm on Shayba b. Wahab al-Jamḥī's head. Later, when the Messenger of God صلى الله عليه وآله came around, he read the Chapter of the Feast (*sūrat al-mā'ida*) for us, so the Messenger of God صلى الله عليه وآله acted upon it and so did we.'

3. From Abū al-Jārūd, from Muḥammad b. 'Alī عليه السلام who said, 'Whoever reads the Chapter of the Feast (*sūrat al-mā'ida*) every Thursday, his faith will not be obscured by transgression, nor will he ever associate anything with God.'

بسم الله الرحمن الرحيم

من سورة المائدة

١. عن زُرارة بن أعيَن، عن أبي جعفر عليه السلام، قال: قال عليُّ بن أبي طالب صلوات الله عليه: نزلت المائدة قبل أن يُقبَضَ النبيّ صلى الله عليه وآله بشهرين أو ثلاثة.

وفي رواية أُخرى: عن زُرارة، عن أبي جعفر عليه السلام، مثله.

٢. عن عيسى بن عبد الله، عن أبيه، عن جدّه، عن عليّ عليه السلام، قال: كان القرآن يَنْسَخ بعضُه بعضًا، وإنّما كان يُؤخَذ من أمر رسول الله صلى الله عليه وآله بآخره، فكان مِن آخر ما نزل عليه سورة المائدة، فنَسَخت ما قبلها، ولم يَنْسَخْها شيء، فلقد نزلت عليه وهو على بغلته الشّهباء، وثَقُل عليها الوحي حتّى وقفت وتدلّى بطنها، حتّى رَأيتُ سُرَّتَها تكادُ تَمَسّ الأرض، وأُغميَ على رسول الله صلى الله عليه وآله حتّى وضع يده على ذُؤابة شيبة بن وهب الجُمَحي، ثمّ رُفع ذلك عن رسول الله صلى الله عليه وآله، فقرأ علينا سورة المائدة، فعَمِل رسول الله صلى الله عليه وآله وعَمِلنا.

٣. عن أبي الجارود، عن محمّد بن علي عليهما السلام، قال: من قرأ سورة المائدة في كلّ يوم خميس، لم يُلبِس إيمانه بظُلم، ولم يُشرِك أبدًا.

4. [From Samāʿa] from Ismāʿīl b. Abī Ziyād al-Sakūnī, from Jaʿfar b. Muḥammad, on his father's authority عليه السلام who said, 'There is no instance of ﴾*O you who believe*﴿ in the Qur'an that is not found in the Torah as "O you poor people."' [5:1]

5. From al-Naḍr b. Suwayd[1], from one of our associates, from 'Abd Allāh b. Sinān who said, 'I asked Abū 'Abd Allāh عليه السلام about God's verse: ﴾*You who believe, fulfil your obligations.*﴿(5:1) He said, "[It means] Your pledges."' There is another narration like it from Ibn Sinān. [5:1]

6. From 'Ikrima that he said, 'Every single time that God, may His mention be exalted, reveals: ﴾*O you who believe*﴿, 'Alī b. Abī Ṭālib عليه السلام is at the forefront of it.' [5:1]

7. From 'Ikrima, from Ibn 'Abbās who said, 'Every single time that the verse: ﴾*O you who believe*﴿ was revealed, 'Alī was its chief and its commander. God has censured the companions of Muḥammad ﷺ elsewhere, but He has only ever mentioned 'Alī with goodness.' [5:1]

8. From Jaʿfar b. Aḥmad[2], from al-'Amrakī b. 'Alī, from 'Alī b. Jaʿfar b. Muḥammad, from his brother Mūsā عليه السلام, from 'Alī b. al-Ḥusayn عليه السلام who said, 'There is no instance of ﴾*O you who believe*﴿ in the Qur'an except it is found in the Torah as "O you poor people."' [5:1]

9. From Muḥammad b. Muslim, from one of the two [Imams al-Bāqir or al-Ṣādiq] that he said regarding God's verse: ﴾*Livestock animals are lawful as food for you*﴿, 'This includes the animal still in the womb at the time that its mother is slaughtered.' [5:1]

---

1 Al-Naḍr b. Suwayd al-Ṣayrafī, a reliable and trustworthy companion of Imam Mūsā al-Kāẓim. See Ḥillī, *Khulāṣat al-aqwāl*, 283 (nr. 1040).

2 There are several narrators in the works of Shīʿī *rijāl* with this name.

٤. عن إسماعيل بن أبي زياد السّكوني، عن جعفر بن محمّد، عن أبيه عليهما السلام، عن عليّ عليه السلام، قال: ليس في القرآن ﴿يَا أَيُّهَا الَّذِينَ آمَنُوا﴾ إلاّ وهي في التوراة: يا أيُّها المساكين.

٥. عن النَّضر بن سُويد، عن بعض أصحابنا، عن عبدالله بن سِنان، قال: سألتُ أبا عبدالله عليه السلام عن قول الله عزّ وجلّ: ﴿يَا أَيُّهَا الَّذِينَ آمَنُوا أَوْفُوا بِالْعُقُودِ﴾، قال: العُهُود.

عن ابن سنان، مثله.

٦. عن عِكْرِمة، أنّه قال: ما أنزل الله جلّ ذكره ﴿يَا أَيُّهَا الَّذِينَ آمَنُوا﴾ إلاّ ورأسها عليّ بن أبي طالب عليه السلام.

٧. عن عِكْرِمة، عن ابن عبّاس، قال: ما نزلت آية ﴿يَا أَيُّهَا الَّذِينَ آمَنُوا﴾ إلاّ وعليّ عليه السلام شريفُها وأميرُها، ولقد عاتب الله أصحاب محمّد عليه وآله السّلام في غير مكان، وما ذَكَر عليّاً عليه السلام إلاّ بخير.

٨. عن جعفر بن أحمد، عن العَمْرَكي بن عليّ، عن عليّ بن جعفر بن محمّد، عن أخيه موسى عليه السلام، عن عليّ بن الحسين عليهما السلام، قال: ليس في القرآن ﴿يَا أَيُّهَا الَّذِينَ آمَنُوا﴾ إلاّ وهي في التوراة: يا أيّها المساكين.

٩. عن محمّد بن مسلم، عن أحدهما عليهما السلام، قال: في قول الله تعالى: ﴿أُحِلَّتْ لَكُمْ بَهِيمَةُ الأَنْعَامِ﴾، قال: هو الذي في البطن، تُذْبَحُ أُمُّه فيكون في بطنها.

10. From Zurāra, from Abū Jaʿfar عليه السلام who said about God's verse: ﴾*Livestock animals are lawful as food for you*﴿, 'They are the foetuses which are still in the cattle's wombs. The Commander of the Faithful عليه السلام used to order the foetuses to be sold.' [5:1]

11. From Aḥmad b. Muḥammad b. Abī Naṣr who said, 'One of our associates narrated from Abū ʿAbd Allāh, regarding God's verse: ﴾*Livestock animals are lawful as food for you*﴿ that he said, "If the foetus in the womb of its mother already has hair or wool, then slaughtering its mother for consumption makes it fit for consumption too."' [5:1]

12. From Wahb b. Wahb[3], from Jaʿfar b. Muḥammad, on his father's authority, that ʿAlī عليه السلام was asked about eating the flesh of elephants, bears, and monkeys, and he replied, 'These are not from among livestock animals that can be consumed.' [5:1]

13. From al-Mufaḍḍal who said, 'I asked al-Ṣādiq عليه السلام about God's verse: ﴾*Livestock animals are lawful as food for you.*﴿ He replied, "The livestock here is the guardian, and the cattle are the believers."' [5:1]

14. From Mūsā b. Bakr, from one of his associates, that Zayd b. ʿAlī once went to Abū Jaʿfar عليه السلام bringing with him letters from the people of Kufa in which they were inviting him to come to them, and informing him of their having gathered [ready to fight] and requesting him to come out to join them. So Abū Jaʿfar عليه السلام said, 'God, Blessed and most High, has made certain things permissible, and He has prohibited certain things; He has provided examples and established certain practices. He has not let the Imam that is knowledgeable about His command be in any obscurity whatsoever about the obedience that God has made incumbent, that he should proceed with an action before its prescribed time, or rise to fight before it has been made permissible. God has said concerning hunting game: ﴾*do not kill game while*

---

3 Abū al-Bakhtarī Wahb b. Wahb b. ʿAbd Allāh b. Zumʿa b. al-Aswad b. al-Muṭṭalib b. ʿAbd al-ʿIzzī (d. *ca.* 200/815), a heavily criticized Sunnī narrator of Imam Jaʿfar al-Ṣādiq who would fabricate many traditions and lie against the Imam who was his step-father. He was appointed as a judge by the Abbasid Caliph Hārūn al-Rashīd. See Ḥillī, *Khulāṣat al-aqwāl*, 414 (nr. 1679); Modarressi, *Tradition and Survival*, 389–91 (nr. 214).

١٠. عن زُرارة، عن أبي جعفر عليه السلام، في قوله تعالى ﴿أُحِلَّتْ لَكُم بَهِيمَةُ الأَنْعَامِ﴾، قال: هي الأجنّة التي في بُطون الأنعام، وقدكان أمير المؤمنين عليه السلام يأمُر ببيع الأجنّة.

١١. عن أحمد بن محمّد بن أبي نصر، قال: روى بعض أصحابنا عن أبي عبد الله عليه السلام، في قول الله تعالى ﴿أُحِلَّتْ لَكُم بَهِيمَةُ الأَنْعَامِ﴾، قال: الجنين في بَطْن أُمّه، إذا أشعر وأوبر، فذكاة أُمّه ذكاته.

١٢. عن وَهْب بن وَهْب، عن جعفر بن محمّد، عن أبيه عليهما السلام: أنّ عليًّا عليه السلام سُئِل عن أكل لحم الفِيل والدُّبّ والقِرد، فقال: ليس هذا من بَهيمة الأنعام التي تُؤكَل.

١٣. عن المُفضّل، قال: سألتُ الصادق عليه السلام عن قول الله تعالى: ﴿أُحِلَّتْ لَكُم بَهِيمَةُ الأَنْعَامِ﴾، قال: البَهيمة هاهُنا الوليّ، والأنعام: المؤمنون.

١٤. عن موسى بن بكر، عن بعض رجاله: أنّ زيد بن عليّ دخل على أبي جعفر عليه السلام ومعه كُتُبٌ من أهل الكوفة يدعونه فيها إلى أنفسهم، ويُخبرونه باجتماعهم، ويأمرونه بالخروج إليهم.

فقال أبو جعفر عليه السلام: إنّ الله تبارك وتعالى أحلّ حلالاً، وحرّم حرامًا، وضرب أمثالاً، وسنّ سُننًا، ولم يجعل الإمام العالم بأمره في شُبهة ممّا فرض الله من الطاعة، أن يسبِقه بأمرٍ قبل محِلّه، أو يُجاهد قبل حُلوله، وقد قال الله تعالى في الصيد: ﴿لاَ تَقْتُلُوا الصَّيْدَ وَأَنْتُمْ حُرُمٌ﴾

you are in the state of consecration [for pilgrimage]﴿ (5:95), so is killing game a greater sin or killing a human being unlawfully? He has designated a prescribed time for everything: ﴾*but when you have completed the rites of pilgrimage you may hunt*﴿, and: ﴾*do not violate the sanctity of God's rites, nor the Sacred Month*﴿ – He has made a certain number of months, of which He has designated four as sacred. He also says: ﴾*you [idolaters] may move freely about the land for four months, but you should bear in mind both that you will not escape God.*﴿ (9:2)' [5:2]

15. From Muḥammad b. 'Abd Allāh, from one of his associates who said, 'I asked Abū 'Abd Allāh ﷺ, "May I be your ransom – why did God forbid the consumption of carrion, blood, and pork?"

So he replied, "God, Blessed and most High, has not forbidden His servants from consuming those things and permitted everything else out of His desire for that which He has prohibited them from – Blessed and Exalted be He – nor is it that He abstains from that which he has permitted them. Rather He has brought all of creation into being, knowing what sustains their bodies and what is good for them, and has made that permissible and allowed it accordingly, as a favour from Him upon them for their benefit. Similarly, He knows what is harmful to them and has thus prohibited it, and forbidden them from it, and only allowed it under duress and only for that particular time when the body can only subsist by means of that thing; and He has commanded them to consume from it only what is necessary for survival and no more."

Then he continued, "As for carrion, no sooner does anyone touch it or eat it than it weakens his body, makes it deteriorate, weakens his energy and leads to infertility; and the one who eats carrion only dies of sudden death.

As for blood, it engenders a burning thirst, hard-heartedness, and a lack of empathy and compassion where the consumer of it cannot be trusted not to kill his own child, his parents, a close friend or whoever keeps his company.

As for pork, God transformed a certain group of people into the form of animals resembling pigs, monkeys and bears and other disfigured forms. Then He prohibited the consumption of anything resembling those so as not to derive any benefit thereby nor make light of His chastisement upon them. As for wine, he has prohibited it because of its effect and its corruption."

فقتل الصيد أعظم، أم قتل النفس الحرام؟ وجعل لكلٍّ مَحِلاً، وقال: ﴿وَإِذَا حَلَلْتُمْ فَاصْطَادُوا﴾، وقال: ﴿لاَ تُحِلُّوا شَعَائِرَ اللهِ وَلاَ الشَّهْرَ الْحَرَامَ﴾ فجَعَل الشُّهور عِدَّةً معلومةً، وجعل منها أربعةً حُرُمًا، وقال: ﴿فَسِيحُوا فِي الأَرْضِ أَرْبَعَةَ أَشْهُرٍ وَاعْلَمُوا أَنَّكُمْ غَيْرُ مُعْجِزِي اللهِ﴾.

١٥. عن محمّد بن عبد الله، عن بعض أصحابه، قال: قلتُ لأبي عبد الله عليه السلام: جُعِلت فداك، لِمَ حرّم الله المَيْتَة والدَّم ولحم الخنزير؟

فقال: إنّ الله تبارك وتعالى لم يُحرّم ذلك على عباده، وأحلّ لهم ما سِواه من رغبةٍ منه تبارك وتعالى فيما حرّم عليهم، ولا زهد فيما أحلّ لهم، ولكنّه خلق الخلق وعَلِم ما يقومُ به أبدانهم وما يُصلحهم، فأحلّه وأباحه تفضّلاً منه عليهم لمصلحتهم، وعَلِم ما يَضُرّهم فنهاهم عنه حرّمه عليهم، ثمّ أباحه للمُضطرّ، وأحلّه لهم في الوقت الّذي لا يقوم بدنه إلاّ به، فأمره أن ينال منه بقدر البُلغة لا غير ذلك.

ثمّ قال: أمّا المَيْتَة، فإنّه لا يدنو منها أحدٌ ولا يأكلها إلاّ ضَعُف بَدَنُه، ونَحَل جِسْمُه، ووَهَنت قُوّتُه، وانقطع نَسْلُه، ولا يموت آكل المَيْتَة إلاّ فُجأة.

وأمّا الدّم، فإنّه يُورِث الكَلَب والقَسْوة للقلب، وقلّة الرأفة والرحمة، لا يُؤمَن أن يَقْتُل ولده ووالديه، ولا يُؤمَن على حميمه، ولا يُؤمَن على من صَحِبه.

وأمّا لحم الخنزير، فإنّ الله مَسَخ قومًا في صُور شتّى شِبه الخنزير والقِرد والدُّبّ، وما كان من الأمساخ، ثمّ نهى عن أكل مِثله، لكيلا ينفع بها، ولا يُستَخَفّ بعقوبته.

Then he said, "The alcoholic is as the idol-worshipper. It will cause him to shake, take away his radiance and make him decrepit. It urges him to make money from unlawful means such as bloodshed and fornication. When he becomes drunk, there is no guarantee that he will not lose his dignity whilst he is out of his senses. Wine makes every evil deed accessible to the one who drinks it."' [5:3]

16. From Zurāra, from Abū Jaʿfar عليه السلام who said, 'Any animal is allowed [for consumption] apart from the pig, one that has died from a violent blow, one that has been gored, or one that has been thrown from a rooftop and died as a result, or that which has been savaged by a predator, and this is God's verse: ﴾*unless you have slaughtered it* [*in the correct manner*].﴿ If you find it to be alive in that its gaze is still darting, its legs are still moving, or its tail is still wagging, and you then slaughter it and make it fit for consumption, then you may eat it.' He continued, 'If you slaughter an animal in the correct manner then put it in fire, or in water, or throw it from a rooftop or a mountain top, as long as you have slaughtered it in the correct manner to begin with, you can eat it.' [5:3]

17. From al-Ḥasan b. ʿAlī al-Washshāʾ, from Abū al-Ḥasan al-Riḍā عليه السلام; he said, 'I heard him say that the animal that has died as a result of a fall or from a violent blow, or that which has been savaged by predators, if you manage to slaughter it [before it dies] then you can eat it.' [5:3]

18. From ʿAyyūq b. Quraṭ, from Abū ʿAbd Allāh عليه السلام regarding God's word: ﴾*any animal strangled*﴿; he said, 'It is an animal that has been strangled by its reins; ﴾*victim of a violent blow*﴿ refers to the sick animal who is not fit to bear the pain of slaughter, who is neither agitated nor does its blood gush out. And ﴾*or of a fall*﴿ is one that has been thrown from a rooftop or another high place, and ﴾*gored*﴿ is one who has been butted by its mate.' [5:3]

وأمّا الخمر، فإنّه حرّمها لفعلها وفسادها، وقال: إنّ مُدمِن الخمر كعابد وثنٍ، ويورثه ارتعاشًا، ويذهب بنُوره، ويَهدِم مُروّته، ويحمله على أن يُكبّ على المحارم من سَفك الدماء وركوب الزّنا، ولا يُؤمَن إذا سكر أن يَثِب على حرمه وهولا يَعقِل ذلك، والخمر لم يرد شاربها إلاّ على شرّ.

١٦. عن زُرارة، عن أبي جعفر ﵇، قال: [كُلْ] كلّ شيء من الحيوان غير الخنزير والنّطيحة والمَوْقُوذة والمُتردّية وما أكل السبع، وهو قول الله ﴿إِلَّا مَا ذَكَّيْتُمْ﴾ فإن أدركتَ شيئًا منها وعين تطرِف، أو قائمة تركُض، أو ذنب يَمْصَع، فذبحت فقد أدركت ذكاته فكُلْه.

قال: وإن ذبحتَ ذبيحةً فأجدتَ الذّبح، فوقعت في النار، أو في الماء، أو من فوق بيت، أو من فوق جبل، إذا كنت قد أجَدتَ الذّبح فكُل.

١٧. عن الحسن بن عليّ الوشّاء، عن أبي الحسن الرضا ﵇، قال: سَمِعته يقول: المتردّية والنّطيحة وما أكل السبع، إذا أدركت ذكاته، فكُله.

١٨. عن عيوق بن قُرط، عن أبي عبد الله ﵇، في قول الله: ﴿الْمُنْخَنِقَةُ﴾.

قال: التي تختنق في رباطها، ﴿وَالْمَوْقُوذَةُ﴾ المريضة التي لا تجد ألم الذّبح، ولا تضطرب، ولا يخرُج لها دم، ﴿وَالْمُتَرَدِّيَةُ﴾ الّتي تردّى من فوق بيت أو نحوه ﴿وَالنَّطِيحَةُ﴾ التي تَنْطَحها صاحبتها.

19. From ʿAmr b. Shimr[4], from Jābir who said, 'Abū Jaʿfar عليه السلام said regarding this verse: ﴾*Today the disbelievers have lost all hope that you will give up your religion. Do not fear them: fear Me*﴿, "The day that the Qā'im عليه السلام will rise the Banū Umayya will lose all hope, for they are the ones who disbelieved and gave up hope in the family of Muḥammad, peace be upon them."' [5:3]

20. From Zurāra, from Abū Jaʿfar عليه السلام who said, 'The last obligation that God revealed was the adherence to the divinely vested authority: ﴾*Today I have perfected your religion for you, completed My blessing upon you, and chosen as your religion Islam:* [*total devotion to God*]﴿, so no other obligations were revealed since then until the Messenger of God ﷺ passed away.' [5:3]

21. From Jaʿfar b. Muḥammad al-Khuzāʿī, on his father's authority who said, 'I heard Abū ʿAbd Allāh عليه السلام say, "When the Messenger of God ﷺ camped at ʿArafāt on Friday, Jibra'īl عليه السلام came to him and said, 'O Muḥammad, God greets you with peace and says to you: "Tell your community: ﴾*Today I have perfected your religion for you, completed My blessing upon you, and chosen as your religion Islam:* [*total devotion to God*]﴿, and I will not reveal anything more to you after this for I have already revealed to you about prayer, alms, fasting and pilgrimage, and this is the fifth, without which I will not accept the other four."' [5:3]

22. From Ibn Udhayna who said, 'I heard Zurāra saying from Abū Jaʿfar عليه السلام that the obligatory acts were revealed one after the other until adherence to the divinely vested authority (*walāya*) was the last of the obligations to come down, when God revealed: ﴾*Today I have perfected your religion for you, completed My blessing upon you, and chosen as your religion Islam:* [*total devotion to God*].﴿ (5:3) Then Abū Jaʿfar said, "God says: I will not send down any other obligatory act after this."' [5:3]

23. From Hishām b. Sālim, from Abū ʿAbd Allāh عليه السلام who said, 'The completion of the blessing is entrance into Paradise.' [5:3]

---

4 Abū ʿAbd Allāh ʿAmr b. Shimr al-Juʿfī, a weak narrator who regularly cites from Jaʿfar al-Ṣādiq. See Ḥillī, *Khulāṣat al-aqwāl*, 378 (nr. 1516); Modarressi, *Tradition and Survival*, 204–5 (nr. 43).

١٩. عن عمرو بن شِمر، عن جابر، قال: قال أبو جعفر عليه السلام في هذه الآية ﴿الْيَوْمَ يَئِسَ الَّذِينَ كَفَرُوا مِن دِينِكُمْ فَلَا تَخْشَوْهُمْ وَاخْشَوْنِ﴾ يوم يقوم القائم عليه السلام يئس بنو اميّة، فهم الذين كفروا، يئسوا من آل محمّد عليهم السلام.

٢٠. عن زُرارة، عن أبي جعفر عليه السلام، قال: آخر فريضة أنزلها الله تعالى الولاية ﴿الْيَوْمَ أَكْمَلْتُ لَكُمْ دِينَكُمْ وَأَتْمَمْتُ عَلَيْكُمْ نِعْمَتِي وَرَضِيتُ لَكُمُ الْإِسْلَامَ دِينًا﴾ فلم يُنزل من الفرائض شيئًا بعدها حتّى قَبَض الله رسوله صلى الله عليه وآله.

٢١. عن جعفر بن محمّد الخُزاعي، عن أبيه، قال: سَمِعتُ أبا عبدالله عليه السلام يقول: لمّا نزل رسول الله صلى الله عليه وآله عرفات يوم الجُمعة، أتاه جبرئيل عليه السلام فقال له: يا محمّد، إنّ الله يقرئك السّلام، ويقول لك: قُل لأُمّتك: ﴿الْيَوْمَ أَكْمَلْتُ لَكُمْ دِينَكُمْ﴾ بولاية عليّ بن أبي طالب ﴿وَأَتْمَمْتُ عَلَيْكُمْ نِعْمَتِي وَرَضِيتُ لَكُمُ الْإِسْلَامَ دِينًا﴾ ولست أُنزل عليكم بعد هذا، قد أنزلت عليكم الصلاة والزكاة والصوم والحجّ، وهي الخامسة، ولست أقبل هذه الأربعة إلاّ بها.

٢٢. عن ابن أُذينة، قال: سَمِعتُ زُرارة، عن أبي جعفر عليه السلام، أنَّ الفريضة كانت تنزل، ثمّ تنزل الفريضة الأُخرى، فكانت الولاية آخر الفرائض، فأنزل الله تعالى ﴿الْيَوْمَ أَكْمَلْتُ لَكُمْ دِينَكُمْ وَأَتْمَمْتُ عَلَيْكُمْ نِعْمَتِي وَرَضِيتُ لَكُمُ الْإِسْلَامَ دِينًا﴾ فقال أبو جعفر عليه السلام: يقول الله: لا أُنزِل عليكم بعد هذه الفريضة فريضة.

٢٣. عن هِشام بن سالم، عن أبي عبدالله عليه السلام، قال: تمام النعمة: دُخُول الجنّة.

24. From Ḥarīz, from Abū 'Abd Allāh ﷺ; he said, 'He was asked about a dog belonging to a Magian but is trained by a Muslim who pronounces God's name, then sends it off to hunt. He replied, "Yes, it can be trained to catch prey, as long as God's name is pronounced over it, there is no problem."' [5:4]

25. From Abū Bakr al-Ḥaḍramī who said, 'I asked Abū 'Abd Allāh ﷺ about the game caught by falcons, hawks, panthers, and dogs. So he replied, "Do not eat from the game of any of them without first making it fit for consumption [in the prescribed manner], apart from dogs." I asked, "What if it has [already] killed it?" He replied, "You can eat it for God says: ﴾[*This includes*] *what you have taught your birds and beasts of prey to catch, teaching them as God has taught you, so eat what they catch for you, but first pronounce God's name over it. Be mindful of God.*﴿"' [5:4]

26. From Abū 'Ubayda, from Abū 'Abd Allāh ﷺ who was asked about a man who dispatches a trained dog and pronounces the name of God before sending it. He said, 'He can eat whatever he catches for him, even if he finds that it has already killed it. However, if he finds another dog with him that has not been trained then he cannot eat from his game.'

I asked, 'What about [the game hunted by] hawks, falcons and eagles?'

He replied, 'If you are assured that it is fit for consumption then you can eat it, but if you do not know whether it is fit for consumption, then do not.'

I asked, 'So the panther is not the same as the dog?'

'No,' he replied, 'only the hunting dog can be trained.' [5:4]

27. From Ismā'īl b. Abī Ziyād al-Sakūnī, from Ja'far b. Muḥammad, on his father's authority, from 'Alī ﷺ who said, 'The panther is among the beasts of prey; and wild dogs, if they are trained, are the same as greyhounds.' [5:4]

28. From Samā'a b. Mihrān, from Abū 'Abd Allāh ﷺ who said, 'My father used to issue rulings and we used to issue rulings, but we were apprehensive about the game caught by falcons and hawks. Now, however, we are no longer apprehensive, and their game is not permissible unless you know it to be fit for consumption; and this is in the book of 'Alī ﷺ that God said: ﴾[*This includes*] *what you have taught your birds and beasts of prey to catch*﴿, and this refers to dogs.' [5:4]

٢٤. عن حَرِيز، عن أبي عبدالله ﵇، قال: سُئِل عن كَلْب المَجُوس يُكَلِّبه المسلم، ويُسمّي ويُرسِله. قال: نعم: إنّه مُكَلَّب، إذا ذكر اسم الله عليه، فلا بأس.

٢٥. عن أبي بكر الحضرمي، قال: سألتُ أبا عبدالله ﵇ عن صيد البُزاة والصُّقور والفُهُود والكلاب، فقال: لا تأكُلْ من صيد شيءٍ منها إلاّ ما ذكّيت إلاّ الكلاب.

قلت: فإن قتله؟ قال: كُل، فإنّ الله يقول: ﴿وَمَا عَلَّمْتُم مِّنَ الْجَوَارِحِ مُكَلِّبِينَ تُعَلِّمُونَهُنَّ مِمَّا عَلَّمَكُمُ اللهُ فَكُلُوا مِمَّا أَمْسَكْنَ عَلَيْكُمْ وَاذْكُرُوا اسْمَ اللهِ عَلَيْهِ﴾.

٢٦. عن أبي عبيدة، عن أبي عبدالله ﵇، عن الرجل سرّح الكلب المُعلّم ويسمّى إذا سرّحه، قال: يأكُلُ ممّا أمسك عليه، وإن أدركه وقتله، وإن وُجِد معه كلبٌ غير مُعَلّم فلا يأكُل منه.

قلت: فالصَّقر والعُقاب والبازِي؟

قال: إن أدركت ذَكاته فكُل منه، وإن لم تُدرِك ذكاته فلا تأكُل منه.

قلت: فالفَهْد ليس بمنزلة الكلب؟

قال: فقال: لا، ليس شيء مُكلَّب إلاّ الكلب.

٢٧. عن إسماعيل بن أبي زياد السّكوني، عن جعفر بن محمّد، عن أبيه، عن عليّ ﵇، قال: الفَهْد من الجَوارح، والكلاب الكُردية إذا عُلّمت فهي بمنزلة السِّلُوقية.

٢٨. عن سَماعة بن مِهران، عن أبي عبدالله ﵇، قال: كان أبي عليه السلام يُفتي، وكنّا نُفتي

29. From Zurāra, from Abū ʿAbd Allāh عليه السلام who said, 'Apart from the game caught by dogs, do not eat what is hunted by panthers, hawks and their like, except what you have established to be fit for consumption, because God says: ﴾*trained to hunt*﴿ – so aside from dogs, the game caught by others must not be eaten unless its fitness for consumption has been established.' [5:4]

30. From al-Ḥalabī, from Abū ʿAbd Allāh عليه السلام that it is mentioned in the book of ʿAlī عليه السلام that God says: ﴾*Except what you have taught your birds and beasts of prey to catch, teaching them as God has taught you*﴿ – 'and these are dogs.' [5:4]

31. From Jamīl, from Abū ʿAbd Allāh عليه السلام who was asked about the game that a dog catches, and which a man leaves aside until it dies [of itself].' He replied, 'Yes, you can eat it, for God says: ﴾*so eat what they catch for you.*﴿' [5:4]

32. From Abū Jamīla, from Abū Ḥanẓala, on his authority about the game that a dog catches and which is found by the man who then takes it, but it dies in its hands – can he eat it?' He replied, 'Yes. God says: ﴾*so eat what they catch for you.*﴿' [5:4]

33. From Abū Baṣīr, from Abū ʿAbd Allāh عليه السلام who said regarding the verse: ﴾[*This includes*] *what you have taught your birds and beasts of prey to catch, teaching them as God has taught you, so eat what they catch for you, but first pronounce God's name over it*﴿, 'There is no problem with eating what the dog has caught as long as the dog himself has not eaten thereof. Thus if the dog has eaten from it before you get it, then do not eat it.' [5:4]

ونحن نخاف في صيد البازِي والصُّقور، فأمّا الآن فإنّا لا نخاف، ولا يَحِلّ صيدها إلاّ أن تُدرَك ذَكاتُه، وإنّه لفي كتاب عليّ عليه السلام: إنَّ الله قال: ﴿وَمَا عَلَّمْتُم مِّنَ الْجَوَارِحِ مُكَلِّبِينَ﴾ فهي الكِلاب.

٢٩. عن زُرارة، عن أبي عبدالله عليه السلام، قال: ما خلا الكلاب ممّا يصيد الفُهود والصُّقور وأشباه ذلك، فلا تأكُلنَّ من صيده إلاّ ما أدركت ذَكاته، لأنَّ الله قال: ﴿مُكَلِّبِينَ﴾ فما خلا الكلاب فليس صيده بالذي يؤكَل إلاّ أن يُدرك ذكاته.

٣٠. عن الحلبي، عن أبي عبدالله عليه السلام، أنَّ في كتاب عليّ عليه السلام قال الله: ﴿وَمَا عَلَّمْتُم مِّنَ الْجَوَارِحِ مُكَلِّبِينَ تُعَلِّمُونَهُنَّ مِمَّا عَلَّمَكُمُ﴾ فهي الكلاب.

٣١. عن جميل، عن أبي عبدالله عليه السلام، أنّه سُئِل عن الصيد يأخُذه الكلب، فيترُكه الرجل حتّى يموت؟ قال: نعم كُل، إنَّ الله يقول: ﴿فَكُلُوا مِمَّا أَمْسَكْنَ عَلَيْكُمْ﴾.

٣٢. عن أبي جميلة، عن ابن حَنْظَلة، عنه عليه السلام، في الصيد يأخُذه الكلب فيُدرِكه الرجل فيأخُذه، ثمّ يموت في يده، أيأكل؟ قال: نعم، إنّ الله يقول: ﴿فَكُلُوا مِمَّا أَمْسَكْنَ عَلَيْكُمْ﴾.

٣٣. عن أبي بصير، عن أبي عبدالله عليه السلام، في قول الله تعالى: ﴿وَمَا عَلَّمْتُم مِّنَ الْجَوَارِحِ مُكَلِّبِينَ تُعَلِّمُونَهُنَّ مِمَّا عَلَّمَكُمُ اللَّهُ فَكُلُوا مِمَّا أَمْسَكْنَ عَلَيْكُمْ وَاذْكُرُوا اسْمَ اللَّهِ عَلَيْهِ﴾.

قال: لا بأس بأكل ما أمسك الكلب ممّا لم يأكُل الكلب منه، فإذا أكل الكلب منه قبل أن تُدرِكه فلا تأكُله.

34. From Rifāʿa, from Abū ʿAbd Allāh عليه السلام who said, 'The panther is included in God's verse: ﴾*trained to hunt*﴿.' [5:4]

35. From Abān b. Taghlib who said, 'I heard Abū ʿAbd Allāh عليه السلام say, "Eat what the dogs catch for you, even if only a third of it remains."' [5:4]

36. From Qutayba al-Aʿshā who said, 'Al-Ḥasan b. al-Mundhir asked Abū ʿAbd Allāh عليه السلام about someone who sends a trustworthy man, either a Christian or a Jew, in charge of his sheep. One of them is afflicted with something so he slaughters her and sells her. So Abū ʿAbd Allāh عليه السلام said, "You should neither eat it nor include it [i.e. the proceeds] in your wealth, because it boils down to pronouncing God's name, and only a Muslim can be trusted to do that."

So a man asked Abū ʿAbd Allāh while I was listening, "So where does God's statement: ﴾*The food of the People of the Book is lawful for you*﴿ (5:5) come in?" So Abū ʿAbd Allāh replied, "My father used to say that that refers to grains and the like."' [5:5]

37. From Hishām b. Sālim, from Abū ʿAbd Allāh عليه السلام regarding the verse of God, Blessed and most High: ﴾*and their food is lawful for you.*﴿ He said, 'Lentils, grains, and other such things – meaning from the People of the Book.' [5:5]

38. From Ibn Sinān, from Abū ʿAbd Allāh عليه السلام who said: ﴾*So are chaste, believing women*﴿ – 'They are the Muslim women.' [5:5]

39. From Masʿada b. Ṣadaqa who reported, 'Abū Jaʿfar عليه السلام was asked about the verse of God, most High: ﴾*as well as chaste women of the people who were given the Scripture before you.*﴿ (5:5) He replied, "It has been abrogated by the verse ﴾*and do not yourselves hold on to marriage ties with disbelieving women.*﴿ (60:10)"' [5:5]

٣٤. عن رفاعة، عن أبي عبدالله عليه السلام، قال: الفَهْد ممّا قال الله ﴿مُكَلِّبِينَ﴾.

٣٥. عن أبان بن تَغْلِب، قال: سَمِعتُ أبا عبدالله عليه السلام يقول: كلّ ما أمسك عليه الكلاب، وإن بقي ثُلثه.

٣٦. عن قُتيبة الأعشى، قال: سأل الحسن بن المُنذر أبا عبدالله عليه السلام: إنّ الرجل يبعثُ في غَنَمه رجلاً أمينًا يكون فيها، نصرانيًا أو يهوديًا، فتقع العارضة فيذبحها ويبيعها؟

فقال أبو عبدالله عليه السلام: لا تأكُلها ولا تُدخِلها في مالِك، فإنّما هو الاسم، ولا يُؤمَن عليه إلاّ المسلم.

فقال رجل لأبي عبدالله عليه السلام وأنا أسمع: فأين قول الله: ﴿وَطَعَامُ الَّذِينَ أُوتُوا الْكِتَابَ حِلٌّ لَّكُمْ﴾ فقال أبو عبدالله عليه السلام: كان أبي عليه السلام يقول: إنّما ذلك الحُبوب وأشباهه.

٣٧. عن هِشام بن سالم، عن أبي عبدالله عليه السلام، في قول الله تبارك وتعالى: ﴿وَطَعَامُكُمْ حِلٌّ لَّهُمْ﴾، قال: العَدَس والحُبوب وأشباه ذلك، يعني [من] أهل الكتاب.

٣٨. عن ابن سِنان، عن أبي عبدالله عليه السلام، قال: ﴿وَالْمُحْصَنَاتُ مِنَ الْمُؤْمِنَاتِ﴾، قال: هُنّ المسلمات.

٣٩. عن مَسْعَدة بن صَدَقة، قال: سُئِل أبو جعفر عليه السلام عن قول الله تعالى: ﴿مِنَ الَّذِينَ أُوتُوا الْكِتَابَ مِن قَبْلِكُمْ﴾، قال: نسختها ﴿وَلَا تُمْسِكُوا بِعِصَمِ الْكَوَافِرِ﴾.

40. From Abū Jamīla, from Abū ʿAbd Allāh ﷺ who said regarding: ﴾*as well as chaste women of the people who were given the Scripture before you*﴿, 'They are the pure, virtuous ones.' [5:5]

41. From the righteous servant [i.e. Imam Mūsā al-Kāẓim]. He said, 'We asked him about His verse: ﴾*as well as chaste women of the people who were given the Scripture before you*﴿ – who are they and what does it mean by their being chaste? He replied, "They are the pure, virtuous ones from amongst their women."' [5:5]

42. From ʿUbayd[a] b. Zurāra who said, 'I asked Abū ʿAbd Allāh ﷺ about the verse of God, Mighty and Exalted: ﴾*The deeds of anyone who rejects faith will come to nothing.*﴿ He replied, "It is to abandon those deeds through which one's faith is attested, such as the abandonment of the prayer without weakness or preoccupation."' He said, 'So I asked him, "Are the grave sins the worst of all transgressions?" He replied, "Yes." So I asked, "Are they worse than abandoning the prayer?" He replied, "If he decidedly abandons the prayer as having nothing to do with him, then it is included among the seven [grave sins]."' [5:5]

43. From Abān b. ʿAbd al-Raḥmān[5] who said, 'I heard Abū ʿAbd Allāh ﷺ say, "All it takes for a man to come out of Islam is for him to entertain an opinion as opposed to the truth, and to hold fast to it." He said: ﴾*The deeds of anyone who rejects faith will come to nothing*﴿, and he said, "The one who rejects faith is one who neither acts according to what God has commanded him nor accepts it."' [5:5]

44. From Muḥammad b. Muslim, from one of the two [Imams al-Bāqir or al-Ṣādiq], regarding God's verse: ﴾*The deeds of anyone who rejects faith will come to nothing.*﴿ He said, "This is to abandon an action to the extent that he gives it up in its entirety." He continued, "Included here is the one who deliberately abandons the prayer, not out of preoccupation or intoxication, meaning sleep."' [5:5]

---

5 Abū ʿAbd Allāh Abān b. ʿAbd al-Raḥmān al-Baṣrī, on whom there is scant information, was a companion of Imam Jaʿfar al-Ṣādiq. See Khūʾī, *Muʿjam*, 1:141 (nr. 32).

٤٠. عن أبي جميلة، عن أبي عبدالله ﷺ، في ﴿وَالْمُحْصَنَاتُ مِنَ الَّذِينَ أُوتُوا الْكِتَابَ مِن قَبْلِكُمْ﴾، قال: هُنّ العَفائف.

٤١. عن العبد الصالح، سألناه عن قوله: ﴿وَالْمُحْصَنَاتُ مِنَ الَّذِينَ أُوتُوا الْكِتَابَ مِن قَبْلِكُمْ﴾ ما هُنّ، وما معنى إحصائهنّ؟ قال: هُنَّ العفائف من نسائهم.

٤٢. عن عُبيد بن زُرارة، قال: سألتُ أبا عبدالله ﷺ عن قول الله عزّ وجلّ: ﴿وَمَن يَكْفُرْ بِالْإِيمَانِ فَقَدْ حَبِطَ عَمَلُهُ﴾، قال: ترك العمل الذي أقرّ به، من ذلك أن يترُك الصلاة من غير سقمٍ ولا شُغل.

قال: قلت له: الكبائر أعظم الذنوب؟ قال: فقال: نعم.

قلت: هي أعظم من ترك الصلاة؟ قال: إذا ترك الصلاة تركًا ليس من أمره، كان داخلاً في واحدة من السبعة.

٤٣. عن أبان بن عبد الرّحمن، قال: سَمِعت أبا عبدالله ﷺ يقول: أدنى ما يخرُج به الرجل من الإسلام أن يرى الرأي بخلاف الحقّ فيقيم عليه، قال: ﴿وَمَن يَكْفُرْ بِالْإِيمَانِ فَقَدْ حَبِطَ عَمَلُهُ﴾، وقل: الذي يكفُر بالإيمان الذي لا يعمل بما أمر الله به، ولا يرضى به.

٤٤. عن محمّد بن مسلم، عن أحدهما عليهما السلام، في قول الله: ﴿وَمَن يَكْفُرْ بِالْإِيمَانِ فَقَدْ حَبِطَ عَمَلُهُ﴾، قال: هو ترك العمل حتّى يَدَعه أجمع: قال: منه الذي يدع الصلاة متعمّدًا، لا من شُغل، ولا من سُكر، يعني النوم.

45. From Jābir, from Abū Jaʿfar عليه السلام. He said, ‘I asked him about the exegesis of this verse: ﴿ *The deeds of anyone who rejects faith will come to nothing.* ﴾ (5:5) “It means the divinely vested authority of ʿAlī عليه السلام, and in the Hereafter he will be of the losers.”’ [5:5]

46. From Hārūn b. Khārija who said, ‘I asked Abū ʿAbd Allāh عليه السلام about God’s verse: ﴿ *The deeds of anyone who rejects faith will come to nothing* ﴾. He said, ‘So he replied, “Included in that is what Zurāra and Abū Ḥanīfa have derived.”’ [5:5]

47. From Abū Bakr b. Ḥazm[6] who said, ‘A man performed the ablution (*wuḍūʾ*) and wiped over his socks, entered the mosque and started praying. At that moment ʿAlī عليه السلام came and stepped on his neck saying, “Damn you for praying without *wuḍūʾ*.”

So he retorted, “ʿUmar b. al-Khaṭṭāb commanded me to do so.”’

He continued, ‘So he, ʿAlī, took him by the hand until they reached him and he said, “Look what this man is saying against you” with a raised voice.

So he, ʿUmar, said, “Yes, I am the one who commanded him to do so. The Messenger of God ﷺ wiped [thus].”

So he, ʿAlī, asked, “Before [the revelation of] *The Chapter of the Feast* or after?”

He replied, “I do not know.”

So he said, “Then how can you issue a ruling when you do not know? The book countermands [wiping on] the socks.”’ [5:6]

48. From al-Muyassar b. Thawbā who said, ‘I heard ʿAlī عليه السلام say, “The book countermands [wiping on] the socks and the face veil.”’ [5:6]

49. From Bukayr b. Aʿyan who said, ‘I asked Abū ʿAbd Allāh عليه السلام about His verse: ﴿ *You who believe, when you get up to pray* ﴾ (5:6) – What does ‘when you get up’ mean? He replied, “When you get up from sleep.” I asked, “Does sleep nullify the *wuḍūʾ*?” He replied, “Yes, if sleep overcomes one’s hearing to such an extent that he can no longer hear sounds.”’ [5:6]

---

6 Abū Bakr b. Ḥazm al-Anṣārī, a close associate and companion of ʿAlī b. Abī Ṭālib. See Khūʾī, *Muʿjam*, 22:70 (nr. 13999).

٤٥. عن جابر، عن أبي جعفر عليه السلام، قال: سألتُه عن تفسير هذه الآية ﴿وَمَنْ يَكْفُرْ بِالْإِيمَانِ فَقَدْ حَبِطَ عَمَلُهُ﴾، [فقال:] يعني بولاية عليّ عليه السلام ﴿وَهُوَ فِي الْآخِرَةِ مِنَ الْخَاسِرِينَ﴾.

٤٦. عن هارون بن خارجة، قال: سألتُ أبا عبدالله عليه السلام عن قول الله: ﴿وَمَنْ يَكْفُرْ بِالْإِيمَانِ فَقَدْ حَبِطَ عَمَلُهُ﴾، قال: فقال: من ذلك ما اشتقّ فيه زُرارة ابن أعين وأبو حنيفة.

٤٧. عن أبي بكر بن حَزْم، قال: توضّأ رجلٌ فمسح على خُفّيه، فدخل المسجد فصلّى فجاء عليّ عليه السلام فوطئ على رقبته، فقال: ويلك تُصلّي على غير وضوء؟ فقال: أمرني عمر بن الخطاب، قال: فأخذ بيده، فانتهى به إليه، فقال: انظُر ما يروي هذا عليك؟ — ورفع صوته — فقال: نعم، أنا أمرته، إنّ رسول الله صلى الله عليه وآله مسح. قال: قبل المائدة أو بعدها؟ قال: لا أدري. قال: فلِمَ تُفتي وأنت لا تدري؟ سبق الكتاب الخُفّين.

٤٨. عن المُيسّر بن ثَوبان، قال: سَمِعت عليّاً عليه السلام يقول: سَبَق الكتاب الخُفّين والخِمار.

٤٩. عن بُكير بن أعْيَن، قال: قلتُ لأبي عبدالله عليه السلام: قوله تعالى: ﴿يَا أَيُّهَا الَّذِينَ آمَنُوا إِذَا قُمْتُمْ إِلَى الصَّلَاةِ﴾ ما معنى إذا قمتم؟ قال: إذا قمتم من النوم.

قلت: ويَنْقُض النوم الوضوء؟ قال: نعم إذا كان نوم يغلِب على السمع، فلا يسمع الصوت.

50. From Bukayr b. Aʿyan, from Abū Jaʿfar عليه السلام regarding God's verse: ﴾ *You who believe, when you get up to pray, wash your faces and your hands up to the elbows* [...]﴿ He said, 'I asked, "What does He mean by that?" He replied, "From sleep."' [5:6]

51. From Zurāra, from Abū Jaʿfar عليه السلام who said regarding God's verse: ﴾ *You who believe, when you are about to pray, wash your faces and your hands up to the elbows, and wipe a part of your heads and your feet* [...]﴿(5:6) 'He must not leave any part of his face unwashed, nor must he leave any part of his hands until the elbows unwashed.' Then they both said, 'Wipe your heads and your feet until the ankles. To wipe part of the head and part of the feet between the ankles and the tips of the toes is sufficient.' He said, 'So I asked, "May God make you prosper – where exactly are the ankles?" He replied, "Right here, meaning the joint just below the leg bone."' [5:6]

52. From Zurāra and Bukayr b. Aʿyan who said, 'We asked Abū Jaʿfar about the *wuḍū'* of the Messenger of God عليه السلام, so he called for a vessel or a bowl filled with water. Then he dipped his right hand into it, took a handful of water and poured it onto his forehead, and washed his face with that. Then he dipped his left hand in and poured the water on his right arm, washing it from the elbow to the hand without taking it back up to the elbow. Then he dipped his right hand in and poured it onto his left arm from the elbow, and did as he did with the right arm. Then he wiped his head and his feet with whatever was left on his palms, without taking any more water. Then he said, "He did not slide his fingers under the strap [of his sandal]."' He continued, 'Then he said, "God says: ﴾ *You who believe, when you are about to pray, wash your faces and your hands up to the elbows*﴿, and then He says: ﴾ *and wipe a part of your heads and your feet, up to the ankles.*﴿ (5:6) So if he wipes a part of his head or a part of his feet between the sides of the ankles and the tips of the toes, it will suffice."

They said, 'We asked, "May God make you prosper – where are the ankles?"

He replied, "Right here, meaning the joint just below the leg bone."

So we asked him, "Is that where it is?"

He replied, "Separate to the leg bone – the ankle is lower than that."

٥٠. عن بُكير بن أعيَن، عن أبي جعفر عليه السلام، في قول الله: ﴿يَا أَيُّهَا الَّذِينَ آمَنُوا إِذَا قُمْتُمْ إِلَى الصَّلَاةِ فَاغْسِلُوا وُجُوهَكُمْ وَأَيْدِيَكُمْ إِلَى الْمَرَافِقِ﴾، قال: قلت: ما عنى بها؟ قال: من النوم.

٥١. عن زُرارة، عن أبي جعفر عليه السلام، في قول الله: ﴿يَا أَيُّهَا الَّذِينَ آمَنُوا إِذَا قُمْتُمْ إِلَى الصَّلَاةِ فَاغْسِلُوا وُجُوهَكُمْ وَأَيْدِيَكُمْ إِلَى الْمَرَافِقِ وَامْسَحُوا بِرُءُوسِكُمْ وَأَرْجُلَكُمْ﴾، قال: ليس له أن يَدَع شيئًا من وجهه إلاّ غسله، وليس له أن يَدَع شيئًا من يديه إلى المرْفقين إلاّ غسله.

ثمّ قال: ﴿وَامْسَحُوا بِرُءُوسِكُمْ وَأَرْجُلَكُمْ إِلَى الْكَعْبَيْنِ﴾ فإذا مسح بشيء من رأسه أو بشيء من قدميه، ما بين كعبيه إلى أطراف أصابعه، فقد أجزأه.

قال: فقلت: أصلحك الله، أين الكعبين؟ قال: هاهنا، يعني المفْصِل دون عَظْم الساق.

٥٢. عن زُرارة وبُكير ابني أعيَن، قالا: سألنا أبا جعفر عليه السلام عن وضوء رسول الله صلى الله عليه وآله، فدعا بطشت — أو تَوْر — فيه ماء، فغمس كفَّه اليمنى، فغرف بها غرفةً، فصبَّها على جبهته، فغسل وجهه بها، ثمّ غمس كفَّه اليُسرى، فأفرغ على يده اليُمنى، فغسل بها ذِراعه من المرْفق إلى الكَفّ، لا يُردّها إلى المرْفِق، ثمّ غمس كفّه اليمنى، فأفرغ بها على ذِراعه الأيسر من المرْفِق، وصنع بها كما صنع باليُمنى، ومسح رأسه بفَضْل كفّيه وقدميه، لم يُحدِث لها ماءً جديدًا، ثمّ قال: ولا يُدخِل أصابعه تحت الشِّراك.

So we said, "May God make you prosper – so a single handful is sufficient for the face, and one for the arm?"

He replied, "Yes, if you manage to wash them both, and two [handfuls] will cover them all sufficiently."' [5:6]

53. From Zurāra who said, 'I said to Abū Ja'far ﵇, "Tell me about the area of the face that must be washed in *wuḍū'* that God has stipulated?"

So he said, "The face that God has commanded to wash, and which no one should wash more or less than – for if he washes more than that he will not be rewarded for it, and if he washes less, then he will be erring – is that part which is covered by the index, the middle finger and the thumb, from the hairline until the chin, and what is covered by a span of two fingers encircling the side of the face. Anything else apart from that is not a part of the face."

I asked, "Are the sideburns not part of the face?"

He replied, "No."'

Zurāra said, 'I then said to Abū Ja'far ﵇, "Can you tell me from where you know that? And also about wiping a part of the head and a part of the feet?"

So he laughed and said, "Zurāra, the Messenger of God ﷺ has said so, the Book of God having revealed it thus from God, since God says: ﴾*wash your faces*﴿, so we know that the whole face needs to be washed. Then He says: ﴾*and your hands up to the elbows*﴿, so He juxtaposed the hands until the elbows to the face, so we know that they must both be washed until the elbows. Then He departed from this statement saying: ﴾*and wipe a part of your heads*﴿, so we know from when He says '*bi-ru'ūsikum*' that a part of the head is to be wiped because of the insertion of *bi*. Then He juxtaposed the feet to the head, just as He had done with the hands to the face, saying: ﴾*and your feet, up to the ankles.*﴿ So we know from His juxtaposition of them to the head that a part of them must also be wiped. The Messenger of God then explained all that for the people, but they lost it.

Then He says: ﴾*and if you can find no water, then take some clean sand and wipe a part of your faces*﴿ and juxtaposed it with: ﴾*and your hands with it.*﴿ So when he absolved the one who cannot find water from *wuḍū'*, He replaced part of the washing with wiping, saying: ﴾*a part of your faces*﴿, then: ﴾*with it*﴿, meaning with that sand, because He knows that that is a

قالا: ثمّ قال: إنّ الله تعالى يقول: ﴿يَا أَيُّهَا الَّذِينَ آمَنُوا إِذَا قُمْتُمْ إِلَى الصَّلَاةِ فَاغْسِلُوا وُجُوهَكُمْ وَأَيْدِيَكُمْ إِلَى الْمَرَافِقِ﴾ فليس له أن يَدَعَ شيئًا من وجهه إلاّ غسله، وأمر بغسل اليدين إلى المرْفقين، فليس ينبغي له أن يَدَعَ من يديه إلى المرْفقين شيئًا إلاّ غسله، لأنّ الله يقول: ﴿فَاغْسِلُوا وُجُوهَكُمْ وَأَيْدِيَكُمْ إِلَى الْمَرَافِقِ وَامْسَحُوا بِرُءُوسِكُمْ وَأَرْجُلَكُمْ إِلَى الْكَعْبَيْنِ﴾ فإذا مسح بشيء من رأسه أو بشيء من قدميه ما بين أطراف الكعبين إلى أطراف الأصابع، فقد أجزأه.

قالا: قلنا: أصلحك الله أين الكعبان؟ قال: هاهنا، يعني المَفْصِل دون عظم الساق.

فقلنا: هذا ما هو؟ قال: من عظم الساق والكعب أسفل من ذلك.

فقلنا: أصلحك الله، فالغرفة الواحدة تُجزي الوجه، وغرفة للذراع؟ قال: نعم، إذا بالغتَ فيهما، والثنتان تأتيان على ذلك كُلّه.

٥٣. عن زُرارة، قال: قلتُ لأبي جعفر عليه السلام: أخبرني عن حدّ الوجه الذي ينبغي له أن يُوَضّأ، الذي قال الله؟

فقال عليه السلام: الوجه الذي أمر الله بغَسله، الذي لا ينبغي لأحد أن يزيد عليه ولا ينْقُص منه، إن زاد عليه لم يُؤجر، وإن نقص منه أثم: ما دارت السبّابة والوسطى والإبهام، من قَصاص الشعر إلى الذّقَن، وما جرت عليه الإصبعان من الوجه مستديرًا فهو من الوجه، وما سوى ذلك فليس من الوجه.

قلت: الصُّدْغ ليس من الوجه؟ قال: لا.

solid which would not flow on the face, as some of that soil will stick to part of the palm and some will not."' [5:6]

54. From Zurāra, from Abū Ja'far ﷺ who said, 'I asked how one should wipe the head? He replied, "God says: ﴾*and wipe a part of your heads*﴿, so that is how you should wipe your head. However, were He to have said: 'wipe your heads' (*imsaḥū ru'ūsakum*), then you would have had to wipe the whole of it."' [5:6]

قال زُرارة: فقلت لأبي جعفر عليه السلام: ألا تخبرني من أين علمت وقلت: إنَّ المسح ببعض الرأس وبعض الرِّجلين؟ فضحك عليه السلام وقال: يا زُرارة، قاله رسول الله صلى الله عليه وآله، وقد نزل به الكتاب من الله، لأنَّ الله قال: ﴿فَاغْسِلُوا وُجُوهَكُمْ﴾ فعرفنا أنّ الوجه كلّه ينبغي له أن يُغْسَل، ثمّ قال: ﴿وَأَيْدِيَكُمْ إِلَى الْمَرَافِقِ﴾ فوصل اليدين إلى المرْفقين بالوجه، فعرفنا أنّهما ينبغي أن يُغسلا إلى المرْفقين، ثمّ فصل بين الكلام، فقال: ﴿وَامْسَحُوا بِرُءُوسِكُمْ﴾ فعلمنا حين قال: ﴿بِرُءُوسِكُمْ﴾ أنَّ المسح ببعض الرأس لمكان الباء، ثمّ وصل الرجلين بالرأس كما وصل اليدين بالوجه، فقال: ﴿وَأَرْجُلَكُمْ إِلَى الْكَعْبَيْنِ﴾ فعرفنا حين وصلهما بالرأس أنَّ المسح على بعضهما، ثمّ فسَّر ذلك رسول الله صلى الله عليه وآله للناس فضيّعوه.

ثمَّ قال: ﴿فَلَمْ تَجِدُوا مَاءً فَتَيَمَّمُوا صَعِيدًا طَيِّبًا فَامْسَحُوا بِوُجُوهِكُمْ﴾ ثمَّ وصل بها ﴿وَأَيْدِيَكُمْ﴾ فلمّا وضع الوضوء عمَّن لم يجد الماء أثبت بعض الغسل مسحًا، لأنّه قال: ﴿بِوُجُوهِكُمْ﴾ ثمّ قال: ﴿مِنْهُ﴾ أي من ذلك التيمّم، لأنّه علِم أنّ ذلك أجمع لا يجرى على الوجه، لأنّه يَعْلَق من ذلك الصعيد ببعض الكفّ، ولا يَعْلَق ببعضها.

٥٤. عن زُرارة، عن أبي جعفر عليه السلام، قال: قلتُ: كيف يُمْسَح الرأس؟ قال: إنَّ الله تعالى يقول: ﴿وَامْسَحُوا بِرُءُوسِكُمْ﴾ فما مسحت من رأسك فهو كذا، ولو قال: امسحوا رؤوسكم، فكان عليك المسح كُلّه.

55. From Ṣafwān who said, 'I asked Abū al-Ḥasan al-Riḍā عليه السلام about God's verse: ﴿*wash your faces and your hands up to the elbows, and wipe a part of your heads and your feet, up to the ankles.*﴾ So he replied, "A man had asked Abū al-Ḥasan [i.e. Imam al-Kāẓim] about that, so he had said, '*The Chapter of the Feast* will suffice you or has sufficed you, meaning in wiping the head and the feet."

So I asked, "But He has said: ﴿*wash your hands up to the elbows*﴾, so how must they be washed?"

He replied, "Like this – that the water should be taken in the right palm, then poured into the left, then he must pour it onto the elbow, then wipe down to the hand."

So I asked him, "Just once?"

So he replied, "He used to do that twice."

I asked, "It would [be enough to] reach the hair?"

He replied, "If he had more he would do so, but if not, then no."' [5:6]

56. From Muyassar, from Abū Ja'far عليه السلام who said, '*Wuḍū'* is only once.' He said, 'He described the ankle as being at the base of the leg.' [5:6]

57. From 'Abd Allāh b. Sulaymān, from Abū Ja'far عليه السلام who said, 'Shall I tell you about God's Messenger's *wuḍū'*?' We replied, 'Yes, please.' So he took a handful of water and poured it onto his face, then he took another handful [of water and poured it onto his face, then took another handful] and poured it onto his right arm, then he took another handful and poured it onto his left arm. Then he wiped his head and his feet. Then he placed his hand on the back of his foot and said, 'This is the back of the foot, and not the ankle,' pointing to the Achilles' tendon. [5:6]

58. In another narration on his authority he said, 'until the Achilles' tendon.' Then he said, 'This is the shin-bone and not the ankle.' [5:6]

٥٥. عن صَفوان، قال: سألتُ أبا الحسن الرضا عليه السلام عن قول الله: ﴿فَاغْسِلُوا وُجُوهَكُمْ وَأَيْدِيَكُمْ إِلَى الْمَرَافِقِ وَامْسَحُوا بِرُءُوسِكُمْ وَأَرْجُلَكُمْ إِلَى الْكَعْبَيْنِ﴾، فقال: قد سأل رجل أبا الحسن عليه السلام عن ذلك؟ فقال: سيكفيك أوكَفَتْك سورة المائدة، يعني المسح على الرأس والرّجلين.

قلتُ: فإنّه قال: ﴿اغْسِلُوا ... أَيْدِيَكُمْ إِلَى الْمَرَافِقِ﴾ فكيف الغَسل؟ قال: هكذا أن يأخُذ الماء بيده اليُمنى، فيصُبَّه في اليُسرى، ثمَّ يُفيضه على المِرْفَق، ثمّ يمسح إلى الكفّ.

قلت له: مرّةً واحدةً؟ فقال: كان يفعل ذلك مرّتين.

قلتُ: يَرُدّ الشعر؟ قال: إذاكان عنده آخر فعل، وإلاّ فلا.

٥٦. عن مُيسّر، عن أبي جعفر عليه السلام، قال: الوضوء واحدة، قال: ووصف الكَعْب في ظهر القَدم.

٥٧. عن عبدالله بن سليمان، عن أبي جعفر عليه السلام، قال: قال: ألا أحكي لكم وضوء رسول الله صلى الله عليه وآله وسلم؟ قلنا: بلى، فأخذ كفّاً من ماء، فصبّه على وجهه، ثمّ أخذ كفّاً آخر فصبَّه على ذِراعه الأيمن، ثمّ أخذ كفّاً آخر فصبَّه على ذِراعه الأيسر، ثمّ مسح رأسه وقدميه، ثمّ وضع يده على ظهر القَدم، ثمّ قال: إنَّ هذا هو الكعب، وأشار بيده إلى العُرقُوب، وليس بالكَعْب.

٥٨. وفي رواية أُخرى عنه، قال: إلى العُرقُوب، فقال: إنّ هذا هو الظُّنْبُوب، وليس بالكَعْب.

59. From ʿAlī b. Abī Ḥamza who said, 'I asked Abū Ibrāhīm عليه السلام [i.e. Imam Mūsā al-Kāẓim] about God's verse: ﴾ *You who believe, when you are about to pray, wash your faces and your hands up to the elbows, and wipe a part of your heads and your feet, up to the ankles.* ﴿ So he replied, "God speaks the truth."

So I asked, "May I be your ransom – how should one perform *wuḍūʾ*?"
He replied, "Each part twice."
I asked, 'Should he wipe [twice too]?"
He replied, "Each part once."
So I asked, "Just the once with water?"
He replied, "Yes."
I asked, "May I be your ransom – what about the feet?"
He said, "Wash them both once."' [5:6]

60. From Muḥammad b. Aḥmad al-Khurāsānī who, without mentioning his source, cited: 'A man came to the Commander of the Faithful عليه السلام and asked him about wiping over the socks, so he kept his gaze down to the ground for a while then looked up and said, 'O man, God, Blessed and most High, has commanded His servants with purification, and has divided this between his limbs. So He kept a part of it [i.e. purification] for the face, a part of it for the hands, a part of it for the head, and a part of it for the feet. If your socks form a part of these limbs, then wipe over them.' [5:6]

61. From Ghālib b. al-Hudhayl[7] who said, 'I asked Abū Jaʿfar عليه السلام about God's verse: ﴾ *and wipe a part of your heads and your feet, up to the ankles* ﴿ – is this downwards or upwards?' So he replied, 'No, it is downwards.' [5:6]

7 Abū al-Hudhayl Ghālib b. al-Hudhayl al-Asadī, about whom there is scant information, was a famous poet and companion of Muḥammad al-Bāqir. See Khūʾī, *Muʿjam*, 14:238 (nr. 9273).

٥٩. عن عليّ بن أبي حمزة، قال: سألتُ أبا إبراهيم ﷺ عن قول الله تعالى: ﴿يَا أَيُّهَا الَّذِينَ آمَنُوا إِذَا قُمْتُمْ إِلَى الصَّلَاةِ﴾ إلى قوله: ﴿إِلَى الْكَعْبَيْنِ﴾

فقال: صدق الله.

قلت: جُعِلتُ فداك، كيف يتوضّأ؟

قال: مرّتين مرّتين.

قلت: يمسح؟

قال: مرّة مرّة. قلت: من الماء مرّة؟

قال: نعم.

قلت: جُعِلت فداك، فالقدمين؟

قال: اغسِلهما غَسلاً.

٦٠. عن محمّد بن أحمد الخُراساني، رفع الحديث، قال: أتى أمير المؤمنين ﷺ رجلٌ، فسأله عن المسح على الخُفّين، فأطرق في الأرض مَليًّا، ثمّ رفع رأسه، فقال: يا هذا، إنّ الله تبارك وتعالى أمر عباده بالطّهارة، وقسّمها على الجوارح فجعل للوجه منه نصيبًا، وجعل لليدين منه نصيبًا، وجعل للرأس منه نصيبًا، وجعل للرجلين منه نصيبًا، فإن كانتا خُفّاك من هذه الأجزاء، فامسح عليها.

٦١. عن غالب بن الهُذيل، قال: سألتُ أبا جعفر ﷺ عن قول الله تعالى: ﴿وَامْسَحُوا بِرُؤُوسِكُمْ وَأَرْجُلَكُمْ إِلَى الْكَعْبَيْنِ﴾ على الخفض هي أم على الرفع؟

فقال: بل هي على الخَفْض.

62. From ʿAbd Allāh b. Khalīfa, otherwise known as al-ʿArīf [or Abū al-ʿArīf] al-Makrānī al-Hamadānī who said, 'Ibn al-Kawwā stood up in the presence of ʿAlī عليه السلام and asked him about wiping over the socks. So he said, 'You are asking me despite the Book of God? God says: ﴾ *You who believe, when you are about to pray, wash your faces and your hands up to the elbows, and wipe a part of your heads and your feet, up to the ankles.* ﴿' So he stood up a second time and asked him the same thing, so he replied the same thing to him three times, reciting this verse to him each time.' [5:6]

63. From al-Ḥasan b. Zayd, from Jaʿfar b. Muḥammad, that ʿAlī عليه السلام went against the majority in their opinion of wiping over the socks during the rule of ʿUmar b. al-Khaṭṭāb. They said, 'We have seen the Prophet صلى الله عليه وآله wiping over the socks.' He said, 'So ʿAlī عليه السلام replied, 'Before the descent of *The Feast* or after it?' So they replied, 'We do not know.' He said, 'Well I do know that the Prophet stopped wiping over the socks when the *Chapter of the Feast* was revealed. For me, wiping on the back of a donkey is better than wiping over socks!' And he recited this verse: ﴾ *You who believe, when you are about to pray, wash your faces and your hands up to the elbows, and wipe a part of your heads and your feet, up to the ankles.* ﴿' [5:6]

64. From Zurāra who said, 'I asked Abū Jaʿfar عليه السلام about *tayammum* (dry ablution). So he said, "ʿAmmār b. Yāsir came to the Prophet صلى الله عليه وآله and said, 'I entered into the state of major impurity and did not have any water.' So he asked, 'So what did you do?' He replied, 'I removed my clothes, then rolled around in the sand.' So he said, 'That is what donkeys do. What God has said is: ﴾ *then find some clean sand and wipe your faces and hands with it.* ﴿'" He continued, 'Then he struck both his hands together on the earth, then wiped one hand over the other on the back of the hand, starting with the right.' [5:6]

65. From Zurāra, from Abū Jaʿfar عليه السلام who said, 'God has made washing the face and the two arms obligatory as well as wiping the head and the feet. So when it came to situations involving travel, sickness and lack [of water], God absolved us of washing and prescribed wiping instead of washing, saying: ﴾ *If any of you is sick or on a journey, or has just relieved himself, or had intimate*

٦٢. عن عبد الله بن خليفة، أبي العريف المُكراني، قال: قام ابن الكوّاء إلى عليّ عليه السلام فسأله عن المسح على الخُفّين؟ فقال: بعد كتاب الله تسألني؟ قال الله تعالى: ﴿يَا أَيُّهَا الَّذِينَ آمَنُوا إِذَا قُمْتُمْ إِلَى الصَّلَاةِ فَاغْسِلُوا﴾ إلى قوله: ﴿الْكَعْبَيْنِ﴾ ثمّ قام إليه ثانية فسأله، فقال له مثل ذلك ثلاث مرّات، كلّ ذلك يتلو عليه هذه الآية.

٦٣. عن الحسن بن زيد، عن جعفر بن محمّد عليه السلام، أنّ عليًا عليه السلام خالف القوم في المسح على الخُفّين على عهد عمر بن الخطاب، قالوا: رأينا النبي صلى الله عليه وآله وسلم يمسح على الخُفّين، قال: فقال عليّ عليه السلام: قبل نزول المائدة أو بعدها؟ فقالوا: لا ندري. قال: ولكن أدري أنّ النبي صلى الله عليه وآله وسلم ترك المسح على الخُفّين حين نزلت المائدة، ولأن أمسح على ظهر حمار أحبّ إليّ من أن أمسح على الخُفّين؛ وتلا هذه الآية ﴿يَا أَيُّهَا الَّذِينَ آمَنُوا إِذَا قُمْتُمْ إِلَى الصَّلَاةِ فَاغْسِلُوا وُجُوهَكُمْ وَأَيْدِيَكُمْ إِلَى الْمَرَافِقِ وَامْسَحُوا بِرُءُوسِكُمْ وَأَرْجُلَكُمْ إِلَى الْكَعْبَيْنِ﴾.

٦٤. عن زُرارة، قال: سألتُ أبا جعفر عليه السلام عن التيمّم، فقال: إنّ عمّار بن ياسر أتى النبي صلى الله عليه وآله وسلم، فقال: أجنبت وليس معي ماء؟ فقال: كيف صنعت يا عمّار؟ قال: نزعت ثيابي، ثمّ تمعّكتُ على الصعيد؟ فقال: هكذا يصنع الحمار، إنّما قال الله تعالى: ﴿فَامْسَحُوا بِوُجُوهِكُمْ وَأَيْدِيكُمْ مِنْهُ﴾ ثمّ وضع يديه جميعًا على الصَّعيد، ثمّ مسحهما، ثمّ مسح من بين عينيه إلى أسفل حاجبيه، ثمّ دلك إحدى يديه بالأُخرى على ظهر الكفّ بدءًا باليُمن.

٦٥. عن زُرارة، عن أبي جعفر عليه السلام، قال: فرض الله الغَسل على الوجه والذراعين، والمسح على الرأس والقدمين، فلمّا جاء حال السفر والمرض والضّرورة، وضع الله الغَسل، وأثبت

contact with a woman, and can find no water, then take some clean sand and wipe a part of your faces and your hands with it. ﴿' [5:6]

66. From Zurāra, from Abū Jaʿfar عليه السلام, regarding His verse: ﴾ *God does not wish to place any burden on you in religion* ﴿ – 'The burden is the constraint.' [5:6]

67. From ʿAbd al-Aʿlā, the protégé of Āl Sām, who said, 'I asked Abū ʿAbd Allāh عليه السلام, "I fell over and my nail got cut off, so I put a poultice on my finger. How do I do *wuḍūʾ* for prayer?" So he عليه السلام replied, "You know that this situation and its like are in the Book of God, Blessed and most High: ﴾ *God does not wish to place any burden on you in religion.* ﴿' [5:6]

68. From Abū Baṣīr, from one of the two [Imams al-Bāqir or al-Ṣādiq] that the head of [the Abbasid Caliph] al-Mahdī would be gifted to Mūsā b. ʿĪsā on a plate. So I said, 'But are not this one and the other one already dead?'

He replied, 'God has said: ﴾ *go into the holy land which God has ordained for you* ﴿, whilst they were not the ones to go into it but rather their children went in.' Or he said, 'Their grandchildren,' and that counted as their entrance therein.

Then I asked, 'So do you consider that what he said about al-Mahdī and Ibn ʿĪsā will transpire in the same way as this?' So he replied, 'It will happen with their children.'

I asked, 'Do you not deny though that what he says about Ibn al-Ḥasan [i.e. the Twelfth Imam] could equally refer to his children?' He replied, 'Yes, that is not the same as this case.' [5:21]

الغَسل مسحًا، فقال: ﴿وَإِن كُنتُم مَّرْضَىٰ أَوْ عَلَىٰ سَفَرٍ أَوْ جَاءَ أَحَدٌ مِّنكُم مِّنَ الْغَائِطِ أَوْ لَامَسْتُمُ النِّسَاءَ﴾ إلى: ﴿وَأَيْدِيكُم مِّنْهُ﴾.

٦٦. عن زُرارة، عن أبي جعفر ﷺ، في قوله تعالى: ﴿مَا يُرِيدُ اللَّهُ لِيَجْعَلَ عَلَيْكُم﴾ في الدين ﴿مِّنْ حَرَجٍ﴾ [٦] والحَرَج: الضيق.

٦٧. عن عبد الأعلى مولى آل سام، قال: قلتُ لأبي عبد الله ﷺ: إنّي عثرت فانقطع ظُفْري: فجعلتُ على إصبعي مرارة، كيف أصنع بالوضوء للصلاة؟ قال: فقال ﷺ: تعرف هذا وأشباهه في كتاب الله تبارك وتعالى: ﴿مَا جَعَلَ﴾ الله ﴿عَلَيْكُمْ فِي الدِّينِ مِنْ حَرَجٍ﴾.

٦٨. عن أبي بصير، عن أحدهما عليهما السلام، أنّ رأس المهدي يُهدى إلى عيسى بن موسى على طبقٍ. قلت: فقد مات هذا وهذا؟!

قال: فقد قال الله: ﴿ادْخُلُوا الْأَرْضَ الْمُقَدَّسَةَ الَّتِي كَتَبَ اللَّهُ لَكُمْ﴾ فلم يَدخُلوها، ودخلها الأبناء — أو قال: أبناء الأبناء — فكان ذلك دخولهم.

فقلت: أو ترى أنَّ الذي قال في المهديّ وفي عيسى يكون مثل هذا؟ فقال: يكون في أولادهم.

فقلت: ما تُنكر أن يكون ما قال في ابن الحسن يكون في ولده؟ قال: ليس ذلك مثل ذا.

69. From Ḥarīz, from one of his associates, from Abū Ja'far ﷺ who said, 'The Messenger of God ﷺ said, "By the One Who holds my soul in His grasp, you will definitely embark upon practices of the people who preceded you, treading in their shoes and doing exactly as they did, such that neither will you miss a step on their path nor will the tradition of the Children of Israel evade you."'

Then Abū Ja'far ﷺ said, 'Mūsā said to his people: ﴾*My people, go into the holy land which God has ordained for you*﴿(5:21), so they retorted to him, and were six hundred in number. ﴾*They said, "Mūsā, there is a fearsome people in this land. We will not go there until they leave. If they leave, then we will enter." Yet two men whom God had blessed among those who were afraid*﴿(5:22–23) – one was Yūsha' b. Nūn and the other Kālib b. Yāfanā.' He said, 'They were both his cousins. ﴾*They said: "Go in to them through the gate and when you go in you will overcome them. If you are true believers, put your trust in God." They said, "Mūsā, we will never enter while they are still there, so you and your Lord go in and fight, and we will stay here."*﴿ (5:23–24)'

He continued, 'Forty thousand people rebelled, whilst Hārūn, his two sons, Yūsha' b. Nūn and Kālib b. Yāfanā submitted. So God called them 'disobedient people' saying: ﴾*Do not grieve over those who disobey.*﴿ (5:26)

So they wandered aimlessly for forty years because they rebelled, and history repeated itself in the same way when the Messenger of God ﷺ passed away – no one adhered to God's command apart from 'Alī, al-Ḥasan, al-Ḥusayn, Salmān, Miqdād and Abū Dharr, and they had to wait forty years until 'Alī rose up to fight those who opposed him.' [5:21–26]

70. From Zurāra, Ḥumrān and Muḥammad b. Muslim, from Abū Ja'far and Abū 'Abd Allāh, peace be upon them both, who said about His verse: ﴾*My people, go into the holy land which God has ordained for you*﴿, 'He did ordain it for them, then cancelled it.' [5:21]

٦٩. عن حَرِيز، عن بعض أصحابه، عن أبي جعفر عليه السلام قال: قال رسول الله صلى الله عليه وآله: والّذي نفسي بيده لتركَبُنّ سُنن من كان قبلكم، حذوَ النعل بالنعل، والقُذّ بالقُذّة، حتّى لا تُخطِئون طريقهم، ولا تخطئكم سُنّة بني إسرائيل.

ثم قال أبو جعفر عليه السلام: قال موسى عليه السلام لقومه: ﴿ادْخُلُوا الأَرْضَ الْمُقَدَّسَةَ الَّتِي كَتَبَ اللهُ لَكُمْ﴾ فردّوا عليه، وكانوا ستّمائة ألف فقالُوا: ﴿يَا مُوسَى إِنَّ فِيهَا قَوْمًا جَبَّارِينَ وَإِنَّا لَنْ نَدْخُلَهَا حَتَّى يَخْرُجُوا مِنْهَا فَإِنْ يَخْرُجُوا مِنْهَا فَإِنَّا دَاخِلُونَ ۞ قَالَ رَجُلَانِ مِنَ الَّذِينَ يَخَافُونَ أَنْعَمَ اللهُ عَلَيْهِمَا﴾ أحدهما يُوشع بن نون، والآخر كالب بن يافنا — قال: وهما ابنا عمّه — فقالا: ﴿ادْخُلُوا عَلَيْهِمُ الْبَابَ فَإِذَا دَخَلْتُمُوهُ﴾ إلى قوله: ﴿إِنَّا هَاهُنَا قَاعِدُونَ﴾.

قال: فعصى أربعون ألفًا — وسَلِم هارون وابناه ويُوشَع بن نُون، وكالب بن يافنا — فسمّاهم الله فاسقين. فقال: ﴿لَا تَأْسَ عَلَى الْقَوْمِ الْفَاسِقِينَ﴾ فتاهوا أربعين سنة، لأنّهم عَصَوا، فكان حَذو النّعل بالنّعل، إنّ رسول الله صلى الله عليه وآله لمّا قُبِض، لم يكن على أمر الله إلاّ عليّ والحسن والحسين وسلمان والمِقداد وأبو ذرّ، فمكثوا أربعين حتّى قام عليّ عليه السلام فقاتل مَن خالفه.

٧٠. عن زُرارة، وَحُمران، ومحمّد بن مسلم، عن أبي جعفر، وأبي عبدالله عليهما السلام، عن قوله: ﴿يَا قَوْمِ ادْخُلُوا الأَرْضَ الْمُقَدَّسَةَ الَّتِي كَتَبَ اللهُ لَكُمْ﴾، قال عليه السلام: كتبها لهم، ثمّ محاها.

71. From Abū Baṣīr who said, 'Abū 'Abd Allāh عليه السلام said to me, "The Children of Israel were commanded to enter the holy land, but they did not enter it until God Himself forbade it to them and their children, and it was their grandchildren who actually entered it."' [5:21]

72. From Ismā'īl al-Ju'fī, from Abū 'Abd Allāh عليه السلام. He said, 'I said to him, "May God make you prosper – ﴿*go into the holy land which God has ordained for you*﴾(5:21) – had He originally ordained it for them?" He replied, "Yes, by God, He had originally ordained it for them, then it became obvious to Him that they would not enter it."' He narrated, 'Then he resumed [the conversation] saying, "The prayer was [originally] two units with God, having ordained it for the traveller thus, and He added two more units for the resident, making them four units."' [5:21]

73. From Mas'ada b. Ṣadaqa, from Abū 'Abd Allāh عليه السلام that he was asked about God's verse: ﴿*go into the holy land which God has ordained for you.*﴾ He said, 'He ordained it for them and then cancelled it. Then He ordained it for their children who entered it, and ﴿*God erases or confirms whatever He wills, and the source of the Scripture is with Him.*﴾ (13:39)' [5:21]

74. From 'Alī b. Asbāṭ, from al-Riḍā عليه السلام. He said, 'I said to him, "The people of Egypt allege that their land is holy."

He replied, "And how is that?"

I replied, "May I be your ransom – they claim that seventy thousand people will be resurrected within their mountains and be made to enter Paradise without accounting."

So he said, "No, by my life, it is not like that. It was only when God was angry with the Children of Israel that He made them enter Egypt, and not until He was pleased with them that He took them out of it and into another land. God had indeed revealed to Mūsā to take Yūsuf's bones out of there too. So Mūsā asked around for someone who might know the whereabouts of the grave, and he was directed to a blind and chronically incapacitated woman. So Mūsā asked her to show him, but she refused unless it was in return for two things for which he could supplicate to God: for Him to remove her chronic incapacity and for Him to grant her the same rank as him in Paradise beside him.

٧١. عن أبي بصير، قال: قال أبو عبد الله عليه السلام لي: إنَّ بني إسرائيل قال لهم: ﴿ادْخُلُوا الأَرْضَ الْمُقَدَّسَةَ﴾ فلم يدخلوها حتى حرّمها عليهم وعلى أبنائهم، وإنّما دخلها أبناء الأبناء.

٧٢. عن إسماعيل الجُعفي، عن أبي عبد الله عليه السلام، قال: قلتُ له: أصلحك الله ﴿ادْخُلُوا الأَرْضَ الْمُقَدَّسَةَ الَّتِي كَتَبَ اللهُ لَكُمْ﴾ أكان كتبها لهم؟ قال: إي والله، لقد كتبها لهم، ثمّ بدا له لا يَدْخُلوها. قال: ثمّ ابتدأ هو فقال: إنَّ الصلاة كانت رَكْعتين عند الله فجعلهما للمسافر، وزاد للمقيم رَكْعتين فجعلها أربعًا.

٧٣. عن مَسْعَدة بن صَدَقة، عن أبي عبد الله عليه السلام، أنّه سُئِل عن قول الله: ﴿ادْخُلُوا الأَرْضَ الْمُقَدَّسَةَ الَّتِي كَتَبَ اللهُ لَكُمْ﴾، قال: كتبها لهم ثمّ محاها، ثمّ كتبها لأبنائهم فدخلوها، والله يمحو ما يشاء ويُثبِت وعنده أُمّ الكتاب.

٧٤. عن عليّ بن أسباط، عن الرضا عليه السلام، قال: قلتُ له: إنَّ أهل مِصْر يَزْعُمون أنَّ بلادهم مُقدَّسة؟ قال: وكيف ذاك؟ قلت: جُعِلت فداك: يَزْعُمون أنّه يُحْشَر في جَبَلهم سبعون ألفًا يَدْخُلون الجنّة بغير حساب.

فقال: لا لَعُمْري، ما ذاك كذلك، وما غَضِب الله على بني إسرائيل إلاّ أدخلهم مِصْرًا، ولا رضي عنهم إلاّ أخرجهم منها إلى غيرها، ولقد أوحى الله إلى موسى عليه السلام أن يخرج عظام يوسف منها، فاستدلَّ موسى عليه السلام على من يَعْرِف موضع القبر، فدُلّ على امرأةٍ عمياءَ زَمِنة، فسألها موسى عليه السلام أنْ تَدُلّه، فأبت إلاّ على خَصلتَين: يدعو

Mūsā thought that was too much, but God revealed to him: 'What is too much here? Give her what she is asking for.'

So he did, and she arranged to meet him at moonrise.

God held the moon at its rising until Mūsā came to his appointment. So she took it out of the Nile in a casket made of marble and Mūsā carried it back."'

He continued, 'Then he said, "The Messenger of God ﷺ said, 'Do not eat from earthenware pots from there [i.e. Egypt], nor wash your heads with its clay, for it engenders disgrace and takes away one's self-respect.'"' [5:21–24]

75. From al-Ḥusayn b. Abī al-'Alā', from Abū 'Abd Allāh عليه السلام; he said, 'He was talking about the people of Egypt, and he mentioned Mūsā's community and their saying: ﴿*you and your Lord go in and fight, and we will stay here.*﴾ (5:24) So God forbade it to them for forty years and made them wander aimlessly. When night fell and they set about on their journey, they called out: "On our way! Let us go!" They continued thus until the sun set, and they had emigrated and found a level plain to settle in. God told the land, "Move them around so that they remain wandering thus," [and they wandered] until the early hours of the morning when they said, "This is water that we have come to, so let's alight." When they woke up in the morning they found themselves in the same dwellings and settlements that they had been in the previous day. So they said to each other, "O people, you are lost and have mistaken the way!" and they continued thus until God allowed them to enter it, having originally ordained it for them.' [5:24]

76. From Dāwūd al-Raqqī who said, 'I heard Abū 'Abd Allāh عليه السلام say, "How blessed the land of Shām is but how bad are the people who live there. And how bad the country of Egypt is – indeed, it is a prison for those whom God was displeased with, and the Children of Israel being made to settle there was for no other reason than their displeasing Him and rebelling against God, because God said: ﴿*go into the holy land which God has ordained for you*﴾ (5:21), meaning Shām. However, they refused to enter it and wandered in Egypt and its desert lands aimlessly for forty years. Then they entered it after forty years." He continued, "Their leaving Egypt and being made to enter into Shām was only after their repentance and God's satisfaction with

الله فيُذهِب بزَمَانَتِها، ويُصيرّها معه في الجنَّة في الدَّرجة الَّتي هو بها، فأعظم ذلك موسى ﴿عليه السلام﴾، فأوحى الله إليه: وما يَعْظُم عليك من هذا؟ أعْطِها ما سألت:

ففعل فوعدته طلوع القمر فحبس الله طُلوع القمر، حتّى جاء موسى لموعده، فأخرجته من النِّيل في سَفَط مَرْمَر فحمله موسى.

قال: ثمّ قال إنّ رسول الله ﷺ قال: لا تأكُلوا في فَخَارِها، ولا تَغْسِلوا رؤوسكم بطِينها، فإنّه يُورِث الذِلَّة، ويذهب بالغِيرة.

٧٥. عن الحسين بن أبي العلاء، عن أبي عبدالله ﴿عليه السلام﴾، قال: ذكر أهل مِصْر، وذكر قوم موسى ﴿عليه السلام﴾ وقولهم: ﴿فَاذْهَبْ أَنتَ وَرَبُّكَ فَقَاتِلَا إِنَّا هَاهُنَا قَاعِدُونَ﴾ فحرّمها الله عليهم أربعين سنة، وتيّههم، فكان إذا كان العشاء وأخذوا في الرّحيل، نادوا: الرحيل الرحيل، الوَحَى الوحَى، فلم يزالوا كذلك حتّى تغيب الشمس، حتّى إذا ارتحلوا واستوَت بهم الأرض، قال الله تعالى للأرض: ديري بهم، فلم يزالوا كذلك حتّى إذا أسحروا وقارب الصُّبح، قالوا: إنّ هذا الماء قد أتيتموه فانْزلوا، فإذا أصبحوا، إذا أبنيتهم ومنازلهم التي كانوا فيها بالأمس، فيقول بعضهم لبعض: يا قوم، لقد ضللتُم وأخطأتم الطريق، فلم يزالوا كذلك حتّى أذِن الله لهم فَدَخلُوها، وقد كان كَتبها لهم.

٧٦. عن داود الرقّي، قال: سَمِعتُ أبا عبدالله ﴿عليه السلام﴾ يقول: كان أبو جعفر ﴿عليه السلام﴾ يقول: نِعم الأرض الشام، وبئس القوم أهلها، وبئس البلاد مصر، أما إنّها سِجن من سَخِط الله عليه، ولم يَكُن دُخُول بني إسرائيل مِصر إلاّ من سَخَطٍ ومعصيةٍ منهم لله، لأنّ الله قال:

them." He added, "Indeed I hate eating anything that has been cooked in earthenware pots from there, nor do I like washing my hair with its clay for fear that its earth will engender disgrace in me and take away my self-respect."' [5:21–24]

77. From Ibn Sinān, from Abū 'Abd Allāh عليه السلام who said with respect to God's verse: ﴿*go into the holy land which God has ordained for you*﴾(5:21), 'He knew that they would rebel and wander the land for forty years, and that they would subsequently enter it after His having forbidden it to them.' [5:21]

78. From Hishām b. Sālim, from Ḥabīb al-Sijistānī, from Abū Ja'far عليه السلام who said, 'When the two sons of Ādam offered a sacrifice and it was accepted from one and not the other – it was accepted from Ḥābīl and not from Qābīl – an intense jealousy overcame him, and he bullied Ḥābīl, continuously ambushing him and trying to corner him on his own until he managed to get him away from Ādam. Then he pounced on him and killed him.'

He continued, 'So when Ādam came to know of Ḥābīl's murder, he grieved over him intensely and a deep sorrow overtook him.' He said, 'So he complained to God of it and God revealed to him saying, "I will grant you a son to take Ḥābīl's place."'

He continued, 'So Ḥawwā' gave birth to a pure and blessed son, and on the seventh day Ādam named him Shīth. Then God revealed to Ādam, "This boy is indeed a gift from Me to you, so call him Hibat Allāh [lit. the gift of God]."' He said, 'So he named him Hibat Allāh.'

He continued, 'So when the end of Ādam's life drew near, God revealed to him, "O Ādam, I will cause you to die and take your soul up to Myself on such and such day, so make a bequest to the best of your offspring, who is the gift that I bestowed upon you. Bequeath him and pass on to him the Names that We have taught you, including the Greatest Name. Place this in a casket for indeed I wish for My earth never to be devoid of a knowledgeable one who knows My knowledge and can rule with My judgement, whom I designate as My proof over My creatures."'

He continued, 'So Ādam gathered all his offspring together, men and women, and said to them, "My children, God has revealed to me that He is going to take my soul up to Himself and has commanded me to make a bequest to the best of my offspring and that this is Hibat Allāh, for God has

﴿ادْخُلُوا الأَرْضَ الْمُقَدَّسَةَ الَّتِي كَتَبَ اللهُ لَكُمْ﴾ يعني الشام، فأبوا أن يَدْخُلوها، فتاهوا في الأرض أربعين سنةً، في مصر وفيَافِيها، ثمّ دَخَلُوها بعد أربعين سنة.

قال: وماكان خُرُوجهم من مِصْر ودخولهم الشام إلاّ من بعد توبتهم، ورضى الله عنهم.

وقال ﷺ: إنّي لأكره أن آكل من شيءٍ طُبخ في فَخّارها، وما أُحبّ أن أغسل رأسي من طِينها مخافة أن تُورثني تُربتها الذُلّ، وتُذهِب بغيرتي.

٧٧. عن ابن سِنان، عن أبي عبد الله ﷺ، في قول الله: ﴿ادْخُلُوا الأَرْضَ الْمُقَدَّسَةَ الَّتِي كَتَبَ اللهُ لَكُمْ﴾، قال: كان في عِلمه أنّهم سيعصون ويتيهون أربعين سنة، ثمّ يَدْخُلونها بعد تحريمه إيّاها عليهم.

٧٨. عن هِشام بن سالم، عن حبيب السّجستاني، عن أبي جعفر ﷺ، قال: لمّا قرّب ابنا آدم القُربان، فتُقُبِّل من أحدهما ولم يُتَقَبل من الآخر - قال: تُقبِّل من هابيل ولم يُتَقَبَّل من قابيل -دخله من ذلك حَسَدٌ شديدٌ، وبغى على هابيل، فلم يَزَل يَرْصُدُه ويتّبع خَلْوَته، حتّى ظَفِر به متنحيًّا عن آدم، فوَثَب عليه فقَتَله، فكان من قِصّتهما ما قد أنبأ الله في كتابه، ممّا كان بينهما من المُحاورة قبل أن يَقْتُله.

قال: فلمّا عَلِم آدم بقتل هابيل جَزِع عليه جَزَعًا شديدًا، ودخله حُزنٌ شديد، قال: فشكا إلى الله ذلك، فأوحى الله إليه: أنّي، واهبٌ لك ذَكَرًا يكون خَلَفًا لك من هابيل. قال: فولدت حوّاء غُلامًا زكيًّا مُباركًا، فلمّا كان يوم السابع سمّاه آدمُ شِيثَ، فأوحى الله إلى آدم: إنّما هذا الغُلام هِبة منّي لك، فسَمِّه هِبة الله، قال: فسمّاه هِبةُ الله.

chosen him for me and you all after me. Listen to him and obey his command, for he is my vicegerent and successor over you."

So they all said, "We will listen to him and obey his command, and we will not oppose him."'

He said, 'So he asked for a casket and did as he was supposed to. Then he placed his knowledge, the Names, and the bequest therein, and transmitted it to Hibat Allāh and commissioned him with it, saying to him, "Be mindful, Hibat Allāh. When I die, wash me, shroud me, pray over me and place me in my grave. When forty days have passed after my death take all my bones out of my grave, gather them and place them inside the casket. Guard it carefully and do not entrust it to anyone else. When your own death approaches and you begin to sense that inside yourself, then take the best of your children, the one who is your closest companion and the most virtuous one of them all from before, and bequeath him in the same way that I bequeathed you. Do not ever leave the earth devoid of a knowledgeable man from amongst us, the people of this household.

My son, God – Blessed and most High – sent me to earth and made me His ambassador on it and His proof over all His creatures. So I have bequeathed you by God's command, and I have designated you a proof of God over all His creatures on His earth after me. So do not leave this world without first leaving behind a proof of God and a vicegerent. Hand the casket and its contents over to him just as I have done unto you. Inform him that there will come a man from my progeny by the name of Nūḥ, whose prophethood will experience flood and drowning. Whoever boards his ship will be saved and whoever lags behind will drown. Make a bequest to your heir to safeguard the casket and its contents, and that when his time of death approaches, to make a bequest to the best, most responsible and most virtuous of his children to him, and to hand the casket and its contents over to him. Every heir should, in turn, place his will in the casket, each one making a bequest to the one after him. And whoever lives to see the prophethood of Nūḥ must board the Ark with him and carry the casket with all its contents onto it, and none must lag behind it.

Hibat Allāh and my children, beware of the wretched Qābīl and his offspring, for you have seen what he did to your brother Ḥābīl, so be on your guard against him and his offspring. Do not marry them, nor mingle with them. Hibat Allāh, you and your brothers and sisters should live at the top

قال: فلمّا دنا أجل آدم عليه السلام أوحى الله إليه: أن يا آدم، إنّي مُتوفّيك، ورافع روحك إليّ يوم كذا وكذا، فأوصِ إلى خير ولدك، وهو هِبتي الذي وَهَبته لك، فأوصِ إليه، وسلّم إليه ما علّمناك من الأسماء والاسم الأعظم، فاجعل ذلك في تابوت، فأنّي أُحبّ أن لا تخلو أرضي من عالمٍ يعلم علمي، ويقضي بحُكمي أجعله حُجّتي على خَلْقي.

قال: فجمع آدم إليه جميع ولده من الرجال والنساء، فقال لهم: يا ولدي، إنّ الله أوحى إليّ أنه رافعٌ إليه روحي، وأمرني أن أُوصي إلى خير ولدي، وأنّه هِبة الله، وإنّ الله اختاره لي ولكم من بعدي، اسمعوا له وأطيعوا أمره، فإنّه وصيّ وخليفتي عليكم، فقالوا جميعًا: نَسمع له، ونُطيع أمره، ولا نخالفه.

قال: فأمر بالتابوت فعُمِل، ثمّ جعل فيه علمه والأسماء والوصيّة، ثمّ دفعه إلى هِبة الله، وتقدّم إليه في ذلك وقال له: انظُر يا هبة الله، إذا أنا مُتُّ فاغسِلني وكفّني، وصلّ عليّ، وأدخلني في حُفرتي، فإذا مضى بعد وفاتي أربعون يومًا، فأخرج عِظامي كُلُّها من حُفرتي، اجمعها جميعًا، ثمّ اجعلها في التابوت، واحتفظ به، ولا تأمَنَنّ عليه أحدًا غيرك، فإذا حضرت وفاتك، وأحسست بذلك من نفسك، فالتمِس خير ولدك، وألزمهم لك صُحبةً، وأفضلهم عندك قبل ذلك، فأوصِ إليه بمثل ما أوصيتُ به إليك، ولا تَدَعنّ الأرض بغير عالمٍ منّا أهل البيت.

يا بنيّ، إنّ الله تبارك وتعالى أهبطني إلى الأرض، وجعلني خليفته فيها، حُجّةً له على خلقه، فقد أوصيتُ إليك بأمر الله، وجعلتك حُجّةً لله على خَلْقه في أرضه بعدي، فلا تَخْرُج من الدنيا حتى تَدَع لله حُجّةً ووصيًّا، وتُسلّم إليه التابوت وما فيه، كما سلّمتُه إليك،

of the mountain far away from him and his children, and let the wretched Qābīl and his children live at the foot of the mountain."'

He continued, 'So when the day came when God had informed him that he would die, Ādam prepared himself for death and yielded before it.' He said, 'The Angel of Death descended upon him, so Ādam said, "O Angel of Death, let me declare my faith and glorify my Lord for what He has done for me before you take my soul." Then Ādam said, "I bear witness that there is no god but God alone without any partner, and I bear witness that I am God's servant and His successor on His earth. He brought me into being out of His Grace and created me with His own Hand when He has not created any other creature apart from me with His Hand and blew His Spirit into me. Then He beautified my form, not having made any other creature like me before. Then He made His angels prostrate before me and taught me all the Names when His angels did not know them. Then He let me reside in His garden, not having designated it as a permanent abode or a dwelling place. He had actually designed me to live on earth for the destiny and plan that He had willed, and He had decreed all that before He even created me. So I went along with His decree and His destiny, and executed His command. Then He forbade me from eating from the tree, but I disobeyed Him and ate from it, but He steadied me after my slip, and pardoned me my sin – so for all the bounties that I have, to Him is due the kind of praise that would complete His satisfaction with me."' He said, 'Then the Angel of Death took his soul, may God's blessings be upon him.'

Then Abū Ja'far said, 'Jibrīl descended with his shroud, his embalmment, and an iron shovel.' He continued, 'Seventy thousand angels also descended with Jibrīl to attend the funeral of Ādam عليه السلام.' He said, 'So Hibat Allāh washed him, and Jibrīl shrouded him and embalmed him, then said, "Hibat Allāh, come forward, pray over your father and perform twenty-five *takbīr* over him." So he laid down Ādam's bier, and Hibat Allāh came forward with Jibrīl standing to his right and angels behind them both. Then he performed the prayer over him and twenty-five *takbīr*, and Jibrīl and the angels followed suit. Then they dug a grave for him with the iron shovel and lowered him into his grave. Jibrīl then said, "Hibat Allāh, this is what you must do for your deceased ones from now onwards, and may the peace, mercy and blessings of God be upon you all, people of the household."'

وأعلمه أنّه سيكون من ذُرّيّتي رجلٌ اسمه نُوح، يكون في نُبوّته الطُّوفان والغَرَق، فمن رَكِب في فُلْكه نجا، ومن تخلّف عن فُلكه غَرق، وأوصِ وصيّك أن يحتفظ بالتابوت وبما فيه، فإذا حضرت وفاته أن يُوصي إلى خير ولده، وألزمهم له، وأفضلهم عنده، وسلّم إليه التابوت وما فيه، وليضع كُلّ وصيّ وصيّته في التابوت، وليُوصِ بذلك بعضهم إلى بعض، فمن أدرك نبوّة نُوح فليَرْكَب معه، وليحمل التابوت وجميع ما فيه في فُلكه، ولا يتخلّف عنه أحد. ويا هبة الله، وأنتم يا ولدي، إيّاكم الملعون قابيل وولده، فقد رأيتم ما فعل بأخيكم هابيل، فاحذروه وولده، ولا تُناكحوهم ولا تُخالطوهم، وكُن أنتَ يا هبة الله وإخوتك وأخواتك في أعلى الجبل، واعزِله وولده، ودَع الملعون قابيل وولده في أسفل الجبل.

قال: فلمّا كان اليوم الذي أخبر الله أنّه متوفّيه فيه، تهيّأ آدم للموت، وأذعن به. قال: وهَبَط عليه مَلَك الموت، فقال آدم: دعني يا مَلَك الموت حتّى أتشهّد، وأُثني على ربّي بما صنع عندي من قبل أن تَقْبِض رُوحي.

فقال آدم: أشهد أن لا إله إلاّ الله، وحده لا شريك له، وأشهد أنّي عبد الله، وخليفته في أرضه، ابتدأني بإحسانه، وخَلَقني بيده، ولم يَخْلُق خلقًا بيده سواي، ونَفَخَ فيّ من رُوحه، ثمّ أجمل صُورتي، ولم يَخْلُق على خَلْقي أحدًا قبلي، ثمّ أسجد لي ملائكته، وعلّمني الأسماء كلّها، ولم يُعلّمها ملائكته، ثمّ أسكنني جنّته، ولم يكن جعلها دارَ قَرارٍ، ولا منزل استيطان، وإنّما خلقني ليُسكنني الأرض، للذي أراد من التقدير والتدبير، وقدّر ذلك كلّه من قبل أن يَخْلُقني، فمضيتُ في قَدَرِه وقضائه ونافذ أمره، ثمّ نهاني أن آكل من الشجرة، فعصيته

Abū Jaʿfar continued saying, 'Then Hibat Allāh led his father's children in obedience to God and according to what his father had bequeathed him, and he stayed away from the children of the wretched Qābīl. When Hibat Allāh's time of death approached he made a bequest to his son, Qaynān, and handed the casket with its contents, Ādam's bones and Ādam's will over to him, and said to him, "If you are the one to witness Nūḥ's prophethood then follow him and carry the casket with you onto his Ark and never lag behind him, for the flood and the drowning will take place during his prophethood. Whoever boards his Ark will be safe and whoever lags behind will drown."'

He continued, 'So Qaynān executed Hibat Allāh's will and led his brothers and his father's children in obedience to God.' He said, 'And when the time of Qaynān's death drew near, he bequeathed his son Mahlāʾīl and handed the casket, its contents and the will over to him. Mahlāʾīl then executed Qaynān's will and followed in his footsteps. When Mahlāʾīl's death drew near, he bequeathed his son, Yarid, and handed the casket with all its contents and the will over to him, and told him of the advent of Nūḥ's prophethood. When the time for Yarid to die drew near, he bequeathed his son, Akhnūkh, who is Idrīs [Enoch]. He handed the casket with all its contents and the will over to him, and Akhnūkh executed Yarid's will. When his end drew near, God revealed to him that, "I am going to take you up to the heavens, and take your soul in the heavens. So make a bequest to your son Kharqāsīl." Kharqāsīl executed Akhnūkh's will. When death came to him, he bequeathed his son, Nūḥ, and handed the casket with all its contents and the will over to him.'

وأكلتُ منها، فأقالني عَثرتي، وصَفح لي عن جُرمي، فله الحمدُ على جميع نِعَمه عندي حمدًا يَكْمُل به رضاه عنّي. قال: فقَبَض مَلَك الموت رُوحه صلوات الله عليه.

فقال أبو جعفر عليه السلام: إنَّ جَبْرَئيل عليه السلام نزل بكَفَن آدم وبحُنُوطه، وبالمِسحاة معه، قال: ونزل مع جَبْرَئيل سبعون ألف مَلَك ليَحْضُروا جنازة آدم عليه السلام، قال: فغسّله هِبة الله، وجَبْرَئيل كفّنه وحنّطه، ثمّ قال: يا هِبة الله، تقدّم فصلِّ على أبيك، وكبِّر عليه خمسًا وعشرين تكبيرةً، فوضع سرير آدم، ثمّ قدّم هِبة الله، وقام جَبْرَئيل عن يمينه، والملائكة خلفهما، فصلّى عليه، وكبّر عليه خمسًا وعشرين تكبيرةً، وانصرف جَبْرَئيل والملائكة فحفروا له بالمِسحاة، ثمّ أدخلوه في حُفرته، ثمّ قال جَبْرَئيل: يا هبة الله، هكذا فافعلوا بموتاكم، والسلام عليكم، ورحمة الله وبركاته عليكم أهل البيت.

فقال أبو جعفر عليه السلام: فقام هِبة الله في ولد أبيه بطاعة الله، وبما أوصاه أبوه، فاعتزل ولد الملعون قابيل، فلمّا حضرت وفاة هِبة الله، أوصى إلى ابنه قينان، وسلَّم إليه التابوت وما فيه، وعظام آدم، ووصيَّة آدم عليه السلام، وقال له: إن أنت أدركت نبوّة نُوح فاتّبعه، واحمِل التابوت معك في فُلكه، ولا تَخَلَّفَنَّ عنه، فإنّ في نبوّته يكون الطّوفان والغَرَق، فمن رَكِب في فُلكه نجا، ومن تخلّف عنه غرِق.

قال: فقام قينان بوصيّة هِبة الله في إخوته وولد أبيه بطاعة الله، قال: فلمّا حضرت قينان الوفاة أوصى إلى مهلائيل، وسلّم إليه التابوت وما فيه والوصيّة، فقام مهلائيل بوصيَّة قينان، وسار بسيرته، فلمّا حضرت مهلائيل الوفاة أوصى إلى ابنه يرد، فسلَّم إليه التابوت وجميع ما فيه والوصيّة، فتقدّم إليه في نبوّة نُوح، فلمّا حضرت وفاة يرد أوصى إلى

He continued, 'The casket remained with Nūḥ until he carried it with him on his Ark, and when death approached Nūḥ, he made a bequest to his son Sām and handed the casket with all its contents and the will over to him.'

Ḥabīb al-Sijistānī said, 'Then Abū Ja'far's account stopped there.' [5:27–32]

79. From Abū Ḥamza al-Thumālī, from Abū Ja'far عليه السلام who said, 'When Ādam ate from the tree, he was sent down to earth. Then Ḥābīl was born to him with his twin sister. Then Qābīl was born with his twin sister. Thereafter Ādam commanded Ḥābīl and Qābīl both to offer a sacrifice. Ḥābīl owned sheep, and Qābīl owned crops. So Ḥābīl offered a ram from among the best of all his sheep, whereas from his crops, Qābīl offered that which was not good enough to bring into his own house. So Ḥābīl's sacrifice was accepted, and Qābīl's was not, and this is as per God's statement: ﴾*[Prophet], tell them the truth about the story of Adam's two sons: each of them offered a sacrifice, and it was accepted from one and not the other. One said, "I will kill you," but the other said, "God only accepts the sacrifice of those who are mindful of Him".*﴿ The sacrifice was consumed by fire, so Qābīl went to the fire and built a house for it, and he is the first to have made buildings to house fire. He said, "I will indeed worship this fire until my sacrifice is accepted."

Then Iblīs, God's enemy, and the one who courses in man's blood in his very veins, came to him and said, "O Qābīl, Ḥābīl's sacrifice has indeed been accepted and yours has not; and if you leave him [alive] he will beget offspring who will boast over your offspring saying, 'We are the sons of the one whose sacrifice was accepted whilst you are the sons of the one whose sacrifice was rejected.' So kill him so that he does not beget any children to boast over your children." So he killed him.

ابنه أخنوخ – وهو إدريس – فسلَّم إليه التابوت وجميع ما فيه والوصيّة، فقام أخنوخ بوصيّة يرد، فلمّا قرُب أجلُه أوحى الله إليه: أنّي رافعك إلى السماء، وقابض روحك في السماء، فأوصِ إلى ابنك خرقاسيل، فقام خرقاسيل بوصيّة أخنوخ، فلمّا حضرته الوفاة أوصى إلى ابنه نُوح، وسلَّم إليه التابوت وجميع ما فيه والوصيّة.

قال: فلم يَزَل التابوت عند نُوح حتّى حمله معه في فُلكه، فلمّا حضرت نوح الوفاة أوصى إلى ابنه سام، وسلَّم التابوت وجميع ما فيه والوصيّة.

قال حبيب السِّجستاني: ثمّ انقطع حديث أبي جعفر عليه السلام عندها.

٧٩. عن أبي حمزة الثُّمالي، عن أبي جعفر عليه السلام، قال: لمّا أكل آدم من الشجرة، أُهبط إلى الأرض، فولد له هابيل وأُخته توأم، ثمّ ولد قابيل وأُخته توأم، ثمّ إنّ آدم عليه السلام أمر هابيل وقابيل أن يُقرّبا قُربانًا، وكان هابيل صاحب غَنَم، وكان قابيل صاحب زَرْع، فقرّب هابيل كَبْشًا من أفضل غَنَمَه، وقرّب قابيل من زرعه ما لم يُكن يُنَقّى، كما أدخل بيته، فتُقُبّل قُربان هابيل، ولم يُتَقَبّل قُربان قابيل، وهو قول الله: ﴿وَاتْلُ عَلَيْهِمْ نَبَأَ ابْنَيْ آدَمَ بِالْحَقِّ إِذْ قَرَّبَا قُرْبَانًا فَتُقُبِّلَ مِنْ أَحَدِهِمَا وَلَمْ يُتَقَبَّلْ مِنَ الْآخَرِ﴾ الآية، وكان القُربان تأكُله النار، فعَمَد قابيل إلى النار فبنى لها بيتًا، وهو أوّل من بنى بيوت النار، فقال: لأعبُدنّ هذه النار حتّى يُتَقَبّل قُرباني.

ثمّ إنّ إبليس عدوّ الله أتاه وهو يجري من ابن آدم مجرى الدم في العُروق، فقال له: يا قابيل، قد تُقُبّل قربان هابيل، ولم يُتَقبّل قُربانك، وإنّك إن تركته يكون له عَقِب يَفْتَخِرون على عَقِبك، ويقولون: نحن أبناء الذي تُقُبّل قُربانه، وأنتم أبناء الذي تُرِك قُربانه، فاقتُله لكي لا يكون له عَقِب يفتخرون على عَقِبك، فقَتَله.

When Qābīl returned to Ādam, he asked him, "Qābīl, where is Ḥābīl?"

So he replied, "Look for him where we offered our sacrifice."

So Ādam rushed there and found Ḥābīl killed, so Ādam said, "Cursed be this earth that accepted the blood of Ḥābīl," and he wept for Ḥābīl for forty nights.

Then Ādam asked his Lord for a son, and a boy was born to him whom he named Hibat Allāh because God had gifted him to him along with his twin sister. So when Ādam's prophethood came to an end and his days were coming to a close, God revealed to him, "Ādam, you have completed your prophethood and your days are coming to an end. Leave behind with your son Hibat Allāh the knowledge that is with you, along with the faith, the Greatest Name, the heirloom of knowledge and the legacy of the knowledge of prophethood for your children after you, for indeed I will never cut off the knowledge, the faith, the Greatest Name, and the legacy of the knowledge of prophethood from your progeny after you until the Day of Resurrection. Nor will I ever leave the earth devoid of a knowledgeable man through whom My creed and My obedience may be known, and to be a source of safety for whoever is born between your time and Nūḥ."

He gave Ādam the good news of Nūḥ saying, "Indeed God will send down a prophet called Nūḥ who will call people towards God, but who will be rejected by his community. So God will destroy them with the flood." There were ten fathers between Ādam and Nūḥ, all of whom were prophets. Ādam bequeathed to Hibat Allāh that whoever ends up meeting him from among you all should have faith in him, follow him, and attest to him, and he will be saved from drowning. Then Ādam was taken ill with the sickness that would cause his death, so he sent for Hibat Allāh and said to him, "If you meet Jibrīl or any of the other angels, pass on my greetings of peace, and say to him, 'O Jibrīl, my father would like to present you the fruits of Paradise as a gift.'"

So Jibrīl replied, "Hibat Allāh, your father has passed away, God's blessings be upon him, and we have only come down to pray over him, so go back home." So he went back and found that Ādam had passed away. So Jibrīl عليه السلام showed him how to wash him until it was time to pray over him. Hibat Allāh said, "Jibrīl, go forward and lead the prayer over Ādam." So Jibrīl replied, "God had indeed commanded us to prostrate before your father, Ādam, when he was in the garden, so it does not befit us now to lead

فلمّا رجع قابيل إلى آدم، قال له: يا قابيل، أين هابيل؟ فقال: اطلبوه حيثُ قرّبنا القُربان، فانطلق آدم فوجد هابيل قتيلاً، فقال آدم: لُعِنتِ من أرضٍ كما قَبلتِ دم هابيل، فبكى آدم على هابيل أربعين ليلة.

ثمّ لإنّ آدم سأل ربّه ولداً، فوُلِد له غُلام فسمّاه هِبة الله، لأنّ الله وَهَبه له وأُخته توأم، فلمّا انقضت نبوّة آدم عليه السلام، واستكمل أيّامُه، أوحى الله تعالى إليه أن يا آدم قد قُضيت نَبوّتك، واستُكمِلت أيّامُك، فاجعل العلم الذي عندك والإيمان والاسم الأكبر وميراث العلم وآثار عِلم النبوة في العَقِب من ذُريّتك، عند هِبة الله ابنك، فإنّي لم أقطع العلم والإيمان والاسم الأعظم وآثار عِلم النبوّة في العَقِب من ذُريّتك إلى يوم القيامة، ولن أدَعَ الأرض إلاّ وفيها عالِمٌ يُعرَف به ديني، وتُعرَف به طاعتي، ويكون نجاةً لمن يُولَد فيما بينك وبين نُوح.

وبَشّر آدم بنُوح، وقال عليه السلام: إنّ الله باعث نبيًّا اسمه نُوح، فإنّه يدعو إلى الله، ويُكذّبه قومه، فيُهلِكهم الله بالطُّوفان، فكان بين آدم ونُوح عشرة آباء، كُلُّهم أنبياء، وأوصى آدم إلى هِبة الله أنّ من أدركه منكم فليُؤمن به، وليتّبعه وليصدّق به، فإنّه يجو من الغَرَق.

ثمّ إنّ آدم مرِض المَرْضَة التي مات فيها، فأرسل هِبة الله فقال له: إن لقيت جبْرَئيل ومن لقيت من الملائكة فاقرأه منّي السلام، وقل له: يا جبْرَئيل، إنّ أبي يستهديك من ثِمار الجنّة. فقال جبْرَئيل: يا هِبة الله، إنّ أباك قد قُبِض صلوات الله عليه، وما نزلنا إلاّ للصلاة عليه فرجع، فوجد آدم قد قُبِض، فأراه جبْرَئيل عليه السلام كيف يغسّله، فغسّله حتّى إذا بلغ الصلاة عليه، قال هِبة الله: يا جبْرَئيل، تقدّم فصلِّ على آدم، فقال له جبْرَئيل: إنّ الله أمرنا أن نَسْجُد لأبيك آدم وهو في الجنّة، فليس لنا أن نَؤُمّ شيئًا من ولده، فتقدّم هِبة

his son in prayer." So Hibat Allāh stepped forward and led the prayer for his father, Ādam, and Jibrīl and the throngs of angels prayed behind him. He performed thirty *takbīr* over him. Then Jibrīl commanded him to omit twenty-five of them, and so the practice today amongst us is five *takbīr*. They used to perform seven and nine *takbīr* over the people who died at Badr.

Then when Hibat Allāh had buried Ādam عليه السلام, Qābīl came to him saying, "Hibat Allāh, I saw that my father Ādam has distinguished you with the knowledge of that which I have not been distinguished with, and this is the same knowledge that your brother Ḥābīl used when his sacrifice was accepted from him. I only killed him so that he would not have a progeny who would boast over my progeny saying, 'We are the sons of the one whose sacrifice was accepted whilst you are the sons of the one whose sacrifice was rejected.' So if you manifest any of this knowledge that my father has distinguished you with, I will kill you just as I killed your brother Ḥābīl."

So Hibat Allāh and his progeny after him remained hiding the knowledge that they possessed, along with the faith, the Greatest Name, the heirloom of prophethood, and the legacy of the knowledge of prophethood, until God sent down Nūḥ, and Hibat Allāh's bequest to his son was made manifest when they looked into Ādam's bequest. They found therein that Nūḥ was to be a prophet of whom Ādam had given the glad tidings. So they believed in him, followed him and attested to him. Ādam had made a bequest to Hibat Allāh to renew the covenant of this bequest at the start of each new year, and that that would be a day of celebration for them. So they prepared themselves for the advent of Nūḥ and the time in which he would come forth. Thus it was in the will of each prophet until God sent down Muḥammad ﷺ.' [5:27–32]

80. Hishām b. al-Ḥakam said that Abū 'Abd Allāh عليه السلام said, 'When God commanded Ādam to make a bequest to Hibat Allāh, he commanded him to conceal it. So that is how the practice of concealing a bequest continued; so he made a bequest to him, and he concealed that.' [5:27–32]

الله فصلّى على أبيه آدم، وجبرَئيل خلفه وجُنُود الملائكة، وكبّر عليه ثَلاثين تكبيرةً، فأمره جَبْرَئيل فرفع من ذلك خمسًا وعشرين تكبيرةً، والسُّنَّة اليوم فينا خمس تكبيرات، وقد كان يُكبّر على أهل بدر تسعًا وسبعًا.

ثمّ إنّ هِبة الله لمّا دفَن آدم عليه السلام أتاه قابيل، فقال: يا هِبة الله، إنّي قد رأيت أبي آدم قد خصّك من العلم بما لم أُخصَّ به أنا، وهو العلم الذي دعا به أخوك هابيل فتُقُبِّل منه قُربانه، وإنّما قَتَلْتُه لكيلا يكون له عَقِب فيفتخرون على عَقِبي، فيقولون: نحن أبناء الذي تُقبِّل منه قربانه، وأنتم أبناء الذي تُرِك قُربانه، وإنّك إن أظهرت من العلم الذي اختصّك به أبوك شيئًا، قَتَلْتُك كما قَتَلتُ أخاك هابيل.

فلَبِثَ هِبة الله والعَقِب من بعده مُسْتَخْفِين بما عندهم من العلم والإيمان والاسم الأكبر ومِيراث النبوّة وآثار العلم والنبوّة، حتّى بعث الله نُوحًا، وظهرت وصيّة هِبة الله حين نظروا في وصية آدم، فوجدوا نُوحًا نبيًّا قد بشّر به أبوهم آدم، فآمنوا به واتّبعوه وصدّقوه، وقد كان آدم أوصى هِبة الله أن يَتَعاهد هذه الوصيّة عند رأس كُلّ سنةٍ، فيكون يوم عيدهم، فيتعاهدون بعث نُوح وزمانه الذي يخرُج فيه، وكذلك في وصيّة كلّ نبيّ حتّى بعث الله محمّدًا صلى الله عليه وآله وسلم.

٨٠. قال هِشام بن الحَكَم: قال أبو عبد الله عليه السلام: لمّا أمر الله آدم أن يُوصي إلى هِبة الله، أمره أن يَسْتُر ذلك، فجَرت السُّنَّة في ذلك بالكِتمان، فأوصى إليه وأسرّ ذلك.

81. From Jābir, from Abū Ja'far عليه السلام who said, 'Qābīl, the son of Ādam, is suspended by his horns in the middle of the sun, and orbits along with it wherever it orbits, in its bitter cold as well as its fierce heat until the Day of Judgement. When the Day of Judgement comes, God will drive him into the Fire.' [5:27–32]

82. From Zurāra, from Abū Ja'far عليه السلام. He said, 'He mentioned the son of Ādam, the murderer, so I asked him, "What is his condition? Is he from among the inmates of the Fire?" So he replied, "Glory be to God – God is far more just than that, and will combine the chastisement of this world and the Hereafter against him."' [5:27–32]

83. From 'Īsā b. 'Abd Allāh al-'Alawī, on his father's authority, on his forefathers' authority, from 'Alī عليه السلام who said, 'The son of Ādam, who killed his own brother was Qābīl, the one who was born in the garden.' [5:27–32]

84. From Sulaymān b. Khālid who said, 'I said to Abū 'Abd Allāh عليه السلام, "May I be your ransom – people allege that Ādam married his daughter to his son." So Abū 'Abd Allāh عليه السلام said, "People have indeed said that, but do you not know, Sulaymān, that the Messenger of God صلى الله عليه وآله said, 'If I knew that Ādam had married his daughter to his son then I would have got Zaynab married to Qāsim, for I would never move away from the creed of Ādam.'"

So I asked, "May I be your ransom – they also allege that Qābīl killed Ḥābīl because they were both contending over their sister?"

So he said, "Sulaymān, how can you say that? Do you not feel ashamed to narrate such a thing against God's prophet, Ādam?"

So I said, "May I be your ransom – then what did Qābīl kill Ḥābīl for?"

٨١. عن جابر، عن أبي جعفر عليه السلام، قال: إنَّ قابيل ابن آدم مُعلَّق بقُرونه في عين الشمس، تَدُور به حيث دارت في زَمْهَرِيرها وحَمِيمها إلى يوم القيامة، فإذا كان يوم القيامة صَيّره الله إلى النار.

٨٢. عن زُرارة، عن أبي جعفر عليه السلام، قال: ذُكر ابن آدم القاتل، قال: فقلتُ له: ما حاله، أمن أهل النار هو؟ فقال: سُبحان الله! الله أعدل من ذلك أن يجمع عليه عقوبة الدنيا وعقوبة الآخرة.

٨٣. عن عيسى بن عبد الله العلوي، عن أبيه، عن آبائه، عن عليّ عليه السلام، قال: إنّ ابن آدم الذي قَتَل أخاه، كان قابيل الذي وُلِد في الجنَّة.

٨٤. عن سُليمان بن خالد، قال: قلتُ لأبي عبد الله عليه السلام: جُعِلت فداك، إنَّ الناس يَزعُمون أنّ آدم زوّج ابنته من ابنه؟

فقال أبو عبد الله عليه السلام: قد قال الناس في ذلك، ولكن يا سليمان، أما عَلِمت أنّ رسول الله صلى الله عليه وآله قال: لو عَلِمت أنّ آدم زوّج ابنته من ابنه، لزوّجت زينب من القاسم، وما كنت لأرغب عن دين آدم.

فقلتُ: جعلتُ فداك، إنَّهم يَزعُمون أنَّ قابيل إنَّما قَتَل هابيل، لأنَّهما تَغايرا على أُختهما؟

فقال له: يا سليمان، تقول هذا! أما تستحيي أن تروي هذا على نبيّ الله آدم؟

فقلتُ: جُعِلت فِداك، ففيم قَتَل قابيل هابيل؟

So he replied, "For the bequest." Then he said to me, "Sulaymān, God, Blessed and most High, revealed to Ādam to transmit the bequest and the Greatest Name to Ḥābīl, whilst Qābīl was older than him. So when Qābīl heard about this, he became angry and said, 'I am more worthy of the honour and the bequest.' So he commanded them both to offer a sacrifice, by God's revelation to him, and so they did. God accepted Ḥābīl's sacrifice, so Qābīl became jealous of him and killed him."

I then asked, "May I be your ransom – so from whom did Ādam's progeny spread? Was there any other female besides Ḥawwā' and any other man beside Ādam?"

So he replied, "Sulaymān, God, Blessed and most High, first granted Ādam a son from Ḥawwā' who was Qābīl, then a son after him – Ḥābīl. When Qābīl came of age, as men do, God brought forth a female Jinn for him, and revealed to Ādam to get her married to Qābīl. So Ādam did that, and Qābīl was pleased and willing. When Ḥābīl came of age, as men do, God brought down a beautiful maiden of paradise for him, and God revealed to Ādam to get her married to Ḥābīl, and so he did. Then Ḥābīl was killed whilst the heavenly maiden was pregnant. The heavenly maiden gave birth to a boy, whom Ādam named Hibat Allāh. Then God revealed to Ādam to transmit the bequest and the Greatest Name to him. Ḥawwā' gave birth to another boy whom Ādam named Shīth b. Ādam. When he came of age as men do, God sent down a heavenly maiden for him and revealed to Ādam to get her married to Shīth b. Ādam. He did so, and the heavenly maiden gave birth to a girl whom Ādam named Ḥawra. When this girl came of age, Ādam got Ḥawra, daughter of Shīth married to Hibat Allāh, son of Ḥābīl; and the progeny of Ādam proliferated from these two. Then Hibat Allāh, son of Ḥābīl, died, and God revealed to Ādam, 'Transfer the bequest, the Greatest Name, the knowledge of prophethood that I have manifested to you, and the Names that I have taught you to Shīth b. Ādam.' This is their story, Sulaymān."' [5:27–32]

فقال: في الوصيَّة، ثمّ قال لي: يا سُليمان، إنَّ الله تبارك وتعالى أوحى إلى آدم: أن يدفع الوصية واسم الله الأعظم إلى هابيل، وكان قابيل أكبر منه، فبلغ ذلك قابيل فغَضِب، فقال: أنا أولى بالكرامة والوصيَّة، فأمرهما أن يُقرّبا قُربانًا بوحي من الله إليه ففعلا، فقَبِلَ الله قُربان هابيل فحَسَده قابيل فقَتَله.

فقلت له: جُعلتُ فداك، فمَّن تناسل ولد آدم، هل كانت أُنثى غير حوّاء، وهل كان ذَكَرٌ غير آدم؟

فقال: يا سليمان، إنَّ الله تبارك وتعالى رَزَق آدم من حوّاء قابيل، وكان ذَكَر ولده من بعده هابيل، فلمّا أدرك قابيل ما يُدرِك الرجال، أظهر الله له جِنّيّة، أوحى إلى آدم أن يُزوّجها قابيل، ففعل ذلك آدم، ورضي بها قابيل وقَنِع، فلمّا أدرك هابيل ما يُدرِك الرجال، أظهر الله له حَوراء، وأوحى الله إلى آدم أن يُزوّجها من هابيل، ففعل ذلك، فقُتِل هابيل والحوراء حامل، فولدت غُلامًا، فسمّاه آدم عليه السلام هبة الله، فأوحى الله إلى آدم عليه السلام أن ادفع إليه الوصيّة واسم الله الأعظم، وولدت حوّاء غُلامًا فسمّاه آدم شِيث بن آدم، فلمّا أدرك ما يُدرِك الرجال، أهبط الله له حوراء، وأوحى إلى آدم أن يُزوّجها من شِيث بن آدم، ففعل فولدت الحَوْراء جارية، فسمّاها آدم حورة، فلمّا أدركت الجارية زوّج آدم حورة بنتِ شيث من هِبة الله بن هابيل، فنَسْل آدم منهما، فمات هِبة الله بن هابيل، فأوحى الله إلى آدم: أن ادْفع الوصيّة واسم الله الأعظم، وما أظهرتك عليه من عِلم النبوّة، وما علّمتك من الأسماء إلى شِيث بن آدم، فهذا حديثهم يا سليمان.

85. From Ḥumrān b. Aʿyan who said, 'I said to Abū ʿAbd Allāh عليه السلام, asking him about God's verse: ﴾ *On account of [his deed], We decreed to the Children of Isrāʾīl that if anyone kills a person – unless in retribution for murder or spreading corruption in the land – it is as if he kills all mankind, while if any saves a life it is as if he saves the lives of all mankind.* ﴿

He replied, "There is a place in the Fire where the most painful chastisement of all culminates, and he will be placed therein."

I asked, "What if he had killed two people?"

He replied, "Understand that there is truly no place with a more severe chastisement than that. It will be intensified for him proportionate to what he had committed."

I asked, "[What about:] ﴾ *while if any saves a life* ﴿?"

He replied, "If he saves someone from drowning, burning, a wild beast or an enemy." Then he fell silent, then turned to me saying, "Its highest level of inner meaning is that he invites a person [to guidance] and the latter responds."' [5:32]

86. From Samāʿa who said, 'I asked about the verse: ﴾ *On account of [his deed], We decreed to the Children of Isrāʾīl that if anyone kills a person – unless in retribution for murder or spreading corruption in the land – it is as if he kills all mankind, while if any saves a life it is as if he saves the lives of all mankind.* ﴿ He replied, "Whoever has taken someone out of deviation and into guidance has indeed saved his life, and whoever has taken someone from guidance and into deviation has indeed killed him."' [5:32]

87. From Ḥanān b. Sadīr, from Abū ʿAbd Allāh عليه السلام, who said about God's verse: ﴾ *If anyone kills a person [...] it is as if he kills all mankind* ﴿, 'There is a valley in Hell reserved for both the one who has killed all mankind as well as the one who has killed a single person.' [5:32]

88. From Muḥammad b. Muslim, from Abū Jaʿfar عليه السلام; 'I asked him about God's verse: ﴾ *If anyone kills a person – unless in retribution for murder or spreading corruption in the land – it is as if he kills all mankind* ﴿, so he said, "There is a seat for him in the Fire [for a killer], and were he to kill all of mankind, there is no worse punishment than that."

٨٥. عن حُمران بن أعْيَن، قال: قلتُ لأبي عبدالله عليه السلام، قول الله تعالى: ﴿مِنْ أَجْلِ ذَٰلِكَ كَتَبْنَا عَلَىٰ بَنِي إِسْرَائِيلَ أَنَّهُ مَن قَتَلَ نَفْسًا بِغَيْرِ نَفْسٍ﴾ إلى قوله: ﴿فَكَأَنَّمَا قَتَلَ النَّاسَ جَمِيعًا﴾؟

قال: منزلةٌ في النّار، إليها انتهى شدَّة عذاب أهل النار جميعًا، فيُجعَل فيها.

قلت: وإن كان قَتَل اثنين؟

قال: ألا ترى أنَّه ليس في النار منزلةٌ أشدّ عذابًا منها؟ قال: يكون يُضاعَف عليه بقَدر ما عَمِل.

قلت: فَمَنْ أحْياها؟ قال: نجّاها من غَرَقٍ أو حَرَقٍ أو سَبُع أو عَدوّ؛ ثمّ سكت، ثمّ التفت إليّ، فقال: تأويلها الأعظم، دعاها فاستجابت له.

٨٦. عن سَماعة، قال: قلتُ: قول الله تعالى: ﴿مَن قَتَلَ نَفْسًا بِغَيْرِ نَفْسٍ أَوْ فَسَادٍ فِي الْأَرْضِ فَكَأَنَّمَا قَتَلَ النَّاسَ جَمِيعًا وَمَنْ أَحْيَاهَا فَكَأَنَّمَا أَحْيَا النَّاسَ جَمِيعًا﴾؟ قال: من أخرجها من ضلالٍ إلى هُدى فقد أحياها، ومن أخرجها من هُدى إلى ضلال فقد قتلها.

٨٧. عن حَنان بن سَدير، عن أبي عبدالله عليه السلام، في قول الله: ﴿مَن قَتَلَ نَفْسًا... فَكَأَنَّمَا أَحْيَا النَّاسَ جَمِيعًا﴾، قال: وادٍ في جهنّم لو قَتَل الناس جميعًا كان فيه، ولو قَتَل نفسًا واحدةً كان فيه.

٨٨. عن محمّد بن مسلم، عن أبي جعفر عليه السلام، قال: سألتُه عن قول الله عزّ وجلّ: ﴿مَن قَتَلَ نَفْسًا بِغَيْرِ نَفْسٍ أَوْ فَسَادٍ فِي الْأَرْضِ فَكَأَنَّمَا قَتَلَ النَّاسَ جَمِيعًا﴾. فقال: له في النار مقعدٌ، لو قتل الناس جميعًا لم يُزَد على ذلك العذاب.

He continued, "Whilst if he saves a life, it is as if he has saved the lives of all mankind, whether it be desisting from killing someone, or saving him from drowning or a fire, or even more significant than all of those – to take someone out of deviation and into guidance."' [5:32]

89. From Abū Baṣīr, from Abū Jaʿfar عليه السلام. He said, 'I asked him about: ﴿ *if any saves a life it is as if he saves the lives of all mankind.* ﴾ He replied, "Whoever removes someone from disbelief and into belief."' [5:32]

90. From Muḥammad b. Muslim, from Abū Jaʿfar عليه السلام who said, 'Whoever takes up arms in one of the major cities and manages to wound people, he must be counterattacked and banished from that city. Whoever takes up arms outside of the major cities, attacks, wounds, and loots property but does not kill is still a warmonger. His punishment is that of a warmonger, and he is to be referred to the Imam. If he wishes, he can either kill him, crucify him, or amputate his hand and foot.'

He continued, 'And if he wages war, kills, and loots property, then the Imam must amputate his hand for the looting, and then hand him over to the family of the murdered. They can then take legal action against him for the property, and kill him.'

Abū ʿUbayda asked him, 'May God make you prosper – what if the victim's family pardon him?' So Abū Jaʿfar عليه السلام replied, 'If they pardon him, then the Imam must kill him, because he waged war, killed and looted.'

Abū ʿUbayda then asked him, 'And if the victim's family wanted to get blood-money from him, then leave him [alive], can they do that?' He replied, 'No, he must be killed.' [5:33]

91. From Abū Ṣāliḥ, from Abū ʿAbd Allāh عليه السلام who said, 'A group of people from Banī Ḍabba came to the Messenger of God ﷺ, so he said to them, "You may stay here with me, and when you are strong enough I will send you out on a campaign."

قال: ﴿وَمَنۡ أَحۡيَاهَا فَكَأَنَّمَا أَحۡيَا ٱلنَّاسَ جَمِيعٗا﴾ لم يَقْتُلها، أو أنجى من غَرَق أو حَرق، وأعظم من ذلك كلّه يُخْرِجها من ضَلالةٍ إلى هُدى.

٨٩. عن أبي بصير، عن أبي جعفر عليه السلام، قال: سألته ﴿وَمَنۡ أَحۡيَاهَا فَكَأَنَّمَا أَحۡيَا ٱلنَّاسَ جَمِيعٗا﴾، قال: من استخرجها من الكُفر إلى الإيمان.

٩٠. عن محمّد بن مسلم، عن أبي جعفر عليه السلام، قال: من شَهَر السلاح في مِصرٍ من الأمصار فعَقَر اقْتُصّ منه، ونُفي من تلك البلدة، ومن شَهَر السلاح في غير الأمصار وضَرَب وعَقَر وأخذ المال ولم يَقتُل فهو محارِب، جزاؤه جزاء المحارِب، وأمره إلى الإمام، إن شاء قتله وصلبه، وإن شاء قطع يده ورجله.

قال: وإن حارب وقتل وأخذ المال، فعلى الإمام أن يقطع يده اليمين بالسرقة، ثمّ يدفعه إلى أولياء المقتول فيتّبعونه بالمال، ثمّ يقتلونه.

فقال له أبو عبيدة: أصلحك الله، أرأيت إن عفا عنه أولياء المقتول؟ فقال أبو جعفر عليه السلام: إن عَفَوا عنه فعلى الإمام أن يَقْتُله، لأنّه قد حارَبَ وقَتَل وسَرَق.

فقال له أبو عبيدة: فإن أراد أولياء المقتول أن يأخُذوا منه الدِّيَة ويَدَعُونه، ألهم ذلك؟ قال: لا، عليه القتل.

٩١. عن أبي صالح، عن أبي عبدالله عليه السلام، قال: قَدِم على رسول الله صلى الله عليه وآله قومٌ من بني ضَبَّة مرضى، فقال لهم رسول الله صلى الله عليه وآله: أقيموا عندي، فإذا قويتم بَعَثْتُكُم في سَرِيَّة.

So they said, “Take us out of Medina.” So he sent them out to the camels used for charity to drink their urine and eat of their dairy products. As soon as they felt better and regained their strength, they killed three of the shepherds and rode the camels away. This news reached the Messenger of God ﷺ and he sent ʿAlī عليه السلام after them. They were in a valley near the land of Yemen, too bewildered to be able to leave from there. So he took them and brought them to the Messenger of God ﷺ, and the verse: ﴾ *Those who wage war against God and His Messenger and strive to spread corruption in the land should be punished by death, crucifixion, the amputation of an alternate hand and foot, or banishment from the land* ﴿ was revealed about them. So the Messenger of God ﷺ chose to amputate alternate hands and feet of theirs.’ [5:33]

92. From Aḥmad b. al-Faḍl al-Khāqānī, from Āl Razīn who said, ‘A highway robbery took place in Jalawlāʾ upon the pilgrims and others who were traversing the main road, and the brigands escaped. News of this reached al-Muʿtaṣim, so he wrote to his worker there saying, “Declare the road to be safe [for travel], and let the brigands attack by permission from the commander of the faithful. Then when the robbers escape, go after them and capture them. If you do not, I will order you to be flogged with a thousand lashes and crucified where the highway robbery took place.”’

He said, ‘So the worker sought them, managed to capture them, and correctly identified them. Then he wrote to al-Muʿtaṣim who had gathered all the jurists, including Ibn Abī Duʾād. Then he asked them all about the ruling on them, whilst Abū Jaʿfar Muḥammad b. al-Riḍā عليه السلام was present there. So they said, “God’s ruling has already come down about them in the verse: ﴾ *Those who wage war against God and His Messenger and strive to spread corruption in the land should be punished by death, crucifixion, the amputation of an alternate hand and foot, or banishment from the land* ﴿, and it is up to the commander of the faithful to decide which of these he chooses concerning them.”

So he turned to Abū Jaʿfar عليه السلام and said to him, “What do you say about how they answered this?” So he said, “These people and the judge have already spoken as the commander of the faithful just heard.” So he insisted, “So now tell me what you think.”

فقالوا: أخرجْنا من المدينة، فبعث بهم إلى إبل الصَّدقة يشربون من أبوالها، يأكلون من ألبانها، فلمّا برئوا واشتدّوا قتلوا ثلاثة نفرٍ كانوا في الإبل، وساقوا الإبل، فبلغ رسول الله ﷺ فبعث إليهم عليّاً عليه السلام، وهم في وادٍ قد تحيّروا، ليس يَقْدِرون أن يَخْرُجوا عنه، قريب من أرض اليمن، فأخذهم فجاء بهم إلى رسول الله ﷺ، ونزلت عليه ﴿إِنَّمَا جَـزَاءُ الَّذِينَ يُحَـارِبُونَ اللَّهَ وَرَسُولَهُ﴾ إلى قوله: ﴿أَوْ يُنفَوْا مِنَ الأَرْضِ﴾، فاختار رسول الله ﷺ قطع أيديهم وأرجلهم من خِلاف.

٩٢. عن أحمد بن الفضل الخاقاني، من آل رَزين، قال: قُطِع الطريق بجَلَولاَء على السابلة من الحُجّاج وغيرهم، وأفلت القُطّاع، فبلغ الخبر المعتصم، فكتب إلى العامل الذي كان بها: أتأمن الطريق بذلك، فقُطع على طرف أُذن أمير المؤمنين، ثمّ انفلت القُطّاع، فإن أنت طلبت هؤلاء وظَفِرت بهم، وإلاّ أمرت بأن تُضْرَب ألف سوط، ثمّ تُصْلَب بحيث قُطع الطريق.

قال: وطلبهم العامل حتّى ظَفِر بهم، واستوثق منهم، ثمّ كتب بذلك إلى المعتصم، فجمع الفقهاء وفيهم ابن أبي دؤاد، ثمّ سأل الآخرين عن الحكم فيهم، وأبو جعفر محمّد بن علي الرضا عليه السلام حاضرٌ، فقالوا: قد سبق حُكم الله فيهم في قوله: ﴿إِنَّمَا جَزَاءُ الَّذِينَ يُحَارِبُونَ اللَّهَ وَرَسُولَهُ وَيَسْعَوْنَ فِي الأَرْضِ فَسَادًا أَنْ يُقَتَّلُوا أَوْ يُصَلَّبُوا أَوْ تُقَطَّعَ أَيْدِيهِمْ وَأَرْجُلُهُمْ مِنْ خِـلَافٍ أَوْ يُنفَوْا مِنَ الأَرْضِ﴾ ولأمير المؤمنين أن يحكم بأيّ ذلك شاء فيهم.

قال: واخْبرني بما عندك. قال: إنّهم قد أضلّوا فيما أفتوا به، والَّذي يجب في ذلك أن يَنْظُر أمير المؤمنين في هؤلاء الذين قطعوا الطريق، فإن كانوا أخافوا السبيل فقط، ولم يَقْتُلوا أحدًا، ولم يأخُذوا مالاً، أمر بإيداعهم الحَبْس، فإنّ ذلك معنى نفيهم من الأرض

He said, "They are mistaken in their ruling. What must be done here is for the commander of the faithful to look into what these brigands did. If they were merely terrorizing people on the road, and neither killed anyone nor looted property, then he must command for a warrant for their arrest, for this is the meaning of their banishment from the land – for their terrorizing on the path. If they terrorized people *and* killed as well, then he must order for them to be killed. If they terrorized, killed and looted property, then he must order for their hands and feet to be amputated alternately, and for them to be crucified after that."

So he wrote to the worker to do exactly that with them.' [5:33]

93. From Burayd b. Muʿāwiya al-ʿIjlī who said, 'A man asked Abū ʿAbd Allāh عليه السلام about God's verse: ﴾ *Those who wage war against God and His Messenger and strive to spread corruption in the land.* ﴿ He replied, "That is up to the Imam to do with him as he wishes." I asked, "So is it entirely at the Imam's discretion?" He replied, "No. It has to fit the crime."' [5:33]

94. From Samāʿa b. Mihrān, from Abū ʿAbd Allāh عليه السلام regarding God's verse: ﴾ *Those who wage war against God and His Messenger and strive to spread corruption in the land should be punished by death, crucifixion, the amputation of an alternate hand and foot, or banishment from the land.* ﴿ He said, 'The ruling on them is at the Imam's discretion, whether he wants to kill, crucify, amputate or banish from the land.' [5:33]

95. From Zurāra, from one of the two [Imams al-Bāqir or al-Ṣādiq] who said regarding the verse: ﴾ *Those who wage war against God and His Messenger and strive to spread corruption in the land should be punished by death, crucifixion, the amputation of an alternate hand and foot, or banishment from the land: a disgrace for them in this world, and then a terrible punishment in the Hereafter* ﴿, 'One must not transact with them, nor bring them food, nor give them charity.' [5:33]

96. From Jamīl b. Darrāj who said, 'I asked Abū ʿAbd Allāh عليه السلام about God's verse: ﴾ *Those who wage war against God and His Messenger and strive to spread corruption in the land should be punished by death, crucifixion, the amputation of an alternate hand and foot, or banishment from the land: a*

بإخافتهم السبيل. وإن كانوا أخافوا السبيل، وقتلوا النفس، أمر بقتلهم، وإن كانوا أخافوا السبيل، وقتلوا النفس، وأخذوا المال، أمر بقطع أيديهم وأرجلهم من خلاف وصلبهم بعد ذلك، قال: فكتب إلى العامل بأن يمثّل ذلك فيهم.

٩٣. عن بُريد بن مُعاوية العِجلي، قال سأل رجل أبا عبدالله عليه السلام عن قول الله: ﴿إِنَّمَا جَزَاءُ الَّذِينَ يُحَارِبُونَ اللَّهَ وَرَسُولَهُ﴾ إلى قوله: ﴿فَسَادًا﴾، قال: ذلك إلى الإمام، يعمل فيه بما شاء.

قلت: ذلك مفوّض إلى الإمام؟ قال: لا، بحقّ الجناية.

٩٤. عن سَماعة بن مِهران، عن أبي عبدالله عليه السلام، في قول الله تعالى: ﴿إِنَّمَا جَزَاءُ الَّذِينَ يُحَارِبُونَ اللَّهَ وَرَسُولَهُ﴾، قال: الإمام في الحكم فيهم بالخِيار، إن شاء قتل: وإن شاء صَلَب، وإن شاء قَطع، وإن شاء نفى من الأرض.

٩٥. عن زُرارة، عن أحدهما عليه السلام، في قوله: ﴿إِنَّمَا جَزَاءُ الَّذِينَ يُحَارِبُونَ اللَّهَ وَرَسُولَهُ﴾ إلى قوله: ﴿أَوْ يُصَلَّبُوا﴾ الآية، قال: لا يُبايع، ولا يُؤتى بطعام، ولا يُتَصَدّق عليه.

٩٦. عن جميل بن دَرّاج، قال: سألتُ أبا عبدالله عليه السلام عن قول الله: ﴿إِنَّمَا جَزَاءُ الَّذِينَ يُحَارِبُونَ اللَّهَ وَرَسُولَهُ﴾ الآية إلى آخرها، أيّ شيءٍ عليهم من هذا الحدّ الذي سمّى؟ قال: ذلك إلى الإمام، إن شاء قطع، وإن شاء صلب، وإن شاء قتل، وإن شاء نفى.

disgrace for them in this world, and then a terrible punishment in the Hereafter﴿ – which one of these punishments listed must be meted out to them? He replied, "That is up to the Imam to decide. He can amputate them if he wishes, or crucify, kill, or banish if he so wishes." I asked, "Banishment to where?" He replied, "From one city to another," and he said, "'Alī ﵇ had banished two men from Kufa to Basra."' [5:33]

97. From Sawra b. Kulayb[8], from Abū Ja'far ﵇; he said, 'I asked: "A man goes out from his house to the mosque in the middle of the night to pray when he is approached by a man who strikes him with a stick and steals his robe." He said, "So how have the people responded to you about this matter previously?" He replied, "They say that this man is not considered a warmonger since someone who wages war is one who operates in disbelieving villages, whereas this is an assault."

So he said, "Which is more important: the sanctity of an Islamic place or a disbelieving place?"' He said, 'I replied, "The Islamic place, of course."

So he said, "These are the very people about whom God says: ﴾*Those who wage war against God and His Messenger and strive to spread corruption in the land should be punished by death, crucifixion, the amputation of an alternate hand and foot, or banishment from the land: a disgrace for them in this world, and then a terrible punishment in the Hereafter.*﴿"' [5:33]

98. In a narration from Samā'a, from Abū 'Abd Allāh ﵇ who said, 'When a man fornicates he must be lashed, and the Imam must banish him from the land in which he was lashed to another land for a year. The same must be done with the man who steals and his hand is amputated.' [5:33]

99. From Abū Isḥāq al-Madā'inī who said, 'I was with Abū al-Ḥasan ﵇ when a man entered and said to him, "May I be your ransom – God says: ﴾*Those who wage war against God and His Messenger and strive to spread corruption in the land should be punished by death, crucifixion, the amputation of an alternate hand and foot, or banishment from the land*﴿" He replied, "Yes, that is exactly what God has said."

8 Sawra b. Kulayb, a narrator from Muḥammad al-Bāqir and Ja'far al-Ṣādiq. His reliability is, however, unascertained. See Ḥillī, *Khulāṣat al-aqwāl*, 165–6 (nr. 480).

قلتُ: النفي إلى أين؟ قال: من مِصر إلى مِصرٍ آخر، وقال: إنَّ علياً عليه السلام قد نفى رجلين من الكوفة إلى البصرة.

٩٧. عن سَورة بن كُليب، عن أبي جعفر عليه السلام، قال: قلتُ: الرجل يخرُج من منزله إلى المسجد يُريد الصلاة ليلاً، فيستقبله رجلٌ فيَضْرِبه بِعصا، ويأخُذ ثوبه؟ قال: فما يقول فيه مَن قِبَلكم؟ قال: يقولون: إنَّ هذا ليس بمُحارب، وإنَّما المحارب في القُرى المُشركيّة، وإنّما هي دَغارة.

قال: فأيّهما أعظم حُرمةً دار الإسلام، أو دار الشرك؟ قال: قلتُ: لا بل دار الإسلام. فقال: هؤلاء من الذين قال الله: ﴿إِنَّمَا جَزَاءُ الَّذِينَ يُحَارِبُونَ اللَّهَ وَرَسُولَهُ﴾ إلى آخر الآية.

٩٨. وفي رواية سَماعة، عن أبي عبد الله عليه السلام، قال: إذا زنى الرجل يُجلَد، وينبغي للإمام أن ينفيه من الأرض التي جُلِد بها إلى غيرها سَنَةً، وكذلك ينبغي للرجل إذا سرق وقُطِعت يده.

٩٩. عن أبي إسحاق المدايني، قال: كنتُ عند أبي الحسن عليه السلام إذ دخل عليه رجلٌ فقال له: جُعِلتُ فداك، إنَّ الله يقول: ﴿إِنَّمَا جَزَاءُ الَّذِينَ يُحَارِبُونَ اللَّهَ وَرَسُولَهُ﴾ إلى ﴿أَوْ يُنفَوْا﴾؟ فقال: هكذا قال الله تعالى.

فقال له: جُعِلتُ فِداك، فأيّ شيءٍ الذي إذا فعله استحقّ واحدةً من هذه الأربع؟

قال: فقال له أبو الحسن عليه السلام: أربع فخُذ أربعًا بأربع، إذا حارب الله ورسوله وسعى في الأرض فسادًا فقَتَل قُتِل وأخذ المال قُتِل وصُلِب، وإن أخذ المال ولم يَقْتُل قُطِعت

So he said to him, "May I be your ransom – what kind of thing is it that would make one merit one of these four were he to commit it?"'

He said, 'So Abū al-Ḥasan ﷺ said to him, "Four [punishments] so consider four [crimes] in their stead. If he wages war against God and His Messenger and strives to spread corruption in the land and kills, then he is to be killed. If he kills and snatches property, then he is killed and crucified. If he steals property but does not kill, his hand and foot are amputated alternately. If he wages war against God and His Messenger, striving to spread corruption in the land but neither kills nor snatches property, then he is to be banished from the land."

So the man asked him, "May I be your ransom – what is the extent of his banishment?"

He replied, "He is to be banished from the city in which he committed the crime to another one. Then the people of that town should be forewarned about him that he has been banished so that they do not entertain him to eat and drink together, nor marry anyone to him. If he leaves that town for another, then they too should be written to similarly, and this is what must be done to him for a year, after which he will repent, being degraded thus."

Then the man asked him, "May I be your ransom – what if he goes to a disbelieving town and enters it?"

He replied, "He would be beheaded if he wished to go to a disbelieving town."' [5:33]

100. In Abū Isḥāq al-Madā'inī's narration from Abū al-Ḥasan al-Riḍā ﷺ, I said, 'What if he heads towards a disbelieving land and enters it?' He replied, 'Its people must be fought.' [5:33]

101. From Abū Baṣīr who said, 'I heard Abū Ja'far ﷺ say, "The enemies of 'Alī are the ones who will abide eternally in the Hellfire; God says: ﴾ *they will be unable to come out of it.* ﴿"' [5:37]

102. From Manṣūr b. Ḥāzim who said, 'I asked Abū 'Abd Allāh ﷺ about: ﴾ *they will be unable to come out of* ﴿ the Fire. He replied, "The enemies of 'Alī are the ones who will abide eternally in the Fire forever and for all eternity."' [5:37]

يده ورِجله من خلاف، وإن حارب الله ورسوله وسعى في الأرض فسادًا ولم يَقْتُل ولم يَأخُذ المال نُفي من الأرض.

فقال له الرجل: جُعِلتُ فِداك، وما حدّ نفيه؟

قال: يُنفى من المِصر الذي فعل فيه ما فعل إلى غيره، ثمّ يُكْتَب إلى أهل ذلك المِصر أن يُنادى عليه بأنّه منفيّ، فلا تُؤاكلوه، ولا تُشاربوه، ولا تناكحوه، فإذا خرج من ذلك المِصر إلى غيره كُتِب إليهم بمثل ذلك، فيفعل به ذلك سنة، فإنّه سيتوب من السنة وهو صاغرٌ.

فقال له الرجل: جُعِلت فداك، فإن أتى أرض الشِرك فدخلها؟ قال: يُضْرَب عُنُقه إن أراد الدُّخول في أرض الشِرك.

١٠٠. وفي رواية أبي إسحاق المدايني، عن أبي الحسن الرضا ﴿عليه السلام﴾، قلتُ: فإن توجّه إلى أرض الشِرك فيَدْخُلها؟ قال: قُوتِل أهلُها.

١٠١. عن أبي بصير، قال: سَمِعتُ أبا جعفر ﴿عليه السلام﴾ يقول: عدوّ عليّ ﴿عليه السلام﴾ هم المُخَلّدون في النار، قال الله: ﴿وَمَا هُم بِخَارِجِينَ مِنْهَا﴾.

١٠٢. عن منصور بن حازم، قال: قلتُ لأبي عبدالله ﴿عليه السلام﴾: ﴿وَمَا هُم بِخَارِجِينَ مِنَ النَّارِ﴾؟ قال أعداء عليّ هم المخلَّدون في النار أبد الآبدين ودهر الداهرين.

103. From Ḥammād b. ʿĪsā, from one of his associates, from Abū ʿAbd Allāh ﷺ, that he was asked about dry ablution (*tayammum*), so he recited this verse: ﴾*Cut off the hands of thieves, whether they are man or woman, as punishment*﴿, and: ﴾*wash your faces and your hands up to the elbows.*﴿(5:6) He said, 'So wipe over your two palms from the point of the amputation.' He said: ﴾*And your Lord is never forgetful.*﴿(19:64)' [5:38]

104. He said, 'Abū Muḥammad wrote to us mentioning from Ibn Abī ʿUmayr, from Ibrāhīm b. ʿAbd al-Ḥamīd, from his Sunni associates, tracing it back to the Commander of the Faithful ﷺ that when he used to amputate the hand of a thief, he used to leave the thumb and the palm. He would be asked, "O Commander of the Faithful, you have left most of the hand?" He said, "So he would reply to them, 'And if he repents, what will he use to do ablution? For indeed God says: ﴾*Cut off the hands of thieves, whether they are man or woman, as punishment for what they have done– a deterrent from God* [...] *But if anyone repents after his wrongdoing and makes amends, God will accept his repentance: God is most forgiving, most merciful.*﴿'" [5:38]

105. From Zurāra, from Abū Jaʿfar ﷺ regarding a man who stole, so his right hand was amputated. Then he stole again, so his left foot was amputated. Then he stole a third time. He said, 'The Commander of the Faithful ﷺ sentenced him to life in prison and said, "I would be too ashamed of my Lord to leave him without a hand with which to clean himself and without a foot on which to walk to fulfil his needs."' He continued, 'When he used to amputate the hand, he would cut it above the joints, and when he amputated the foot, it would be cut below the ankle.' He said, 'He was never negligent about any aspect of legal punishments.' [5:38]

106. From Samāʿa, from Abū ʿAbd Allāh ﷺ that he said, 'When the thief is arrested, the middle of his hand is to be amputated. If he repeats the crime, then he is to be cut from the middle of the foot. If he reoffends, then he is to be imprisoned. And if he steals in prison, then he must be killed.' [5:38]

١٠٣. عن حمّاد بن عيسى، عن بعض أصحابه، عن أبي عبد الله ﵇، أنّه سُئِل عن التيمّم، فتلا هذه الآية ﴿وَالسَّارِقُ وَالسَّارِقَةُ فَاقْطَعُوا أَيْدِيَهُمَا جَزَاءً﴾، وقال: ﴿فَاغْسِلُوا وُجُوهَكُمْ وَأَيْدِيَكُمْ إِلَى الْمَرَافِقِ﴾، قال: فامْسح على كفّيك من حيث موضع القطع، قال: ﴿وَمَا كَانَ رَبُّكَ نَسِيًّا﴾.

١٠٤. قال: وكتب إلينا أبو محمّد يذكُر عن أبن أبي عمير، عن إبراهيم بن عبد الحميد، عن عامّة أصحابه، يرفعه إلى أمير المؤمنين ﵇، أنّه كان إذا قطع السارق، ترك له الإبهام والراحة.

فقيل له: يا أمير المؤمنين، تركت عامّة يده؟ قال: فقال لهم: فإن تاب، فبأيّ شيءٍ يتوضّأ؟ لأنّ الله يقول: ﴿وَالسَّارِقُ وَالسَّارِقَةُ فَاقْطَعُوا أَيْدِيَهُمَا جَزَاءً بِمَا كَسَبَا نَكَالًا مِنَ اللَّهِ ... فَمَنْ تَابَ مِنْ بَعْدِ ظُلْمِهِ وَأَصْلَحَ فَإِنَّ اللَّهَ يَتُوبُ عَلَيْهِ إِنَّ اللَّهَ غَفُورٌ رَحِيمٌ﴾.

١٠٥. عن زُرارة، عن أبي جعفر ﵇، عن رجلٍ سَرَق فقُطِعت يده اليُمنى، ثمّ سَرَق فقُطِعت رِجله اليُسرى، ثمّ سرق الثالثة، قال: كان أمير المؤمنين ﵇ يُخلّده في السِّجن، ويقول: إنّي لأَستحيي من ربّي أن أدعه بلا يد يستنظف بها، ولا رجل يمشي بها إلى حاجته، قال: وكان إذا قطع اليد قطعها دون المفْصِل، وإذا قطع الرِجل قطعها دون الكَعْبين، قال: وكان لا يرى أن يُغْفَل عن شيءٍ من الحدود.

١٠٦. عن سَماعة، عن أبي عبد الله ﵇، أنّه قال: إذا أُخذ السارق قُطِع من وسط الكفّ، فإن عاد قُطِعت رجله من وسط القدم، فإن عاد استُودِع السجن، فإن سرق في السجن قُتِل.

107. From al-Sakūnī, from Jaʿfar b. Muḥammad, on his father's authority, from ʿAlī that a thief was once brought before him, so he amputated his hand. Then he was brought before him again, so he amputated his left foot. Then he was brought before him a third time, so he said, 'I am truly too ashamed of my Lord to not leave him a hand with which to eat, drink and clean himself after relieving himself, nor a foot to walk with. So flog him and imprison him, covering his expenses from the treasury.' [5:38]

108. From Jamīl, from one of our associates, from one of the two [Imams al-Bāqir or al-Ṣādiq] that he said, 'The thief is not amputated unless he persists with stealing twice and goes back to stealing again, and he is not to be amputated without a testimony.' [5:38]

109. From al-Sakūnī, from Jaʿfar on his father's authority, peace be upon them both. He said, 'Only the one who breaks into a house or breaks a lock must be amputated.' [5:38]

110. From Zurqān, Ibn Abī Du'ād's very close friend and associate who said, 'Ibn Abī Du'ād was returning one day from al-Muʿtaṣim's palace, sorrowful. So I asked him about it, and he said, "Today I wished that I had already died twenty years ago."' He said, 'I asked him, "Why is that?"

He replied, "Because of what happened today with that black man Abū Jaʿfar Muḥammad b. ʿAlī b. Mūsā [i.e. Imam al-Jawād] right in front of the commander of the faithful, al-Muʿtaṣim."'

He said, 'I asked him, "What happened?"

He replied, "A thief confessed to his crime of stealing and asked the Caliph to absolve him by castigating him with the due punishment. So he gathered all the jurists together in his council, and Muḥammad b. ʿAlī عليه السلام was also present there. So we were asked about the point from which the amputation should commence. So I said, 'From the wrist.' He asked, 'What is the proof for that?' I said, 'Because the hand consists of the palm and the fingers until the wrist, because of God's statement about dry ablution: ﴾*and wipe a part of your faces and your hands with it*﴿(5:6); and a group of people agreed with me about that.

Others said, 'It must be cut from the elbow.'

He asked, 'What is it that indicates to that?'

١٠٧. عن السّكوني، عن جعفر بن محمّد، عن أبيه، عن عليّ ﷺ، أنّه أُتي بسارق فقَطَع يده، ثمّ أُتي به مرةً أُخرى فقَطعَ رِجله اليسرى، ثمّ أُتي به ثالثة، فقال: إنّي لأَستحيي من ربّي أنْ لا أدع له يدًا يأكُل بها، ويشرب بها، ويستنجي بها، ورِجلاً يمشي عليها،فجلَدَه واستودعَه السِجن، وأنفق عليه من بيت المال.

١٠٨. عن جميل، عن بعض أصحابنا، عن أحدهما ﷺ، أنّه قال: لا يُقْطَع السارق حتّى يُقِرّ بالسرقة مرّتين، فإن رجع ضَمِن السَّرقة، ولم يُقْطَع إذا لم يَكُن له شُهُود.

١٠٩. عن السّكوني، عن جعفر، عن أبيه ﷺ، قال: لا يُقْطَع إلاّ من نَقَب بيتًا، أوكسر قُفلاً.

١١٠. عن زُرقان صاحب ابن أبي دؤاد وصديقه بشدّة، قال: رجع ابن أبي دؤاد ذات يوم من عند المعتصم وهو مغتمّ، فقلت له في ذلك، فقال: وددتُ اليوم أنّي قد مُتُّ منذ عشرين سنة. قال: قلت له: ولِمَ ذاك؟ قال: لِما كان من هذا الأسود أبي جعفر محمّد بن عليّ بن موسى اليوم بين يدي أمير المؤمنين المعتصم.

قال: قلتُ له: وكيف كان ذلك؟ قال: إنَّ سارقًا أقرّ على نفسه بالسرقة، وسأل الخليفة تطهيره بإقامة الحدّ عليه،فجمع لذلك الفُقهاء في مجلسه، وقد أحضر محمّد ابن عليّ، فسألنا عن القطع، في أي موضع يجب أن يُقْطَع. قال: فقلتُ: من الكُرسُوع.

قال: وما الحُجَّة في ذلك؟ قال: قلتُ: لأنَّ اليد هي الأصابع والكفّ إلى الكُرسُوع، لقول الله تعالى في التيمّم: ﴿فَامْسَحُوا بِوُجُوهِكُمْ وَأَيْدِيكُمْ﴾ واتّفق معي على ذلك قوم.

They replied, 'Because of when God says: ﴾*Wash ... your hands up to the elbows*﴿ whilst washing. This shows that the hand extends all the way to the elbow.'"

He said, "Then he turned to Muḥammad b. 'Alī ﷺ and asked, 'What do you say about this, O Abū Ja'far?'

So he replied, 'The people have already spoken about it, O commander of the faithful.'

He said, 'Let me decide if they have spoken or not. What do you say?'

He replied, 'Absolve me from this, O commander of the faithful.'

He said, 'I swear by God against you if you do not inform me of your opinion on the matter.'

So he said, 'If you are going to swear by God against me, then I will tell you that they are mistaken about that practice, for the amputation must be from the joints at the base of the fingers, and the palm must be left alone.'

He asked, 'And what is the proof for that?'

He replied, 'The Messenger of God, peace be upon him and his family, said, "Prostration is incumbent upon seven parts of the body: the face, the two hands, the two knees, and the two feet." So if you cut his hand off from the wrist or the elbow, then he will be left with no hand with which to prostrate. God, Blessed and most High, has said: ﴾*the places of prostration are for God alone*﴿ meaning these seven parts of the body that he prostrates with ﴾*so do not pray to anyone other than God.*﴿(72:18) Whatever is for God cannot be cut off."

He continued, 'So Mu'taṣim was impressed with that, and ordered for the thief's hand to be amputated from the finger joints above the palm.'

Ibn Abī Du'ād said, 'I was mortified and wished that I were not alive.'

Zurqān narrated, "Ibn Abī Du'ād said, 'I went to al-Mu'taṣim three days later and said, "Advising the commander of the faithful is a duty that is incumbent upon me, and I must convey what I know to him lest I enter the Fire as a result of it."

He asked, "What is it?"

I replied, "When the commander of the faithful summons together to his council all the jurists and scholars from among his subjects to discuss a pressing matter of religion, and asks them about the ruling for it, and they inform him of their opinions, in the presence of members of his family, his generals, ministers and scribes as well as members of the public listening in

وقال آخرون: بل يجب القطع من المِرْفق، قال: وما الدليل على ذلك؟ قالوا: لأنَّ الله لمّا قال: ﴿وَأَيْدِيَكُمْ إِلَى الْمَرَافِقِ﴾ في الغسل،دلّ ذلك على أنّ حدّ اليد هو المِرْفق.

قال: فالتفت إلى محمّد بن علي، فقال: ما تقول في هذا، يا أبا جعفر؟ فقال: قد تكلّم القوم فيه، يا أمير المؤمنين، قال: دعني ممّا تكلّموا به، أيّ شيءٍ عندك؟ قال: أعفني عن هذا، يا أمير المؤمنين.

قال: أقسمت عليك بالله لمّا أخبرتَ بما عندك فيه. فقال: أمّا إذا أقسمت عليّ بالله، إنّي أقول إنّهم أخطئوا فيه السُّنَّة، فإنّ القطع يجب أن يكون من مَفْصِل أُصول الأصابع، فيُتْرَك الكَفّ.

قال: وما الحُجَّة في ذلك؟ قال: قول رسول الله صلّى الله عليه وآله وسلّم: «السُّجودُ على سبعة أعضاء: الوجه، واليدين، والرُّكبتين، والرجلين» فإذا قطعت يده من الكُرْسُوع أو المِرْفق، لم يبقَ له يدٌ يَسْجُد عليها، وقال الله تبارك وتعالى: ﴿وَأَنَّ الْمَسَاجِدَ لِلَّهِ﴾ يعني به هذه الأعضاء السبعة التي يُسْجَد عليها ﴿فَلَا تَدْعُوا مَعَ اللَّهِ أَحَدًا﴾، وماكان لله لم يُقْطَع.

قال: فأعجب المعتصم ذلك، وأمر بقطع يد السارق من مَفْصِل الأصابع دون الكفّ. قال ابن أبي دؤاد: قامت قيامتي وتمنّيتُ أنّي لم أكُ حيًّا.

قال زُرقان: إنّ ابن أبي دؤاد قال: صِرتُ إلى المعتصم بعد ثلاثة، فقلت: إنَّ نصيحة أمير المؤمنين عليّ واجبة، وأنا أُكلّمه بما أعلم أنّي أدخُل به النار. قال: وما هو؟

قلت: إذا جمع أمير المؤمنين في مجلسه فُقهاء رعيّته وعلماءهم لأمرٍ واقعٍ من أُمور الدين، فسألهم عن الحكم فيه، فأخبروه بما عندهم من الحكم في ذلك، وقد حضر المجلس

from behind the door. Then he leaves all of their statements in favour of the opinion of a man whom a constituency of this community believe to be their Imam, claiming that he is worthier of this position than them. Then he goes on to accept his ruling over the ruling of the jurists?"'

He continued, 'So his face changed colour, and he took note of what I had just alerted him to saying, "May God reward you well for your advice."'

He continued, 'On the fourth day, he commanded one of his ministerial scribes to invite him [i.e. the Imam] to his house. He did so, but he refused saying: "You know that I do not attend your gatherings."

So he replied, "I am, in fact, inviting you to a meal and would appreciate it if you would grace me with your presence in entering my home so that I may be blessed thereby. So and so from among the caliph's ministers will gladly come and fetch you."

So he went to his house and when he ate there, he sensed poison in his food. So he called for his horse, even while the host was asking him to stay on. He replied, "My leaving your house is better for you." He عليه السلام survived that day and night, and then died.' [5:38]

111. From Sulaymān b. Khālid who said, 'I heard Abū 'Abd Allāh عليه السلام say, "When God wills something good for His servant, He places a white spot inside his heart, opens the ears of his heart and assigns an angel to him to guide his steps. When God wills something bad for His servant, He places a black spot inside his heart and blocks the ears of his heart and assigns a devil to him to mislead him." Then he recited this verse: ﴾ *When God wishes to guide someone, He opens their breast to Islam; when He wishes to lead them astray, He closes and constricts their breast as if they were climbing up to the skies. That is how God makes the foulness of those who do not believe rebound against them* ﴿ (6:125), and he said: ﴾ *Those against whom your Lord's sentence is passed will not believe* ﴿ (10:96) and: ﴾ *These are the ones whose hearts God does not intend to cleanse.* ﴿' [5:41]

112. From al-Ḥasan b. 'Alī al-Washshā', from al-Riḍā عليه السلام. He said, 'I heard him say, "The profit from selling a dog is unlawful, and unlawful earnings merit the Fire."' [5:42]

أهل بيته وقُوّاده ووزراؤه وكُتّابه، وقد تسامع الناس بذلك من وراء بابه، ثمّ أقاويلهم كُلّهم لقول رجلٍ يقول شَطْر هذه الأُمّة بإمامته، ويَدَّعون أنه أولى منه بمقامه، ثمّ يحكم بحكمه دون حُكم الفُقهاء؟!

قال: فتغيَّر لونُه، وانتبه لما نبَّهته له، وقال: جزاك الله عن نصيحتك خيرًا.

قال: فأمر يوم الرابع فلانًا من كُتّاب وزرائه بأن يدعوه إلى منزله، فدعاه فأبى أن يجيبه، وقال: قد عَلِمتَ أنّي لا أحضُر مجالسكم. فقال: إنّي إنّما أدعوك إلى الطعام، وأُحبُّ أن تطأ ثيابي، وتدخل منزلي، فأتبرّك بذلك، وقد أحبّ فلان ابن فلان من وزراء الخليفة لقاءك؛ فصار إليه فلمّا أطعَمَ منها أحسّ السمَّ فدعا بدابّته، فسأله ربّ المنزل أن يُقيم، قال: خُروجي من دارك خيرٌ لك، فلم يزَل يومه ذلك وليله في خِلْفةٍ حتّى قُبِض عليه السلام.

١١١. عن سليمان بن خالد، قال: سَمِعتُ أبا عبد الله عليه السلام يقول: إنَّ الله إذا أراد بعبدٍ خيرًا نَكت في قلبه نُكتةً بيضاء، وفتح مسامع قلبه، ووكَّل به مَلَكًا يُسدّده، وإذا أراد الله بعبد سوءًا نَكَت في قلبه نُكتةً سوداء وسدّ مسامع قلبه، ووكَّل به شيطانًا يُضِلُّه، ثمّ تلا هذه الآية ﴿فَمَنْ يُرِدِ اللهُ أَنْ يَهْدِيَهُ يَشْرَحْ صَدْرَهُ لِلإِسْلاَمِ وَمَنْ يُرِدْ أَنْ يُضِلَّهُ يَجْعَلْ صَدْرَهُ ضَيِّقًا حَرَجًا﴾ الآية، وقال: ﴿إِنَّ الَّذِينَ حَقَّتْ عَلَيْهِمْ كَلِمَةُ رَبِّكَ لاَ يُؤْمِنُونَ﴾ وقال: ﴿أُولَئِكَ الَّذِينَ لَمْ يُرِدِ اللهُ أَنْ يُطَهِّرَ قُلُوبَهُمْ﴾.

١١٢. عن الحسن بن علي الوشّاء، عن الرضا عليه السلام، قال: سَمِعتُه يقول: ثَمَن الكَلْب سُحْتٌ، والسُّحتُ في النار.

113. From Samā'a b. Mihrān, from Abū 'Abd Allāh and Abū al-Ḥasan Mūsā, peace be upon them both, who said, 'Unlawful gains are of many kinds, some of which are: the cupping practitioner (who earns from unlawful means), the prostitute's charge and the sale of wine. As for bribing in the course of justice, that is disbelief in God.' [5:42]

114. From Jarrāḥ al-Madā'inī[9], from Abū 'Abd Allāh عليه السلام who said, 'One of the unlawful gains is bribery in the course of justice.' Also from him, 'And the prostitute's payment.' [5:42]

115. From Muḥammad b. Muslim, from Abū 'Abd Allāh عليه السلام who said, 'The [earnings from the] sale of a dog who is not used for hunting is unlawful.' He also said, 'There is no problem in the sale of a cat.' [5:42]

116. From 'Ammār b. Marwān who said, 'I asked Abū 'Abd Allāh عليه السلام about unlawful gains from war booty, so he replied, "Anything that is defrauded from the Imam is unlawful, as well as the unlawful consumption of the property of the orphan. Unlawful gains are of many kinds, including the profit made from the properties of oppressive governors, the charges of the judges and corrupt individuals, and the sale of wine, spirits, intoxicants and usury after they have been declared unlawful. As for the bribes given in the course of justice, O 'Ammār, that is disbelief in God and His Messenger."' [5:42]

117. From al-Sakūnī, from Abū Ja'far, on his father's authority, peace be upon them both, that he used to forbid the eating of walnuts that children brought home from their gambles saying, 'They are unlawful gains.' [5:42]

118. With the same chain of transmission on his father's authority, from 'Alī عليه السلام, that he said, 'Unlawful gains include the sale of carrion, dogs, wine, pork, the prostitute's payment, the bribe in the course of justice and the fortune-teller's fee.' [5:42]

---

9 Al-Jarrāḥ al-Madā'inī, a companion of the fifth and sixth Imams. See Khū'ī, *Mu'jam*, 4:359–60 (nr. 2086); Modarressi, *Tradition and Survival*, 309 (nr. 121).

١١٣. عن سَماعة بن مِهران، عن أبي عبدالله وأبي الحسن موسى عليه السلام، قال: السُّحت أنواع كثيرة، منها: كسب الحجّام، وأجر الزانية، وثمن الخَمر، فأما الرِّشا في الحُكم فهو الكُفر بالله.

١١٤. عن جرّاح المَدايني، عن أبي عبدالله عليه السلام، قال: مِن أكل السُّحت: الرَّشْوة في الحُكم، وعنه عليه السلام: ومَهر البغيّ.

١١٥. عن محمّد بن مسلم، عن أبي عبدالله عليه السلام، قال: ثَمَن الكلب الذي لا يصيد سُحتٌ، وقال: لا بأس بثمن الهِرّة.

١١٦. عن عمّار بن مَروان، قال: سألتُ أبا عبدالله عليه السلام عن الغُلول. فقال: كلُّ شيءٍ غُلّ عن الإمام فهو السُّحت، وأكلُ مال اليتيم شبهه، والسُّحت أنواعُ كثيرةٌ، منها ما أُصيب من أعمال الولاة الظَّلَمَة، ومنها أُجور القضاة، وأُجور الفواجر، وثَمَن الخمر، والنبيذ المُسكر، والرِّبا بعد البيّنة، فأمّا الرِّشا في الأحكام يا عمّار، فإنّ ذلك الكفر بالله وبرسوله.

١١٧. عن السَّكوني، عن جعفر، عن أبيه عليه السلام أنّه كان ينهى عن الجَوزِ الذي يجيء به الصبيان من القمار أن يُؤكَل، وقال: هو السُّحت.

١١٨. وبإسناده عن أبيه، عن علي عليه السلام، أنّه قال: إنّ السُّحت ثَمَن الميْتَة، وثَمَن الكلب، وثَمَن الخمر، ومَهْر البغيّ، والرَّشوة في الحُكم، وأجر الكاهِن.

119. From Mālik al-Juhnī[10] who said, 'Abū Ja'far عليه السلام said: ﴿ *We revealed the Torah with guidance and light, and the prophets, who had submitted to God, judged according to it for the Jews. So did the rabbis and the scholars in accordance with that part of God's Scripture which they were entrusted to preserve.* ﴾' He said, 'It came down regarding us.' [5:44]

120. From Abū 'Amr al-Zubayrī, from Abū 'Abd Allāh عليه السلام, 'Among the prerequisites of Imamate are purification and immaculacy from sins and grave acts of disobedience that are necessarily punishable by the Fire. Then enlightening knowledge of everything to do with the community's needs as regards the permissible and the prohibited, knowledge of the Scripture: both the general aspects of it as well as the specific, the decisive and the ambiguous, the minute details of its contents, its unique inner meanings and its abrogating and abrogated verses.' I asked, 'What is the proof that it can only be an Imam who is knowledgeable about these things that you mentioned?' He replied, 'God's statement about those whom God Himself has permitted rulership to and those who are worthy of it: ﴿ *We revealed the Torah with guidance and light, and the prophets, who had submitted to God, judged according to it for the Jews. So did the rabbis and the scholars* [...] ﴾ So these are the leaders who nurture people with their knowledge aside from the prophets. The scholars are the people of knowledge, different to the rabbis.' Then He informed us saying: ﴿ *in accordance with that part of God's Scripture which they were entrusted to preserve.* ﴾ He did not say 'which they carried.' [5:44]

121. From 'Abd Allāh b. Muskān, from Abū 'Abd Allāh عليه السلام, on his father's authority, from his forefathers, peace be upon them, who said, 'The Messenger of God صلى الله عليه وآله said, "Whoever passes an oppressive judgement against someone regarding a mere two dirhams then forces it upon him, this verse applies to him: ﴿ *those who do not judge according to what God has sent down are rejecting* [*God's teachings*]. ﴾" So I asked, "O son of God's Messenger, how would he force him?" He replied, "He may have a whip or a prison by which to coerce him, so if he accepts his judgement, then fine. However, if he does not, then he harms him with his whip or incarcerates him in his prison."' [5:44]

10 On whom there is little information; see Ḥillī, *Khulāṣat al-aqwāl*, 411 (nr. 1665).

١١٩. عن مالك الجُهني، قال: قال أبو جعفر عليه السلام: ﴿إِنَّا أَنزَلْنَا التَّوْرَاةَ فِيهَا هُدًى وَنُورٌ﴾ إلى قوله: ﴿بِمَا اسْتُحْفِظُوا مِن كِتَابِ اللَّهِ﴾، قال: فينا نزلت.

١٢٠. عن أبي عمرو الزبيري، عن أبي عبدالله عليه السلام: أنَّ ممّا أستُحِقَّت به الإمامة: التطهير، والطهارة من الذنوب والمعاصي الموبقة الّتي تُوجب النار، ثمّ العِلم المنُوّر. بجميع ما تحتاج إليه الأُمّة من حلالها وحرامها، والعلم بكتابها خاصّه، وعامّه، والمُحكم والمُتشابه، ودقائق علمه، وغرائب تأويله، وناسخه ومنسوخه.

قلت: وما الحُجَّة بأنَّ الإمام لا يكون إلاّ عالمًا بهذه الأشياء الذي ذكرت؟

قال: قول الله في من أذِن الله لهم في الحُكومة وجعلهم أهلها: ﴿إِنَّا أَنزَلْنَا التَّوْرَاةَ فِيهَا هُدًى وَنُورٌ يَحْكُمُ بِهَا النَّبِيُّونَ الَّذِينَ أَسْلَمُوا لِلَّذِينَ هَادُوا وَالرَّبَّانِيُّونَ وَالْأَحْبَارُ﴾ فهذه الأئمّة دون الأنبياء الذين يرثون الناس بعلمهم، وأمّا الأحبار فهم العُلماء دون الربّانيّين، ثمّ أخبر فقال: ﴿بِمَا اسْتُحْفِظُوا مِن كِتَابِ اللَّهِ وَكَانُوا عَلَيْهِ شُهَدَاءَ﴾ ولم يَقُل بما حملوا منه.

١٢١. عن عبدالله بن مُسكان، عن أبي عبدالله، عن أبيه، عن آبائه عليهم السلام، قال: قال رسول الله صلى الله عليه وآله وسلم: من حكم في دِرهَمين حُكم جَور ثمّ جبر عليه، كان من أهل هذه الآية ﴿وَمَن لَّمْ يَحْكُم بِمَا أَنزَلَ اللَّهُ فَأُولَٰئِكَ هُمُ الْكَافِرُونَ﴾.

فقلتُ: يا ابن رسول الله: وكيف: [يجبُرُ] عليه؟ قال: يكون له سَوط وسِجن فيحكُم عليه، فإن رضي بحكومته، وإلاّ ضَرَبه بسَوطه وحَبَسه في سِجنه.

122. From Abū Baṣīr, from Abū ʿAbd Allāh عليه السلام who said, 'Whoever judges regarding a mere two dirhams contrary to what God has revealed has indeed rejected [His teachings], and whoever judges regarding two dirhams and makes a mistake in his judgement has rejected [His teachings].' [5:44]

123. From Abū Baṣīr b. ʿAlī, from Abū ʿAbd Allāh عليه السلام. He said, 'I heard him say, "Whoever judges regarding a mere two dirhams contrary to what God has revealed is indeed a disbeliever in God, the Great."' [5:44]

124. From one of his associates who said, 'I heard ʿAmmār say from the pulpit in Kufa, "There are three that bear witness against ʿUthmān that he is a disbeliever, and I am the fourth, and I will name the four. Then he read these verses from the *Chapter of the Feast*: ﴿*those who do not judge according to what God has sent down are rejecting* [*God's teachings*] [...] *they are doing grave wrong*﴾ ﴿*they are the lawbreakers.*﴾(5:47)"' [5:44]

125. From Abū Baṣīr, from Abū Jaʿfar عليه السلام who said, "Alī عليه السلام said, "Whoever judges regarding a mere two dirhams contrary to what God has revealed has indeed rejected [His teachings]."' [5:44]

126. From Ibn Sinān, from Abū ʿAbd Allāh عليه السلام who said, 'The Commander of the Faithful عليه السلام, in the case of the blood money payable for a nose that had been cut clean off, ruled for one hundred camels to be paid: thirty suckling she-camels not more than three years old, thirty suckling she-camels not more than two years old, twenty camels of six years of age, and twenty male suckling camels. The blood money payable for an eye that had been gouged was fifty camels; for a penis that was cut from the glans, accidentally and not intentionally, was one hundred camels, as was the case for a leg that had been cut. Similarly, the blood money for a hand cut off was fifty camels, and fifty camels too for an ear that was cut clean off.' He continued, 'And that did not apply to wounds or to punitive measures used to discipline slaves, which someone vested with justice from among you, meaning an Imam, must judge separately.' He said: ﴿*those who do not judge according to what God has sent down are rejecting* [*God's teachings*].﴾' [5:44]

١٢٢. عن أبي بصير، عن أبي عبد الله ﵇، قال: من حَكَمَ في دِرْهَمين بغير ما أنزل الله فقد كفر، ومن حكم في دِرْهَمين فأخطأ كفر.

١٢٣. عن أبي بصير بن علي، عن أبي عبد الله ﵇، قال: سَمِعتُه يقول: من حَكَمَ في دِرْهَمين بغير ما أنزل الله، فهو كافر بالله العظيم.

١٢٤. عن بعض أصحابه، قال: سَمِعتُ عمّارًا يقول على مِنبَر الكوفة: ثلاثة يَشْهَدون على عُثمان أنّه كافر، وأنا الرابع، وأنا أُسمّي الأربعة، ثمّ قرأ هؤلاء الآيات في المائدة ﴿وَمَنْ لَمْ يَحْكُمْ بِمَا أَنْزَلَ اللهُ فَأُولَئِكَ هُمُ الْكَافِرُونَ﴾ و ﴿...الظَّالِمُونَ﴾ و ﴿...الْفَاسِقُونَ﴾.

١٢٥. عن أبي بصير، عن أبي جعفر ﵇، قال: قال عليّ ﵇: من قضى في دِرْهَمين بغير ما أنزل الله، فقد كفر.

١٢٦. عن ابن سِنان، عن أبي عبد الله ﵇، قال: قضى أمير المؤمنين ﵇ في دِيَةِ الأنف إذا استؤصل مائة من الإبل: ثلاثون حِقّة، وثَلاثون بنت لَبُون، وعشرون بنت مَخاض، وعشرون ابن لَبُون ذَكَر، ودِيَة العين إذا فُقِئت خمسون من الإبل، ودِيَة ذَكَر الرجل إذا قُطع من الحَشَفة مائة من الإبل، على أسباب الخطأ دون العَمْد، وكذلك دِيَة الرِّجل، وكذلك دِيَة اليد إذا قُطِعت خمسون من الإبل، وكذلك دِيَة الأُذن إذا قُطِعت فَجُدِعت خمسون من الإبل.

قال: وما كان ذلك من جُرُوح أو تَنكيل فيَحْكُم به ذو عدل منكم، يعني به الإمام، قال: ﴿وَمَنْ لَمْ يَحْكُمْ بِمَا أَنْزَلَ اللهُ فَأُولَئِكَ هُمُ الْكَافِرُونَ﴾.

127. From Ibn Sinān, from Abū ʿAbd Allāh عليه السلام who said, 'The blood money for a nose that has been cut clean off is one hundred camels, for an eye that has been gouged out it is fifty camels, for a hand that has been cut off, fifty camels. For a penis that has been cut off, it is one hundred camels and for an ear that has been cut clean off, fifty camels. Other injuries such as wounds, exemplary punishments, the finger and the like are to be judged individually by one vested with justice from among you, and ﴾*those who do not judge according to what God has sent down are rejecting* [*God's teachings*].﴿' [5:44]

128. From Abū al-ʿAbbās, from Abū ʿAbd Allāh عليه السلام who said, 'Whoever judges regarding a mere two dirhams contrary to what God has revealed has indeed rejected [His teachings].' I asked, 'Would he have rejected everything that God has revealed or only what He has revealed to Muḥammad صلى الله عليه وآله specifically?' He said, 'Woe unto you! If he rejects what was revealed to Muḥammad صلى الله عليه وآله, is that not tantamount to rejecting all that God has revealed?' [5:44]

129. From Ḥafṣ b. Ghiyāth, from Jaʿfar b. Muḥammad عليه السلام who said, 'God sent Muḥammad down with five swords. One of these swords is sheathed: it is up to others to draw it and up to us to issue the ruling. This sheathed sword is the one with which retaliations are executed. God, Mighty and Exalted, says: ﴾*a life for a life, an eye for an eye, a nose for a nose, an ear for an ear, a tooth for a tooth, an equal wound for a wound: if anyone forgoes this out of charity, it will serve as atonement for his bad deeds. Those who do not judge according to what God has revealed are doing grave wrong.*﴿ So drawing the sword is up to the family of the victim, and issuing the ruling for it is up to us.' [5:45]

130. From Abū Baṣīr who said, 'I asked Abū ʿAbd Allāh عليه السلام about: ﴾*If anyone forgoes this out of charity, it will serve as atonement for his bad deeds.*﴿ He said, "It atones for his bad deeds in proportion to the injury that he forwent."' [5:45]

١٢٧. عن ابن سِنان، عن أبي عبدالله عليه السلام، قال: دِيَة الأنف إذا استؤصل مائة من الإبل، والعين إذا فُقِئت خمسون من الإبل، واليد إذا قُطِعت خمسون من الإبل، وفي الذَّكَر إذا قُطِع مائة من الإبل، وفي الأُذن إذا جُدعت خمسون من الإبل، وما كان من ذلك جُروحًا دون المثُلات، والإصْبَع وشِبهه، يحكُم به ذو عدلٍ منكم ﴿وَمَنْ لَمْ يَحْكُمْ بِمَا أَنْزَلَ اللهُ فَأُولَئِكَ هُمُ الْكَافِرُونَ﴾.

١٢٨. عن أبي العباس، عن أبي عبدالله عليه السلام، قال: من حَكَم في دِرْهَمين بغير ما أنزل الله، فقد كفر.

قلت: كَفَر بما أنزل الله، أو بما أُنزِل على محمّد صلى الله عليه وآله وسلم؟ قال: ويلك إذا كفر بما أُنزِل على محمّد صلى الله عليه وآله وسلم، أليس قد كَفَر بما أنزل الله؟

١٢٩. عن حَفص بن غِياث، عن جعفر بن محمّد عليه السلام، قال: إنّ الله بعث محمّدًا صلى الله عليه وآله وسلم بخمسة أسياف، سيف منها مغمود سلّه إلى غيرنا وحُكمه إلينا، فأمّا السيف المغمود فهو الذي يُقام به القِصاص، قال الله جلّ وجهه: ﴿النَّفْسَ بِالنَّفْسِ﴾ الآية، فسلّه إلى أولياء المقتول، وحُكمه إلينا.

١٣٠. عن أبي بصير، قال: سألتُ أبا عبدالله عليه السلام ﴿فَمَنْ تَصَدَّقَ بِهِ فَهُوَ كَفَّارَةٌ لَهُ﴾؟ قال: يُكَفَّر عنه من ذُنوبه بقدر ما عفا من جِراحٍ أو غيره.

131. From Abū Jamīla, from one of his associates, from one of the two [Imams al-Bāqir or al-Ṣādiq] who said, 'God set aside an obligatory share of the *khums* for the family of Muḥammad ﷺ, but Abū Bakr refused to give them their share out of jealousy and animosity, when God had said: ﴾*Those who do not judge according to what God has revealed are doing grave wrong.*﴿ Abū Bakr was the first to deny the family of Muḥammad, peace be upon them, their right; he oppressed them and turned people against them. When Abū Bakr died, 'Umar succeeded him with neither consensus from the Muslims nor consent from the family of Muḥammad ﷺ. So 'Umar carried on, in the same way, not giving the family of Muḥammad their right, and did exactly as Abū Bakr did.' [5:45]

132. From Sulaymān b. Khālid, from Abū 'Abd Allāh عليه السلام who said, 'Neither the Jew nor the Christian nor the Magian must be judged by other than God's law. God says: ﴾*so judge between them according to what God has sent down.*﴿' [5:49]

133. From Abū Baṣīr, from Abū Ja'far عليه السلام who said, 'The law is of two types: God's law and pre-Islamic pagan law.' Then he said: ﴾*Is there any better judge than God for those of firm faith?*﴿ He continued, 'So bear witness that Zayd [ibn Thābit] had judged according to pagan law, i.e. concerning the incumbent duties.' [5:50]

134. From Dāwūd al-Raqqī who said, 'A man asked Abū 'Abd Allāh عليه السلام in my presence about God's verse: ﴾*But God may well bring about a triumph or some other event of His own making: then they will rue the secrets they harboured in their hearts.*﴿ So he replied, "This refers to the destruction of the Banī Umayya seven days after Zayd's body was burnt."' [5:52]

١٣١. عن أبي جميلة، عن بعض أصحابه، عن أحدهما ﴿عليه السلام﴾، قال: قد فرض الله في الخُمس نصيبًا لآل محمّد ﷺ، فأبى أبو بكر أن يُعطيهم نصيبهم حَسَدًا وعَداوةً، وقد قال الله: ﴿وَمَن لَّمْ يَحْكُم بِمَا أَنزَلَ اللّٰهُ فَأُولَٰئِكَ هُمُ الْفَاسِقُونَ﴾ وكان أبو بكر أوّل من منع آل محمّد ﴿عليه السلام﴾ حقّهم، وظَلَمهم، وحمل الناس على رقابهم، ولمّا قُبِض أبو بكر استخلف عمر على غير شورى من المسلمين، ولا رضا من آل محمّد ﷺ، فعاش عمر بذلك لم يُعطِ آل محمّد حقّهم، وصنع ما صنع أبو بكر.

١٣٢. عن سليمان بن خالد، عن أبي عبدالله ﴿عليه السلام﴾، قال: لا يُحلَّف اليهوديّ ولا النصرانيّ، ولا المجوسيّ بغير الله، إنّ الله يقول: ﴿فَاحْكُم بَيْنَهُم بِمَا أَنزَلَ اللّٰهُ﴾.

١٣٣. عن أبي بصير، عن أبي جعفر ﴿عليه السلام﴾، قال: إنّ الحكم حُكمان: حُكم الله، وحكم الجاهليّة، ثم قال: ﴿وَمَنْ أَحْسَنُ مِنَ اللّٰهِ حُكْمًا لِّقَوْمٍ يُوقِنُونَ﴾، قال: فأشهد أنّ زيدًا قد حَكَم بحُكم الجاهلية، يعني في الفرايض.

١٣٤. عن داود الرّقي، قال: سأل أبا عبدالله ﴿عليه السلام﴾ رجل وأنا حاضر، عن قول الله سبحانه وتعالى: ﴿فَعَسَى اللّٰهُ أَن يَأْتِيَ بِالْفَتْحِ أَوْ أَمْرٍ مِّنْ عِندِهِ فَيُصْبِحُوا عَلَىٰ مَا أَسَرُّوا فِي أَنفُسِهِمْ نَادِمِينَ﴾.

فقال: أذِن في هلاك بني أُميّة بعد إحراق زيد بسبعة أيّام.

135. From Abū Baṣīr who said, 'Abū Ja'far ﷺ says that al-Ḥakam b. 'Utayba, Salama, Kathīr al-Nawwā', Abū al-Miqdām, and al-Tammār, meaning Sālim, have led many people astray from those who were misled by these people; and they are among those about whom God says: ﴿*Some people say, "We believe in God and the Last Day," when really they do not believe*﴾(2:8) and they are among those about whom God says: ﴿*they swore by God using their strongest oaths that they were with you. All they did was in vain: they have lost everything.*﴾' [5:53]

136. From Sulaymān b. Hārūn[11] who said, 'I said to him that some of these '*Ijla* claim that the sword belonging to the Messenger of God is now in the possession of 'Abd Allāh b. al-Ḥasan.' So he said, 'By God, neither they nor their father have ever seen it from one of their two eyes unless his father noticed it with al-Ḥusayn ﷺ. It is preserved for the one vested with this authority, so do not go right nor left for by God, the position is clear. By God, if all the inhabitants of the sky and the earth were to come together to turn this authority away from the places wherein God has placed it, they would not be able to. If all of the people were to reject faith such that no one remained, God would bring about a people who would be worthy of this position.' Then he continued, 'Have you not heard God's statement: ﴿*You who believe, if any of you go back on your faith, God will soon replace you with people He loves and who love Him, people who are humble towards the believers, hard on the disbelievers*﴾ until he had finished that verse and recited another verse: ﴿*Even if these people now disbelieve in them, We have entrusted them to others who do not disbelieve.*﴾(6:89) Then he said that this verse referred specifically to the people about whom that verse applied to.' [5:54]

11 Sulaymān b. Hārūn, on whom there is scant information. See Khū'ī, *Mu'jam*, 9:297 (nr. 5526).

١٣٥. عن أبي بصير، قال: أبو جعفر عليه السلام يقول: إنّ الحكم بن عُتيبة وسَلَمة، وكثير النّواء، وأبا المِقدام، والتمّار - يعني سالمًا - أضلّوا كثيرًا ممّن ضلّ من هؤلاء الناس، وإنّهم ممّن قال الله: ﴿وَمِنَ النَّاسِ مَنْ يَقُولُ آمَنَّا بِاللَّهِ وَبِالْيَوْمِ الْآخِرِ وَمَا هُمْ بِمُؤْمِنِينَ﴾ وإنّهم ممّن قال الله: ﴿أَقْسَمُوا بِاللَّهِ جَهْدَ أَيْمَانِهِمْ﴾ يحلفون بالله ﴿إِنَّهُمْ لَمَعَكُمْ حَبِطَتْ أَعْمَالُهُمْ فَأَصْبَحُوا خَاسِرِينَ﴾.

١٣٦. عن سُليمان بن هارون، قال: قلتُ له: إنّ بعض هذه العِجلَة يقولون: إنّ سيف رسول الله صلى الله عليه وآله وسلم عند عبدالله بن الحسن؟

فقال: والله ما رآه هو ولا أبوه بواحدةٍ من عينيه، إلاّ أن يكون رآه أبوه الحسين عليه السلام، وإنّ صاحب هذا الأمر محفوظٌ له، فلا تذهبنّ يمينًا ولا شمالاً، فإنّ الأمر والله واضحٌ، والله لو أنّ أهل السماء والأرض اجتمعوا على أن يحوّلوا هذا الأمر من موضعه الذي وضعه الله فيه ما استطاعوا، ولو أنّ الناس كفروا جميعًا حتّى لا يبقى أحدٌ لجَاء الله لهذا الأمر بأهلٍ يكونون من أهله.

ثم قال: أما تسمع الله يقول: ﴿يَا أَيُّهَا الَّذِينَ آمَنُوا مَنْ يَرْتَدَّ مِنْكُمْ عَنْ دِينِهِ فَسَوْفَ يَأْتِي اللَّهُ بِقَوْمٍ يُحِبُّهُمْ وَيُحِبُّونَهُ أَذِلَّةٍ عَلَى الْمُؤْمِنِينَ أَعِزَّةٍ عَلَى الْكَافِرِينَ﴾؟ حتّى فرغ من الآية - وقال في آية أُخرى: ﴿فَإِنْ يَكْفُرْ بِهَا هَؤُلَاءِ فَقَدْ وَكَّلْنَا بِهَا قَوْمًا لَيْسُوا بِهَا بِكَافِرِينَ﴾ ثمّ قال: إنّ أهل هذه الآية هم أهل تلك الآية.

137. From one of his associates, from a man, from Abū ʿAbd Allāh عليه السلام. He said, 'I asked him about this verse: ﴾ *God will soon replace you with people He loves and who love Him, people who are humble towards the believers, hard on the disbelievers.* ﴿ He replied, "The protégés."' [5:54]

138. From Khālid b. Yazīd[12], from al-Maʿmar b. al-Makkī, from Isḥāq b. ʿAbd Allāh b. Muḥammad b. ʿAlī b. al-Ḥusayn, from al-Ḥasan b. Zayd, from his father Zayd b. al-Ḥasan, on his grandfather's authority عليه السلام who said, 'I heard ʿAmmār b. Yāsir say, "A beggar came and stood before ʿAlī b. Abī Ṭālib while he was bowing in his supererogatory prayer, so he removed his ring and gave it to the beggar. So when the Messenger of God صلى الله عليه وآله came, he informed him of that and this verse was revealed to the Prophet صلى الله عليه وآله: ﴾ *Your guardian is only God, His Messenger, and the believers who maintain the prayer and pay the prescribed alms while bowing down in worship.* ﴿ So the Messenger of God صلى الله عليه وآله recited it to us, then he said, "For whosoever I am master, ʿAlī is his master. O God, protect whoever adheres to him and oppose whoever opposes him."' [5:55]

139. From Ibn Abī Yaʿfūr who said, 'I said to Abū ʿAbd Allāh عليه السلام, "I present to you my faith with which I believe in God." He said, "Hand it over." I said, "I bear witness that there is no god but God, and I bear witness that Muḥammad صلى الله عليه وآله is the Messenger of God, and I attest to that which he brought from God."' He continued, 'Then I listed the Imams to him until I reached Abū Jaʿfar. Then I said, "And I attest to you the same way that I believe in them." So he said, "I forbid you from mentioning my name outside in public."'

Abān said that Ibn Abī Yaʿfūr said, 'I also said to him along with my first statement, "And I proclaim that they are the ones about whom God says in the Qur'an: ﴾ *You who believe, obey God and the Messenger, and those in authority among you.* ﴿(4:59)" So Abū ʿAbd Allāh said, "Now recite the verse after it?"

So I said, "May I be your ransom – which verse?"

---

12 Khālid b. Yazīd al-Bajalī, about whom there is scant information. See Khūʾī, *Muʿjam*, 8:43 (nr. 4234).

١٣٧. عن بعض أصحابه، عن رجل، عن أبي عبد الله عليه السلام، قال: سألتُه عن هذه الآية ﴿فَسَوْفَ يَأْتِي اللَّهُ بِقَوْمٍ يُحِبُّهُمْ وَيُحِبُّونَهُ أَذِلَّةٍ عَلَى الْمُؤْمِنِينَ أَعِزَّةٍ عَلَى الْكَافِرِينَ﴾ قال: الموالي.

١٣٨. عن خالد بن يزيد، عن المَعْمَر بن المكّي، عن إسحاق بن عبد الله ابن محمّد بن علي بن الحسين عليه السلام، عن الحسن بن زيد، عن أبيه زيد بن الحسن، عن جدّه عليه السلام، قال: سَمِعتُ عمّار بن ياسر يقول: وقف لعليّ بن أبي طالب عليه السلام سائلٌ وهو راكع في صلاة تطوُّع، فنزع خاتَمَه، فأعطاه السائل، فأتى رسول الله صلى الله عليه وآله، فأعلمه بذلك، فنزل على النبيّ صلى الله عليه وآله هذه الآية ﴿إِنَّمَا وَلِيُّكُمُ اللَّهُ وَرَسُولُهُ وَالَّذِينَ آمَنُوا الَّذِينَ يُقِيمُونَ الصَّلَاةَ وَيُؤْتُونَ الزَّكَاةَ وَهُمْ رَاكِعُونَ﴾ فقرأها رسول الله صلى الله عليه وآله علينا، ثم قال: «من كنتُ مولاه، فعليٌّ مولاه، اللّهم والِ من والاه، وعادِ من عاداه».

١٣٩. عن ابن أبي يعفور، قال: قلتُ لأبي عبد الله عليه السلام: أعرِض عليك ديني الذي أدينُ الله به؟ قال: هاته. قلتُ: أشهد أن لا إله إلاّ الله، وأشهد أنّ محمّدًا رسول الله، وأُقِرّ بما جاء به من عند الله، قال: ثمّ وصفتُ له الأئمّة حتّى انتهيتُ إلى أبي جعفر عليه السلام، قلتُ: وأُقِرّ بك ما أقول فيهم، فقال: أنهاك أن تذهب باسمي في الناس.

قال أبان: قال ابن أبي يعفور: قلتُ له مع الكلام الأوّل: وأزعُم أنّهم الذين قال الله في القرآن ﴿أَطِيعُوا اللَّهَ وَأَطِيعُوا الرَّسُولَ وَأُولِي الْأَمْرِ مِنْكُمْ﴾. فقال أبو عبد الله عليه السلام: والآية الأُخرى فاقرأ.

قال: قلتُ له: جُعِلت فِداك، أيّ آية؟

He replied: ﴾*Your guardian is only God, His Messenger, and the believers who maintain the prayer and pay the prescribed alms while bowing down in worship.*﴿

Then he said, "May God have mercy on you."

He said, 'I asked, "Are you saying may God have mercy on you for [acknowledging] this authority?"

He replied, "May God have mercy on you for [acknowledging] this authority."' [5:55]

140. From Abū Ḥamza, from Abū Ja'far عليه السلام who said, 'Whilst the Messenger of God, peace be upon him and his family, was sitting in his house, there was a Jewish man with him – or he said five Jews and among them was – 'Abd Allāh b. Sallām, when this verse was revealed: ﴾*Your guardian is only God, His Messenger, and the believers who maintain the prayer and pay the prescribed alms while bowing down in worship.*﴿ So the Messenger of God ﷺ left them in his house and went out to the mosque, and there was a beggar there. The Messenger of God ﷺ asked him, "Did anyone give you something in charity?" He replied, "Yes, that man praying over there." It was 'Alī عليه السلام.' [5:55]

141. From al-Mufaḍḍal b. Ṣāliḥ, from one of his associates, from one of the two [Imams al-Bāqir or al-Ṣādiq] who said, 'When this verse was revealed: ﴾*Your guardian is only God, His Messenger, and the believers who maintain the prayer and pay the prescribed alms while bowing down in worship*﴿, it was challenging for the Prophet ﷺ and he feared that the Quraysh would belie him, so God revealed: ﴾*Messenger, proclaim everything that has been sent down to you from your Lord – if you do not, then you will not have communicated His message – and God will protect you from people. God does not guide those who defy Him.*﴿(5:67) So he undertook that on the day of Ghadīr Khumm.' [5:55]

142. From Abū Jamīla, from one of his associates, from one of the two [Imams al-Bāqir or al-Ṣādiq] who said, 'The Messenger of God ﷺ said, "Indeed, God has revealed to me to love four people: 'Alī, Abū Dharr, Salmān, and al-Miqdād."'

قال: ﴿إِنَّمَا وَلِيُّكُمُ اللَّهُ وَرَسُولُهُ وَالَّذِينَ آمَنُوا الَّذِينَ يُقِيمُونَ الصَّلَاةَ وَيُؤْتُونَ الزَّكَاةَ وَهُمْ رَاكِعُونَ﴾.

قال: فقال: رَحِمك الله. قال: قلت: تقول: رحمك الله على هذا الأمر؟ قال: فقال: رَحِمك الله على هذا الأمر.

١٤٠. عن أبي حمزة، عن أبي جعفر عليه السلام، قال: بينا رسول الله صلى الله عليه وآله جالسٌ في بيته، وعنده نفرٌ من اليهود — أو قال: خمسة من اليهود — فيهم عبد الله بن سلاّم، فنزلت هذه الآية: ﴿إِنَّمَا وَلِيُّكُمُ اللَّهُ وَرَسُولُهُ وَالَّذِينَ آمَنُوا الَّذِينَ يُقِيمُونَ الصَّلَاةَ وَيُؤْتُونَ الزَّكَاةَ وَهُمْ رَاكِعُونَ﴾ فتركهم رسول الله صلى الله عليه وآله في منزله، وخرج إلى المسجد، فإذا بسائلٍ، فقال له رسول الله صلى الله عليه وآله: أصَدّق عليك أحدٌ بشيءٍ؟ قال: نعم، هو ذاك المُصلّي، فإذا هو عليّ عليه السلام.

١٤١. عن المفضَّل بن صالح، عن بعض أصحابه، عن أحدهما عليه السلام، قال: إنّه لمّا نزلت هذه الآية ﴿إِنَّمَا وَلِيُّكُمُ اللَّهُ وَرَسُولُهُ وَالَّذِينَ آمَنُوا﴾ شقّ ذلك على النبيّ صلى الله عليه وآله، وخشي أن تُكذّبه قُريش، فأنزل الله ﴿يَا أَيُّهَا الرَّسُولُ بَلِّغْ مَا أُنزِلَ إِلَيْكَ مِن رَّبِّكَ﴾ الآية، فقام بذلك يوم غدير خُمّ.

١٤٢. عن أبي جميلة، عن بعض أصحابه، عن أحدهما عليه السلام، قال: إنّ رسول الله صلى الله عليه وآله قال: إنّ الله أوحى إليّ أن أُحبّ أربعةً: عليًا، وأبا ذرّ، وسلمان، والمِقداد.

فقلتُ: ألا فما كان من كَثْرة الناس، أما كان أحدٌ يعرِف هذا الأمر؟ فقال: بلى ثلاثة.

So I said, 'Indeed! However, from all those people at the time, did no one know about this authority?' So he replied, 'Yes three people did.'

I asked, 'These verses that were revealed: ﴾*Your guardian is only God, His Messenger, and the believers* [...]﴿ and: ﴾*obey God and the Messenger, and those in authority among you*﴿ – did no one ask whom they were revealed about?' So he replied, 'For the very reason that it had come to them, they did not ask.' [5:55]

143. From al-Mufaḍḍal, from Abū Jaʿfar عليه السلام, about His verse: ﴾*Your guardian is only God, His Messenger, and the believers...*﴿, he said, 'They are the Imams, peace be upon them.' [5:55]

144. From Ṣafwān al-Jammāl who said, 'Abū ʿAbd Allāh عليه السلام said, "When this verse of authority came down the Messenger of God ﷺ called for canopies, all the canopies at Ghadīr Khumm. So they were swept, and the call for prayer was made to gather everyone.

Then he said, 'O people! Is not the authority I have over the believers greater than the authority they have over their own selves?' They replied, 'Of course.' He said, 'Then for whomsoever I am master, ʿAlī is his master. My Lord, protect whoever adheres to him and oppose whoever opposes him.'

Then he ordered the people to pay allegiance to him, and the people did so. Not a single person approached without paying allegiance to him, and he did not speak until Abū Bakr came forth, whereupon he said, 'Abū Bakr, pay allegiance to ʿAlī's authority.' So he replied, 'From God or His Messenger?' So he replied, 'From God as well as His Messenger.' Then ʿUmar came, so he said, 'Pay allegiance to ʿAlī's authority.' So he said, 'From God or His Messenger?' So he replied, 'From God as well as His Messenger.' Then he turned away indignantly, and when they both met he said to Abū Bakr, 'He is certainly pulling the top of his cousin's arms up very high.'

Then he quickly rushed out from the camp, but it was not long before he returned to the Prophet again, peace be upon him and his family, saying, 'O Messenger of God ﷺ, I left the camp to fulfil a need when I saw a man wearing white clothes, and I have never seen someone more handsome than him. He had the most beautiful face and the most pleasant smell of all. And

قلتُ: هذه الآيات التي أُنزِلت ﴿إِنَّمَا وَلِيُّكُمُ اللهُ وَرَسُولُهُ وَالَّذِينَ آمَنُوا﴾ وقوله: ﴿أَطِيعُوا اللهَ وَأَطِيعُوا الرَّسُولَ وَأُولِي الأَمْرِ مِنكُمْ﴾، أما كان أحدٌ يسأل فيمَ نزلت؟ فقال: من ثمَّ أتاهم، لم يكونوا يسألون.

١٤٣. عن المفضَّل، عن أبي جعفر عليه السلام، في قوله: ﴿إِنَّمَا وَلِيُّكُمُ اللهُ وَرَسُولُهُ وَالَّذِينَ آمَنُوا﴾، قال: هم الأئمّة عليهم السلام.

١٤٤. عن صَفوان الجمّال، قال: قال أبو عبد الله عليه السلام: لمّا نزلت هذه الآية بالولاية، أمر رسول الله صلى الله عليه وآله بالدَّوحات، دَوحات غدير خُمّ، فَقُمّت، ثمّ نودي الصلاة جامعة.

ثمّ قال: أيُّها الناس، ألستُ أولى بالمؤمنين من أنفسهم؟ قالوا: بلى. قال: فمن كنتُ مولاه فعليّ مولاه، ربِّ والِ من والاه، وعادِ من عاداه.

ثمّ أمر الناس ببيعته، وبايعه الناس، لا يجيء أحدٌ إلاّ بايعه، ولا يتكلّم، حتّى جاء أبو بكر، فقال: يا أبا بكر، بايع عليًّا بالولاية. فقال: من الله، أو من رسوله؟ فقال: من الله ومن رسوله. ثمّ جاء عمر فقال: بايع عليًّا بالولاية. فقال: من الله، أو من رسوله؟ فقال: من الله ومن رسوله. ثم ثنّى عطفيه فالتقيا، فقال لأبي بكر: لشَدَّ ما يرفع بضَبْعي ابن عمّه!

ثمّ خرج هاربًا من العسكر، فما لَبث أن رجع إلى النبيّ عليه وآله السلام فقال: يا رسول الله، إنّي خرجتُ من العسكر لحاجةٍ، فرأيتُ رجلاً عليه ثِياب بِيض لم أرَ أحسن منه، والرجل من أحسن الناس وجهًا، وأطيبهم ريحًا، فقال: لقد عَقَد رسول الله صلى الله عليه وآله لعليّ عقدًا لا يحُلّه إلاّ كافر.

he said, "The Messenger of God ﷺ has made a pact with 'Alī that only a disbeliever would reject."'

So he said, "Umar, do you know who that was?' He replied, 'No.' He said, 'That was Jibra'īl عليه السلام, so beware lest you be the first to reject it and to disbelieve as a result.'"

Then Abū 'Abd Allāh عليه السلام said, "Twelve thousand men had attended Ghadīr and borne witness to 'Alī b. Abī Ṭālib عليه السلام, and yet he was not able to take his right even though one of you need only have wealth and two witnesses to be able to take your right. The party of God are the victorious ones regarding 'Alī عليه السلام."' [5:55]

145. From Abū Baṣīr who said, 'I said to Abū 'Abd Allāh عليه السلام, "'Umar b. Rayāḥ claims that you have said that there is no divorce without clear evidence."'

He said, 'So he replied, "I am not the one who has said that, rather it is God, Blessed and most High, who says it. By God, were we to issue rulings to you unjustly, we would be worse off than you all. Indeed, God says: ﴾ *Why do their rabbis and scholars not forbid them* ﴿"' [5:63]

146. From Hishām al-Mishraqī[13], from Abū al-Ḥasan al-Khurāsānī [i.e. al-Riḍā] عليه السلام. He said, 'Indeed, God is as He has described Himself: Unique, Self-subsisting, Light.' Then he said, ﴾ *Truly, God's Hands are open wide.* ﴿

So I asked him, 'Does He have hands like these?', pointing to my hand and his. So he said, 'If He were thus, He would be a created being.' [5:64]

147. From Ya'qūb b. Shu'ayb who said, 'I asked Abū 'Abd Allāh عليه السلام about God's verse: ﴾ *The Jews have said, "God is tight-fisted," but it is they who are tight-fisted.* ﴿' He said, 'So he said to me, "Not only that, but they also said that His Hands are [tied] to His Neck, but He said, "He has rid Himself of all things."

In another narration about this statement of theirs: "He has rid Himself of all command."' [5:64]

13 Hishām b. Ibrāhīm al-Mashriqī, a reliable companion of Imam Ja'far al-Ṣādiq. See Khū'ī, *Mu'jam*, 20:291–3 (nr. 13349).

فقال ﷺ: يا عمر، أتدري من ذاك؟ قال: لا. قال: ذاك جَبْرَئيل عليه السلام، فاحْذَر أن تكون أوّل من تَحُلّه فتكفُر.

ثم قال أبو عبدالله عليه السلام: لقد حضر الغدير اثنا عشر ألف رجلٍ يشهدون لعليّ ابن أبي طالب عليه السلام، فما قَدَر على أخذ حقّه، وإنّ أحدكم يكون له المال، وله شاهدان، فيأخذ حقه ﴿فَإِنَّ حِزْبَ اللهِ هُمُ الْغَالِبُونَ﴾ في عليّ عليه السلام.

١٤٥. عن أبي بصير، قال: قلتُ لأبي عبدالله عليه السلام: إنّ عمر بن رياح زَعَم أنّك قلت: لا طلاق إلاّ ببيّنة؟

قال: فقال: ما أنا قُلته، بل الله تبارك وتعالى يقوله، إنّا والله لوكُنّا نُفتيكم بالجَور، لكُنّا أشدّ منكم، إنّ الله يقول: ﴿لَوْلاَ يَنْهَاهُمُ الرَّبَّانِيُّونَ وَالأَحْبَارُ﴾.

١٤٦. عن هِشام المِشْرَقيّ، عن أبي الحسين الخُراساني عليه السلام، قال: إنّ الله كما وصف نفسه أحدٌ صَمَدٌ نورٌ، ثمّ قال: ﴿بَلْ يَدَاهُ مَبْسُوطَتَانِ﴾.

فقلت له: أفله يدان هكذا – وأشرت بيدي إلى يده – فقال: لوكان هكذا، كان مخلوقًا.

١٤٧. عن يعقوب بن شُعيب، قال: سألتُ أبا عبدالله عليه السلام عن قول الله: ﴿وَقَالَتِ الْيَهُودُ يَدُ اللهِ مَغْلُولَةٌ غُلَّتْ أَيْدِيهِمْ﴾. قال: فقال: لا كذا – وقال بيده إلى عُنُقه – ولكنّهم يقولون ويعنون أنّ الله قد فرغ من الأشياء.

وفي رواية أُخرى عنه: يعنون أنه فَرَغ من الأمر.

148. From Ḥammād, on his authority about God's verse: ﴾*God is tight-fisted*﴿, 'They meant that He had rid Himself of every existing being. They are cursed for what they said. God, Mighty and Exalted, says: ﴾*Truly, God's Hands are open wide.*﴿' [5:64]

149. From Jābir, from Abū Jaʿfar عليه السلام, about God's verse: ﴾*Whenever they kindle the fire of war, God will put it out.*﴿ 'Whenever one of the tyrants wishes to destroy the family of Muḥammad, peace be upon them, God will shatter him.' [5:64]

150. From Muḥammad b. Muslim, from Abū Jaʿfar عليه السلام who said regarding God's verse: ﴾*If only they had upheld the Torah and the Gospel and what was sent down to them from their Lord, they would have been given abundance from above and from below*﴿, 'Divine authority (*walāya*).' [5:66]

151. From Abū al-Ṣahbā' (or al-Ṣahbān) al-Bakrī[14] who said, 'I heard ʿAlī b. Abī Ṭālib عليه السلام invite the exilarch and the archbishop and said, "I am going to ask you about a matter that I know better than both of you, so do not hide it from me." Then he called the archbishop and said, "I implore you, by God, who sent down the Injīl to ʿIṣā, and placed blessings at his disposal such that he could cure the blind and the leper, remove eye pain and give life to the dead. He made birds for you out of clay and would inform you of all that you ate and stored away."

So he replied, "The above is all true."

Then ʿAlī عليه السلام asked, "How many factions did the Children of Israel split into after ʿĪsā?" So he replied, "By God, there was only one group."

So ʿAlī عليه السلام said, "You are lying, by God, save Whom there is no god. ʿĪsā's community split up into seventy-two factions, all of whom will be in the Fire except one. Indeed, God says: ﴾*There is an upright group among them, but evil is what many of them do*﴿, so this is the one that shall be saved."' [5:66]

---

14 His name appears as Ibn al-Ṣahbān and Ibn al-Ṣahbāʿ in the various editions of ʿAyyāshī's *tafsīr*, but this appears to be a distortion of Abu al-Ṣahbā' or Ṣuhayb al-Bakrī al-Baṣrī, the client of Ibn ʿAbbās. See Jamāl al-Dīn al-Mazzī, *Tahdhīb al-kāmāl fī asmā' al-rijāl* (Beirut: Mu'assasat al-risāla, 1985), 13:241; Muḥammad b. Ismāʿīl al-Bukhārī, *al-Tārīkh al-kabīr* (Beirut: Dār al-kutub al-ʿilmiyya, n.d.) 4:315.

١٤٨. عن حمّاد، عنه، في قول الله: ﴿يَدُ اللَّهِ مَغْلُولَةٌ﴾ يعنون أنّه قد فرغ ممّا هو كائن، لُعِنوا بما قالوا، قال الله عزّ وجلّ ﴿بَلْ يَدَاهُ مَبْسُوطَتَانِ﴾.

١٤٩. عن جابر، عن أبي جعفر عليه السلام في قوله: ﴿كُلَّمَا أَوْقَدُوا نَارًا لِّلْحَرْبِ أَطْفَأَهَا اللَّهُ﴾، قال: كلّما أراد جبّار من الجبابرة هَلَكة آل محمد عليهم السلام قصمه الله.

١٥٠. عن محمّد بن مسلم، عن أبي جعفر عليه السلام، في قول الله تعالى: ﴿وَلَوْ أَنَّهُمْ أَقَامُوا التَّوْرَاةَ وَالْإِنجِيلَ وَمَا أُنزِلَ إِلَيْهِم مِّن رَّبِّهِمْ﴾ قال: الولاية.

١٥١. عن أبي الصّهباء البكري، قال: سَمِعتُ علي بن أبي طالب عليه السلام دعا رأس الجَالُوت وأسقُف النصارى فقال: إنّي سائلكما عن أمرٍ، وأنا أعلم به منكما، فلا تكتُماني. ثمّ دعا أسقُف النصارى، فقال: أنشدك بالله الذي أنزل الإنجيل على عيسى، وجعل على رِجله البَرَكة، وكان يُبرئ الأكمه والأبرص، وأزال ألم العين، وأحيي الميت، وصنع لكم من الطين طيورًا، وأنبأكم بما تأكُلون وما تَدّخرون. فقال: دون هذا صدق.

فقال عليّ عليه السلام: بكم افترقت بنو إسرائيل بعد عيسى، فقال: لا والله إلاّ فرقة واحدة.

قال عليّ عليه السلام: كَذَبت والله الذي لا إله إلاّ هو، لقد افترقت أُمّة عيسى على أثنين وسبعين فِرقة كُلّها في النار إلاّ فرقة واحدة، إنّ الله يقول: ﴿أُمَّةٌ مُّقْتَصِدَةٌ وَكَثِيرٌ مِّنْهُمْ سَاءَ مَا﴾ كانوا ﴿يَعْمَلُونَ﴾ فهذه الّتي تنجو.

152. From Zayd b. Aslam, from Anas b. Mālik who said, ‘The Messenger of God ﷺ used to say, “The community of Mūsā split up into seventy-one groups, seventy of which will be in the Fire and one in Paradise. The community of ʿĪsā split up into seventy-two groups, seventy-one of them in the Fire and one in Paradise; and my community will surpass both of these by one extra group, of which one will go to Paradise and seventy-two in the Fire.”

They asked, “Who are they, O Messenger of God?” He replied, “The masses, the masses.”

Yaʿqūb b. Zayd said that ʿAlī b. Abī Ṭālib, whenever he used to narrate this narration from the Messenger of God ﷺ he would recite from the Qurʾan: ﴾*If only the People of the Book would believe and be mindful of God, We would take away their sins and bring them into the Gardens of Delight. If only they had upheld the Torah and the Gospel and what was sent down to them from their Lord, they would have been given abundance from above and from below: there is an upright group among them, but evil is what many of them do.*﴿ He would also recite: ﴾*Among those We created are a group of people who guide with truth and act justly according to it*﴿(7:181), meaning the community of Muḥammad ﷺ.’ [5:66]

153. From Abū Ṣāliḥ, from Ibn ʿAbbās and Jābir b. ʿAbd Allāh who both said, ‘God, exalted be He, commanded His Prophet Muḥammad ﷺ to appoint ʿAlī ؑ as a guiding authority for people, and to inform them of his authority. However, the Messenger of God ﷺ feared that they would say: ‘He has brought his own cousin!’, and that they would rebel against him thereat. So God revealed to him: ﴾*Messenger, proclaim everything that has been sent down to you from your Lord – if you do not, then you will not have communicated His message – and God will protect you from the people.*﴿ So the Messenger of God ﷺ established his authority on the day of Ghadīr Khumm.’ [5:67]

154. From Ḥanān b. Sadīr, on his father’s authority, from Abū Jaʿfar ؑ who said, ‘When Jibraʾīl ؑ revealed to the Messenger of God ﷺ during the farewell pilgrimage to announce the authority of ʿAlī b. Abī Ṭālib ؑ, saying: ﴾*Messenger, proclaim everything that has been sent down to you from your Lord – if you do not, then you will not have communicated His message – and God will protect you from the people. God does not guide those who defy Him*﴿, the

١٥٢. عن زيد بن أسلم، عن أنس بن مالك، قال: كان رسول الله ﷺ يقول: تفرّقت أُمّة موسى على إحدى وسبعين مِلّة، سبعون منها في النار، وواحدة في الجنّة، وتفرّقت أُمّة عيسى على اثنين وسبعين فِرقة، إحدى وسبعون فِرقة في النار، وواحدة في الجنّة، وتعلو أُمّتي على الفِرقتين جميعًا بملّة، واحدة في الجنّة، وثنتان وسبعون في النار.

قالوا: مَنْ هم، يا رسول الله؟ قال: الجماعات الجماعات.

قال يعقوب بن زيد: كان عليُّ بن أبي طالب عليه السلام إذا حدّث بهذا الحديث عن رسول الله ﷺ، تلا فيه قرآنًا ﴿وَلَوْ أَنَّ أَهْلَ الْكِتَابِ آمَنُوا وَاتَّقَوْا لَكَفَّرْنَا عَنْهُمْ سَيِّئَاتِهِمْ﴾ إلى قوله: ﴿سَاءَ مَا يَعْمَلُونَ﴾ وتلا أيضًا و﴿وَمِمَّنْ خَلَقْنَا أُمَّةٌ يَهْدُونَ بِالْحَقِّ وَبِهِ يَعْدِلُونَ﴾ يعني أُمّة محمد ﷺ.

١٥٣. عن أبي صالح، عن ابن عبّاس وجابر بن عبدالله، قالا: أمر الله محمّدًا ﷺ أن ينصب عليًّا عليه السلام للنّاس ليُخبرهم بولايته، فتخوّف رسول الله ﷺ أن يقولوا: جاء بابن عمّه، وأن يَطْغوا في ذلك عليه، فأوحى الله إليه ﴿يَا أَيُّهَا الرَّسُولُ بَلِّغْ مَا أُنْزِلَ إِلَيْكَ مِنْ رَبِّكَ وَإِنْ لَمْ تَفْعَلْ فَمَا بَلَّغْتَ رِسَالَتَهُ وَاللَّهُ يَعْصِمُكَ مِنَ النَّاسِ﴾ فقام رسول الله ﷺ بولايته يوم غدير خُمّ.

١٥٤. عن حَنان بن سَدير، عن أبيه، عن أبي جعفر عليه السلام، قال: لمّا نزل جبْرَئيل عليه السلام على رسول الله ﷺ في حجّة الوَداع بإعلان أمر عليّ بن أبي طالب عليه السلام ﴿يَا أَيُّهَا الرَّسُولُ بَلِّغْ مَا أُنْزِلَ إِلَيْكَ مِنْ رَبِّكَ﴾ إلى آخر الآية، قال: فمكث النبي ﷺ ثلاثًا حتّى أتى الجُحفة، فلم يأخذ بيده فَرَقًا من الناس.

Prophet ﷺ tarried for three days until he arrived at Juḥfa and had not yet taken him up by the hand for fear of the people.

So when they settled at Juḥfa on the day of al-Ghadīr and reached a place called Mahya'a, he called out: "Prayer in congregation!" So the people gathered together and the Prophet ﷺ asked, "Who is more authoritative over you than your own selves?"' He said, 'So they loudly proclaimed: "God and His Messenger." Then he asked them a second time, "Who is more authoritative over you than your own selves?"' He said, 'So they said: "God and His Messenger." Then he asked them a third time and they replied, "God and His Messenger." So he took 'Alī عليه السلام by the hand and said, "For whomsoever I am master, then 'Alī is his master. O God, protect whoever adheres to him and oppose whoever opposes him. Assist whoever assists him and thwart whoever abandons him, for indeed, he is a part of me and I of him. He is to me as Hārūn was to Mūsā, except that there is no prophet after me.'"' [5:67]

155. From 'Umar b. Yazīd who said, 'Abū 'Abd Allāh عليه السلام initiated [the conversation] saying, "What 'Alī b. Abī Ṭālib faced, O Abū Ḥafṣ, was most surprising. He had ten thousand witnesses but yet was not able to take his right, whereas a man needs only two witnesses to do so. The Messenger of God ﷺ left Medina to go for Hajj with five thousand people, and when he was returning from Mecca, five thousand more from the inhabitants of Mecca escorted him back.

When they arrived at Juḥfa, Jibra'īl came down with the [revelation of the] sacred authority of 'Alī. This revelation about his authority had actually come down at Mina, but the Messenger of God ﷺ was prevented from establishing it due to the stance of the people. So he said: ﴾*Messenger, proclaim everything that has been sent down to you from your Lord – if you do not, then you will not have communicated His message – and God will protect you from the people*﴿ from what you were apprehensive about in Mina." So the Messenger of God ﷺ ordered for the palm canopies to be swept. A man from among the people said, 'By God, he is surely going to bring you a catastrophe.'"' I asked 'Umar [ibn Yazīd], 'Who was this man?' So he replied, 'al-Ḥabashī.' [5:67]

فلمّا نزل الجُحفة يوم الغدير في مكان يقال له مَهْيَعة، نادى: الصَّلاة جامعة، فاجتمع الناس، فقال النبي ﷺ: من أولى بكم من أنفسكم؟ قال: فجَهَروا فقالوا: الله ورسوله. ثمّ قال لهم الثانية، فقالوا: الله ورسوله، ثمّ قال لهم الثالثة، فقالوا: الله ورسوله، فأخذ بيد علي عليه السلام، فقال: من كنتُ مولاهُ فعليٌّ مولاه، اللّهمّ والِ من والاهُ، وعادِ من عاداهُ، وانصُر من نصره، واخذُل من خذله، فإنّه منّي، وأنا منه، وهو منّي بمنزلة هارون من موسى، إلاّ أنه لا نبيَّ من بعدي.

١٥٥. عن عمر بن يزيد، قال: قال أبو عبدالله عليه السلام ابتداءً منه: العَجَبُ — يا أبا حَفْص — لِمَا لقي عليّ بن أبي طالب عليه السلام، أنّه كان له عَشَرة آلاف شاهد، فلم يقدِر على أخذ حقّه، والرجل يأخُذ حقَّه بشاهدين، إنَّ رسول الله ﷺ خرج من المدينة حاجًّا، ومعه خمسة آلاف، ورَجَع من مكّة وقد شيّعه خمسة آلاف من أهل مكّة.

فلمّا انتهى إلى الجُحفة نزل جبْرَئيل عليه السلام بولاية عليّ عليه السلام، وقد كانت نزلت ولايته بمِنىً، وامتنع رسول الله ﷺ من القيام بها لمكان الناس، فقال تعالى: ﴿يَا أَيُّهَا الرَّسُولُ بَلِّغْ مَا أُنزِلَ إِلَيْكَ مِن رَّبِّكَ وَإِن لَّمْ تَفْعَلْ فَمَا بَلَّغْتَ رِسَالَتَهُ وَاللَّهُ يَعْصِمُكَ مِنَ النَّاسِ﴾ ممّا كَرِهْتَ بمِنى، فأمر رسول الله ﷺ فقُمّت السَّمُرات فقال رجلٌ من الناس: أما والله ليأتينّكم بداهيةٍ.

فقلت لعمر: من الرجل؟ فقال: الحبشيّ.

156. From Abū al-Jārūd Ziyād b. al-Mundhir, the author of *al-Damdama al-Jārūdiyya*, who said, 'I was with Abū Ja'far Muḥammad b. 'Alī عليه السلام at al-Abṭaḥ while he was talking to people, when a man from Basra known as 'Uthmān, the short-sighted one, who used to narrate from al-Ḥasan al-Baṣrī came up to him and said, "O son of God's Messenger, may I be your ransom – al-Ḥasan al-Baṣrī narrates a tradition to us that claims that this verse was revealed regarding a certain man, but he does not inform us who this man is: ﴾*Messenger, proclaim everything that has been sent down to you from your Lord – if you do not, then you will not have communicated His message*﴿, implying that: Do you fear people when God will surely protect you from the people?"

So Abū Ja'far عليه السلام said, "What is wrong with him? May God not accept his debt to him, meaning his prayers. Indeed, he could have told you about him if he had so wished. Jibra'īl descended upon the Messenger of God ﷺ and said to him, 'Indeed your Lord, Blessed and most High, commands you to detail the daily prayer for your community,' and he outlined the prayer to him in detail, furnishing the evidence for it, and the Messenger of God ﷺ demonstrated it to his community in turn providing proof for it.

Then he came and said to him, 'God, Blessed and most High, commands you to detail everything about alms-giving to your community just like you did with the prayer.' So he explained the alms-giving and the evidence for it, and the Messenger of God ﷺ explained the alms-giving to his community and furnished the evidence thereof.

Then Jibra'īl came to him saying, 'God, Blessed and most High, commands you to explain the fasting to your community just like you explained the prayer and alms to them; that the month of Ramadan comes in between Sha'bān and Shawwāl, such and such must be done therein and such and such must be avoided', and he explained the fasting to him and the evidence for it. So the Messenger of God ﷺ outlined the fasting to his community and gave them the evidence for it.

Then he came to him and said, 'God, Blessed and most High, commands you to explain the Hajj to your community, just like you explained their prayer, their alms-giving and their fasting to them'; and he explained to him everything about Hajj and furnished the evidence for it. So the Messenger of God ﷺ detailed the Hajj for his community and gave them evidence for it.

Then he came to him and said, 'God, Blessed and most High, commands you to explain to your people about their guardian exactly as you did with

١٥٦. عن زياد بن المُنذر أبي الجارود، صاحب الدمدمة الجارودية، قال: كنتُ عند أبي جعفر محمّد بن علي عليه السلام بالأبطح، وهو يحدّث الناس، فقام إليه رجلٌ من أهل البصرة، يقال له عثمان الأعشى، كان يروي عن الحسن البصري، فقال: يابن رسول الله، جُعِلت فداك، إنّ الحسن البصري يُحدّثنا حديثًا يزعُم أنّ هذه الآية نزلت في رجل، ولا يُخبرنا مَن الرجل ﴿يَا أَيُّهَا الرَّسُولُ بَلِّغْ مَا أُنزِلَ إِلَيْكَ مِن رَّبِّكَ وَإِن لَّمْ تَفْعَلْ فَمَا بَلَّغْتَ رِسَالَتَهُ﴾ تفسيرها: أتخشى الناس فالله يَعْصِمك من الناس؟

فقال أبو جعفر عليه السلام: ما له لا قضى الله دينه — يعني صلاته — أما إن لو شاء أن يُخبِر به خبّر به، إنَّ جبْرَئيل عليه السلام هَبَط على رسول الله صلى الله عليه وآله، فقال له: إنّ ربك تبارك وتعالى يأمُرك أن تَدُلّ أُمّتك على صلاتهم، فدلّه على الصلاة، واحتجّ بها عليه، فدلّ رسول الله صلى الله عليه وآله أُمّته عليه، واحتجّ بها عليهم.

ثمّ أتاه، فقال: إنّ الله تبارك وتعالى يأمُرك أن تَدُلّ أُمّتك من زكاتهم على مِثل ما دَلَلْتَهُم عليه من صلاتهم، فدلّه على الزكاة، واحتجّ بها عليه، فدلّ رسول الله صلى الله عليه وآله أُمّته على الزكاة، واحتجّ بها عليهم.

ثمّ أتاه جبْرَئيل فقال: إنّ الله تبارك وتعالى يأمُرك أن تدُلّ أُمّتك من صيامهم على مِثل ما دَلَلْتَهُم عليه من صلاتهم وزكاتهم، شهر رمضان بين شعبان وشوّال، يُؤتى فيه كذا، ويُجتَنَب فيه كذا، فدلّه على الصيام، واحتجّ به عليه، فدلّ رسول الله صلى الله عليه وآله أُمّته على الصيام، واحتجّ به عليهم.

their prayer, their alms-giving, their fasting and their Hajj.' So the Messenger of God ﷺ said, 'My Lord, my community have only recently left the era of pagan ignorance.' So God revealed: ﴾*Messenger, proclaim everything that has been sent down to you from your Lord – if you do not, then you will not have communicated His message.*﴿ Its interpretation was: 'Do you fear people when God will protect you from the people?'

So the Messenger of God ﷺ stood up and took 'Alī b. Abī Ṭālib by the hand, and raised it saying, 'For whomsoever I am master, then 'Alī is his master. O God, protect whoever adheres to him, oppose whoever opposes him, assist whoever assists him, thwart whoever abandons him, love whoever loves him and despise whoever despises him.'" [5:67]

157. From Abū al-Jārūd, from Abū Ja'far عليه السلام who said, 'When God revealed to His Prophet: ﴾*Messenger, proclaim everything that has been sent down to you from your Lord – if you do not, then you will not have communicated His message – and God will protect you from the people. God does not guide those who defy Him*﴿, the Messenger of God ﷺ took Alī by the hand and said, "O people, every single one of the prophets who came before me lived his life on earth then God called him back so he answered, and I am almost being called, and I too will answer. I am responsible, and you are all responsible too, so what do you say to that?"

They said, "We bear witness that you have proclaimed, advised and fulfilled all that was upon you, so may God give you the best reward that he has ever given the messengers." So he said, "O God, bear witness to this!"

ثمّ أتاه فقال: إنَّ الله تبارك وتعالى يأمُرك أن تَدُلّ أُمّتك في حجّهم على مثل ما دَلَلْتَهُم عليه في صلاتهم وزكاتهم وصيامهم، فدلَّه على الحج، واحتجَّ به عليه، فدلَّ رسول الله ﷺ أمّته على الحجّ، واحتجّ به عليهم.

ثمّ أتاه فقال: إنَّ الله تبارك وتعالى يأمُرك أن تدُلَّ أُمّتك مَن وليّهم، على مثل ما دَلَلْتَهُم عليه في صلاتهم وزكاتهم وصيامهم وحجّهم.

قال: فقال رسول الله ﷺ: ربّ أُمّتي حديثو عهد بجاهلية، فأنزل الله تعالى: ﴿يَا أَيُّهَا الرَّسُولُ بَلِّغْ مَا أُنزِلَ إِلَيْكَ مِن رَّبِّكَ وَإِن لَّمْ تَفْعَلْ فَمَا بَلَّغْتَ رِسَالَتَهُ﴾ تفسيرها: أتخشى الناس، فالله يَعْصِمك من الناس.

فقام رسول الله ﷺ، فأخذ بيد عليّ بن أبي طالب عليه السلام فرفعها، فقال: من كنتُ مولاهُ فعليّ مولاه، اللّهم والِ من والاه، وعادِ من عاداه، وانصُر من نصره، واخذُل من خذَله، وأحبّ من أحبّه، وأبغض من أبغضه.

١٥٧. عن أبي الجارود، عن أبي جعفر عليه السلام، قال: لمّا أنزل الله على نبيه ﷺ ﴿يَا أَيُّهَا الرَّسُولُ بَلِّغْ مَا أُنزِلَ إِلَيْكَ مِن رَّبِّكَ وَإِن لَّمْ تَفْعَلْ فَمَا بَلَّغْتَ رِسَالَتَهُ وَاللَّهُ يَعْصِمُكَ مِنَ النَّاسِ إِنَّ اللَّهَ لَا يَهْدِي الْقَوْمَ الْكَافِرِينَ﴾، قال: فأخذ رسول الله ﷺ بيد عليّ عليه السلام فقال: يا أيُّها الناس، إنّه لم يكن نبيّ من الأنبياء ممّن كان قبلُ، إلاّ وقدعمّرثمّ دعاه الله فأجابه، وأُوشِك أن أُدعى فأُجيب، وأنا مسؤول، وأنتم مسؤولون، فما أنتم قائلون؟

قالوا: نشهد أنّك قد بلَّغت ونصحت، وأدَّيت ما عليك،فجزاك الله أفضل ما جزى المرسلين. فقال: اللّهم اشهَد.

Then he said, "O Muslims, the one who witnesses this should tell the one absent that I am entrusting whoever has faith in me and believes in me with the sacred authority of ʿAlī, to the extent that ʿAlī's authority is my authority [and my authority is my Lord's authority]. Who knows how much more time my Lord has kept for me whilst He has commanded me to proclaim it to you." Then he said three times, "Did you all hear?" A man spoke up, "Yes, we have heard, O Messenger of God."' [5:67]

158. From Ḥumrān b. Aʿyan, from Abū Jaʿfar عليه السلام regarding God's verse: ﴾ *Say, "People of the Book, you have no true basis* [*for your religion*] *unless you uphold the Torah, the Gospel, and that which has been sent down to you from your Lord," but what has been sent down to you* [*Prophet*] *from your Lord is sure to increase many of them in their insolence and defiance.* ﴿ He said, 'This is the sacred authority of the Commander of the Faithful عليه السلام.' [5:68]

159. From Khālid b. Yazīd, from one of his associates, from Abū ʿAbd Allāh regarding God's verse: '﴾ *They thought no harm could come to them* ﴿ whilst the Messenger of God was in their midst, then they ﴾ *became blind and deaf* ﴿ when the Messenger of God صلى الله عليه وآله was taken from this world. Then ﴾ *God turned to them in mercy* ﴿ when the Commander of the Faithful عليه السلام rose up.' He said, 'Then they ﴾ *became blind and deaf again* ﴿ until this very hour.' [5:71]

160. From Zurāra who said, 'I wrote to Abū ʿAbd Allāh عليه السلام along with some of our associates regarding that which the people narrate from the Messenger of God صلى الله عليه وآله, that Hell is obligatory for whoever associates anything with God, and whoever does not associate anything with God, Paradise becomes obligatory for him. He replied, "Whoever associates anything with God, that association is evident, as per God's statement: ﴾ *If anyone associates others with God, God will forbid him from the Garden.* ﴿" As for his saying that whoever does not associate anything with God, Paradise becomes obligatory for him, Abū ʿAbd Allāh عليه السلام said, "This is the [correct] view: it is whoever does not disobey God."' [5:72]

ثمّ قال: يا معشر المسلمين، ليُبلّغ الشاهد الغائب، أُوصي من آمن بي وصدّقني بولاية عليّ ﷺ، ألا إنّ ولاية عليّ ولايتي عَهْدًا عَهِد إليّ ربي، وأمرني أن أُبلّغكموه. ثمّ قال: هل سَمِعتم؟ — ثلاث مرّات يقولها — فقال قائل: قد سَمِعنا يا رسول الله.

١٥٨. عن حُمران بن أعْيَن، عن أبي جعفر ﷺ، في قول الله: ﴿يَا أَهْلَ الْكِتَابِ لَسْتُمْ عَلَى شَيْءٍ حَتَّى تُقِيمُوا التَّوْرَاةَ وَالإِنْجِيلَ وَمَا أُنْزِلَ إِلَيْكُمْ مِنْ رَبِّكُمْ وَلَيَزِيدَنَّ كَثِيرًا مِنْهُمْ مَا أُنْزِلَ إِلَيْكَ مِنْ رَبِّكَ طُغْيَانًا وَكُفْرًا﴾، قال: هو ولاية أمير المؤمنين ﷺ.

١٥٩. عن خالد بن يزيد، عن بعض أصحابه، عن أبي عبد الله ﷺ، في قول الله تعالى: ﴿وَحَسِبُوا أَلاَّ تَكُونَ فِتْنَةٌ﴾، قال: حيث كان رسول الله ﷺ بين أظهرهم ثمّ عَمُوا وصَمّوا حيث قُبِض رسول الله ﷺ، ثمّ تاب الله عليهم حيث قام أمير المؤمنين ﷺ، قال: ثمّ عَمُوا وصَمّوا إلى الساعة.

١٦٠. عن زُرارة، قال: كتبتُ إلى أبي عبد الله ﷺ مع بعض أصحابنا فيما يروي الناس عن النبيّ ﷺ، أنّه «من أشرك بالله فقد وجبت له النار، ومن لم يُشرِك بالله فقد وجبت له الجنّة». قال: أمّا من أشرك بالله فهذا الشّرك البيّن، وهو قول الله: ﴿مَنْ يُشْرِكْ بِاللهِ فَقَدْ حَرَّمَ اللهُ عَلَيْهِ الْجَنَّةَ﴾، وأمّا قوله: «من لم يُشرِك بالله فقد وجبت له الجنّة» قال أبو عبد الله ﷺ: ها هنا النظر، هو من لم يعصِ الله.

161. From Aḥmad b. Khālid, on his father's authority, citing an infallible without mentioning his source, regarding God's verse: ﴾ *his mother was a virtuous woman; both ate food.* ﴿ He said, 'They used to have bowel movements.' [5:75]

162. From Abū 'Ubayda, from Abū 'Abd Allāh عليه السلام who said: ﴾ *Those Children of Isrā'īl who defied* [*God*] *were rejected through the words of Dāwūd, and 'Īsā, son of Maryam.* ﴿ He said, 'They were called pigs by Dāwūd and apes by 'Īsā b. Maryam.' [5:78]

163. From Muḥammad b. al-Haytham al-Tamīmī[15], from Abū 'Abd Allāh عليه السلام regarding His verse: ﴾ *They did not forbid each other from the wrong that they used to do. How vile their deeds were!* ﴿

He said, 'Even though they did not enter their meeting places or sit in their gatherings, they would still laugh with them and socialise intimately with them.' [5:79]

164. From Marwān, from one of our associates, from Abū 'Abd Allāh عليه السلام. He said, 'He mentioned the Christians and their enmity, and read God's verse: ﴾ *for there are among them people devoted to learning and ascetics. These people are not given to arrogance.* ﴿ He said, "Those were people between the time of 'Īsā and Muḥammad, who were waiting for the advent of Muḥammad صلى الله عليه وآله."' [5:82]

165. From 'Abd Allāh b. Sinān who said, 'I asked him about a man who threatens to divorce his wife [as an oath] or expel his slaves if they drink something prohibited and made impermissible. So he replied, "As for what is prohibited, it is not binding, whether he swears an oath or not. As for what is permissible, it cannot be abandoned, for it is not up to him to forbid that which God has made permissible because God says: ﴾ *You who believe, do not forbid the good things God has made lawful to you.* ﴿ So his oath is not binding on the permissible either."' [5:87]

15 Muḥammad b. al-Haytham b. 'Urwa al-Tamīmī, a reliable narrator of Imam Ja'far al-Ṣādiq's traditions. See Ḥillī, *Khulāṣat al-aqwāl*, 263 (nr. 924).

١٦١. عن أحمد بن خالد، عن أبيه، رفعه، في قول الله: ﴿وَأُمُّهُۥ صِدِّيقَةٞۖ كَانَا يَأۡكُلَانِ ٱلطَّعَامَۗ﴾، قال: كانا يتغوّطان.

١٦٢. عن أبي عبيدة، عن أبي عبدالله ﵇، قال: ﴿لُعِنَ ٱلَّذِينَ كَفَرُواْ مِنۢ بَنِيٓ إِسۡرَٰٓءِيلَ عَلَىٰ لِسَانِ دَاوُۥدَ وَعِيسَى ٱبۡنِ مَرۡيَمَۚ﴾، قال: الخنازير على لسان داود، والقردة على لسان عيسى بن مريم ﵇.

١٦٣. عن محمّد بن الهيثم التميمي، عن أبي عبدالله ﵇، في قوله تعالى: ﴿كَانُواْ لَا يَتَنَاهَوۡنَ عَن مُّنكَرٖ فَعَلُوهُۚ لَبِئۡسَ مَا كَانُواْ يَفۡعَلُونَ﴾.

قال: أما إنّهم لم يكونوا يَدخُلون مَداخلهم ولا يجلِسون مجالسهم، ولكن كانوا إذا لَقُوهم ضَحِكوا في وُجوههم وأنِسُوا بهم.

١٦٤. عن مَروان، عن بعض أصحابنا، عن أبي عبدالله ﵇، قال: ذكر النصارى وعداوتهم، فقال: قول الله: ﴿ذَٰلِكَ بِأَنَّ مِنۡهُمۡ قِسِّيسِينَ وَرُهۡبَانٗا وَأَنَّهُمۡ لَا يَسۡتَكۡبِرُونَ﴾.

قال: أُولئك كانوا قومًا بين عيسى ومحمّد، يَنتَظِرون مجيء محمّد ﷺ.

١٦٥. عن عبدالله بن سِنان، قال: سألتُهُ عن رجلٍ قال: امرأته طالق، أو مماليكه أحرار، إن شَرِبت حرامًا ولا حلالاً. فقال: أمّا الحرام فلا يَقرَبه حَلَفَ أو لم يحلِف، وأمّا الحلال فلا يَترُكه، فإنّه ليس له أن يحرِّم ما أحلَّ الله، لأنّ الله يقول: ﴿يَٰٓأَيُّهَا ٱلَّذِينَ ءَامَنُواْ لَا تُحَرِّمُواْ طَيِّبَٰتِ مَآ أَحَلَّ ٱللَّهُ لَكُمۡ﴾ فليس عليه شيءٌ في يمينه من الحلال.

166. From ʿAbd Allāh b. Sinān, from Abū ʿAbd Allāh عليه السلام who said, 'God's saying: ﴾*God does not take you [to task] for what is thoughtless in your oaths*﴿; this is when a man says: "No, by God!", or "By God, of course!" whilst his heart does not avow anything.'

167. In another narration from Muḥammad b. Muslim, he said, 'While he does not avow it.' [5:89]

168. From Isḥāq b. ʿAmmār who said, 'I asked Abū al-Ḥasan عليه السلام about: ﴾*to feed ten poor people with food equivalent to what you would normally give your own families, or to clothe them*﴿, or to feed sixty poor people. Can he give that altogether [to one person]? He replied, "No, rather he should give each person as God has stipulated."'

He said, 'I asked, "So the man should give to his relatives if they are needy?" He replied, "Yes."

I asked, "Can he still give it to them if they are weak but not adherents of the authority of the Imams?" He replied, "Yes, and the adherents of *walāya* are more beloved to me."' [5:89]

169. From Muḥammad b. Muslim, from one of the two [Imams al-Bāqir or al-Ṣādiq] who said, '[The atonement] for breaking an oath is feeding ten poor people. Do you not see that He says: ﴾*the atonement for breaking an oath is to feed ten poor people with food equivalent to what you would normally give your own families, or to clothe them, or to set free a slave – if a person cannot find the means, he should fast for three days.*﴿ Perhaps your own family's provision per person comes to less than a *mudd* (a measure of food). However, one should calculate and set aside one *mudd* of flour, water, and dough per person. As for their clothing, if it coincides with winter then clothing suitable for that, and if it coincides with summer then clothe them accordingly. Each poor person should have trousers and an overshirt, and for women it should be that which covers all that is prohibited to be left uncovered: trousers, a head covering and an overgarment; and to fast for three days – if one wishes to fast instead. However, the fast should be performed with your own body and not through your wealth or other means.' [5:89]

١٦٦. عن عبدالله بن سِنان، عن أبي عبدالله ﴿عليه السلام﴾، قال: قول الله: ﴿لَا يُؤَاخِذُكُمُ اللَّهُ بِاللَّغْوِ فِي أَيْمَانِكُمْ﴾ قال: هو قول الرجل: لا والله، وبلى والله، ولا يَعْقِد قلبُهُ على شيء.

١٦٧. وفي رواية أُخرى عن محمّد بن مسلم، قال: ولا يَعْقِد عليها.

١٦٨. عن إسحاق بن عمّار، قال: سألتُ أبا الحسن ﴿عليه السلام﴾ عن إطْعام عَشَرَةِ مَساكينَ مِنْ أَوْسَطِ ما تُطْعِمُونَ أَهْلِيكُمْ أَوْ كِسْوَتُهُمْ، أو إطعام ستّين مسكينًا، أيُجْمَع ذلك؟ فقال: لا، ولكن يُعطى إنسان إنسان، كما قال الله.

قال: قلتُ: فيُعطي الرجل قرابته، إذا كانوا محتاجين؟ قال: نعم.

قلت: فيُعطيها إذا كانوا ضُعفاء من غير أهل الولاية؟ فقال: نعم، وأهل الولاية أحبّ إليّ.

١٦٩. عن محمّد بن مسلم، عن أحدهما ﴿عليه السلام﴾، قال في اليمين في إطعام عَشَرة مساكين: ألا ترى أنّه يقول: ﴿مِنْ أَوْسَطِ مَا تُطْعِمُونَ أَهْلِيكُمْ أَوْ كِسْوَتُهُمْ أَوْ تَحْرِيرُ رَقَبَةٍ فَمَنْ لَمْ يَجِدْ فَصِيَامُ ثَلَاثَةِ أَيَّامٍ﴾ فلعلّ أهلك أن يكون قُوتُهم لكُلّ إنسان دون المُدّ، ولكن يحسب في طحنه ومائه وعجينه، فإذا هو يُجزي لكُلّ إنسانٍ مُدّ، وأمّا كُسوتهم فإن وافقت به الشتاء فكُسوته، وإن وافقت به الصيف فكُسوته، لكُلّ مسكين إزارٌ ورِداء، وللمرأة ما يُواري ما يَحْرُمُ منها: إزارٌ وخِمارٌ دِرعٌ، وصوم ثلاثة أيّام، إن شئت أن تصوم، إنّما الصوم من جَسَدك، ليس من مالك ولا غيره.

170. From Samā'a b. Mihrān, from Abū 'Abd Allāh عليه السلام who said, 'I asked him about God's verse: ﴾*with food equivalent to what you would normally give your own families*﴿ as atonement for breaking an oath. He replied, "What your own family eats to satisfy them for one day; and one *mudd* per poor person was suitable according to him."

I asked, "[What about]:﴾*or to clothe them*﴿?" He replied, "Two garments for each man."' [5:89]

171. From Abū Baṣīr who said, 'I asked Abū Ja'far عليه السلام about God's verse: ﴾*with food equivalent to what you would normally give your own families.*﴿ He said, "The same provision as your own dependents and the provision of that time was one *mudd*." I asked, "What about their clothing?" He replied, "One garment."' [5:89]

172. From Ibrāhīm b. 'Abd al-Ḥamīd, from Abū Ibrāhīm عليه السلام [i.e. Imam Mūsā al-Kāẓim]. He said, 'I asked him about feeding ten poor people or sixty poor people – can that be combined and given to one individual? He replied, "No. Give it to each person separately as God has said."' He said, 'I asked, "Can a man give it to his relatives?" He replied, "Yes."' He said, 'I asked, "Can he give it to incapacitated women who are not adherents of the authority (*walāya*) [of the Imams]?" He replied, "Yes, though adherents of the *walāya* are more beloved to me."' [5:89]

173. From Ibn Sinān, from Abū 'Abd Allāh عليه السلام who said, 'The atonement for breaking an oath is to give every poor person a *mudd* of food equivalent to what feeds a person from your own family per day. A *mudd* of wheat should include its grinding and baking for each poor person; or it is to clothe them with two garments.' [5:89]

١٧٠ . عن سَماعة بن مِهران، عن أبي عبدالله عليه السلام، قال: سألتُه عن قول الله: ﴿مِنْ أَوْسَطِ مَا تُطْعِمُونَ أَهْلِيكُمْ أَوْ كِسْوَتُهُمْ﴾ في كفّارة اليمين. قال: ما يأكُل أهل البيت يُشبِعهم يوم، وكان يُعجِبه مُدّ لكلّ مسكين.

قلت: ﴿أَوْ كِسْوَتُهُمْ﴾؟ قال: ثوبين لكُلّ رجل.

١٧١ . عن أبي بصير، قال: سألتُ أبا جعفر عليه السلام عن قول الله ﴿مِنْ أَوْسَطِ مَا تُطْعِمُونَ أَهْلِيكُمْ﴾، قال: قُوت عيالك، والقوت يومئذٍ مُدّ.

قلت: ﴿أَوْ كِسْوَتُهُمْ﴾، قال: ثوب.

١٧٢ . عن إبراهيم بن عبد الحميد، عن أبي إبراهيم عليه السلام، قال: سألتُه عن إطعام عشرة مساكين، أو ستّين مسكينًا، أيُجمَع ذلك لإنسانٍ واحد؟ قال: لا، أعطِه واحدًا واحدًا، كما قال الله.

قال: قلت: أفيُعطيه الرجل قرابته؟ قال: نعم.

قال: قلت: أفيُعطيه الضُّعفاء من النساء من غير أهل الولاية؟ قال: أهل الولاية أحبُّ إليَّ.

١٧٣ . عن ابن سِنان، عن أبي عبدالله عليه السلام، قال في كفّارة اليمين: يُعطى كلّ مسكين مُدًّا، على قدر ما يقوت إنسانًا من أهلك في كُلّ يوم، وقال: مُدّ من حِنطة يكون فيه طَحنه، وحَطَبه على كُلّ مِسكين، أوكُسوتهم ثوبين.

174. In another narration on his authority, 'Two garments for every man; or to set a slave free from among the helpless people, in situations where you must set a slave free.' [5:89]

175. From Zurāra, from Abū 'Abd Allāh عليه السلام who said, 'The atonement for breaking an oath is to set a slave free, or ﴾*to feed ten poor people with food equivalent to what you would normally give your own families*﴿ with condiments, the norm of which would be oil and vinegar, and superior to that bread and meat. The offering should be one *mudd* per person, and the clothing should be two garments. Whoever cannot afford this must fast for three days. God says: ﴾*If a person cannot find the means, he should fast for three days.*﴿ He must fast them consecutively. In the atonement for breaking an oath, one is allowed to set a boy slave free, whereas in the atonement for murder, it can only be someone who professes the unity of God [i.e. a Muslim].' [5:89]

176. From al-Ḥalabī, from Abū 'Abd Allāh عليه السلام, that the atonement for breaking an oath is to feed ten poor people, for each one two *mudd*: one of wheat and one of flour, enough to fit in both hands; or to clothe them with two garments per person; or to free a slave. He has a choice as to which of the three he would like to do, and if he does not have the means to do any of these three, then fasting for three days is obligatory for him. [5:89]

177. From Abū Ḥamza, from Abū Ja'far عليه السلام. He said, 'I heard him say, "God has authorized man with the power to choose when it comes to the atonement for breaking an oath just as he has authorized the Imam regarding [the punishment for] a warmonger, to do as he wills." He also said, "Whenever the word 'or' occurs in the Qur'an, man has a choice therein."' [5:89]

١٧٤. وفي رواية أُخرى عنه: ثوبين لكُلّ رجلٍ، والرَّقَبة تُعتق من المستضعفين في الذي يجب عليك فيه رَقَبة.

١٧٥. عن زُرارة، عن أبي عبدالله ﷺ، قال في كفّارة اليمين: عِتق رَقَبة، أو إطعام عشرة مساكين من أوسط ما تُطعِمون أهليكم، والإدام، والوسط: الخَلّ والزيت، وأرفعه: الخبز واللَّحم، والصَّدقة مُدّ مُدّ لكلِّ مسكين، والكُسوة ثوبان، فمن لم يجد فعليه الصيام، يقول الله: ﴿فَمَن لَّمْ يَجِدْ فَصِيَامُ ثَلَاثَةِ أَيَّامٍ﴾ ويصومهنّ متتابعًا، ويجوز في عِتق الكفّارة الوَلَد، ولا يجوز في عِتق القتل إلاّ مُقِرّة بالتوحيد.

١٧٦. عن الحلبي، عن أبي عبدالله ﷺ، في كفّارة اليمين: يُطعِم عَشَرة مساكين، لكُلّ مسكين مُدّ من حِنطة، ومُدّ من دقيق، وحَفْنَة، أوكُسوتهم لكلّ إنسان ثوبان، أو عِتق رَقَبة، وهو في ذلك بالخِيار، أيّ الثَلاثة شاء صنع: فإن لم يَقْدِر على واحدةٍ من الثَلاث، فالصّيام عليه واجب، صيام ثَلاثة أيّام.

١٧٧. عن أبي حمزة، عن أبي جعفر ﷺ، قال: سَمِعته يقول: إنّ الله فوّض إلى الناس في كفّارة اليمين، كما فوّض إلى الإمام في المُحارب أن يصنع ما يشاء، وقال كُلّ شيء في القرآن (أو) فصاحبه فيه بالخِيار.

178. From al-Zuhrī, from ʿAlī b. al-Ḥusayn عليه السلام who said, ʿFasting for three days as atonement for breaking an oath is obligatory for one who does not have the means to feed others. God says: ﴾*If a person cannot find the means, he should fast for three days. This is the atonement for breaking your oaths.*﴿ This is all consequential and not a separate option.ʾ [5:89]

179. From Isḥāq b. ʿAmmār, from Abū ʿAbd Allāh عليه السلام. He said, ʿHe was asked about the atonement for breaking an oath, regarding God's verse: ﴾*if a person cannot find the means, he should fast for three days*﴿ – what are the criteria for not having the means? What if a man begs for a living and hence acquires the means? So he replied, "If he does not have an extra day's worth of food in addition to his family's daily provision, then he does not have the means." He also said, "Fasting must be done for three days without a break in between them."ʾ [5:89]

180. From Abū Khālid al-Qammāṭ[16] that he heard Abū ʿAbd Allāh عليه السلام say about the atonement for breaking an oath, ʿWhoever has the means to feed is not supposed to fast. Feed ten poor people a *mudd*'s worth of food each, and if he cannot afford it then he must fast for three days or free a slave or clothe [people]. Clothing should be two garments, or feeding ten poor people – whichever one of those he undertakes will absolve him.ʾ [5:89]

181. ʿAlī b. Abī Ḥamza said from Abū ʿAbd Allāh عليه السلام that he said, ʿIf he does not have the means then he should fast for three consecutive days, and the feeding of ten poor people is a *mudd* per person.ʾ [5:89]

182. From al-Ḥalabī, from Abū ʿAbd Allāh عليه السلام who said, ʿFasting for three days as atonement for breaking an oath must be done on consecutive days without a break in between them.ʾ He also said, ʿAll fasting can be split up except for the three days of fasting as atonement for an oath, for God says: ﴾*he should fast for three days*﴿ consecutively.ʾ [5:89]

16 Abū Khālid Yazīd al-Qammāṭ, a reliable transmitter of Imam Jaʿfar al-Ṣādiq's traditions. See Ḥillī, *Khulāṣat al-aqwāl*, 295 (nr. 1099); Modarressi, *Tradition and Survival*, 399 (nr. 226).

١٧٨. عن الزُّهري، عن علي بن الحسين ﵇، قال: صيام ثَلاثة أيّام في كَفّارة اليمين واجبٌ لمن لم يجد الإطعام، قال الله تعالى: ﴿فَصِيَامُ ثَلَاثَةِ أَيَّامٍ ذَلِكَ كَفَّارَةُ أَيْمَانِكُمْ إِذَا حَلَفْتُمْ﴾ كُلّ ذلك متتابع، ليس بمُتَفرّقٍ.

١٧٩. عن إسحاق بن عمّار، عن أبي عبدالله ﵇، قال: سُئل عن كفّارة اليمين في قول الله: ﴿فَمَنْ لَمْ يَجِدْ فَصِيَامُ ثَلَاثَةِ أَيَّامٍ﴾، ما حدّ من لم يجد، فهذا الرجل يسأل في كفّه وهو يَجِد؟

فقال: إذا لم يكن عنده فضل يومه عن قُوت عياله فهولا يجد، وقال: الصيام ثَلاثة أيّام، لا يُفرّق بينهنّ.

١٨٠. عن أبي خالد القمّاط، أنّه سَمِع أبا عبدالله ﵇ يقول في كَفّارة اليمين: من كان له ما يُطعِم فليس له أن يصوم، أطعم عَشَرة مساكين مُدّاً مُدّاً، فإن لم يجد فصيام ثَلاثة أيّام، أو عِتق رَقَبة، أوكُسوة، والكُسوة ثوبان، أيّ ذلك فعل أجزأ عنه.

١٨١. قال عليّ بن أبي حمزة، عن أبي عبدالله ﵇، قال: فإن لم يجد فصيام ثَلاثة أيّام متواليات، وإطعام عشرة مساكين مُدّ مُدّ.

١٨٢. عن الحلبي، عن أبي عبدالله ﵇، قال: صيام ثَلاثة أيّام في كَفّارة اليمين متتابعات لا يفصل بينهنّ. قال: وقال: كُلّ صيام يُفرّق إلاّ صيام ثَلاثة أيّام في كَفّارة اليمين، فإنّ الله يقول: ﴿فَصِيَامُ ثَلَاثَةِ أَيَّامٍ﴾ مُتَتابِعات.

183. From Abū al-Ḥasan al-Riḍā. He said, 'He says, "Gambling is wagering."' [5:90]

184. From Abū al-Ḥasan al-Riḍā عليه السلام. He said, 'I heard him say, "Chess, backgammon, mancala, and everything that one can wager on is gambling."' [5:90]

185. From Hishām b. Sālim, from Abū 'Abd Allāh عليه السلام. He said, 'I heard him say, "When Ḥamza b. 'Abd al-Muṭṭalib and his comrades were drunk on a wine called al-Sukruka, they reminisced together about camel hump-meat. So Ḥamza asked them, 'How can we get some?' So they replied, 'There is a she-camel belonging to your nephew 'Alī.' So he went out and slaughtered it. Then he cut out its liver and hump and brought them inside to them."

He continued, "'Alī approached and saw his she-camel and was greatly upset by that. They told him, 'Your uncle Ḥamza has done that.'

He said, 'So he went to the Prophet ﷺ and complained to him about it."

He continued, "So the Messenger of God ﷺ went with him, and Ḥamza was alerted: 'That is the Messenger of God ﷺ at the door.' So Ḥamza came out in a fury, and when the Messenger of God ﷺ saw him with an angry face, he left, and Ḥamza said to him, 'If the son of Abū Ṭālib wished to drive you along with reins, he could do so.' Then Ḥamza went into his house, and the Prophet ﷺ left."

He said, "And this was before [the Battle of] Uḥud."

He continued, "So God revealed the prohibition of wine, and the Messenger of God ﷺ ordered for all their bottles to be brought, which were poured out."

He said, "Then the people were called upon to march out to Uḥud, so the Messenger of God ﷺ went out, as well as the people, and Ḥamza went out too and positioned himself aside from the Prophet ﷺ." He said, "So when everyone had expressed their sincere affection for one another before the battle, Ḥamza went out to attack the enemy until he was victorious. Then when he came back to his position, the people said to him, 'O uncle of the Messenger of God, how could you go out to fight while the Messenger of God ﷺ may still be harbouring something against you?' Then he went to attack a second time until he disappeared among the people, then returned to his position. So they said to him, 'O uncle of the Messenger of God, how could you go out to fight while the Messenger of God ﷺ may still be

١٨٣. عن أبي الحسن الرضا عليه السلام، قال: يقول: المَيسر: هو القِمار.

١٨٤. عن أبي الحسن الرضا عليه السلام، قال: سَمِعتُه يقول: إنّ الشِّطْرَنج والنَّرد وأربعة عشر، وكُلّ ما قُومِر عليه منها، فهو مَيسِر.

١٨٥. عن هِشام بن سالم، عن أبي عبد الله عليه السلام، قال: سَمِعتُه يقول: بينما حمزة بن عبد المطّلب عليه السلام وأصحاب له على شَرَابٍ لهم، يقال له السُّكُرْكَة، قال: فتَذَاكروا السَّديف فقال لهم حمزة: كيف لنا به؟ فقالوا: هذه ناقة ابن أخيك عليّ، فخرج إليها فَنَحَرها، ثمّ أخذ كَبِدها وسَنَامها، فأدخله عليهم.

قال: وأقبل عليّ عليه السلام فأبصر ناقته، فدخله من ذلك، فقالوا له: عمّك حمزة صنع هذا، قال: فذهب إلى النبيّ صلى الله عليه وآله، فشكا ذلك إليه، قال: فأقبل معه رسول الله صلى الله عليه وآله فقيل لحمزة: هذا رسول الله بالباب. قال: فخرج حمزة وهو مُغضِب، فلمّا رأى رسول الله صلى الله عليه وآله الغَضَب في وجهه انصرف.

قال: فقال له حمزة: لو أراد ابن أبي طالب أن يَقُودك بزمامٍ فَعَل، فدخل حمزة منزله، وانصرف النبيّ صلى الله عليه وآله، قال: وكان قبل أُحد، قال: فأنزل الله تحريم الخمر، فأمر رسول الله صلى الله عليه وآله بآنيتهم فأُكفئت.

قال: فنُودي في الناس بالخُروج إلى أُحد، فخرج رسول الله صلى الله عليه وآله، وخرج الناس، وخرج حمزة، فوقف ناحيةً من النّبيّ صلى الله عليه وآله، قال: فلمّا تصافّوا حمل حمزة في النّاسِ حتّى غاب فيهم، ثمّ رجع إلى موقفه، فقال له الناس: الله الله يا عمّ رسول الله، أن تذهب وفي

harbouring something against you?' So he went up to the Prophet ﷺ, and when he saw him approaching him, he went up to him and hugged him, and the Messenger of God kissed him between his eyes." He said, "Then he went to attack the enemy and Ḥamza was martyred, may God have mercy on him. So the Messenger of God ﷺ shrouded him in a woollen cloth with black and white stripes (*al-nimra*)."

Then Abū 'Abd Allāh said, "It was like this curtain on my door. It was such that when he covered his face with it, his feet would be uncovered, and when he went to cover his feet, his face would show." He said, "So he covered his face with it and placed leaves from the *ikhdhir* plant on his feet." He said, "So the people fled and 'Alī عليه السلام remained standing, and the Messenger of God asked him, 'What were you doing, 'Alī?' He replied, 'O Messenger of God, I was standing firm on the battlefield.' So he said, 'I thought as much.'" He said, "And the Messenger of God ﷺ said, 'I implore you, my Lord, for what You have promised me, for truly if You willed they [i.e. the idols] would never again be venerated.'"' [5:90]

186. From Abū al-Ṣabbāḥ, from Abū 'Abd Allāh عليه السلام. He said, 'I asked him about *nabīdh* and wine – are they considered the same? He replied, "No, *nabīdh* is not equal to wine. God has prohibited wine, both a little of it as well as a lot, just as He has prohibited carrion, blood, and pork, and the Prophet ﷺ prohibited the intoxicating drinks. Whatever the Messenger of God ﷺ prohibits has been prohibited by God Himself." I asked, "I wonder how the Messenger of God ﷺ used to deal with wine-drinking?" So he said, "He used to beat them with slippers, more or less, every time a drunkard was brought before him. Then the people continued to increase the number of lashes until it stopped at eighty. 'Alī عليه السلام informed 'Umar of that."' [5:90]

نفس رسول الله ﷺ عليك شيء. فأقبل إلى النبيّ ﷺ، فلمّا رآه مقبلاً نحوه، أقبل إليه فعانقه، وقبّل رسول الله ﷺ ما بين عينيه، قال: ثمّ حمل على الناس فاستُشْهد حمزة رحِمه الله، وكفّنه رسول الله ﷺ في نَمِرة.

ثمّ قال أبو عبد الله عليه السلام: نحوٌ من سِتر بابي هذا، فكان إذا غُطّي بها وجهه انكشف رِجلاه، وإذا غُطّي رجلاه انكشف وجهه، قال: فغُطّي بها وجهُه، وجُعِل على رجليه إذْخِر.

قال: فانهزم الناسَ وبقي عليّ عليه السلام، فقال له رسول الله ﷺ: يا عليّ، ما صنعت؟ قال: يا رسول الله، لَزِمت الأرض. فقال: ذلك الظّن بك. قال: وقال رسول الله ﷺ: أنشدك يا ربّ ما وعدتني، فإنّك إن شئت لم تُعْبَد.

١٨٦. عن أبي الصبّاح، عن أبي عبد الله عليه السلام، قال: سألتُهُ عن النبيذ والخمر، بمنزلة واحدة هما؟ قال: لا، إنَّ النبيذ ليس بمنزلة الخمر، إنَّ الله حرّم الخمر قليلها وكثيرها، كما حرّم الميْتَة والدم ولحم الخنزير، وحرّم النبي ﷺ من الأشربة المُسكِر، وما حرّم رسول الله ﷺ فقد حرّمه الله.

قلت أرأيت رسول الله ﷺ كيف كان يَضرِب في الخمر؟ فقال: كان يضرِب بالنِّعال، ويزيد كُلّما أُتي بالشارب، ثمّ لم يَزَل الناس يزيدون حتّى وقف على ثمانين، أشار بذلك عليّ عليه السلام على عمر.

187. From ʿAbd Allāh b. Jundab, from whoever reported it from Abū ʿAbd Allāh عليه السلام who said, 'Chess is gambling, and backgammon is gambling.' [5:90]

188. From Ismāʿīl al-Juʿfī, from Abū Jaʿfar عليه السلام who said, 'Chess and backgammon are gambling.' [5:90]

189. From Yāsir, the servant, from al-Riḍā عليه السلام. He said, 'I asked him about gambling. He said, "The deposit from each thing." He said, "The bread and the deposit that is placed by the gamblers [as pawns], be it cash or anything else."' [5:90]

190. From Hishām, from the reliable narrator, who without mentioning his source said that Abū ʿAbd Allāh عليه السلام was once told, 'It has been narrated on your authority that [according to you] intoxicants and gambling, idolatrous practices, and [divining with] arrows all refer to certain men.' So he replied, 'God does not address His creatures in a way that they cannot comprehend.' [5:90]

191. From ʿAbd Allāh b. Sinān, from Abū ʿAbd Allāh عليه السلام who said, 'Quddāma b. Maẓʿūn was brought before ʿUmar b. al-Khaṭṭāb having drunk wine for the punishment to be meted out to him. So he in turn asked ʿAlī عليه السلام and ordered him to flog him with eighty lashes.

So Quddāma said, "O Commander of the Faithful, I should not get even a single lash because I am of those whom this verse applies to: ﴾*There will be no blame upon those who believe and do righteous deeds in regards to what they have consumed* [*in the past*]﴿" and he recited the whole verse to completion. So ʿAlī عليه السلام said to him, "You are wrong! You are not among the addressees of this verse. What they consumed was permissible for them, and they only ate and drank what was permissible for them at the time."'

192. There is a similar narration from Ibn Sinān, from Abū ʿAbd Allāh عليه السلام with the addition of: 'They only ate and drank what God had made permissible for them.' Then he said, 'When the drunkard drinks, he does not even know what he is eating and drinking. So flog him with eighty lashes.' [5:93]

١٨٧. عن عبدالله بن جُندب، عمَّن أخبره، عن أبي عبدالله ﵇، قال: الشِّطْرَنج مَيْسِر، والنَّرْد مَيْسِر.

١٨٨. عن إسماعيل الجُعفي، عن أبي جعفر ﵇، قال: الشِّطْرَنج والنَّرد مَيْسِر.

١٨٩. عن ياسر الخادم، عن الرضا ﵇، قال: سألتُهُ عن المَيْسِر، قال: الثّقل من كُلّ شيءٍ، قال الحسين: والثّقل: ما يُخْرَج بين المتَراهِنَين من الدَّراهم وغيره.

١٩٠. عن هِشام، عن الثِّقَة، رفعه، عن أبي عبدالله ﵇، أنّه قيل له: رُوي عنكم أنّ الخمر والميسر والأنصاب والأزلام رجالٌ؟ فقال: ماكان الله ليُخاطِب خَلْقه بما لا يَعْقِلون.

١٩١. عن عبدالله بن سِنان، عن أبي عبدالله ﵇، قال: أُتي عمر بن الخطّاب بقُدامة بن مَظْعُون وقد شَرِب الخمر، وقامت عليه البيّنة، فسأل عليّاً ﵇، فأمره أن يجْلِده ثمانين.

فقال قُدامة: يا أمير المؤمنين، ليس عليَّ جلدٌ، أنا من أهل هذه الآية ﴿لَيْسَ عَلَى الَّذِينَ آمَنُوا وَعَمِلُوا الصَّالِحَاتِ جُنَاحٌ فِيمَا طَعِمُوا﴾ فقرأ الآية حتّى استتمّها. فقال له عليّ ﵇: كَذَبت، لست من أهل هذه الآية، ما طعم أهلها فهو لهم حلالٌ، وليس يأْكُلون ولا يَشْرَبُون إلاّ ما يحلّ لهم.

١٩٢. عن ابن سِنان، عن أبي عبدالله ﵇ مثله، وزاد فيه: وليس يأْكُلون ولا يَشْربون إلاّ ما أحلَّ الله لهم. ثمّ قال: إنَّ الشارب إذا ما شَرِب، لم يَدْرِ ما يأْكُل ولا ما يشرَب، فاجْلِدُوه ثمانين جلدةً.

193. From Abū al-Rabīʿ, from Abū ʿAbd Allāh عليه السلام, who said about *nabīdh* and wine, ʿ*Nabīdh* is not the same as wine. God prohibited wine in and of itself, so both a little as well as a lot of it is forbidden, just as He has prohibited carrion, blood, and pork. The Messenger of God ﷺ banned the drinking of every intoxicant, so whatever the Messenger of God ﷺ prohibits has been prohibited by God Himself.'

I asked, 'So how did the Messenger of God ﷺ deal with wine-drinking?'

So he said, 'He used to beat them with slippers, more or less. After that the people used to increase or decrease the beatings without a fixed amount until ʿAlī b. Abī Ṭālib عليه السلام fixed it to eighty lashes for the wine-drinker, whereby he flogged Quddāma b. Maẓʿūn.'

He continued, 'So Quddāma said, "I should not get a single lash, I am among the addressees of this verse: ﴿ *There will be no blame upon those who believe and do righteous deeds in regards to what they have consumed* [*in the past*] *so long as they are mindful of God, and believe* ﴾" So he said to him, "You are wrong! You are not among them. Those people were not consuming the forbidden."

Then ʿAlī عليه السلام said, "When the drunkard drinks, he becomes drunk and does not even know what he is saying or doing." The Messenger of God ﷺ, when a drunkard was brought before him, he would beat him. If he was brought before him a second time, he would beat him again. And if he was brought a third time, he was killed.'

I asked, 'What if the drinker of *nabīdh* drinks something else that intoxicates him?'

He replied, 'He must be flogged with eighty lashes, and the third time he does it, he is to be killed, just as a drinker of wine would be killed.'

I asked, 'What if a wine-drinker drinks *nabīdh* and gets drunk from it – is he flogged eighty lashes?'

He replied, 'No, less than that; but everything that intoxicates man in large amounts is prohibited even in small amounts.' [5:93]

١٩٣. عن أبي الربيع، عن أبي عبدالله عليه السلام، في الخمر والنبيذ، قال: إنَّ النبيذ ليست بمنزلة الخمر، إنَّ الله حرَّم الخمر بعينها، فقليلها وكثيرها حرام، كما حرّم الميْتَة والدم ولحم الخنزير، وحرّم رسول الله صلى الله عليه وآله الشَّراب من كُلّ مُسكِر، فما حرّمه رسول الله صلى الله عليه وآله فقد حرّمه الله.

قلت: فكيف كان ضَرَب رسول الله صلى الله عليه وآله في الخمر؟

فقال: كان يضرِب بالنَّعل، ويَزيد ويَنقِص، وكان الناس بعد ذلك يَزيدون ويُنقِصون ليس بحدٍّ محدود حتّى وقف عليّ بن أبي طالب عليه السلام في شارب الخمر على ثمانين جلدة، حيث ضَرَب قُدامة بن مَظْعُون.

قال: فقال قُدامة: ليس عليَّ جلدٌ، أنا من أهل هذه الآية ﴿لَيْسَ عَلَى الَّذِينَ آمَنُوا وَعَمِلُوا الصَّالِحَاتِ جُنَاحٌ فِيمَا طَعِمُوا إِذَا مَا اتَّقَوْا وَآمَنُوا﴾ فقال له: كَذَبت، ما أنت منهم، إن أولئك كانوا لا يشربون حرامًا.

ثمّ قال عليّ عليه السلام: إنّ الشارب إذا شَرِب فسَكِر، لم يدرِ ما يقول وما يصنع، وكان رسول الله صلى الله عليه وآله إذا أُتي بشارب الخمر ضربه، فإذا أُتي به ثانيةً ضربه، فإذا أُتي به ثالثةً ضرب عُنُقه.

قلت: فإن أخذ شارب نبيذ مُسكر قد انتشى منه؟

قال: يُضرَب ثمانين جلدةً، فإن أخذ ثالثةً قُتِل كما يُقتَل شارب الخمر.

قلت: إن أُخِذ شارب الخمر نبيذ مُسكر سَكِر منه، أيُجلَد ثمانين؟

قال: لا، دون ذلك، كلّ ما أسكر كثيره، فقليله حرام.

194. From Ḥarīz, from Abū ʿAbd Allāh عليه السلام who said, ʻIf a man in the state of ritual consecration (*iḥrām*) kills a dove, its penalty is an ewe. If he kills chicks, then a camel. If he steps on an egg and breaks it, then he must pay money. All of this is to be offered as charity in Mecca and Mina, as per God's statement in His Book: ﴾*God is sure to test you with game within reach of your hands*﴿ – meaning eggs and chicks – ﴾*and your spears*﴿ – meaning full-grown mother birds.' [5:94]

195. From Samāʿa, from Abū ʿAbd Allāh عليه السلام regarding God's verse: ﴾*God is sure to test you with game*﴿ He said, ʻGod tests them with wild animals that they can surmount from anywhere.' [5:94]

196. From Muʿāwiya b. ʿAmmār, from Abū ʿAbd Allāh عليه السلام regarding God's verse: ﴾*God is sure to test you with game within reach of your hands and spears.*﴿ He said, ʻWild animals gathered around the Messenger of God ﷺ during the *ʿumra* of Ḥudaybiyya within reach of their hands and their spears so that God may test them.' [5:94]

197. In al-Ḥalabī's narration on his authority, ʻGame gathered around them from all sides, coming near them to such proximity that they were within reach of their hands and spears, so that God could test them thereby.' [5:94]

198. From Zurāra, from Abū Jaʿfar عليه السلام regarding God's verse: ﴾*Do not kill game while you are in the state of consecration* [*for pilgrimage*]. *If someone does so intentionally the penalty is an offering of a domestic animal brought to the Kaʿba, equivalent.*﴿ He said, ʻWhoever kills an ostrich, then [the penalty is] a full-grown she-camel or cow. Whoever kills a donkey or similar animal, then he must offer a cow; and whoever kills a deer must offer an ewe. They are to be brought to the Kaʿba and sacrificed as an obligation due. If it is during the Hajj, then it is done at Mina where people carry out the sacrifice, and if it is during *ʿumra* then he sacrifices at Mecca. If he wishes, he can leave it until he buys it after coming back, and sacrifice it then and that would absolve him.' [5:95]

١٩٤. عن حَريز، عن أبي عبدالله عليه السلام، قال: إذا قتل الرجل المحُرِم حمامةً ففيها شاة، فإن قتل فرخًا ففيه حَمَل، فإن وَطِئ بيضةً فكسَرها فعليه دِرْهَم، كلُّ هذا يتصدّق بمكّة ومِنى، وهو قوله الله في كتابه: ﴿لَيَبْلُوَنَّكُمُ اللَّهُ بِشَيْءٍ مِنَ الصَّيْدِ تَنَالُهُ﴾ البيض والفِراخ ﴿وَرِمَاحُكُمْ﴾ الأمّهات الكِبار.

١٩٥. عن سَماعة، عن أبي عبدالله عليه السلام، قول الله: ﴿لَيَبْلُوَنَّكُمُ اللَّهُ بِشَيْءٍ مِنَ الصَّيْدِ﴾، قال: ابتلاهم الله بالوحش، فرَكِبهم من كُلّ مكان.

١٩٦. عن معاوية بن عمّار، عن أبي عبدالله عليه السلام، في قول الله: ﴿لَيَبْلُوَنَّكُمُ اللَّهُ بِشَيْءٍ مِنَ الصَّيْدِ تَنَالُهُ أَيْدِيكُمْ وَرِمَاحُكُمْ﴾، قال: حشر لرسول الله صلى الله عليه وآله الوحوش حتّى نالتها أيديهم ورماحهم في عُمرة الحُديبية، ليبلوهم الله به.

١٩٧. وفي رواية الحلبي عنه: حُشِر عليهم الصيد من كلّ مكان حتّى دنا منهم، فنالته أيديهم ورماحهم، ليَبْلُوَنّكم الله به.

١٩٨. عن زُرارة، عن أبي جعفر عليه السلام، في قول الله تعالى: ﴿لَا تَقْتُلُوا الصَّيْدَ وَأَنْتُمْ حُرُمٌ وَمَنْ قَتَلَهُ مِنْكُمْ مُتَعَمِّدًا فَجَزَاءٌ مِثْلُ مَا قَتَلَ مِنَ النَّعَمِ﴾.

قال: من أصاب نَعامة فبَدَنة، ومن أصاب حِمارًا أو شِبهه فعليه بَقَرة، ومن أصاب ظَبيًا فعليه شاة، بالغ الكعبة حقًّا واجبًا عليه أن يَنْحَر، إن كان في حجّ فبمنى حيث يَنْحَر الناس، وإن كان في عُمرة نَحَر بمكّة، وإن شاء تَركه حتّى يَشتريه بعد ما يقدم فيَنْحَره، فإنّه يُجزي عنه.

199. From Abū al-Ṣabbāh al-Kinānī, from Abū ʿAbd Allāh عليه السلام who said about God's verse: ﴿*If someone does so intentionally the penalty is an offering of a domestic animal brought to the Kaʿba, equivalent*﴾, 'For a deer, it is an ewe as well as for a dove and its like; for chicks, the same number of lambs; for a wild donkey, a cow; and for an ostrich, a full-grown sacrificial animal.' [5:95]

200. From Ayyūb b. Nūḥ[17]: 'For an ostrich, [the penalty is] a full-grown she-camel or cow; and for a cow, it is a cow.'

201. In a narration by Ḥarīz, from Zurāra he said, 'I asked Abū Jaʿfar عليه السلام about God's verse: ﴿*as judged by two just men among you.*﴾ He said, "The just man is the Messenger of God صلى الله عليه وآله and the Imam after him." Then he said, "And this is one of the places where the scribes made a mistake."' [5:95]

202. From Muḥammad b. Muslim, from Abū Jaʿfar عليه السلام regarding God's verse: ﴿*as judged by two just men among you*﴾, 'It refers to one man, meaning the Imam عليه السلام.' [5:95]

203. From Ibn Sinān, from Abū ʿAbd Allāh عليه السلام who said, 'The Commander of the Faithful عليه السلام, concerning the laws of retaliation when it came to injuries and exemplary punishments, ruled that where two just men from among you are to judge, it means the Imam.' [5:95]

204. From Zurāra who said, 'I heard Abū Jaʿfar عليه السلام say: ﴿*as judged by two just men among you.*﴾ He said, "That is the Messenger of God صلى الله عليه وآله and the Imam after him. So if the Imam judges, then that suffices you."' [5:95]

---

17 Abū al-Ḥusayn Ayyūb b. Nūḥ b. Darrāj al-Nakhaʿī, a reliable and trustworthy representative of the eighth Imam who was known for his piety and asceticism. His father, Nūḥ b. Darrāj, was a judge in Kufa. See Ḥillī, *Khulāṣat al-aqwāl*, 59 (nr. 58).

١٩٩. عن أبي الصبّاح الكِناني، عن أبي عبدالله عليه السلام، في قول الله: ﴿وَمَن قَتَلَهُ مِنكُم مُتَعَمِّدًا فَجَزَاءٌ مِثْلُ مَا قَتَلَ مِنَ النَّعَمِ﴾.

قال: في الظبي شاة، وفي الحَمامة وأشباهها، وإن كانت فِراخًا فعِدّتها من الحُملان، وفي حِمار وحشٍ بقرة، وفي النّعامة جَزور.

٢٠٠. عن أيّوب بن نُوح: وفي النّعامة بَدَنة، وفي البَقَرة بَقَرة.

٢٠١. وفي رواية حَريز، عن زُرارة، قال: سألتُ أبا جعفر عليه السلام عن قول الله تعالى: ﴿يَحْكُمُ بِهِ ذَوَا عَدْلٍ مِنكُمْ﴾، قال: العدل: رسول الله صلى الله عليه وآله والإمام من بعده، ثمّ قال: وهذا ممّا أخطأت به الكُتّاب.

٢٠٢. عن محمّد بن مسلم، عن أبي جعفر عليه السلام، في قوله الله: ﴿يَحْكُمُ بِهِ ذَوَا عَدْلٍ مِنكُمْ﴾ يعني رجلاً واحدًا، يعني الإمام عليه السلام.

٢٠٣. عن ابن سِنان، عن أبي عبدالله عليه السلام، قال: قضي أمير المؤمنين عليه السلام في الدِّيات ماكان من ذلك من جُروحٍ أو تنكيلٍ، فيحكُم به ذوا عدلٍ منكم، يعنى الإمام.

٢٠٤. عن زُرارة، قال: سَمِعتُ أبا جعفر عليه السلام يقول: ﴿يَحْكُمُ بِهِ ذَوَا عَدْلٍ مِنكُمْ﴾، قال: ذلك رسول الله صلى الله عليه وآله والإمام من بعده، فإذا حَكَم به الإمام فَحَسْبُك.

205. From al-Zuhrī, from ʿAlī b. al-Ḥusayn عليه السلام who said, 'Fasting as a penalty for hunting is obligatory. God, Blessed and most High, says: ﴾*If someone does so intentionally the penalty is an offering of a domestic animal brought to the Kaʿba, equivalent – as judged by two just men among you – to the one he has killed; alternatively, he may atone by feeding the needy or by fasting an equivalent number of days.*﴿

Do you know how the balance of those fasts is worked out, Zuhrī?' So I replied, 'No.' He said, 'He should get the game valued. Then he should get an amount of wheat equivalent to that value. Then he should measure the number of cubits covered by that amount of wheat, and fast one day for each half-cubit.' [5:95]

206. From Dāwūd b. Sirḥān, from Abū ʿAbd Allāh عليه السلام who said, 'Whoever kills game while in the state of consecration, if it is an ostrich, then he must offer a full-grown she-camel or cow [as penalty]; for a wild donkey – a cow, and for a deer – an ewe, as judged by two just men among you.'

He added, 'His judgement would be to rule based on what he sees whether to enforce the penalty or the fasting. God says: ﴾*an offering of a domestic animal brought to the Kaʿba*﴿, and fasting for one who cannot afford a sacrificial animal, so he must instead fast for three days: the day before the *tarwiya*, the day of *tarwiya*, and the day of *ʿarafa*.' [5:95]

207. From ʿAbd Allāh b. Sinān, from Abū ʿAbd Allāh عليه السلام. He said, 'I asked him about God's statement regarding one who intentionally kills game while in the state of consecration: ﴾*If someone does so intentionally the penalty is an offering of a domestic animal brought to the Kaʿba, equivalent - as judged by two just men among you - to the one he has killed; alternatively, he may atone by feeding the needy or by fasting an equivalent number of days*﴿ – what is that?'

So he replied, 'He considers the penalty that he has to offer for that which he killed, so he can either sacrifice that or get it valued and buy food with it to feed the poor, allowing one *mudd* per person, or he can calculate how many people that would feed and fast one day per poor person.' [5:95]

٢٠٥. عن الزُّهري، عن عليّ بن الحسين عليهما السلام، قال: صومُ جزاء الصيد واجبٌ، قال الله تبارك وتعالى: ﴿وَمَن قَتَلَهُ مِنكُم مُّتَعَمِّدًا فَجَزَاءٌ مِّثْلُ مَا قَتَلَ مِنَ النَّعَمِ يَحْكُمُ بِهِ ذَوَا عَدْلٍ مِّنكُمْ هَدْيًا بَالِغَ الْكَعْبَةِ أَوْ كَفَّارَةٌ طَعَامُ مَسَاكِينَ أَوْ عَدْلُ ذَٰلِكَ صِيَامًا﴾.

أوَ تدري كيف يكون عدل ذاك صياماً، يا زُهري؟ فقلت: لا. قال: يُقوّم الصيد، قال: ثمّ يفضّ القِيمة على البُرّ، ثم يُكال ذلك البُرّ أصواعًا، فيصوم لكُلّ نصف صاعٍ يومًا.

٢٠٦. عن داود بن سِرحان، عن أبي عبدالله عليه السلام، قال: مَن قتل مِن النَّعم وهو مُحرِم نَعَامة، فعليه بَدَنة، ومن حِمار وحشٍ بَقَرة، ومن الظَّبي شاة، يحكُم به ذوا عدلٍ منكم.

وقال: عَدْله أن يحكُم بما رأى من الحكم أو صيام، يقول الله: ﴿هَدْيًا بَالِغَ الْكَعْبَةِ﴾ والصّيام لمن لم يَجد الهدي، فصيام ثَلاثة أيّام قبل التَّروية بيومٍ، ويوم التَّروية، ويوم عَرَفة.

٢٠٧. عن عبدالله بن سِنان، عن أبي عبدالله عليه السلام، قال: سألتُهُ عن قول الله فيمن قتل صيدًا متعمّدًا وهو مُحرِم: ﴿مُّتَعَمِّدًا فَجَزَاءٌ مِّثْلُ مَا قَتَلَ مِنَ النَّعَمِ يَحْكُمُ بِهِ ذَوَا عَدْلٍ مِّنكُمْ هَدْيًا بَالِغَ الْكَعْبَةِ أَوْ كَفَّارَةٌ طَعَامُ مَسَاكِينَ أَوْ عَدْلُ ذَٰلِكَ صِيَامًا﴾ ما هو؟

فقال: ينظر إلى الذي عليه بجزاء ما قتل، فإمّا أن يهديه، وإمّا أن يُقوّم فيشتري به طعامًا، فيُطعمه، يُطعم كُلّ مسكين مُدّاً، وإمّا أن يَنْظُر كم يبلُغ عدد ذلك من المساكين، فيصوم مكان كُلّ مسكين يومًا.

208. From 'Abd Allāh b. Bukayr, from one of his associates, from Abū 'Abd Allāh ﵇, about the verse of God, Mighty and Exalted: ﴾*or by fasting an equivalent number of days.*﴿ He said, 'He should value the sacrificial animal regarding food, then fast one day per *mudd* of food. If the total number of *mudd* exceeds two months, then he need not fast more than that.' [5:95]

209. In Muḥammad b. Muslim's narration from one of the two [Imams al-Bāqir or al-Ṣādiq] regarding the verse: ﴾*or by fasting an equivalent number of days*﴿, he said, 'The balance of the value of the sacrificial animal is to be offered to charity, and if he does not have the means, then he must fast according to the amount of food allowing a day per poor person.' [5:95]

210. From Muḥammad b. Muslim, from one of the two [Imams], he said, 'I asked him about God's verse: ﴾*but if anyone re-offends, God will take vengeance on him.*﴿ He replied, 'There was once a man who took a fox while in the state of ritual consecration, and began to bring some fire close to the fox's nose. The fox began to screech and defecated. His companions were trying to stop him from what he was doing, so then he let him go. While the man was sleeping, a snake came and entered his backside and made him defecate just as he had tortured the fox. Then it came out and went off.' Another narration says that it came out from him.' [5:95]

211. From al-Ḥalabī, from Abū 'Abd Allāh ﵇ who said, 'If a man in the state of consecration kills game within the sacred area, then he must pay the penalty for it by giving charity to the poor. If he reoffends and kills game again, he does not have to pay the penalty, but God will take vengeance on him.' [5:95]

٢٠٨. عن عبدالله بن بُكير، عن بعض أصحابه، عن أبي عبدالله عليه السلام، في قول الله عزَّ وجلَّ: ﴿أَوْ عَدْلُ ذَٰلِكَ صِيَامًا﴾. قال: يُقوَّم ثمن الهدي طعامًا، ثمَّ يصوم لكلّ مُدّ يومًا، فإن زادت الأمداد على شهرين، فليس عليه أكثر من ذلك.

٢٠٩. وفي رواية محمّد بن مسلم، عن أحدهما عليهما السلام: ﴿أَوْ عَدْلُ ذَٰلِكَ صِيَامًا﴾ قال: عَدْل الهدي ما بَلَغَ يتصدّق به، فإن لم يكُن عنده فليَصُم بقَدر ما بَلَغ، لكُلّ طعام مسكين يومًا.

٢١٠. عن محمّد بن مسلم، عن أحدهما عليهما السلام، قال سألتُهُ عن قول الله: ﴿وَمَنْ عَادَ فَيَنْتَقِمُ اللَّهُ مِنْهُ﴾.

قال: إنَّ رجلاً أخذ ثعلبًا وهو مُحرِم فجعل يُقدّم النار إلى أنف الثعلب، وجعل الثعلب يصيح ويُحِدث من استه، وجعل أصحابه ينْهونه عمّا يصنع، ثمّ أرسله بعد ذلك، فبينا الرجل نائمٌ إذا جاءت حيَّة، فدخلت في دُبره، فجعل يُحِدث من استه، كما عذَّب الثعلب، ثمّ خَلّته فانطلق.

وفي رواية أخرى: ثمّ خَلَّت عنه.

٢١١. عن الحَلَبي، عن أبي عبدالله عليه السلام، قال: المُحرِم إذا قتَل الصيد في الحِلّ، فعليه جزاؤه، يتصدَّق بالصيد على مسكين، فإن عاد وقتَل صيدًا لم يَكُن عليه جزاؤه، فينتقم الله منه.

212. In another narration from al-Ḥalabī, on his authority, about a man in the state of consecration killing game, he said, 'He must pay the penalty, and if he re-offends then he is one about whom God says: ﴾*God will take vengeance on him*﴿, and he does not have to pay the penalty again.' [5:95]

213. From Ḥarīz, from Abū ʿAbd Allāh عليه السلام who said, ﴾*It is permitted for you to catch and eat seafood – an enjoyment for you.*﴿ He said, 'The briny food that they eat thereof.'

And he said, 'There is a distinction between them: every bird that lives in the forest, lays eggs on dry land, which hatch on dry land count as land game. Birds that live on land but lay eggs in the sea that hatch in the sea are considered seafood.' [5:96]

214. From Zayd al-Shaḥḥām, from Abū ʿAbd Allāh عليه السلام. He said, 'I asked him about God's verse: ﴾*It is permitted for you to catch and eat seafood – an enjoyment for you and the traveller.*﴿ He replied, 'These are the briny fish and what they subsist on too; and even if is not briny, it is an enjoyment.' [5:96]

215. From Abān b. Taghlib who said, 'I asked Abū ʿAbd Allāh عليه السلام about: ﴾*God has made the Kaʿba – the Sacred House – a means of support for people.*﴿ He said, "God has made it for their religion as well as a means of livelihood for them."' [5:97]

216. From Aḥmad b. Muḥammad who said, 'I wrote to Abū al-Ḥasan al-Riḍā عليه السلام, so he wrote at the end [of his reply], "Have you still not stopped asking so many questions, for you seem to refuse to restrain yourselves. People before you perished as a result of their abundant questioning of everything, so God, Blessed and most High, said: ﴾*You who believe, do not ask about matters which, if made known to you, might make things difficult for you – if you ask about them while the Qurʾān is being revealed, they will be made known to you – for God has kept silent about them: God is most forgiving and forbearing. Before you, some people asked about things, and then came to disbelieve in them.*﴿"' [5:101]

٢١٢. وفي رواية أخرى، عن الحلبي، عنه: في محرم أصاب صيداً، قال: عليه الكَفّارة، فإن عاد فهو ممّن قال الله: ﴿فَيَنتَقِمُ اللهُ مِنْهُ﴾ وليس عليه كفّارة.

٢١٣. عن حَرِيز، عن أبي عبد الله ﷺ، قال: ﴿أُحِلَّ لَكُمْ صَيْدُ الْبَحْرِ وَطَعَامُهُ مَتَاعًا لَكُمْ﴾، قال: مالحه الذي يأكلون.

وقال: فَصْلُ ما بينهما: كُلّ طير يكون في الآجام يَبيض في البرّ، ويُفرخ في البرّ، فهو من صيد البرّ، وما كان من طيرٍ يكون في البرّ، ويبيض في البحر، ويفرخ في البحر، فهو من صيد البحر.

٢١٤. عن زيد الشَّحّام، عن أبي عبد الله ﷺ، قال: سألتُه عن قول الله: ﴿أُحِلَّ لَكُمْ صَيْدُ الْبَحْرِ وَطَعَامُهُ مَتَاعًا لَكُمْ وَلِلسَّيَّارَةِ﴾، قال: هي الحيتان المالح، وما تزوّدت منه أيضاً، وإن لم يكُن مالحًا فهو مَتاع.

٢١٥. عن أبان بن تَغْلِب، قال: قلتُ لأبي عبد الله ﷺ: ﴿جَعَلَ اللهُ الْكَعْبَةَ الْبَيْتَ الْحَرَامَ قِيَامًا لِلنَّاسِ﴾؟، قال: جعلها الله لدينهم ومعايشهم.

٢١٦. عن أحمد بن محمّد، قال: كتبتُ إلى أبي الحسن الرضا ﷺ، وكتب في آخره: أولم تُنْهَوا عن كَثْرة المسائل؟ فأبيتم أن تنتهوا، إيّاكم وذاك، فإنّما هَلَك من كان قبلكم بكَثْرة سؤالهم، فقال الله تبارك وتعالى: ﴿يا أَيُّهَا الَّذِينَ آمَنُوا لاَ تَسْأَلُوا عَنْ أَشْيَاءَ﴾ إلى قوله ﴿كَافِرِينَ﴾.

217. From Muḥammad b. Muslim, from Abū ʿAbd Allāh عليه السلام regarding God's verse: ﴾*God did not institute the dedication of such things as baḥīra, sāʾiba, waṣīla, or ḥām to idols.*﴿ He said, 'The people during pre-Islamic pagan ignorance, when a she-camel gave birth to twins would say: This is a *waṣīla*, and would not allow it to be slaughtered for consumption. If it gave birth to ten, they would term it *sāʾiba*, and would not allow it to be ridden or eaten. The *ḥām* was a male camel that they would not be allowed to eat. So God revealed that indeed God does not forbid any such thing.' [5:103]

218. From Abū al-Rabīʿ who said, 'Abū ʿAbd Allāh عليه السلام was asked about the *sāʾiba*.' He replied, "This is in reference to when a man sets his slave free then says to him, 'Go wherever you want, and I will have nothing to do with your inheritance, and I am no longer responsible on your account; and and this is witnessed by a witness."' [5:103]

219. From ʿAmmār b. Abī al-Aḥwaṣ who said, ' I asked Abū Jaʿfar عليه السلام about the *sāʾiba*. He replied, "Look in the Qurʾan, wherever it refers to ﴾*setting a slave free*﴿[4:92], that is what the *sāʾiba* is, ʿAmmār, one who has no one among people to fend for him apart from God. Whoever has only God to fend for him is under the protection of the Messenger of God, peace be upon him and his family. And whoever is fended for by the Messenger of God is also fended for by the Imam. He is his legal guardian for criminal offences and executor of his inheritance."' [5:103]

220. He said, 'Abū ʿAbd Allāh عليه السلام said that the *baḥīra* was when an animal gave birth to its young who in turn gave birth too, its ears would be slit.' [5:103]

221. From Abū Usāma from Abū ʿAbd Allāh عليه السلام. He said, 'I asked him about God's verse: ﴾*You who believe, when death approaches any of you, let two just men from among you act as witnesses to the making of a bequest or two men from another people if you are journeying in the land when death approaches.*﴿ He replied, "They are two disbelievers."

I said, "So what about God's words: ﴾*two just men*﴿?" He replied, "Two Muslims."' [5:106]

٢١٧. عن محمّد بن مسلم، عن أبي عبدالله عليه السلام، في قول الله: ﴿مَا جَعَلَ اللَّهُ مِن بَحِيرَةٍ وَلَا سَائِبَةٍ وَلَا وَصِيلَةٍ وَلَا حَامٍ﴾، قال: وإنّ أهل الجاهلية كانوا إذا وَلَدتِ الناقة ولدين في بطنٍ قالوا: وَصَلَت، فلا يستحلّون ذبحها، ولا أكلها، وإذا وَلَدت عشرًا جعلوها سائبةً، فلا يستحلّون ظهرها ولا أكلها، والحَام: فحل الإبل، لم يكونوا يَسْتَحِلّونه، فأنزل الله أنّ الله لم يحرّم شيئًا من هذا.

٢١٨. عن أبي الربيع، قال: سُئِل أبو عبدالله عليه السلام عن السائِبة؟ قال: هو الرجل يعتِقُ غُلامه، ثمّ يقول له: اذهب حيث شئت، وليس لي من ميراثك شيءٌ، ولا عليّ من جريرتك شيء، ويُشهِدُ على ذلك شاهدًا.

٢١٩. عن عمّار بن أبي الأحوص، قال: سألتُ أبا جعفر عليه السلام عن السائبة، قال: انظُر في القرآن، فما كان منه ﴿فَتَحْرِيرُ رَقَبَةٍ﴾. فتلك يا عمّار السائبة التي لا ولاء لأحدٍ من الناس عليها إلاّ الله، فما كان ولاؤه لله فهو لرسول الله عليه وآله السلام، وما كان ولاؤه لرسول الله صلى الله عليه وآله وسلم فإنّ ولاءه للإمام، وجنايته على الإمام، وميراثه له عليه السلام.

٢٢٠. قال: وقال أبو عبدالله عليه السلام: البحيرة إذا وَلَدَتْ وَوَلَدَ وَلَدُها بُحِرت.

٢٢١. عن أبي أسامة، عن أبي عبدالله عليه السلام، قال: سألتُهُ عن قول الله عزّ وجلّ: ﴿يَا أَيُّهَا الَّذِينَ آمَنُوا شَهَادَةُ بَيْنِكُمْ إِذَا حَضَرَ أَحَدَكُمُ الْمَوْتُ﴾، قال: هما كافران.

قلت: فيقول الله تعالى: ﴿ذَوَا عَدْلٍ مِنكُمْ﴾، قال: مسلمان.

222. From Zayd al-Shaḥḥām, from Abū ʿAbd Allāh عليه السلام. He said, 'I asked him about God's verse: ﴾ *You who believe, when death approaches any of you, let two just men from among you act as witnesses to the making of a bequest or two men from another people if you are journeying in the land when death approaches.* ﴿ So he replied, "They would be two disbelievers."' [5:106]

223. From ʿAlī b. Sālim, from a man who said, 'I asked Abū ʿAbd Allāh عليه السلام about God's verse: ﴾ *You who believe, when death approaches any of you, let two just men from among you act as witnesses to the making of a bequest or two men from another people if you are journeying in the land when death approaches.* ﴿ So he replied, "Those from among you are the two Muslims, and those from another people would be the People of the Book. If you cannot find anyone from the People of the Book, then from the Magians, because the Messenger of God ﷺ said, 'Uphold the same practice with the Magians as you do with the People of the Book with regards to the poll tax (*jizya*).'" He continued, "That is if a man died in a foreign land and there are no Muslims. Then he [i.e. his guardian] should get two men from the People of the Book to act as witnesses who are to be kept back after the prayer, and be made to swear by God: ﴾ *We will not sell our testimony for any price, even if a close relative is involved. We will not hide God's testimony, for then we should be doing wrong.* ﴿ And that is if the deceased's guardian has any doubt about their testimony. ﴾ *If it is discovered that these two are guilty* [*of perjury*] ﴿, then he can say that they have given a false testimony but he cannot reject their testimonies until two other witnesses come to replace the first two witnesses, ﴾ *and swear by God, "Our testimony is truer than theirs. We have said nothing but the truth, for that would make us wrongdoers."* ﴿ When he does that, then he can reject the testimony of the first two, and the testimony of the other two witnesses is valid. God says: ﴾ *that will make it more likely that they will give true and proper testimony, or fear that their oaths might be refuted by others afterwards.* ﴿"' [5:106]

٢٢٢. عن زيد الشحّام، عن أبي عبد الله ، قال: سألتُه عن قول الله: ﴿يَا أَيُّهَا الَّذِينَ آمَنُوا شَهَادَةُ بَيْنِكُمْ﴾ إلى: ﴿أَوْ آخَرَانِ مِنْ غَيْرِكُمْ﴾، فقال: هما كافران.

٢٢٣. عن عليّ بن سالم، عن رجل، قال: سألتُ أبا عبد الله عن قول الله: ﴿يَا أَيُّهَا الَّذِينَ آمَنُوا شَهَادَةُ بَيْنِكُمْ إِذَا حَضَرَ أَحَدَكُمُ الْمَوْتُ حِينَ الْوَصِيَّةِ اثْنَانِ ذَوَا عَدْلٍ مِنْكُمْ أَوْ آخَرَانِ مِنْ غَيْرِكُمْ﴾.

فقال: اللّذان منكم مسلمان، واللّذان من غيركم من أهل الكتاب، فإن لم تَجِدُوا من أهل الكتاب فمن المَجُوس، لأنّ رسول الله قال: «وسنّوا في المَجُوس سُنّةَ أهل الكتاب في الجِزية».

قال: وذلك إذا مات الرجل بأرض غُربةٍ، فلم يَجِد مُسْلِمَين، أشهد رجلين من أهل الكتاب، يُحْبِسان من بعد الصلاة، فيُقْسِمان بالله ﴿لَا نَشْتَرِي بِهِ ثَمَنًا﴾ قليلاً ﴿وَلَوْ كَانَ ذَا قُرْبَى وَلَا نَكْتُمُ شَهَادَةَ اللَّهِ إِنَّا إِذًا لَمِنَ الْآثِمِينَ﴾.

قال: وذلك إن ارتاب وليّ الميت في شهادتهما ﴿فَإِنْ عُثِرَ عَلَى أَنَّهُمَا اسْتَحَقَّا إِثْمًا﴾ يقول شَهِدا بالباطل، فليس له أن يَنْقُض شهادتهما حتّى يجيء شاهدان فيقومان مقام الشاهدين الأوّلين ﴿فَيُقْسِمَانِ بِاللَّهِ لَشَهَادَتُنَا أَحَقُّ مِنْ شَهَادَتِهِمَا وَمَا اعْتَدَيْنَا إِنَّا إِذًا لَمِنَ الظَّالِمِينَ﴾ فإذا فعل ذلك نقض شهادة الأوّلين، وجازت شهادة الآخرين، يقول الله تعالى: ﴿ذَلِكَ أَدْنَى أَنْ يَأْتُوا بِالشَّهَادَةِ عَلَى وَجْهِهَا أَوْ يَخَافُوا أَنْ تُرَدَّ أَيْمَانٌ بَعْدَ أَيْمَانِهِمْ﴾.

224. From [Muḥammad] Ibn al-Fuḍayl, from Abū al-Ḥasan عليه السلام. He said, ‘I asked him about God’s verse: ﴿*when death approaches any of you, let two just men from among you act as witnesses to the making of a bequest or two men from another people* [...].﴾ He replied, “Those from among you who are Muslims, and those from another people are the People of the Book. If you do not find anyone from the People of the Book, then from the Magians, because the Messenger of God صلى الله عليه وآله said, ‘Uphold the same practice with them as you do with the People of the Book. That means that when a Muslim man dies in a foreign land, then two Muslim men are sought after and made to bear witness over his bequest, and if he does not find Muslims to act as witnesses then two men from the People of the Book.”’ Ḥumrān said that Abū ʿAbd Allāh عليه السلام said, ‘Those from another people are from the People of the Book, and that is only when a Muslim man dies in a foreign land, seeks two Muslims to act as witnesses over the bequest and does not find any Muslims, then he can get two *dhimmī* men from the People of the Book, well-regarded among their fellow compatriots.’ [5:106]

225. From Yazīd al-Kanāsī[18] who said, ‘I asked Abū Jaʿfar عليه السلام about this verse: ﴿*On the Day when God assembles all the messengers and asks, “What response did you receive?” They will say, “We do not have that knowledge.”*﴾ He replied, “He will ask, ‘What response did you receive regarding your vicegerents that you left behind to succeed you over your communities?’ They will say, ‘We do not have knowledge about what they did after us.’”’ [5:109]

226. From Muḥammad b. Yūsuf al-Ṣanʿānī[19], on his father’s authority who said, ‘I asked Abū Jaʿfar عليه السلام about the verse: ﴿*How I inspired the disciples.*﴾ He replied, “They were inspired.”’ [5:111]

227. From Yaḥyā al-Ḥalabī, regarding His phrase: ﴿*can your Lord* [...]﴾ He said, ‘I read it as: ﴿*can you unto your Lord*﴾, meaning “can you request your Lord.”’ [5:112]

---

18 Abū Khālid Yazīd al-Kanāsī, on whom there is scant information, was a transmitter of Imam Muḥammad al-Bāqir’s traditions. See Khūʾī, *Muʿjam*, 21:131 (nr. 13716).

19 Muḥammad b. Yūsuf al-Ṣanʿānī, described by al-ʿAllāma al-Ḥillī as a reliable narrator of the sixth Imam’s traditions. See Ḥillī, *Khulāṣat al-aqwāl*, 261 (nr. 914).

٢٢٤ . عن ابن الفُضيل، عن أبي الحسن عليه السلام، قال: سألتُهُ عن قول الله تعالى: ﴿إِذَا حَضَرَ أَحَدَكُمُ الْمَوْتُ حِينَ الْوَصِيَّةِ اثْنَانِ ذَوَا عَدْلٍ مِنْكُمْ أَوْ آخَرَانِ مِنْ غَيْرِكُمْ﴾.

قال: اللّذان منكم مسلمان، واللّذان من غيركم من أهل الكتاب، فإن لم تَجِدوا من أهل الكتاب فمن المَجُوس، لأنَّ رسول الله صلى الله عليه وآله قال: «سُنّوا بهم سُنَّة أهل الكتاب» وذلك إذا مات الرجل بأرض غربةٍ فلم يجد مُسْلِمَين يُشْهِدهما، فرجلين من أهل الكتاب.

قال حُمران: قال أبو عبد الله عليه السلام: واللّذان من غيركم من أهل الكتاب، وإنَّما ذلك إذا مات الرجل المسلم في أرض غُربة، فطلب رجلين مُسْلِمَين يُشْهِدهما على وصيّته فلم يَجِد مُسْلِمين، فليُشهِد رجلين ذِمّيّين من أهل الكتاب، مَرْضِيّين عند أصحابهما.

٢٢٥ . عن يزيد الكُناسي، قال: سألتُ أبا جعفر عليه السلام عن هذه الآية ﴿يَوْمَ يَجْمَعُ اللهُ الرُّسُلَ فَيَقُولُ مَاذَا أُجِبْتُمْ قَالُوا لَا عِلْمَ لَنَا﴾.

قال: يقول: ماذا أُجِبتم في أوصيائكم الذين خلَّفتم على أُمّتكم؟ قال: فيقولون: لا علم لنا بما فعلوا من بعدنا.

٢٢٦ . عن محمّد بن يوسف الصنعاني، عن أبيه، قال: سألتُ أبا جعفر عليه السلام عن قوله تعالى: ﴿أَوْحَيْتُ إِلَى الْحَوَارِيِّينَ﴾، قال عليه السلام: أُلهِموا.

٢٢٧ . عن يحيى الحلبي، في قوله تعالى: ﴿هَلْ يَسْتَطِيعُ رَبُّكَ﴾، قال: قراءتها (هل تستطيع ربَّك) يعني: هل تستطيع أن تدعو ربّك.

228. From ʿĪsā al-ʿAlawī, on his father's authority, from Abū Jaʿfar ﷺ who said, 'The feast-table that was sent down to the Children of Israel was suspended with golden ropes, and on it were nine spreads and nine loaves of bread.' [5:112–115]

229. From al-Fayḍ b. al-Mukhtār[20] who said, 'I heard Abū ʿAbd Allāh ﷺ say, "When the feast was sent down to ʿĪsā, the disciples said: 'Do not eat from it until he has given you permission.' But one man from among them ate from it, so some of the disciples said, 'O Spirit of God, so-and-so has eaten from it.' So ʿĪsā asked him, 'Did you eat from it?' He replied, 'No.' So the disciples said, 'Yes he did, by God, O Spirit of God. He definitely ate from it.' So ʿĪsā said to him, 'Believe your brother and believe your sight.'" [5:112–115]

230. From ʿĪsā al-ʿAlawī, on his father's authority, from Abū Jaʿfar ﷺ who said, 'The feast that was sent down to the Children of Israel was suspended with golden ropes on which were loaves of bread of nine different colours.' [5:112–115]

231. From al-Fuḍayl b. Yasār, from Abū al-Ḥasan ﷺ who said, 'The pigs from the community of ʿĪsā asked for the descent of the feast, then did not even believe in it, so God transformed them into pigs.' [5:112–115]

232. From ʿAbd al-Ṣamad b. Bundār[21], who said, 'I heard Abū al-Ḥasan ﷺ say, "Pigs were originally a community of heedless people – they rejected the feast and were thus transformed into pigs."' [5:112–115]

233. From Thaʿlaba b. Maymūn from one of our associates, from Abū Jaʿfar ﷺ regarding the words of God, Blessed and most High, to ʿĪsā: ﴾*Did you say to people, "Take me and my mother as two gods alongside God"?*﴿ He said, 'He had not said that, but would say it in the future. When God knew something

20 Fayḍ b. al-Mukhtār al-Khathʿamī, a reliable narrator of the fifth, sixth and seventh Imams. See Ḥillī, *Khulāṣat al-aqwāl*, 230 (nr. 775).

21 ʿAbd al-Ṣamad b. Bundār, on whom there is almost nothing. See Khūʾī, *Muʿjam*, 11:26 (nr. 6529).

٢٢٨. عن عيسى العلوي، عن أبيه، عن أبي جعفر عليه السلام، قال: المائدة التي نزلت على بني إسرائيل مُدلاّة بسلاسل من ذَهَبٍ، عليها تسعة أَخْوِنَة، وتسعة أرغفة.

٢٢٩. عن الفَيض بن المختار، قال: سَمِعتُ أبا عبد الله عليه السلام، يقول: لما أُنزِلت المائدة على عيسى عليه السلام قال للحَواريّين: لا تأكُلوا منها حتّى آذَن لكم. فأكل منها رجلٌ منهم، فقال بعض الحَواريّين: يا رُوح الله، أكل منها فلان. فقال له عيسى عليه السلام: أكلت منها؟ قال له: لا. فقال الحَواريُّون: بلى واللهِ يا رُوح الله، لقد أكل منها. فقال له عيسى عليه السلام: صَدِّق أخاك، وكذِّب بَصَرك.

٢٣٠. عن عيسى العلوي، عن أبيه، عن أبي جعفر عليه السلام، قال: المائدة التي نزلت على بني إسرائيل مُدلاّة بسلاسل من ذهبٍ، عليها تسعة ألوان وتسعة أرغفة.

٢٣١. عن الفُضيل بن يَسَار، عن أبي الحسن عليه السلام، قال: إنّ الخنازير من قوم عيسى عليه السلام سألوا نُزُول المائدة، فلم يُؤمنوا بها، فمسخهم الله خَنَازِير.

٢٣٢. عن عبد الصمد بن بُندار، قال: سَمِعتُ أبا الحسن عليه السلام يقول: كانت الخنازير قومٌ من القَصّارين، كَذّبوا بالمائدة، فمُسِخوا خَنَازِيرَ.

٢٣٣. عن ثَعْلَبة بن ميمون، عن بعض أصحابنا، عن أبي جعفر عليه السلام، في قول الله تبارك وتعالى لعيسى عليه السلام: ﴿أَأَنتَ قُلْتَ لِلنَّاسِ اتَّخِذُونِي وَأُمِّيَ إِلَٰهَيْنِ مِن دُونِ اللَّهِ﴾، قال: لم يَقُله وسيقوله، إنّ الله إذا عَلِم أنّ شيئاً كائن، أخبر عنه خبر ما قد كان.

to be, He informed him about it as if it was something that had already happened.' [5:116]

234. From Sulaymān b. Khālid who said, 'I asked Abū 'Abd Allāh ﷺ about God's words to 'Īsā: ﴿*Did you say to people, "Take me and my mother as two gods alongside God"?*﴾ – did God really say that?' So he replied, 'When God wills something to be, he relates it before it happens as if it has already happened.' [5:116]

235. From Jābir al-Ju'fī , from Abū 'Abd Allāh ﷺ regarding the exegesis of this verse: ﴿*You know all that is within me, though I do not know what is within You, You alone have full knowledge of things unseen.*﴾ He said, 'The Greatest Name [of God] consists of seventy-three letters, and the Lord, Blessed and most High, has hidden Himself away from it by a single letter. Thus no one knows what is within Him, Mighty and Exalted. He gave Ādam seventy-two letters, which the prophets after him inherited from each other until they came to 'Īsā. So that is what 'Īsā's statement means: ﴿*You know all that is within me*﴾ referring to the seventy-two letters of the Greatest Name. He says: You are the One Who has taught them to me, so You know them, but I do not know what is within You.' He says: 'Because You have hidden Yourself from Your creatures with that one letter, no one can know what is within You.' [5:116]

236. From 'Abd Allāh b. Bushayr[22], from Abū 'Abd Allāh ﷺ who said, "Īsā had two letters in his possession which he used; Mūsā had four, Ibrāhīm had six, Nūḥ eight, and Ādam, twenty-five. The Messenger of God ﷺ had the sum of all of those. God's Name consists of seventy-three letters, of which the Messenger of God ﷺ had seventy-two, and one was hidden from him.' [5:116]

---

22 'Abd Allāh b. Bushayr al-Khath'amī, on whom there is scant information, was a narrator of Imam Ja'far al-Ṣādiq's traditions. His reliability, though, is somewhat uncertain. See Khū'ī, *Mu'jam*, 11:127 (nr. 6739).

٢٣٤. عن سُليمان بن خالد، قال: قلتُ لأبي عبدالله عليه السلام: قول الله لعيسى عليه السلام: ﴿أَأَنتَ قُلْتَ لِلنَّاسِ اتَّخِذُونِي وَأُمِّيَ إِلَـٰهَيْنِ مِن دُونِ اللَّهِ﴾، قال الله بهذا الكلام؟ فقال: إنّ الله إذا أراد أمرًا أن يكون، قصّه قبل أن يكون، كأن قد كان.

٢٣٥. عن جابر الجُعفي، عن أبي جعفر عليه السلام في تفسير هذه الآية ﴿تَعْلَمُ مَا فِي نَفْسِي وَلَا أَعْلَمُ مَا فِي نَفْسِكَ إِنَّكَ أَنتَ عَلَّامُ الْغُيُوبِ﴾. قال: إنّ الاسم الأكبر ثلاثة وسبعون حرفًا، فاحتجب الربُّ تبارك وتعالى منها بحرف، فمن ثمّ لا يعلم أحدٌ ما في نفسه عزّ وجلّ، أعطى آدم اثنين وسبعين حرفًا، فتوارثها الأنبياء حتّى صارت إلى عيسى عليه السلام، فذلك قول عيسى عليه السلام ﴿تَعْلَمُ مَا فِي نَفْسِي﴾ يعني اثنين وسبعين حرفًا من الاسم الأكبر، يقول: أنت علّمْتَنيها، فأنت تَعْلَمها ﴿وَلَا أَعْلَمُ مَا فِي نَفْسِكَ﴾ يقول: لأنّك احتجبت من خلقك بذلك الحرف، فلا يعلم أحدٌ ما في نفسك.

٢٣٦. عن عبدالله بن بشير، عن أبي عبدالله عليه السلام، قال: كان مع عيسى عليه السلام حرفان يعمل بهما، وكان مع موسى أربعة، وكان مع إبراهيم ستّة، وكان مع نُوح ثمانية، وكان مع آدم خمسة وعشرون، وجمع ذلك كلّه لرسول الله صلى الله عليه وآله، إنّ اسم الله ثلاثة وسبعون حرفًا، كان مع رسول الله صلى الله عليه وآله اثنان وسبعون حرفًا، وحُجِب عنه واحد.

Livestock

6. Livestock

1. From Abū Baṣīr who said, 'I heard Abū 'Abd Allāh عليه السلام say, 'The Chapter of Livestock (*sūrat al-an'ām*) was revealed all at once and spread forth by seventy thousand angels when it was revealed to the Messenger of God صلى الله عليه وآله. They magnified it and venerated it, for God's name, Blessed and most High, is contained within it at seventy different places. If people were to know the virtue that lies in reading it they would never leave it.'

Then Abū 'Abd Allāh عليه السلام said, 'Whoever has a need that he wants God to fulfil should perform four units of prayer with the Chapter of the Opening (*sūrat al-fātiḥa*) and the Chapter of Livestock (*sūrat al-an'ām*) [in each unit]. Once he has completed the recitation of these chapters, he should say within his prayer:

'O Generous One, O Generous One, O Generous One. O Magnificent One, O Magnificent One, O Magnificent One. O One Who is more magnificent than any other.

O Hearer of the supplication. O One Who remains unchanged by the days and the nights, bless Muḥammad and the family of Muḥammad, and have mercy on my incapacity, my poverty, my deprivation and my destitution, for You know of them better than myself, and You are more aware of my need.

O One Who had mercy on Ya'qūb in his advanced years, when He returned the light of his eyes, Yūsuf, back to him.

O One Who had mercy on Ayyūb after he was struck with his affliction.

O One Who had mercy on Muḥammad صلى الله عليه وآله by giving refuge to him as an orphan and helping him against the tyrants and rebels of the Quraysh, and gave him the upper hand over them.

O Helper, O Helper, O Helper.'

بِسْمِ اللَّهِ الرَّحْمَٰنِ الرَّحِيمِ

من سورة الأنعام

١. عن أبي بصير، قال: سَمِعتُ أبا عبد الله عليه السلام يقول: إنَّ سورة الأنعام نَزَلَت جُملةً واحدةً، وشيّعها سبعون ألف مَلَكٍ حين أُنزِلت على رسول الله صلى الله عليه وآله، فَعَظّموها وبجّلوها، فإنَّ اسم الله تبارك وتعالى فيها في سبعين مَوضِعًا، ولو يعلم الناس بما في قراءتها من الفَضْل ما تَرَكُوها.

ثمّ قال أبو عبد الله عليه السلام: مَن كان له إلى الله حاجةٌ يُريد قضاءها، فليُصلّ أربع ركَعات بفاتحة الكتاب والأنعام، فليقل في صلاته إذا فرغ من القراءة «يا كَرِيمُ، يا كَرِيمُ، يا كَرِيمُ، يا عَظِيمُ، يا عَظِيمُ، يا عَظِيمُ، يا أعْظَمَ مِن كُلّ عَظيم، يا سَمِيعَ الدُّعاء، يا مَن لا تُغيّره الأيّام والليالي، صَلِّ على مُحمّد، وارْحَمْ ضَعْفي وفَقْري، وفَاقَتي ومَسْكَنَتي، فإنّك أعلمُ بها منّي، وأنت أعلمُ بحاجَتي، يا مَن رَحِم الشيخَ يَعْقُوبَ حِين رَدّ عليه يُوسُفَ قُرّة عَينِه، يا مَن رَحِم أيّوب بعد حُلُولِ بَلائه، يا مَن رَحِمَ مُحمّدًا صلى الله عليه وآله، ومِن اليُتْم آواه، ونَصَرهُ على جَبابِرةِ قُريش وطَوَاغِيتها وأمْكَنَهُ منهم، يا مُغيثُ، يا مُغِيثُ، يا مُغيثُ» يقوله مرارًا.

فوالّذي نفسي بيده، لو دَعَوت بها بعد ما تُصلّي هذه الصلاة في دبُر هذه السورة ثمّ سألتَ الله جميع حوائجك ما بَخِل عليك، ولأعطاكَ ذلك إن شاء الله.

He should say this several times. By He who holds my soul in His Grasp, if you were to call upon God with this supplication after reciting this chapter when you perform this prayer, then ask for all of your needs, He would not withhold anything from you, and would grant you that if God wills.'

2. From Abū Ṣāliḥ, from Ibn ʿAbbās who said, 'Whoever recites the Chapter of Livestock (*sūrat al-anʿām*) every night will be among those who are safeguarded on the Day of Resurrection, and he will never see the Fire directly.'

3. Abū ʿAbd Allāh عليه السلام also said, 'The Chapter of Livestock (*sūrat al-anʿām*) came down all at once, and was spread forth by seventy thousand angels until it was revealed to Muḥammad ﷺ. So they magnified it and venerated it, for God's Name is contained within it at seventy different places. If people were to know the virtue that lies in reciting it, they would not leave it.'

4. From Jaʿfar b. Aḥmad from al-ʿAmrakī [b. ʿAlī][1] from al-ʿUbaydī from Yūnus b. ʿAbd al-Raḥmān from ʿAlī b. Jaʿfar from Abū Ibrāhīm who said, 'Every prayer has two times, one of which is on Friday at noon.' Then he recited this verse: ﴾*Praise belongs to God who created the heavens and the earth and made darkness and light; yet the disbelievers set up equals to their Lord!*﴿ He said, 'They equate darkness with light, and oppression with justice.' [6:1]

5. From Masʿada b. Ṣadaqa, from Abū ʿAbd Allāh عليه السلام regarding His verse: ﴾*then specified a term [for you] and another fixed time, known only to Him.*﴿ He said, 'The term which is unfixed is provisional, and it can be hastened by God and delayed as He wills. The fixed term, however, is the one that He wills to descend on the Night of Destiny and other such occasions.' He continued, 'So that is the purport of God's statement: ﴾*they cannot hasten it, nor, when their time comes, will they be able to delay it for a single moment.*﴿ (7:34)' [6:2]

---

1 Abū Muḥammad al-ʿAmrakī b. ʿAlī al-Būfakī, a reliable and trustworthy scholar of Nishapur. On him, see Ḥillī, *Khulāṣat al-aqwāl*, 227 (nr. 764).

٢. عن أبي صالح، عن ابن عباس، قال: مَن قرأ سورة الأنعام في كُلّ ليلةٍ، كان من الآمنين يوم القيامة، ولم يرَ النار بعينه أبدًا.

٣. وقال أبو عبد الله عليه السلام: نزلت سورة الأنعام جُملةً واحدةً، شيّعها سبعون ألف مَلَك حتّى أُنزِلت على محمّد صلى الله عليه وآله، فعَظّموها وبجّلوها، فإنّ اسم الله فيها في سبعين موضعًا، ولو يعلم الناس ما في قراءتها من الفضل ما تَركُوها.

قوله تعالى: ﴿الْحَمْدُ لِلَّهِ الَّذِي خَلَقَ السَّمَاوَاتِ وَالْأَرْضَ﴾.

٤. جعفر بن أحمد، عن العَمْرَكي بن علي، عن العبيدي، عن يونس بن عبد الرّحمن، عن عليّ بن جعفر، عن أبي إبراهيم عليه السلام قال: لكُلّ صلاة وقتان، وقت يوم الجمعة زوال الشمس، ثمّ تلا هذه الآية ﴿الْحَمْدُ لِلَّهِ الَّذِي خَلَقَ السَّمَاوَاتِ وَالْأَرْضَ وَجَعَلَ الظُّلُمَاتِ وَالنُّورَ ثُمَّ الَّذِينَ كَفَرُوا بِرَبِّهِمْ يَعْدِلُونَ﴾ قال: يَعْدِلُون بين الظُّلمات والنُور، وبين الجَور والعَدل.

٥. عن مَسْعَدة بن صَدَقة، عن أبي عبد الله عليه السلام، في قوله: ﴿ثُمَّ قَضَى أَجَلًا وَأَجَلٌ مُسَمًّى عِنْدَهُ﴾.

قال: الأجل الذي غير مُسمّى موقوفٌ، يُقدّم منه ما شاء، ويؤخّر منه ما شاء، وأمّا الأجل المُسمّى فهو الذي ينزل ممّا يُريد أن يكون من ليلة القَدر إلى مثلها من قابل، فذلك قول الله ﴿فَإِذَا جَاءَ أَجَلُهُمْ لَا يَسْتَأْخِرُونَ سَاعَةً وَلَا يَسْتَقْدِمُونَ﴾.

6. From Ḥumrān, from Abū ʿAbd Allāh عليه السلام. He said, 'I asked him about God's verse: ﴾ *then specified a term* [*for you*] *and another fixed time, known only to Him.* ﴿ He replied, "The fixed term is the one that has been specified to the Angel of Death on that night, and this is as per God's verse: ﴾ *when their time comes, then they can neither delay nor hasten it, even for a moment.* ﴿ (10:49; 16:61) This [verse, 6:2] is the one specified to the Angel of Death on the Night of Destiny, and the other one is left at His discretion. If He wills, He can hasten it, and if He wills, He can delay it."' [6:2]

7. From Ḥumrān who said, 'I asked Abū ʿAbd Allāh عليه السلام about God's verse: ﴾ *then specified a term* [*for you*] *and another fixed time, known only to Him.* ﴿ So he replied, "There are two terms: a provisional term with which God does as He pleases, and a fixed term."' [6:2]

8. Ḥumrān's narration on his عليه السلام authority: 'As for the term that has not been fixed by Him it is provisional, and He can hasten it as He pleases and delay it as He pleases. The fixed term, however, is the one that is defined on the Night of Destiny.' [6:2]

9. From al-Ḥuṣayn, from Abū ʿAbd Allāh عليه السلام who said regarding God's verse: ﴾ *then specified a term* [*for you*] *and another fixed time, known only to Him* ﴿, 'The first term is the one that He has consigned to the angels, the messengers, and the prophets, and the fixed term known only to Him is the one that God has kept hidden from His creatures.' [6:2]

10. From ʿAbd Allāh b. Abī Yaʿfūr who said, 'Abū ʿAbd Allāh عليه السلام said, "They confounded others, and God would confound them, that is why God says: ﴾ *We would have surely confounded them, in regard to* [*the truth of*] *what they confound.* ﴿"' [6:9]

11. From Hishām al-Mishraqī who said, 'I wrote to Abū al-Ḥasan al-Khurāsānī عليه السلام about a man who was asking about the different meanings of *tawḥīd*. He said to me, "What would you say if they asked you to tell them about God and whether He is something or nothing?"'

He replied, 'I would say, "God has established Himself as being something by saying: ﴾ *Say, 'What thing is greatest as witness?' Say,* 'God*!*

٦. عن حُمران، عن أبي عبد الله عليه السلام، قال: سألتُهُ عن قول الله تعالى: ﴿ثُمَّ قَضَىٰ أَجَلًا وَأَجَلٌ مُّسَمًّى عِندَهُ﴾. قال: المسمّى ما سُمّي لمَلَك الموت في تلك الليلة، وهو الذي قال الله تعالى: ﴿فَإِذَا جَاءَ أَجَلُهُمْ لَا يَسْتَأْخِرُونَ سَاعَةً وَلَا يَسْتَقْدِمُونَ﴾ وهو الذي سُمّي لمَلَكَ المَوت في ليلة القَدْر، والآخَر له فيه المشيّة، إن شاء قدّمه وإن شاء أخّره.

٧. عن حُمران، قال: سألتُ أبا عبد الله عليه السلام، عن قول الله﴿ قَضَىٰ أَجَلًا وَأَجَلٌ مُّسَمًّى﴾ قال: فقال: هما أجلان: أجلٌ موقوفٌ يصنع الله ما يشاء، وأجلٌ محتوم.

٨. وفي رواية حُمران عنه: أمّا الأجل الذي غير مُسمّى عنده، فهو أجل موقوف، يُقدّم فيه ما يشاء، ويؤخّر فيه ما يشاء، وأمّا الأجل المُسمّى، فهو الذي يُسمّى في ليلة القَدْر.

٩. عن حُصين، عن أبي عبد الله عليه السلام، في قوله: ﴿قَضَىٰ أَجَلًا وَأَجَلٌ مُّسَمًّى﴾، قال: الأجل الأوّل هو ما نبذه إلى الملائكة والرُّسل والأنبياء، والأجل المُسمّى عنده هو الذي ستره الله عن الخلائق.

١٠. عن عبد الله بن أبي يعفور، قال: قال أبو عبد الله عليه السلام: لَبَسُوا عليهم لَبَس الله عليهم، فإنّ الله يقول: ﴿وَلَلَبَسْنَا عَلَيْهِم مَّا يَلْبِسُونَ﴾.

١١. عن هِشام المِشْرَقي، قال: كتبت إلى أبي الحسن الخُراساني عليه السلام: رجلٌ يسأل عن معانٍ في التوحيد. قال: فقال لي: ما تقول إذا قالوا لك: أخبرنا عن الله، شيء هو أم لا شيء؟

[*He is*] *witness between me and you'*﴾ – and I do not say that He is a 'thing' like other things nor do we say that God is a body."'

So he said, "And what weakens this argument: that God is a body unlike other bodies, but that nothing resembles Him from all of His creations?"

He continued, 'So he عليه السلام replied, "People adhere to three opinions when it comes to God's unity: the opinion of denial, the opinion of anthropomorphism, and the opinion of affirming [His Being] without anthropomorphism. Neither is the opinion of denial admissible nor that of anthropomorphism, because nothing can be like God. The solution in all that is the third way, which is the affirmation of His Being without likening Him to anything else. He is as He has described Himself: One, Independent, Light."' [6:19]

12. From Zurāra and Ḥumrān, from Abū Jaʿfar and Abū ʿAbd Allāh, peace be upon them both, who said regarding God's verse: ﴿*And this Qurʾān has been revealed to me that I may warn thereby you and whomever it may reach*﴾, 'It refers to the Imams after him, and they warn people thereby.' [6:19]

13. From Abū Khālid al-Kābulī who said, 'I asked Abū Jaʿfar عليه السلام about: ﴿*And this Qurʾān has been revealed to me that I may warn thereby you and whomever it may reach*﴾ – what did He mean by the words: ﴿*and whomever it may reach*﴾? So he replied, "Whomsoever *he* may reach, being an Imam from the progeny of the successors, so that he may warn through the Qurʾan just as the Messenger of God ﷺ warned people thereby."' [6:19]

14. From ʿAbd Allāh b. Bukayr, from Muḥammad, from Abū Jaʿfar عليه السلام about God's verse: ﴿*that I may warn thereby you and whomever it may reach*﴾, he said, "Alī عليه السلام was among those whom it reached.' [6:19]

قال: فقلتُ: إنّ الله أثبت نفسه شيئًا، فقال: ﴿قُلْ أَيُّ شَيْءٍ أَكْبَرُ شَهَادَةً قُلِ اللَّهُ شَهِيدٌ بَيْنِي وَبَيْنَكُمْ﴾ لا أقول شيئًا كالأشياء، أو نقول إنّ الله جِسم.

فقال: وما الذي يَضْعُف فيه من هذا، إنّ الله جِسمٌ لا كالأجسام، ولا يُشبِهه شيء من المخلوقين.

قال: ثمّ قال: إنّ للنّاس في التوحيد ثلاثة مذاهب: مذهب نفي، ومذهب تشبيه، ومذهب إثبات بغير تشبيه، فمذهب النفي لا يجوز، ومذهب التشبيه لا يجوز، وذلك أنّ الله لا يُشبهه شيء، والسبيل في ذلك الطريقة الثالثة، وذلك أنّه مُثبت لا يُشبهه شيء، وهو كما وصف نفسه أحدٌ صَمَدٌ نُورٌ.

١٢. عن زُرارة وحُمران، عن أبي جعفر، وأبي عبدالله عليه السلام، في قوله: ﴿وَأُوحِيَ إِلَيَّ هَٰذَا الْقُرْآنُ لِأُنذِرَكُم بِهِ وَمَن بَلَغَ﴾ يعني الأئمّة من بعده، وهم يُنْذِرون به الناس.

١٣. عن أبي خالد الكابُلي، قال: قلتُ لأبي جعفر عليه السلام: ﴿وَأُوحِيَ إِلَيَّ هَٰذَا الْقُرْآنُ لِأُنذِرَكُم بِهِ وَمَن بَلَغَ﴾ حقيقة أيّ شيء عنى بقوله ﴿وَمَن بَلَغَ﴾؟ قال: فقال: من بَلَغ أن يكون إمامًا من ذُرّيّة الأوصياء، فهو يُنْذِر بالقرآن كما أنذر به رسول الله صلى الله عليه وآله وسلم.

١٤. عن عبدالله بن بُكير، عن محمّد، عن أبي جعفر عليه السلام، في قول الله ﴿لِأُنذِرَكُم بِهِ وَمَن بَلَغَ﴾، قال: عليّ عليه السلام ممّن بَلَغ.

15. From Hishām b. Sālim, from Abū ʿAbd Allāh عليه السلام who said, 'On the Day of Resurrection, God shall pardon in a way that no one could have imagined, such that even the polytheists will say: ﴾*By God, our Lord, we have not set up partners beside Him!'*﴿ [6:23]

16. From Abū Maʿmar al-Saʿdī who said, 'A man came to ʿAlī عليه السلام and said, "O Commander of the Faithful, I have doubts about God's revealed Book." So ʿAlī عليه السلام said to him, "May your mother be bereaved of you! How can you doubt in God's revealed Book?"

So the man said to him, "Because I find that some parts of the book rebut other parts of it, and they contradict each other."

He said, "So bring forth that which you have doubts in."

So he said, "Since God says: ﴾*On the Day when the Spirit and the angels stand in rows, they will not speak except for those to whom the Lord of Mercy gives permission, who will say only what is right,*﴿(78:38) then when they are made to speak, God says: ﴾*they will only say, 'By God, our Lord, we have not set up partners beside Him!'*﴿ and: ﴾*on the Day of Resurrection, you will reject and curse one another*﴿(29:25) and: ﴾*This is how it will really be: the inhabitants of the Fire will blame one another in this way*﴿(38:64) and: ﴾*God will say, 'Do not argue in My presence. I sent you a warning,*﴿(50:28) and: ﴾*On that Day We shall seal up their mouths, but their hands will speak to Us, and their feet bear witness to everything they have done.*﴿(36:65) So one minute they speak, and the next they do not speak; and here you have the skins and the hands and feet being made to speak, and there you have nothing being able to speak except those to whom the Merciful gives permission, who will say only what is right. So how is that possible, Commander of the Faithful?"

So he said to him, "All of that [which you have mentioned] does not happen in a single occurrence, but rather at various points during that Day whose length will be fifty thousand years. God will first gather all His creatures together in one place, where they will recognise each other. They will talk to each other, seek each other's forgiveness – those that displayed obedience to the messengers and their followers, and assisted each other in righteousness and piety in the world. The disobedient lot from among those who displayed their transgression in this world and aided and abetted each other in oppression and enmity in this life will curse each other. The arrogant ones too, as well as the helpless ones – they will curse and reject each

١٥. عن هِشام بن سالم، عن أبي عبد الله عليه السلام، قال: إنّ الله يعفو يوم القيامة عفوًا لا يَخْطِر على بال أحدٍ، حتّى يقول أهلُ الشّرك: ﴿وَاللهِ رَبِّنَا مَا كُنَّا مُشْرِكِينَ﴾.

١٦. عن أبي مَعْمَر السّعدي، قال أتى عليًّا عليه السلام رجلٌ فقال: يا أمير المؤمنين، إنّي شَكَكْتُ في كتاب الله المُنْزَل، فقال له عليّ عليه السلام: ثَكِلَتْك أُمُّك، وكيف شَكَكت في كتاب الله المُنْزَل؟

فقال له الرجل: لأنّي وجدتُ الكتاب يُكذّب بعضُهُ بعضًا، ويَنْقُض بعضُه بعضًا.

قال: فهات الذي شَكَكت فيه.

فقال: لأنّ الله يقول: ﴿يَوْمَ يَقُومُ الرُّوحُ وَالْمَلَائِكَةُ صَفًّا لَا يَتَكَلَّمُونَ إِلَّا مَنْ أَذِنَ لَهُ الرَّحْمَنُ وَقَالَ صَوَابًا﴾ ويقول حيث استنطقوا، فقالوا: ﴿وَاللهِ رَبِّنَا مَا كُنَّا مُشْرِكِينَ﴾، فصوابٌ ذلك؟ ويقول: ﴿يَوْمَ الْقِيَامَةِ يَكْفُرُ بَعْضُكُمْ بِبَعْضٍ وَيَلْعَنُ بَعْضُكُمْ بَعْضًا﴾، ويقول: ﴿إِنَّ ذَلِكَ لَحَقٌّ تَخَاصُمُ أَهْلِ النَّارِ﴾، ويقول: ﴿وَلَا تَخْتَصِمُوا لَدَيَّ﴾، ويقول: ﴿الْيَوْمَ نَخْتِمُ عَلَى أَفْوَاهِهِمْ وَتُكَلِّمُنَا أَيْدِيهِمْ وَتَشْهَدُ أَرْجُلُهُمْ بِمَا كَانُوا يَكْسِبُونَ﴾ فمرّةً يتكلّمون، ومرّةً لا يتكلّمون، ومرّةً يُنْطِق الجُلُود والأيدي والأرجُل، ومرّةً لا يتكلّمون إلاّ من أذِن له الرحمن وقال صوابًا، فأنّى ذلك يا أمير المؤمنين؟

فقال له عليّ عليه السلام: إنّ ذلك ليس في موطنٍ واحدٍ، هي في مواطن في ذلك اليوم الذي مقداره خمسون ألف سنة، فجمع الله الخلائق في ذلك اليوم في موطنٍ يتعارفون فيه، فيُكلّم بعضُهم بعضًا، ويستغفر بعضهم لبعضٍ، أولئك الذين بَدَت منهم الطاعة من الرُّسل والأتباع، وتعاونوا على البرّ والتقوى في دار الدُّنيا، ويَلْعَن أهل المعاصي بعضُهم

other. Then they will be gathered to a place where they will run away from each other, as per God's statement: ﴾*On the Day man will flee from his own brother, his mother, his father, his wife, his children*﴿ – if they had collaborated in wrongdoing and animosity in this world ﴾*each of them will be absorbed in concerns of their own on that Day.*﴿(80:34–37)

Then they will be gathered at a place wherein they will weep, and if those cries were to be heard by the inhabitants of this world they would all be petrified and would flee away from their lifestyles; the mountains themselves would crack open, except for what God wills. They will continue to cry until they shed tears of blood.

Then they will be gathered at a place where they will be made to speak, and they will say: ﴾*'By* God, *our Lord, we have not set up partners beside Him!'*﴿ not admitting to what they had done. So their mouths will be sealed shut, and instead their hands, feet, and their skins will be made to speak – and they will speak, bearing witness to every act of disobedience that emanated from them.

Then the seal will be lifted from their mouths, and they will interrogate their own skins, hands, and feet: ﴾*Why did you give testimony against us?*﴿ They will reply: ﴾*God, who makes all things speak, made us speak.*﴿(41:21) Thereafter they will be gathered in a place where everyone will try to speak, but none shall be able except those to whom the Merciful gives permission, and who will speak only what is right. They will then be gathered to a place in which they will quarrel with each other, and debts will be extracted from one another as per the Qur'anic statements. All that will take place before the Account, and when the accounting begins each person will be absorbed with his own account. We ask God for the blessing of that Day."' [6:23–24]

بعضًا من الذين بَدَت منهم المعاصي في دار الدُّنيا، وتَعَاونوا على الظُّلم والعُدوان في دار الدُّنيا، والمُسْتَكبِرون منهم، والمُسْتَضْعَفون يَلْعَن بعضُهم بعضًا، ويُكفِّر بعضُهم بعضًا.

ثُمّ يُجْمَعُون في موطنٍ يفِرّ بعضهم من بعض، وذلك قوله: ﴿يَوْمَ يَفِرُّ الْمَرْءُ مِنْ أَخِيهِ ۝ وَأُمِّهِ وَأَبِيهِ ۝ وَصَاحِبَتِهِ وَبَنِيهِ﴾ إذا تعاونوا على الظُّلم والعُدوان في دار الدنيا ﴿لِكُلِّ امْرِئٍ مِنْهُمْ يَوْمَئِذٍ شَأْنٌ يُغْنِيهِ﴾.

ثمّ يُجْمَعُون في موطن يبكون فيه، فلو أنّ تلك الأصوات بَدَت لأهل الدنيا لأذهلت جميع الخلائق عن معايشهم، وصَدَّعت الجبال، إلاّ ما شاء الله، فلا يَزالون يَبْكُون حتّى يَبْكُون الدم.

ثمّ يَجْتَمِعون في موطن يُسْتَنْطَقُون فيه، فيقولون: ﴿وَاللَّهِ رَبِّنَا مَا كُنَّا مُشْرِكِينَ﴾ ولا يُقِرّون بما عَمِلوا، فيُخْتَم على أفواههم، وتُسْتَنْطَق الأيدي والأرجل والجُلُود، فتَنْطِق، فتشهد بكُلّ معصيةٍ بَدَت منهم، ثمّ يُرْفَع الخاتَم عن ألسنتهم، فيقولون لجُلُودهم وأيديهم وأرجلهم ﴿لِمَ شَهِدْتُمْ عَلَيْنَا﴾؟ فتقول: ﴿أَنْطَقَنَا اللَّهُ الَّذِي أَنْطَقَ كُلَّ شَيْءٍ﴾.

ثمّ يَجْتَمِعُون في موطنٍ يُسْتَنْطَق فيه جميعُ الخلائق، فلا يتكلّم أحدٌ إلاّ من أذِن له الرّحمن وقال صوابًا.

ويَجْتَمِعُون في موطنٍ يَخْتَصِمون فيه، ويُدان لبعض الخلائق من بعض، وهو القول، وذلك كُلُّه قبل الحساب، فإذا أُخِذ بالحسابِ، شُغِل كُلٌّ بما لديه، نسأل الله بَرَكَةَ ذلك اليوم.

17. From Muḥammad b. Muslim, from Ja'far b. Muḥammad, on his father's authority, on his grandfather's authority who said, 'The Commander of the Faithful ﷺ said in his sermon, "So when they are made to stand in front of it, they will say: ﴿*'If only we could be sent back, we would not reject the revelations of our Lord, but be among the believers.' No! The truth they used to hide will become all too clear to them. Even if they were brought back, they would only return to the very thing that was forbidden to them – they are such liars!*﴾"' [6:27–28]

18. From 'Uthmān b. 'Īsā, from one of his associates who reported on his authority that he said, 'God said to water: be fresh and sweet; from you I will create My Paradise and the people of My obedience.' Then He said to the water: 'Be briny and bitter; from you I will create My Fire and the people of disobedience to Me.' Then He poured both waters on the clay, then took a handful with this one, which is right, and created them into particle-like creatures. Then He asked them to bear witness over their own selves: 'Am I not your Lord whom you are obligated to obey?' They replied, 'Of course.' So He said to fire: 'Be fire!' and it was a blazing fire. Then He said to them: 'Fall into it.' So some of them rushed towards it while others moved slowly, and some of them did not leave their seats. When they felt its heat they returned, and not one of them entered it again.

Then He took a handful from this one and created them into particle-like creatures, just like the others. Thereafter He made them bear witness over their own selves just like the others had done previously. Then He said to them: 'Fall into this fire.' So some of them moved slowly, some rushed in, and some bolted in the blink of an eye. They all fell into it. Then He said, 'Now come out of it safe and sound.' So they came out of it unscathed.

So the others said, 'Ignore our first attempt so that we may do as they did.' He said, 'Very well, I will ignore it.' So some of them rushed in, some of them moved slowly, and some of them did not even leave their seats, exactly as they had done the first time round. That is the purport of His verse: ﴿*Even if they were brought back, they would only return to the very thing that was forbidden to them– they are such liars!*﴾' [6:28]

١٧. عن محمّد بن مسلم، عن جعفر بن محمّد، عن أبيه، عن جدّه عليه السلام، قال: قال أمير المؤمنين عليه السلام في خُطبته: فلمّا وَقَفُوا عليها قالوا: ﴿يَا لَيْتَنَا نُرَدُّ وَلاَ نُكَذِّبَ بِآيَاتِ رَبِّنَا وَنَكُونَ مِنَ الْمُؤْمِنِينَ﴾ إلى قوله: ﴿وَإِنَّهُمْ لَكَاذِبُونَ﴾.

١٨. عن عثمان بن عيسى، عن بعض أصحابه، عنه عليه السلام، قال: إنَّ الله تعالى قال للماء: كُن عَذْبًا فُراتًا، أَخْلُق منك جنّتي وأهل طاعتي، وقال للماء: كُن مِلحًا أُجاجًا، أَخْلُق منك ناري وأهل معصيتي، فأجرى الماءين على الطِّين، ثمّ قَبَض قبضةً بهذه — وهي يمين — فخلقهم خَلْقًا كالذرّ، ثمّ أشهدهم على أنفسهم: ألستُ بربكم وعليكم طاعتي؟ قالوا: بلى. فقال للنار: كُوني نارًا؛ فإذا نار تأجّجُ، وقال لهم: قَعُوا فيها، فمنهم من أسرع، ومنهم من أبطأ في السعي، ومنهم من لم يَرِم مجلسه، فلمّا وجدوا حرّها رجعوا، فلم يَدْخُلها منهم أحد.

ثمّ قبض قبضةً بهذه، فخلقهم خلقًا مثل الذرّ، مثل أُولئك، ثمّ أشهدهم على أنفسهم مثل ما أشهد الآخرين، ثمّ قال لهم: قَعُوا في هذه النار، فمنهم من أبطأ ومنهم من أسرع، ومنهم من مرّ بطرف العين، فوقعوا فيها كُلّهم، فقال: اخْرُجوا منها سالمين؛ فخرجوا لم يُصِبهم شيء، وقال الآخرون: يا ربّنا: أَقِلْنا نفعل كما فعلوا، قال: قد أَقَلْتُكم؛ فمنهم من أسرع في السعي، ومنهم من أبطأ، ومنهم من لم يَرِم مجلسه، مثل ما صنعوا في المرَّة الأُولى، فذلك قوله: ﴿وَلَوْ رُدُّوا لَعَادُوا لِمَا نُهُوا عَنْهُ وَإِنَّهُمْ لَكَاذِبُونَ﴾.

19. From Khālid, from Abū ʻAbd Allāh عليه السلام who said: ﴾*Even if they were brought back, they would only return to the very thing that was forbidden to them*﴿ – ʻIndeed they are rejected from the beginning.' [6:28]

20. From ʻAmmār b. Maytham[2], from Abū ʻAbd Allāh who said, ʻA man recited this verse in the presence of the Commander of the Faithful عليه السلام: ﴾*It is not you they disbelieve: the evildoers reject God's signs*﴿, so he said, "Yes actually, they did disbelieve in him. By God, they disbelieved in him in the worst manner, but it was subtle. ﴾*It is not you they disbelieve*﴿ means that they cannot bring forth a falsehood with which to disbelieve in your right."' [6:33]

21. From al-Ḥusayn b. al-Mundhir, from Abū ʻAbd Allāh عليه السلام who said regarding His verse: ﴾*It is not you they disbelieve*﴿, 'They are not able to disprove your words.' [6:33]

22. From Abū al-Ḥasan ʻAlī b. Muḥammad عليه السلام, that Qanbar, the client of the Commander of the Faithful, was brought before al-Ḥajjāj b. Yūsuf who asked him, 'What did you use to carry out for ʻAlī b. Abī Ṭālib عليه السلام?' He said, 'I used to help him perform his minor ablution (*wuḍū'*).'

So he asked, 'What would he say upon completing his *wuḍū'*?' He said, 'He used to recite this verse: ﴾*So, when they had forgotten the warning that they had been reminded of, We opened the gates to everything for them. Then, as they revelled in what they had been given, We struck them suddenly and they were dumbfounded. The evildoers were wiped out: Praise be to God, the Lord of the Worlds!*﴿

So al-Ḥajjāj asked, 'He would interpret it as applying to us?' So he said, 'Yes.' Then he asked, 'What are you going to do when I kill you?' He replied, 'I will rejoice, and you will remain wretched!' So he ordered for him to be killed.' [6:44–45]

2 Most likely a transcription error for ʻImrān b. Maytham b. Yaḥyā al-Asadī.

١٩. عن خالد، عن أبي عبدالله ﵇، قال: ﴿وَلَوْ رُدُّوا لَعَادُوا لِمَا نُهُوا عَنْهُ﴾ أنَّهم مَلْعُونون في الأصل.

٢٠. عن عمّار بن ميثم، عن أبي عبدالله ﵇، قال: قرأ رجلٌ عند أمير المؤمنين ﵇ ﴿فَإِنَّهُمْ لاَ يُكَذِّبُونَكَ وَلَكِنَّ الظَّالِمِينَ بِآيَاتِ اللهِ يَجْحَدُونَ﴾، فقال: بلى، والله لقد كذّبوه أشدّ التكذيب، ولكنّها مخفّفة: (لاَ يَكْذِبُونَك) لا يأتون بباطلٍ يُكْذِبون به حقّك.

٢١. عن الحسين بن المُنذِر، عن أبي عبدالله ﵇، في قوله: ﴿فَإِنَّهُمْ لاَ يُكَذِّبُونَكَ﴾، قال: لا يستطيعون إبطال قولك.

٢٢. عن أبي الحسن علي بن محمّد ﵇: أنّ قَنْبَرًا مولى أمير المؤمنين ﵇ أُدخل على الحجّاج بن يوسف، فقال له: ما الّذي كنتَ تلي من أمر عليّ بن أبي طالب؟ قال: كنتُ أُوضّئه.

فقال له: ما كان يقول إذا فرغ من وُضُوئه؟ قال: كان يتلو هذه الآية ﴿فَلَمَّا نَسُوا مَا ذُكِّرُوا بِهِ فَتَحْنَا عَلَيْهِمْ أَبْوَابَ كُلِّ شَيْءٍ حَتَّى إِذَا فَرِحُوا بِمَا أُوتُوا أَخَذْنَاهُمْ بَغْتَةً فَإِذَا هُمْ مُبْلِسُونَ ۞ فَقُطِعَ دَابِرُ الْقَوْمِ الَّذِينَ ظَلَمُوا وَالْحَمْدُ لِلَّهِ رَبِّ الْعَالَمِينَ﴾.

فقال الحجّاج: كان يتأوّلها علينا؟ فقال: نعم. فقال: ما أنت صانع إذا ضَرَبْتُ عِلاوتك؟ قال: إذًا أسعَدُ وتَشْقَى، فأمر به.

23. From Abū Ḥamza al-Thumālī, from Abū Ja'far عليه السلام who said regarding God's verse: ﴾*So, when they had forgotten the warning that they had been reminded of*﴿, 'When they abandoned the sacred authority of 'Alī عليه السلام having previously been commanded to it, ﴾*We struck them suddenly and they were dumbfounded. The evildoers were wiped out: Praise be to God, the Lord of the Worlds!*﴿' He said, 'This was revealed about the progeny of al-'Abbās.' [6:44–45]

24. From Manṣūr b. Yūnus, from a man, from Abū 'Abd Allāh عليه السلام who said regarding God's verse: ﴾*So, when they had forgotten the warning that they had been reminded of, We opened the gates to everything for them. Then, as they revelled in what they had been given, We struck them suddenly and they were dumbfounded*﴿, 'The Banū Umayya were struck suddenly, and the Banū 'Abbās will be struck publicly.' [6:44–45]

25. From al-Fuḍayl b. 'Iyāḍ[3] who said, 'I asked Abū 'Abd Allāh عليه السلام: Who is defined as a 'pious' person? So he replied, "The one who refrains from God's prohibitions and shuns them. If he is not cautious against dubious things, he will fall into prohibited things without even realising. If he sees wrong being done but does not forbid it whilst having the capability to do so, then he has in effect deemed God's disobedience palatable. Whoever accepts for God to be disobeyed, however, challenges God with enmity; and whoever accepts an evildoer to remain in power has indeed liked for God to be disobeyed. God, Blessed and most High, has praised Himself with the destruction of the evildoers saying: ﴾*The evildoers were wiped out: Praise be to God, the Lord of the Worlds!*﴿"' [6:44–45]

26. From al-Aṣbagh b. Nubāta who said, 'Whilst 'Alī عليه السلام was delivering the sermon on Friday from the pulpit, al-Ash'ath b. Qays came in stepping over the people to get to the front, saying, "O Commander of the Faithful, the foreigners[4] are obstructing me from your face."' He said, 'So 'Alī عليه السلام said,

---

3 Abū 'Alī al-Fuḍayl b. 'Iyāḍ b. Mas'ūd al-Tamīmī al-Yarbū'ī al-Marwazī (d. 187/803) of Basra was a reliable Sunnī ascetic and narrator of Imam Ja'far al-Ṣādiq's traditions. See Ḥillī, *Khulāṣat al-aqwāl*, 387 (nr. 1554); Modarressi, *Tradition and Survival*, 223–4 (nr. 61).

4 The manuscripts quote the word *al-ḥamd* here which can either mean, literally, 'the praise' or may refer to the opening chapter of the Qur'an, *al-fātiḥa*. But in any case, neither of

٢٣. عن أبي حمزة الثّمالي، عن أبي جعفر عليه السلام، في قول الله: ﴿فَلَمَّا نَسُوا مَا ذُكِّرُوا بِهِ﴾، قال: لمّا تركوا ولاية علي عليه السلام وقد أُمروا بها ﴿أَخَذْنَاهُم بَغْتَةً فَإِذَا هُم مُّبْلِسُونَ ۝ فَقُطِعَ دَابِرُ الْقَوْمِ الَّذِينَ ظَلَمُوا وَالْحَمْدُ لِلَّهِ رَبِّ الْعَالَمِينَ﴾ قال: نزلت في ولد العباس.

٢٤. عن منصور بن يُونس، عن رجلٍ، عن أبي عبدالله عليه السلام، في قول الله: ﴿فَلَمَّا نَسُوا مَا ذُكِّرُوا بِهِ﴾ إلى قوله: ﴿فَإِذَا هُم مُّبْلِسُونَ﴾، قال: أخَذَ بني أُميّة بَغْتَةً، ويُؤخَذُ بنو العباس جَهْرَةً.

٢٥. عن الفُضيل بن عياض، قال: سألتُ أبا عبدالله عليه السلام عن الوَرَع من الناس. فقال: الذي يَتورَّع من محارم الله، ويجتنب هؤلاء، وإذا لم يتّقِ الشُّبهات وقع في الحرام وهو لا يَعْرِفه، وإذا رأى المُنكَر فلم يُنكِره وهو يَقْدِر عليه، فقد أحبّ أن يُعصَى الله، ومن أحبّ أن يُعصى الله فقد بارز الله بالعَداوة، ومن أحبّ بقاء الظالم فقد أحبّ أن يُعصى الله، إنّ الله تبارك وتعالى حَمِد نفسه على هلاك الظالمين، فقال: ﴿فَقُطِعَ دَابِرُ الْقَوْمِ الَّذِينَ ظَلَمُوا وَالْحَمْدُ لِلَّهِ رَبِّ الْعَالَمِينَ﴾.

٢٦. عن الأصبغ بن نُباتة، قال: بينا عليّ عليه السلام يخطُب يوم الجمعة على المِنبَر بجاء الأشعث بن قيس يتخطّى رِقاب الناس، فقال: يا أمير المؤمنين، حالت الحمراء بيني وبين وجهك. قال: فقال عليّ عليه السلام: ما لي وما للضّياطِرة، أطرُد قومًا غدَوا أوّل النهار يَطْلُبُون رزق الله، وآخر النهار ذَكَرُوا الله، أفأطرُدهم فأكون من الظالمين؟!

"What do I have to do with these self-important people? I repel people who spend the first part of the day in the quest for God's sustenance then eventually remember God at the end of the day. Should I not repel them lest I be included among the wrongdoers?"' [6:45]

27. From Abū 'Amr al-Zubayrī, from Abū 'Abd Allāh ﷺ who said, 'May God have mercy on the servant who repents before death, for repentance purifies one from the filth of sin and saves one from the brink of destruction. God has made it incumbent upon Himself towards His righteous servants saying: ﴾*Your Lord has taken it on Himself to be merciful: if any of you has foolishly done a bad deed, and afterwards repented and mended his ways, God is most Forgiving and most Merciful.*﴿(6:54) ﴾*Yet anyone who does evil or wrongs his own soul and then asks God for forgiveness will find Him most forgiving and merciful.*﴿(4:110)' [6:54]

28. From Abū Rabī' al-Shāmī who said, 'I asked Abū 'Abd Allāh ﷺ about God's verse: ﴾*No leaf falls without His knowledge nor is there a single grain in the darkness of the earth, or anything, fresh or withered, that is not written in a clear Record.*﴿ He said, "The leaf is a miscarried foetus and the grain is a child. The darkness of the earth is the wombs; the fresh is that which lives and the withered is that which is miscarried; and all that is in a clear Record."' [6:59]

29. From al-Ḥusayn b. Khālid who said, 'I asked Abū al-Ḥasan ﷺ about God's verse: ﴾*No leaf falls without His knowledge nor is there a single grain in the darkness of the earth, or anything, fresh or withered, that is not written in a clear Record.*﴿ So he replied, "The leaf is the miscarried foetus that falls from its mother's womb before it is born and takes the first breath of life."'

He said, 'So I asked him about the words: ﴾*nor is there a single grain.*﴿

He replied, "That refers to the child in its mother's womb which was implanted but was miscarried before birth."'

He said, 'I asked about the words: ﴾*or anything, fresh.*﴿

---

these meanings makes much sense and is most probably a transcription error. According to Ibn Abī al-Ḥadīd, author of *Sharḥ Nahj al-Balāgha*, it should be *al-ḥumarā'*, meaning the foreigners or non-Arabs.

٢٧. عن أبي عمرو الزُبيري، عن أبي عبد الله عليه السلام، قال: رحِمَ الله عبدًا تاب إلى الله قبل الموت، فإنّ التوبة مُطهّرة من دَنَس الخطيئة، ومُنقِذة من شَفَا الهلَكة، فرض الله بها على نفسه لعباده الصالحين، فقال: ﴿كَتَبَ رَبُّكُمْ عَلَىٰ نَفْسِهِ الرَّحْمَةَ أَنَّهُ مَنْ عَمِلَ مِنكُمْ سُوءًا بِجَهَالَةٍ ثُمَّ تَابَ مِنْ بَعْدِهِ وَأَصْلَحَ فَأَنَّهُ غَفُورٌ رَحِيمٌ﴾ ﴿وَمَنْ يَعْمَلْ سُوءًا أَوْ يَظْلِمْ نَفْسَهُ ثُمَّ يَسْتَغْفِرِ اللَّهَ يَجِدِ اللَّهَ غَفُورًا رَحِيمًا﴾.

٢٨. عن أبي الربيع الشامي، قال: سألتُ أبا عبد الله عليه السلام عن قول الله تعالى: ﴿وَمَا تَسْقُطُ مِنْ وَرَقَةٍ إِلَّا يَعْلَمُهَا﴾ إلى قوله: ﴿إِلَّا فِي كِتَابٍ مُبِينٍ﴾ قال: الورقة: السِّقط، والحبَّة: الولد، وظُلُمات الأرض: الأرحام، والرَّطب: ما يحيا، واليابس: ما يَغيض، وكلّ ذلك في كتابٍ مبين.

٢٩. عن الحسين بن خالد، قال: سألتُ أبا الحسن عليه السلام عن قول الله جلّ وعزّ: ﴿وَمَا تَسْقُطُ مِنْ وَرَقَةٍ إِلَّا يَعْلَمُهَا وَلَا حَبَّةٍ فِي ظُلُمَاتِ الْأَرْضِ وَلَا رَطْبٍ وَلَا يَابِسٍ إِلَّا فِي كِتَابٍ مُبِينٍ﴾ فقال: الوَرَقة: السِّقط، يَسْقُط من بطن أُمّه من قبل أن يُهِلَّ الولد.

قال: فقلتُ: وقوله: ﴿وَلَا حَبَّةٍ﴾؟ قال: يعني الولد في بطن أُمّه إذ أهلَّ، ويُسقِط من قبل الولادة.

قال: قلتُ: قوله: ﴿وَلَا رَطْبٍ﴾؟ قال: يعني المُضْغَة إذا أُسكنت في الرَّحم، قبل أن يتِمّ خَلْقُها، قبل أن ينتقل.

He replied, "That refers to the embryo which became stuck in the womb before it had been fully formed and before moving on."'

He said, 'Then I asked about the words: ﴾ *or withered.* ﴿

He replied, "The fully-formed child."'

He said, 'I asked, "What about: ﴾ *written in a clear Record* ﴿?"

He replied, "In a clear guide."' [6:59]

30. From Dāwūd b. Farqad, from Abū ʿAbd Allāh عليه السلام. He said, 'Marwān b. al-Ḥakam came to Medina.' He continued, 'He stretched himself out on the bed, and there was a protégé of al-Ḥusayn present there, so he said: ﴾ *Then they will all be returned to God, their true Lord. The Judgement truly belongs to Him, and He is the swiftest of reckoners.* ﴿'

So al-Ḥusayn asked his protégé: "What did this one say to you when he entered?" He replied, "He stretched himself out on the bed, and recited: ﴾ *Then they will all be returned to God, their true Lord. The Judgement truly belongs to Him, and He is the swiftest of reckoners.* ﴿ So al-Ḥusayn عليه السلام said, "Indeed! By God, my companions and I will be returned to Paradise, and him and his companions to the Fire."' [6:62]

31. From Ribʿī b. ʿAbd Allāh, from whoever mentioned it on Abū Jaʿfar's authority regarding God's verse: ﴾ *When you come across people who speak with scorn about Our revelations* [...]. ﴿ He said, 'Speaking [ignorantly] about God and disputation about the Qur'an, ﴾ *then turn away from them until they move on to another topic.* ﴿' He said, 'Among such people are the story-tellers.' [6:68]

32. From Abū Baṣīr who said, 'I asked Abū ʿAbd Allāh عليه السلام about God's verse: ﴾ *Remember when Ibrāhīm said to his father, Āzar.* ﴿ He replied, "His father's name was Āzar."' [6:74]

33. From Zurāra who said, 'I asked Abū ʿAbd Allāh عليه السلام about God's verse: ﴾ *In this way We showed Ibrāhīm* [*God's*] *mighty dominion over the heavens and the earth, so that he might be a firm believer.* ﴿ He replied, "The earth was unveiled for him so that he could see all that was in it, as well as the heavens and all that lives therein, the angel that carries it, the Throne and all that is upon it."' [6:75]

قال: قلتُ قوله: ﴿وَلَا يَابِسٍ﴾؟ قال: الولد التامّ. قال: قلت: ﴿فِي كِتَابٍ مُبِينٍ﴾؟ قال: في إمام مبين.

٣٠. عن داود بن فَرقد، عن أبي عبدالله عليه السلام، قال: دخل مَروان بن الحَكَم المدينة، فاستلقى على السرير، وثمّ مولى للحسين عليه السلام: فقال: ﴿رُدُّوا إِلَى اللهِ مَوْلَاهُمُ الْحَقِّ... وَهُوَ أَسْرَعُ الْحَاسِبِينَ﴾.

قال: فقال الحسين عليه السلام لمولاه: ماذا قال هذا حين دخل؟ قال: استلقى على السرير فقرأ ﴿رُدُّوا إِلَى اللهِ مَوْلَاهُمُ﴾ إلى قوله: ﴿الْحَاسِبِينَ﴾. قال: فقال الحسين عليه السلام: نعم والله، رُدِدتُ أنا وأصحابي إلى الجنّة، ورُدَّ هو وأصحابه إلى النار.

٣١. عن رِبعي بن عبدالله، عمّن ذكره، عن أبي جعفر عليه السلام، في قول الله تعالى: ﴿وَإِذَا رَأَيْتَ الَّذِينَ يَخُوضُونَ فِي آيَاتِنَا﴾، قال: الكلام في الله، والجِدال في القرآن ﴿فَأَعْرِضْ عَنْهُمْ حَتَّىٰ يَخُوضُوا فِي حَدِيثٍ غَيْرِهِ﴾، قال: منه القُصّاص.

٣٢. عن أبي بصير، قال: سألتُ أبا عبدالله عليه السلام عن قول الله: ﴿وَإِذْ قَالَ إِبْرَاهِيمُ لِأَبِيهِ آزَرَ﴾، قال: كان اسم أبيه آزر.

٣٣. عن زُرارة، قال: سألتُ أبا عبدالله عليه السلام عن قول الله سبحانه وتعالى: ﴿وَكَذَٰلِكَ نُرِي إِبْرَاهِيمَ مَلَكُوتَ السَّمَاوَاتِ وَالْأَرْضِ وَلِيَكُونَ مِنَ الْمُوقِنِينَ﴾. قال: كُشِطَ له عن الأرض حتّى رآها وما فيها، والسماء وما فيها، والمَلَك الذي يحمِلها، والعَرْش وما عليه.

34. From ʿAbd al-Raḥīm al-Quṣayr[5], from Abū Jaʿfar ﷺ who said regarding God's verse: ﴾*In this way We showed Ibrāhīm* [*God's*] *mighty dominion over the heavens and the earth*﴿, 'The seven heavens were unveiled for him such that he could see the seventh heaven and all that was in it, as well as the seven earths and their contents. The same thing was done for Muḥammad ﷺ and Ibrāhīm ﷺ, and indeed the same was done for your companion too.' [6:75]

35. From Zurāra, from Abū Jaʿfar and Abū ʿAbd Allāh, peace be upon them both, regarding God's verse: ﴾*In this way We showed Ibrāhīm* [*God's*] *mighty dominion over the heavens and the earth, so that he might be a firm believer.*﴿ Abū Jaʿfar said, 'The heavens were unveiled for him such that he could see the Throne and what was on it.' He said, 'The heavens, the earth, the Throne, and the Seat of Sovereignty.'

And Abū ʿAbd Allāh ﷺ said, 'The earth was unveiled for him such that he could see it as well as the sky and its contents, the angel that bears it, and the Seat of Sovereignty and what is upon it.' [6:75]

36. In another narration on Zurāra's authority, from Abū Jaʿfar ﷺ about: ﴾*In this way We showed Ibrāhīm* [*God's*] *mighty dominion over the heavens and the earth*﴿, he said, 'He granted his eyes a certain power that pierced through the heavens and saw what was in it. He saw the Throne and what was upon it as well as the earth and all that was under it.' [6:75]

37. From Abū Baṣīr, from Abū ʿAbd Allāh ﷺ who said, 'When he was shown the dominion of the heavens and the earth, he turned and saw a man fornicating. So he invoked God's chastisement on him, and he died. Then he saw another, and he invoked the same and he too died. Then he saw three more, invoked God, and they too died. So God revealed to him saying, "O Ibrāhīm, your invocation is always answered so do not invoke Me against My servants, for indeed if I had willed I would not have created them. I have created people of three different types: 1) a servant to worship Me and never associate

5 ʿAbd al-Raḥīm al-Quṣayr, a client of the Banū Asad, was a companion of Imam Jaʿfar al-Ṣādiq who had also met his father, Imam Muḥammad al-Bāqir, and his son, Imam Mūsā b. Jaʿfar. See Khūʾī, *Muʿjam*, 11:12–4 (nr. 6500).

٣٤. عن عبد الرّحيم القَصير، عن أبي جعفر عليه السلام، في قول الله: ﴿وَكَذَٰلِكَ نُرِي إِبْرَاهِيمَ مَلَكُوتَ السَّمَاوَاتِ وَالْأَرْضِ﴾. قال: كُشِطَ له السّماوات السبع حتّى نَظَر إلى السماء السابعة وما فيها، والأرضين السبع وما فيهنّ، وفُعِل بمحمّد صلى الله عليه وآله كما فُعِل بإبراهيم عليه السلام، وإنّي لأرى صاحبكم قد فُعِل به مثل ذلك.

٣٥. عن زُرارة، عن أبي جعفر وأبي عبدالله عليه السلام، في قول الله: ﴿وَكَذَٰلِكَ نُرِي إِبْرَاهِيمَ مَلَكُوتَ السَّمَاوَاتِ وَالْأَرْضِ وَلِيَكُونَ مِنَ الْمُوقِنِينَ﴾. فقال أبو جعفر عليه السلام: كُشِطَ له عن السّماوات حتّى نَظَرَ إلى العرش وما عليه، قال: والسّماوات والأرض والعرش والكرسيّ.

فقال: أبو عبدالله عليه السلام: كُشِطَ له عن الأرض حتّى رآها، وعن السماء وما فيها، والمَلَك الذي يَحمِلها، والكُرسيّ وما عليه.

٣٦. وفي رواية أُخرى، عن زُرارة، عن أبي جعفر عليه السلام: ﴿وَكَذَٰلِكَ نُرِي إِبْرَاهِيمَ مَلَكُوتَ السَّمَاوَاتِ وَالْأَرْضِ﴾، قال: أُعطي بَصَرُه من القوّة ما نَفَذَ السّماوات فرآى ما فيها، ورأى العرش وما فوقه، ورأى ما في الأرض وما تحتها.

٣٧. عن أبي بصير، عن أبي عبدالله عليه السلام، قال: إنّ إبراهيم عليه السلام لمّا رأى ملكوت السماوات والأرض التفت فرأى رجلاً يزني، فدعا عليه فمات، ثمّ رأى آخر فدعا عليه فمات، حتّى رأى ثلاثةً فدعا عليهم فماتوا، فأوحى الله سبحانه إليه: أنْ يا إبراهيم، إنَّ دعوتَك مُجابةٌ، فلا تدعُ على عبادي، فإنّي لو شِئتُ لم أَخْلُقْهُم، إنّي خَلَقتُ خَلْقي على ثلاثة أصنافٍ: عبد

anything with Me, and whom I then reward; 2) a servant who worships other than Me but even then, He will not escape from Me; and 3) a servant who worships other than Me but from whose loins I create one who will worship Me."' [6:75]

38. From Muḥammad b. Muslim, from one of the two Imams [al-Bāqir or al-Ṣādiq] who said regarding Ibrāhīm عليه السلام when he saw the stars, that he said, 'He was looking for his Lord and never touched disbelief. Whoever from among the people thinks like that is of his calibre.' [6:75]

39. From Abū 'Ubayda, from Abū Ja'far عليه السلام who said with regard to Ibrāhīm's statement, may God's blessings be upon him: ﴾*If my Lord does not guide me, I shall be one of those who go astray*﴿, 'It means people in general towards the covenant.' [6:77]

40. From Abān b. 'Uthmān[6], from whoever mentioned it to him on their authority, that one of the accounts about Ibrāhīm عليه السلام was that he was born during the time of Nimrūd b. Kan'ān. By that time four rulers had ruled the earth, two of whom were believers and two disbelievers: Sulaymān b. Dāwūd and Dhū'l Qarnayn, and Nimrūd b. Kan'ān and Bakht Naṣr. Nimrūd had been told: 'This year a baby boy will be born who will destroy you all, your religion and your idols.' So he ordered midwives to monitor the women and commanded for any male infant born in that year to be killed.

However, Ibrāhīm's mother carried him in her back and not in her belly, and when she had given birth to him she placed him in an underground den and covered it up. He grew up much faster than other boys, and she had made him promise [not to come out until then].

Then Ibrāhīm عليه السلام came out of the den, and saw the planet Venus never having seen a more beautiful star than it, so he said, 'This is my Lord.'

6 Abū 'Abd Allāh Abān b. 'Uthmān al-Aḥmar in a report cited by Kishshī was apparently a follower of the heterodox movement known as the Nāwūsiyya, named thus after their eponymous founder 'Abd Allāh b. Nāwūs al-Miṣrī. The group acknowledges the divine authority (*walāya*) of the first six Imams only, believing that Imam Ja'far al-Ṣādiq is the Mahdī and therefore still alive. Though considered deviant in his beliefs, Abān is nonetheless regarded a reliable narrator of the Imams' traditions. See Ḥillī, *Khulāṣat al-aqwāl*, 74 (nr. 121); Modarressi, *Tradition and Survival*, 129–31 (nr. 1).

يَعْبُدُني لا يُشرِكُ بي شيئًا فأُثِيبه، وعبد يَعْبُدُ غيري فلن يَفُوتني، وعبد يَعْبُدُ غيري فأُخرِج من صُلْبِهِ مَن يَعْبُدُني.

٣٨. عن محمّد بن مسلم، عن أحدهما عليه السلام، قال في إبراهيم عليه السلام، إذ رأى كوكبًا، قال: إنّما كان طالبًا لربّه ولم يَبْلُغ كُفرًا، وإنّه من فكّر من الناس في مثل ذلك فإنّه بمنزلته.

٣٩. عن أبي عبيدة، عن أبي جعفر عليه السلام، في قول إبراهيم صلوات الله عليه: ﴿لَئِن لَّمْ يَهْدِنِي رَبِّي لَأَكُونَنَّ مِنَ الْقَوْمِ الضَّالِّينَ﴾ أي ناسٍ للمِيثاق.

٤٠. عن أبان بن عثمان، عمّن ذكره عنهم عليهم السلام، أنّه كان من حديث إبراهيم عليه السلام أنّه وُلِد في زمان نمْرُود بن كَنْعان، وكان قد مَلَكَ الأرض أربعة، مؤمنان وكافران: سليمان بن داود، وذو القَرنين، ونُمْرُود بن كَنْعان وبُخْت نصَّر، وأنّه قيل لنُمْرُود: إنّه يُولَدُ العام غُلامٌ يكون هلاككم وهلاك دينكم وهلاك أصنامكم على يديه، وأنّه وَضَعَ القوابل على النساء، وأمر أن لا يُولد هذه السنة ذكرٌ إلاّ قتلوه.

وإنَّ إبراهيم عليه السلام حملته أُمّه في ظهرها، ولم تَحمِله في بطنها، وأنّه لمّا وضعته أدخلته سَرَبًا ووضعت عليه غِطاءً، وإنّه كان يشِبّ شبًّا لا يَشِبُّه الصِّبيان، وكانت تعاهده.

فخرج إبراهيم عليه السلام من السَّرب، فرأى الزُّهَرَة، ولم يَرَ كوكبًا أحسن منها، فقال: هذا ربّي، فلم يَلبَث أن طَلَع القمر، فلمّا رآه، قال: هذا أعظم، هذا ربّي، فلمّا أفل، قال: لا أُحِبُّ الآفلين، فلمّا رأى النهار وطَلَعت الشمس، قال: هذا ربّي، أكبر ممّا رأيت، فلمّا أفلت قالَ:

However it was not long before the moon rose, and when he saw it it astonished him, and he said, 'This is greater, this is my Lord.' But when it set he said, 'I do not like things that set.' When he witnessed daytime and the sun rose, he said, 'This is my Lord. This is bigger than anything I have seen.' When it set, however, he said: ﴾*If my Lord does not guide me, I shall be one of those who go astray. I have turned my face as a true believer towards Him who created the heavens and the earth. I am not one of the polytheists.*﴿ [6:77–79]

41. From Ḥujr who said that al-ʿAlā b. Sayāba wrote to Abū ʿAbd Allāh عليه السلام asking him about Ibrāhīm's words: ﴾*'This is my Lord'*﴿ – and that whoever would say such a thing today would be deemed a polytheist by us. He replied, 'There was no polytheism on Ibrāhīm's part, rather it was in the quest for his Lord; and it would be polytheism from anyone other than him.' [6:78]

42. From Muḥammad b. Ḥumrān who said, 'I asked Abū ʿAbd Allāh عليه السلام about God's words when we are being informed about Ibrāhīm عليه السلام: ﴾*'This is my Lord.'*﴿ He replied, "He did not conclude anything thereby; he meant something other than what he uttered."' [6:78]

43. From Muḥammad b. Muslim, from Abū ʿAbd Allāh عليه السلام who said regarding God's verse: ﴾*It is those who have faith, and do not mix their faith with wrongdoing.*﴿ 'Both from within as well as what Zurāra and his associates have invented.' [6:82]

44. From Abū Baṣīr who said, 'I said to him, "Shayṭān is really pushing me in my old age, causing me to despair." He replied, "Tell him: 'You lie, you disbeliever and polytheist! I believe in my Lord; I pray, fast and glorify Him, and I do not mix up my faith with wrongdoing."' [6:82]

45. From Jābir al-Juʿfī, from whoever narrated it to him. He said, 'When the Messenger of God ﷺ was on one of his travels, he saw a black man in the distance and he said, "This man has never known a friend."

So when he approached nearer, he greeted him. So the Messenger of God ﷺ asked him, "Where is your good self headed?"

He replied, "I am headed for Yathrib."

He asked, "And what do you want there?"

﴿لَئِن لَّمْ يَهْدِنِي رَبِّي لَأَكُونَنَّ مِنَ الْقَوْمِ الضَّالِّينَ ۞ إِنِّي وَجَّهْتُ وَجْهِيَ لِلَّذِي فَطَرَ السَّمَاوَاتِ وَالْأَرْضَ حَنِيفًا﴾ مُسلمًا ﴿وَمَا أَنَا مِنَ الْمُشْرِكِينَ﴾.

٤١. عن حُجر، قال أرسل العلاء بن سَيَابة يسأل أبا عبدالله عليه السلام عن قول إبراهيم عليه السلام: ﴿هَٰذَا رَبِّي﴾ وقال: إنّه من قال هذا اليوم فهو عندنا مشرك؟ فقال عليه السلام: لم يكُن من إبراهيم شِركٌ، إنّما كان في طَلَب ربّه وهو من غيره شِركٌ.

٤٢. عن محمّد بن حُمران، قال: سألتُ أبا عبدالله عليه السلام عن قول الله فيما أخبر عن إبراهيم عليه السلام: ﴿هَٰذَا رَبِّي﴾، قال: لم يَبْلُغ به شيئًا، أراد غير الذي قال.

٤٣. عن محمّد بن مسلم، عن أبي عبدالله عليه السلام، في قول الله: ﴿الَّذِينَ آمَنُوا وَلَمْ يَلْبِسُوا إِيمَانَهُم بِظُلْمٍ﴾، منه وما أحدث زُرارة وأصحابه.

٤٤. عن أبي بصير، قال: قلتُ له: إنّه قد ألحّ عليّ الشيطان عند كِبَر سِنّي يُقَنِّطني. قال: قل: كَذَبتَ يا كافر يا مُشرِك، إنّي أُؤمِنُ بِربّي، وأُصَلّي له، وأَصوم، وأُثني عليه، ولا أُلْبِسُ إيماني بظُلمٍ.

٤٥. عن جابر الجُعفي، عمَّن حدَّثه، قال: بينا رسول الله صلى الله عليه وآله في مسيرٍ له إذ رأى سوادًا من بعيد، فقال: هذا سوادٌ لا عَهْد له بأنيس، فلمّا سلّم، فقال له رسول الله صلى الله عليه وآله: أين أراد الرجل؟

قال: أراد يثرب.

قال: وما أردت بها؟ قال: أردتُ محمّدًا.

He replied, "I want to meet Muḥammad."

He replied, "I am Muḥammad."

He said, "By the One Who has sent you with the truth, I have not seen a single soul for seven days, nor have I eaten anything except for that which my riding beast eats thereof."'

He said, 'So he proposed Islam to him, and he became a Muslim.'

He said, 'Then his mount bit him, and he died. He was ordered to be washed and shrouded, then the Prophet prayed over him.'

He continued, 'When he was placed in his grave, he said, "He was among those who had faith and did not mix up their faith with wrongdoing."' [6:82]

46. From Abū Baṣīr, from Abū ʿAbd Allāh عليه السلام. He said, 'I asked him: ﴾*those who have faith, and do not mix their faith with wrongdoing*﴿ – Is fornication part of this? He replied, "I seek refuge in God from such people. No, but it is a sin, and if he repents then God will accept his repentance." He also said, "The one who fornicates regularly, steals and drinks wine is just like the idol-worshipper."' [6:82]

47. Yaʿqūb b. Shuʿayb, on his authority, about His verse: ﴾*and do not mix their faith with wrongdoing*﴿, that he said, 'Misguidance and beyond.' [6:82]

48. Abū Baṣīr, on his authority regarding: ﴾*with wrongdoing*﴿, he said, 'With doubt.' [6:82]

49. From ʿAbd al-Raḥmān b. Kathīr al-Hāshimī, from Abū ʿAbd Allāh عليه السلام who said regarding His verse: ﴾*those who have faith, and do not mix their faith with wrongdoing*﴿, 'They have faith in the sacred authority that Muḥammad صلى الله عليه وآله has come with and they do not mix it up with the authority of so-and-so and so-and-so, for that would be mixing with wrongdoing.' He added, 'As for faith, not all of it is prone to division, but it does disintegrate little by little.' I asked, 'Is there a state between misguidance and disbelief?' He replied, 'Faith has many ropes indeed.' [6:82]

قال: فأنا محمّد. قال: والذي بعثك بالحقّ، ما رأيت إنسانًا مذ سبعة أيّام، ولا طعمتُ طعامًا إلاّ ما تناول منه دابّتي.

قال: فَعَرَضَ عليه الإسلام فأسلم، قال: فعضّته راحلته فمات، وأمر به فغُسِّل وكُفِّن، ثمّ صلّى عليه النبيّ صلّى الله عليه وآله وسلّم.

قال: فلمّا وُضِع في اللّحد قال: هذا من الّذين آمنوا ولم يَلْبِسوا إيمانَهُم بظُلمٍ.

٤٦. عن أبي بصير، عن أبي عبدالله عليه السلام، قال: قلتُ له: ﴿الَّذِينَ آمَنُوا وَلَمْ يَلْبِسُوا إِيمَانَهُمْ بِظُلْمٍ﴾ الزنا منه؟ قال: أعوذ بالله من أُولئك، لا ولكنّه ذنبٌ، إذا تاب تاب الله عليه.

قال: مُدمن الزِّنا والسَّرقة وشارب الخمر كعابد الوثن.

٤٧. يعقوب بن شُعيب، عنه عليه السلام، في قوله تعالى: ﴿وَلَمْ يَلْبِسُوا إِيمَانَهُمْ بِظُلْمٍ﴾، قال: الضَّلال فما فوقه.

٤٨. أبو بصير، عنه عليه السلام: ﴿بِظُلْمٍ﴾، قال: بشكٍّ.

٤٩. عن عبد الرّحمن بن كَثير الهاشمي، عن أبي عبدالله عليه السلام، في قوله تعالى: ﴿الَّذِينَ آمَنُوا وَلَمْ يَلْبِسُوا إِيمَانَهُمْ بِظُلْمٍ﴾، قال: آمنوا بما جاء به محمّد صلّى الله عليه وآله وسلّم من الولاية، ولم يَخْلُطوها بولاية فلان وفلان، فهو اللَّبس بظُلم.

وقال: أمّا الإيمان فليس يتبعَّض كُلّه، ولكن يتبعّض قليلاً قليلاً.

قلت: بين الضَّلال والكُفر منزلةٌ؟ قال: ما أكثر عُرى الإيمان!

50. From Abū Baṣīr who said, 'I asked him about God's verse: ﴾*those who have faith, and do not mix their faith with wrongdoing*﴿. He replied, "We seek refuge in God, O Abū Baṣīr, that you should ever be one of those who mix up their faith with wrongdoing." Then he said, "Those are the Kharijites and their associates."' [6:82]

51. From Muḥammad b. al-Fuḍayl, from al-Thumālī, from Abū Jaʿfar عليه السلام regarding His verse: ﴾*We gave him Isḥāq and Yaʿqūb, each of whom We guided*﴿, 'That we may deposit it [the *walāya*] with the people of his household ﴾*as We had guided Nūḥ before*﴿, that we may deposit it with the people of his household. So He commanded the later generations of prophets that came before Ibrāhīm, and Ibrāhīm himself.' [6:84]

52. From Bashīr al-Dahhān, from Abū ʿAbd Allāh عليه السلام who said, 'By God, God traced ʿĪsā b. Maryam's ancestry back to Ibrāhīm عليه السلام in the Qur'an before the Chapter of Women (*sūrat al-nisā'*).' Then he recited: ﴾*and among his descendants were Dāwūd, Sulaymān* [...]﴿ until the end of the two verses, mentioning ʿĪsā عليه السلام. [6:84]

53. From Abū Ḥarb b. Abī al-Aswad who said, 'Al-Ḥajjāj sent a message to Yaḥyā b. Maʿmar saying, "I have heard that you claim that al-Ḥasan and al-Ḥusayn are counted among the progeny of the Prophet صلى الله عليه وآله and that you can find them in God's Book; and I have read God's Book from cover to cover and have not found it."

He replied, "Have you not read the Chapter of the Livestock: ﴾*and among his descendants were Dāwūd, Sulaymān, Ayyūb, Yūsuf, Mūsā, and Hārūn – in this way We reward those who do good – Zakariyyā, Yaḥyā, ʿĪsā*﴿?"

He continued, "Is ʿĪsā not included in the progeny of Ibrāhīm even though he had no father." He replied, "You are right."' [6:84]

54. From Muḥammad b. Ḥumrān who said, 'I was with Abū ʿAbd Allāh when a man came and said to him, "O Abū ʿAbd Allāh, is it not shocking that ʿĪsā b. Zayd b. ʿAlī claims that ʿAlī عليه السلام was only appointed to leadership publicly, and you never know but he could have actually been worshipping seventy other idols besides God."'

٥٠. عن أبي بصير، قال: سألتُهُ عليه السلام عن قول الله ﴿الَّذِينَ آمَنُوا وَلَمْ يَلْبِسُوا إِيمَانَهُم بِظُلْمٍ﴾، قال: نَعوذُ بالله يا أبا بصير أن تكون ممّن لَبَس إيمانه بظُلم، ثمّ قال: أُولئك الخوارج وأصحابهم.

٥١. عن محمّد بن الفُضيل، عن الثُّمالي، عن أبي جعفر عليه السلام، في قوله تعالى: ﴿وَوَهَبْنَا لَهُ إِسْحَاقَ وَيَعْقُوبَ كُلًّا هَدَيْنَا﴾ لنَجْعَلَها في أهل بيته ﴿وَنُوحًا هَدَيْنَا مِن قَبْلُ﴾ لنجعلها في أهل بيته، فآمن العَقِب من ذُريَّة الأنبياء من كان قبل إبراهيم لإبراهيم عليه السلام.

٥٢. عن بشير الدهّان، عن أبي عبدالله عليه السلام، قال: والله لقد نَسَب الله عيسى بن مريم في القرآن إلى إبراهيم عليه السلام من قبل النِّساء، ثمّ تلا عليه السلام ﴿وَمِن ذُرِّيَّتِهِ دَاوُودَ وَسُلَيْمَانَ﴾ إلى آخر الآيتين، وذَكَر عيسى عليه السلام.

٥٣. عن أبي حَرْب بن أبي الأسود، قال: أرسل الحجّاج إلى يحيى بن مَعْمَر، قال: بلغني أنّك تزْعُم أنّ الحسن والحسين من ذُريّة النبيّ، تَجِده في كتاب الله؟ وقد قرأتُ كتاب الله من أوّله إلى آخره فلم أجده.

قال: أليس تقرأ سورة الأنعام ﴿وَمِن ذُرِّيَّتِهِ دَاوُودَ وَسُلَيْمَانَ﴾ حتّى بلغ ﴿وَيَحْيَىٰ وَعِيسَىٰ﴾، قال: أليس عيسى من ذُريَّة إبراهيم عليه السلام، وليس له أب؟ قال: صدقت.

٥٤. عن محمّد بن حُمران، قال: كنتُ عند أبي عبدالله عليه السلام فجاءه رجلٌ، وقال له: يا أبا عبدالله، ما يُتعجَّب من عيسى بن زيد بن عليّ، يزْعُم أنّه ما يتولّى عليًّا عليه السلام إلاّ على الظاهر، وما يدري لعلّه كان يَعْبُد سبعين إلهًا من دون الله!

He said, 'So he said, "So what do I do with that? God says: ﴾*Even if these people now disbelieve in them, We have entrusted them to others who do not disbelieve,*﴿" and he motioned with his hand towards us. So I said, "By God, we understand it."' [6:89]

55. From al-ʿAbbās b. Hilāl, from al-Riḍā ﷺ that a man came to ʿAbd Allāh b. al-Ḥasan[7] when he was at al-Sabāla[8] and asked him about the Hajj. So he said to him, 'There is Jaʿfar b. Muḥammad who has appointed himself for that, so ask him.' So the man approached Jaʿfar ﷺ and asked him, so he said to him, 'I saw you standing with ʿAbd Allāh b. al-Ḥasan – what did he say to you?'

He replied, 'I asked him so he told me to come to you saying, "There is Jaʿfar b. Muḥammad, who has appointed himself for that."

So Jaʿfar ﷺ said, "Yes, I am one of those about whom God has said in His Book: ﴾*Those were the people that God guided,* [*Prophet*], *so follow their guidance.*﴿ Ask whatever you want." So the man asked, and he informed him about everything that he asked him.' [6:90]

56. From Ibn Sinān, from Sulaymān b. Hārūn who said, 'By God, even if all the inhabitants of the heavens and the earth were to come together to turn this authority away from the rightful place that God has appropriated it, they would never be able to. If all the people were to reject faith altogether such that not a single one remained, He would bring forth a people who would be worthy of this authority.' Then he continued, 'Have you not heard God's statement: ﴾*You who believe, if any of you go back on your faith, God will soon replace you with people He loves and who love Him, people who are*

7 ʿAbd Allāh b. al-Ḥasan b. Abī Ṭālib, known as al-Maḥḍ (the pureblooded). Shaykh al-Ṭūsī lists him among the companions of Imam Jaʿfar al-Ṣādiq. He was known as al-Maḥḍ because his father was al-Ḥasan b. al-Ḥasan, the grandson of the Prophet, while his mother was Fāṭima bt. al-Ḥusayn, and he used to resemble the Messenger of God. He was the chieftain of the Banū Hāshim and used to be in charge of the alms of ʿAlī after his father, al-Ḥasan. According to the biographical reports about him, he was a very reputable and noble man, and held a favourable position with the Umayyad Caliph ʿUmar b. ʿAbd al-ʿAzīz. The Caliph al-Manṣūr, however, kept him imprisoned for several years because of his two sons Muḥammad (*al-nafs al-zakiyya*) and Ibrāhīm, and had him transferred later on to Kufa where it is said he died in prison. See Ziriklī, *al-Aʿlām*, 4:78.

8 Al-Sabāla or Sibāl is a place between Basra and Medina; see Baghdādī, *Marāṣid al-iṭlāʿ*, 2:688.

قال: فقال: وما أصنع؟ قال الله تعالى: ﴿فَإِن يَكْفُرْ بِهَا هَٰؤُلَاءِ فَقَدْ وَكَّلْنَا بِهَا قَوْمًا لَّيْسُوا بِهَا بِكَافِرِينَ﴾ وأومأ بيده إلينا. فقلت: نَعْقِلها والله.

٥٥. عن العباس بن هلال، عن الرضا عليه السلام: أنّ رجلاً أتى عبد الله بن الحسن وهو بالسَّيالة، فسأله عن الحجّ، فقال له: هذاك جعفر بن محمّد، قد نصب نفسه لهذا فاسأله، فأقبل الرجل إلى جعفر عليه السلام فسأله، فقال له: قد رأيتك واقفًا على عبد الله بن الحسن، فما قال لك.

قال: سألته فأمرني أن آتيك، وقال: هذاك جعفر بن محمّد، قد نَصَب نفسه لهذا.

فقال جعفر عليه السلام: نعم، أنا من الذين قال الله تعالى في كتابه: ﴿أُولَٰئِكَ الَّذِينَ هَدَى اللَّهُ فَبِهُدَاهُمُ اقْتَدِهِ﴾ سَل عمّا شِئت، فسأله الرجل، فأنبأه عن جميع ما سأله.

٥٦. عن ابن سِنان، عن سليمان بن هارون، قال: والله لو أنّ أهل السماء والأرض اجتمعوا على أن يُحَوّلوا هذا الأمر من موضعه الذي وضعه الله فيه ما استطاعوا، ولو أنّ الناس كَفَرُوا جميعًا حتّى لا يبقى أحدٌ لجاء [الله] لهذا الأمر بأهلٍ يكونون هم أهله، ثمّ قال: أما تسمع الله يقول: ﴿يَا أَيُّهَا الَّذِينَ آمَنُوا مَن يَرْتَدَّ مِنكُمْ عَن دِينِهِ﴾ الآية، وقال في آية أُخرى: ﴿فَإِن يَكْفُرْ بِهَا هَٰؤُلَاءِ فَقَدْ وَكَّلْنَا بِهَا قَوْمًا لَّيْسُوا بِهَا بِكَافِرِينَ﴾؟ ثمّ قال: أما إنّ أهل هذه الآية هم أهل تلك الآية.

humble towards the believers, hard on the disbelievers, and who strive in God's way without fearing anyone's reproach. Such is God's favour. He grants it to whoever He will. God has endless bounty and knowledge ﴿?(5:54) He has also said in another verse: ﴾*Even if these people now disbelieve in them, We have entrusted them to others who do not disbelieve.* ﴿' He then said, 'Indeed the very people whom this verse applies to are the same ones meant in that one too.' [6:89]

57. From al-Thumālī, from Abū Ja'far عليه السلام who said, 'God, Blessed and most High, has said in His Book: ﴾*as We had guided Nūḥ before, and among his descendants were Dāwūd, Sulaymān, Ayyūb, Yūsuf, Mūsā, and Hārūn – in this way We reward those who do good – Zakariyyā, Yaḥyā, 'Īsā, and Ilyās – every one of them was righteous – Ismā'īl, Elisha, Yūnus, and Lūṭ. We favoured each one of them over other people, and also some of their forefathers, their off-spring, and their brothers: We chose them and guided them on a straight path. Such is God's guidance, with which He guides whichever of His servants He will. If they had associated other gods with Him, all their deeds would have come to nothing. Those are the ones to whom We gave the Scripture, wisdom, and prophethood. Even if these people now disbelieve in them, We have entrusted them to others who do not disbelieve,* [...] ﴿(6:84–89) So He is the one who has entrusted this favour unto the people of his household, the brothers, and the progeny. This is God's statement. If your community rejects it, He says: I have indeed entrusted the faith that I have sent you with to the people of your household, and they will never reject it. I will never let the faith that I sent you with get lost, even after the passing of the people of your household who will come after you, the scholars of your religion, the executors of My authority after you, and the extractors of the knowledge of the religion – [this religion] which contains no lie therein, no sin, no burden, no arrogance and no dissemblance.' [6:84–89]

58. From 'Abd Allāh b. Sinān who said, 'I asked Abū 'Abd Allāh عليه السلام about God's verse: ﴾*Say, 'Who was it who sent down the Scripture, which Mūsā brought as a light and a guide to people, which you made into separate sheets, showing some but hiding many?'* ﴿ He replied, "They used to hide what they wished and show only that which they wished."' [6:91]

٥٧ . عن الثُّمالي، عن أبي جعفر عليه السلام، قال: قال الله تبارك وتعالى في كتابه: ﴿وَنُوحًا هَدَيْنَا مِنْ قَبْلُ وَمِنْ ذُرِّيَّتِهِ دَاوُودَ﴾ إلى قوله: ﴿أُولَئِكَ الَّذِينَ آتَيْنَاهُمُ الْكِتَابَ وَالْحُكْمَ وَالنُّبُوَّةَ﴾ إلى قوله: ﴿بِهَا بِكَافِرِينَ﴾ فإنّه من وَكَّل بالفضل من أهل بيته والإخوان والذُّرِيَّة، وهو قول الله: إن يَكْفُر به أُمّتك، يقول: فقد وكَّلت أهل بيتك بالإيمان الذي أرسلتك به فلا يَكْفُرون به أبدًا، ولا أُضيّع الإيمان الذي أرسلتك به من أهل بيتك بعدك، عُلماء أُمّتك، وولاة أمري بعدك، وأهل استنباط عِلْمِ الدِّين، ليس فيه كَذِبٌ، ولا إثمٌ، ولا وِزرٌ، ولا بَطَرٌ، ولا رياءٌ.

٥٨ . عن عبدالله بن سِنان، قال: سألتُ أبا عبدالله عليه السلام: عن قول الله تعالى: ﴿قُلْ مَنْ أَنْزَلَ الْكِتَابَ الَّذِي جَاءَ بِهِ مُوسَى نُورًا وَهُدًى لِلنَّاسِ تَجْعَلُونَهُ قَرَاطِيسَ تُبْدُونَهَا﴾، قال: كانوا يَكْتُمون ما شاءوا ويُبدُون ما شاءوا.

59. In another narration on his authority عليه السلام he said, 'They used to hide some in their separate sheets, then show only whatever they wished and hide what they wished.' And he said, 'Every scripture that has been revealed is with the People of Knowledge.' [6:91]

60. From al-Ḥusayn b. Saʿīd[9], from one of the two [al-Ṣādiq or al-Bāqir]. He said, 'I asked him about God's verse: ﴾ *or claims, 'A revelation has come to me,' when no revelation has been sent to him.* ﴿ He replied, "It was revealed about Ibn Abī Sarḥ whom ʿUthmān b. ʿAffān had dispatched to work in Egypt. He was one of those whose life the Messenger of God صلى الله عليه وآله had spared on the day of the Conquest of Mecca, and he used to be a scribe for the Messenger of God صلى الله عليه وآله. Once, when God revealed to him: ﴾*for verily God is the Mighty, the Wise*﴿, he wrote: ﴾*for verily God is the all-Knowing, the Wise.*﴿ Ibn Abī Sarḥ used to tell the hypocrites, 'I say the exact thing that he brings [afterwards], and he does not differ from me.' So God revealed what He did about him."' [6:93]

61. From Abū Baṣīr, from Abū Jaʿfar عليه السلام regarding: ﴾ *Who could be more wicked than someone who invents a lie against God, or claims, 'A revelation has come to me,' when no revelation has been sent to him, or says, 'I too can reveal something equal to God's revelation'?* ﴿ He said, 'One who claims the Imamate for himself aside from the rightful Imam.' [6:93]

62. From Sallām, from Abū Jaʿfar عليه السلام who said regarding the verse: ﴾ *Today you will be repaid with a humiliating punishment*﴿, 'Thirst on the Day of Resurrection.' [6:93]

63. From al-Fuḍayl who said, 'I heard Abū ʿAbd Allāh comment on His verse: ﴾*Give up your souls. Today you will be repaid with a humiliating punishment* [...]﴿ he said, 'Thirst.' [6:93]

---

9 This is most likely a reference to al-Ḥusayn b. Saʿīd b. Ḥammād b. Mihrān al-Ahwāzī, the manumitted slave of Imam ʿAlī b. al-Ḥusayn, who is a highly regarded companion and narrator of Shīʿī traditions having known and met five of the Imams from the Ahl al-Bayt. Born in Kufa, he travelled with his brother al-Ḥasan b. Saʿīd to Ahwāz and then finally to Qom where he died. See Ḥillī, *Khulāṣat al-aqwāl*, 114 (nr. 278); Khūʾī, *Muʿjam*, 2265–91 (nr. 3424).

٥٩. وفي رواية أُخرى عنه عليه السلام، قال: كانوا يَكْتُبون في القَراطِيس، ثمّ يبُدون ما شاءوا، ويُخفون ما شاءوا، وقال: كُلّ كتابٍ أُنزل، فهو عند أهل العلم.

٦٠. عن الحسين بن سعيد، عن أحدهما عليه السلام، قال: سألتُهُ عن قول الله: ﴿أَوْ قَالَ أُوحِيَ إِلَيَّ وَلَمْ يُوحَ إِلَيْهِ شَيْءٌ﴾، قال: نزلت في ابن أبي سَرْح، الذي كان عثمان بن عفّان استعمله على مِصر، وهو ممّن كان رسول الله صلى الله عليه وآله يوم فتح مكّة هَدَر دمه، وكان يكتُبُ لرسول الله صلى الله عليه وآله، فإذا أنزل الله عليه ﴿فَإِنَّ اللهَ عَزِيزٌ حَكِيمٌ﴾ كتب: فإنّ الله عليم حكيم. وقد كان ابن أبي سَرْح يقول للمنافقين: إنّي لأقول الشيء مثل ما يجيء به هو، فما يُغيّر عليَّ، فأنزل الله فيه الذي أنزل.

٦١. عن أبي بصير، عن أبي جعفر عليه السلام ﴿وَمَنْ أَظْلَمُ مِمَّنِ افْتَرَىٰ عَلَى اللهِ كَذِبًا أَوْ قَالَ أُوحِيَ إِلَيَّ وَلَمْ يُوحَ إِلَيْهِ شَيْءٌ وَمَنْ قَالَ سَأُنزِلُ مِثْلَ مَا أَنزَلَ اللهُ﴾، قال: من ادّعى الإمامة دون الإمام عليه السلام.

٦٢. عن سلاّم، عن أبي جعفر عليه السلام، في قوله: ﴿الْيَوْمَ تُجْزَوْنَ عَذَابَ الْهُونِ﴾ قال: العَطَش يوم القيامة.

٦٣. عن الفُضيل، قال: سَمِعتُ أبا عبدالله عليه السلام، في قوله تعالى: ﴿أَخْرِجُوا أَنفُسَكُمُ الْيَوْمَ تُجْزَوْنَ عَذَابَ الْهُونِ﴾. قال: العَطَش.

64. From Ṣāliḥ b. Sahl who, without mentioning his source, cited Abū ʿAbd Allāh عليه السلام as having stated regarding God's verse: ﴾*It is God who splits open the seed and the fruit stone*﴿, 'The seed represents that which loves Him and the fruit stone that which turns away from the truth and does not accept Him.' [6:95]

65. From al-Mufaḍḍal who said, 'I heard Abū ʿAbd Allāh عليه السلام say about His verse: ﴾*It is God who splits open the seed and the fruit stone*﴿, "The seed is the believer, as per His statement: ﴾*I showered you with My love*﴿;(20:39) and the fruit stone is the disbeliever who turns away from the truth and does not accept it."' [6:95]

66. From ʿAbd Allāh b. al-Faḍl al-Nawfalī[10], from whoever referenced Abū Jaʿfar عليه السلام as having said, 'When you go out to seek your livelihoods, do so during the daytime, for God has placed demureness in the eyes. When you consort with your wives, however, do so at night, for God has said: ﴾*He makes the night for rest.*﴿' [6:96]

67. From al-Ḥasan b. ʿAlī b. Bint Ilyās[11] who said, 'I heard Abū al-Ḥasan al-Riḍā عليه السلام say, "Indeed, God has made the night for rest and He has made women for rest; and it is a prophetic practice to consort with them at night and to serve food."' [6:96]

68. From ʿAlī b. ʿUqba, on his father's authority from Abū ʿAbd Allāh عليه السلام who said, 'Consort with your wives in the night for indeed God has made it a time for rest, and do not go out to seek your livelihoods in the night for it is dark.' [6:96]

69. From Abū Baṣīr, from Abū Jaʿfar عليه السلام. He said, 'I asked about: ﴾*It is He who first produced you from a single soul, then gave you a place to settle and a resting place.*﴿

---

10 ʿAbd Allāh b. al-Faḍl b. ʿAbd Allāh b. al-Ḥārith b. Nawfal b. ʿAbd al-Muṭṭalib al-Nawfalī, a trustworthy narrator of Imam Muḥammad al-Bāqir's traditions. See Ḥillī, *Khulāṣat al-aqwāl*, 202 (nr. 633).

11 According to Khūʾī, al-Ḥasan b. ʿAlī b. Bint Ilyās is the same individual as al-Ḥasan b. ʿAlī b. Ziyād al-Washshāʾ. See Khūʾī, *Muʿjam*, 6:30 (nr. 2951).

٦٤. عن صالح بن سهل، رفعه إلى أبي عبدالله ﵇، في قول الله: ﴿فَالِقُ الْحَبِّ وَالنَّوَى﴾ الحبُّ: ما أحبَّه، والنَّوى: ما نأى عن الحقّ فلم يَقْبَله.

٦٥. عن المفَضّل، قال: سألتُ أبا عبدالله ﵇ عن قوله ﴿فَالِقُ الْحَبِّ وَالنَّوَى﴾، قال: الحبّ: المؤمن، وذلك قوله: ﴿وَأَلْقَيْتُ عَلَيْكَ مَحَبَّةً مِنِّي﴾، والنّوى: هو الكافر الذي نأى عن الحقّ فلم يَقْبَله.

٦٦. عن عبدالله بن الفضل النَّوفلي، عمَّن رفعه إلى أبي جعفر ﵇، قال: إذا طَلَبتم الحوائج فاطلبوها بالنهار، فإنَّ الله جعل الحياء في العينين، وإذا تزوَّجتم فتزوَّجوا بالليل، فأن الله جَعل اللّيل سَكَناً.

٦٧. عن الحسن بن علي ابن بنت إلياس، قال: سَمِعتُ أبا الحسن الرضا ﵇ يقول: إنّ الله جعل اللّيل سَكَناً، وجعل النساءَ سَكَناً، ومن السُّنّة التزويج بالليل، وإطعام الطعام.

٦٨. عن عليّ بن عُقبة، عن أبيه، عن أبي عبدالله ﵇، قال: تزوَّجوا بالليل، فإنَّ الله جعله سَكَناً، ولا تَطْلُبوا الحوائج بالليل، فإنّه مُظلِم.

٦٩. عن أبي بصير، عن أبي جعفر ﵇، قال: قلت: ﴿وَهُوَ الَّذِي أَنْشَأَكُمْ مِنْ نَفْسٍ وَاحِدَةٍ فَمُسْتَقَرٌّ وَمُسْتَوْدَعٌ﴾؟

قال: ما يقول أهل بلدك الذي أنت فيه؟ قال: قلت: يقولون: مُسْتَقَرٌّ في الرَّحِم، ومُسْتَودَع في الصُّلْب.

He said, "What do the people of the town where you live say about it?"' He said, 'I replied, "They say that the settling place is in the womb and the resting place in the loins."

So he said, "They are wrong. The settling place is when faith settles in the heart and can never again leave, and the resting place is when faith rests there for some time then vacates it. Zubayr was one of those."' [6:98]

70. From Jaʿfar b. Marwān[12] who said, 'Zubayr unsheathed his sword on the day that the Prophet ﷺ passed away saying, "I will not sheathe it again until I have sworn allegiance to ʿAlī." Subsequently he unsheathed his sword to fight ʿAlī; so he was one of those who was stripped of faith. So first he walked in the glow of its light then God snatched it away from him.' [6:98]

71. From Saʿīd b. Abī al-Aṣbagh[13] who said, 'I heard Abū ʿAbd Allāh عليه السلام say when he was asked about the settling place and the resting place, "The settling place is in the womb whereas the resting place is in the loins. It may also be the settling place of faith before it is snatched away. Zubayr had walked in the glow and light of faith until the Messenger of God ﷺ passed away to the extent that he used to walk with a drawn sword saying, 'We will not swear allegiance to any person or individual save ʿAlī.'"' [6:98]

72. From Muḥammad b. al-Fuḍayl, from Abū al-Ḥasan عليه السلام who said regarding his verse: ﴾*It is He who first produced you from a single soul, then gave you a place to settle and a resting place*﴿, 'Whatever faith is settled is settled [in the heart] until the Day of Resurrection [or forever], and whatever is resting [temporarily] will be snatched away by God before death.' [6:98]

73. From Ṣafwān who said, 'Abū al-Ḥasan عليه السلام was talking to me whilst Muḥammad b. al-Khalaf was seated there, and he asked me, "Has Yaḥyā b. al-Qāsim, the shoemaker, died?" So I replied to him, "Yes, and Zurʿa has also died." So he said, "Jaʿfar عليه السلام used to say: ﴾*then gave you a place to settle and a resting place*﴿ – the settling refers to people who have been granted faith

---

12 There is no individual with this name in either Ḥillī's *Khulāṣat al-aqwāl* or Khūʾī's *Muʿjam*. It is possible that this is a transcription error for Jaʿfar b. Muḥammad b. Marwān.

13 There is no record of this individual in either Ḥillī's *Khulāṣat al-aqwāl* or Khūʾī's *Muʿjam*.

فقال: كَذَبوا، المُسْتقَرّ: ما استقرّ الإيمان في قلبه، فلا يُنْزَع منه أبدًا، والمُسْتَودَع: الذي يُسْتَودَع الإيمان زمانًا، ثمّ يُسْلَبه، وقد كان الزبير منهم.

٧٠. عن جعفر بن مَروان، قال: إنّ الزبير اخترط سيفه يوم قُبِض النبيّ ﷺ وقال: لا أغْمِده حتّى أُبايع لعليّ عليه السلام، ثمّ اخترط سيفه فضارب عليًّا عليه السلام، فكان ممّن أُعير الإيمان، فمشى في ضوء نُوره، ثمّ سَلَبه الله إيّاه.

٧١. عن سعيد بن أبي الأصبغ، قال: سَمِعتُ أبا عبدالله عليه السلام وهو يسأل عن مُسْتَقَرّ ومُسْتَودَع، قال: مُسْتَقَرّ في الرَّحِم، ومُسْتَودَع في الصُّلْب، وقد يكون مُسْتَودَع الإيمان ثمّ يُنْزَع منه، ولقد مشى الزبير في ضوء الإيمان ونُوره حين قُبِض رسول الله ﷺ حتّى مشى بالسيف وهو يقول: لا نُبايع إلاّ عليًّا.

٧٢. عن محمّد بن الفُضيل، عن أبي الحسن عليه السلام: ﴿هُوَ الَّذِي أَنْشَأَكُمْ مِنْ نَفْسٍ وَاحِدَةٍ فَمُسْتَقَرٌّ وَمُسْتَوْدَعٌ﴾، قال: ما كان من الإيمان المُستَقَرّ فُمستَقَرّ إلى يوم القيامة، أو أبدًا، وما كان مُسْتَودَعًا سَلَبه الله قبل الممات.

٧٣. عن صَفوان، قال: سألني أبو الحسن عليه السلام ومحمّد بن خَلَف جالسٌ، فقال لي: مات يحيى بن القاسم الحذّاء؟ فقلت له: نعم، ومات زُرعة. فقال: كان جعفر عليه السلام يقول: ﴿فَمُسْتَقَرٌّ وَمُسْتَوْدَعٌ﴾ فالمُستَقَرّ: قومٌ يُعْطَون الإيمان ويَسْتَقِرّ في قلوبهم، والمُسْتَودَع: قومٌ يُعْطَون الإيمان ثمّ يُسْلَبونه.

and it settles in their hearts, and the resting place to people who have been granted faith, but it is then snatched away from them."' [6:98]

74. From the first Abū al-Ḥasan [i.e. al-Kāẓim]. He said, 'I asked him about God's verse: ﴾*then gave you a place to settle and a resting place.*﴿ He said, "The settling place is firm faith whereas the resting place is the provisional one."' [6:98]

75. From Aḥmad b. Muḥammad who said, 'The second Abū al-Ḥasan [i.e. al-Riḍā] was expressing his stance to me regarding the doubts he had about the Banū Zurayq, so he said to me, raising his voice, "O Aḥmad!" I replied, "At your service." He said, "When the Messenger of God ﷺ was taken from this world the people did their utmost to extinguish God's light, but God would accept nothing other than the extension of His light through the Commander of the Faithful. When Abū al-Ḥasan [i.e. Imam al-Kāẓim] passed away, Ibn Abī Ḥamza[14] and his companions did their utmost to extinguish God's light, but God would accept nothing other than the extension of His light.

The people of truth are such that when someone enters in their midst they rejoice, but if someone leaves their midst they do not grieve over him because they have conviction in their stance. The people of falsehood, however, are such that when someone joins them they rejoice, but when he leaves their fold they grieve on his account, and that is because they doubt in their own stance. God says: ﴾*then gave you a place to settle and a resting place.*﴿"' He continued, 'Then Abū ʿAbd Allāh عليه السلام said, "The settling place is firm, whereas the resting place is provisional."' [6:98]

76. From Muḥammad b. Muslim who said, 'I heard him say, "God created people with unwavering belief, and He created people with unwavering disbelief; and between them both He created people in whom He deposited

14 This refers to Abū al-Ḥasan ʿAlī b. Abī Ḥamza [=Sālim] al-Baṭāʾinī, who narrated from Imam al-Ṣādiq and Imam al-Kāẓim, but after his death refused to acknowledge the Imamate of Imam al-Riḍā due to his nefarious greed for the wealth that had been in his care whilst he had been one of Imam al-Kāẓim's treasurers. He is variously described in the books of *rijāl* as a liar and a cursed individual. See Ḥillī, *Khulāṣat al-aqwāl*, 362–3 (nr. 1326); Modarressi, *Tradition and Survival*, 183–7 (nr. 32); Tustarī, *Qāmūs al-rijāl* (Qum: Muʾassasat al-nashr al-islāmī al-tābiʿa li-jamāʿat al-mudarrisīn, 1995), 7:268 (no. 4984).

٧٤. عن أبي الحسن الأوّل عليه السلام، قال: سألتُهُ عن قول الله: ﴿فَمُسْتَقَرٌّ وَمُسْتَوْدَعٌ﴾، قال: المُستَقَرّ: الإيمان الثابت، والمُسْتودَع: المُعَار.

٧٥. عن أحمد بن محمّد، قال: وقف عليَّ أبو الحسن الثاني عليه السلام في بني زُرَيق، فقال لي وهو رافعٌ صوته: يا أحمد. قلت: لبّيك. قال: إنّه لمّا قُبِض رسول الله صلى الله عليه وآله جَهَد الناس على إطفاء نُور الله، فأبى الله إلاّ أن يُتِمَّ نُوره بأمير المؤمنين عليه السلام، فلمّا تُوُفّي أبو الحسن عليه السلام جَهَد ابن أبي حمزة وأصحابه على إطفاء نُور الله، فأبى الله إلاّ أن يُتِمَّ نُوره.

وإنَّ أهل الحقّ إذا دَخل فيهم داخِلٌ سُرُّوا به، وإذا خَرَج منهم خارجٌ لم يَجْزَعُوا عليه، وذلك أنّهم على يقين من أمرهم، وإنّ أهل الباطل إذا دخل فيهم داخِلٌ سُرُّوا به، وإذا خرج منهم خارجٌ جَزِعوا عليه، وذلك أنّهم على شكٍّ من أمرهم، إنَّ الله يقول: ﴿فَمُسْتَقَرٌّ وَمُسْتَوْدَعٌ﴾، قال: ثمّ قال أبو عبد الله عليه السلام: المُسْتَقَرّ: الثابت، والمُسْتَودَع: المُعَار.

٧٦. عن محمّد بن مسلم، قال: سَمِعتُه يقول: إنَّ الله خَلَق خَلْقًا للإيمان لا زوال له، وخَلَق خَلْقًا للكُفر لا زوال له، وخَلَق خَلْقًا بين ذلك فاستودع بعضهم الإيمان، فإن شاء أن يُتِمّه لهم أتمّه، وإن شاء أن يَسْلِبَهم إيّاه سَلَبهم.

belief, and if He so wills He completes it for them, and if He wills, he takes it away from them."' [6:98]

77. From Sadīr who said, 'I heard Ḥumrān asking Abū Jaʿfar ﵇ about the words of God, Mighty and Exalted: ﴾ *The Creator of the heavens and earth.* ﴿ So Abū Jaʿfar ﵇ replied him, "He originated all things with His knowledge without any prototype, and He originated the heavens and the earth without any prior heavens and earths. Have you not heard His statement: ﴾ *And His Rule extends over the waters too.* ﴿[(11:7)]"' [6:101]

78. From Abū Ḥamza al-Thumālī, from ʿAlī b. al-Ḥusayn ﵇. He said, 'I heard him say, "God is not described in His decisive revealed scripture – our Lord is far above description. How can one who is indefinable be described when He apprehends the sights whilst no sights can perceive Him, and He is the all-Subtle, the all-Aware."' [6:103]

79. From al-Ashʿath b. Ḥātim who said, 'Dhū al-Riyāsatayn[15] said, "I said to Abū al-Ḥasan al-Riḍā ﵇: 'May I be your ransom – can you tell me about what the people differ on as regards seeing [God]. Some people say that He cannot be seen.'

So he replied, 'O Abū al-ʿAbbās, whoever describes God contrary to how He describes Himself commits a great slander against God. God has said: ﴾ *The sights cannot apprehend Him, yet He apprehends the sights. He is the all-Subtle, the all-Aware.* ﴿ These sights are not the eyes. Rather they are the sights of the heart, such that even the imaginations cannot perceive Him nor apprehend how He is.'" [6:103]

---

15 The editors of the Arabic edition name him as Abū al-ʿAbbās al-Faḍl b. Sahl al-Sarkhasī, a close companion of the Abbasid Caliph al-Ma'mūn. When al-Ma'mūn assumed the caliphate, he appointed al-Sarkhasī as prime minister as well as commander of the army, hence the title Dhū al-Riyāsatayn, the one in charge of both the ministry and the army. Both his birth and death were in Sarkhas, and he was killed whilst in the bath by a group of people commissioned by al-Ma'mūn who could not tolerate his command. He was, by all accounts, an intelligent, decisive and eloquent man. See Ziriklī, *al-Aʿlām*, 5:149.

٧٧. عن سَدير، قال: سَمِعتُ حُمران يسأل أبا جعفر عليه السلام عن قول الله عزّ وجلّ: ﴿بَدِيعُ السَّمَوَاتِ وَالأَرْضِ﴾، فقال له أبو جعفر عليه السلام: ابتدع الأشياء كُلّها بعِلْمه على غير مثال كان، وابتدع السماوات والأرضين ولم يكن قبلهنّ سماوات ولا أرَضُون، أما تسمع قوله: ﴿وَكَانَ عَرْشُهُ عَلَى الْمَاءِ﴾؟

٧٨. عن أبي حمزة الثُّمالي، عن علي بن الحسين عليه السلام، قال سَمِعته يقول: لا يُوصَف الله بمُحكم وَحْيه، عَظُم ربُّنا عن الصِّفة، كيف يُوصف من لا يُحَدُّ! وهو يُدرِك الأبصار، ولا تُدركه الأبصار، وهو اللطيف الخبير.

٧٩. عن الأشعث بن حاتم، قال: قال ذو الرياستين: قلت لأبي الحسن الرضا عليه السلام: جُعِلت فداك، أخبِرني عمّا اختلف فيه الناس من الرُؤية، فقال بعضهم: لا يُرى.

فقال: يا أبا العباس، من وَصَف الله بخلاف ما وَصَف به نفسه فقد أعظم الفِرية على الله، قال الله: ﴿لَا تُدْرِكُهُ الأَبْصَارُ وَهُوَ يُدْرِكُ الأَبْصَارَ وَهُوَ اللَّطِيفُ الْخَبِيرُ﴾ هذه الأبصار ليست هي الأعْيُن، إنّما هي الأبصار التي في القلوب، لا يقع عليه الأوهام، ولا يُدْرَك كيف هو.

80. From ʿUmar al-Ṭayālisī, from Abū ʿAbd Allāh عليه السلام. He said, ʻI asked him about God's command: ﴾*[Believers], do not revile those they call on beside God in case they, in their hostility and ignorance, revile God.*﴿

So he replied, "O ʿUmar, have you seen anyone reviling God?"ʼ He said, ʻI replied, "May God make me your ransom – how do you mean?" He said, "Whoever reviles the vicegerent of God has indeed reviled God."ʼ [6:108]

81. From Zurāra, Ḥumrān and Muḥammad b. Muslim, from Abū Jaʿfar and Abū ʿAbd Allāh, peace be upon them both, about God's statement: ﴾*We would make their hearts and their eyes turn away just as they did not believe the first time, and leave them to flounder in their obstinacy.*﴿ ʻAs for His words: ﴾*just as they did not believe the first time*﴿, they refer to when He took the pledge from them.ʼ [6:110]

82. From Yūnus b. Ẓibyān who said, ʻI heard Abū ʿAbd Allāh عليه السلام say, "When God wills for an Imam to have an Imam born unto him, he is granted seven leaves from Paradise, so he eats them before consorting [with his wife]." He continued, "When he is conceived in the womb he hears speech from within his mother's belly. When she gives birth to him, He raises a pillar of light for him from the heavens to the earth, and he sees all that is between them. On his forearm is written: ﴾*The word of your Lord is complete in its truth and justice.*﴿"

Abū ʿAbd Allāh[16] said, "When this narration came up, al-Washshāʾ said, ʻI will not narrate this for you so do not transmit it [to others] on my authority.ʼ"ʼ [6:115]

83. From Yūnus b. Ẓibyān, from Abū ʿAbd Allāh عليه السلام who said, ʻWhen God wants to take the soul of an Imam and create an Imam after him, He sends down a droplet from beneath the Throne down to the earth, directing it at a fruit or vegetable.ʼ He continued, ʻThe Imam eats that fruit or vegetable, from which God then creates the seed for the Imam that will take his place.ʼ

He continued, ʻSo from that droplet, God creates a seed in the loins, which then moves on to the womb and stays there for forty days. After forty

16 Abū ʿAbd Allāh here is not the Imam but rather Aḥmad b. Muḥammad al-Sayārī; see Khūʾī, *Muʿjam*, 2:282.

٨٠ . عن عُمر الطيالسي، عن أبي عبد الله عليه السلام، قال: سألتُهُ عن قول الله: ﴿وَلَا تَسُبُّوا الَّذِينَ يَدْعُونَ مِن دُونِ اللَّهِ فَيَسُبُّوا اللَّهَ عَدْوًا بِغَيْرِ عِلْمٍ﴾.

قال: فقال: يا عُمر، هل رأيت أحدًا يَسُبّ الله؟ قال: فقلت: جعلني الله فداك، فكيف؟ قال: من سَبّ وليّ الله فقد سَبّ الله.

٨١ . عن زُرارة وحُمران ومحمّد بن مسلم، عن أبي جعفر وأبي عبد الله عليه السلام، عن قول الله تعالى: ﴿وَنُقَلِّبُ أَفْئِدَتَهُمْ وَأَبْصَارَهُمْ﴾ إلى آخر الآية: أمّا قوله: ﴿كَمَا لَمْ يُؤْمِنُوا بِهِ أَوَّلَ مَرَّةٍ﴾ فإنّه حين أخذ عليهم المِيثاق.

٨٢ . عن يُونس بن ظِبيان، قال: سَمِعتُ أبا عبد الله عليه السلام يقول: إنَّ الإمام إذا أراد الله أن يُحْمَل له بإمام، أُتي بسبع وَرَقات من الجنّة، فأكلهنَّ قبل أن يُواقِع، قال: فإذا وَقَع في الرَّحم سَمِع الكلام في بطن أُمّه، فإذا وضعته رُفِع له عمودٌ من نُور ما بين السماء والأرض، يَرَى ما بين المشرق والمغرب، وكُتِب على عَضُدِه ﴿وَتَمَّتْ كَلِمَتُ رَبِّكَ صِدْقًا وَعَدْلًا﴾.

قال أبو عبد الله: قال الوشّاء حين مرّ هذا الحديث: لا أروي لكم هذا، لا تُحَدِّثوا عنّي.

٨٣ . عن يُونس بن ظِبيان، عن أبي عبد الله عليه السلام، قال: إذا أراد الله أن يَقبض روح إمام ويَخْلُق بعده إمامًا، أنزل قَطرةً من تحت العرش إلى الأرض، يُلقيها على ثَمَرةٍ أو بَقْلةٍ، قال: فيأكُل تلك الثَّمرة، أو تلك البَقْلَة الإمام الذي يَخْلُق الله منه نُطفة الإمام الذي يقوم من بعده.

قال: فيَخْلُق الله من تلك القَطرة نُطفةً في الصُّلب، ثمّ يصير إلى الرَّحم، فيمكُث فيه أربعين يومًا، فإذا مضى له أربعون يومًا سَمِع الصوت، فإذا مضى له أربعة أشهر كُتِب على

days have passed, he begins to hear. Then after four months have passed, it is written on his right forearm: ﴾ *The word of your Lord is complete in its truth and justice. No one can change His words: He is the all-Hearing, the all-Knowing.* ﴿ When he comes out into the world, he is granted wisdom, adorned with judiciousness and a dignified bearing, clothed with reverence, and a lamp of guidance is designated for him, through which he knows people's conscience and sees their deeds.' [6:115]

84. From 'Umar b. Ḥanẓala regarding the verse of God, Blessed and most High: ﴾ *So [believers] eat any [animal] over which God's name has been pronounced* ﴿ – 'As for the Magians, it is not allowed for they are not from among the People of the Book. There is no problem with the Jews and the Christians if they pronounce God's name.' [6:118]

85. From Muḥammad b. Muslim: He said, 'I asked him whether the man could slaughter the animal whilst reciting either *lā ilāha illa Llāh* (There is no god but God), or *subḥān Allāh* (Glory be to God), or *al-ḥamdu li-Llāh* (All praise is due to God) or *Allāhu akbar* (God is greater)? He replied, "All of that counts as names of God."' [6:118]

86. From Ibn Sinān, from Abū 'Abd Allāh عليه السلام. He said, 'I asked him whether one could eat meat slaughtered by a woman or a slave? He replied, "Yes, if the woman is Muslim and she pronounces God's name over it, the meat slaughtered by her is permissible. If the slave is strong enough to carry out the slaughter and pronounces God's name, then the meat slaughtered by him is permissible. If a Muslim man forgets to pronounce God's name, there is no problem with eating it, as long as you do not have doubts about him [i.e. his being a Muslim]."' [6:118]

87. From Ḥumrān who said, 'I heard Abū 'Abd Allāh عليه السلام say about the meat slaughtered by an enemy [of the Shī'a] and a Jew – he said, "Do not eat the meat he slaughters until you hear him pronouncing God's name. Have you not heard God's words: ﴾ *do not eat anything over which God's name has not been pronounced.* ﴿"' [6:121]

عضُدِه الأيمن ﴿وَتَمَّتْ كَلِمَتُ رَبِّكَ صِدْقًا وَعَدْلًا لَا مُبَدِّلَ لِكَلِمَاتِهِ وَهُوَ السَّمِيعُ الْعَلِيمُ﴾ فإذا خرج إلى الأرض أوتي الحِكمة، وزُيِّن بالحلم والوَقار، وأُلبِس الهَيبة، وجُعِل له مِصباحٌ من نُور، فعرف به الضمير، ويرى به أعمال العباد.

٨٤. عن عمر بن حنظلة، في قول الله تبارك وتعالى: ﴿فَكُلُوا مِمَّا ذُكِرَ اسْمُ اللَّهِ عَلَيْهِ﴾، قال: أمّا المَجوس فلا، فليسوا من أهل الكتاب، وأمّا اليهود والنصارى فلا بأس إذا سمّوا.

٨٥. عن محمّد بن مسلم، قال: سألتُهُ عن الرجل يَذْبَحَ الذبيحة فيُهَلّل، أو يُسبّح، أو يُحَمّد، أو يُكَبّر؟ قال: هذا كُلّه من أسماء الله.

٨٦. عن ابن سِنان، عن أبي عبدالله عليه السلام، قال: سألتُهُ عن ذبيحة المرأة والغُلام، هل تُؤكَل؟ قال: نعم، إذا كانت المرأةُ مسلمةً، وذكرت اسم الله حَلَّت ذَبيحتها، وإذا كان الغُلامُ قويًّا على الذَّبح وذَكَر اسم الله حلَّت ذَبيحته، وإذا كان الرجُلُ مُسلمًا فنسي أن يُسمّي فلا بأس بأكْلِهِ، إذا لم تتَّهِمه.

٨٧. عن حُمران، قال: سَمِعتُ أبا عبدالله عليه السلام يقول في ذبيحة الناصب واليهودي، قال: لا تأكل ذبيحته حتّى تسمعه يذكُر اسم الله، أما سَمِعت قول الله: ﴿وَلَا تَأْكُلُوا مِمَّا لَمْ يُذْكَرِ اسْمُ اللَّهِ عَلَيْهِ﴾؟

88. From Dāwūd b. Farqad who said, 'I said to Abū 'Abd Allāh عليه السلام, "May I be your ransom – I was praying at the graveside when a man from behind me said: ﴾***Do you want to guide those God has left to stray***﴿, ﴾***when God Himself has rejected them because of what they have done?***﴿(4:88)"

I turned around, for he had reversed the order of this verse, using it against me; and not knowing who it was, I said: ﴾*The evil ones incite their followers to argue with you: if you listen to them, you too will become idolaters*﴿; and it turned out to be Hārūn b. Sa'd.'[17]

He continued, 'So Abū 'Abd Allāh عليه السلام laughed and said, "So you gave the right answer, then" – or he said, "[Correct] speech by God's permission."' [6:121]

89. From Burayd al-'Ijlī, from Abū Ja'far عليه السلام who said: ﴾*Is a dead person brought back to life by Us, and given light with which to walk among people* [...]﴿ He said, 'The dead person is one who does not recognise this lofty position.' He said, 'Do you know what the meaning of 'dead person' is?'

He said, 'I replied: May I be your ransom – no.'

He said, 'The dead person is the one who does not know anything, so we bring him back to life through this authority and give him a light with which to walk among people.' He said, 'An Imam whom he can follow.'

He continued the verse: ﴾*comparable to someone trapped in deep darkness who cannot escape?*﴿ He said, 'Comparable to these people who do not know their Imam.' [6:122]

90. In another narration from Burayd al-'Ijlī he said, 'I asked Abū Ja'far عليه السلام about God's verse: ﴾*Is a dead person brought back to life by Us, and given light with which to walk among people* [...]﴿ He replied, "The dead person is one who does not recognise this lofty position, meaning this authority; ﴾*and given light*﴿ is an Imam whom he can follow, meaning 'Alī b. Abī Ṭālib عليه السلام." I said, "What about His words: ﴾*comparable to someone trapped in deep darkness who cannot escape?*﴿" So he replied, "Whereas this is how these people who do not know anything are."' [6:122]

---

17 Hārūn b. Sa'd al-'Ijlī al-Kūfī was the leader of the 'Ijliyya sect of the *ghulāt* extremists. There are various reports that condemn him and allude to his corrupt beliefs. See Khū'ī, *Mu'jam*, 19:226 and Tustarī, *Qāmūs al-rijāl*, 10:471 (nr. 8136).

٨٨. عن داود بن فَرْقَد، قال: قلتُ لأبي عبد الله ﷺ: جُعِلت فِداك، كنتُ أُصلّي عند القبر، وإذا رجلٌ خلفي يقول: ﴿أَتُرِيدُونَ أَن تَهْدُوا مَنْ أَضَلَّ اللَّهُ﴾ ﴿وَاللَّهُ أَرْكَسَهُم بِمَا كَسَبُوا﴾.

قال: فالتفت إليه، وقد تأوّل عليَّ هذه الآية، وما أدري من هو، وأنا أقول: ﴿وَإِنَّ الشَّيَاطِينَ لَيُوحُونَ إِلَىٰ أَوْلِيَائِهِمْ لِيُجَادِلُوكُمْ وَإِنْ أَطَعْتُمُوهُمْ إِنَّكُمْ لَمُشْرِكُونَ﴾ فإذا هو هارون بن سعد.

قال: فضَحِك أبو عبد الله ﷺ، ثمّ قال: إذاً أصَبْتَ الجواب — أو قال: الكلام — بإذن الله.

٨٩. عن بُريد العجلي، عن أبي جعفر ﷺ، قال: قال: ﴿أَوَمَن كَانَ مَيْتًا فَأَحْيَيْنَاهُ وَجَعَلْنَا لَهُ نُورًا يَمْشِي بِهِ فِي النَّاسِ﴾، قال: الميتُ الذي لا يعرِف هذا الشأن.

قال: أتدري ما يعني مَيْتًا؟ قال: قلتُ: جُعِلت فِداك، لا.

قال: الميّت الذي لا يعرف شيئًا ﴿فَأَحْيَيْنَاهُ﴾ بهذا الأمر ﴿وَجَعَلْنَا لَهُ نُورًا يَمْشِي بِهِ فِي النَّاسِ﴾، قال: إمامًا يأتمّ به. قال: ﴿كَمَن مَّثَلُهُ فِي الظُّلُمَاتِ لَيْسَ بِخَارِجٍ مِّنْهَا﴾، قال ﷺ: كمَثَل هذا الخَلْق الذي لا يَعْرِفون الإمام.

٩٠. وفي رواية أُخرى، عن بُريد العِجلي، قال: سألتُ أبا جعفر ﷺ عن قول الله: ﴿أَوَمَن كَانَ مَيْتًا فَأَحْيَيْنَاهُ وَجَعَلْنَا لَهُ نُورًا يَمْشِي بِهِ فِي النَّاسِ﴾، قال: الميّتُ الذي لا

91. From Ṣafwān, from Ibn Sinān who said, 'I heard him say, "You are the worthiest of people when it comes to piety. You visit the sick and attend funerals. Other people go here and there whilst you go where God Himself goes. God knows best where He places His message."' [6:124]

92. From Abū Baṣīr, from Abū Ja'far عليه السلام who said, 'God does not grant victory over an oppressor except by means of another oppressor, and that is the purport of His verse: ﴾*In this way, We make some evildoers have power over others through their misdeeds.*﴿' [6:129]

93. From Abū Jamīla, from 'Abd Allāh b. Abī Ja'far عليه السلام, from his brother who said, 'Deep inside the heart there is a quivering that seeks the truth, and when it finds it, it feels content as a result of it.' Then he recited: ﴾*When God wishes to guide someone, He opens their breast to Islam, and when He wishes to lead them astray, He closes and constricts their breast as if they were climbing up to the skies.*﴿ [6:125]

94. From Sulaymān b. Khālid who said, 'I have heard Abū 'Abd Allāh عليه السلام say, "When God wishes goodness for a servant, He places a white spot inside his heart and opens up the heart to be receptive, and he places an angel in charge of him who remedies his shortcomings. However, when God wishes bad for a servant, He places a black spot inside his heart, and causes the receptivity in his heart to close up, and He places a devil in charge of him who leads him astray." Then he recited this verse: ﴾*When God wishes to guide someone, He opens their breast to Islam, and when He wishes to lead them astray, He closes and constricts their breast as if they were climbing up to the skies.*﴿

Sulaymān b. Khālid also narrated it on his authority with the wording: 'a spot of light' instead of 'a white spot.' [6:125]

يعرف هذا الشأن، يعني هذا الأمر ﴿وَجَعَلْنَا لَهُ نُورًا﴾ إماماً يأتمّ به، يعني عليّ بن أبي طالب عليه السلام.

قلتُ: فقوله: ﴿كَمَن مَّثَلُهُ فِي الظُّلُمَاتِ لَيْسَ بِخَارِجٍ مِّنْهَا﴾؟ فقال بيده هكذا، هذا الخَلْق الذين لا يعرِفون شيئًا.

٩١. عن صفوان، عن ابن سِنان، قال: سَمِعتُه يقول: أنتم أحقّ الناس بالوَرَع، عُودُوا المرضى، وشَيّعوا الجَنَائز، إنّ النّاس ذهبوا كذا وكذا وذهبتم حيث ذهب الله، الله أعلم حيث يَجْعَل رِسالَتَه.

٩٢. عن أبي بصير، عن أبي جعفر عليه السلام، قال: ما انتصر الله من ظالم إلاّ بظالِم، وذلك قول الله تعالى: ﴿وَكَذَٰلِكَ نُوَلِّي بَعْضَ الظَّالِمِينَ بَعْضًا بِمَا كَانُوا يَكْسِبُونَ﴾.

٩٣. عن أبي جميلة، عن عبد الله بن أبي جعفر عليه السلام، عن أخيه عليه السلام، قال: إنّ للقلب تَلَجْلجًا في الجَوف يَطلُب الحقّ، فإذا أصابه اطمأنّ به، وقرأ ﴿فَمَن يُرِدِ اللَّهُ أَن يَهْدِيَهُ يَشْرَحْ صَدْرَهُ لِلْإِسْلَامِ وَمَن يُرِدْ أَن يُضِلَّهُ يَجْعَلْ صَدْرَهُ ضَيِّقًا حَرَجًا كَأَنَّمَا يَصَّعَّدُ فِي السَّمَاءِ﴾.

٩٤. عن سُليمان بن خالد، قال: قد سَمِعت أبا عبد الله عليه السلام يقول: إنّ الله إذا أراد بعبدٍ خيرًا نَكَت في قلبه نُكتةً بيضاء، وفَتَح مسامع قَلبه، ووكّل به مَلَكًا يُسَدّده، وإذا أراد بعبدٍ سُوءًا نَكَت في قلبه نُكتةً سوداء، وسدّ عليه مسامع قلبه، ووكّل به شيطانًا يُظلّه، ثمّ تلا هذه

95. From Abū Baṣīr, from Khaythama who said, 'I heard Abū Ja'far ﷺ say, "The heart fluctuates from its position up to the throat so long as it has not yet found the truth, and when it does find the truth it rests." Then he closed his fingers together and recited this verse: ﴾ *When God wishes to guide someone, He opens their breast to Islam, and when He wishes to lead them astray, He closes and constricts their breast as if they were climbing up to the skies.* ﴿'

He said, 'Abū 'Abd Allāh also said to Mūsā b. Ashyam, "Do you know what constriction is?" He replied, "No." So he showed him with his hand by closing up his fingers into a fist such that nothing could penetrate nor exit from it.' [6:125]

96. From Abū Baṣīr, from Abū 'Abd Allāh ﷺ who said regarding His verse: ﴾ *That is how God makes the foulness of those who do not believe rebound against them* ﴿, 'This is doubt.' [6:125]

97. From al-Ḥasan b. 'Alī, from al-Riḍā ﷺ. He said, 'I asked him about God's verse: ﴾ *pay what is due on the day of harvest.* ﴿ He replied, "A bundle or two of dry and green herbs that you can give to whoever comes to you."' [6:141]

98. He also said, 'The Messenger of God ﷺ prohibited harvesting at night.' [6:141]

99. From Hāshim b. al-Muthannā[18] who said, 'I asked Abū 'Abd Allāh ﷺ about: ﴾ *pay what is due on the day of harvest.* ﴿ He said, "Give to whoever comes to you [even a polytheist]."' [6:141]

18 Hāshim b. al-Muthannā al-Ḥannāṭ al-Kūfī, a reliable and trustworthy companion of Imam Ja'far al-Ṣādiq. See Khū'ī, *Mu'jam*, 20:269–71 (nr. 13298).

الآية ﴿ فَمَنْ يُرِدِ اللهُ أَنْ يَهدِيَهُ يَشْرَحْ صَدْرَهُ لِلإِسْلَامِ وَمَنْ يُرِدْ أَنْ يُضِلَّهُ يَجْعَلْ صَدْرَهُ ضَيِّقًا حَرَجًا ﴾ الآية.

ورواه سليمان بن خالد عنه: نَكتة من نُور، ولم يقل: بيضاء.

٩٥. عن أبي بصير، عن خَيثمة، قال: سَمِعتُ أبا جعفر عليه السلام يقول: إنّ القلب ينقلب من لَدُن مَوْضِعه إلى حَنْجرته ما لم يُصِب الحقّ، فإذا أصاب الحقّ قرّ، ثمّ ضمّ أصابعه، ثمّ قرأ هذه الآية ﴿ فَمَنْ يُرِدِ اللهُ أَنْ يَهدِيَهُ يَشْرَحْ صَدْرَهُ لِلإِسْلَامِ وَمَنْ يُرِدْ أَنْ يُضِلَّهُ يَجْعَلْ صَدْرَهُ ضَيِّقًا حَرَجًا ﴾.

قال: وقال أبو عبد الله عليه السلام لموسى بن أشْيَم: أتدري ما الحَرَج؟ قال: قلتُ: لا. فقال بيده وضمّ أصابعه كالشيء المُصْمَتَ الذي لا يَدْخُل فيه شيء، ولا يَخْرُج منه شيء.

٩٦. عن أبي بصير، عن أبي عبد الله عليه السلام، في قوله تعالى: ﴿ كَذَلِكَ يَجْعَلُ اللهُ الرِّجْسَ عَلَى الَّذِينَ لَا يُؤْمِنُونَ ﴾، قال: هو الشّكّ.

٩٧. عن الحسن بن علي، عن الرضا عليه السلام، قال: سألتُهُ عن قول الله عزّ وجلّ ﴿ وَآتُوا حَقَّهُ يَوْمَ حَصَادِهِ ﴾، قال عليه السلام: الضِّغْث والاثنين، تُعطي من حَضَرك.

٩٨. وقال: نهى رسول الله صلى الله عليه وآله عن الحَصَاد بالليل.

٩٩. عن هشام بن المثنَى، قال: قلتُ لأبي عبد الله عليه السلام: قوله: ﴿ وَآتُوا حَقَّهُ يَوْمَ حَصَادِهِ ﴾؟ قال: أعطِ من حَضَرك من مُشركٍ أو غيره.

100. From ʿAbd Allāh b. Sinān, from Abū ʿAbd Allāh عليه السلام. He said, 'I asked him about His verse: ﴾*pay what is due on the day of harvest.*﴿ He replied, "Give to [whoever comes to you] the Muslims, and if no one but a polytheist comes, then give it to him."' [6:141]

101. From Muʿāwiya b. Maysara[19]. He said, 'I heard Abū ʿAbd Allāh عليه السلام say, "Vegetation has two dues: one that is due to be taken from it, and one due to be given away. The due that is taken is the tithe [one-tenth] or half of it, whereas regarding the due to be given away, He says: ﴾*pay what is due on the day of harvest.*﴿ So you should give away bundle by bundle until it runs out."' [6:141]

102. In a narration of ʿAbd Allāh b. Sinān, on his authority, he said, 'Give out from it to the paupers who come to you, even if none but a polytheist comes.' [6:141]

103. From Zurāra b. Aʿyan and Muḥammad b. Muslim, from Abū Jaʿfar and Abū ʿAbd Allāh, peace be upon them both, about His verse: ﴾*pay what is due on the day of harvest.*﴿ They said, 'Give out bundles from the ears of corn [a handful or two from them].' [6:141]

104. From Zurāra, Muḥammad b. Muslim, and Abū Baṣīr from Abū Jaʿfar عليه السلام regarding God's statement: ﴾*pay what is due on the day of harvest.*﴿

He said, 'This is different to charity. He should give out of it to each pauper, bunch after bunch, and also from the surplus pieces of dates by the handfuls until they run out, keeping aside a specific share for the one who weighs and values the dates. He should leave aside the *muʿāfāra* and the *umm juʿrūr* and not value them.[20] He should leave aside a cluster, two or even three clusters of dates for the guard who stands watch by the wall, for his supervision and guarding.' [6:141]

---

19 Muʿāwiya b. Maysara b. Sharīḥ b. al-Ḥārith al-Kindī al-Qāḍī, a companion of Imam Jaʿfar al-Ṣādiq. See Khūʾī, *Muʿjam*, 13:239–40 (nr. 12493).

20 These are dates of the lowest quality because of their dryness.

١٠٠. عن عبدالله بن سِنان، عن أبي عبدالله ﵇، قال: سألتُهُ عن قوله: ﴿وَآتُوا حَقَّهُ يَوْمَ حَصَادِهِ﴾، قال: أعطِ من حَضَرك من المسلمين، وإن لم يَحْضُرك إلاّ مُشرِك فأعْطِه.

١٠١. عن معاوية بن مَيْسَرة، قال: سَمِعتُ أبا عبدالله ﵇ يقول: إنّ في الزَّرع حَقَّين: حقٌّ تُؤخذُ به، وحقٌّ تُعطيه، فأمّا الذي تُؤخذ به فالعُشْر ونِصف العُشْر، وأمّا الحَقّ الذي تُعطيه فإنّه يقول: ﴿وَآتُوا حَقَّهُ يَوْمَ حَصَادِهِ﴾ فالضِغْث تُعطيه ثمّ الضِغْث حتى تَفْرُغ.

١٠٢. وفي رواية عبدالله بن سِنان، عنه ﵇ قال: تُعطي منه المساكين الذين يَحْضُرونك، ولو لم يَحْضُرك إلاّ مُشرِك.

١٠٣. عن زُرارة وحُمران بن أعْيَن ومحمّد بن مسلم، عن أبي جعفر وأبي عبدالله عليهما السلام، في قوله ﴿وَآتُوا حَقَّهُ يَوْمَ حَصَادِهِ﴾، قالا: تُعطي منه الضِغْث، تقبِضُ من السُّنْبُل قبضةً والقبضة.

١٠٤. عن زُرارة ومحمّد بن مسلم وأبي بصير، عن أبي جعفر ﵇، في قول الله تعالى: ﴿وَآتُوا حَقَّهُ يَوْمَ حَصَادِهِ﴾.

قال: هذا من غير الصدقة، يُعطى منه المسكين والمسكين القبضةَ بعد القَبضة، ومن الجِداد الحَفْنَة ثمّ الحَفْنَة حتّى يَفْرُغ، ويترُك للخارِص أجرًا معلومًا، ويترُك من النخل مُعافارة وأُمّ جُعْرُور لا يُخْرَصان، ويَترُك للحارس يكون في الحائط العِذْق والعِذْقان والثَلاثة لنَظَره وحِفظه له.

105. From Muḥammad b. Muslim, from Abū Jaʿfar ﵇ who said, 'Harvesting and reaping should not be undertaken in the night. God says: ﴾*pay what is due on the day of harvest but do not be wasteful: God does not like wasteful people.*﴿' He continued, '*x* son of *y* al-Anṣārī – he named him – had crops, and whenever he reaped them, he would give them away such that he and his family would be left with nothing, so God designated that as a waste.' [6:141]

106. From Aḥmad b. Muḥammad, from Abū al-Ḥasan al-Riḍā ﵇ who said, 'Wastefulness in harvesting and reaping is when someone gives away in charity with both hands full. When my father would visit any of these [plantations] and he saw any of his servants giving away with both palms full, he would shout at him, saying, "Give with one hand, one handful, after another handful; one bunch followed by another bunch of ears of corn."' [6:141]

107. From Samāʿa, from Abū ʿAbd Allāh ﵇ who said regarding His verse: ﴾*pay what is due on the day of harvest*﴿, 'Its due on the day of harvest is obligatory upon you. A handful taken from it or a bunch from the ears of corn given away to one who comes to you as a beggar does not count as the alms-tax. Harvesting and reaping must not be undertaken at night, for God says: ﴾*the day of harvest,*﴿ for when you harvest it in the night, no one is going to come to your door to beg nor is it bright enough [to do so] in the night.' [6:141]

108. From Samāʿa, from Abū ʿAbd Allāh ﵇, on his father's authority, on the Prophet's authority that he used to detest for date-palms to be cut at night, and for crops to be reaped at night, for God says: ﴾*pay what is due on the day of harvest.*﴿ He was asked, 'O Prophet of God, what is its due?' He replied, 'Give out of it to the pauper and the beggar.' [6:141]

١٠٥. عن محمّد بن مسلم، عن أبي جعفر عليه السلام، قال لا يكون الحَصاد والجِداد بالليل، إنّ الله يقول: ﴿وَآتُواْ حَقَّهُ يَوْمَ حَصَادِهِ وَلاَ تُسْرِفُواْ إِنَّهُ لاَ يُحِبُّ الْمُسْرِفِينَ﴾. قال: كان فلان بن فلان الأنصاري - سمّاه - وكان له حَرْثٌ، وكان إذا جِذَّهُ تَصدّق به، وبقي هو وعياله بغير شيءٍ،فجعل الله ذلك سَرَفًا.

١٠٦. عن أحمد بن محمّد، عن أبي الحسن الرضا عليه السلام [كان أبي عليه السلام]، يقول: من الاسراف في الحَصاد والجِذاذ، أن يَصّدّق الرجل بكفّيه جميعًا، وكان أبي عليه السلام إذا حَضَر شيئًا من هذا فرأى أحدًا من غِلمانه تَصَدَّق بكفّيه صاح به: أعطِ بيدٍ واحدةٍ، القبضة بعد القبضة، والضِّغث بعد الضِّغْث من السُّنْبُل.

١٠٧. عن سَماعة، عن أبي عبدالله عليه السلام، في قوله: ﴿وَآتُواْ حَقَّهُ يَوْمَ حَصَادِهِ﴾. قال: حقّه يوم حَصاده عليك واجبٌ، وليس من الزكاة، تقبِضُ منه القَبْضَة والضِّغْث من السُّنْبُل لمن يَحْضُرك من السوّال، لا يُحصَدُ بالليل، ولا يُجَذُّ بالليل، إنَّ الله يقول: ﴿يَوْمَ حَصَادِهِ﴾ فاذا أنت حَصَدته بالليل لم يَحْضُرك سُوَّال، ولا يُضَحّى بالليل.

١٠٨. عن سَماعة، عن أبي عبدالله عليه السلام، عن أبيه، عن النبيّ صلى الله عليه وآله وسلم، أنّه كان يكره أن يُصرَم النَّخل بالليل، وأن يُحصَد الزَّرع بالليل، لأنَّ الله تعالى يقول: ﴿وَآتُواْ حَقَّهُ يَوْمَ حَصَادِهِ﴾، قيل: يا نبيّ الله، وما حقّه؟ قال: ناول منه المسكين والسائل.

109. From al-Jarrāḥ al-Madā'inī, from Abū ʿAbd Allāh عليه السلام who said regarding God's statement: ﴾*pay what is due on the day of harvest*﴿, 'Give out of it to the paupers who come to your door, taking bunch after bunch in your hand until it runs out.' [6:141]

110. From Muḥammad b. Muslim, from Abū Jaʿfar عليه السلام who said, 'Crops must not be harvested at night for God says: ﴾*pay what is due on the day of harvest*﴿, and its due is a bundle of ears of corn.' [6:141]

111. From Muḥammad al-Ḥalabī, from Abū ʿAbd Allāh عليه السلام from Abū Jaʿfar عليه السلام from ʿAlī b. al-Ḥusayn, may God's blessings be upon him, that he said to his treasurer when he found him having cut one of his date-palms in the middle of the night, 'Do not do that. Do you not know that the Messenger of God صلى الله عليه وآله forbade harvesting and reaping at night?'

He would also say: 'Give a bundle of it to one who comes to beg from you, for that is his due on the day of harvest.' [6:141]

112. From Abū Baṣīr, from Abū ʿAbd Allāh عليه السلام regarding His verse: ﴾*pay what is due on the day of harvest*﴿ – how should it be given? He replied, 'Take a bundle in your hand and pronounce the name of God on it in truth.' He said, 'I asked, "And what is due on the day of harvest?"

He replied, "A bundle that you can give to whoever comes to you from among the *khāṣṣa* [i.e. the Shīʿa]."' [6:141]

113. From al-Ḥalabī, from Abū ʿAbd Allāh عليه السلام. He said, 'I asked him about God's statement: ﴾*pay what is due on the day of harvest*﴿ – how should it be given? He replied, "Take a bundle in your hand and give it away to pauper after pauper until it runs out. With dates, give handful after handful until it runs out."' [6:141]

١٠٩. عن جرّاح المدائني، عن أبي عبدالله ﵇، في قول الله: ﴿وَآتُوا حَقَّهُ يَوْمَ حَصَادِهِ﴾، قال: تُعطي منه المساكين الذين يَحْضُرونك، تأخُذ بيدك القَبْضَة والقبْضَة حتّى تَفرُغ.

١١٠. عن محمّد بن مسلم، عن أبي جعفر ﵇، قال: لا يكون الجِداد والحصاد بالليل، إنّ الله يقول: ﴿وَآتُوا حَقَّهُ يَوْمَ حَصَادِهِ﴾ وحقّه في شيءٍ ضِغْث، يعني من السُّنْبُل.

١١١. عن محمّد الحلبي، عن أبي عبدالله، عن أبي جعفر، عن عليّ بن الحسين صلوات الله وسلامه عليهم، أنّه قال ﵇ لقَهْرَمانه، ووجده قد جَذّ نخلاً له من آخر اللّيل، فقال له: لا تفعل، ألم تعلم أنّ رسول الله صلى الله عليه وآله وسلّم نهى عن الجِذاذ والحَصاد بالليل.

وكان يقول: الضِّغْث تُعطيه من يسأل فذلك حقّه يوم حَصاده.

١١٢. عن أبي بصير، عن أبي عبدالله ﵇، في قوله: ﴿وَآتُوا حَقَّهُ يَوْمَ حَصَادِهِ﴾ كيف يُعطى؟ قال: تَقْبِض بيدك الضِّغْث، فسمّاه الله حقّاً.

قال: قلتُ: وما حقّه يوم حَصاده؟ قال: الضِّغْث تُناوله من حَضَرك من أهل الخاصّة.

١١٣. عن الحلبي، عن أبي عبدالله ﵇، قال: سألتُهُ عن قول الله تعالى: ﴿وَآتُوا حَقَّهُ يَوْمَ حَصَادِهِ﴾ كيف يُعطى؟

قال: تَقْبِض بيدك الضِّغْث فتُعطيه المسكين، ثمّ المسكين حتّى تفرُغ، وعند الصِّرام الحَفْنَة ثمّ الحَفنة حتّى تفرُغ منه.

114. From Abū al-Jārūd Ziyād b. al-Mundhir who said, 'Abū Ja'far ﷺ said: ﴿*pay what is due on the day of harvest*﴾, 'A bundle from each plot that you must give away to the paupers.' [6:141]

115. From Ayyūb b. Nūḥ b. Darrāj who said, 'I asked the third Abū al-Ḥasan [i.e. Imam 'Alī al-Naqī] about the buffalo, informing him that the people of Iraq considered it to be a mutant. So he replied, "Have you not heard God's verse: ﴿*And a pair of camels and a pair of cattle.*﴾

I wrote to Abū al-Ḥasan ﷺ after my return from Khurasan asking him about what Ayyūb had narrated to me regarding the buffalo, and he wrote back saying the same thing that he told you."' [6:143]

116. From Dāwūd al-Raqqī who said, 'One of the Kharijites asked me about this verse from God's Book: ﴿*a pair of sheep and a pair of goats – ask them* [*Prophet*], *'Has He forbidden the two males, the two females, or the young in the wombs of the two females? Tell me based on knowledge if you are telling the truth.' And a pair of camels and a pair of cattle* [...]﴾ – "What is it exactly that God has made permissible and what is it that God has forbidden?" I did not know anything about it, so I went to Abū 'Abd Allāh ﷺ whilst on Hajj, and told him about what had transpired.

So he replied, "God, Blessed and most High, has made the meat of desert camels permissible for consumption and has forbidden the meat of the wild Bactrian camels. He has permitted the meat of domestic cattle and has forbidden mountain cattle."

So I went back to the man and informed him of this answer. So he said to me, "So this thing has been brought on camelback all the way from Hijaz from a man from among the Basran peddlers[21] [i.e. Kharijites]."' [6:143–144]

117. From Ṣafwān al-Jammāl who said, 'On my trade route to Egypt, I had a Kharijite friend who came to visit me as I was leaving for Hajj, and he asked me, "Have you heard anything from Ja'far b. Muḥammad ﷺ about the verse of God, Mighty and Exalted: ﴿[*God gave you*] *eight animals, in* [*four*] *pairs: a pair of sheep and a pair of goats - ask them* [*Prophet*], *'Has He forbidden the*

21 *Shāriya*, peddlers or salesmen. This was a nickname given to a group of Kharijites because of their saying, 'We have sold our souls to God's obedience.'

١١٤. عن أبي الجارود زياد بن المُنذر، قال: قال أبو جعفر عليه السلام: ﴿وَآتُوا حَقَّهُ يَوْمَ حَصَادِهِ﴾، قال: الضِغْث من المكان بعد المكان تُعطي المسكين.

١١٥. عن أيّوب بن نوح بن درّاج، قال: سألت أبا الحسن الثالث عليه السلام عن الجاموس، وأعلمته أنّ أهل العراق يقولون: إنّه مِسخٌ، فقال عليه السلام: أوَما سَمِعتَ قول الله تعالى: ﴿وَمِنَ الْإِبِلِ اثْنَيْنِ وَمِنَ الْبَقَرِ اثْنَيْنِ﴾.

وكتبتُ إلى أبي الحسن عليه السلام بعد مقدمي خُراسان، أسأله عمّا حدّثني به أيوب في الجامُوس، فكتب عليه السلام: هو ما قال لك.

١١٦. عن داود الرقّي، قال: سألني بعض الخوارج عن هذه الآية في كتاب الله ﴿مِنَ الضَّأْنِ اثْنَيْنِ وَمِنَ الْمَعْزِ اثْنَيْنِ قُلْ آلذَّكَرَيْنِ حَرَّمَ أَمِ الْأُنْثَيَيْنِ... ۞ وَمِنَ الْإِبِلِ ... وَمِنَ الْبَقَرِ اثْنَيْنِ﴾ ما الّذي أحلّ الله من ذلك، وما الّذي حرّم الله؟ فلم يكن عندي فيه شيء، فدخلتُ على أبي عبد الله عليه السلام وأنا حاجّ، فأخبرته بما كان.

فقال: إنّ الله تبارك وتعالى أحلّ في الأُضحيّة بمنى الإبل العِراب، وحرّم فيها البَخَاتي، وأحلَّ البقرة الأهليّة أن يُضحّى بها، وحرّم الجبليّة. فانصرفت إلى الرجل، فأخبرته بهذا الجواب، فقال لي: هذا شيءٌ حَمَلَته الإبل من الحِجاز، عن رجلٍ من البصريّين من الشارية.

١١٧. عن صفوان الجمّال، قال: كان متجري إلى مِصر، وكان لي بها صديقٌ من الخوارج، فأتاني وقت خروجي إلى الحجّ، فقال لي: هل سَمِعتَ من جعفر بن محمّد عليهما السلام في قول الله عزّ وجلّ: ﴿ثَمَانِيَةَ أَزْوَاجٍ مِنَ الضَّأْنِ اثْنَيْنِ وَمِنَ الْمَعْزِ اثْنَيْنِ قُلْ

two males, the two females, or the young in the wombs of the two females? Tell me based on knowledge if you are telling the truth.' And a pair of camels and a pair of cattle [...] ﴾ – which of them has He permitted and which of them has He prohibited?" I replied, "I have not heard anything from him about this." So he said to me, "Since you are travelling there, I would like it if you could ask him about that."'

He said, 'So I completed my Hajj and went to visit Abū ʿAbd Allāh عليه السلام and asked him about the Kharijite's query. So he said to me, "He has prohibited the mountainous sheep and the goats and permitted the domestic ones, meaning their meat for consumption. He has also permitted the meat of desert camels and domestic cattle, and prohibited mountainous cattle and Bactrian camels from consumption."'

He said, 'So when I returned, I informed him of this, so he said, "Were it not for the bloodshed caused by his grandfather, I would not follow any other Imam save him."' [6:143–144]

118. From Ḥarīz, from Abū ʿAbd Allāh عليه السلام. He said, 'He was asked about birds of prey and wild beasts, whereupon I mentioned porcupines, bats, donkeys, mules and horses.

So he said, "Nothing is prohibited except for that which God Himself has prohibited in His Book. The Messenger of God ﷺ had forbidden the consumption of donkey-meat on the day of Khaybar, but he did that because of their disregard and overconsumption of it to extinction, but donkey-meat is not prohibited in itself." And he recited this verse: ﴿ *[Prophet], say, 'In all that has been revealed to me, I find nothing forbidden for people to eat, except for carrion, flowing blood, pig's meat – it is loathsome – or a sinful offering over which any name other than God's has been invoked.'* ﴾ [6:145]

آلذَّكَرَيْنِ حَرَّمَ أَمِ الأُنثَيَيْنِ أَمَّا اشْتَمَلَتْ عَلَيْهِ أَرْحَامُ الأُنثَيَيْنِ... وَمِنَ الإِبْلِ اثْنَيْنِ وَمِنَ الْبَقَرِ اثْنَيْنِ﴾ أيّاً أحلّ، وأيّاً حرّم؟

قلتُ: ما سَمِعت منه في هذا شيئًا، فقال لي: أنت على الخُروج، فأُحبُّ أن تسأله عن ذلك.

قال: فحَجَجْتُ فدخلتُ على أبي عبدالله عليه السلام، فسألته عن مسألة الخارجي، فقال عليه السلام لي: حرّم من الضأن ومن المعز الجَبَليّة، وأحلّ الاهليّة – يعني في الأضاحي – وأحلّ من الإبل العِراب، ومن البقر الأهليّة، وحرّم من البقر الجَبليّة، ومن الإبل البَخاتي – يعني في الأضاحي – قال: فلمّا انصرفتُ أخبرته، فقال: أمّا إنّهُ لولا ما إهراق جَدُّه من الدّماء، ما اتّخذت إمامًا غيره.

١١٨. عن حَريز، عن أبي عبدالله عليه السلام، قال: سُئل عن سِباع الطير والوَحْش، حتّى ذكر القَنافِذ، والوَطْوَاط، والحَمير، والبِغال، والخَيل.

فقال عليه السلام: ليس الحرام إلاّ ما حرّم الله في كتابه، وقد نهى رسول الله صلى الله عليه وآله وسلّم يوم خيبر عن أكل لحوم الحمير، وإنّما نهاهم من أجل ظَهْرهم أن يُفنوه، وليس الحمير بحرام، وقال قرأ هذه الآيات: ﴿قُل لاَّ أَجِدُ فِي مَا أُوحِيَ إِلَيَّ مُحَرَّمًا عَلَى طَاعِمٍ يَطْعَمُهُ إِلاَّ أَن يَكُونَ مَيْتَةً أَوْ دَمًا مَّسْفُوحًا أَوْ لَحْمَ خِنزِيرٍ فَإِنَّهُ رِجْسٌ أَوْ فِسْقًا أُهِلَّ لِغَيْرِ اللهِ بِهِ﴾.

119. From Muḥammad b. Muslim, from Abū Ja'far عليه السلام. He said, 'Al-Mughīra's companions used to write to me requesting me to ask him about catfish, eel, knife fish and scale-less fish and whether they were prohibited or not.'

He said, 'So I asked him about that and he said, "Muḥammad, read this verse that is in the Chapter of the Livestock: ﴿*[Prophet], say, 'In all that has been revealed to me, I find nothing forbidden for people to eat, except for carrion, flowing blood, pig's meat.*﴾"'

He said, 'So I read it until the end and he said, "The prohibited things are only that which God has prohibited in His Book, but they used to seek out exceptions, and so we dispense them."' [6:145]

120. From Zurāra who said, 'I asked Abū Ja'far عليه السلام about the catfish. So he asked, "What is a catfish?" So I described it to him, so he said: ﴿*[Prophet], say, 'In all that has been revealed to me, I find nothing forbidden for people to eat, except for carrion, flowing blood, pig's meat – it is loathsome – or a sinful offering over which any name other than God's has been invoked.' But if someone is forced by hunger, rather than desire or excess, then God is most forgiving and most merciful.*﴾ Then he said, "God has not prohibited any animal from consumption in the Qur'an apart from the pig itself, and anything from the ocean that contains no scales is disapproved of for consumption."

I asked, "What are scales?" He said, "They are like leaves. And this is not prohibited – only disapproved of."' [6:145]

121. From Muḥammad al-Ḥalabī, from Abū 'Abd Allāh عليه السلام who said, 'He forbade the Children of Israel from eating every animal with claws, and the fat [of cattle] except what is on their backs and in their intestines, or that which is intermingled with bones.' [6:146]

122. From al-Ḥusayn who said, 'I heard Abū Ṭālib al-Qummī narrate from Sadīr, from Abū 'Abd Allāh عليه السلام who said, "We are God's conclusive argument against everyone under the sky and on the face of the earth."' [6:149]

١١٩. عن محمّد بن مسلم، عن أبي جعفر عليه السلام، قال: قد كان أصحاب المُغيرة يكْتُبون إليّ أن أسأله عن الجِرّي، والمَارماهي، والزِّمّير، وما ليس له قِشْرٌ من السّمك، أحرام هو أم لا؟

قال: فسألتُه عن ذلك، فقال: يا محمّد، اقرأ هذه الآية التي في الأنعام ﴿قُل لاَّ أَجِدُ فِي مَا أُوحِيَ إِلَيَّ مُحَرَّمًا عَلَى طَاعِمٍ يَطْعَمُهُ إِلاَّ أَن يَكُونَ مَيْتَةً أَوْ دَمًا مَّسْفُوحًا أَوْ لَحْمَ خِنزِيرٍ﴾، قال: فقرأتها حتّى فرغت منها، فقال: إنّما الحرام ما حرّم الله في كتابه، ولكنّهم كانوا يَعافُون أشياء، فنحن نَعافُها.

١٢٠. عن زُرارة، قال: سألتُ أبا جعفر عليه السلام عن الجِرّي، فقال: وما الجِرّي؟ فَنَعَتُّه له، قال: فقال: ﴿لا أَجِدُ فِي مَا أُوحِيَ إِلَيَّ مُحَرَّمًا عَلَى طَاعِمٍ يَطْعَمُهُ﴾ إلى آخر الآية.

ثمّ قال: لم يُحرّم الله شيئًا من الحيوان في القرآن إلاّ الخِنزير بعينه، ويُكْرَه كلّ شيءٍ من البحر ليس فيه قِشر.

قال: قلتُ: وا القِشر؟ قال: الذي مثل الوَرَق، وليس هو بحرام، إنّما هو مكروه.

١٢١. عن محمّد الحلبي، عن أبي عبد الله عليه السلام، قال: حرّم على بني إسرائيل كلّ ذي ظُفُر والشُّحوم إلاّ ما حملت ظُهورهما أو الحَوَايا أو ما اختلط بعظم.

١٢٢. الحسين، قال: سَمِعتُ أبا طالب القُمّي يروي عن سَدير، عن أبي عبد الله عليه السلام، قال: نحن الحُجّة البالغة على من دون السماء وفوق الأرض.

123. From Abū Baṣīr who said, 'I was sitting with Abū Ja'far عليه السلام while he was reclining on his bed when he recited the decisive verses of the Chapter of Livestock, which have not been abrogated by any other verses. He said, "It has been proliferated by seventy thousand angels: ﴾*Say, 'Come! I will tell you what your Lord has really forbidden you. Do not ascribe anything as a partner to Him.*﴿"' [6:151]

124. From 'Amr b. Abī al-Miqdām, on his father's authority, from 'Alī b. al-Ḥusayn, may God's blessings be upon him. He said: '﴾*committing obscenities, whether openly or in secret*﴿ – The open obscenity refers to marrying the wife of one's father, and the secret obscenity is fornication.' [6:151]

125. From Burayd al-'Ijlī, from Abū Ja'far عليه السلام who said: ﴾*This is My path, leading straight, so follow it, and do not follow other ways: they will lead you away from it.*﴿ He asked, 'Do you know what the meaning of ﴾*My straight path*﴿ is?'

I replied, 'No.'

He said, 'The sacred authority of 'Alī and his successors.' Then he asked, 'And do you know what ﴾*so follow it*﴿ refers to?'

I said, 'No.'

So he said, 'It refers to 'Alī b. Abī Ṭālib, may God's blessings be upon him.' He then asked me, 'And do you know what ﴾*do not follow other ways: they will lead you away from it*﴿ means?'

I replied, 'No.'

He said, '*x* and *y*'s authority, by God!' Then he asked, 'And do you know what ﴾*they will lead you away from it*﴿ refers to?'

I said, 'No.'

He said, 'It refers to the way of 'Alī عليه السلام.' [6:153]

١٢٣. عن أبي بصير، قال: كنتُ جالسًا عند أبي جعفر عليه السلام، وهو مُتّكئ على فِراشه، إذ قرأ الآيات المُحكمات الّتي لم يَنْسَخْهُنّ شيءٌ من الأنعام، قال: شيّعها سبعون ألف ملك ﴿قُلْ تَعَالَوْاْ أَتْلُ مَا حَرَّمَ رَبُّكُمْ عَلَيْكُمْ أَلاَّ تُشْرِكُواْ بِهِ شَيْئًا﴾.

١٢٤. عن عمرو بن أبي المِقدام، عن أبيه، عن عليّ بن الحسين صلوات الله عليه، قال: ﴿الْفَوَاحِشَ مَا ظَهَرَ مِنْهَا وَمَا بَطَنَ﴾، قال: ما ظَهَر منها نِكاح امرأة الأب، وما بطن الزِّنا.

١٢٥. عن بُريد العِجلي، عن أبي جعفر عليه السلام، قال: ﴿وَأَنَّ هَـذَا صِرَاطِي مُسْتَقِيمًا فَاتَّبِعُوهُ وَلاَ تَتَّبِعُواْ السُّبُلَ فَتَفَرَّقَ بِكُمْ عَن سَبِيلِهِ﴾، قال: أتدري ما يعني بـ ﴿صِرَاطِي مُسْتَقِيمًا﴾؟ قلت: لا، قال: ولاية عليّ والأوصياء عليهم السلام.

قال: وتدري ما يعني ﴿فَاتَّبِعُوه﴾؟

قال: قلت: لا.

قال: يعني عليّ بن أبي طالب صلوات الله عليه. قال: وتدري ما يعني ﴿وَلاَ تَتَّبِعُواْ السُّبُلَ فَتَفَرَّقَ بِكُمْ عَن سَبِيلِهِ﴾؟

قلت: لا.

قال: ولاية فلان وفلان والله. قال: وتدري ما يعني ﴿فَتَفَرَّقَ بِكُمْ عَن سَبِيلِهِ﴾؟

قلت: لا.

قال: يعني سبيل عليّ عليه السلام.

126. From Saʿd, from Abū Jaʿfar عليه السلام regarding: ﴿*This is My path, leading straight, so follow it*﴾, he said, 'The family of Muḥammad ﷺ is the path that leads to Him.' [6:153]

127. From Masʿada b. Ṣadaqa, from Abū Jaʿfar Muḥammad b. ʿAlī, on his father's authority, on his grandfather's authority, peace be upon them both. He said, 'The Commander of the Faithful عليه السلام said, "People are on the verge of giving up their striving and the door of repentance will be blocked for them, and ﴿*no soul will profit from faith if it had none before, or it had not already earned some good through its faith.*﴾"' [6:158]

128. From Zurāra, Ḥumrān and Muḥammad b. Muslim, from Abū Jaʿfar and Abū ʿAbd Allāh, peace be upon them both, regarding His verse: ﴿*But on the Day that some of your Lord's signs come, no soul will profit from faith* [...]﴾ He said, 'The rising of the sun from the west, the emergence of the Animal[22] and Dajjāl, while man will persist [in wrongdoing] and not strive upon his faith, then the signs will come and his faith will not profit him.' [6:158]

129. From Ḥafṣ b. Ghiyāth, from Jaʿfar b. Muḥammad عليه السلام who said, 'A man asked my father عليه السلام about the Commander of the Faithful's battles, and this man was one of our devotees.'

He said, 'So Abū Jaʿfar said, "God sent Muḥammad ﷺ with five swords: three of these have been drawn and will not be sheathed until the war has ended. And the war will not end until the sun rises from the west. But when the sun does rise from the west, all the people will have faith on that day; ﴿*But on the Day that some of your Lord's signs come, no soul will profit from faith if it had none before, or has not already earned some good through its faith.*﴾"' [6:158]

---

22 One of the signs of the reappearance of the Twelfth Imam narrated in Imāmī *ḥadīth* literature is the emergence of the 'Animal' (*al-dābba*) from the region between Ṣafā and Marwa, or between the corner of the Kaʿba and Maqām Ibrāhīm, as mentioned in al-Mufaḍḍal b. ʿUmar's narration. It will inform the believer that s/he is a believer, while it will tell the infidel that s/he is a disbeliever.

١٢٦ . عن سعد، عن أبي جعفر عليه السلام ﴿وَأَنَّ هَـٰذَا صِرَاطِي مُسْتَقِيمًا فَاتَّبِعُوهُ﴾، قال: آل محمّد عليهم السلام الصِّراط الذي دَلّ عليه.

١٢٧ . عن مَسْعَدة بن صَدَقة، عن أبي جعفر محمّد بن علي، عن أبيه، عن جدّه عليهم السلام، قال: قال أمير المؤمنين عليه السلام: إنّ الناس يُوشِكُون أن يَنْقَطِع بهم العمل، ويُسَدّ عليهم باب التوبة، فلا يَنفعُ نَفسًا، إيمانُها لم تَكُن آمنت من قبلُ أوكسبت في إيمانها خيرًا.

١٢٨ . عن زُرارة وحُمران ومحمّد بن مسلم، عن أبي جعفر وأبي عبدالله عليهما السلام، في قوله ﴿يَوْمَ يَأْتِي بَعْضُ آيَاتِ رَبِّكَ لَا يَنفَعُ نَفْسًا إِيمَانُهَا﴾.

قال: طُلُوع الشمس من المغرب، وخُروج الدابّةَ والدّجّال، والرجل يكون مُصِرًّا، ولم يَعمَل على الإيمان ثمّ تجيءُ الآيات فلا يَنْفَعُه إيمانه.

١٢٩ . عن حَفْص بن غِياث، عن جعفر بن محمّد عليهما السلام، قال: سأل رجل أبي عليه السلام عن حروب أمير المؤمنين عليه السلام، وكان السائل من مُحبّينا.

قال: فقال أبو جعفر عليه السلام: إنّ الله بعث محمّدًا صلى الله عليه وآله وسلم بخمسة أسياف، ثَلاثة منها شاهرة لا تُغمَد إلاّ أن تَضَع الحرب أوزارها، ولن تَضَع الحرب أوزارها حتّى تَطْلُع الشمس من مَغْرِبها، فاذا طلعت الشمس من مغربها، آمن الناس كلّهم في ذلك اليوم، فيومئذٍ ﴿لَا يَنفَعُ نَفْسًا إِيمَانُهَا لَمْ تَكُنْ آمَنَتْ مِن قَبْلُ أَوْ كَسَبَتْ فِي إِيمَانِهَا خَيْرًا﴾.

130. From 'Amr b. Shimr, from one of the two Imams regarding His verse: ﴾*or has not already earned some good through its faith.*﴿ He said, 'The believer – wrongdoings will come between him and his faith as a result of his many sins and his lack of good deeds, so he will not have earned much good from his faith.' [6:158]

131. From Kulayb al-Ṣaydāwī[23] who said, 'I asked Abū 'Abd Allāh عليه السلام about God's statement: ﴾*As for those who have divided their religion and broken up into factions.*﴿ Then he said, "Alī used to recite it as "those who have departed from their religion."' Then he said, 'By God, the masses have departed from their religion.' [6:159]

132. From al-Sakūnī, from Ja'far b. Muḥammad, on his father's authority, peace be upon them both, who said, 'The Messenger of God صلى الله عليه وآله said, "Whoever fasts three days in a month and then is subsequently asked if he is fasting the whole month, if he replies, 'Yes,' he would be telling the truth, because God says: ﴾*Whoever has done a good deed will have it ten times to his credit.*﴿"' [6:160]

133. From Zurāra and Muḥammad b. Muslim, from Abū Ja'far and Abū 'Abd Allāh, peace be upon them both. They said, 'We asked them about His verse: ﴾*Whoever has done a good deed will have it ten times to his credit*﴿ – is that for Muslims who are weak? They replied, "No, rather it is for the believers. God has a right to be compassionate towards them."' [6:160]

134. From al-Ḥusayn b. Sa'īd who, without mentioning his source, cited the Commander of the Faithful عليه السلام as having said, 'Fasting in the month of perseverance [i.e. Ramadan] and three days in each month removes anxieties from the hearts, and fasting for three days every month equates to fasting for a lifetime: ﴾*Whoever has done a good deed will have it ten times to his credit.*﴿' [6:160]

---

23 Kulayb b. Mu'āwiya al-Ṣaydāwī, about whom there are differing opinions as to his reliability, was a companion of Imam Ja'far al-Ṣādiq. See Ḥillī, *Khulāṣat al-aqwāl*, 232 (nr. 793); Modarressi, *Tradition and Survival*, 315 (nr. 130).

١٣٠ . عن عمرو بن شِمر، عن أحدهما عليهما السلام، في قوله تعالى: ﴿أَوْ كَسَبَتْ فِي إِيمَانِهَا خَيْرًا﴾، قال: المؤمن، حالت المعاصي بينه وبين إيمانه، وكَثرت ذُنوبه وقلّت حَسَناته، فلم يَكْسِب في إيمانه خيرًا.

١٣١ . عن كُليب الصيداوي، قال: سألتُ أبا عبدالله عليه السلام عن قول الله تعالى: ﴿إِنَّ الَّذِينَ فَرَّقُوا دِينَهُمْ وَكَانُوا شِيَعًا﴾، ثمّ قال: كان عليّ عليه السلام يقرأها: (فَارَقُوا دِيْنَهُم)، ثمّ قال: فارق والله القوم دينهم.

١٣٢ . عن السّكوني، عن جعفر بن محمّد، عن أبيه عليهما السلام، قال: قال رسول الله صلى الله عليه وآله وسلم: من صام ثلاثة أيّام في الشهر، فقيل له: أنت صائمٌ الشهر كلّه؟ فقال: نعم، صَدَق، لأنّه تعالى قال: ﴿مَن جَاءَ بِالْحَسَنَةِ فَلَهُ عَشْرُ أَمْثَالِهَا﴾.

١٣٣ . عن زُرارة وحُمران ومحمّد بن مسلم، عن أبي جعفر وأبي عبدالله عليهما السلام، قالوا: سألناهما عن قوله: ﴿مَن جَاءَ بِالْحَسَنَةِ فَلَهُ عَشْرُ أَمْثَالِهَا﴾ أهي لضُعفاء المسلمين؟ قالا: لا، ولكنّها للمؤمنين، وإنّه لحقٌّ على الله تعالى أن يَرحمهم.

١٣٤ . عن الحسين بن سعيد، يرفعه، عن أمير المؤمنين عليه السلام، قال: صيام شهر الصبر وثلاثة أيّام في كلّ شهر، يُذهِبن بَلابِل الصُّدور، وصيام ثلاثة أيّام في كلّ شهر صيام الدهر ﴿مَن جَاءَ بِالْحَسَنَةِ فَلَهُ عَشْرُ أَمْثَالِهَا﴾.

135. From one of our associates, from Aḥmad b. Muḥammad who said, ‘I asked him how to go about fasting for the whole year?’ So he replied, ‘By fasting for three days in each month: one Thursday in ten days, one Wednesday in ten days, another Thursday in ten days, and the Wednesday should be between two Thursdays. God says: ﴾ *Whoever has done a good deed will have it ten times to his credit.* ﴿ Three fasts per month equate to fasting for a lifetime.’ [6:160]

136. From ‘Alī b. ‘Ammār who said, ‘Abū ‘Abd Allāh عليه السلام said: ﴾ *Whoever has done a good deed will have it ten times to his credit.* ﴿ This includes fasting for three days each month.’ [6:160]

137. Muḥammad b. ‘Īsā said in Sudayf’s report from Muḥammad b. Alī – and I have never seen a Muḥammadan quite like him before – saying ‘The good deed that God meant here is the adherence to our sacred authority as the Family of the Prophet’s Household (*ahl al-bayt*); and the bad deed is enmity towards us, the Family of the Prophet’s Household.’ [6:160]

138. From Muḥammad b. Ḥakīm[24], from Abū Ja‘far عليه السلام who said, ‘Whoever intends to fast then goes to visit his brother who offers him something to eat that will break his fast, then let him break his fast and give him that pleasure, for that day of his will be counted as ten days’ worth, as per God’s statement: ﴾ *Whoever has done a good deed will have it ten times to his credit.* ﴿’ [6:160]

139. From Zurāra, from Abū ‘Abd Allāh عليه السلام who said, ‘God, Blessed and most High, has designated three favours for Ādam’s children: He has decreed that whoever intends to do a good deed but does not actually do it gets [the reward of] a good deed written for him. And whoever intends to do a good deed and does it, gets it written ten times to his credit. Whoever intends a bad deed but does not commit it, it is not recorded against him, and whoever intends a bad deed and commits it, it is recorded against him as a single

24 Abū Ja‘far Muḥammad b. Ḥakīm was an expert dialectician in the field of dogmatic disputation (*kalām*). He was, according to some reports, ordered by Imam ‘Alī b. Mūsā al-Riḍā to sit in the Prophet’s mosque at Medina and dispute the followers of other schools of thought. See Ḥillī, *Khulāṣat al-aqwāl*, 253 (nr. 863); Khū’ī, *Mu‘jam*, 17: 36–9 (nr. 10647); Modarressi, *Tradition and Survival*, 341–2 (nr. 151).

١٣٥ . عن بعض أصحابنا، عن أحمد بن محمّد، قال: سألتُهُ كيف يصنع في الصوم صوم السُنّة؟ فقال: صوم ثلاثة أيّام في الشهر: خميس من عشر، وأربعاء من عشر، وخميس من عشر، الأربعاء بين خميسين، إنَّ الله تعالى يقول: ﴿مَن جَاءَ بِالْحَسَنَةِ فَلَهُ عَشْرُ أَمْثَالِهَا﴾ ثلاثة أيّام في الشهر صوم دهر.

١٣٦ . عن علي بن عمّار، قال: قال أبو عبد الله عليه السلام: ﴿مَن جَاءَ بِالْحَسَنَةِ فَلَهُ عَشْرُ أَمْثَالِهَا﴾ من ذلك صيام ثلاثة أيّام من كُلّ شهر.

١٣٧ . قال محمّد بن عيسى: في رواية سُدَيف، عن محمّد بن عليّ عليهما السلام — وما رأيت محمّديًا مثله قطّ -: الحسنة التي عنى الله ولايتنا أهل البيت، والسّيئة عَداوتنا أهل البيت.

١٣٨ . عن محمّد بن حكيم، عن أبي جعفر عليه السلام، قال: من نوى الصوم ثمّ دخل على أخيه فسأله أن يُفْطِر عنده فليُفْطِر، وليُدخِل عليه السُّرور، فإنّه يُحسَب له بذلك اليوم عَشَرة أيّام، وهو قول الله: ﴿مَن جَاءَ بِالْحَسَنَةِ فَلَهُ عَشْرُ أَمْثَالِهَا وَمَن جَاءَ بِالسَّيِّئَةِ فَلَا يُجْزَىٰ إِلَّا مِثْلَهَا﴾.

١٣٩ . عن زُرارة، عن أبي عبد الله عليه السلام، قال: إنَّ الله تبارك وتعالى جعل لآدم عليه السلام ثلاث خِصال في ذُرِيّته: جعل لهم أنَّ مَن همَّ منهم بحسنة ولم يعملها كُتِب له حسنة، ومن همَّ بحسنةٍ فعَمِلها كُتِب له بها عشر حسنات، ومن همَّ بالسيئة ولم يعملها لا تُكتَب عليه، ومن عَمِلها كُتِبت عليه سّيئة واحدة، وجعل لهم التوبة حتّى يَبْلُغ النفس حَنْجَرَة الرجل.

bad deed and He keeps the door of repentance open for him until his very last breath.

Upon this, Iblīs said, "My Lord, You have given Ādam three favours, so give me the same as him too." So He said, "I will. For every child born unto him, you will have one too. I will let you course in them like the blood in their veins, and I will let you take up their hearts as your abodes and your homes." So Iblīs said, "That will suffice me, my Lord."' [6:160]

140. From Zurāra, on his authority: ﴾*Whoever has done a good deed will have it ten times to his credit.*﴿ He said, 'The one who curses these two every morning whenever he remembers them, God will write down seventy good deeds for him, wipe out ten bad deeds, and raise him ten degrees in rank.' [6:160]

141. From 'Abd Allāh al-Ḥalabī, from Abū 'Abd Allāh ﷺ, from the Commander of the Faithful ﷺ who said, 'Fasting in the month of perseverance [i.e. Ramadan] and three days in each month removes anxieties from the hearts, and fasting for three days every month equates to fasting for a lifetime: ﴾*Whoever has done a good deed will have it ten times to his credit.*﴿' [6:160]

142. From 'Alī b. al-Ḥasan who said, 'I found written in the book of Isḥāq b. 'Umar or in my father's book – and I do not know, but he might have heard it from Ibn Yasār on his father's authority, from Abū 'Abd Allāh ﷺ that he said, "Yasār, do you have any idea what three days of fasting signifies?"

He said, 'I replied, "May I be your ransom, I do not know." He said, "They were given to the Messenger of God ﷺ as he was passing away – [They are]: the first Thursday from the beginning of the month, a Wednesday in the middle of the month, and a Thursday at the end of it. That is God's statement: ﴾*Whoever has done a good deed will have it ten times to his credit.*﴿ So he would be fasting for a lifetime without breaking it."

Then he said, "There is no one I envy more than the fasting person constantly engaged in God's obedience, walking about whilst hungry for food and thirsty for drink. Indeed, the fast maintains, protects and nurtures the body."' [6:160]

فقال إبليس: يا ربّ، جعلت لآدم ثلاث خِصال، فاجعلْ لي مثل ما جعلتَ له.

فقال: قد جعلتُ لك لا يُولد له مولود إلاّ ولد لك مثله، وجعلتُ لك أن تجري منهم مجرى الدم في العُروق، وجعلتُ لك أن جعلتُ صدورهم أوطانًا ومساكنَ لك.

فقال إبليس: يا ربّ حسبي.

١٤٠. عن زُرارة، عنه عليه السلام ﴿مَن جَاءَ بِالْحَسَنَةِ فَلَهُ عَشْرُ أَمْثَالِهَا﴾، قال: من ذَكَرهما فلعنهما كُلّ غَداةٍ، كَتَب الله له سبعين حسنة، ومحا عنه عشر سيّئات، ورَفَع له عشر درجات.

١٤١. عن عبدالله الحلبي، عن أبي عبدالله عليه السلام، عن أمير المؤمنين عليه السلام، قال: صيام شهر الصبر، وثلاثة أيّام في الشهر، يُذهِبُ بلابِل الصدور، وصيام ثلاثة أيّام في الشهر صوم الدهر، إنّ الله يقول: ﴿مَن جَاءَ بِالْحَسَنَةِ فَلَهُ عَشْرُ أَمْثَالِهَا﴾.

١٤٢. علي بن الحسن، قال: وجدتُ في كتاب إسحاق بن عمر، [أو] في كتاب أبي — وما أدري — سَمِعه عن ابن يَسار، عن أبيه، عن أبي عبدالله عليه السلام، قال: يا يَسار، تدري ما صيام ثلاثة أيّام؟

قال: قلتُ: جُعِلت فداك، ما أدري.

قال: أتي بها إلى رسول الله صلى الله عليه وآله حين قُبِض، أوّل خميس من أوّل الشهر، وأربعاء في أوسطه، وخميس في آخره، ذلك قول الله: ﴿مَن جَاءَ بِالْحَسَنَةِ فَلَهُ عَشْرُ أَمْثَالِهَا﴾ هو الدهر صائم لا يُفطِر.

143. From Zurāra, from Abū Ja'far ﷺ, 'The upright religion has not disregarded anything such that even guidelines for clipping nails, trimming the moustache and circumcision are included therein.' [6:161]

144. From Jābir al-Ju'fī, from Muḥammad b. 'Alī ﷺ who said, 'There is no one from among the community of Muḥammad who still adheres to the religion of Ibrāhīm other than us and our Shī'a.' [6:161]

145. From Ṭalḥa b. Zayd[25], from Ja'far b. Muḥammad, on his father's authority, on his forefathers' authority, from 'Alī ﷺ who said, 'The Messenger of God ﷺ said, "God, Mighty and Exalted, sent His friend with the upright religion, and He commanded him to trim the moustache, clip his nails, shave the armpits and the pubic region, and to circumcise."' [6:161]

146. From 'Imrān b. Maytham who said, 'I heard al-Ḥusayn b. 'Alī ﷺ say, "No one is on the creed of Ibrāhīm apart from ourselves and our Shī'a, and the rest of people have disassociated themselves from it."' [6:161]

147. From Abū Baṣīr, from Abū 'Abd Allāh ﷺ who said, 'We do not say that there is only one rank, for God says: ﴾ *and raises some of you above others in rank.* ﴿ Rather, people outdo each other through their good deeds.' [6:165]

25 Abū al-Khazraj Ṭalḥa b. Zayd al-Nahdī al-Shāmī, a Sunnī transmitter but nonetheless reliable narrator of Imam Ja'far al-Ṣādiq's traditions. See Ḥillī, *Khulāṣat al-aqwāl*, 361 (nr. 1424); Modarressi, *Tradition and Survival*, 375–6 (nr. 199).

ثمّ قال: ما أغْبَط عندي الصائم! يَظَلُّ في طاعة الله، ويمسي يشتهي الطعام والشراب، إنّ الصوم ناصِرٌ للجسد، حافِظٌ وراعٍ له.

١٤٣. عن زُرارة، عن أبي جعفر عليه السلام: ما أبقت الحنيفيّة شيئًا حتّى إنَّ منها قصَّ الشارب والأظفار، والأخذ من الشارب، والختان.

١٤٤. عن جابر الجُعفي، عن محمّد بن علي عليهما السلام، قال: ما من أحدٍ من هذه الأُمّة يَدين بدينِ إبراهيم عليه السلام غيرنا وشيعتنا.

١٤٥. عن طلحة بن زيد، عن جعفر بن محمّد، عن أبيه، عن آبائه، عن علي عليهم السلام، قال: قال رسول الله صلى الله عليه وآله: إنّ الله عزّ وجلّ بعث خليله بالحنيفيّة، وأمره بأخذ الشارِب، وقصّ الأظفار، ونَتْف الإبط، وحلق العانة، والخِتان.

١٤٦. عن عمران بن مِيثم، قال: سَمِعتُ الحسين بن عليّ صلوات الله عليه، يقول: ما أحدٌ على ملّة إبراهيم عليه السلام إلاّ نحن وشيعتنا، وسائر الناس منها براء.

١٤٧. عن أبي بصير، عن أبي عبدالله عليه السلام، قال: لا نقول درجة واحدة، إنَّ الله يقول: ﴿دَرَجَاتٌ بَعْضُهَا فَوْقَ بَعْضٍ﴾. إنّما تفاضل القوم بالأعمال.

The Heights

7. The Heights

1. From Abū Baṣīr, from Abū ʿAbd Allāh عليه السلام who said, 'Whoever reads the Chapter of the Heights (*sūrat al-aʿrāf*) every month will be included among those who will have nothing to fear nor grieve about on the Day of Resurrection. If one recites it every Friday, he will be among those who will not be made to account on the Day of Resurrection.' Then Abū ʿAbd Allāh عليه السلام said, 'Indeed in it are decisive verses, so never stop reading it, reciting it and putting it into practice, for it will be a witness in front of God on the Day of Resurrection in favour of whoever recited it.'

2. From Abū Jumuʿa Raḥma b. Ṣadaqa who said, 'A man from the Banū Umayya who was a heretic came to Jaʿfar b. Muḥammad عليه السلام and asked him about God's word in His Book: ﴾*Alif Lām Mīm Ṣād*﴿ and what He means by that, what mention there is in that of the permissible and prohibited things, and what benefit people can derive thereof.'

He said, 'That man was speaking rudely to Jaʿfar b. Muḥammad عليه السلام so he said, "Are you done with your wretchedness? The *Alif* represents the number one, the *Lām* thirty, the *Mīm* forty, and the *Ṣād* ninety – how many is that in total?"

So the man replied, "One hundred and sixty-one."

So Jaʿfar b. Muḥammad عليه السلام said to him, "As soon as the year 161 comes to an end the reign of your companions [i.e. the Umayyad rulers] shall finish with it.'"

He said, 'So we waited and no sooner had the year 161 finished than on the day of ʿĀshūrā, the black-robed ones[1] entered Kufa and their kingdom collapsed.' [7:1]

---

1 Referring to the Abbasid Caliphs, who were reputed for their black clothing and flags.

بِسْمِ اللَّهِ الرَّحْمَٰنِ الرَّحِيمِ

من سورة الأعراف

١. عن أبي بصير، عن أبي عبد الله عليه السلام، قال: من قرأ سورة الأعراف في كُلّ شهر، كان يوم القيامة من الذين لا خوفٌ عليهم ولا يحزنون، فإن قرأها في كلّ جمعة كان ممّن لا يُحاسَب يوم القيامة.

ثمّ قال أبو عبد الله عليه السلام: أما إنَّ فيها آيًا محكمةً، فلا تَدَعُوا قِراءتها وتلاوتها والقيام بها، فإنّها تَشهَد يوم القيامة لمن قرأها عند ربّه.

٢. عن أبي جمعة رَحمَة بن صَدَقة، قال: أتى رجلٌ من بني أميّة — وكان زنديقًا — جعفر بن محمّد عليه السلام، فقال له: قول الله في كتابه: ﴿المص﴾ أيّ شيءٍ أراد بهذا، وأيّ شيء فيه من الحلال والحرام، وأيّ شيءٍ في ذا مما ينتفع به الناس؟

قال: فأغلظ ذلك جعفر بن محمّد عليه السلام، فقال: أمسِك ويحك: الألف واحد، واللاّم ثلاثون، والميم أربعون، والصاد تسعون، كم معك؟ فقال الرجل: مائة وإحدى وستّون.

فقال له جعفر بن محمّد عليه السلام: إذا انقضت سنة إحدى وستّين ومائة ينقضي ملك أصحابك.

قال: فنظرنا، فلمّا انقضت إحدى وستّون ومائة يوم عاشوراء، دخل المسوّدة الكوفة، وذهب مُلكهم.

3. From Khaythama al-Juʿfī from Abū Lubayd al-Makhzūmī who said, 'Abū Jaʿfar عليه السلام said, "Abū Lubayd, twelve people from the progeny of al-ʿAbbās will rule, and four of them after the eighth one will be killed. One of them will be afflicted with a blood-filled lump in his throat which will cause him to die. This group will have short lives, with a short-lived rein and impudent characters. Among them will be the debaucher known as al-Hādī, as well as al-Nāṭiq and al-Ghāwī.

Abū Lubayd, the disconnected letters of the Qur'an contain a comprehensive knowledge – God, Blessed and most High, revealed ﴾*Alif Lām Mīm*﴿ and Muḥammad ﷺ rose until His light was manifest and His words established. He was born on that particular day when one hundred and three years had passed since the seventh millennium."

Then he continued, "This has been elucidated in God's book through the disconnected letters if you count them without repetition. There is not a single letter of these disconnected letters that does not count the passage of days until the Qā'im from the Banu Hāshim [comes] when they have come to pass." Then he said, "The *Alif* represents the number one, the *Lām* thirty, the *Mīm* forty, and the *Ṣād* ninety. That makes one hundred and sixty-one. The beginning of al-Ḥusayn b. ʿAlī's uprising was marked by: ﴾*Alif Lām Mīm* [...]﴿

When the time for it comes, the insurgent from the progeny of al-ʿAbbās will rise to power upon ﴾*Alif Lām Mīm Ṣād.*﴿ Our Qā'im will rise when those days pass, with ﴾*Alif Lām Rā*﴿(10:1) so grasp this well, be alert to it and conceal it."' [7:1]

4. From Masʿada b. Ṣadaqa, from Abū ʿAbd Allāh عليه السلام who said, 'The Commander of the Faithful عليه السلام said in his sermon that God said: ﴾*Follow what has been sent down to you from your Lord; do not follow other masters beside Him. How seldom you take heed!*﴿ So there is great victory in following what has been sent down to you from your Lord, and manifest error in abandoning it.' [7:3]

٣. خَيثَمة الجُعفي، عن أبي لبيد المخزومي، قال: قال أبو جعفر عليه السلام يا أبا لبيد، إنّه يملكُ من ولد العباس اثنا عشر، يُقتَل بعد الثامن منهم أربعةٌ، فتُصيب أحدهم الذُّبحَة فتَذبحَه هم فِئةٌ قصيرةٌ أعمارُهم، قليلةٌ مُدَّتهم، خَبيثةٌ سِيرتُهُم، منهم الفُويسق المُلقّب بالهادي، والناطِق، والغاوي.

يا أبا لبيد، إنّ في حروف القرآن المقَطَّعة لعلمًا جمًّا، إنّ الله تبارك وتعالى أنزل ﴿الٓمٓ ۞ ذَٰلِكَ الْكِتَـٰبُ﴾. فقام محمّد صلى الله عليه وآله حتّى ظهر نُورُه، وثبتت كَلِمتُهُ، ووُلِد يوم وُلِد، وقد مضى من الألف السابع مائة سنة وثلاثين سنين.

ثمّ قال: وتبيانه في كتاب الله في الحروف المقَطَّعة إذا عددتها من غير تكرار، وليس من حروفٍ مُقَطَّعة حرفٌ ينقضي أيّامُه إلاّ وقائم من بني هاشم عند انقضائه. ثمّ قال: الألف واحد، واللاّم ثلاثون، والميم أربعون، والصاد تسعون، فذلك مائة وإحدى وستّون، ثمّ كان بدو خُروج الحسين بن عليّ عليه السلام ﴿الٓمٓ﴾.

فلمّا بلغت مُدّته قام قائم ولد العباس عند ﴿الٓمٓصٓ﴾ ويقوم قائمنا عليه السلام عند انقضائها بـ ﴿الٓر﴾ . فافهَم ذلك وَعِه واكتُمهُ.

٤. عن مَسعَدة بن صَدَقة، عن أبي عبدالله عليه السلام، قال: قال أمير المؤمنين عليه السلام في خُطبته: قال الله: ﴿اتَّبِعُوا مَـا أُنـزِلَ إِلَيْكُم مِّن رَّبِّكُمْ وَلَا تَتَّبِعُوا مِن دُونِهِ أَوْلِيَـاءَ قَلِيلًا مَّا تَـذَكَّرُونَ﴾ ففي اتّباع ما جاءكم من الله الفَوز العظيم، وفي تركه الخَطأ المُبين.

5. From Dāwūd b. Farqad, from Abū ʿAbd Allāh عليه السلام who said, 'The angels used to consider Iblīs to be one of them, but in God's knowledge he was not one of them, and God drew out the bigotry that was in his heart when he said, ﴾ *You created me from fire and him from clay.* ﴿' [7:12]

6. From Abū Baṣīr, from Abū ʿAbd Allāh عليه السلام who said, 'The path that Iblīs referred to when he said: ﴾ *I will lie in wait for them all on Your straight path. I will come at them – from their front and their back, from their right and their left – and You will find that most of them are ungrateful* ﴿ is ʿAlī عليه السلام.' [7:16–17]

7. From Zurāra who said, 'I asked Abū Jaʿfar عليه السلام about God's words: ﴾ *I will lie in wait for them all on Your straight path. I will come at them – from their front and their back, from their right and their left – and You will find that most of them are ungrateful.* ﴿ He replied, "Zurāra, indeed it is you and your companions that he will target since he has already got the better of the others."' [7:16–17]

8. From Mūsā b. Muḥammad b. ʿAlī, from his brother, the third Abū al-Ḥasan [i.e. Imam ʿAlī al-Naqī] who said, 'The tree that God forbade Ādam and his wife from eating from was the tree of jealousy. He required of them not to look enviously at those of His creatures whom He had favoured over him. However, God did not find that firm resolve in him.' [7:19]

9. From Jamīl b. Darrāj, from one of our associates, from one of the two [al-Bāqir or al-Ṣādiq]. He said, 'I asked him how God could take Ādam to task for forgetting. So he replied, "He did not forget though – how could he forget when he was reminded of it when Iblīs said: ﴾ *Your Lord only forbade you this tree to prevent you becoming angels or immortals.* ﴿"' [7:20]

10. From Masʿada b. Ṣadaqa, from Abū ʿAbd Allāh عليه السلام referring it to the Prophet صلى الله عليه وآله that once when Mūsā had ascended to the heavens on business of the daily prayer (*ṣalāt*), he asked his Lord to let him meet his father Ādam, so He did. Mūsā said to him, 'O Ādam, you are the one that God created with His own Hand, into whom He blew His Spirit, before whom His angels prostrated, for whom He opened His Garden, whom He made to reside in His vicinity, and who He spoke to before that. Then He forbade you from

٥. عن داود بن فرقد، عن أبي عبد الله عليه السلام، قال: إنّ الملائكة كانوا يحسبون أنّ إبليس منهم، وكان في عِلم الله أنّه ليس منهم، فاستخرج الله ما في نفسه بالحميّة، فقال: ﴿خَلَقْتَنِي مِن نَّارٍ وَخَلَقْتَهُ مِن طِينٍ﴾.

٦. عن أبي بصير، عن أبي عبد الله عليه السلام، قال: الصّراط الذي قال إبليس: ﴿لَأَقْعُدَنَّ لَهُمْ صِرَاطَكَ الْمُسْتَقِيمَ ۞ ثُمَّ لَآتِيَنَّهُم مِّن بَيْنِ أَيْدِيهِمْ﴾ الآية، وهو عليّ عليه السلام.

٧. عن زُرارة، قال: سألتُ أبا جعفر عليه السلام عن قول الله عزّ وجلّ ﴿لَأَقْعُدَنَّ لَهُمْ صِرَاطَكَ الْمُسْتَقِيمَ﴾ إلى ﴿شَاكِرِينَ﴾، قال: يا زُرارة، إنّما صَمَدَ لك ولأصحابك، وأمّا الآخرون فقد فَرَغ منهم.

٨. عن موسى بن محمّد بن عليّ، عن أخيه أبي الحسن الثالث عليه السلام، قال: الشجرة التي نهى الله آدم زوجته أن يأكُلا منها شَجَرة الحَسَد، عَهد إليهما أن لا ينظُرا إلى من فضّل عليه وعلى خلائقه بعين الحسد، ولم يَجِد له عَزمًا.

٩. عن جميل بن دَرّاج، عن بعض أصحابنا، عن أحدهما عليهما السلام، قال: سألتُهُ كيف أخذ الله آدم عليه السلام بالنسيان؟ فقال: إنّه لم يَنسَ، وكيف ينسى وهو يُذكّرُه، ويقول له إبليس: ﴿مَا نَهَاكُمَا رَبُّكُمَا عَنْ هَٰذِهِ الشَّجَرَةِ إِلَّا أَن تَكُونَا مَلَكَيْنِ أَوْ تَكُونَا مِنَ الْخَالِدِينَ﴾.

١٠. عن مَسعَدة بن صَدَقة، عن أبي عبد الله عليه السلام، رفعه إلى النبيّ صلى الله عليه وآله وسلم: أنّ موسى عليه السلام سأل ربّه أن يجمع بينه وبين أبيه آدم عليه السلام حيث عَرَج إلى السماء في أمر الصلاة ففعل، فقال

one single tree, but you could not be patient with it until you were made to descend to the earth as a result of it. So could you not control yourself from it that Iblīs was able to entice you and you obeyed him? For then surely you are the one who caused us to be expelled from the Garden through your disobedience?'

So Ādam said to him, 'Be gentle with your father, my son, for the tribulation that he faced with regard to this tree. [My son], my enemy approached me with cunning and deception, swearing by God that in his counselling me he was naught but a sincere adviser, and he said to me pretending to advise: "By your status, O Ādam, I am so upset."

I asked, "Why?"

He said, "I have grown attached to you and your closeness to me, and now you are going to leave this place to somewhere that you are going to hate."

So I asked him, "What is the solution then?"

He replied, "Well, the solution is right here with you. Shall I show you the tree of immortality and a kingdom that will never perish? You and your wife can eat from it and you will both become immortal and live in the Garden with me forever."

He swore by God, lying to me that he was a sincere adviser. I did not imagine, Mūsā, that anyone could swear by God dishonestly, so I trusted in his oath. This is my excuse. So tell me, my son, can you find anything in that which God has revealed to you that suggests that my mistake already existed before I was created?'

So Mūsā said to him, 'A long time before that.'

The Messenger of God ﷺ said, 'So Ādam convinced Mūsā.' He said that three times. [7:21]

11. From 'Abd Allāh b. Sinān who said, 'Abū 'Abd Allāh عليه السلام was asked while I was present how many years Ādam and his wife lived in the Garden before their mistake caused them to be expelled from it. So he replied, "God, Blessed and most High, blew His Spirit into Ādam after noon on Friday, then He brought his wife into being from his lowest rib. Then He made his angels prostrate before him and made him live in His Garden from that same day. By God, he did not stay there for longer than six hours of that day before he disobeyed God. So God expelled them from it after sunset. They did not

له موسى عليه السلام: يا آدم، أنت الذي خلقك الله بيده، ونَفَخ فيك من رُوحه، وأسجد لك ملائكته، وأباح لك جنّته، وأسكنك جِواره، وكلّمك قُبُلاً، ثمّ نهاك عن شجرةٍ واحدةٍ، فلم تصبِر عنها، حتّى أُهبِطتَ إلى الأرض بسببها، فلم تستطع أن تضبِط نفسك عنها، حتّى أغراك إبليس فأطعته، فأنت الذي أخرجتنا من الجنّة بمعصيتك.

فقال له آدم عليه السلام: ارفِق بأبيك - أي بُنَيّ - محنةَ ما لقي في أمر هذه الشجرة، يا بُنَيّ إنّ عدوّي أتاني من وجه المكر والخَديعة، فحلف لي بالله أنّه في مشورته، عليّ لمن الناصحين، وذلك أنّه مُستَنصِحًا: إنّي لشأنك يا آدم لمغمُوم، قلتُ: وكيف؟ قال: قد كنتُ أنِستُ بك وبقُربك مِنّي، وأنت تخرَج ممّا أنت فيه إلى ما ستَكرَهه.

فقلت له: وما الحِيلة؟

فقال: إنّ الحِيلة هو ذا هو معك، أفلا أدُلّك على شجرة الخُلد ومُلك لا يبلى؟ فكُلا منها أنت وزَوجُك فتصيرا معي في الجنّة أبدًا من الخالدين، وحلف لي بالله كاذبًا أنّه لَمِن الناصحين، ولم أظُنّ - يا موسى - أنّ أحدًا يحلِف بالله كاذبًا، فوَثِقتُ بيمينه، فهذا عُذري، فأخبرني يا بُنَيّ هل تجد فيما أنزل الله إليك أنّ خطيئتي كائنةٌ من قبل أن أخلَق؟

قال له موسى: بدهرٍ طويل.

قال رسول الله صلى الله عليه وآله: فحجّ آدم موسى، قال ذلك ثلاثًا.

١١. عن عبد الله بن سِنان، قال: سُئِل أبو عبد الله عليه السلام - وأنا حاضرٌ - كم لَبِث آدم وزوجته في الجنّة حتّى أخرجَتْهما منها خطيئتُهما؟ فقال: إنّ الله تبارك وتعالى نفخ في آدم رُوحه بعد زوال الشمس من يوم الجمعة، ثمّ برَأ زوجته من أسفل أضلاعه، ثمّ أسجد له

even spend the night therein and were made to go out into the threshold of the Garden until they awoke in the morning and their nakedness became exposed to them, and their Lord called out to them: ﴾*Did I not forbid you from approaching that tree?*﴿ So Ādam felt ashamed in front of his Lord and abased himself, saying, 'Our Lord, we have wronged ourselves and admit to our sins, so please forgive us.' God said to them both, 'Get down from My heavens unto My earth, for a disobedient one cannot remain in My vicinity: neither in My Garden nor My heavens.'"

Then Abū 'Abd Allāh عليه السلام said, "As soon as Ādam ate from the tree he remembered that this was the one that God had forbidden him from, and he regretted it so he went to move away from the tree, but it grabbed him by the head and pulled him towards itself saying, 'You did not [think you could] escape before you had eaten from me, did you?'" [7:20–22]

12. From one of our associates, from Abū 'Abd Allāh عليه السلام regarding God's verse: ﴾*Their nakedness became exposed to them.*﴿ He said, 'Their nakedness was not exposed to them before, and now it was – meaning that it used to be within.' [7:22]

13. From Zurāra, Ḥumrān and Muḥammad b. Muslim, from Abū Ja'far and Abū 'Abd Allāh, peace be upon them both, who said regarding His words: ﴾*Children of Ādam* [...]﴿ 'It is a general address.' [7:26]

14. From Mas'ada b. Ṣadaqa, from Abū 'Abd Allāh عليه السلام: 'Whoever claims that God commands wrongdoing and disgraceful deeds has indeed lied about God. Whoever claims that good and evil are independent of His Will have taken God out of His authority. And whoever claims that transgressions can be carried out without His Power has indeed lied about God, and whoever lies about God, God will make Him enter the Fire.' [7:28]

ملائكته، وأسكنه جنّته من يومه ذلك، فوالله ما استقرّ فيها إلاّ ستّ ساعات في يومه ذلك حتّى عصى الله، فأخرَجَهما اللهُ منها بعد غُروب الشمس، وما باتا فيها وصُيِّرا بفِناء الجنّة حتّى أصبحا، فبَدَت لهما سَوآتهما، وناداهما ربُّهما: ألم أنهكُما عن تِلكُما الشجرة؟! فاستحيا آدم من ربّه وخَضَع، وقال: ربَّنا ظَلَمنا أنفُسَنا، واعتَرَفنا بذُنوبنا، فاغفِر لنا. قال الله لهما: اهبِطا من سماواتي إلى الأرض، فإنّه لا يُجاورني في جنّتي عاصٍ، ولا في سماواتي.

ثمّ قال أبو عبد الله عليه السلام: إنّ آدم لما أكل من الشجرة ذَكر ما نهاهُ الله عنها فنَدِم، فذهب ليتنحّى من الشجرة، فأخذت الشجرة برأسه فجرّته إليها، وقالت له: أفلا كان فِرارك من قَبل أن تأكُل منّي.

١٢. عن بعض أصحابنا، عن أبي عبد الله عليه السلام، في قول الله تعالى: ﴿بَدَتْ لَهُمَا سَوْآتُهُمَا﴾، قال: كانت سَوآتهما لا تبدو لهما فبَدَت، يعني كانت من داخل.

١٣. عن زُرارة وحمران ومحمّد بن مسلم، عن أبي جعفر وأبي عبد الله عليهما السلام، عن قوله تعالى: ﴿يَا بَنِي آدَمَ﴾، قالا: هي عامّة.

١٤. عن مَسعدة بن صَدَقة، عن أبي عبد الله عليه السلام قال: من زَعَم أنّ الله أمر بالسُّوء والفَحشاء فقد كَذَب على الله، ومن زَعَم أنّ الخير والشرّ بغير مَشيّة منه فقد أخرج الله من سُلطانه، ومن زَعَم أنّ المعاصي عُمِلت بغير قُوّة الله فقد كَذَب على الله، ومن كَذَب على الله أدخَلَه الله النار.

15. From Muḥammad b. Manṣūr, from al-ʿAbd al-Ṣāliḥ عليه السلام [i.e. Imam al-Kāẓim]. He said, 'I asked him about God's verse: ﴾*Yet when [these people] do something disgraceful, they say, 'We found our forefathers doing this,' and, 'God has commanded us to do this.' Say [Prophet], 'God does not command disgraceful deeds. How can you say about God things that you do not know [to be true]?'*﴿ So he replied, "Have you ever seen anyone claiming that God has commanded us to fornicate, drink wine, and other such prohibited acts?"

So I replied, "No."

He asked, "So what are these disgraceful acts which they claim God has commanded?"

I said, "God and His vicegerent know best."

So he said, "This comes from despotic leaders – they claim that God has commanded them to be leaders over people, and this is God's response to them. He is informing us that they have lied about Him, and this is what He calls ﴾*disgraceful deeds*﴿."' [7:28]

16. From Abū Baṣīr, from Abū ʿAbd Allāh عليه السلام. He said, 'I heard him say, 'Whoever claims that God commands disgraceful deeds has indeed lied about God. And whoever claims that good and evil can be attributed to Him has indeed lied about God.' [7:28]

17. From Abū Baṣīr, from one of the two [Imams al-Bāqir or al-Ṣādiq] who said regarding God's verse: ﴾*Direct your worship straight to Him wherever you pray*﴿, 'It is towards the *qibla*.' [7:29]

18. From al-Ḥusayn b. Mihrān, from Abū ʿAbd Allāh عليه السلام who said about His verse: ﴾*Direct your worship straight to Him wherever you pray*﴿, 'It means the Imams.' [7:29]

19. From Zurāra, Ḥumrān and Muḥammad b. Muslim, from Abū Jaʿfar and Abū ʿAbd Allāh عليه السلام who said about His verse: ﴾*Direct your worship straight to Him wherever you pray*﴿: 'Mosques are recent; they have actually been commanded to direct their worship towards the Sacred Mosque.' [7:29]

١٥. عن محمّد بن منصور، عن عبد صالح عليه السلام، قال: سألتُه عن قول الله تعالى: ﴿وَإِذَا فَعَلُوا فَاحِشَةً﴾ إلى قوله: ﴿أَتَقُولُونَ عَلَى اللَّهِ مَا لَا تَعْلَمُونَ﴾. فقال: أرأيت أحدًا يَزعُم أنّ الله أمرنا بالزِّنا وشُرب الخَمر وشيءٍ من هذه المحارم؟ فقلت: لا.

فقال: ما هذه الفاحشة الّتي يدّعون أنّ الله أمر بها. فقلت: الله أعلم ووليّه.

فقال: إنّ هذا من أئمّة الجَور، ادّعوا أنّ الله أمرهم بالائتمام بهم، فردّ الله ذلك عليهم، فأخبرنا أنّهم قد قالوا عليه الكَذِب، فسمّى ذلك منهم فاحشةً.

١٦. عن أبي بصير، عن أبي عبد الله عليه السلام، قال: سَمِعتُه يقول: من زَعَم أنَّ الله يأمُر بالفحشاء، فقد كَذَب على الله، ومن زَعَم أنَّ الخير والشرّ إليه، فقد كَذَبَ على الله.

١٧. عن أبي بصير، عن أحدهما عليهما السلام، في قول الله تعالى: ﴿وَأَقِيمُوا وُجُوهَكُمْ عِندَ كُلِّ مَسْجِدٍ﴾، قال: هو إلى القِبلة.

١٨. عن الحسين بن مِهران، عن أبي عبد الله عليه السلام، في قوله: ﴿وَأَقِيمُوا وُجُوهَكُمْ عِندَ كُلِّ مَسْجِدٍ﴾، قال: يعني الأئمّة.

١٩. عن زُرارة وحُمران ومحمّد بن مسلم، عن أبي جعفر وأبي عبد الله عليهما السلام، عن قوله: ﴿وَأَقِيمُوا وُجُوهَكُمْ عِندَ كُلِّ مَسْجِدٍ﴾. قال: مساجد مُحدَثة، فأُمِروا أن يُقيموا وجوههم شَطر المسجد الحرام.

20. From Abū Baṣīr, from one of the two [Imams al-Bāqir or al-Ṣādiq] who said, 'It means towards the *qibla* which is absolutely and thoroughly free of idol-worship.' [7:29]

21. From Muḥammad b. al-Fuḍayl, from Abū al-Ḥasan al-Riḍā عليه السلام who said regarding the verse: ﴾*put on your adornment on every occasion of prayer*﴿, 'This refers to clothing.' [7:31]

22. From al-Ḥusayn b. Mihrān, from Abū 'Abd Allāh عليه السلام who said regarding the verse: ﴾*put on your adornment on every occasion of prayer*﴿, 'It means the Imams.' [7:31]

23. From Abān b. Taghlib who said, 'Abū 'Abd Allāh عليه السلام said, "Do you really think that the one to whom God has given [more], He has simply done so out of His high esteem for him, and likewise withheld from the one to whom He has given less simply out of His contempt for him? No! Rather all wealth belongs to God, and He entrusts it to man as a deposit. He allows them to eat and drink from it purposefully, to clothe themselves, marry and travel around by means of it purposefully. Then they are to remit the rest of it to the poor believers to help them get on their two feet. Whoever does this has indeed eaten, drunk, travelled and married in a permissible manner. Whoever exceeds that, however, it becomes prohibited for him."

Then he said: ﴾*but do not be extravagant: God does not like extravagant people.*﴿ Do you think God has entrusted wealth to a man for him to have it entirely at his disposal and buy a horse for ten thousand dirhams when a twenty-dirham horse would have sufficed him? Or for him to buy a maid-servant for one thousand dinars when a maid-servant of twenty dinars would have been fine?" He then said: ﴾*but do not be extravagant: God does not like extravagant people.*﴿' [7:31]

24. From Zurāra, from Abū Ja'far عليه السلام. He said, 'I asked him about God's verse: ﴾*put on your adornment on every occasion of prayer.*﴿ He said, "On the night of *'arafa*."' [7:31]

٢٠. أبو بصير، عن أحدهما عليهما السلام، قال: هو إلى القِبلة ليس فيها عِبادة الأوثان، خالصًا مخلصًا.

٢١. عن محمّد بن الفُضيل، عن أبي الحسن الرضا ﵇، في قول الله: ﴿خُذُوا زِينَتَكُمْ عِندَ كُلِّ مَسْجِدٍ﴾، قال: هي الثِّياب.

٢٢. عن الحسين بن مِهران، عن أبي عبد الله ﵇، في قول الله تعالى: ﴿خُذُوا زِينَتَكُمْ عِندَ كُلِّ مَسْجِدٍ﴾، قال: يعني الأئمّة.

٢٣. عن أبان بن تغلِب، قال: قال أبو عبد الله ﵇: أترى الله أعطى مَن أعطى مِن كرامته عليه، ومنع مَن منع مِن هوانٍ به عليه؟ لا، ولكنّ المال مال الله يَضَعَه عند الرجل ودائع، وجوّز لهم أن يأكُلوا قصدًا، ويَشرَبوا قصدًا، ويَلبَسُوا قصدًا، ويَنكِحوا قصدًا، ويَركَبُوا قَصدًا، ويَعُودوا بما سوى ذلك على فُقراء المؤمنين ويَلُمّوا به شَعَثَهم، فمَن فعل ذلك كان ما يأكُل حلالاً، ويشرب حلالاً، ويركب ويَنكِح حلالاً، ومن عدا ذلك كان عليه حرامًا.

ثمّ قال: ﴿وَلَا تُسْرِفُوا إِنَّهُ لَا يُحِبُّ الْمُسْرِفِينَ﴾ أترى الله ائتمن رجُلاً على مالٍ، خوّل له أن يشتري فَرَسًا بعشرة آلاف دِرهَم، ويُجزيه فَرَسٌ بعشرين دِرهَمًا؟! ويشتري جاريةً بألف دينار، ويُجزيه جاريةٌ بعشرين دينارًا؟! وقال: ﴿وَلَا تُسْرِفُوا إِنَّهُ لَا يُحِبُّ الْمُسْرِفِينَ﴾.

٢٤. عن زُرارة، عن أبي جعفر ﵇، قال: سألتُهُ عن قول الله تعالى: ﴿خُذُوا زِينَتَكُمْ عِندَ كُلِّ مَسْجِدٍ﴾، قال: عَشيّة عَرَفَة.

25. From Abū Baṣīr, from Abū ʿAbd Allāh ﵇. He said, ʻI asked him about: ﴾*put on your adornment on every occasion of prayer.*﴿ He said, "It is to comb your hair for every obligatory and supererogatory prayer."ʼ [7:31]

26. From ʿAmmār al-Nawfilī, on his father's authority who said, ʻI heard Abū al-Ḥasan say, "Combing the hair takes away disease." He said, "Abū ʿAbd Allāh ﵇ used to keep a comb in the mosque with which he would comb his hair whenever he finished praying."ʼ [7:31]

27. From al-Muḥāmilī, from one of our associates, from Abū ʿAbd Allāh ﵇ who said regarding God's verse ﴾*put on your adornment on every occasion of prayer*﴿: ʻThe garments on the two ʿĪds and on Fridays.ʼ [7:31]

28. From Hārūn b. Khārija who said, ʻAbū ʿAbd Allāh ﵇ said, "Whoever asks people for something when he has enough provision for that day is considered among those who are extravagant."ʼ [7:31]

29. From Khaythama b. Abī Khaythama who said, ʻWhen al-Ḥasan b. ʿAlī ﵇ used to stand for prayer he would wear the best of his clothes. So he was once asked, "O son of God's Messenger, why do you wear your best clothes?" Imam Ḥasan replied, "God, most High, is beautiful and loves beauty, so I beautify myself for my Lord, for He says: ﴾*put on your adornment on every occasion of prayer*﴿, so I love wearing the best of my clothes."ʼ [7:31]

30. From al-Ḥakam b. ʿUtayba who said, ʻI saw Abū Jaʿfar ﵇ wearing a red loincloth once so I was staring at him, whereupon he said [to me], "Abū Muḥammad, there is nothing wrong with wearing this." Then he recited: ﴾*Say* [*Prophet*], *ʻWho has forbidden the adornment and the nourishment God has provided for His servants?ʼ*﴿ʼ [7:32]

٢٥. عن أبي بصير، عن أبي عبدالله عليه السلام، قال: سألتُهُ: ﴿خُذُوا زِينَتَكُمْ عِندَ كُلِّ مَسْجِدٍ﴾، قال: هو المِشط عند كُلّ صلاة فريضة ونافلة.

٢٦. عن عمّار النّوفلي، عن أبيه، قال: سَمِعتُ أبا الحسن عليه السلام يقول: المِشط يذهب بالوَباء، قال: وكان لأبي عبدالله عليه السلام مِشطٌ في المسجد يَتَمشَّط به إذا فَرَغ من صلاته.

٢٧. عن المحاملي، عن بعض أصحابه، عن أبي عبدالله عليه السلام، في قول الله تعالى: ﴿خُذُوا زِينَتَكُمْ عِندَ كُلِّ مَسْجِدٍ﴾، قال: الأردية في العِيدين والجُمُعة.

٢٨. عن هارون بن خارجة، قال: قال أبو عبدالله عليه السلام: مَن سأل الناس شيئًا وعنده ما يَقُوته يومه فهو من المُسرِفين.

٢٩. عن خَيثمة بن أبي خَيثمة، قال: كان الحسين بن عليّ عليهما السلام إذا قام إلى الصّلاة لَبِس أجود ثِيابه، فقيل له: يا بن رسول الله، لِمَ تلبَس أجود ثِيابك؟ فقال عليه السلام: إنَّ الله تعالى جميلٌ يُحِبُّ الجمال، فأتجمّل لربّي، وهو يقول: ﴿خُذُوا زِينَتَكُمْ عِندَ كُلِّ مَسْجِدٍ﴾ فأُحِبُّ أن ألبس أجود ثيابي.

٣٠. عن الحَكَم بن عُتيبة، قال: رأيتُ أبا جعفر عليه السلام وعليه إزار أحمر، قال: فاحددتُ النظر إليه، فقال: يا أبا محمّد، إنَّ هذا ليس به بأس، ثمّ تلا: ﴿قُلْ مَنْ حَرَّمَ زِينَةَ اللهِ الَّتِي أَخْرَجَ لِعِبَادِهِ وَالطَّيِّبَاتِ مِنَ الرِّزْقِ﴾.

31. From al-Washshā' from al-Riḍā عليه السلام who said, "Alī b. al-Husayn عليه السلام used to wear a long robe, a printed silk shawl and a cap, and he sold the shawl and gave its value to charity saying: ﴾*Say* [*Prophet*], *'Who has forbidden the adornment and the nourishment God has provided for His servants?'*﴿' [7:32]

32. From Yūsuf b. Ibrāhīm who said, 'I visited Abū 'Abd Allāh عليه السلام wearing a long silk robe and a green silken cape, and he looked at me, so I asked, "May I be your ransom – I am wearing a silk robe and a silk cape – what is your opinion on that?"

So he replied, "There is nothing wrong with silk."

I asked, "And the silken tassels?"

He said, "There is no problem with it. Al-Ḥusayn b. 'Alī عليه السلام was wearing a silken robe when he was struck." Then he continued, "When the Commander of the Faithful عليه السلام dispatched 'Abd Allāh b. 'Abbās to the Kharijites, he wore the best clothing, perfumed himself with the best fragrance, and rode on his finest horse. So he went out to them and was met favourably by them saying: 'Ibn 'Abbās, you are the best person among us all for you have come to us dressed and equipped with clothing and a ride fit for mighty rulers.' So he recited this verse: ﴾*Say* [*Prophet*], *'Who has forbidden the adornment and the nourishment God has provided for His servants?'*﴿ Wear good clothes and beautify yourself, for God is beautiful and loves beauty, so long as it is permissible."' [7:32]

33. From al-'Abbās b. Hilāl al-Shāmī [who said, 'Abū al-Ḥasan said] on the authority Abū al-Ḥasan al-Riḍā عليه السلام. He said, 'I said: "May I be your ransom – is it not more admirable for people to eat coarse unwholesome food, wear rough clothing and abase themselves." He replied, "Do you not know that Yūsuf b. Ya'qūb عليه السلام, a prophet and the son of a prophet, used to wear cloaks of silken brocade embroidered with gold when he was sitting in the assemblies of Pharaoh's household? He ruled over the people, and although they were not in need of his clothing, what they did need was his fairness. Similarly what is needed from the Imam is that when he speaks, he speaks the truth; when he makes a promise, he fulfils it; and when he rules, he does so with justice. God has not forbidden any permissible (*ḥalāl*) food or drink. He has only forbidden what is prohibited (*ḥarām*), be it a little or a lot, having said:

٣١. عن الوشّاء، عن الرضا عليه السلام، قال: كان عليّ بن الحسين عليهما السلام يلبَس الجُبَّة المِطرَف الخَزّ، والقَلَنسُوة ويبيع المِطرَف، ويَتَصَدّق بثمنه، ويقول: ﴿قُلْ مَنْ حَرَّمَ زِينَةَ اللهِ الَّتِي أَخْرَجَ لِعِبَادِهِ وَالطَّيِّبَاتِ مِنَ الرِّزْقِ﴾.

٣٢. عن يوسف بن إبراهيم، قال: دخلتُ على أبي عبدالله عليه السلام وعليّ جُبَّة خَزٍّ وطَيلَسان خَزّ، فنظر إليّ، فقلت: جُعِلتُ فِداك، عليّ جُبَّة خَزٍّ وطَيلَسان خَزٍّ، ما تقول فيه؟

فقال: وما بأس بالخَزّ.

قلت: وسَداه إبريسم؟

فقال: لا بأس به، فقد أُصيب الحسين بن عليّ عليه السلام وعليه جُبّة خَزّ.

ثمّ قال: إنّ عبدالله بن عبّاس لمّا بعثه أمير المؤمنين عليه السلام إلى الخَوارج لَبِس أفضل ثِيابه، وتَطَيَّب بأطيب طِيبه، وركِب أفضل مَراكِبه، فخرج إليهم فواقفهم، فقالوا: يا بن عبّاس، بينا أنت خير الناس، إذ أتيتنا في لباس من لباس الجَبابرة ومَراكِبهم! فتلا هذه الآية: ﴿قُلْ مَنْ حَرَّمَ زِينَةَ اللهِ الَّتِي أَخْرَجَ لِعِبَادِهِ وَالطَّيِّبَاتِ مِنَ الرِّزْقِ﴾ ألبسُ وأتَجَمّلُ، فإنّ الله جميلٌ يُحِبّ الجمال، وليكُن من حَلال.

٣٣. عن العبّاس بن هلال الشامي، عن أبي الحسن الرضا عليه السلام، قال: قلتُ: جُعِلتُ فداك، ما أعجَبَ إلى النّاس مَن يأكُل الجَشِب ويَلبَس الخَشِن ويَتَخَشّع! قال: أما عَلِمتَ أنّ يوسف بن يعقوب عليهما السلام نبيّ ابن نبيّ، كان يَلبَس أقبية الدِّيباج مَزرُورةً بالذهب، ويجلس في مجالس آل فِرعون يحكم؟ فلم يحتج الناسُ إلى لباسه، وإنّما احتاجوا إلى قِسطه، وإنّما

﴾*Say* [*Prophet*], *'Who has forbidden the adornment and the nourishment God has provided for His servants?'*﴿"' [7:32]

34. From Aḥmad b. Muḥammad, from Abū al-Ḥasan عليه السلام who said, "Alī b. al-Ḥusayn, peace be upon them both, used to wear a robe of five hundred dinars and a shawl of fifty dinars that he would wear throughout the winter. Then when winter was over, he would sell it and give the money away in charity.' [7:32]

35. In a report of 'Umar b. 'Alī from his father 'Alī b. al-Ḥusayn عليه السلام that he used to buy a silken cloak of fifty dinars then give it away to charity when summer came, and saw no problem with doing that saying: ﴾*Say* [*Prophet*], *'Who has forbidden the adornment and the nourishment God has provided for His servants?'*﴿ [7:32]

36. From Muḥammad b. Manṣūr who said, 'I asked al-'Abd al-Ṣāliḥ [i.e. Imam Mūsā al-Kāẓim] about God's statement: ﴾*Say* [*Prophet*], *'My Lord only forbids disgraceful deeds – whether they be open or hidden.'*﴿ He said, "The Qur'an has a manifest and a hidden aspect, so everything that He has forbidden therein is manifest, the hidden aspect of them being the oppressive leaders. Everything that He has made permissible in the Book is manifest, and the hidden aspect of these are the rightful leaders."' [7:33]

37. From 'Alī b. Ḥamza who said, 'I heard Abū 'Abd Allāh عليه السلام say, "The Messenger of God صلى الله عليه وآله said: 'There is no one more fervently protective than God, Blessed and most High. Who can be more protective than the One who has forbidden all disgraceful deeds – whether they be open or hidden?'" [7:33]

يُحتاجُ من الإمام إلى أنّ إذا قال صَدَق، وإذا وَعَد أنجز، وإذا حَكَم عدل، إنّ الله لم يُحَرّم طعامًا ولا شرابًا من حلال، وإنّما حَرّم الحرام قلّ أوكثُر، وقد قال: ﴿قُلْ مَنْ حَرَّمَ زِينَةَ اللَّهِ الَّتِي أَخْرَجَ لِعِبَادِهِ وَالطَّيِّبَاتِ مِنَ الرِّزْقِ﴾.

٣٤. عن أحمد بن محمّد، عن أبي الحسن عليه السلام، قال: كان عليّ بن الحسين عليهما السلام يَلْبس بخمسمائة دينار، والمِطرَف بخمسين دينارًا يشتوفيه، فإذا ذهب الشتاء باعه وتصدّق بثمنه.

٣٥. وفي خبرعمر بن علي، عن أبيه عليّ بن الحسين عليه السلام، أنّه كان يشتري الكِساء الخَزّ بخمسين دينارًا، فإذا صاف تَصَدّق به، لا يَرَى بذلك بأسًا ويقول: ﴿قُلْ مَنْ حَرَّمَ زِينَةَ اللَّهِ الَّتِي أَخْرَجَ لِعِبَادِهِ وَالطَّيِّبَاتِ مِنَ الرِّزْقِ﴾.

٣٦. عن محمّد بن منصور، قال: سألتُ عبدًا صالحًا عليه السلام عن قول الله عزّ وجلّ: ﴿إِنَّمَا حَرَّمَ رَبِّيَ الْفَوَاحِشَ مَا ظَهَرَ مِنْهَا وَمَا بَطَنَ﴾. قال: إنّ القرآن له ظهرٌ وبطنٌ، فجميع ما حرّم في الكتاب هو في الظاهر، والباطن من ذلك أئمّة الجَوْر، وجميع ما أحلّ في الكتاب هو في الظاهر، والباطن من ذلك أئمّة الحقّ.

٣٧. عن عليّ بن أبي حمزة، قال: سَمِعتُ أبا عبدالله عليه السلام يقول: قال رسول الله صلى الله عليه وسلم: ما مِن أحدٍ أغير مِن الله تبارك وتعالى، ومَن أغير ممّن حرّم الفَواحش ما ظَهَر منها وما بَطَن؟

38. From ʿAlī b. Yaqṭīn who said, ʿAl-Mahdī[2] asked Abū al-Ḥasan عليه السلام [i.e. Imam al-Kāẓim] about alcohol and whether it was actually prohibited (*ḥarām*) in God's Book, since the people knew of its disallowance but not of its prohibition per se. So Abū al-Ḥasan replied to him, "Of course it is prohibited." He asked, "Where exactly in God's Book is it prohibited, Abū al-Ḥasan?"

So he replied, "The statement of God, Blessed and most High: ﴾*Say* [*Prophet*], *'My Lord only forbids disgraceful deeds – whether they be open or hidden – and sin and unjustified aggression.*﴿ As for His words ﴾*whether they be open*﴿ it refers to overt fornication and the raising of banners that the corrupt people of pagan pre-Islamic times used to do. His words ﴾*or hidden*﴿ refer to marrying their fathers' widows, for in the times before the Prophet ﷺ was sent down, if a man died leaving his wife behind his son would inherit her and marry her if she was not his mother; and God prohibited that. The ﴾*sin*﴿ is alcohol itself, for God has said elsewhere: ﴾*They ask you* [*Prophet*] *about intoxicants and gambling: say, 'There is great sin in both, and some benefit for people: the sin is greater than the benefit.'*﴿(2:219) So the 'sin' in God's Book is alcohol and gambling is backgammon [and chess], and their sin is great as God has said. His word ﴾aggression﴿ is fornication in private."

So al-Mahdī said, "By God, this is a Hashimite juristic verdict."' [7:33]

39. From Abū ʿAbd Allāh عليه السلام who said regarding His verse ﴾*There is a time set for every people: they cannot hasten it, nor, when it comes, will they be able to delay it for a single moment*﴿: 'This is what has been assigned to the Angel of Death عليه السلام.' [7:34]

40. From Manṣūr b. Yūnus, from a man, from Abū ʿAbd Allāh عليه السلام who said regarding God's verse ﴾*The gates of Heaven will not be open to those who rejected Our revelations and arrogantly spurned them; even if a thick rope were to pass through the eye of a needle they would not enter the Garden*﴿: 'It was revealed about Ṭalḥa and Zubayr, and the camel that belonged to them.' [7:40]

2 This refers to Muḥammad b. ʿAbd Allāh b. Muḥammad b. ʿAlī b. ʿAbd Allāh b. ʿAbbās, better known as al-Mahdī, the third Abbasid Caliph.

٣٨. عن عليّ بن يقطين، قال: سأل المهديّ أبا الحسن عليه السلام عن الخمر، هل هي مُحرّمة في كتاب الله، فإنّ الناس يَعرِفون النهي، ولا يَعرِفون التحريم؟ فقال له أبو الحسن عليه السلام: بل هي محرّمة.

قال: في أيّ موضع هي محرّمة بكتاب الله، يا أبا الحسن؟

قال: قول الله تبارك وتعالى: ﴿قُلْ إِنَّمَا حَرَّمَ رَبِّيَ الْفَوَاحِشَ مَا ظَهَرَ مِنْهَا وَمَا بَطَنَ وَالْإِثْمَ وَالْبَغْيَ بِغَيْرِ الْحَقِّ﴾، فأمّا قوله: ﴿مَا ظَهَرَ مِنْهَا﴾ فيعني الزِنا المُعلن، ونصب الرايات التي كانت تَرفعُها الفواجِر في الجاهلية، وأمّا قوله: ﴿وَمَا بَطَنَ﴾ يعني ما نكح من الآباء، فإنّ الناس كانوا قبل أن يُبعَث النبي صلى الله عليه وآله إذا كان للرجل زوجةٌ ومات عنها، تزوّجها ابنه من بعده، إذا لم تكن أُمّه، فحرم الله ذلك، وأمّا الإثم فإنّها الخمر بعينها، وقد قال الله في موضع آخر: ﴿يَسْأَلُونَكَ عَنِ الْخَمْرِ وَالْمَيْسِرِ قُلْ فِيهِمَا إِثْمٌ كَبِيرٌ وَمَنَافِعُ لِلنَّاسِ﴾

فأمّا الإثم في كتاب الله فهي الخمر، والمَيسر فهي النَّرد، وإثمهما كبيرٌ كما قال الله، وأمّا قوله: ﴿الْبَغْيَ﴾ فهو الزِنا سِرّاً.

قال: فقال المهديّ: هذه والله فتوًى هاشميّة.

٣٩. عن أبي عبد الله عليه السلام، في قوله: ﴿إِذَا جَاءَ أَجَلُهُمْ فَلَا يَسْتَأْخِرُونَ سَاعَةً وَلَا يَسْتَقْدِمُونَ﴾، قال: هو الذي يُسمّى لملَك الموت عليه السلام.

٤٠. عن منصُور بن يُونُس، عن رجُلٍ، عن أبي عبد الله عليه السلام، في قول الله تعالى: ﴿إِنَّ الَّذِينَ كَذَّبُوا بِآيَاتِنَا وَاسْتَكْبَرُوا عَنْهَا لَا تُفَتَّحُ لَهُمْ أَبْوَابُ السَّمَاءِ وَلَا يَدْخُلُونَ الْجَنَّةَ حَتَّى يَلِجَ الْجَمَلُ فِي سَمِّ الْخِيَاطِ﴾ نزلت في طَلحة والزُّبير، والجمَل جَملهم.

41. From Muḥammad b. al-Fuḍayl, from Abū al-Ḥasan al-Riḍā عليه السلام regarding His verse ﴾*A caller will proclaim from their midst, 'God's rejection* [*hangs*] *over the evildoers'*﴿: 'The caller is the Commander of the Faithful عليه السلام.' [7:44]

42. From Masʿada b. Ṣadaqa, from Jaʿfar b. Muḥammad, on his father's authority, on his grandfather's authority, from ʿAlī عليه السلام that he said, 'I am the chief of the believers, the pioneer of the foremost ones, and the successor of the Messenger of the Lord of the Worlds. I am the denominator [of people] between the Garden and the Fire, and I am in charge of the heights.' [7:46]

43. From Hilqām, from Abū Jaʿfar عليه السلام. He said, 'I asked him about God's verse: ﴾*men on its heights recognizing each group by their marks*﴿ – what does He mean when saying ﴾*men on its heights*﴿? He replied, "Do you not know of any cognizant men who oversee your tribes and know exactly about any good or bad man there is among them?" I replied, "Yes." He said, "Well then, we are those men who know each group by their marks."' [7:46]

44. From Zādhān, from Salmān who said, 'I heard the Messenger of God صلى الله عليه وآله say to ʿAlī عليه السلام more than ten times, "O ʿAlī, you and the successors after you are the heights between the Garden and the Fire, and none shall enter the Garden except those who recognize you and you recognize them. None shall enter the Fire except those who reject you and are in turn rejected by you."' [7:46]

45. From Saʿd b. Ṭarīf, from Abū Jaʿfar عليه السلام who said about this verse: ﴾*men on its heights recognizing each group by their marks*﴿, 'O Saʿd, they are the family of Muḥammad صلى الله عليه وآله; none shall enter the Garden save one who recognizes them and they recognize him, and none shall enter the Fire except one who rejected them and is, in turn, rejected by them.' [7:46]

٤١. عن محمّد بن الفُضيل، عن أبي الحسن الرضا عليه السلام، في قوله: ﴿فَأَذَّنَ مُؤَذِّنٌ بَيْنَهُمْ أَنْ لَعْنَةُ اللهِ عَلَى الظَّالِمِينَ﴾، قال: المؤَذِّن أمير المؤمنين عليه السلام.

٤٢. عن مَسعَدة بن صَدَقة، عن جعفر بن محمّد، عن أبيه، عن جدّه، عن عليّ عليه السلام، قال: أنا يَعسُوب المؤمنين، وأنا أوّل السابقين، وخليفة رسول ربّ العالمين، وأنا قسيمُ الجنّة والنار، وأنا صاحب الأعراف.

٤٣. عن هِلقام، عن أبي جعفر عليه السلام، قال: سألتُهُ عن قول الله تعالى: ﴿وَعَلَى الأَعْرَافِ رِجَالٌ يَعْرِفُونَ كُلاًّ بِسِيمَاهُمْ﴾ ما يعني بقوله: ﴿وَعَلَى الأَعْرَافِ رِجَالٌ﴾؟ قال: ألستم تعرِفون عليكم عُرفاء على قبائلكم، ليعرِفوا من فيها من صالح أو طالح؟ قلتُ: بلى، قال: فنحن أُولئك الرجال الذين يعرِفون كُلاًّ بسيماهم.

٤٤. عن زاذان، عن سلمان، قال: سَمِعتُ رسول الله صلّى الله عليه وآله يقول لعليّ عليه السلام أكثر من عشر مرّات، يا عليّ، إنّك والأوصياء من بعدك أعرافُ بين الجنّة والنار، لا يدخُل الجنّة إلاّ من عَرَفكم وعَرَفتموه، ولا يَدخُل النار إلاّ من أنكركم وأنكَرتُموه.

٤٥. عن سعد بن طريف، عن أبي جعفر عليه السلام، في هذه الآية ﴿وَعَلَى الأَعْرَافِ رِجَالٌ يَعْرِفُونَ كُلاًّ بِسِيمَاهُمْ﴾، قال: يا سعد، هم آل محمّد عليهم السلام، لا يَدخُل الجنّة إلاّ من عَرَفهم وعَرَفوه، ولا يَدخُل النار إلاّ من أنكرهم وأنكروه.

46. From al-Ṭayyār, from Abū ʿAbd Allāh عليه السلام. He said, ʿI asked him, "What is the function of the people of the heights?" He replied, "When someone has an equal amount of good deeds and misdeeds. If He [i.e. God] admits them into the Garden, then it is by His mercy; and if He chastises them, then He would not be wronging them."ʾ [7:46]

47. From Karrām who said, ʿI heard Abū ʿAbd Allāh عليه السلام say, "On the Day of Resurrection seven domes of light will come forth made of white and green rubies, in each dome the Imam of that time, who will be surrounded by the people of his time, both the good and the bad, until they stop at the gate of the Garden. The first to emerge forth from it will be the master of that dome, who will distinguish between his loyal adherents and his enemies. Then he will approach his enemies and say, 'You are the ones who swore that God would never bless these people.' 'Now enter the Garden fearlessly today,' he will say to his companions, at which moment the wrongdoers' faces will darken, and he will separate his companions towards the Garden saying: ﴾*Our Lord, do not let us join the evildoers!*﴿

When the people of the second dome see the small number of people entering the Garden and the large numbers entering the Fire, they will fear lest they are made to enter it too, and that is the meaning of the phrase: ﴾*they will not have entered, but they will be hoping.*﴿"ʾ [7:46–47]

48. From al-Thumālī who said, ʿAbū Jaʿfar was asked about God's verse: ﴾*men on its heights recognizing each group by their marks.*﴿ So Abū Jaʿfar said, "We are the heights, and God is only acknowledged by means of recognizing us; we are the heights whereby none can enter the Garden save one who recognizes us and we recognize him, and whereby none will enter the Fire except the one who rejects us and is in turn rejected by us. That is because God could have willed for people to acknowledge Him by Himself, but He has made us His means, His path and His gate to be entered through."ʾ [7:46]

٤٦. عن الطيّار، عن أبي عبدالله عليه السلام، قال: قلتُ له: أيّ شيءٍ أصحاب الأعراف؟ قال: استوت الحسنات والسيّئات، فإن أدخلهم الجنّة فبرحمته، وإن عذّبهم لم يَظلِمهم.

٤٧. عن كَرّام، قال: سَمِعتُ أبا عبدالله عليه السلام يقول: إذا كان يوم القيامة أقبل سبعُ قِباب من نُور يواقيت خُضر وبيض، في كُلّ قبّة إمامُ دهره، قد احتفّ به أهل دهره بَرُّها وفاجِرُها حتّى يقفوا بباب الجنَّة، فيَطّلع أوّلُها صاحب قُبّةٍ إطّلاعةً فيُميِّز أهل ولايته وعدوّه، ثمّ يُقبِل على عدّوه فيقول: أنتم الذين أقسمتم لا ينالهم الله برحمة؟ ادخُلُوا الجنّة، لا خوف عليكم اليوم، يقول لأصحابه فتَسوَدّ وجوه الظالمين، فيميز أصحابه إلى الجنَّة، وهم يقولون: ﴿رَبَّنَا لَا تَجۡعَلۡنَا مَعَ ٱلۡقَوۡمِ ٱلظَّٰلِمِينَ﴾.

فإذا نَظَر أهل القُبّة الثانية إلى قِلّة من يَدخُل الجنَّة وكَثْرة من يدخُل النار، خافوا أن لا يَدخُلوها، وذلك قوله تعالى: ﴿لَمۡ يَدۡخُلُوهَا وَهُمۡ يَطۡمَعُونَ﴾.

٤٨. عن الثُّمالي، قال: سُئل أبو جعفر عليه السلام عن قول الله: ﴿وَعَلَى ٱلۡأَعۡرَافِ رِجَالٞ يَعۡرِفُونَ كُلَّۢا بِسِيمَىٰهُمۡ﴾. فقال أبو جعفر عليه السلام: نحن الأعراف الذين لا يُعرَف الله إلاّ بسبب معرفتنا، ونحن الأعراف الذين لا يدخُل الجنَّة إلاّ من عَرَفَنا وعَرَفْناه، ولا يَدخُل النار إلاّ من أنكرَنا وأنكرْناه، وذلك بأنّ الله لو شاء أن يُعرِّف الناس نفسه لعَرّفهم، ولكنّه جعلنا سببه وسبيله، وبابه الذي يؤتى منه.

49. From Ibrāhīm b. ʿAbd al-Ḥamīd, from one of the two [al-Bāqir or al-Ṣādiq] who said, 'The people of Hell will die thirsty and shall go into their graves thirsty, they shall [be raised thirsty] and will enter the Fire thirsty. So they will look up towards their relatives in the Garden and say: ﴾ *Give us some water, or any of the sustenance God has granted you!* ﴿" [7:50]

50. From al-Zuhrī, from Abū ʿAbd Allāh عليه السلام who said, ﴾ *The day of distress calls between people* ﴿ (40:32) is the day when the inmates of the Fire will call out to the people in the Garden to pour some water down on them. [7:50]

51. From Muyassar, from Abū Jaʿfar عليه السلام who said about His verse ﴾ *do not corrupt the earth after it has been set right* ﴿: 'The earth used to be corrupt so he set it right through His Prophet صلى الله عليه وآله and said: ﴾ *do not corrupt the earth after it has been set right.* ﴿' [7:56]

52. From Aḥmad b. Muḥammad, from Abū al-Ḥasan al-Riḍā عليه السلام. He said, 'I heard him say, "How excellent is patience and waiting for relief! Have you not heard al-ʿAbd al-Ṣāliḥ [i.e. Imam Mūsā al-Kāẓim] say: ﴾ *Just wait; I too am waiting.* ﴿"' [7:71]

53. From Yaḥyā b. al-Musāwir al-Hamadānī[3], on his father's authority, that a man from among the people of Shām came to ʿAlī b. al-Ḥusayn عليه السلام and asked, 'Are you ʿAlī b. al-Ḥusayn?'

He replied, 'Yes.'

He asked, 'So your father is the one who killed the believers?'

So ʿAlī b. al-Ḥusayn wept, then wiped his eyes and said, 'Woe unto you! How can you assert so confidently that my father killed the believers?'

He replied, 'By his own words: "Our brothers oppressed us indeed, so we fought them on account of their oppression."'

He retorted, 'Woe unto you – do you not read the Qurʾan?'

He replied, 'I do.'

3 Abū Zakariyya Yaḥyā b. [al-]Musāwir al-Tamīmī, an acquaintance of the fifth, sixth, seventh and eighth Imams about whom there is scant information. See Khūʾī, *Muʿjam* 21:96–7 (nr. 13617).

٤٩. عن إبراهيم بن عبد الحميد، عن أحدهما عليهما السلام، قال: إنَّ أهل النار يموتون عطاشى، ويَدخَلون قبورهم عطاشى ويُحْشَرون عطاشى، ويَدخُلون جهنَّمَ عطاشى، فتُرفع لهم قراباتهم من الجنَّة، فيقولون: ﴿أَفِيضُوا عَلَيْنَا مِنَ الْمَاءِ أَوْ مِمَّا رَزَقَكُمُ اللَّهُ﴾.

٥٠. عن الزُّهري، عن أبي عبد الله عليه السلام يقول: يَومَ التَّنادِ يوم ينادي أهل النار أهل الجنة: أن أفيضوا علينا من الماء.

٥١. عن مُيسّر، عن أبي جعفر عليه السلام، في قوله تعالى: ﴿وَلَا تُفْسِدُوا فِي الْأَرْضِ بَعْدَ إِصْلَاحِهَا﴾. قال: إنّ الأرض كانت فاسدةً، فأصْلَحَها الله بنبيِّه صلى الله عليه وسلم، فقال: ﴿وَلَا تُفْسِدُوا فِي الْأَرْضِ بَعْدَ إِصْلَاحِهَا﴾.

٥٢. عن أحمد بن محمّد، عن أبي الحسن الرضا عليه السلام، قال: سَمِعتُه يقول: ما أحسن الصبر وانتظار الفرج! أما سَمِعت قول العبد الصالح: ﴿فَانْتَظِرُوا إِنِّي مَعَكُمْ مِنَ الْمُنْتَظِرِينَ﴾؟

٥٣. عن يحيى بن المُساور الهمداني، عن أبيه: جاء رجلٌ من أهل الشام إلى عليّ بن الحسين عليه السلام، فقال: أنت عليّ بن الحسين؟ قال: نعم. قال: أبوك الذي قَتَل المؤمنين؟ فبكى عليّ بن الحسين عليهما السلام، ثمّ مسح عينيه، فقال: ويلك! كيف قطعتَ على أبي أنّه قَتَل المؤمنين.

قال: قوله: «إخواننا قد بَغَوا علينا، فقاتلناهم على بغيهم».

فقال: ويلك أما تقرأ القرآن؟

He said, 'So God says: ﴾*To the people of Midian We sent their brother, Shu'ayb*﴿ and: ﴾*To the people of Thamūd We sent their brother, Ṣāliḥ*﴿ – so were they their brothers in faith or their brothers by kin?'

The man replied to him, 'Their brothers by kin, of course.'

He said, 'So these were their brothers by kin too and not their brothers in faith.'

He said, 'You have given me solace, may God give you solace too.' [7:73]

54. From Abū Ḥamza al-Thumālī, from Abū Ja'far Muḥammad b. 'Alī عليه السلام who said, 'The Messenger of God صلى الله عليه وآله asked Jibra'īl, "How did the destruction of the community of Ṣāliḥ come about?"

He replied, "O Muḥammad, Ṣāliḥ began his mission amongst his people when he was sixteen years old and stayed with them until the age of one hundred and twenty without a positive response from them."

He continued, "They used to worship seventy idols instead of God, and when he saw them doing that, he said: 'My people, I was sent to you when I was sixteen years old, and now I have reached a hundred and twenty years. I propose two solutions to you if you agree: I will ask your idols to fulfil something for me that I usually ask my God to fulfil, and if they manage to do so, then He will fulfil whatever you ask of Him. If, when I ask your gods, they respond to me and fulfil whatever I ask of them, I will leave you to be, for now I have grown weary of you and you of me.'

So they said, 'You have been fair, Ṣāliḥ.' They then agreed on the day that they would all go out to do this."

He continued, "So they set out with their idols on their backs, then laid out their food and drink and ate and drank. After they had finished they called him out and said, 'Ṣāliḥ, now ask.' So Ṣāliḥ called out to their biggest idol, asking them what its name was, so they informed him of its name. He called it by its name, but it did not reply.

So Ṣāliḥ asked, 'Why does it not reply?'

They suggested for him to call another one, so he called each one of them by name in turn, but not one of them replied.

He said, 'My people, you saw how I called your idols but none of them responded to me, so now you may ask me something that I can request from my God, and He will respond to you immediately.'

قال: بلى.

قال: فقد قال الله: ﴿وَإِلَىٰ مَدْيَنَ أَخَاهُمْ شُعَيْبًا﴾ ﴿وَإِلَىٰ ثَمُودَ أَخَاهُمْ صَالِحًا﴾ فكانوا إخوانهم في دينهم، أو في عشيرتهم؟

قال له الرجل: لا، بل في عشيرتهم.

قال: فهؤلاء إخوانهم في عشيرتهم، وليسوا إخوانهم في دينهم.

قال: فرّجت عنّي، فرّج الله عنك.

٥٤. عن أبي حمزة الثُّمالي، عن أبي جعفر محمّد بن عليّ عليهما السلام، قال: إنَّ رسول الله صلى الله عليه وسلم سأل جَبرَئيل عليه السلام: كيف كان مَهلَك قوم صالح؟ فقال: يا محمّد، إنَّ صالحًا بُعِث إلى قومه وهو ابن ستّ عشرة سنة، فلَبِث فيهم حتّى بلغ عشرين ومائة سنة لا يجيبونه إلى خير.

قال: وكان لهم سبعون صنمًا يَعبُدونها من دون الله، فلمّا رأى ذلك منهم قال: يا قوم، إنّي قد بُعِثت إليكم وأنا ابن ستّ عشرة سنة، وقد بلغت عشرين ومائة سنة، وأنا أعرِض عليكم أمرين، إن شئتم فسلوني حتّى أسأل إلهي فيجيبكم فيما تسألوني، وإن شئتم سألتُ آلهتكم، فإن أجابتني بالذي أسألها خرجتُ عنكم، فقد شنأتكم وشنأتموني.

فقالوا: قد أنصفتَ يا صالح، فاتّعدوا ليومٍ يخرُجون فيه.

قال: فخرجوا بأصنامهم إلى ظهرهم، ثمّ قرّبوا طعامهم وشرابهم، فأكلوا وشَرِبوا، فلمّا أن فرَغوا دعوه فقالوا: يا صالح، سَل. فدعا صالح كبير أصنامهم، فقال: ما اسم هذا؟

So they went up to their idols saying, 'What is wrong with you? Why did you not respond to Ṣāliḥ?' They of course did not reply, so they said, 'Ṣālīh, leave us for a little while with our idols.'"

He continued, "They threw the picnic blanket that they had spread out previously as well as their containers, and rolled around in the dirt. Then they said to them, 'If you do not respond to Ṣāliḥ today, we will really be put to shame.'"

He said, "Then they called him saying, 'Come, Ṣāliḥ, and ask them now.'

So he asked them but they still did not respond.

He said to them, 'My people, this is the way it is. The day is almost over, and I do not think your gods are going to answer me, so why do you not ask me instead that I may supplicate to my God and He will answer you immediately.'

So seventy men were appointed to do that from among their elders, their chieftains as well as their trainees. They said, 'We are now ready to ask you, Ṣāliḥ.'

He asked, 'Are all these people satisfied with you [as their representatives]?'

They replied, 'Yes. If these people follow you, then so will the rest of us.' They said, 'Ṣāliḥ, we will now ask you, and if your Lord answers you we will follow you, and respond to you, and all the people of our village will follow you too.'

So Ṣāliḥ said to them, 'Ask me whatever you wish.'"

He continued, "So Ṣāliḥ set off with them until they ended up at the mountain, where they said, 'Ṣāliḥ, ask your Lord to immediately bring out for us a bright red, shaggy, fully-pregnant she-camel.'(In a narration by Muḥammad b. Nuṣayr, it was a red, shaggy she-camel coming out of a slope between the two sides [of the mountain]).

He replied, 'You have asked me something that would be impossible for me to do, but is easy for my Lord.' So he asked God for just that, and the mountain cracked open with a crack so loud that it could drive people almost mad upon hearing it. Then the mountain groaned like a woman in childbirth, then it was not long before her head emerged from that crack. Then her neck straightened up and came out, and then the rest of her body. Then she stood straight on the ground.

فأخبروه باسمه، فناداه باسمه، فلم يُجِب، فقال صالح: ما له لا يُجيب؟ فقالوا له: ادعُ غيره، فدعاها كلّها بأسمائها، فلم يُجبه واحدٌ منهم.

فقال: يا قوم، قد تَرَون [أنّي] قد دعوتُ أصنامكم فلم تُجبني، فسلوني حتّى أدعو إلهي فيُجيبكم الساعة، فأقبلوا على أصنامهم، فقالوا لها: ما بالكنّ لا تُجبن صالحًا؟ فلم تُجب، فقالوا: يا صالح، تنحّ عنّا، ودَعنا وأصنامنا قليلاً، قال: فرَمَوا بتلك البُسط التي بَسَطُوها، وبتلك الآنية، وتمرَّغوا في التُّراب، وقالوا لها: لئن لم تُجبن صالحًا اليوم لنُفضحَنّ.

قال: ثمّ دَعَوه، فقالوا: يا صالح، تَعال فسلْها؛ فعاد فسألها فلم تُجِبه، فقال: إنّما أراد صالح أن تُجيبه وتُكلّمه بالجواب. قال: فقال لهم: يا قوم، هوذا تَرَون قد ذهب النهار، ولا أرى آلهتكم تجيبني، فسلُوني حتّى أدعو إلهي، فيُجيبكم الساعة.

قال: فانتدب له منهم سبعون رجلاً من كُبرائهم وعُظمائهم والمنظور إليهم منهم، فقالوا: يا صالح، نحن نسألك، قال: فكلُّ هؤلاء يَرضُون بكم؟ قالوا: نعم، فإن أجابوك هؤلاء أجبناك. قالوا: يا صالح، نحن نسألك، فإن أجابوك ربّك اتّبعناك وأجبناك، وتابعك جميع أهل قريتنا. فقال لهم صالح: سَلُوني ما شئتم.

فقالوا: انطلق بنا إلى هذا الجبل — وكان الجبل قريبًا منهم — حتّى نسألك عنده، قال: فانطلق، فانطلقوا معه، فلمّا انتهوا إلى الجبل، قالوا: يا صالح، سَل ربّك أن يُخرج لنا الساعة من هذا الجبل ناقةً حمراء شقراء وبْراء عَشراء — وفي رواية محمّد بن نصير: حمراء شَعراء، بين جنبيها مِيل -.

When they saw that they said, 'O Ṣāliḥ, how quickly your Lord answered! Now ask him to bring her young out for us.'

So he asked God for that, and she gave birth, and her young one started crawling around her.

He said to them, 'My people, is there anything left after this?'

They said, 'No. Come back with us to our people to inform them of what we have seen and they will believe in you.'"

He continued, "So they returned, but the seventy men had not even reached them and sixty-four of them changed their minds and said that it had been magic. Only six of them remained saying, 'What we have seen is the truth.'

He continued, 'The people discussed at length and they went back belying what they had seen, except for the six.' Then one of those six started doubting too, and he was one of the ones who hamstrung her in the end."'

Muḥammad b. Nuṣayr[4] added in his narration saying, 'Ibn Maḥbūb said that when narrating this report to a man from among our associates named Saʿīd b. Yazīd, "He informed me that he had seen the mountain from which it had come out in Shām, and he saw that there was a split in the side of the mountain and a mark left there and that there was a slope between this mountain and the next."' [7:73–79]

55. From Yazīd b. Thābit[5] who said, 'A man asked the Commander of the Faithful عليه السلام: "Can women be entered from behind?" He replied, "May God's damnation descend upon you! Have you not heard God says: ﴾*Do you commit an outrage none in the world ever committed before you?!*﴿"' [7:80]

4 Muḥammad b. Nuṣayr was one of ʿAyyāshī's teachers and sources.

5 Yazīd b. Thābit, on whom there is hardly any biographical information. See Khūʾī, *Muʿjam* 21:116 (nr. 13669).

قال: قد سألتموني شيئًا يَعظُم عليّ، ويَهُون على ربّي، فسأل الله ذلك، فانصَدَع الجبل صَدعًا كادت تطيرُ منه العُقول لمّا سَمِعوا صوته، قال: واضطرب الجبل كما تَضطَرِب المرأة عند المَخاض، ثمّ لم يُعجلهم إلاّ ورأسها قد طَلع عليهم من ذلك الصَّدع، فما استتمّت رقبتها حتّى اجترّت، ثمّ خرج سائر جسدها، ثمّ استوت على الأرض قائمةً، فلمّا رأوا ذلك قالوا: يا صالح، ما أسرع ما أجابك ربُّك! فسَله أن يُخرج لنا فَصيلها.

قال: فسأل الله ذلك فرَمَتْ به، فدبَّ حولها، فقال لهم: يا قوم، أبَقِيَ شيءٌ؟ قالوا: لا، انطلق بنا إلى قومنا نُخبِرهم ما رأينا ويُؤمنوا بك.

قال: فرَجَعوا فلم يَبلُغ السبعون إليهم حتّى ارتدّ منهم أربعة وستُّون رجلاً، وقالوا: سِحرٌ، وثبت الستَّة، وقالوا: الحقُّ ما رأينا. قال: فكثر كلام القوم، ورجَعوا مُكذِّبين إلاّ الستّة، ثمّ ارتاب من الستّة واحدٌ، فكان فيمن عَقَرها.

وزاد محمّد بن نصير في حديثه: قال [ابن محبوب: فحدّثتُ بهذا الحديث رجلاً من أصحابنا، يقال له:] سعيد بن يزيد: فأخبرني أنّه رأى الجبل الذي خرجت منه بالشام، فرأى جنبها قد حكَّ الجبل، فأثَّر جنبها فيه، وجبل آخر بينه وبين هذا ميل.

٥٥. عن يزيد بن ثابت، قال: سأل رجلٌ أمير المؤمنين عليه السلام أيُؤتى النساء في أدبارهنّ؟ فقال: سَفُلتَ سفَّل الله بك، أما سَمِعت الله يقول: ﴿أَتَأْتُونَ الْفَاحِشَةَ مَا سَبَقَكُمْ بِهَا مِنْ أَحَدٍ مِنَ الْعَالَمِينَ﴾.

56. From ʿAbd al-Raḥmān b. al-Ḥajjāj who said, 'I heard Abū ʿAbd Allāh عليه السلام remark when someone mentioned entering women from their backsides in his presence: "I do not know of any verse in the Qurʾan that has permitted this apart from one: ﴿*You lust after men rather than women! You transgress all bounds!*﴾"' [7:81]

57. From al-Ḥusayn b. ʿAlī, from Abū ʿAbd Allāh عليه السلام. He said, 'I heard him say, "Damn these Qadariyya – they read this verse: ﴿*apart from his wife whom We decreed to stay behind.*﴾(27:57) Damn them – who else could decree that for her apart from God, Blessed and most High?"' [7:83]

58. From Ṣafwān al-Jammāl who said, 'I was praying behind Abū ʿAbd Allāh عليه السلام when he bowed his head and said, "O God do not let me feel secure against Your plan." Then he said audibly, ﴿*Only the losers feel secure against God's plan.*﴾' [7:99]

59. From Abū Dharr who said, 'He said: "By God, from among all those who made the covenant with God, none of them honoured their commitment to Him apart from the Household of His Prophet and a small group of their followers. This is the meaning of the verse: ﴿*We found that most of them did not honour their commitments; We found that most of them were defiant*﴾ and: ﴿*though most people do not believe.*﴾(13:1)" [7:102]

60. He said, 'Al-Ḥusayn b. al-Ḥakam al-Wāsiṭī said, "I wrote to one of the righteous ones complaining of doubt, so he said, 'Doubt can only pertain to unknown things. Once conviction has come, however, then there is no more room for doubt, for God says: ﴿*We found that most of them did not honour their commitments; We found that most of them were defiant.*﴾ It was revealed about those who persisted in their doubts.'"' [7:102]

61. From ʿĀṣim al-Miṣrī[6] who, without mentioning his source, cited one of the Imams as having said, 'Pharaoh had built seven cities to protect him from Mūsā عليه السلام and had placed thickets and jungles between each of them filled

6 This is most likely a transcription error for ʿĀṣim b. Sulaymān al-Baṣrī, who is better known as al-Kūzī.

٥٦. عن عبد الرّحمن بن الحجّاج، قال: سَمِعتُ أبا عبدالله ﵇ ذكر عنده إتيان النساء في أدبارهنّ، فقال: ما أعلم آية في القرآن أحلّت ذلك إلاّ واحدة ﴿إِنَّكُمْ لَتَأْتُونَ الرِّجَالَ شَهْوَةً مِنْ دُونِ النِّسَاءِ﴾ الآية.

٥٧. عن الحسين بن عليّ، عن أبي عبدالله ﵇، قال: سَمِعتُه يقول: يا ويح هذه القدرية، إنّما يقرءون هذه الآية ﴿إِلاَّ امْرَأَتَهُ قَدَّرْنَاهَا مِنَ الْغَابِرِينَ﴾
ويحهم من قدّرها إلاّ الله تبارك وتعالى.

٥٨. عن صفوان الجمّال، قال: صلّيت خلف أبي عبدالله ﵇ فأطرق، ثمّ قال: اللّهم لا تُؤمِنّي مكرك، ثمّ جهر فقال: ﴿فَلاَ يَأْمَنُ مَكْرَ اللهِ إِلاَّ الْقَوْمُ الْخَاسِرُونَ﴾.

٥٩. عن أبي ذرّ، قال: قال: والله ما صدق أحدٌ ممّن أخذ الله ميثاقه فوفى بعهد الله غير أهل بيت نبيّهم، وعِصابة قليلة من شيعتهم، وذلك قول الله تعالى: ﴿وَمَا وَجَدْنَا لأَكْثَرِهِمْ مِنْ عَهْدٍ وَإِنْ وَجَدْنَا أَكْثَرَهُمْ لَفَاسِقِينَ﴾، وقوله: ﴿وَلَكِنَّ أَكْثَرَ النَّاسِ لاَ يَعْلَمُونَ﴾.

٦٠. قال: وقال الحسين بن الحكم الواسطي: كتبتُ إلى بعض الصالحين أشكو الشّك، فقال: إنّما الشكّ فيما لا يُعرَف، فإذا جاء اليقين فلا شكّ، يقول الله: ﴿وَمَا وَجَدْنَا لِأَكْثَرِهِمْ مِنْ عَهْدٍ وَإِنْ وَجَدْنَا أَكْثَرَهُمْ لَفَاسِقِينَ﴾ نزلت في الشُّكّاك.

٦١. عن عاصم المِصري، رفعه، قال: إنّ فِرعون بنى سبع مدائن يتحصّن فيها من موسى ﵇، وجعل فيما بينها آجامًا وغِياضًا، وجعل فيها الأُسد ليتحصّن بها من موسى ﵇. قال:

with lions to protect him from Mūsā. When God dispatched Mūsā to Pharaoh, he entered one of the cities, and as soon as the lions saw him they began to wag their tails and retreated tamely. Every single city he entered thereafter opened its doors to him until he ended up at Pharaoh's palace, wherein he was present. He stood at the gate wearing a woolen cloak and had his staff with him. When the doorman came out, Mūsā said to him, "Tell Pharaoh that I would like to see him," but he did not pay any attention to him. So Mūsā said to him, "I am the messenger of the Lord of the Universe," but he again paid no attention to him.

Thus Mūsā remained, continuing to seek permission to enter, and after he had insisted for a while the man said to him, "Could the Lord of the Universe find no one else to send besides you?"

So Mūsā lost his temper and struck the door with his staff such that every single door between him and Pharaoh opened until Pharaoh himself could see him from his assembly.

He said, "Admit him in."

So he entered into a large domed hall with a dome higher than eighty cubits in height, and said, "I am indeed the messenger of the Lord of the Universe sent to you."

He retorted, "Then show me a sign if you are telling the truth."

So he threw down his staff, which split into two forks. Suddenly it turned into a python, one half of its mouth on the ground and the other at the top of the dome.

So Pharaoh looked inside it and saw it blazing with fire as it lunged towards him. Pharaoh lost control of his bowels and screamed: "Mūsā! Take it away!"' [7:103–107]

62. From Yūnus b. Ẓibyān who said, 'He said that when Mūsā and Hārūn entered Pharaoh's assembly none of his courtiers on that particular day were of illegitimate birth; they were all born in wedlock. Were there to have been a single illegitimate person present there, he would have commanded for these two to be killed. But instead they said: '﴾*Delay him and his brother for a while*﴿; and they told him to take his time and think about it.' Then he [i.e. the Imam] placed his hand on his chest and said, 'It is the same thing with us – it is only the ones of illegitimate birth that are intent on [killing] us.' [7:111]

فلمّا بعث الله موسى عليه السلام إلى فِرعون فدخل المدينة، فلمّا رآه الأُسد تبصبصت وولّت مدبرة، قال: ثمّ لم يأتِ إلاّ انفتح له بابها، حتّى انتهى إلى قَصر فِرعون الذي هو فيه، قال: فقعَد على بابه، وعليه مِدرَعةٌ من صُوف ومعه عصاه، فلمّا خرج الآذِن قال له موسى عليه السلام: استأذِن لي على فِرعون. فلم يلتفِت إليه، قال: فقال له موسى عليه السلام: إنّي رسول ربّ العالمين. قال فلم يلتفِت إليه.

قال: فمَكَث بذلك ما شاء الله يسأله أن يستأذن له، قال: فلمّا أكثر عليه، قال له: أما وَجَد ربّ العالمين من يُرسِله غيرك؟

قال: فغَضِب موسى عليه السلام وضرب الباب بعصاه، فلم يبقَ بينه وبين فِرعون باب إلاّ انفتح، حتّى نظر إليه فِرعون وهو في مجلسه، فقال: أدخلوه.

قال: فَدَخَل عليه وهو في قُبَّةٍ له مرتفعةٍ كثيرة الارتفاع، ثمانون ذراعًا، قال: فقال: إنّي رسول ربّ العالمين إليك. قال: فقال: فأتِ بآيةٍ إن كُنتَ مِن الصادقين.

قال: فألقى عصاه، وكان لها شُعبتان. قال: فإذا هي حَيَّة، قد وقع إحدى الشعبتين في الأرض، والشُعبة الأُخرى في أعلى القُبّة، قال: فنظر فِرعون إلى جَوفها وهو يلتهبُ نِيرانًا، قال: وأهوَت إليه، فأحدث وصاح: يا موسى، خُذها.

٦٢. عن يُونس بن ظِبيان، قال: قال عليه السلام: إنّ موسى وهارون حين دخلا على فِرعون، لم يكُن في جُلسائه يومئذٍ ولد سِفاح، كانوا ولد نِكاح كلّهم، ولوكان فيهم ولد سِفاح لأمر بقتلهما، فقالوا: ﴿أَرْجِهْ وَأَخَاهُ﴾ وأمروه بالتأنّي والنَّظر، ثمّ وَضَع عليه السلام يده على صدره، فقال: وكذلك نحن لا يَنزِع إلينا إلاّ كُلّ خبيث الولادة.

63. From Mūsā b. Bakr, from Abū ʿAbd Allāh عليه السلام who said, 'I bear witness that the Murji'a are on the creed of those who said: ﴿*Delay him and his brother for a while, and send messengers to all the cities.*﴾' [7:111]

64. From Muḥammad b. ʿAlī عليه السلام who said, 'Mūsā's staff originally belonged to Ādam, and was passed down to Shuʿayb and then to Mūsā, the son of ʿImrān. It frightened them all and devoured their fakery, doing exactly as it was commanded to do. It had a mouth of two forks: one on the ground and the other on the ceiling with forty cubits between them, devouring with its tongue all that they had conjured up.' [7:117]

65. From ʿAmmār al-Sābāṭī who said, 'I heard Abū ʿAbd Allāh عليه السلام say, "The earth belongs to God, He gives it as their own to whichever of His servants He chooses." He continued, "And whatever belongs to God belongs to His Messenger, and whatever belongs to His Messenger belongs to the Imam after the Messenger of God صلى الله عليه وآله."' [7:129]

66. From Abū Khālid al-Kābulī, from Abū Jaʿfar عليه السلام who said, 'We found written in the book of ʿAlī عليه السلام that the earth belongs to God, and He will give it to whichever of His servants He chooses, and that the outcome will be in favour of those who are God-conscious, and that my Household and I are the ones to whom God has given the earth as theirs. We are the God-conscious ones, and the whole earth belongs to us. So whoever from among the Muslims revives a land and makes it flourish should remit its due to the Imam from among my Household, and he can have whatever he needs to consume from it. If, however, he abandons it after having cultivated it, and subsequently another Muslim takes it up, cultivates it and revives it again after him, then he is more entitled to it than the one who had abandoned it. He too should remit what is due from it to the Imam from my Household, and keep whatever he consumes thereof until the Qā'im of my Household reappears with the sword. He will occupy it and guard it, expelling them from it just as the Messenger of God صلى الله عليه وآله used to possess it exclusively, apart from that which the Shīʿa own. He will disassociate from them [the wrongdoers] and leave the earth in their hands [i.e. the God-conscious ones] instead.' [7:129]

٦٣. عن موسى بن بكر، عن أبي عبدالله عليه السلام، قال: أشهدُ أنّ المُرجئة على دين الذين قالوا: ﴿أَرْجِهْ وَأَخَاهُ وَأَرْسِلْ فِي الْمَدَائِنِ حَاشِرِينَ﴾.

٦٤. عن محمّد بن عليّ عليه السلام، قال: كانت عصا موسى لآدم عليهما السلام، فصارت إلى شُعيب عليه السلام، ثمّ صارت إلى موسى بن عِمران عليه السلام، وإنّها لتَروّع وَتلقَف ما يأفِكُون، وتَصنَع ما تُؤمَر، يُفتَح لها شُعبتان، إحداهما في الأرض، والأخرى في السقف، وبينهما أربعون ذراعًا، تلقف ما يأفِكُون بلسانها.

٦٥. عن عمّار الساباطي، قال: سَمِعتُ أبا عبدالله عليه السلام يقول: إنّ الأرض لله يُورثها من يشاء من عباده، قال: فما كان لله فهو لرسوله، وما كان لرسول الله فهو للإمام بعد رسول الله صلى الله عليه وآله وسلم.

٦٦. عن أبي خالد الكابُلي، عن أبي جعفر عليه السلام، قال: وجدنا في كتاب عليّ عليه السلام: ﴿إِنَّ الْأَرْضَ لِلَّهِ يُورِثُهَا مَنْ يَشَاءُ مِنْ عِبَادِهِ وَالْعَاقِبَةُ لِلْمُتَّقِينَ﴾ أنا وأهل بيتي الّذين أورثنا الله الأرض، ونحن المتّقون، والأرض كلّها لنا، فمن أحيا أرضًا من المسلمين فعمّرها فليؤدّ خَراجها إلى الإمام من أهل بيتي، وله ما أكل منها، فإن تَرَكها وأخربها بعدما عمّرها، فأخذها رجلٌ من المسلمين بعده فعمَّرها وأحياها، فهو أحقُّ به من الذي تَرَكها، فليؤدّ خَراجها إلى الإمام من أهل بيتي، وله ما أكل منها حتّى يظهر القائم من أهل بيتي بالسيف، فيحوزها ويمنعها، ويُخرِجهم عنها، كما حواها رسول الله صلى الله عليه وآله وسلم ومنعها، إلاّ ماكان في أيدي شيعتنا، فإنّه يُقاطِعهم ويترُك الأرض في أيديهم.

67. From Muḥammad b. Qays, from Abū ʿAbd Allāh عليه السلام. He said, 'I asked: "What was the flood?" He replied, "It was a flood of water along with the plague."' [7:133]

68. From Muḥammad b. ʿAlī, from Abū ʿAbd Allāh who informed me from Sulaymān, from al-Riḍā عليه السلام who said regarding His verse ﴿ *if you relieve us of the plague, we will believe you* ﴾: 'It was a plague of ice.' He added, 'Khurasan is a land of plague.' [7:134]

69. From Muḥammad al-Ḥalabī, from Abū ʿAbd Allāh عليه السلام who said regarding His verse ﴿ *We appointed thirty nights for Mūsā, then added ten more* ﴾: 'With ten more from the month of Dhū al-Ḥijja, which is an incomplete month [i.e. of 29 days].' [Then he listed them] until he ended up at the month of Shaʿbān, and said, 'That too is incomplete, not a full [thirty days].' [7:142]

70. From al-Fuḍayl b. Yasār who said, 'I asked Abū Jaʿfar عليه السلام, "May I be your ransom – can you give us an exact time frame for these people?" So he replied, "God's knowledge contradicts the knowledge of those who fix exact timings. Have you not heard God say: ﴿ *We appointed thirty nights for Mūsā, then added ten more: the term set by his Lord was completed in forty nights* ﴾? Mūsā himself did not know about those extra ten nights and nor the Children of Israel. When he told them thus, they said, 'Mūsā lied and Mūsā broke his promise.' So when you speak to them, say: 'God and His Messenger speak the truth, and you will be rewarded twice.'" [7:142]

71. From al-Fuḍayl b. Yasār, from Abū Jaʿfar عليه السلام who said, 'When Mūsā left to go and meet his Lord and promised them thirty days, and when afterwards God increased the term beyond thirty days, his people said, "Mūsā broke his promise to us," and hence they did what they did.'

From Muḥammad b. ʿAlī b. al-Ḥanafiyya that he said the same thing. [7:142]

٦٧. عن محمّد بن قيس، عن أبي عبدالله عليه السلام، قال: قلتُ: ما الطُّوفان؟ قال: هو طُوفان الماء والطّاعون.

٦٨. عن محمّد بن علي، عن أبي عبدالله، أنبأني عن سليمان عن الرضا عليه السلام في قوله تعالى: ﴿لَئِن كَشَفْتَ عَنَّا الرِّجْزَ لَنُؤْمِنَنَّ لَكَ﴾، قال: الرِّجز: هو الثّلج، ثمّ قال: خُراسان بلاد رِجز.

٦٩. عن محمّد الحلبي، عن أبي عبدالله عليه السلام في قوله: ﴿وَوَاعَدْنَا مُوسَىٰ ثَلَاثِينَ لَيْلَةً وَأَتْمَمْنَاهَا بِعَشْرٍ﴾، قال: بعشر ذي الحجّة ناقصة حتّى انتهى إلى شعبان فقال: ناقِصٌ لا يَتِمّ.

٧٠. عن الفُضيل بن يَسار، قال: قلتُ لأبي جعفر عليه السلام: جُعِلتُ فِداك، وقِّت لنا وقتًا فيهم.

فقال: إنّ الله خالف علمه علم المُوقِّتين، أما سَمِعت الله يقول: ﴿وَوَاعَدْنَا مُوسَىٰ ثَلَاثِينَ لَيْلَةً﴾ إلى ﴿أَرْبَعِينَ لَيْلَةً﴾؟ أما إنّ موسى لم يَكُن يعلم بتلك العشر، ولا بنو إسرائيل، فلمّا حدّثهم قالوا: كَذَب موسى، وأَخْلَفَنا موسى؛ فإن حُدِّثتُم به فقولوا: صَدَق الله ورسوله، تُؤجَروا مرّتَين.

٧١. عن الفُضيل بن يَسار، عن أبي جعفر عليه السلام، قال: إنّ موسى عليه السلام لمّا خرَجَ وافدًا إلى ربّه وأعدهم ثلاثين يومًا، فلمّا زاده الله الثّلاثين عشرًا قال قومه: أَخْلَفَنا موسى، فصَنَعوا ما صَنَعوا.

عن محمّد بن علي بن الحنفية، أنّه قال مثل ذلك.

72. From Abū Baṣīr, from Abū Jaʿfar عليه السلام and Abū ʿAbd Allāh عليه السلام that he said, ʿWhen Mūsā asked his Lord, Blessed and most High: ﴾*ʿMy Lord, show Yourself to me: let me see You!' He said, ʿYou will never see Me, but look at that mountain: if it remains standing firm, you will see Me,'* [...]﴿ He continued, ʿSo when Mūsā climbed to the top of the mountain, the gates of the heavens opened up and the angels came forth in their throngs with poles in their hands and halos of light on their heads, passing by him, throng after throng saying, "O son of ʿImrān, stand firm for you have asked for a gargantuan thing indeed."' He continued, ʿMūsā was still standing when our Lord – exalted be His might – manifested Himself and caused the mountain to crumble, and Mūsā fell unconscious. When God returned his soul back to him he came to his senses, and ﴾*he said, ʿGlory be to You! To You I turn in repentance! I am the first to believe!'*﴿' [7:143]

73. Ibn Abī ʿUmayr said, ʿA number of our associates narrated to me: "Fire surrounded him such that he could not escape from the terror of what he saw." This man narrated from one of his protégés saying, "He must have either been suspended in that state of unconsciousness three times, or it may have been manifest to him before that point since his soul would have returned to him by then."' [7:143]

74. From Abū Baṣīr who said, ʿI heard Abū ʿAbd Allāh عليه السلام say, "When Mūsā b. ʿImrān عليه السلام asked his Lord to let him see Him, God made him promise to stay in one spot. Then He commanded the angels to pass by him, horde after horde, with lightning, thunder, wind and thunderbolts. Every time a horde of angels passed, he would shake violently, lift his head up and ask: ʿIs my Lord among you?' And the reply would come: ʿHe is coming, but you have asked a gargantuan thing indeed, O son of ʿImrān.'"' [7:143]

75. From Ḥafṣ b. Ghiyāth who said, ʿI heard Abū ʿAbd Allāh عليه السلام say about His verse ﴾*and when his Lord revealed Himself to the mountain, He made it crumble: Mūsā fell down unconscious*﴿: "The mountain sunk into the sea and it will remain submerged until the Hour."' [7:143]

٧٢. عن أبي بصير، عن أبي جعفر وأبي عبد الله عليهما السلام، قال: لمّا سأل موسى عليه السلام ربّه تبارك وتعالى: ﴿قَالَ رَبِّ أَرِنِي أَنظُرْ إِلَيْكَ قَالَ لَن تَرَانِي وَلَٰكِنِ انظُرْ إِلَى الْجَبَلِ فَإِنِ اسْتَقَرَّ مَكَانَهُ فَسَوْفَ تَرَانِي﴾، قال: فلمّا صَعِد موسى عليه السلام على الجبل، فُتِحت أبواب السماء، وأقبلت الملائكة أفواجًا في أيديهم العُمُد، وفي رأسها النُّور، يَمُرُّون به فوجًا بعد فَوج، يقولون: يا بن عِمران، اثبُت فقد سألت عظيمًا، قال: فلم يَزَل موسى عليه السلام واقفًا حتّى تجلّى ربّنا جلّ جلاله، فجعل الجَبَل دَكًّا، وخرّ موسى صَعِقًا، فلمّا أن ردّ الله إليه رُوحه أفاق ﴿قَالَ سُبْحَانَكَ تُبْتُ إِلَيْكَ وَأَنَا أَوَّلُ الْمُؤْمِنِينَ﴾.

٧٣. قال ابن أبي عُمير: وحدَّثني عدَّة من أصحابنا: أنّ النار أحاطت به حتّى لا يَهرُب لهول ما رأى. قال: وروى هذا الرجل عن بعض مواليه، قال: ينبغي أن يُنتَظَر بالمَصعُوق ثلاثًا، أو يتبيّن قبل ذلك، لأنّه ربما رُدّ عليه رُوحه.

٧٤. عن أبي بصير، قال: سَمِعتُ أبا عبد الله عليه السلام يقول: إنّ موسى بن عِمران عليه السلام لمّا سأل ربه النّظر إليه وعده الله أن يَقعُد في موضع، ثمّ أمر الملائكة، أن تمرُّ عليه موكِبًا موكِبًا بالبَرق والرَّعد والرّيح والصَّواعق، فكلَّما مَرّ به مَوكبٌ من المَواكب ارتعدت فرائصه، فيرفع رأسه، فيسأل: أفيكم ربّي؟ فيُجاب: هوآتٍ، وقد سألت عظيمًا يا بن عِمران.

٧٥. عن حَفص بن غِياث، قال: سَمِعتُ أبا عبد الله عليه السلام يقول في قوله تعالى: ﴿فَلَمَّا تَجَلَّىٰ رَبُّهُ لِلْجَبَلِ جَعَلَهُ دَكًّا وَخَرَّ مُوسَىٰ صَعِقًا﴾، قال: ساخَ الجبلُ في البَحر، فهو يهوي حتّى الساعة.

76. In another narration, fire surrounded Mūsā so that he would not escape from the terror of what he would see. He said, 'When Mūsā fell unconscious he actually died. So when God returned his soul to him, he came to his senses and said: ﴾*Glory be to You! To You I turn in repentance! I am the first to believe!*﴿' [7:143]

77. From Abū Ḥamza, from Abū 'Abd Allāh عليه السلام who said, 'It is written in [the book] *al-Jafr* that when God, Blessed and most High, revealed the tablets unto Mūsā عليه السلام, He expounded to him therein every single thing that has ever been and ever will be until the Hour.[7] When the end of Mūsā's appointed days approached, God revealed to him to hide the tablets away for safe keeping inside a mountain called Zīna, for they were an adornment from the Garden. So Mūsā came to the mountain, which split open for him. He placed the wrapped-up tablets therein and as soon as he did, the mountain encapsulated them. They remained thus in the mountain until God sent His Prophet Muḥammad ﷺ down.

A caravan of people once set out from Yemen, headed towards the Messenger ﷺ when they ended up at this mountain and it opened up, and the wrapped-up tablets came out from it as intact as Mūsā had placed them therein. So the people took them, and as soon as their hands held them God cast a deep fear into their hearts making them unable to look at them, and they were terrified of them until they brought them to the Messenger of God ﷺ. God sent Jibra'īl down to His Prophet to inform him of the matter of these people and what had afflicted them.

When they approached the Prophet ﷺ he initiated the conversation and asked them about that which they had found. They said, "How do you know what we found?"

He replied, "My Lord informed me about it – they are the tablets."

---

7 According to narrations, *al-Jafr* is an esoteric book compiled (according to Shī'ī belief) by 'Alī b. Abī Ṭālib. The first mention of the book is associated with the sixth Imam Ja'far al-Ṣādiq. According to al-Ḥasan al-Saffār in *Baṣā'ir al-darajāt* there are two types of *jafr*: the white *jafr* and red *jafr*. The white *jafr* contains the previous scriptures; namely the Psalms, Torah and Injīl and even the scrolls of Abraham. The red *jafr* is a leather sack containing the weapons of the Prophet. All these are said to have been inherited by Imam 'Alī and passed down to the Imams after him.

٧٦. وفي رواية أخرى: أنّ النّار أحاطت بموسى عليه السلام لئلاّ يَهرُب لِهَول ما رأى، وقال: لمّا خرّ موسى صَعِقًا مات، فلمّا أن ردّ الله رُوحه أفاق، فقال: سُبحانك تُبت إليك وأنا أوّل المؤمنين.

٧٧. عن أبي حمزة، عن أبي عبد الله عليه السلام، قال في الجَفر: إنّ الله تبارك وتعالى لمّا أنزل الألواح على موسى عليه السلام، أنزلها عليه وفيها تِبيان كُلّ شيءٍ كان أو هو كائن، إلى أن تقوم الساعة، فلمّا انقضت أيّام موسى عليه السلام أوحى الله إليه: أن استَودِع الألواح؛ وهي زَبَرجَدَةٌ من الجَنّة، جَبلاً يقال له زينة، فأتى موسى الجبلَ، فانشق له الجبلُ، فجعل فيه الألواح مَلفُوفةً، فلمّا جَعَلها فيه انطَبق الجبلُ عليها، فلم تَزَل في الجبل حتّى بَعَث الله نبيّه محمّدًا صلى الله عليه وآله، فأقبل رَكبٌ من اليمن يُريدون الرسول صلى الله عليه وآله، فلمّا انتهوا إلى الجبل أنفَرَج الجبلُ وخرجت الألواحُ ملفوفة كما وَضَعها موسى عليه السلام، فأخذها القوم، فلمّا وقعت في أيديهم ألقى الله في قلوبهم أن لا يَنظُروا إليها، وهابوها حتّى يأتُوا بها رسول الله صلى الله عليه وآله، وأنزل الله جبرَئيل عليه السلام على نبيّه صلى الله عليه وآله، فأخبره بأمر القوم، وبالّذي أصابوه.

فلمّا قَدِموا على النبيّ صلى الله عليه وآله وسلّموا عليه ابتدأهم، فسألهم عمّا وَجَدوا فقالوا: وما عِلمُك بما وَجَدنا؟ قال: أخبرني به ربّي، وهو الألواح. قالوا: نشهد أنّك لرسول الله، فأخرَجُوها فوَضَعُوها إليه، فنظر إليها، وقولها وكَتَبها بالعِبراني، ثمّ دعا أمير المؤمنين عليه السلام فقال: دُونك هذه ففيها علم الأوّلين وعلم الآخرين، وهي ألواح موسى عليه السلام، وقد أمرني ربّي أن أدفعها إليك.

فقال: لستُ أُحسِن قراءتها.

They exclaimed, "We bear witness that you are indeed the Messenger of God," and they took them out and gave them to him. He looked at them and read them, and they were written in Hebrew.

Then he called the Commander of the Faithful عليه السلام saying, "Take these, for they contain the knowledge of the first and the last ones. They are Mūsā's tablets, and my Lord has commanded me to give them to you."

He replied, "O Messenger of God, I am not able to read them."

He said, "Jibra'īl has commanded me to tell you to place them under your head tonight and when you awake in the morning, you will know how to read them."

So he placed them under his head, and when he woke up God had taught him all that they contained. Then the Messenger of God صلى الله عليه وآله commanded him to transcribe it all, which he did on sheep hide, and this is what [the book of] *al-Jafr* is. It contains the knowledge of the first and last people, and we have it with us along with the tablets and the staff of Mūsā. We have inherited from the prophets, peace be upon them all.'

He continued, 'Abū Ja'far عليه السلام then said, "That rock which safeguarded Mūsā's tablets is to be found under a tree in the valley known as such and such."' [7:145]

78. From Muḥammad b. Sābiq b. Ṭalḥa al-Anṣārī[8] who said, 'One of the things that Hārūn [al-Rashīd] asked Abū al-Ḥasan Mūsā [al-Kāẓim] عليه السلام when he was brought before him was: "What is this abode?"

He replied, "This is the abode of the corrupt ones."

He [the narrator] said, 'Then he [the Imam] read: ﴿*I will keep distracted from My signs those who behave arrogantly on Earth without any right, and who, even if they see every sign, will not believe in them; they will not take the way of right guidance if they see it, but will take the way of error if they see that*﴾, meaning that even if they see every sign, they will not believe in it and refuse to take the path of guidance when they see it.'

So Hārūn asked him, "So who does the abode belong to then?"

He replied, "It is a joy for our Shī'a and a trial for others."

He asked, "So why does the proprietor of the abode not take it back?"

8 We were unable to identify this individual.

قال: إنّ جَبرَئيل، أمرني أن آمرك أن تَضَعها تحت رأسك ليلتك هذه، فإنّك تُصبح وقد عَلمت قراءتها، قال: فجعلها تحت رأسه، فأصبح وقد علّمه الله كلّ شيء فيها، فأمره رسول الله ﷺ بنسخها، فنسخها في جِلدٍ وهو الجَفر، وفيه علم الأوّلين والآخرين، وهو عندنا، والألواح عندنا، وعصا موسى عندنا، ونحن وَرِثنا النبّيين صلّى الله عليهم أجمعين.

قال: قال أبو جعفر عليه السلام: تلك الصَخرة التي حَفَظت ألواح موسى تحت شجرةٍ في وادٍ يُعرَف بكذا.

٧٨. عن محمّد بن سابق بن طلحة الأنصاري، قال: كان ممّا قال هارون لأبي الحسن موسى عليه السلام حين اُدخل عليه: ما هذه الدار؟

قال: هذه دار الفاسقين.

قال: وقرأ ﴿سَأَصْرِفُ عَنْ آيَاتِيَ الَّذِينَ يَتَكَبَّرُونَ فِي الأَرْضِ بِغَيْرِ الْحَقِّ... وَإِنْ يَرَوْا سَبِيلَ الْغَيِّ يَتَّخِذُوهُ سَبِيلاً﴾ يعني وإن يَرَوا كُلّ آيةٍ لا يُؤمنوا بها، وإن يروا سبيل الرشد لا يتّخذوه سبيلاً.

فقال له هارون: فدارُ من هي؟

قال: هي لشيعتنا فترة، ولغيرهم فتنة.

قال: فما بال صاحب الدار لا يأخُذها؟

قال: اُخِذت منهم عامرة، ولا يأخُذها إلاّ مَعْمُورة.

He replied, "It was taken from them whilst it was still thriving, and he will not take it back until it has been fully restored."' [7:146]

79. From Muḥammad b. Abī Ḥamza, from whoever mentioned it from Abū ʿAbd Allāh عليه السلام about God's verse: ﴾*In his absence, Mūsā's people took to worshipping a mere shape that made sounds like a cow – a calf made from their jewellery.*﴿ 'Mūsā said, "My Lord, who caused the statue to make the sound?" So God replied, "I did, Mūsā." So Mūsā said, ﴾*This is only a trial from You – through it, You cause whoever You will to stray and guide whoever You will.*﴿ (7:155)' [7:148]

80. From Ibn Muskān, from al-Waṣṣāf, from Abū Jaʿfar عليه السلام who said, 'One of the conversations that Mūsā had with God was that he asked, "My Lord, this Sāmirī made the calf, but who made the sound that came from it?"' He said, 'So God revealed to him, "Mūsā, that is My test so do not probe into it."' [7:148]

81. From Ismāʿīl b. ʿAbd al-ʿAzīz, from Abū ʿAbd Allāh عليه السلام who added, 'Whereby Mūsā said: "You are the chief of all wise ones."' [7:148]

82. From Muḥammad b. Abī Ḥamza, from whoever mentioned it from Abū ʿAbd Allāh عليه السلام who said, 'When God, Blessed and most High, informed Mūsā that his people had taken to worshipping a mooing calf, he had not yet witnessed it with his own eyes. However, when he saw them his anger intensified and he threw the tablets down from his hand.' Then Abū ʿAbd Allāh said, 'Seeing something is better than hearing about it.' [7:150]

83. From Dāwūd b. Farqad who said, 'Abū ʿAbd Allāh عليه السلام said, "I petitioned my Lord for a need I had so I went to the mosque [to supplicate] for it at high-noon, since this is what I do when I have something that needs to be granted. While I was praying in the garden a man stood by my head."

He said, "I asked him: 'Which people does your good self come from?' He replied: 'From the people of Kufa.'"

٧٩. عن محمّد بن أبي حمزة، عمّن ذكره، عن أبي عبدالله عليه السلام، في قول الله تعالى: ﴿وَاتَّخَذَ قَوْمُ مُوسَى مِنْ بَعْدِهِ مِنْ حُلِيِّهِمْ عِجْلاً جَسَدًا لَهُ خُوَارٌ﴾ فقال موسى: يا ربّ ومن أخار الصّنم؟ فقال الله: أنا يا موسى أخرته. فقال: موسى: ﴿إِنْ هِيَ إِلاَّ فِتْنَتُكَ تُضِلُّ بِهَا مَنْ تَشَاءُ وَتَهْدِي مَنْ تَشَاءُ﴾.

٨٠. عن ابن مُسكان، عن الوصاف، عن أبي جعفر عليه السلام، قال: إنّ فيما ناجى الله موسى عليه السلام أن قال: يا ربّ، هذا السّامري صَنَع العِجل، فالخُوار مَن صَنَعه؟ قال: فأوحى الله إليه: يا موسى، إنّ تلك فِتنتي فلا تفحص عنها.

٨١. عن إسماعيل بن عبد العزيز، عن أبي عبدالله عليه السلام، قال: حيث قال موسى عليه السلام: أنت أبو الحُكماء.

٨٢. عن محمّد بن أبي حمزة، عمّن ذكره، عن أبي عبدالله عليه السلام، قال: إنّ الله تبارك وتعالى لمّا أخبر موسى عليه السلام أنّ قومه اتّخذوا عِجلاً له خُوار، فلم يَقَع منه موقع العِيان، فلمّا رآهم اشتدّ غضبه، فألقى الألواح من يده، فقال أبو عبدالله عليه السلام: وللرؤية فضلٌ على الخَبَر.

٨٣. عن داود بن فَرقد، قال: قال أبو عبدالله عليه السلام: عَرَضَت لي إلى ربّي حاجة، فهجّرت فيها إلى المسجد، وكذلك أفعل إذا عرَضَت لي الحاجة، فبينا أنا أُصلّي في الرّوضة إذا رجلٌ على رأسي، قال: فقلتُ: ممّنَ الرجل؟

فقال: من أهل الكوفة.

He said, "I asked: 'From which people exactly?'

He replied: 'From Aslam.'"

He said, "So I asked: 'From which people, to be precise?'

He replied, 'From the Zaydīs.'"

He said, "I asked: 'O brother from Aslam, whom do you know from among them?'

He replied: 'I know the best of them, their chief, their guide and the most virtuous one from among them: Hārūn b. Saʿd.'

I said: 'O brother from Aslam, that one is the head of the *ʿIjliyya* as you have heard God say: ﴾*Those who took to worshipping the calf will be afflicted by their Lord's wrath, and by disgrace in this life.*﴿[9] The true Zaydī is Muḥammad b. Sālim, the cane-seller.'"' [7:152]

84. From al-Ḥārith b. al-Mughīra, from Abū ʿAbd Allāh عليه السلام. He said, 'I said to him, "ʿAbd Allāh b. ʿAjalān when he was suffering from his terminal illness stated that he would not die but he died." He replied, "May God not give him insight into any of his sins – where else can he go? Mūsā chose seventy men from his community, and when they were seized by the trembling he exclaimed, 'My Lord! My companions!' He said, 'I will substitute them for you with people who are better for you than them.' So he said, 'Indeed, I already know them and have sensed their aura.'" He said, "So God sent prophets down for him."' [7:155]

85. A similar narration has been quoted from Abān b. ʿUthmān, from al-Ḥārith, save that it mentions them as having been seized by thunderbolts rather than the trembling. [7:155]

86. From Abū Baṣīr, from Abū Jaʿfar عليه السلام who said, 'When Mūsā conversed with His Lord, God revealed to Him: "O Mūsā, I have indeed tested your people."

He asked, "Through what, my Lord?"

He replied, "Through the Sāmirī – he has made a calf for them out of their jewellery."

9 The *ʿIjliyya* were a sect belonging to the *ghulāt* extremists. There may also be a play on words here as *ʿijl* also means calf, and refers to those who worshipped the golden calf.

قال: قلت: ممّن الرجل؟ قال: من أسلم.

قال: فقلت: ممّن الرجل؟ قال: من الزيدية.

قال: قلت: يا أخا أسلم، مَن تعرِف منهم؟

قال: أعرِف خيّرهم وسيّدهم ورشيدهم وأفضلهم هارون بن سعد.

قلت: يا أخا أسلم، ذلك رأسُ العِجليّة، أما سَمِعت الله يقول: ﴿إِنَّ الَّذِينَ اتَّخَذُوا الْعِجْلَ سَيَنَالُهُمْ غَضَبٌ مِنْ رَبِّهِمْ وَذِلَّةٌ فِي الْحَيَاةِ الدُّنْيَا﴾ وإنّما الزيديّ حقّاً محمّد بن سالم بياع القَصَب.

٨٤. عن الحارث بن المُغيرة، عن أبي عبدالله عليه السلام، قال: قلتُ له: إنّ عبدالله بن عجلان قال في مرضه الذي مات فيه: إنّه لا يموت فمات، فقال: لا عرّفه الله شيئًا من ذُنوبه، أين ذهب؟ إنّ موسى اختار سبعين رجلاً من قومه، فلمّا أَخَذَتهم الرَّجفة قال: ربّ أصحابي أصحابي. قال: إنّي أُبَدِّلك بهم من هو خيرٌ لك منهم. فقال: إنّي عَرفتُهم ووجدتُ رِيحهم، قال: فبعثهم الله له أنبياء.

٨٥. عن أبان بن عثمان، عن الحارث: مثله، إلاّ أنّه ذَكَر: فلمّا أخذتهم الصّاعِقة، ولم يَذكُر الرَّجفَة.

٨٦. عن أبي بصير، عن أبي جعفر عليه السلام، قال: لمّا ناجى موسى ربَّه أوحى الله إليه: أن يا موسى قد فتنتُ قومك. قال: وبماذا يا ربُّ؟ قال: بالسامريّ، صاغ لهم من حُليّهم عِجلاً، قال: يا ربّ إنّ حُليَّهم لا يُحتمل أن يُصاغ منه غزال وتِمثال وعِجل، فيكف فتَنتهم؟ قال: صاع

He said, "My Lord, but their jewellery cannot possibly be made into a gazelle or statue or calf, so how have You tested them?"

He replied, "He made a calf with a mooing sound for them."

He said, "My Lord, but who made it moo?"

He replied, "I did."

Thereupon Mūsā said, ﴾ *This is only a trial from You– through it, You cause whoever You will to stray and guide whoever You will.* ﴿' [7:155]

87. From ʿAlī b. Asbāṭ who said, 'I asked Abū Jaʿfar عليه السلام, "Why was the Prophet صلى الله عليه وآله called *ummī* (unlettered)?" He replied, "It relates to Mecca, going back to God's statement: ﴾ *and for you to warn the Mother of Cities (umm al-qurā) and all around it* ﴿(42:7). And *umm al-qurā* is Mecca; so that is why he has been called *ummī*."' [7:157]

88. From al-Ṯhumālī, from Abū Jaʿfar عليه السلام who said regarding His words ﴾ *they find described* ﴿: 'It means that the Jews and the Christians can find Muḥammad's name and attributes written in the Torah and the Gospel, commanding them to do right and forbidding them from wrongdoing.' [7:157]

89. From Abū Baṣīr regarding God's verse: ﴾ *So it is those who believe him, honour and help him, and who follow the light which has been sent down with him, who will succeed.* ﴿ Abū Jaʿfar عليه السلام said, 'The light is ʿAlī عليه السلام.' [7:157]

90. From ʿAbd Allāh b. Sinān, from Abū ʿAbd Allāh عليه السلام who said about God's verse: ﴾ *There is a group among the people of Mūsā who guide with truth, and who act justly according to it* ﴿; he said, 'The people of Mūsā are the people of submission (*islām*).' [7:159]

91. From al-Mufaḍḍal b. ʿUmar, from Abū ʿAbd Allāh عليه السلام who said, 'When the Qāʾim from the family of Muḥammad rises, he will draw out twenty-seven men from behind the Kaʿba: fifteen from the people of Mūsā who judged with truth and acted justly according to it, seven from the companions of the

لهم عِجلاً لُخَارَ، قال: يا ربّ، ومن أخاره؟ قال: أنا. قال عندها موسى: ﴿إِنْ هِيَ إِلاَّ فِتْنَتُكَ تُضِلُّ بِهَا مَنْ تَشَاءُ وَتَهْدِي مَنْ تَشَاءُ﴾.

٨٧. عن علي بن أسباط، قال: قلتُ لأبي جعفر عليه السلام: لِمَ سُمّيَ النبيّ الأُمّي؟ قال: نُسِب إلى مكّة، وذلك من قول الله: ﴿لِتُنْذِرَ أُمَّ الْقُرَى وَمَنْ حَوْلَهَا﴾ وأُمّ القُرى مكّة، فقيل أُمّي لذلك.

٨٨. عن الثّمالي، عن أبي جعفر عليه السلام، قال: قوله: ﴿يَجِدُونَهُ﴾ يعني اليهود والنصارى، صفة محمّد واسمه ﴿مَكْتُوبًا عِنْدَهُمْ فِي التَّوْرَاةِ وَالإِنْجِيلِ يَأْمُرُهُمْ بِالْمَعْرُوفِ وَيَنْهَاهُمْ عَنِ الْمُنْكَرِ﴾.

٨٩. عن أبي بصير، في قول الله: ﴿فَالَّذِينَ آمَنُوا بِهِ وَعَزَّرُوهُ وَنَصَرُوهُ وَاتَّبَعُوا النُّورَ الَّذِي أُنْزِلَ مَعَهُ﴾، قال أبو جعفر عليه السلام: النُّور: عليّ عليه السلام.

٩٠. عن عبدالله بن سِنان، عن أبي عبدالله عليه السلام، في قول الله تعالى: ﴿وَمِنْ قَوْمِ مُوسَى أُمَّةٌ يَهْدُونَ بِالْحَقِّ وَبِهِ يَعْدِلُونَ﴾، فقال: قوم موسى هم أهل الإسلام.

٩١. عن المفضّل بن عمر، عن أبي عبدالله عليه السلام، قال: إذا قام قائم آل محمّد استخرج من ظهر الكعبة سبعة وعشرين رجلاً، خمسة عشر من قوم موسى عليه السلام الذين يَقضُون بالحقّ وبه يَعدِلون، وسبعة من أصحاب الكهف، ويُوشعَ وصيّ موسى، ومؤمن آل فِرعون، وسلمان الفارسي، وأبا دُجانة الأنصاري، ومالك الأشتر.

cave, Joshua (Mūsā's successor), the believer from Pharaoh's family, Salmān al-Fārsī (the Persian), Abū Dujāna al-Anṣārī[10] and Mālik al-Ashtar.' [7:159]

92. From Abū al-Ṣahbā' al-Bakrī who said, 'I heard 'Alī b. Abī Ṭālib ﷺ when he was inviting the Jewish exilarch and the Christian archbishop. He said, "I am going to ask you about something that I know better than you both, so do not conceal from me, O Exilarch, by the One who revealed the Torah unto Mūsā and how he fed you manna and quails, made a dry path for you in the sea, made twelve springs gush forth from the rock of Mount Sinai – one spring for each tribe of the Children of Israel. Rather inform me – how many groups did the Children of Israel split into after Mūsā?" He replied, "A single group."

He retorted, "You are lying, by the One apart from Whom there is no god but He. They split up into seventy-one groups, all of which are in the Fire except for one, for God says: ﴾ *There is a group among the people of Mūsā who guide with truth, and who act justly according to it.* ﴿ This is the saved one.' [7:159]

93. From al-Aṣbagh b. Nubāta, from 'Alī b. Abī Ṭālib ﷺ who said, 'There was a town by the sea, so [the inhabitants of the town] said to their prophet: "If He is real, then let our Lord transform us into eels. Now this town was in the middle of the sea and it sank in the night, and every single man from among them was [transformed into] a black eel whose mouth could engulf a boat."' [7:163]

94. From Abū 'Ubayda, from Abū Ja'far ﷺ who said, 'We found written in the Commander of the Faithful's book that a community from among the inhabitants of Ayla[11] were descended from the people of Thamūd and that the fish

10 This is Simāk b. Kharasha al-Khazrajī al-Bayāḍī al-Anṣārī, better known as Abu Dujāna, who was a companion of the Prophet. He is remembered in the sources as a brave warrior who was present at Badr and stood firm in the Battle of Uḥud. He was inflicted with many wounds and was martyred in Yamāma in the year 11/632. See Ziriklī, *Kitāb al-a'lām* (Beirut: Dār al-'ilm li-l-malāyīn, 1986), 3:138.

11 Ayla was a town on the banks of the Red Sea near Shām, or between Shām and Ḥijāz, and it was the town of Jews who transgressed with the Sabbath. See 'Abd al-Mu'min al-Baghdādī, *Marāṣid al-iṭlā' 'alā asmā' al-amkina wa-l-buqā'*. (Beirut: Dār al-ma'rifa, 1953), 1:138.

٩٢. عن أبي الصَّهباء البكري، قال: سَمِعتُ عليّ بن أبي طالب عليه السلام ودعا رأس الجالوت وأسقُف النصارى، فقال: إنّي سائلكما عن أمرٍ، وأنا أعلم به منكما، فلا تكتُماني يا رأس الجالوت بالذي أنزل التوراة على موسى، وأطعمكم المنّ والسلوى، وضرب لكم في البحر طريقًا يَبَسًا، وفجّر لكم من الحَجَر الطُّوري اثنتي عشرة عينًا، لكلّ سِبطٍ من بني إسرائيل عينًا، إلاّ ما أخبرتني على كم افترقت بنو إسرائيل بعد موسى؟ فقال: فِرقة واحدة.

فقال: كَذَبت، والذي لا إله غيره، لقد افترقت على إحدى وسبعين فِرقة كُلّها في النار إلاّ واحدة، فإنّ الله يقول: ﴿وَمِن قَوۡمِ مُوسَىٰٓ أُمَّةٞ يَهۡدُونَ بِٱلۡحَقِّ وَبِهِۦ يَعۡدِلُونَ﴾ فهذه التي تنجو.

٩٣. عن الأصبغ بن نُباتة، عن عليّ بن أبي طالب عليه السلام، قال: كانت مدينة حاضرة البحر، فقالوا لنبيّهم: إن كان صادقًا فليُحوّلنا ربّنا جِرّيثًا، فإذا المدينة في وَسَط البحر قَدْ غَرِقت من الليل، وإذا كلّ رجلٍ منهم مسوداً جِرّيثًا يدخُل الراكب في فيها.

٩٤. عن أبي عبيدة، عن أبي جعفر عليه السلام، قال: وجدنا في كتاب أمير المؤمنين عليه السلام: أنّ قومًا من أهل أَيْلَة من قوم ثَمود، وأنّ الحِيتان كانت سبقت إليهم يوم السبت، لِيَختَبِر الله طاعتهم في ذلك، فشَرَعت لهم يوم سبتهم في ناديهم وقُدّام أبوابهم، في أنهارهم وسواقيهم، فَتَبادروا إليها، فأخذوا يصطادونها ويأكُلونها، فلَبِثوا بذلك ما شاء الله، لا ينهاهم الأحبار ولا ينهاهم العلماء من صَيدها.

would race to them on the Sabbath so that God might test their obedience. So they would surface for them on the Sabbath while they were in their meeting houses in front of their doors, in their rivers and their marketplaces. So they rushed towards them and began to catch them and eat them. They continued to do this for a time that only God knows how long, and neither their rabbis nor their scholars forbade them from fishing.

Then Shayṭān insinuated to a faction from among them, "You have only been prohibited from eating them on the Sabbath, not from catching them." So they would catch them on the Sabbath and eat them on the other days.

One faction from among them said, "Now we can freely catch them." Another faction broke away from them towards the right and said, "God, God! Indeed, we forbid you from eliciting God's consequences if you persist in going against His command." Another faction broke away from them towards the left and remained silent, not admonishing them. This faction which did not admonish them said to the other, ﴾*'Why do you bother preaching to people God will destroy, or at least punish severely?'*﴿

And the faction which had admonished them replied, ﴾*'In order to be free from your Lord's blame, and so that they may perhaps take heed.'*﴿ God said: ﴾*When they ignored* [*the warning*] *they were given*﴿, meaning that when they disregarded what they had been admonished about and persisted in their wrongdoing, the faction that had admonished them said, "No, by God. We cannot have you living amongst us, and we will not let you stay the night in this town of yours in which you have disobeyed God, for fear that He will descend an affliction upon you." So they stayed close to the town and slept under the open sky.

When God's friends, the ones who had obeyed his command, woke up, they went to check on the condition of the disobedient lot. They went to the gate of the town and found it to be silent. So they knocked on it, but received no answer and nor did they hear a whisper from anyone. They proceeded to place a ladder against the town wall, then made a man climb and look over it beyond the town. He looked and there were the people, like apes, screeching. The man said to his companions, "My people! By God, I see something strange!"

They asked, "What can you see?"

He said, "I can see the people as apes, screeching, and they have tails."' He continued, 'Then they broke the gate and entered the town. The apes

ثمّ إنّ الشيطان أوحى إلى طائفةٍ منهم: إنّما نُهيتم عن أكلها يوم السبت، ولم تُنهوا عن صَيدها، فاصطادوا يوم السبت وأكلوها فيما سِوى ذلك من الأيّام.

فقالت طائفة منهم: الآن نَصطادها، وانحازت طائفةٌ منهم ذات اليمين، وقالوا: الله الله، إنّا نَهَيناكم عن عُقُوبة الله أن تَعرِضوا لخِلاف أمره، واعتزلت طائفةٌ منهم ذات اليَسار، فَسَكتت فلم تعِظهم، وقالت الطائفة التي لم تَعِظهم: ﴿لِمَ تَعِظُونَ قَوۡمًا ٱللَّهُ مُهۡلِكُهُمۡ أَوۡ مُعَذِّبُهُمۡ عَذَابٗا شَدِيدٗا﴾.

وقالت الطائفة التي وَعَظتْهُم: ﴿مَعۡذِرَةً إِلَىٰ رَبِّكُمۡ وَلَعَلَّهُمۡ يَتَّقُونَ﴾، قال الله: ﴿فَلَمَّا نَسُواْ مَا ذُكِّرُواْ بِهِۦ﴾ يعني لمّا تَرَكُوا مَا وُعِظُوا به ومَضَوا على الخطيئة، قالت الطائفة الّتي وعظتهم: لا والله، لا نُجامعكم ولا نُبايتكم الليلَ في مدينتكم هذه الّتي عصيتم الله فيها، مخافة أن ينزِل بكم البلاء، فنزلوا قريبًا من المدينة، فباتُوا تحت السماء.

فلمّا أصبح أولياء الله المطيعون لأمر الله، غَدَوا لِيَنظُروا ما حال أهل المعصية، فأتَوا باب المدينة، فإذا هو مُصمَت، فَدقّوه فلم يُجابوا، ولم يَسمَعوا منها حِسّ أحدٍ، فَوَضَعُوا سُلّمًا على سُور المدينة، ثمّ أصعَدوا رجلاً منهم، فأشرف على المدينة فنظر فإذا هو بالقوم قِردةً يتَعاوون، فقال الرجل لأصحابه: يا قوم، أرى والله عَجَبًا. فقالوا: وما ترى؟ قال: أرى القوم قِرَدة يتعاوون، لهم أذناب. قال: فكسروا الباب ودخلوا المدينة. قال: وعرفت القردة أنسابها من الإنس، ولم تعرِف الإنس أنسابها من القِردة، قال: فقال القوم للقِردة: ألم ننهكم؟

recognized their human relatives, but the humans could not recognize them from among the apes.'

He said, 'Then the people said to the apes, "Did we not forbid you?"'

Then the Commander of the Faithful said, 'By the One Who splits the seed and originates people, indeed I know their relatives from this very community. They neither denounce wrongdoing nor are they protective [over those who commit it], rather they have ignored what they have been commanded to do, and have hence become divided in themselves. God has said: ﴾*Away with those evildoing people!*﴿(23:41). And God says: ﴾ *When they ignored [the warning] they were given, We saved those who forbade evil, and punished the wrongdoers severely because of their disobedience.* ﴿' [7:163–166]

95. From 'Alī b. 'Uqba[12], from a man, from Abū 'Abd Allāh عليه السلام who said, 'The Jews were commanded to abstain [from fishing] on Friday, but they disregarded Friday and abstained on Saturday instead.' [7:163]

96. From al-Aṣbagh, from 'Alī عليه السلام who said, 'There were two communities who were transformed from the Children of Israel. The one that took to the sea were [transformed into] catfish, and the one that lived on land were [transformed into] lizards.' [7:163–166]

97. From Hārūn b. 'Ubayd[13] who, without mentioning his source, cited one of them as having said, 'Some people came to the Commander of the Faithful عليه السلام in Kufa and said to him, "O Commander of the Faithful. These catfish are being sold in our markets."

So the Commander of the Faithful عليه السلام laughed and said, "Stand up so I can show you something strange, and do not speak anything but positive about your vicegerent." So they got up and went with him until they came to the seashore. There he spat into it and said a few words, and suddenly there was a catfish lifting its head out of the water with its mouth open. The Commander of the Faithful said to it, "Who are you? Woe unto you and your

12 Abū al-Ḥasan 'Alī b. 'Uqba b. Khālid, a reliable and trustworthy companion of Imam Ja'far al-Ṣādiq. See Ḥillī, *Khulāṣat al-aqwāl*, 189 (nr. 570); Modarressi, *Tradition and Survival*, 193–4 (nr. 37).

13 We were unable to identify this individual.

قال: فقال أمير المؤمنين عليه السلام: والذي فَلَق الحَبّة وبرأ النَّسمَة، إنّي لأعرف أنسابها من هذه الأُمّة، لا يُنكرون ولا يُغيّرون، بل تركوا ما أُمِروا به، وقد قال الله تعالى: ﴿ فَبُعْدًا لِلْقَوْمِ الظَّالِمِينَ ﴾، وقال الله: ﴿ أَنْجَيْنَا الَّذِينَ يَنْهَوْنَ عَنِ السُّوءِ وَأَخَذْنَا الَّذِينَ ظَلَمُوا بِعَذَابٍ بَئِيسٍ بِمَا كَانُوا يَفْسُقُونَ ﴾.

٩٥. عن عليّ بن عُقبة، عن رجلٍ، عن أبي عبد الله عليه السلام، قال: إنّ اليهود أُمِروا بالإمساك يوم الجمعة، فتَركُوا يوم الجمعة، فأمسكوا يوم السبت.

٩٦. عن الأصبغ، عن عليّ عليه السلام، قال: أُمّتان تابعنا من بني إسرائيل: فأمّا التي أخذت البحر فهي الجَراري، وأمّا التي أخذت البرّ فهي الضِباب.

٩٧. عن هارون بن عبيد، رفعه إلى أحدهم عليهم السلام، قال: جاء قومٌ إلى أمير المؤمنين عليه السلام بالكُوفة، وقالوا له: يا أمير المؤمنين، إنّ هذه الجَراري تُباع في أسواقنا؟

قال: فَتَبسّم أمير المؤمنين عليه السلام ضاحكًا، ثمّ قال: قُوموا لأُريكم عَجَبًا، ولا تقولوا في وصيّكم إلاّ خيرًا، فقاموا معه فأتوا شاطئ بحرٍ، فَتَفَل فيه تفلةً، وتَكَلّم بكلماتٍ، فإذا بجِرِّيّة رافعة رأسها، فاتحة فاها، فقال أمير المؤمنين عليه السلام: من أنت؟ الويل لك ولقومك! فقالت: نحن من أهل القرية التي كانت حاضرة البحر، إذ يقول الله في كتابه: ﴿ إِذْ تَأْتِيهِمْ حِيتَانُهُمْ يَوْمَ سَبْتِهِمْ شُرَّعًا ﴾ الآية، فعرض الله علينا ولايتك فقعدنا عنها فمَسَخنا الله، فبعضنا في البرّ، وبعضنا في البحر، فأمّا الذين في البحر فنحن الجَراري، وأمّا الذين في البرّ فالضَّبّ واليَربوع.

community!" So it replied, "We are from the inhabitants of the town which was by the sea, about which God says in His Book: ﴾*how its people broke the Sabbath when their fish surfaced for them only on that day never on weekdays – We tested them in this way: because of their disobedience.*﴿ God suggested to us to adhere to your guardianship (*walāya*) but we desisted from it, so God transformed us. Some of us are on land and some of us are in the sea. As for the ones in the sea, it is us, the catfish; and the ones on land are the lizards and the jerboas."'

He said, 'Then the Commander of the Faithful عليه السلام turned to us and said, "Did you hear what it said?" We said, "Yes, By God." He said, "By the One Who sent Muḥammad with prophethood, they menstruate just like your women do."' [7:163–166]

98. From Ṭalḥa b. Zayd, from Ja'far b. Muḥammad, on his father's authority regarding God's verse: ﴾*And when Our command came*﴿, ﴾*We saved those who forbade evil.*﴿ He said, 'The community was divided into three groups: a group who forbade evil and distanced themselves from it; a group who remained impartial though they did not commit the sins themselves; and a group who committed the sins. So none was saved from chastisement except for those who forbade evil.'

Ja'far عليه السلام said, 'I asked Abū Ja'far عليه السلام, "What happened to those who remained impartial and did not commit the sins?" Abū Ja'far replied, "I heard that they became tiny particles."' [7:165–166]

99. From Isḥāq b. 'Abd al-'Azīz[14], from the first Abū al-Ḥasan [i.e. al-Kāẓim] عليه السلام who said, 'God specifically addresses His servants in two verses of His Book to not deny that which they do not know about, and to not speak about that which they have no knowledge.' Then he read: ﴾*But they deny that which they do not comprehend*﴿(10:39) and: ﴾*Was a pledge not taken from them, written in the Scripture, to say nothing but the truth about God?*﴿' [7:169]

14 Abū al-Safātij Isḥāq b. 'Abd al-'Azīz, a reporter of the fifth and sixth Imams' traditions concerning whom there are mixed opinions among Shī'a *rijāl* authors. See Ḥillī, *Khulāṣat al-aqwāl*, 319 (nr. 1250).

قال: ثمّ التفت أمير المؤمنين عليه السلام إلينا، فقال: أسمِعتم مقالتها؟ قلنا: اللّهُمّ نعم. قال: والذي بعث محمّدًا صلى الله عليه وآله بالنبّوة لتَحيض كما تَحيض نِساؤكم.

٩٨. عن طلحة بن زيد، عن جعفر بن محمّد، عن أبيه عليهما السلام، في قول الله: فلمّا جَاءَ أمرنا ﴿أَنْجَيْنَا الَّذِينَ يَنْهَوْنَ عَنِ السُّوءِ﴾. قال: افترق القوم ثلاث فِرق، فِرقة انتهت واعتزلت، وفِرقة أقامت ولم تُقارف الذَنُوب، وفِرقة اقترفت الذُّنوب، فلم تنجُ من العذاب إلاّ من انتهت.

قال جعفر عليه السلام: قلت لأبي جعفر عليه السلام: ما صنع بالذي أقاموا ولم يُقارفوا الذُّنوب؟ قال أبو جعفر عليه السلام: بلغني أنّهم صاروا ذَرًّا.

٩٩. عن إسحاق بن عبد العزيز، عن أبي الحسن الأوّل عليه السلام، قال: إنّ الله خَصّ عباده بآيتين من كتابه: أن لا يكذبوا بما لا يَعلَمون، أو يقولوا بما لا يَعلمون، وقرأ: ﴿بَلْ كَذَّبُوا بِمَا لَمْ يُحِيطُوا بِعِلْمِهِ﴾، وقال: ﴿أَلَمْ يُؤْخَذْ عَلَيْهِمْ مِيثَاقُ الْكِتَابِ أَنْ لَا يَقُولُوا عَلَى اللَّهِ إِلَّا الْحَقَّ﴾.

100. From Isḥāq: 'Abū 'Abd Allāh عليه السلام said, "God specifically commands humans in two verses in His Book to refrain from speaking about God unless it is with knowledge, and to not reject without knowledge. Was a pledge not taken from them, written in the Scripture, to say nothing but the truth about God? He has said, ﴿*But they deny that which they do not comprehend, and whose explanation has not yet come to them.*﴾(10:39)"' [7:169]

101. From Isḥāq b. 'Ammār, from Abū 'Abd Allāh عليه السلام. He said, 'I asked him, "Can one place his hand on his arm during the prayer?" He replied, "There is no problem with that. When the Children of Israel would enter the state of prayer, they would stand limp and languid as if they were dead, so God revealed to His Prophet صلى الله عليه وآله: 'Hold on to what I have given you with strength, and when you enter the state of prayer, do so with strength and determination.' Then he repeated it for seeking livelihood, so when you seek your livelihood, do so with strength."' [7:171]

102. In a narration of Isḥāq b. 'Ammār, on his authority regarding God's words ﴿*Hold on with strength to what We have given you*﴾: 'Is it a strength in the body or strength in the heart?' He replied, 'In both of them, together.' [7:171]

103. From Muḥammad b. Ḥamza[15], from whoever informed him from Abū 'Abd Allāh عليه السلام regarding God's verse: ﴿*Hold on with strength to what We have given you.*﴾: He said, '[It refers to] the prostration, and to placing the hands on the knees in the prayer.' [7:171]

104. From Rifā'a who said, 'I asked Abū 'Abd Allāh عليه السلام about God's verse: ﴿*[Prophet], when your Lord took out the offspring from the loins of the Children of Ādam* [...]﴾. He said, "God took the proof against all of His creatures on the day of the covenant like this" – and he gripped his hand.' [7:172]

105. From Abū Baṣīr who said, 'I asked Abū 'Abd Allāh عليه السلام: "How did they reply Him whilst they were particles?" He said, "He put in them such a thing whereby when He asked them, they were able to answer Him, meaning regarding the covenant."' [7:172]

---

15 There are multiple individuals with this name in books of Shī'a *rijāl*.

١٠٠. عن إسحاق، قال أبو عبد الله عليه السلام: خَصّ الله الخلق في آيتين من كتاب الله: أن لا يقولوا على الله إلاّ بعلمٍ، ولا يَرُدّوا إلاّ بعلم [قال الله عزّ وجلّ:] ﴿أَلَمْ يُؤْخَذْ عَلَيْهِم مِّيثَاقُ الْكِتَابِ أَن لَّا يَقُولُوا عَلَى اللَّهِ إِلَّا الْحَقَّ﴾، وقال: ﴿بَلْ كَذَّبُوا بِمَا لَمْ يُحِيطُوا بِعِلْمِهِ وَلَمَّا يَأْتِهِمْ تَأْوِيلُهُ﴾.

١٠١. عن إسحاق بن عمّار، عن أبي عبد الله عليه السلام، قال: قلتُ له: أيضَعَ الرجلُ يده على ذِراعه في الصلاة؟ قال: لا بأس إنّ بني إسرائيل كانوا إذا دخلوا في الصلاة دخلوا متماوتين كأنّهم موتى، فأنزل الله على نبيّه صلى الله عليه وآله: خُذ ما آتيتُك بقُوّة، فإذا دخلت الصلاة فادخُل فيها بجَلَدٍ وقُوّة، ثمّ ذكرها في طلب الرزق، فإذا طلبت الرزق فاطلُبه بقُوّة.

١٠٢. وفي رواية إسحاق بن عمّار، عنه عليه السلام، في قول الله: ﴿خُذُوا مَا آتَيْنَاكُم بِقُوَّةٍ﴾ أقوّة في الأبدان، أم قوّة في القلوب؟ قال: فيهما جميعًا.

١٠٣. عن محمّد بن حمزة، عمّن أخبره، عن أبي عبد الله عليه السلام، في قول الله: ﴿خُذُوا مَا آتَيْنَاكُم بِقُوَّةٍ﴾، قال: السُّجود ووضع اليدين على الرُّكبتين في الصلاة.

١٠٤. عن رِفاعة، قال: سألتُ أبا عبد الله عليه السلام عن قول الله تعالى: ﴿وَإِذْ أَخَذَ رَبُّكَ مِن بَنِي آدَمَ مِن ظُهُورِهِمْ ذُرِّيَّتَهُمْ﴾، قال: نعم أخذ الله الحُجّة على جميع خلقه يوم المِيثاق هكذا، وقَبَض يده.

١٠٥. عن أبي بصير، قال: قلتُ لأبي عبد الله عليه السلام: كيف أجابوه وهم ذَرّ؟ قال: جعل فيهم ما إذا سألهم أجابوه، يعني في المِيثاق.

106. From 'Ubayd Allāh al-Ḥalabī, from Abū Ja'far and Abū 'Abd Allāh, peace be upon them both, who said, "Umar went for Hajj the very first year that he was caliph; and the *muhājirūn* (migrants from Mecca) and the *anṣār* (Medinan helpers) also went for Hajj that same year, as did 'Alī along with al-Ḥasan and al-Ḥusayn, peace be upon them both, and 'Abd Allāh b. Ja'far.' He said, 'So when 'Abd Allāh entered into the state of *iḥrām* he wore a loincloth and shawl made of hemp and dyed with hemp clay. Then he came and 'Umar was staring at him while he was reciting the *talbiya*, clad in the loincloth and shawl and walking next to 'Alī عليه السلام.

So 'Umar said from behind them, "What is this innovation in the Holy Sanctuary?"

'Alī عليه السلام turned to him and said, "'Umar, it is not appropriate for anyone to teach us the prophetic practice."

So 'Umar said to him, "You are right, Abū al-Ḥasan. By God, I did not know that you all include them."'

He continued, 'And that was just one incident on that journey of theirs. When they entered Mecca, they circumambulated the House and 'Umar greeted the [Black] Stone with peace, and said, "Indeed, by God, I know that you are a mere stone that can neither harm nor benefit. Were it not for the fact that the Messenger of God ﷺ greeted you, I would not greet you."

So 'Alī عليه السلام said to him, "No need, O Abū Ḥafṣ, do not do it then, for the Messenger of God only greeted it because of a specific feature that he knew. If you were to read the Qur'an and knew what others know of its inner meaning, you too would have known that indeed it can harm as well as benefit. It has two eyes, two lips, and an eloquent tongue that bears witness to whoever fulfils his pledge to it."

So 'Umar said to him, "Then find that for me in God's Book, O Abū al-Ḥasan."

So 'Alī said, "His words, Blessed and most High: ﴿ *When your Lord took out the offspring from the loins of the Children of Ādam and made them bear witness about themselves, He said, 'Am I not your Lord?' and they replied, 'Yes, we bear witness.'* ﴾ When they attested obediently to the fact that He was their Lord and that they were His servants, He took the pledge from them to go for pilgrimage to His Sacred House. Then God created a parchment more delicate than water and said to the Pen: 'Write down My creatures' pledge to My Sacred House.' So the Pen wrote down the pledges of the Children

١٠٦. عن عبيد الله الحلبي، عن أبي جعفر وأبي عبد الله عليما السلام، قالا: حجّ عمر أوّل سنة حجّ وهو خليفة، فحجّ تلك السنة المهاجرون والأنصار، وكان عليّ عليه السلام قد حجّ في تلك السنة بالحسن والحسين عليهم السلام وبعبد الله ابن جعفر. قال: فلمّا أحرم عبدُ الله لَبس إزارًا ورداء مُمَشّقين – مَصبُوغَين بطِين المَشق – ثمّ أتى فنظر إليه عمر وهو يُلبّي وعليه الإزار والرِّداء، وهو يسير إلى جنب عليّ عليه السلام، فقال عمر من خلفتهم: ما هذه البدعة التي في الحَرَم؟

فالتفت إليه عليّ عليه السلام، فقال له: يا عمر، لا ينبغي لأحدٍ أن يُعلّمنا السُّنّة.

فقال عمر: صدقت يا أبا الحسن، لا والله ما علِمتُ أنّكم هم.

قال: فكانت تلك واحدة في سفرتهم تلك، فلمّا دخلوا مكّة طافوا بالبيت، فاستلم عمر الحجَرَ، وقال: أما والله إنّي لأعلم أنك حَجَرٌ لا تَضُرّ ولا تنفع، ولولا أنّ رسول الله صلى الله عليه وآله استلمك ما استلمتك.

فقال عليّ عليه السلام: مه يا أبا حَفص، لا تفعل فإنّ رسول الله صلى الله عليه وآله لم يستلم إلاّ لأمرٍ قد علِمه، ولو قرأتَ القرآن فَعلِمتَ من تأويله ما عَلِم غيرك لعَلمتَ أنّه يَضرّ وينفع، وله عينان وشَفتان ولسان ذَلِق يشهد لمن وافاه بالموافاة. قال: فقال له عمر: فأوجدني ذلك من كتاب الله، يا أبا الحسن.

فقال عليّ عليه السلام: قوله تبارك وتعالى ﴿وَإِذْ أَخَذَ رَبُّكَ مِنْ بَنِي آدَمَ مِنْ ظُهُورِهِمْ ذُرِّيَّتَهُمْ وَأَشْهَدَهُمْ عَلَى أَنْفُسِهِمْ أَلَسْتُ بِرَبِّكُمْ قَالُوا بَلَى شَهِدْنَا﴾ فلمّا أقرّوا بالطاعة بأنه الربّ وهم العباد، أخذ عليهم المِيثاق بالحجّ إلى بيته الحرام، ثمّ خلق الله رَقًّا

of Ādam on the parchment. Then the Stone was told to open its mouth, so it opened it and swallowed up the parchment. Then He said to the Stone, 'Guard it and bear witness to the pledge of My servants.' So the Stone descended in obedience to God. O 'Umar, is it not the case that when we greet the Stone, we say: 'This is my trust that I am fulfilling and my covenant that I had pledged, so that you may bear witness that I have fulfilled it'?'"

So 'Umar replied, "Yes, by God."

So 'Alī عليه السلام said to him, "Well that is where it comes from."' [7:172]

107. From al-Ḥalabī who said, 'I asked him why He has designated the greeting of the Stone? He replied, "When God took the covenant from the Children of Ādam, He called the Stone from the Garden and commanded it to swallow the covenant. So it bears witness for whoever fulfils it faithfully."' [7:172]

108. From Ṣāliḥ b. Sahl, from Abū 'Abd Allāh عليه السلام who said, 'One of the Quraysh asked the Messenger of God صلى الله عليه وآله: "What did you precede the rest of the prophets in if you were sent after them and as the seal to them all?" He replied, "Indeed I was the first one to attest to my Lord, and the first one to respond when God took the pledge from the prophets and made them bear witness over their own souls asking: 'Am I not your Lord?' And they said, 'Yes, of course.' Well, I was the first one to say, 'Yes, of course' and I preceded them in attesting to God."' [7:172]

109. From Zurāra who said, 'I asked Abū 'Abd Allāh عليه السلام about God's verse: ﴿ *When your Lord took out the offspring from the loins of the Children of Ādam and made them bear witness about themselves, He said, 'Am I not your Lord?' and they replied, 'Yes, we bear witness.'* ﴾ He said, "Muḥammad, peace be upon him and his family, was the first one to say: 'Yes, of course.'" I asked, "Was it a physical witnessing?" He replied, "Yes, and that recognition was established in their hearts and they forgot that covenant, but they will remember it afterwards. Were it not for that no one would ever know who his Creator is nor who sustains him."' [7:172]

110. From Zurāra, that a man asked Abū 'Abd Allāh عليه السلام about God's verse ﴿ *When your Lord took out the offspring from the loins of the Children of Ādam* [...] ﴾: He said, within earshot of his father, 'My father narrated to me that God,

أرقّ من الماء، وقال للقلم: اكْتُب موافاة خلقي ببيتي الحرام، فكتب القلم موافاة بني آدم في الرقّ، ثمّ قيل للحَجَر: افتح فاك، ففتحته فالقمه الرَّقّ، ثمّ قال للحَجَر: احفظ واشهد لعبادي بالموافاة، فهَبَط الحَجَر مُطيعًا لله. يا عمر، أو ليس إذا استلمت الحَجَر قلت: أمانتي أدّيتها، ومِيثاقي تعاهدته، لتشهد لي بالموافاة؟

فقال عمر: اللّهمّ نعم.

فقال له عليّ عليه السلام: من ذلك.

١٠٧. عن الحلبي، قال: سألتهُ عليه السلام لِمَ جُعِل استلام الحجر؟ قال: إنَّ الله حيث أخذ المِيثاق من بني آدم، دعا الحَجَر من الجنَّة، وأمره والتقم المِيثاق، فهو يَشهَد لمن وافاه بالوفاء.

١٠٨. عن صالح بن سهل، عن أبي عبدالله عليه السلام، قال: إنَّ بعض قُريش قال لرسول الله صلى الله عليه وآله: بأيّ شيءٍ سبقت الأنبياء وأنت بُعِثت آخرهم وخاتمهم؟ فقال: إنّي كنتُ أوّل من أقرّ بربّي، وأوّل من أجاب حيث أخذ الله ميثاق النبيّين وأشهدهم على أنفسهم: ألست بربّكم؟ قالوا: بلى، فكنتُ أوّل من قال: بلى، فسبقتهم إلى الإقرار بالله.

١٠٩. عن زُرارة، قال: سألتُ أبا عبدالله عليه السلام عن قول الله تعالى: ﴿وَإِذْ أَخَذَ رَبُّكَ مِنۢ بَنِيٓ ءَادَمَ مِن ظُهُورِهِمْ﴾ إلى: ﴿قَالُوا بَلَىٰ﴾، قال: كان محمّد عليه وآله السلام أوّل من قال: بلى.

قلت: كانت رُؤية مُعاينة؟ قال: أثبت المعرفة في قُلُوبهم، وأنسَوا ذلك المِيثاق، وسَيَذكُرونه بعد، ولولا ذلك لم يدرِ أحدٌ مَن خالقه، ولا مَن يَرزُقه.

most High, took a handful of the same earth that He created Ādam from and poured some sweet freshwater on it. Then he left it for forty mornings. Then He poured some briny seawater onto it and left it for forty mornings. When the clay had fermented, He – Blessed and most High – took it and kneaded it thoroughly. Then – this is as he narrated it – He opened His Palms and they all emerged like tiny ants from His Right and His Left. So He commanded them all to plunge into the Fire. The people of the right went in and it cooled down and became safe for them, but the people of the left refused to go into it.' [7:172]

111. From Abū Baṣīr, from Abū 'Abd Allāh عليه السلام regarding God's verse: ﴿*'Am I not your Lord?'*﴾ – 'Did they reply verbally?' He said, 'Yes, and they also said it with their hearts.' I asked, 'So how exactly were they able to do that on that day?' He replied, 'He made them into whatever was necessary for that.' [7:172]

112. From Zurāra who said, 'I asked Abū Ja'far عليه السلام about God's verse ﴿*[Prophet], when your Lord took out the offspring from the loins of the Children of Ādam and made them bear witness about themselves.*﴾ He replied, "God took out from Ādam's loins all his offspring until the Day of Judgement, so they all came out in a particle-like state. He introduced Himself and showed Himself to them; and were it not for that, not a single person would know his Lord. This is as per His statement: ﴿*If you ask them who created the heavens and earth, they are sure to say, 'God.'*﴾(31:25)"' [7:172]

113. From Zurāra, from Abū Ja'far عليه السلام. He said, 'I asked him about the verse ﴿*[Prophet], when your Lord took out the offspring from the loins of the Children of Ādam and made them bear witness about themselves, He said, 'Am I not your Lord?' and they replied, 'Yes, we bear witness.'*﴾' He continued, 'So he said, "That inner cognizance [of God] was established but they have forgotten the incident [though they will remember it]. Were it not for that, not a single person would know who his Creator is nor who his Sustainer is."' [7:172]

١١٠. عن زُرارة: أنَّ رجلاً سأل أبا عبدالله عليه السلام عن قول الله: ﴿وَإِذْ أَخَذَ رَبُّكَ مِنْ بَنِي آدَمَ مِنْ ظُهُورِهِمْ ذُرِّيَّتَهُمْ﴾. فقال عليه السلام – وأبوه يسمع –: حدَّثني أبي أنّ الله تعالى قَبَض قَبضةً من تُراب التُّربة التي خَلَق منها آدم عليه السلام، فصَبّ عليها الماء العَذب الفُرات، فتَرَكها أربعين صباحًا، ثمّ صَبّ عليها الماء المالح الأُجاج، فتركها أربعين صباحًا، فلمّا اختمرت الطِّينة أخذها تبارك وتعالى فَعَركها عَركًا شديدًا، ثمّ هكذا – حكى بسط كفّيه – فخرجوا كالذرّ من يمينه وشماله، فأمرهم جميعًا أن يَقعُوا في النار، فدخل أصحاب اليمين، فصارت عليهم بَردًا وسَلامًا، وأبى أصحاب الشمال أن يَدخُلوها.

١١١. عن أبي بصير، عن أبي عبدالله عليه السلام، في قول الله تبارك وتعالى: ﴿أَلَسْتُ بِرَبِّكُمْ قَالُوا بَلَى﴾ قالوا بألسنتهم؟ قال: نعم، وقالوا بقلوبهم. فقلت: وأيّ شيّء كانوا يومئذٍ؟ قال: صنع منهم ما اكتفى به.

١١٢. عن زُرارة، قال: سألتُ أبا جعفر عليه السلام عن قول الله: ﴿وَإِذْ أَخَذَ رَبُّكَ مِنْ بَنِي آدَمَ﴾ إلى ﴿أَنْفُسِهِمْ﴾. قال: أخرج الله من ظهر آدم ذُرّيته إلى يوم القيامة،فخرجوا كالذّرّ، فعَرفهم نفسه، وأراهم نفسه، ولولا ذلك ما عَرَف أحدٌ ربّه، وذلك قوله: ﴿وَلَئِنْ سَأَلْتَهُمْ مَنْ خَلَقَ السَّمَاوَاتِ وَالْأَرْضَ لَيَقُولُنَّ اللَّهُ﴾.

١١٣. عن زُرارة، عن أبي جعفر عليه السلام، قال: قلت له: ﴿وَإِذْ أَخَذَ رَبُّكَ مِنْ بَنِي آدَمَ﴾ إلى ﴿شَهِدْنَا﴾، قال: ثمّ قال: ثبتت المعرفة، ونَسَوا الموقف وسَيَذكُرونه، ولولا ذلك لم يَدرِ أحدٌ مَن خالِقه، ولا مَن رازقه.

114. From Jābir who said, 'I asked Abū Jaʿfar عليه السلام: "When was the Commander of the Faithful given the appellation of the Commander of the Faithful?" He replied, "By God, this verse came down to Muḥammad صلى الله عليه وآله: ﴾***and made them bear witness about themselves, He said, 'Am I not your Lord, and is Muḥammad, the Messenger of God, not your prophet, and is ʿAlī not the Commander of the Faithful?'***﴿ So by God, God Himself called Him 'the Commander of the Faithful."' [7:172*]

115. From Jābir who said, 'Abū Jaʿfar عليه السلام said to me, "Jābir, if the ignorant people were to know when the Commander of the Faithful ʿAlī was called thus, they would not deny his right."' He said, 'I asked, "May I be your ransom – when was he called that?" He said to me, "His verse: ﴾*[Prophet], when your Lord took out the offspring from the loins of the Children of Ādam and made them bear witness about themselves, He said, 'Am I not your Lord,* ***and is Muḥammad, the Messenger of God, not your prophet, and is ʿAlī not the Commander of the Faithful?'***﴿' He said, 'He then said to me, "Jābir, by God, this is exactly as Muḥammad صلى الله عليه وآله brought it."' [7:172]

116. From Ibn Muskān, from one of his associates, from Abū Jaʿfar عليه السلام who said, 'The Messenger of God صلى الله عليه وآله said, "My community was shown to me during the covenant. The first to believe in me was ʿAlī, and he was the first to have faith in me when my mission started, and he is the most uprightly honest (*al-ṣiddīq*) and the distinguisher (*al-fārūq*) who separates truth from falsehood."' [7:172]

117. From al-Aṣbagh b. Nubāta, from ʿAlī عليه السلام. He said, 'Ibn al-Kawwāʾ came to him and said, "O Commander of the Faithful, tell us about whether God, Blessed and most High, has ever spoken to any human before Mūsā?"

So ʿAlī said, "God spoke to all His creatures, both good and bad, and they even replied Him."

Ibn al-Kawwāʾ was taken aback by this and did not know about it, so he asked him, "How was that, Commander of the Faithful?"

So he said to him, "Do we not read God's Book when he says to His Prophet: ﴾*When your Lord took out the offspring from the loins of the Children of Ādam and made them bear witness about themselves, He said, 'Am I not your Lord?' and they replied, 'Yes, we bear witness.'*﴿ So He made them hear

١١٤. عن جابر، قال: قلتُ لأبي جعفر عليه السلام: من سمّى أمير المؤمنين أمير المؤمنين؟ قال: قال: والله نزلت هذه الآية على محمّد صلى الله عليه وآله: ﴿وَأَشْهَدَهُمْ عَلَىٰٓ أَنفُسِهِمْ أَلَسْتُ بِرَبِّكُمْ﴾ وأنّ محمّدًا رسول الله، وأنّ عليًّا أمير المؤمنين، فسمّاه الله — والله — أمير المؤمنين.

١١٥. عن جابر، قال: قال لي أبو جعفر عليه السلام: يا جابر، لو يعلم الجُهّال متى سُمّي أمير المؤمنين عليّ عليه السلام لم يُنكِروا حقَّه. قال: قلتُ: جُعِلت فِداك، متى سمّي؟ فقال لي: قوله: ﴿وَإِذْ أَخَذَ رَبُّكَ مِنۢ بَنِىٓ ءَادَمَ﴾ إلى ﴿أَلَسْتُ بِرَبِّكُمْ﴾ وأنّ محمداً رَسُول الله، وأنّ عليًّا أمير المؤمنين. قال: ثمّ قال لي: يا جابر، هكذا والله جاء بها محمّد صلى الله عليه وآله.

١١٦. عن ابن مُسكان، عن بعض أصحابه، عن أبي جعفر عليه السلام، قال: قال رسول الله صلى الله عليه وآله: إنَّ أمّتي عُرِضت عليّ في المِيثاق، فكان أوّل من آمن بي عليّ، وهو أوّل من صَدّقني حين بُعِثتُ، وهو الصِّدّيق الأكبر، والفاروق يَفرُق بين الحقّ والباطل.

١١٧. عن الأصبغ بن نُباتة، عن عليّ عليه السلام قال: أتاه ابن الكوّاء، فقال: يا أمير المؤمنين، أخبِرني عن الله تبارك وتعالى، هل كَلَّم أحدًا من ولد آدم قبل موسى عليه السلام؟

فقال عليّ عليه السلام: قد كلَّم الله جميع خَلقه بَرّهم وفاجِرهم، ورَدُّوا عليه الجَواب، فثَقُل ذلك على ابن الكوّاء ولم يَعرِفه.

فقال له: كيف كان ذلك يا أمير المؤمنين؟

فقال له: أو ما تقرأ كتاب الله إذ يقول لنبيّه صلى الله عليه وآله: ﴿وَإِذْ أَخَذَ رَبُّكَ مِنۢ بَنِىٓ ءَادَمَ مِن ظُهُورِهِمْ ذُرِّيَّتَهُمْ وَأَشْهَدَهُمْ عَلَىٰٓ أَنفُسِهِمْ أَلَسْتُ بِرَبِّكُمْ قَالُوا بَلَىٰ﴾؟ فقد

His speech and they replied to Him too, as you can hear in God's statement: ﴾*and they replied, 'Yes.'*﴿. He said to them: 'Indeed, I am God. There is no god but Me, the most Beneficent, most Merciful.' So they professed obedience to Him and to His Lordship. He singled out the messengers, prophets and successors, and commanded the creatures to obey them, and they pledged to do so in the covenant. When they attested to all that, the angels said, "We have borne witness over you, O Children of Ādam, lest you say on the Day of Judgement: 'Indeed we were oblivious of this.'"' [7:172]

118. Abū Baṣīr said, 'I said to Abū 'Abd Allāh عليه السلام, "Tell me about the particles when He made them bear witness about themselves, saying: 'Am I not your Lord?' and they replied: 'Yes.' Some of them concealed contrary to what they manifested, however." I continued, "How did they know what speech was when they were asked: 'Am I not your Lord?'" He replied, "God placed in them that which enabled them to respond to Him when they were asked."' [7:172]

119. From Sulaymān al-Labbān (the milkman) who said, 'Abū Ja'far عليه السلام said, "Do you know what the similitude of al-Mughīra b. Sa'īd is?" I replied, "No." He said, "It is as the similitude of Bal'am who was given the Greatest Name, regarding which God says ﴾*the man to whom We gave Our messages: he sloughed them off, so Satan took him as his follower and he became one of the perverse.*﴿"' [7:175]

120. From Muḥammad b. Abī Zayd al-Rāzī[16], from whoever mentioned it from al-Riḍā عليه السلام who said, 'When a hardship befalls you, use us to seek out God's aid, and this is God's statement: ﴾*The Most Excellent Names belong to God: use them to call on Him.*﴿ Abū 'Abd Allāh said, "By God, we are the Most Excellent Names, which will not be accepted from anyone save when accompanied with acknowledgement of us."' He said, 'So use them to call on Him.' [7:180]

16 Muḥammad b. Abī Zayd al-Rāzī, a companion of the ninth and tenth Imams about whom there is scant information. See Khū'ī, *Mu'jam* 15:255 (nr. 10010).

أسمعهم كلامه وردّوا عليه الجَواب، كما تسمع في قول الله يا بن الكوّاء: ﴿ قَالُوا بَلَى ﴾، فقال لهم: إنّي أنا الله لا إله إلاّ أنا، وأنا الرّحمن، فأقرّوا له بالطاعة والرُّبوبية، وميّز الرُّسل والأنبياء والأوصياء، وأمر الخَلق بطاعتهم، فأقرّوا بذلك في المِيثاق، فقالت الملائكة عند إقرارهم بذلك: شَهِدنا عليكم يا بني آدم أن تَقُولوا يوم القيامة: إنّا كُنّا عن هذا غافلين.

١١٨. قال أبو بصير: قلتُ لأبي عبدالله ﷺ: أخبرني عن الذَرّ حيث أشهدهم على أنفسهم ألست بربّكم؟ قالوا: بلى؛ وأسرّ بعضهم خلاف ما أظهر. قلت: كيف عَلِموا القول حيث قيل لهم: ألست بربّكم؟ قال: إنّ الله جعل فيهم ما إذا سألهم أجابوه.

١١٩. عن سليمان اللبّان، قال: قال أبو جعفر ﷺ: أتدري ما مَثَل المغيرة ابن سعيد؟ قال: قلت: لا. قال: مَثَله مَثَل بَلعم الذي أُوتي الاسم الأعظم الذي قال الله تعالى: ﴿ آتَيْنَاهُ آيَاتِنَا فَانسَلَخَ مِنْهَا فَأَتْبَعَهُ الشَّيْطَانُ فَكَانَ مِنَ الْغَاوِينَ ﴾.

١٢٠. عن محمّد بن أبي زيد الرازي، عمَّن ذكره عن الرضا ﷺ، قال: إذا نزلت بكم شِدّة، فاستعينوا بنا على الله، وهو قول الله تعالى: ﴿ وَلِلَّهِ الْأَسْمَاءُ الْحُسْنَى فَادْعُوهُ بِهَا ﴾، قال: قال أبو عبدالله ﷺ: نحن والله الأسماء الحسنى الذي لا يُقبَل من أحدٍ بمعرفتنا، قال: فادعوه بها.

121. From Ḥumrān from Abū Ja'far ﵇ who said regarding God's verse ﴾*Among those We created are a group of people who guide with truth and act justly according to it*﴿: 'They are the Imams.' [7:181]

122. Muḥammad b. 'Ajalān also said on his authority, 'We are those [people].' [7:181]

123. From Abū al-Ṣahbā' al-Bakrī who said, 'I heard the Commander of the Faithful ﵇ say, "By the One Who holds my life in His Hand, this community will most certainly split into seventy-three groups, and every one of those will end up in the Fire except for one. ﴾*Among those We created are a group of people who guide with truth and act justly according to it.*﴿ So this is the one that will be saved from this community."' [7:181]

124. From Ya'qūb b. Zayd[17] who said, 'The Commander of the Faithful ﵇ said, ﴾*Among those We created are a group of people who guide with truth and act justly according to it.*﴿ He said, "This refers to Muḥammad 's community."' [7:181]

125. From Khalaf b. Ḥammād[18], from a man, from Abū 'Abd Allāh ﵇ who said, 'God says in His Book: ﴾*if I had knowledge of what is hidden, I would have abundant good things and no harm could touch me*﴿, meaning poverty.' [7:188]

126. From Zurāra, from Abū Ja'far ﵇. He said, 'I heard him say, ﴾*and yet when He gives them a good child they ascribe partners to Him in what He had granted them*﴿ – This was Ādam and Ḥawwā', but their ascription of anything to God did not occur in their worship but rather in their obedience."'

Another narration says: 'It was not an ascription of partnership to God in His worship.' [7:190]

---

17 We were unable to identify this individual.

18 Khalaf b. Ḥammād b. Nāshir b. al-Musayyab, generally regarded a reliable transmitter of the narrations of the sixth and seventh Imams. See Ḥillī, *Khulāṣat al-aqwāl*, 139 (nr. 381).

١٢١. عن حمران، عن أبي جعفر ﷺ، في قول الله تعالى: ﴿وَمِمَّنْ خَلَقْنَا أُمَّةٌ يَهْدُونَ بِالْحَقِّ وَبِهِ يَعْدِلُونَ﴾، قال: هم الأئمّة.

١٢٢. وقال محمّد بن عجلان، عنه ﷺ: نحن هم.

١٢٣. عن أبي الصهباء البكري، قال: سَمِعتُ أمير المؤمنين ﷺ يقول: والذي نفسي بيده، لتُفرّقنّ هذه الأمّة على ثلاث وسبعين فرقة، كلُّها في النّار إلاّ فِرقة واحدة ﴿وَمِمَّنْ خَلَقْنَا أُمَّةٌ يَهْدُونَ بِالْحَقِّ وَبِهِ يَعْدِلُونَ﴾ فهذه التي تنجو من الأمّة.

١٢٤. عن يعقوب بن زيد، قال: قال أمير المؤمنين ﷺ: ﴿وَمِمَّنْ خَلَقْنَا أُمَّةٌ يَهْدُونَ بِالْحَقِّ وَبِهِ يَعْدِلُونَ﴾، قال: يعني أمّة محمّد ﷺ.

١٢٥. عن خلف بن حمّاد، عن رجل، عن أبي عبد الله ﷺ، قال: إنّ الله يقول في كتابه: ﴿وَلَوْ كُنْتُ أَعْلَمُ الْغَيْبَ لَاسْتَكْثَرْتُ مِنَ الْخَيْرِ وَمَا مَسَّنِيَ السُّوءُ﴾ يعني الفقر.

١٢٦. عن زُرارة، عن أبي جعفر ﷺ، قال سَمِعتُه يقول: ﴿فَلَمَّا آتَاهُمَا صَالِحًا جَعَلَا لَهُ شُرَكَاءَ فِيمَا آتَاهُمَا﴾، قال: هو آدم وحوّاء، إنّما كان شِركهما شِرك طاعة، وليس شِرك عبادة.

وفي رواية أخرى: ولم يكن شِرك عبادة.

127. From al-Ḥasan b. ʿAlī b. al-Nuʿmān, on his father's authority, from whoever heard Abū ʿAbd Allāh عليه السلام say, 'God trained His Messenger صلى الله عليه وآله saying, "O Muḥammad, ﴾*Adopt* [*a policy of*] *excusing* [*people*], *bid what is right and turn away from those who are ignorant.*﴿"' He said, 'Accept from them at face value, and what has been simplified; and a policy of moderate tolerance.' [7:199]

128. From ʿAbd al-Aʿlā, from Abū ʿAbd Allāh عليه السلام: ﴾*Adopt* [*a policy of*] *excusing* [*people*], *bid what is right*﴿ – he said: 'Through guardianship ﴾*and turn away from those who are ignorant*﴿ [of it], meaning the guardianship.' [7:199]

129. From Zayd b. Abī Usāma, from Abū ʿAbd Allāh عليه السلام. He said, 'I asked him about God's verse: ﴾*When those who are God-wary are touched by an insinuation from Satan, they remember* [*God*] *and immediately they can see* [*straight*].﴿ He said, "It is when the servant thinks of committing a sin but he remembers [God] and abandons it."' [7:201]

130. From ʿAlī b. Abī Ḥamza, from Abū ʿAbd Allāh عليه السلام. He said, 'I asked him about God's verse: ﴾*When those who are God-wary are touched by an insinuation from Satan, they remember* [*God*] *and immediately they can see* [*straight*]﴿ – what is that insinuation?' So he replied, 'It is the misdeed that the servant intends to commit, but then he remembers God and can perceive, and so he desists.' [7:201]

131. Abū Baṣīr, on his authority that he said, 'It is the man who intends to commit a sin but then remembers and abandons it.' [7:201]

132. From Zurāra, 'Abū Jaʿfar عليه السلام said, ﴾*When the Qurʾān is recited*﴿ in the obligatory prayer behind the imam ﴾*pay attention and listen quietly so that you may be given mercy.*﴿' [7:204]

133. From Zurāra who said, 'I heard Abū ʿAbd Allāh عليه السلام say, "It is obligatory to listen quietly to the Qurʾan, both during the prayer as well as other times; and when the Qurʾan is recited you must pay attention and listen quietly."' [7:204]

١٢٧. عن الحسن بن عليّ بن النعمان، عن أبيه، عمّن سَمِع أبا عبدالله عليه السلام وهو يقول: إنّ الله أدّب رسوله صلى الله عليه وآله فقال: يا محمّد ﴿خُذِ الْعَفْوَ وَأْمُرْ بِالْعُرْفِ وَأَعْرِضْ عَنِ الْجَاهِلِينَ﴾ قال: خُذ منهم ما ظَهَر وما تيسّر، والعَفو: الوَسط.

١٢٨. عن عبد الأعلى، عن أبي عبدالله عليه السلام، في قول الله تعالى: ﴿خُذِ الْعَفْوَ وَأْمُرْ بِالْعُرْفِ﴾، قال: بالولاية ﴿وَأَعْرِضْ عَنِ الْجَاهِلِينَ﴾، قال: عنها يعني الولاية.

١٢٩. عن زيد أبي أُسامة، عن أبي عبدالله عليه السلام، قال: سألتُه عن قول الله: ﴿إِنَّ الَّذِينَ اتَّقَوْا إِذَا مَسَّهُمْ طَائِفٌ مِنَ الشَّيْطَانِ تَذَكَّرُوا فَإِذَا هُمْ مُبْصِرُونَ﴾، قال: هو الذّنب يَهُمّ به العبد فيَتَذكّر فيَدَعُه.

١٣٠. عن عليّ بن أبي حمزة، عن أبي عبدالله عليه السلام، قال: سألتُه عن قول الله: ﴿إِنَّ الَّذِينَ اتَّقَوْا إِذَا مَسَّهُمْ طَائِفٌ مِنَ الشَّيْطَانِ تَذَكَّرُوا فَإِذَا هُمْ مُبْصِرُونَ﴾ ما ذلك الطائف؟ فقال: هو السيّئ يهُمّ العبد به، ثمّ يذكُر الله فيُبصِر ويُقصِر.

١٣١. أبو بصير، عنه عليه السلام، قال: هو الرجُل يَهُمّ بالذنب ثمّ يَتَذكّر فيدَعه.

١٣٢. عن زُرارة قال: قال أبو جعفر عليه السلام: ﴿وَإِذَا قُرِئَ الْقُرْآنُ﴾ في الفريضة خَلف الإمام ﴿فَاسْتَمِعُوا لَهُ وَأَنْصِتُوا لَعَلَّكُمْ تُرْحَمُونَ﴾.

١٣٣. عن زُرارة، قال: سَمِعتُ أبا عبدالله عليه السلام، يقول: يجب الإنصات للقرآن في الصلاة وفي غيرها، وإذا قُرِئ عندك القرآن وجب عليك الإنصات والاستماع.

134. From Abū Kahmas, from Abū ʿAbd Allāh عليه السلام who said, ʿIbn al-Kawwāʾ recited the following behind the Commander of the Faithful عليه السلام: ﴿*If you ascribe any partner to God, all your work will come to nothing: you will be one of the losers.*﴾(39:65) So the Commander of the Faithful listened to him quietly.ʾ [7:204]

135. From Zurāra, from one of the two [al-Bāqir or al-Ṣādiq] who said, ʻThe angel can only write down that which he hears himself; and God says: ﴿*remember your Lord inwardly, in all humility and awe.*﴾ʾ He said, ʻHe does not know the reward for that remembrance within the servant's soul due to its great esteem with God.ʾ He also said, ʻWhen you are praying behind an imam and he is continuing the recitation, listen quietly and glorify [God] inwardly.ʾ [7:205]

136. From Ibrāhīm b. ʿAbd al-Ḥamīd who, without mentioning his source, said, ʻThe Messenger of God ﷺ said, ʻ﴿*Remember your Lord inwardly*﴾ meaning abasedly, ﴿*in all humility and awe*﴾ meaning in fear of His chastisement, ﴿*without raising your voice*﴾ meaning without using a loud voice in the recitation, ﴿*in the mornings and in the evenings*﴾ meaning during the day as well as in the evening.ʾ [7:205]

137. From al-Ḥusayn b. al-Mukhtār[19], from Abū ʿAbd Allāh عليه السلام who said with regard to God's verse: ﴿*Remember your Lord inwardly, in all humility and awe, without raising your voice, in the mornings and in the evenings*﴾, ʻIn the evening, say: "There is not god but God, He alone and without a partner. To Him belongs the kingdom and to Him belongs all Praise. He gives life and causes to die, [and He causes to die and revives], and He has power over all things."ʾ

I asked, ʻWhat about: ﴿*all good in His Hand*﴾?ʾ He replied, ʻOf course all good is in His Hand, but say exactly as I say it, ten times. "And I seek refuge in God, the all-Hearing, the Omniscient, from the goading of the devils, and I seek refuge in you, my Lord, lest they should come near me. Indeed,

19 Abū ʿAbd Allāh al-Ḥusayn b. al-Mukhtār al-Qalānisī, a Wāqifī companion of Imam Mūsā al-Kāẓim. See Ḥillī, *Khulāṣat al-aqwāl*, 337–8 (nr. 1332); Modarressi, *Tradition and Survival*, 277 (nr. 97).

١٣٤. عن أبي كَهْمَس، عن أبي عبدالله عليه السلام، قال: قرأ ابن الكوّاء خلف أمير المؤمنين عليه السلام: ﴿لَئِنْ أَشْرَكْتَ لَيَحْبَطَنَّ عَمَلُكَ وَلَتَكُونَنَّ مِنَ الْخَاسِرِينَ﴾ فأنصت له أمير المؤمنين.

١٣٥. عن زُرارة، عن أحدهما عليهما السلام، قال: لا يكتُبُ المَلَكُ إلاّ ما أسمع نفسه، وقال الله: ﴿وَاذْكُرْ رَبَّكَ فِي نَفْسِكَ تَضَرُّعًا وَخِيفَةً﴾ قال: لا يَعلَمُ ثواب ذلك الذِّكر في نفس العبد لعظمته إلاّ الله، وقال: إذا كُنتَ خلف إمام تأتمّ به، فأنصِت وسبّح في نفسك.

١٣٦. عن إبراهيم بن عبد الحميد، يرفعه، قال: قال رسول الله صلى الله عليه وآله: ﴿وَاذْكُرْ رَبَّكَ فِي نَفْسِكَ تَضَرُّعًا﴾ يعني مستكينًا ﴿وَخِيفَةً﴾ يعني خوفًا من عذابه ﴿وَدُونَ الْجَهْرِ مِنَ الْقَوْلِ﴾ يعني دون الجهر من القراءة ﴿بِالْغُدُوِّ وَالْآصَالِ﴾ يعني بالغداة والعشي.

١٣٧. عن الحسين بن المختار، عن أبي عبدالله عليه السلام، في قول الله تعالى: ﴿وَاذْكُرْ رَبَّكَ فِي نَفْسِكَ تَضَرُّعًا وَخِيفَةً وَدُونَ الْجَهْرِ مِنَ الْقَوْلِ بِالْغُدُوِّ وَالْآصَالِ﴾. قال: تقول عند المساء: «لا إله إلا الله، وحده لا شريك له، له الملك وله الحمد، يُحيي ويميت، ويميت ويحيي، وهو على كل شيء قدير».

قلت: ﴿بِيَدِهِ الْخَيْرُ﴾؟ قال: إنّ بيده الخير، ولكن قل كما أقول لك عشر مرّات» «وأعوذ بالله السميع العليم من همزات الشياطين، وأعوذ بك ربّ أن يحضرون، إنّ الله هو السميع العليم» عشر مرّات حين تطلع الشمس، وعشر مرّات حين تغرب.

God is the all-Hearing, the Omniscient" – ten times at sunrise and ten times at sunset.' [7:205]

138. From Muḥammad b. Marwān, from one of his associates who said, 'Ja'far b. Muḥammad عليه السلام said, "Seek refuge in God, the all-Hearing, the Omniscient, from the outcast Shayṭān, and I seek refuge in God lest they should come near me – indeed God is the all-Hearing, the Omniscient. And say: 'There is no god but God, He alone and without a partner. To Him belongs the kingdom and to Him belongs all Praise. He gives life and causes to die, [and He causes to die and revives], and He has power over all things.'

So a man asked him, "Is this obligatory?" He replied, "Yes, it is obligatory, and defined. Say it before sunrise and before sunset ten times. If you fail to do it for some reason, then make up for it by saying it in the night and during the day instead."' [7:205–206]

١٣٨. عن محمّد بن مروان، عن بعض أصحابه، قال: قال جعفر بن محمّد عليه السلام: «أستعيذ بالله السميع العليم من الشيطان الرجيم، وأعوذ بالله أن يحضرون، أنّ الله هو السميع العليم» وقل: «لا إله إلا الله، وحده لا شريك له، له الملك وله الحمد، يحيي ويميت، ويميت ويحيي، وهو على كل شيء قدير».

فقال له رجلٌ: مفروض هو؟ قال: نعم مفروض، هو محدود، تقوله قبل طلوع الشمس وقبل الغروب عشر مرّات، فإن فاتك شيء منها فاقْضه من الليل والنهار.

The Battle Gains

8. The Battle Gains[1]

1. From Abū Baṣīr, from Abū ʿAbd Allāh عليه السلام. He said, 'I heard him say, "Hypocrisy will never infect one who recites the Chapter of the Impunity (*sūrat al-barāʿa*) and the Chapter of the Battle Gains (*sūrat al-anfāl*) every month, and he will be among the followers (*shīʿa*) of the Commander of the Faithful عليه السلام in truth. On the Day of Judgement, he will be eating from the feasts of the Garden with his followers until people finish giving their account."'

2. In another narration on his authority: "Every month, hypocrisy will never infect him, and he will be among the followers of the Commander of the Faithful عليه السلام in truth."

3. From Muḥammad b. Muslim who said, 'I heard Abū Jaʿfar عليه السلام say, "In the Chapter of the Battle Gains is the cutting off of noses."'

4. From Ḥarīz, from Abū ʿAbd Allāh عليه السلام. He said, 'I asked him (or he was asked) about the battle gains, so he said, "Any village whose inhabitants had been annihilated or displaced from it, whereupon it became war booty, half of it would be divided among the people and the other half was for the Messenger."' [8:1]

---

1 Throughout this section there are three different words that feature in the *ḥadīth*s about battle gains: namely *anfāl*, *ghanīma*, and *fay'*. Although they are sometimes used interchangeably, *anfāl* and *fay'* are usually taken to denote property that has been confiscated without fighting or violence, i.e. through raids of abandoned villages or when the enemy would surrender without military action; whereas *ghanīma* refers specifically to the booty or spoils gained during or after the battle from the enemy camp.

بسم الله الرحمن الرحيم

من سورة الأنفال

١. عن أبي بصير، عن أبي عبد الله عليه السلام، قال: سمعته يقول: من قرأ سورة براءة والأنفال في كلّ شهر، لم يدخُله نفاق أبدًا، وكان من شيعة أمير المؤمنين عليه السلام حقًّا، وأكل يوم القيامة من موائد الجنّة مع شيعته حتى يفرغ الناس من الحساب.

٢. وفي رواية أخرى عنه: ... في كلّ شهر، لم يدخله نفاق أبدًا، وكان من شيعة أمير المؤمنين عليه السلام حقًّا.

٣. عن محمّد بن مسلم، قال: سمعتُ أبا جعفر عليه السلام يقول: في سورة الأنفال جدع الأنوف.

٤. عن حريز، عن أبي عبد الله عليه السلام، قال: سألتُه — أو سُئِل — عن الأنفال، فقال: كلّ قرية يُهلك أهلها، أو يجلُون عنها، فهي نفل، نصفُها يُقسّم بين الناس، ونصفها للرسول.

5. From Zurāra, from Abū Jaʿfar ﷷ who said, 'The battle gains are those places that have not been raided by horses or riders [i.e. uncharted territory].' [8:1]

6. From ʿAbd Allāh b. Sinān, from Abū ʿAbd Allāh ﷷ. He said, 'I asked him about the battle gains. He said, "These are the villages that have been deserted by their inhabitants who have perished, and have consequently become dilapidated, so they belong to God and the Messenger."' [8:1]

7. From Muḥammad b. Muslim, from Abū Jaʿfar ﷷ. He said, 'I heard him say, "The booty and the battle gains are those that are taken from a land in which there has been no bloodshed, nor that in which good people reside, nor people who have signed treaties. It also includes those that are captured from desolate places and the depths of the valleys. This all constitutes booty and belongs to God and the Messenger. And whatever belongs to God belongs to His Messenger, and He places it at his disposal; and it belongs to the Imam after the Messenger."' [8:1]

8. From Bashīr al-Dahhān [the tanner] who said, 'I heard Abū ʿAbd Allāh ﷷ say, "God has obligated our obedience in His Book, so people cannot allow themselves to remain ignorant of us. The surplus from the profits is due unto us, the battle gains belong to us, and to us refer the contexts of the Qur'an."' [8:1]

9. From Abū Ibrāhīm who said, 'I asked him about the battle gains, so he said, "Whichever place has been abandoned by its inhabitants – those are the battle gains and they belong to us."' [8:1]

10. From Abū Usāma Zayd, from Abū ʿAbd Allāh ﷷ. He said, 'I asked him about the battle gains so he said, "It is any dilapidated place and any place that has not been trampled on by horses and camels."'

Another narration on his authority adds: "The Messenger of God ﷺ has authority over it." [8:1]

11. From Abū Baṣīr who said, 'I heard Abū Jaʿfar ﷷ say, "The battle gains belong to us." I asked, 'And what are the battle gains?' He replied, 'They

٥. عن زرارة، عن أبي جعفر عليه السلام، قال: الأنفال ما لم يُوجَف عليه بِخيلٍ ولا ركاب.

٦. عن عبدالله بن سنان، عن أبي عبدالله عليه السلام، قال: سألتُه عن الأنفال: قال: هي القُرى التي قد جلا أهلُها وهلكوا فخرِبت، فهي لله وللرسول.

٧. عن محمّد بن مسلم، عن أبي جعفر عليه السلام، قال سمعتُه يقول: إنّ الفيء والأنفال: ماكان من أرضٍ لم يكن فيها هِراقة دم، أو قوم صالَحُوا، أو قوم أعطُوا بأيديهم، وماكان من أرض خَرِبةٍ أو بُطون الأودية، فهذا كلّه من الفيء، فهذا لله وللرسول، فماكان لله فهو لرسوله يضعه حيث يشاء، وهو للإمام من بعد الرسول.

٨. عن بشير الدهان، قال: سمعتُ أبا عبدالله عليه السلام يقول: إنّ الله فرض طاعتنا في كتابه، فلا يسع النّاس جهلُنا، لنا صفو المال، ولنا الأنفال، ولنا قرائن القرآن.

٩. عن أبي إبراهيم عليه السلام، قال: سألتُه عن الأنفال؟ فقال: ماكان من أرضٍ باد أهلها، فذلك الأنفال، فهو لنا.

١٠. عن أبي أسامة زيد، عن أبي عبدالله عليه السلام، قال: سألته عن الأنفال، فقال: هو كلّ أرضٍ خَرِبةٍ، وكلّ أرض لم يُوجف عليها بخيلٍ ولا ركاب. وزاد في رواية أخرى عنه: عليها رسول الله صلى الله عليه وآله وسلم.

١١. عن أبي بصير، قال: سمعتُ أبا جعفر عليه السلام: يقول: لنا الأنفال.

include the mines and the thickets, any piece of land that has no proprietor, and any whose inhabitants have deserted it; so it belongs to us.'' [8:1]

12. In another narration from one of the two [al-Bāqir or al-Ṣādiq] from Abān b. Taghlib from Abū ʿAbd Allāh عليه السلام who said, 'Whoever dies leaving behind neither protégé nor heir is referred to by this verse: ﴾ *They ask you* [*Prophet*] *about* [*distributing*] *the battle gains. Say, 'The battle gains belong to God and His Messenger.'* ﴿' [8:1]

13. In a narration by Ibn Sinān, he said, 'This refers to the village that has become dilapidated, its inhabitants having deserted it and perished, and it belongs to God and the Messenger.' [8:1]

14. In a narration by Ibn Sinān and Muḥammad al-Ḥalabī, on his authority عليه السلام he said, 'Whoever dies without leaving a next of kin, then whatever belonged to him is considered part of the *anfāl*.' [8:1]

15. In a narration by Zurāra on his authority, that he said, 'Any place that has been deserted by its inhabitants without having been attacked by horses, foot soldiers or riders is considered battle gains for God and the Messenger.' [8:1]

16. From al-Thumālī, from Abū Jaʿfar عليه السلام. He said, 'I heard him talking about the kings that persecute people [confiscating their chattel], that these are part of war booty, battle gains and the like.' [8:1]

17. In another narration from al-Thumālī. He said, 'I asked Abū Jaʿfar عليه السلام about God's verse: ﴾ *They ask you* [*Prophet*] *about* [*distributing*] *the battle gains.* ﴿' He said, "Whatever belonged to the kings now belongs to the Imam."' [8:1]

قلتُ: وما الأنفال؟ قال: منها المعادن والآجام، وكلّ أرضٍ لا ربّ لها، وكلّ أرضٍ باد أهلُها، فهو لنا.

١٢. وفي رواية أخرى، عن أحدهما، عن أبان بن تغلب، عن أبي عبد الله عليه السلام، قال: كلّ من مات لا مولى له ولا وَرَثة، فهو من أهل هذه الآية: ﴿يَسْأَلُونَكَ عَنِ الأَنْفَالِ قُلِ الأَنْفَالُ لِلَّهِ وَالرَّسُولِ﴾.

١٣. وفي رواية ابن سنان، قال عليه السلام: هي القرية التي قد جلا أهلُها وهلَكوا فخَرِبت، فهي لله وللرسول.

١٤. وفي رواية ابن سنان ومحمّد الحلبي عنه عليه السلام، قال: من مات وليس له مولى، فماله من الأنفال.

١٥. وفي رواية زُرارة عنه عليه السلام، قال: هي كلّ أرضٍ جلا أهلُها من غير أن يحمِل عليها بخيلٍ ولا رِجال ولا ركاب، فهي نفل لله وللرسول.

١٦. عن الثمالي، عن أبي جعفر عليه السلام، قال: سمعتُه يقول في الملوك الذين يقطعون الناس: هي من الفَيء والأنفال وأشباه ذلك.

١٧. وفي رواية أخرى، عن الثمالي، قال سألتُ أبا جعفر عليه السلام عن قول الله تعالى: ﴿يَسْأَلُونَكَ عَنِ الأَنْفَالِ﴾، قال: ما كان للملوك فهو للإمام.

18. From Samā'a b. Mihrān. He said, 'I asked him about the battle gains. He said, "Any desolate place and things that used to belong to kings. That is specifically for the Imam and people have no share in that." He said, "And also among these are islands that have not been trampled by horses or camels [i.e. uncharted territory]."' [8:1]

19. From Bashīr al-Dahhān who said, 'We were at Abū 'Abd Allāh's house once when it was full of people, and he said to us, "You love us, but they despise us. You maintain relations with us whilst they cut us off. You acquaint yourselves with us whilst they reject [us], and this is the truth. God adopted Muḥammad as a servant before he took him as a messenger, just as 'Alī was a servant who sincerely advised for the sake of God, so God made him an advisor, and he loved God, so God loved him; and love for us is evident in God's Book. The surplus of the profits is due unto us; the battle gains belong to us, and we are the people whose obedience God has made incumbent. However, you follow someone whom even the people can find no excuse for his ignorance, whilst the Messenger of God ﷺ had said, 'Whoever dies without following an Imam, then his death is one of pagan ignorance.' So obedience is incumbent upon you for surely you have seen 'Alī's companions."' [8:1]

20. From al-Thumālī, from Abū Ja'far عليه السلام about: ﴾*They ask you* [*Prophet*] *about* [*distributing*] *the battle gains.*﴿ He said, 'Whatever belonged to the kings now belongs to the Imam.'

I said, 'But they distribute away whatever they own to their children, their women, their relatives and noblemen, to the extent that even eunuchs have been mentioned [as their recipients].'

Then I did not say anything further about that until he said, 'He is given anything between a single dirham and one hundred and one thousand dirhams.' Then he said, ﴾*This is our giving, so bestow or withhold without account.*﴿(38:39). [8:1]

١٨. عن سماعة بن مهران، قال: سألتُه عن الأنفال؟ قال: كلّ أرضٍ خرِبة، وأشياء كانت تكون للملوك، فذلك خالص للإمام، ليس للنّاس فيه سهم، قال: ومنها (البحرين) لم يوجف [عليها] بخيلٍ ولا ركاب.

١٩. عن بشير الدهّان، قال: كنّا عند أبي عبد الله عليه السلام والبيت غاصّ بأهله، فقال لنا: أحبَبتم وأبغَض الناس، ووصلتُم وقطَع الناس، وعرفَتم وأنكر الناس، وهو الحق، وإنّ الله اتّخذ محمّدًا عبدًا قبل أن يتّخذه رسولاً، وأنّ عليًّا عبدٌ نصح لله فنصحه، وأحبّ الله فأحبّه، وحقّنا بيّن في كتاب الله، لنا صفو المال، ولنا الأنفال، ونحن قوم فرَض الله طاعتنا، وإنّكم لتأتمّون بمن لا يُعذَر الناسُ بجهالته، وقد قال رسول الله صلّى الله عليه وآله: «من مات وليس له إمام يأتمّ به، فميتته جاهلية»، فعليكم بالطاعة، فقد رأيتم أصحاب عليّ عليه السلام.

٢٠. عن الثّمالي، عن أبي جعفر عليه السلام ﴿يَسْأَلُونَكَ عَنِ الْأَنفَالِ﴾، قال: ما كان للملوك فهو للإمام.

قلتُ: فإنّهم يُقطِعون ما في أيديهم أولادهم ونساءهم وذوي قرابتهم وأشرافهم حتّى بلغ ذكر من الخِصيان، فجعلت لا أقول في ذلك شيئًا إلاّ قال: وذلك، حتّى قال: يُعطى منه ما بين الدرهم إلى المائة والألف، ثمّ قال: ﴿هَٰذَا عَطَاؤُنَا فَامْنُنْ أَوْ أَمْسِكْ بِغَيْرِ حِسَابٍ﴾.

21. From Dāwūd b. Farqad who said, 'I said to Abū ʿAbd Allāh عليه السلام, "We have heard that the Messenger of God صلى الله عليه وآله assigned all that the Euphrates irrigated to ʿAlī عليه السلام?" He replied, "Yes. And what is it that the Euphrates irrigated? Most of what the Euphrates irrigated was battle gains." I asked, "What are the battle gains?" He replied, "The depths of the valleys, the mountains tops, the thickets, the mines, any uncharted territory that has not been trampled by horses or riders, any barren land whose inhabitants have deserted it, and the chattel usurped by the kings."' [8:1]

22. From Abū Maryam al-Anṣārī who said, 'I asked Abū ʿAbd Allāh عليه السلام about His verse: ﴿*They ask you* [*Prophet*] *about* [*distributing*] *the battle gains. Say, 'The battle gains belong to God and His Messenger.'*﴾ He replied, "One share belongs to God and one to the Messenger."'

He said, 'I asked him, "So who does God's share go to?" He replied, "To the Muslims."' [8:1]

23. From Muḥammad b. Yaḥyā al-Khathʿamī, from Abū ʿAbd Allāh عليه السلام who said regarding His verse: ﴿*Remember how God promised you* [*believers*] *that one of the two enemy groups would fall to you: you wanted the unarmed group to be yours* [...]﴾, 'The armed group would be the one fighting.' [8:7]

24. From Jābir who said, 'I asked Abū Jaʿfar عليه السلام about the exegesis of this verse of God's: ﴿*but God desires to confirm the Truth with His words, and to root out the disbelievers.*﴾ Abū Jaʿfar عليه السلام said, "Its exegesis in its inward meaning is that ﴿*God desires*﴾ means there is something He desires but that He has not done it yet. As for His words ﴿*to confirm the Truth with His words*﴾, it means for him to confirm the truth of Muḥammad's household. And His statement ﴿*with His words*﴾ refers to ʿAlī; he is God's words as regards the inward.

As for His statement ﴿*and to root out the disbelievers*﴾, they are the Banū Umayya. They are the disbelievers whom God will root out. His words ﴿*to prove the Truth to be true*﴾ mean to confirm the truth of Muḥammad's Household when the Qāʾim عليه السلام rises; and His words ﴿*and* [*to prove*] *the false*﴾, to be ﴿*false*﴾ means that when the Qāʾim rises he will prove the falsehood of the Banū Ummaya, and that is [the meaning of] His statement:

٢١ . عن داود بن فرقد، قال: قلتُ لأبي عبدالله عليه السلام: بلغَنا أنّ رسول الله صلى الله عليه وآله أقطع عليًّا عليه السلام ما سقى الفرات؟ قال: بطون الأودية ورؤوس الجبال والآجام والمَعادن، وكلّ أرضٍ لم يُوجف عليها بخيلٍ ولا ركاب، وكلّ أرضٍ مَيتةٍ قد جلا أهلها، وقطائع المُلوك.

٢٢ . عن أبي مريم الأنصاري، قال: سألتُ أبا عبدالله عليه السلام عن قوله: ﴿يَسْأَلُونَكَ عَنِ الأَنْفَالِ قُلِ الأَنْفَالُ لِلَّهِ وَالرَّسُولِ﴾، قال: سهمٌ لله، وسهمٌ للرسول.

قال: قلت: فلمن سهم الله؟ فقال: للمسلمين.

٢٣ . عن محمّد بن يحيى الخثعمي، عن أبي عبدالله عليه السلام، في قوله تعالى: ﴿وَإِذْ يَعِدُكُمُ اللَّهُ إِحْدَى الطَّائِفَتَيْنِ أَنَّهَا لَكُمْ وَتَوَدُّونَ أَنَّ غَيْرَ ذَاتِ الشَّوْكَةِ تَكُونُ لَكُمْ﴾، فقال عليه السلام: الشوكة التي فيها القِتال.

٢٤ . عن جابر، قال: سألتُ أبا جعفر عليه السلام عن تفسير هذه الآية في قول الله: ﴿وَيُرِيدُ اللَّهُ أَنْ يُحِقَّ الْحَقَّ بِكَلِمَاتِهِ وَيَقْطَعَ دَابِرَ الْكَافِرِينَ﴾. قال أبو جعفر عليه السلام: تفسيرها في الباطن يريد الله، فإنه شيء يريده ولم يفعله بعد، وأمّا قوله: ﴿يُحِقَّ الْحَقَّ بِكَلِمَاتِهِ﴾ فإنه يعني يحقّ حقّ آل محمّد، وأما قوله: ﴿بِكَلِمَاتِهِ﴾ قال: كلماته في الباطن عليّ، هو كلمة الله في الباطن.

وأما قوله: ﴿وَيَقْطَعَ دَابِرَ الْكَافِرِينَ﴾ فهم بنو أميّة، هم الكافرون، يقطع الله دابرهم، وأما قوله: ﴿لِيُحِقَّ الْحَقَّ﴾ فإنه يعني لِيُحقّ حقّ آل محمّد حين يقوم القائم عليه السلام، وأمّا قوله:

﴾*to prove the Truth to be true, and the false to be false, much as the guilty might dislike it.*﴿"' [8:7–8]

25. From Jābir, from Abū 'Abd Allāh, Ja'far b. Muḥammad عليه السلام. He said, 'I asked him about the inner meaning of this verse: ﴾*and sent down water from the sky to cleanse you, to remove Satan's pollution from you, to make your hearts strong and your feet firm.*﴿ He replied, "The inner meaning of the sky is the Messenger of God, the water is 'Alī عليه السلام – God designated 'Alī through the Messenger of God صلى الله عليه وآله, so that is [the meaning of] His statement: ﴾*water from the sky to cleanse you*﴿, that being 'Alī, through whom God cleanses the heart of whoever adheres to him. As for His words ﴾*to remove Satan's pollution from you*﴿, whoever adheres to 'Alī, he removes filth away from him and strengthens his heart, and ﴾*make your hearts strong and your feet firm*﴿, and indeed, it refers to 'Alī. Whoever adheres to 'Alī's guardianship, God strengthens his heart through 'Alī and makes his feet firm on his guardianship."' [8:11]

26. From Muḥammad b. Yūsuf who said, 'My father informed me saying, "I asked Abū Ja'far عليه السلام about: ﴾*Your Lord revealed to the angels: 'I am with you.'*﴿ He replied, 'Inspiration.'"' [8:12]

27. From a man, from Abū 'Abd Allāh عليه السلام who said regarding God's verse ﴾*to remove Satan's pollution from you*﴿: 'The doubt that enters into people does not enter us.' [8:11]

28. From Abū Baṣīr, from Abū 'Abd Allāh عليه السلام on his father's authority, on his grandfather's authority, on his forefathers' authority who said, 'The Commander of the Faithful عليه السلام said, "Drink the water from the sky as it cleanses the body and repels illnesses. God says: ﴾*and sent down water from the sky to cleanse you, to remove Satan's pollution from you, to make your hearts strong and your feet firm.*﴿"' [8:11]

﴿وَيُبْطِلَ الْبَاطِلَ﴾ يعني القائم، فإذا قام بطل باطِل بني أميّة، وذلك ﴿لِيُحِقَّ الْحَقَّ وَيُبْطِلَ الْبَاطِلَ وَلَوْ كَرِهَ الْمُجْرِمُونَ﴾.

٢٥. عن جابر، عن أبي عبدالله جعفر بن محمّد عليه السلام، قال: سألتُه عن هذه الآية في البطن ﴿وَيُنَزِّلُ عَلَيْكُمْ مِنَ السَّمَاءِ مَاءً لِيُطَهِّرَكُمْ بِهِ وَيُذْهِبَ عَنْكُمْ رِجْزَ الشَّيْطَانِ وَلِيَرْبِطَ عَلَى قُلُوبِكُمْ وَيُثَبِّتَ بِهِ الْأَقْدَامَ﴾. قال: السماء في الباطن رسول الله صلى الله عليه وآله، والماء عليّ عليه السلام، جعل الله عليًّا عليه السلام من رسول الله صلى الله عليه وآله. فذلك قوله: ﴿مَاءً لِيُطَهِّرَكُمْ بِهِ﴾ فذلك عليّ يطهّر الله به قلب من والاه، وأمّا قوله: ﴿وَيُذْهِبَ عَنْكُمْ رِجْزَ الشَّيْطَانِ﴾ مَن والى عليًّا عليه السلام يُذهِب الرّجز عنه، ويُقوّي قلبه و ﴿وَلِيَرْبِطَ عَلَى قُلُوبِكُمْ وَيُثَبِّتَ بِهِ الْأَقْدَامَ﴾ فإنّه يعني عليًّا عليه السلام، مَن والى عليًّا تربط الله على قلبه بعليّ، فيثبت على ولايته.

٢٦. عن محمّد بن يوسف، قال: أخبرني أبي، قال: سألتُ أبا جعفر عليه السلام فقلتُ: ﴿إِذْ يُوحِي رَبُّكَ إِلَى الْمَلَائِكَةِ أَنِّي مَعَكُمْ﴾ قال: إلهام.

٢٧. عن رجل، عن أبي عبدالله عليه السلام، في قول الله: ﴿وَيُذْهِبَ عَنْكُمْ رِجْزَ الشَّيْطَانِ﴾، قال: لا يدخُلنا ما يدخُل الناس من الشكّ.

29. From Zurāra, from one of the two [al-Bāqir or al-Ṣādiq]. He said, 'I asked: Was al-Zubayr present at the [Battle of] Badr?' He replied, "Yes, but he fled on the day of [the Battle of] the Camel, for if he had fought the believers, then he would have surely perished by fighting them; and if he had fought the disbelievers then he has already incurred God's wrath for previously turning his back on them."' [8:15]

30. From Abū Jaʿfar عليه السلام: 'What was the matter with the Commander of the Faithful that he did not fight in the face of all that was perpetrated against him?' So he replied, 'Due to that which God already knew would happen to the Commander of the Faithful عليه السلام in that he would fight whilst having no more than three bands of men with him; so could he fight? Have you not heard the words of God, Mighty and Exalted: ﴾*Believers, when you meet the disbelievers in battle, never turn your backs on them* [...] until *a wretched destination!*﴿? so how could the Commander of the Faithful fight after that? On that day, there were indeed no more than three bands of believers with him.' [8:15]

31. From Abū Usāma Zayd al-Shaḥḥām who said, 'I said to Abū al-Ḥasan عليه السلام, "May I be your ransom – they are asking what prevented ʿAlī from standing up for his right if the right was indeed his?" He replied, "God has not tasked anyone with this save His Prophet ﷺ. He said to him: ﴾*So [Prophet] fight in God's way. You are accountable only for yourself*﴿(4:84), whereas to others He said: ﴾*unless maneuvering to fight or to join a fighting group*﴿, so ʿAlī did not find such a group, and if he had found one he would have fought." Then he said, "Were Jaʿfar and Ḥamza alive, not even two men would have remained."' He said, '﴾*unless maneuvering to fight or to join a fighting group*﴿ – he said, 'He pushes them back incessantly, wishing to charge against them, or ﴾*to join [a fighting group]*﴿ meaning to join his companions later without experiencing any defeat. So whoever flees in such a manner and allows his companions to go forward [to fight], then he has indeed incurred God's wrath.' [8:16]

٢٨. عن أبي بصير، عن أبي عبد الله عليه السلام، عن أبيه، عن جدّه، عن آبائه، قال: قال أمير المؤمنين عليه السلام: اشربوا ماء السماء، فإنّه يُطهّر البدن، ويدفع الأسقام، قال الله تعالى: ﴿وَيُنَزِّلُ عَلَيْكُمْ مِنَ السَّمَاءِ مَاءً لِيُطَهِّرَكُمْ بِهِ﴾ إلى قوله ﴿وَيُثَبِّتَ بِهِ الْأَقْدَامَ﴾.

٢٩. عن زرارة، عن أحدهما عليه السلام، قال: قلتُ: الزبير شهد بدرًا؟ قال: نعم، ولكنّه فرّ يوم الجمل، فإن كان قاتل المؤمنين فقد هلَك بقتاله إيّاهم، وإن كان قاتل كُفّارًا فقد باء بغضبٍ من الله حين ولاّهم دُبره.

٣٠. عن أبي جعفر عليه السلام ما شأن أمير المؤمنين عليه السلام حين رَكِب منه ما رَكِب لم يُقاتِل؟ فقال: الذي سبق في علم الله أن يكون، ما كان لأمير المؤمنين عليه السلام أن يُقاتِل وليس معه إلاّ ثلاثة رهطٍ، فكيف يُقاتِل؟ ألم تسمعْ قول الله جلّ وعزّ: ﴿يَا أَيُّهَا الَّذِينَ آمَنُوا إِذَا لَقِيتُمُ الَّذِينَ كَفَرُوا زَحْفًا﴾ إلى ﴿وَبِئْسَ الْمَصِيرُ﴾، فكيف يُقاتِل أمير المؤمنين بعد هذا؟ وإنّما هو يومئذٍ ليس معه مؤمنٌ غير ثلاثة رَهط.

٣١. عن أبي أسامة زيد الشحّام، قال: قلتُ لأبي الحسن عليه السلام: جُعِلت فِداك، إنّهم يقولون: ما منع عليًّا إن كان له حقّ أن يقوم بحقّه؟ فقال: إنّ الله لم يُكلّف هذا أحدًا إلاّ نبيّه عليه وآله السلام، قال: ﴿فَقَاتِلْ فِي سَبِيلِ اللَّهِ لَا تُكَلَّفُ إِلَّا نَفْسَكَ﴾، وقال لغيره: ﴿إِلَّا مُتَحَرِّفًا لِقِتَالٍ أَوْ مُتَحَيِّزًا إِلَى فِئَةٍ﴾ فعليّ عليه السلام لم يجد فئةً، ولو وجد فئةً لقاتل.

32. From Muḥammad b. Kulayb al-Asadī, on his father's authority who said, 'I asked Abū ʿAbd Allāh عليه السلام about God's statement ﴾*and when you* [*Prophet*] *threw* [*sand at them*] *it was not your throw* [*that defeated them*] *but God's*﴿: He replied, "Alī عليه السلام handed the Messenger of God صلى الله عليه وآله the handful [of sand] that he threw.' [8:17]

33. In another narration on his authority, "Alī gave him the handful of sand, so he used that to throw.' [8:17]

34. From ʿAmr b. Abī al-Miqdām, from ʿAlī b. al-Ḥusayn عليه السلام who said, "Alī b. Abī Ṭālib, may God honour him, handed the Messenger of God صلى الله عليه وآله a handful of sand which he threw in the faces of the polytheists, so God said: ﴾*and when you* [*Prophet*] *threw* [*sand at them*] *it was not your throw* [*that defeated them*] *but God's.*﴿' [8:17]

35. From Ḥamza b. al-Ṭayyār[2], from Abū ʿAbd Allāh عليه السلام about God's statement: ﴾*God intervenes between a man and his heart.*﴿ He said, 'It is for someone to desire something with his hearing, his sight, his tongue and his hand, but when he comes face to face with the object of his desire, no sooner does he approach it than his heart is repulsed and does not allow him to approach it, knowing that what it contains is not right.' [8:24]

36. In a narration of Hishām's on his authority, that he said, 'He intervenes between him and between his acknowledgement of falsehood as the truth.' [8:24]

37. From Ḥamza b. al-Ṭayyār, from Abū ʿAbd Allāh عليه السلام [about]: ﴾*Know that God intervenes between a man and his heart.*﴿ He said, 'It is for someone to desire something with his hearing, his sight, his tongue and his hand, but no sooner does he comes face to face with any part of it than he does not approach it without his heart being repulsed by it, even though he used to

2 Ḥamza b. al-Ṭayyār, on whom there are differing accounts, was a narrator of the seventh Imam's traditions. There is some disagreement about whether Ḥamza ever met Imam Jaʿfar al-Ṣādiq and if, therefore, he was ever praised by him as reported in some traditions. See Ḥillī, *Khulāṣat al-aqwāl*, 120 (nr. 305 and fn. 1).

ثمّ قال: لو كان جعفر وحمزة حيّين، إنّما بقي رجلان؛ قال مُتطرّدًا يريد الكرّة عليهم، أو متحيّزًا — يعني متأخّرًا — إلى أصحابه من غير هزيمةٍ، فمن انهزم حتّى يجوز صفّ أصحابه، فقد باء بِغضبٍ من الله.

٣٢. عن محمّد بن كليب الأسدي، عن أبيه، قال: سألتُ أبا عبد الله عليه السلام عن قول الله: ﴿وَمَا رَمَيْتَ إِذْ رَمَيْتَ وَلَكِنَّ اللَّهَ رَمَى﴾، قال عليّ عليه السلام ناول رسول الله صلى الله عليه وآله القَبضة التي رمى بها.

٣٣. وفي خبر آخر، عنه: أنّ عليًّا عليه السلام ناوله قبضةً من تُرابٍ، فرمى بها.

٣٤. عن عمرو بن أبي المقدام، عن عليّ بن الحسين عليه السلام قال: ناول رسول الله صلى الله عليه وآله عليّ بن أبي طالب كرّم الله وجهه القبضةَ من التُّراب الّتي رمى بها في وجوه المُشركين، فقال الله: ﴿وَمَا رَمَيْتَ إِذْ رَمَيْتَ وَلَكِنَّ اللَّهَ رَمَى﴾.

٣٥. عن حمزة بن الطيّار، عن أبي عبد الله عليه السلام، في قول الله: ﴿يَحُولُ بَيْنَ الْمَرْءِ وَقَلْبِهِ﴾. قال: هو أن يشتهي الشيء بسمعه وببصره ولسانه ويده، أمّا إن هو غشي شيئًا مما يشتهي، فإنّه لا يأتيه إلاّ وقلبه مُنكِرٌ، لا يقبل الذي يأتي، يعرف أن الحقّ ليس فيه.

٣٦. وفي خبر هشام، عنه عليه السلام، قال: يَحُول بينه وبين أن يعلم أنّ الباطل حقّ.

desire it. He does not accept it, knowing that that is not where the truth lies.' [8:24]

38. From Jābir, from Abū Jaʿfar عليه السلام who said, 'Whatever man desires with his heart, his hearing and his sight whereby his soul does not yearn for anything else besides that, then indeed that thing has intervened between himself and his heart.' [8:24]

39. In Yūnus b. ʿAbd al-Raḥmān's narration from Abū ʿAbd Allāh عليه السلام he said, 'The heart can never be convinced that the truth is false, and nor can it ever be convinced that falsehood is true.' [8:24]

40. From ʿAbd al-Raḥmān b. Sālim, on his authority عليه السلام that he said regarding His verse ﴾*Beware of discord that does not exclusively harm the wrongdoers among you*﴿: 'After God took His Prophet up unto Himself, the people were afflicted with such discord that they abandoned ʿAlī and swore allegiance to someone else. This is the discord that they were afflicted with whilst the Messenger of God عليه السلام had previously commanded them to follow ʿAlī and the successors from Muḥammad's Household, peace be upon them.' [8:25]

41. From Ismāʿīl al-Suddī, from al-Bahī: ﴾*Beware of discord that does not exclusively harm the wrongdoers among you.*﴿ He said, 'I was informed that they are the people [who instigated the Battle] of the Camel.' [8:25]

42. From Zurāra, Ḥumrān and Muḥammad b. Muslim, from one of the two [al-Bāqir or al-Ṣādiq] that the Quraysh gathered together, and members of each clan came out. Then they set off for Dār al-Nadwa to consult each other on what they should do about the Messenger of God, peace be upon him and his family. There they found an old man standing by the door, so they approached it to enter and he said, 'Let me come in with you.'

They asked, 'Who are you, old man?'

He replied, 'I am an elder from the tribe of Banū Muḍarr, and I have an opinion that I would like to express to you.'

So they entered, sat down and started discussing while he too sat with them. They decided all together that they would expel him [i.e. Muḥammad ﷺ].

٣٧. عن حمزة بن الطيّار، عن أبي عبد الله عليه السلام ﴿وَاعْلَمُوا أَنَّ اللَّهَ يَحُولُ بَيْنَ الْمَرْءِ وَقَلْبِهِ﴾. قال: هو أن يشتهي الشيء بسمعه وبصره ولسانه ويده، أمّا إنّه لا يغشى شيئًا منها، وإن كان يشتهيه، فإنّه لا يأتيه إلاّ وقلبه مُنكِر، لا يقبل الذي يأتي، يعرِف أنّ الحقّ ليس فيه.

٣٨. عن جابر، عن أبي جعفر عليه السلام، قال: هذا الشيء يشتهيه الرجل بقلبه وسمعه وبصره، لا تَتوقُ نفسه إلى غير ذلك، فقد حِيل بينه وبين قلبه إلى ذلك الشيء.

٣٩. وفي خبر يونس بن عمّار عن أبي عبد الله عليه السلام قال لا يستيقن القلب أنّ الحقّ باطلٌ أبدًا، ولا يستيقن أنّ الباطل حقّ أبدًا.

٤٠. عن عبد الرحمن بن سالم، عنه عليه السلام، في قوله تعالى: ﴿وَاتَّقُوا فِتْنَةً لَا تُصِيبَنَّ الَّذِينَ ظَلَمُوا مِنْكُمْ خَاصَّةً﴾. قال: أصابت الناسُ فتنةٌ بعد ما قَبَض الله نبيّه صلى الله عليه وآله وسلم حتّى تركوا عليًّا عليه السلام وبايعوا غيره، وهي الفتنة التي فُتِنوا بها، وقد أمرهم رسول الله صلى الله عليه وآله وسلم باتّباع عليّ والأوصياء من آل محمّد صلى الله عليه وآله وسلم.

٤١. عن إسماعيل السُّدّي، عن البَهيّ ﴿وَاتَّقُوا فِتْنَةً لَا تُصِيبَنَّ الَّذِينَ ظَلَمُوا مِنْكُمْ خَاصَّةً﴾ قال: أُخبِرت أنّهم أصحاب الجمل.

٤٢. عن زُرارة ومحمّد بن مسلم، عن أحدهما عليه السلام: أنّ قريشًا اجتمعت فخرج من كُلّ بطن أُناس، ثمّ انطلقوا إلى دار النَّدوة لِيتشاوروا فيما يصنعون برسول الله عليه وآله السلام، فإذا هم بشيخٍ قائمٍ على الباب، فإذا ذهبوا إليه ليدخلوا قال: أدخلوني معكم. قالوا: ومن أنت،

He said, 'This is not an idea in your favour, for if you expel him he can attract more people to fight against you.'

So they said, 'You are right. This is not a good idea.' Then they discussed again and decided to imprison him.

He said, 'This is not the solution. If you do that, [remember that] Muḥammad is a soft-spoken man; he has already corrupted your children and your servants against you, and what will any of you gain by having your brother, your son and your wife leave you?' Then they discussed further and concluded that they would kill him, and that a swordsman from each clan would come out and strike him with their swords all together by the Ka'ba.

Then he recited the verse: ﴾*Remember* [*Prophet*] *when the disbelievers plotted to take you captive, kill, or expel you. They schemed and so did God: He is the best of schemers.*﴿' [8:30]

43. From Zurāra and Ḥumrān, from Abū Ja'far عليه السلام and Abū 'Abd Allāh عليه السلام about His statement: ﴾*And God is the best of schemers.*﴿ He said, 'The Messenger of God used to face enormous hardship from his people, such that they even came to him one day when he was in prostration and threw sheep entrails on him. So his daughter came up to him while he was still prostrating and had not yet lifted his head up. She removed them from him and wiped him clean. Thereafter, God showed him something that he loved; he was at Badr whilst [previously] he had had no more than a single horseman with him, then on the Day of the Conquest [of Mecca] there were twelve thousand of them, causing Abū Sufyān and the polytheists to appeal to him for aid. Then the Commander of the Faithful faced hardship, tribulation, and rallying against him whilst he had no one of his calibre to help him – Ḥamza had been killed on the day of Uḥud, and Ja'far had been killed on the day of the Battle of the Trench.' [8:30]

يا شيخ؟ قال: أنا شيخٌ من مُضَر، ولي رأيٌ أُشير به عليكم. فدخلوا وجلسُوا وتشاوروا وهو جالسٌ، وأجمعوا أمرهم على أن يُخرِجوه، فقال: ليس هذا لكم برأيٍ، إن أخرجتموه أجلب عليكم الناس فقاتلوكم، قالوا: صدّقتَ ما هذا برأي.

ثمّ تشاوروا، فأجمعوا أمرهم على أن يُوثِقوه، قال: هذا ليس بالرأي، إن فعلتُم هذا — ومحمّد رجل حُلو اللسان — أفسد عليكم أبناءكم وخَدَمكم، وما ينفع أحدكم إذا فارقه أخوه وابنه أو امرأته.

ثمّ تشاوروا، فأجمعوا أمرهم على أن يقتلوه، يُخرِجون من كلّ بطنٍ منهم بشاب، فيضرِبونه بأسيافهم جميعًا عند الكعبة، ثمّ قرأ الآية ﴿وَإِذْ يَمْكُرُ بِكَ الَّذِينَ كَفَرُوا لِيُثْبِتُوكَ أَوْ يَقْتُلُوكَ﴾ إلى آخر الآية.

٤٣. عن زُرارة وحُمران، عن أبي جعفر عليه السلام وأبي عبد الله عليه السلام، في قوله: ﴿وَاللَّهُ خَيْرُ الْمَاكِرِينَ﴾. قال: إنّ رسول الله صلى الله عليه وآله قد كان لقي من قومه بلاءً شديدًا، حتّى أتوه ذات يومٍ وهو ساجد، حتّى طَرَحُوا عليه رَحِم شاةٍ، فأتته ابنته وهو ساجدٌ لم يرفع رأسه، فرفعته عنه ومسحته، ثمّ أراه الله بعد ذلك الذي يُحبّ، إنّه كان ببدرٍ وليس معه غير فارسٍ واحدٍ، ثمّ كان معه يوم الفتح اثنا عشر ألفًا، حتّى جعل أبو سفيان والمشركون يستغيثون، ثمّ لقي أمير المؤمنين عليه السلام من الشدّة والبلاء والتظاهر عليه، ولم يكن معه أحدٌ من قومه بمنزلته، أمّا حمزة فَقُتِل يوم أُحد، وأمّا جعفر فقُتِل يوم مُؤتة.

44. From ʿAbd Allāh b. Muḥammad al-Juʿfī[3] who said, 'I heard Abū Jaʿfar عليه السلام say, "The Messenger of God ﷺ and the seeking of forgiveness are two fortresses for you from chastisement. The greater of the fortresses has passed away and only seeking forgiveness is left, so do it abundantly for indeed it saves one from sins. And if you want, read ﴾*But God would not send them punishment while you* [*Prophet*] *are in their midst, nor would He punish them if they sought forgiveness.*﴿"' [8:33]

45. From Ḥanān, on his father's authority, on Abū Jaʿfar's authority who said, 'The Messenger of God – may God's blessings be on him and his family – said once when he was with a few of his companions, "My staying in your midst is good for you as is my departing from you." So Jābir b. ʿAbd Allāh al-Anṣārī stood up and said, "O Messenger of God, regarding your staying in our midst being good for us, we understand that. But how is your departing good for us?"

He replied, "Regarding my stay in your midst, God says: ﴾*But God would not send them punishment while you* [*Prophet*] *are in their midst, nor would He punish them if they sought forgiveness*﴿, punishing them by the sword. As for my departing from you, it is good for you because your deeds will be exposed to me every Monday and Thursday. Whatever good befalls you, praise God for it, and whatever evil befalls you, seek God's forgiveness."' [8:33]

46. From Ibrāhīm b. ʿUmar al-Yamānī, citing whoever narrated it from Abū ʿAbd Allāh عليه السلام regarding God's verse: ﴾*When they debar people from the Sacred Mosque, although they are not its* [*rightful*] *guardians?*﴿ meaning that the polytheists were not the guardians of the [Sacred] House, ﴾*Only those mindful of God are its rightful guardians*﴿, where they had more right to it than the polytheists. ﴾*Their prayers before the House are nothing but whistling and clapping*﴿ – he said, 'Wolf-whistles and clapping.' [8:34–35]

3 ʿAbd Allāh b. Muḥammad al-Juʿfī, a weak narrator according Ḥillī. See Ḥillī, *Khulāṣat al-aqwāl*, 373 (nr. 1483).

٤٤. عن عبدالله بن محمّد الجُعفي، قال: سمعتُ أبا جعفرٍ عليه السلام يقول: كان رسول الله صلى الله عليه وآله والاستغفار حِصنين حَصِينين لكُم من العذاب، فمضى أكبر الحِصنين، وبقي الاستغفار، فأكثروا منه، فإنّه مَمحاة للذنوب، وإن شئتم فاقرؤوا ﴿وَمَا كَانَ اللَّهُ لِيُعَذِّبَهُمْ وَأَنْتَ فِيهِمْ وَمَا كَانَ اللَّهُ مُعَذِّبَهُمْ وَهُمْ يَسْتَغْفِرُونَ﴾.

٤٥. عن حنان، عن أبيه، عن أبي جعفر عليه السلام، قال: قال رسول الله صلوات الله عليه وآله وهو في نفرٍ من أصحابه: إنّ مقامي بين أظهركم خيرٌ لكم، وإنّ مفارقتي إيّاكم خيرٌ لكم. فقام إليه جابر بن عبدالله الأنصاري، فقال: يا رسول الله، أمّا مقامك بين أظهرنا خيرٌ لنا فقد عرفنا، فكيف يكون مُفارقتك إيّانا خيرًا لنا؟

فقال: أمّا مقامي بين أظهركم، فإنّ الله يقول: ﴿وَمَا كَانَ اللَّهُ لِيُعَذِّبَهُمْ وَأَنْتَ فِيهِمْ وَمَا كَانَ اللَّهُ مُعَذِّبَهُمْ وَهُمْ يَسْتَغْفِرُونَ﴾ فعذّبهم بالسيف، وأمّا مفارقتي إيّاكم فهو خيرٌ لكم، لأنّ أعمالكم تُعرَض عليّ كلّ اثنين وخميس، فما كان من حسنٍ حَمِدَت الله عليه، وما كان من سيّء استغفرت الله لكم.

٤٦. عن إبراهيم بن عمر اليماني، عمّن ذكره، عن أبي عبدالله عليه السلام، في قول الله تعالى: ﴿وَهُمْ يَصُدُّونَ عَنِ الْمَسْجِدِ الْحَرَامِ وَمَا كَانُوا أَوْلِيَاءَهُ﴾ يعني أولياء البيت، يعني المشركين ﴿إِنْ أَوْلِيَاؤُهُ إِلَّا الْمُتَّقُونَ﴾ حيثما كانوا هم أولى به من المشركين ﴿وَمَا كَانَ صَلَاتُهُمْ عِنْدَ الْبَيْتِ إِلَّا مُكَاءً وَتَصْدِيَةً﴾ قال: التّصفير والتّصفيق.

47. From ʿAlī b. Darrāj al-Asadī who said, 'I entered in the presence of Abū Jaʿfar ﷺ and said to him, "I used to work for the Banū Umayya and acquired much wealth [as a result] and presumed that this was not lawful for me. He said, 'Have you asked anyone else about this besides me?

He said, 'I replied, "Yes, I have, and I was told: 'Your family, your wealth and everything is prohibited for you.' [Is that right?]"

He said, "It is not as they said to you."

He said, 'I asked, "May I be your ransom – am I eligible for pardon?" He replied, "Yes, your pardon is in God's Book: ﴾*[Prophet], tell the disbelievers that if they desist their past will be forgiven.*﴿"' [8:38]

48. From Zurāra who said, 'Abū ʿAbd Allāh ﷺ said, "My father was asked about God's statements: ﴾*Fight all the polytheists as they fight you all until there is no more persecution, and all worship is devoted to God alone.*﴿ He said, 'The interpretation of this verse has not been fulfilled yet. And if our Qā'im were to rise after it, then those who meet him will surely see that it is the actualisation of the interpretation of this verse; and the religion of Muḥammad ﷺ will most surely materialise, just as nightfall draws in [eventually] until there will be no polytheism left on the face of the earth as God has said.'"' [8:39]

49. From ʿAbd al-Aʿlā al-Ḥalabī who said, 'Abū Jaʿfar ﷺ said, "The master of this authority [i.e. the Twelfth Imam] will have an occultation in one of these mountain passes," pointing in the direction of Dhī Ṭuwā. "Until there are only two nights remaining before his emergence, the special servant at his disposal will come out to meet some of his companions, and he will ask: 'How many of you are here?'

They will reply: 'Approximately forty men.'

He will then ask: 'How would you feel if you were to see your master?'

And they will say: 'By God, if only the mountains would take us in, we would reside therein with him.'

Then he will come to them from the opposite side and say to them, 'Indicate to our contemporaries and the good people from amongst your clans.' So they will point them out to him, and he will set off with them until they come to their master, and he will meet them the following night."

Then Abū Jaʿfar said, "By God, it is as if I can see him leaning against the [Black] Stone beseeching God for his right, then saying: 'O people, whoever

٤٧ . عن عليّ بن درّاج الأسدي، قال: دخلتُ على أبي جعفر عليه السلام، فقلتُ له: إنّي كنتُ عاملاً لبني أميّة، فأصبت مالاً كثيرًا، فظننتُ أنّ ذلك لا يحِلّ لي؟ قال: فسألتَ عن ذلك غيري؟

قال: قلتُ: قد سألتُ، فقيل لي: إنّ أهلك ومالك وكلّ شيء لك حرام.

قال: ليس كما قالوا لك.

قلتُ: جُعِلت فداك، فلي توبة؟ قال: نعم، توبتُك في كتاب الله ﴿قُل لِّلَّذِينَ كَفَرُوٓا۟ إِن يَنتَهُوا۟ يُغْفَرْ لَهُم مَّا قَدْ سَلَفَ﴾.

٤٨ . عن زُرارة، قال: قال أبو عبد الله عليه السلام: سُئِل أبي عليه السلام عن قول الله: ﴿وَقَـٰتِلُوا۟ ٱلْمُشْرِكِينَ كَآفَّةً كَمَا يُقَـٰتِلُونَكُمْ كَآفَّةً﴾ حتّى لا يكون مشرك ﴿وَيَكُونَ ٱلدِّينُ كُلُّهُۥ لِلَّهِ﴾. فقال: إنّه لم يجئ تأويل هذه الآية، ولو قد قام قائمُنا بعد سيرى مَن يُدركه ما يكون من تأويل هذه الآية، وليبلُغنّ دين محمّد صلّى الله عليه وآله ما بلغ اللّيل حتّى لا يكون شِرك على ظَهر الأرض كما قال الله.

٤٩ . عن عبد الأعلى الحلبي، قال: قال أبو جعفر عليه السلام: يكون لصاحب هذا الأمر غيبةٌ في بعض هذه الشِّعاب — ثمّ أومأ بيده إلى ناحية ذي طُوى — حتّى إذا كان قبل خُروجه بليلتين انتهى المولى الذي يكون بين يديه حتّى يلقى بعض أصحابه، فيقول: كم أنتم هاهنا؟ فيقولون: نحو من أربعين رجلاً. فيقول: كيف أنتم لو قد رأيتُم صاحبكم؟ فيقولون: والله لو يأوي بنا الجبال لأوَيناها معه، ثمّ يأتيهم من القابلة، فيقول لهم: أشيروا إلى ذوي أسنانكم وأخياركم عشرة. فيُشيرون إليهم، فينطلق بهم حتّى يأتوا صاحبهم، ويَعِدهم إلى الليلة التي تليها.

disputes with me about God, then know that I am the worthiest of people with respect to God; and whoever disputes with me about Ādam, then I am the worthiest of all people [to claim proximity] to Ādam. O people, whoever disputes with me about Nūḥ, I am the worthiest of people to Nūḥ. O people, whoever disputes with me about Ibrāhīm, then I am the worthiest of people to Ibrāhīm. O people, whoever disputes with me about Mūsā, I am the worthiest of people with respect to Mūsā. O people, whoever disputes with me regarding ʿĪsā, then I am the worthiest of people to ʿĪsā. O people, whoever disputes with me about Muḥammad, then I am the worthiest of all people with respect to Muḥammad ﷺ. O people, whoever disputes with me about God's Book, then I am the worthiest of people to God's Book.' Then he will end up at the Station [of Ibrāhīm] and perform two units of prayer there, then beseech God for his right."

Abū Jaʿfar continued, "By God, he is the distressed one in God's Book, as per God's words: ﴾ *Who is it that answers the distressed when he calls upon Him and removes his suffering, who makes you successors in the earth?* ﴿(27:62). Jibra'īl will be on the spout [on the roof of the Kaʿba] in the form of a white bird and will be the first one to pay allegiance to him; and three hundred and ten odd men will pledge allegiance to him too."'

He continued, 'Abū Jaʿfar عليه السلام said, "Whoever will have embarked on the journey [to him] will arrive at that moment, and whoever has not yet set off on the journey will be missing from his bed." Then he said, "By God, this is as per ʿAlī b. Abī Ṭālib's statement: "The ones missing from their beds," and as per God's statement: ﴾ *race to do good deeds and wherever you are, God will bring you together.* ﴿(2:148) The companions of the Qā'im will number some three hundred and ten odd men."

He then said, "By God, they are the determined group that God has mentioned in His Book: ﴾ *If We defer their punishment for a determined time* [...]﴿ (11:18) They will gather together at one particular time like scattered clouds gathering in autumn. Then in the morning he will invite all people to God's Book and the Sunna of His Prophet ﷺ. A simple man will respond to him, and he will place him in charge of Mecca. Then he will march ahead and receive the news that his agent has been killed. He will then go back to them and kill the murderers, not exceeding the limits at all, i.e. by taking captives. He will set off again calling people to God's Book, the Sunna of His Prophet, peace be upon him and his family, adherence to the guardianship of ʿAlī b.

ثمّ قال أبو جعفر عليه السلام: والله لكأنّي أنظر إليه، وقد أسند ظهره إلى الحجر، ثمّ يُنشِد الله حقّه، ثمّ يقول: يا أيّها الناس، من يُحاجّني في الله فأنا أولى الناس بالله، ومن يُحاجّني في آدم فأنا أولى الناس بآدم. يا أيّها الناس، من يُحاجّني في نوح فأنا أولى الناس بنوح. يا أيّها الناس، من يُحاجَّني في إبراهيم فأنا أولى الناس بإبراهيم. يا أيّها الناس، من يُحاجّني في موسى فأنا أولى الناس بموسى. يا أيّها الناس، من يحاجّني في عيسى فانا أولى الناس بعيسي، يا أيّها الناس، من يحاجَّني في محمّد فأنا أولى النّاس بمحمّد صلى الله عليه وآله، يا أيّها الناس من يُحاجَّني في كتاب الله فأنا أولى الناس بكتاب الله، ثمّ ينتهي إلى المقام فيُصلّي ركعتين، ثمّ يُنشد الله حقّه.

قال أبو جعفر عليه السلام: هو والله المضطرّ في كتاب الله، وهو قول الله: ﴿أَمَّن يُجِيبُ ٱلْمُضْطَرَّ إِذَا دَعَاهُ وَيَكْشِفُ ٱلسُّوٓءَ وَيَجْعَلُكُمْ خُلَفَآءَ ٱلْأَرْضِ﴾ وجبرائيل على الميزاب في صورة طائر أبيض، فيكون أوّل خلق الله يبايعه جبرئيل، ويبايعه الثلاثمائة والبضعة عشر رجلاً.

قال أبو جعفر عليه السلام: فمن ابتُلي في المَسير، وافاه في تلك الساعة، ومن لم يُبتَل بالمسير فُقِد عن فِراشه، ثمّ قال: هو والله قول عليّ بن أبي طالب عليه السلام: المفقودون عن فُرشهم، وهو قول الله: ﴿فَٱسْتَبِقُوا ٱلْخَيْرَٰتِ أَيْنَ مَا تَكُونُوا يَأْتِ بِكُمُ ٱللَّهُ جَمِيعًا﴾ أصحاب القائم الثلاثمائة وبضعة عشر رجلاً.

قال: هُم والله الأمّة المعدودة التي قال الله في كتابه: ﴿وَلَئِنْ أَخَّرْنَا عَنْهُمُ ٱلْعَذَابَ إِلَىٰٓ أُمَّةٍ مَّعْدُودَةٍ﴾، قال: يجمعون في ساعةٍ واحدةٍ قزَعًا كقزَع الخريف، فيصبح بمكّة،

Abī Ṭālib ﷺ and disassociation from his enemies. He will not appoint anyone else until he reaches the desert.

Thereafter Sufyānī's army will come out towards him, and God will command the earth which will grab them from under their feet. This is as per God's statement: ﴿*[Prophet], if you could only see their terror! There will be no escape when they are seized from a nearby place; they will say, 'Now we believe in it* [...]﴾(34:51–52) meaning [they believe] in the Qā'im from Muḥammad's family; ﴿*when they had rejected it all in the past*﴾ meaning they had denied the Qā'im from Muḥammad's family, until the end of the chapter. None but two men from among them will remain alive, known as Watr and Wutayr from Murād. Their faces will be inverted back to front, and they will be walking backwards. They will inform people of what happened to their companions. Then he will enter Medina causing the Quraysh to hide from him at that moment, as per 'Alī b. Abī Ṭālib's words: "By God, the Quraysh are blood-thirsty" – meaning that they only have one stance, which is to slaughter and massacre whomsoever they rule and whomsoever the sun shines or does not shine on. Then he will do something, and when he does it the Quraysh will say, "Take us to these rebels. By God, if he were a Muḥammadan he would not have done that, and if he were an 'Alawī he would not have done that, and if he were a Fāṭimī he would not have done that."

God will allow him to fight them, and he will kill the combatants and capture their progeny. After that he will set off again until he reaches al-Shaqara, and he will receive news that they have killed his agent. He will go back to them and kill them in such a manner that the Battle of al-Harra will look like nothing in comparison. He will then set off inviting people to God's Book, the Sunnah of His Prophet, adherence to the guardianship of 'Alī b. Abī Ṭālib ﷺ and disassociation from his enemies, until he will reach al-Tha'labiyya. A descendant of his own father will come to him. He will be the strongest of people physically and the most courageous of them, besides the master of this authority himself. He will say, "You over there! What are you doing? By God, you are driving people away like cattle. Can this truly be by the commission of the Messenger of God ﷺ or something else?"

So the agent in charge of allegiance will say, "By God, either you calm down, or I will strike you between the eyes."

فيدعو الناس إلى كتاب الله وسُنّة نبيّه صلى الله عليه وآله، فيجيبه نفرٌ يسير، ويستعمل على مكّة، ثمّ يسير فيبلُغه أن قد قُتِل عامِلُه، فيرجع إليهم فيقتُل المقُاتلة، لا يزيد على ذلك شيئًا، يعني السّبي.

ثمّ ينطلق فيدعو النّاس إلى كتاب الله وسُنّة نبيّه عليه وآله السلام، والولاية لعليّ بن أبي طالب عليه السلام، والبراءة من عدوّه، ولا يُسمّي أحدًا حتّى ينتهي إلى البيداء، فيخرُج إليه جيش السُّفياني، فيأمُر الله الأرض، فتأخُذهم من تحت أقدامهم، وهو قول الله: ﴿وَلَوْ تَرَىٰ إِذْ فَزِعُوا فَلَا فَوْتَ وَأُخِذُوا مِن مَّكَانٍ قَرِيبٍ ۞ وَقَالُوا آمَنَّا بِهِ﴾ يعني بقائم آل محمّد ﴿وَقَدْ كَفَرُوا بِهِ﴾ يعني بقائم آل محمّد إلى آخر السورة، ولا يبقى منهم إلاّ رجلان، يقال لهما: وتر ووتير من مُراد، وجوههما في أقفيتهما يمشيان القَهقَرى، يُخبِران الناس بما فعل بأصحابهما.

ثمّ يدخُل المدينة، فتغيب عنهم عند ذلك قريش، وهو قول عليّ بن أبي طالب عليه السلام: والله لودّت قريش أنّ عندها موقفًا واحدًا جزرَ جَزُور بكلّ ما ملكت وكلّ ما طلعَت عليه الشمس أو غَرَبت. ثمّ يُحدِث حَدَثًا، فإذا هو فعل ذلك، قالت قريش: اخرجوا بنا إلى هذه الطاغية، فوالله أن لو كان محمّديًا ما فعل، ولو كان علويًّا ما فعل، ولو كان فاطميًّا ما فعل، فيمنحه الله أكتافهم، فَيَقتُل المقُاتلة ويسبي الذُّرّية، ثمّ ينطلق حتى ينزل الشقرة، فيبلّغه أنهم قد قتلوا عامله، فيرجع إليهم فيقتلهم مقتلة ليس قتل الحرّة إلها بشيءٍ.

ثمّ ينطلق يدعو الناس إلى كتاب الله وسُنّة نبيّه، والولاية لعليّ بن أبي طالب عليه السلام، والبراءة من عدوّه، حتّى إذا بلغ إلى الثعلبية قام إليه رجلٌ من صُلب أبيه، وهو من أشدّ الناس ببدنه، وأشجعهم بقلبه، ما خلا صاحب هذا الأمر، فيقول: يا هذا ما تصنع؟

The Qā'im ﷺ will say to him, "Be quiet." "Yes, by God. I have God's Messenger's commissioning with me. Hand me the casket, O man," and he will give it to him. He will then read out to him the Messenger of God's mission statement.

He [the man] will say, "May God sacrifice me for you – give me your head that I may kiss it." So he will give him his head and he will kiss him between the eyes, saying, "May God sacrifice me for you - renew our allegiance." Then their allegiance will be renewed."'

Abū Ja'far ﷺ continued, "It is as if I can see them advancing from Najaf to Kufa, three hundred and ten men or so, with hearts as hard as iron blocks, with Jibra'īl to his right and Mikā'īl to his left. Their awe precedes them by the span of a month and follows in their wake by a month. God will reinforce them with five thousand swooping angels until they ascend into Najaf. He will say to his companions, 'Spend this night of yours in worship.' Thus, they will spend the night, bowing and prostrating, making entreaties to God submissively until morning.

He will say, 'Let us take the path of al-Nukhayla for Kufa has a fortified army.'"

I asked: "A fortified army?"

He replied, "Yes, by God. Then he will reach the mosque of Ibrāhīm ﷺ in al-Nukhayla, where he will perform two units of prayer. The Murji'ites and others from the Sufyānī camp from the people of Kufa will come out towards him, and will tell his companions: 'Move away from him.' Then he will say: 'Attack them!'"

Abū Ja'far ﷺ continued, "By God, not even a ditch on their side will live to tell the tale. Then he will enter Kufa and every single believer will either be present there or will rush there, as per Commander of the Faithful 'Alī's words. Then he will say to his companions, 'March towards these tyrants.' Then he will invite him to the Book of God and the Sunnah of His Prophet ﷺ, and Sufyānī will offer an entreaty of peace to him. So the tribe of Kalb, being their uncles, will say, 'What is this you are doing? By God, we will never pledge allegiance to you upon this.'

He will retort, 'What am I doing?'

And they will say, 'Go and approach him,' so he will approach him.

Then the Qa'im ﷺ will say to him, 'You had better be on your guard, for I have fulfilled my duty to you and I will fight you.'

فوالله إنّك لتُجفل الناس إجفال النَّعَم، أفبعَهدٍ من رسول الله ﷺ، أم بماذا؟ فيقول المولى الذي ولي البيعة: والله لتَسكُتَنَّ أو لأضرِبَنّ الذي فيه عيناك.

فيقول القائم عليه السلام: اسكُت يا فلان، إي والله إنّ معي عهدًا من رسول الله ﷺ، هات لي يا فلان العيبة -- أو الطيبة، أو الزنفليجة -- فيأتيه بها، فيُقرئه العهد من رسول الله ﷺ، فيقول: جعلني الله فداك، أعطني رأسك أُقبِّله، فيُعطيه رأسه، فيُقبِّله بين عينيه، ثمّ يقول: جعلني الله فِداك، جَدِّد لنا بيعةً، فيُجدِّد لهم بيعةً.

قال أبو جعفر عليه السلام: لكأنّي أنظُر إليهم مُصعدين من نَجَف الكُوفة ثلاثمائة وبضعة عشر رجلاً، كأنّ قلوبهم زُبر الحديد، جَبرئيل عن يمينه، وميكائيل عن يساره، يسيرُ الرُّعب أمامه شهرًا، وخلفه شهرًا، أمدَّه الله بخمسة آلاف من الملائكة مُسوّمين، حتّى إذا صَعِد النجف، قال لأصحابه: تَعَبّدُوا ليلتكم هذه، فيَبيتون بين راكعٍ وساجدٍ، يَتَضرّعون إلى الله، حتّى إذا أصبح قال: خُذوا بنا طريق النُّخيلة، وعلى الكوفة جُندٌ مُجنّد.

قلتُ: جُندٌ مُجنّد؟ قال: أي والله، حتّى ينتهي إلى مسجد إبراهيم عليه السلام بالنخيلة، فيُصلّي فيه ركعتين، فيخرُج إليه من كان بالكوفة من مُرجئها وغيرهم من جيش السُّفياني، فيقول لأصحابه: استطردوا لهم، ثمّ يقول: كرُّوا عليهم، قال أبو جعفر عليه السلام: ولا يجوز والله الخَندق منهم مُخبِرٌ.

ثمّ يدخُل الكوفة، فلا يبقى مؤمن إلاّ كان فيها أو حنّ إليها، وهو قول أمير المؤمنين عليّ عليه السلام، ثمّ يقول لأصحابه سيروا إلى هذه الطّاغية، فيدعوه إلى كتاب الله وسُنّة نبيّه ﷺ، فيُعطيه السُّفياني من البيعة سِلمًا، فيقول له كَلب، وهم أخواله: ما هذا؟ ما

The next morning he will fight them and God will permit him to kill them. He will take Sufyānī captive, then proceed to slaughter him with his own hands. Then he will send a contingent of horsemen to the Roman Empire to draw out the remaining Banū Umayya. When they arrive at the Roman Empire, they will say, 'Bring out our fellow countrymen that you are harbouring.' They will refuse, saying, 'We will not.'

Then the horsemen will say, 'By God, we would fight you if only we were commanded to do so.'

Then they will set off, back to their master and recount everything for him, upon which he will say, 'Go forth and make them bring out their associates, for indeed they have already been brought a mighty proof,' which is God's statement: ﴾*Do not try to escape. Go back to your homes and the pleasure you revelled in so that you may be questioned*﴿(21:13) referring to the treasures that you used to hoard. ﴾*They said, 'Woe to us! We were wrong!' and that cry of theirs did not cease until We made them burnt-off stubble.*﴿(21:14–15) No one will live to tell the tale. Then he will return to Kufa and dispatch the three hundred and ten or so men to all regions far and wide, and he will swipe his hand between their shoulders and over their chests so that they are never incapacitated out in the open; and no land will remain without the announcement of the testimony that there is no god but God, the One and Only and without partner, and that Muḥammad is the Messenger of God, and this is His statement: ﴾*Everyone in the heavens and earth submits to Him, willingly or unwillingly; they will all be returned to Him.*﴿(3:83) The master of this authority will not accept the *jizya* poll tax like the Messenger of God ﷺ had accepted, and this is God's statement: ﴾*[Believers], fight them until there is no more persecution, and all worship is devoted to God alone.*﴿"

Then Abū Jaʿfar عليه السلام said, "By God, they will fight until the oneness of God is established and nothing is associated with him, and until a frail old woman can come out from the East and travel to the West without anyone stopping her, and God can draw the seedlings out from the earth and send the rains down from the sky, and the people [willingly] take out the land tax incumbent upon them to the Mahdī عليه السلام, and God gives ampleness to our followers (*shīʿa*) – and were it not for him, whatever good fortune were to come their way they would squander it.

While the master of this authority will pass some rulings and speak about some prophetic practices, a group of dissenters will come out of the mosque

صنعت؟ والله ما نبايعك على هذا أبدًا. فيقول: ما أصنع؟ فيقولون: استقبله فيستقبله، ثمّ يقول له القائم ﷺ: خُذ حِذرك، فإنّني أدّيت إليك، وأنا مُقاتلك. فيُصبح فيُقاتلهم، فيمنحه الله أكتافهم، ويأخُذ السُّفياني أسيرًا، فينطلق به ويذبحه بيده. ثمّ يُرسِل جَريدةَ خَيلٍ إلى الرُّوم، فيستحضرون بقيّة بني أُميّة، فإذا انتهوا إلى الرُّوم قالوا: اخرجُوا إلينا أهل مِلّتنا عندكم، فيأبَون ويَقولون: واللهِ لا نفعل.

فتقول الجَريدة: واللهِ لو أمرنا لقاتلناكم. ثمّ ينطلِقون إلى صاحبهم، فيعرِضون ذلك عليه، فيقول: انطلقوا فأخرجوا إليهم أصحابهم، فإنّ هؤلاء قد أتوا بسُلطان عظيم، وهو قول الله: ﴿فَلَمَّا أَحَسُّوا بَأْسَنَا إِذَا هُم مِّنْهَا يَرْكُضُونَ ۝ لَا تَرْكُضُوا وَارْجِعُوا إِلَىٰ مَا أُتْرِفْتُمْ فِيهِ وَمَسَاكِنِكُمْ لَعَلَّكُمْ تُسْأَلُونَ﴾، قال: يعني الكنوز التي كُنتم تكنِزون ﴿قَالُوا يَا وَيْلَنَا إِنَّا كُنَّا ظَالِمِينَ ۝ فَمَا زَالَت تِّلْكَ دَعْوَاهُمْ حَتَّىٰ جَعَلْنَاهُمْ حَصِيدًا خَامِدِينَ﴾ لا يبقى منهم مُخبِر.

ثمّ يرجع إلى الكوفة، فيبعث الثلاثمائة والبِضعة عشر رجلاً إلى الآفاق كلّها، فيمسَح بين أكتافهم وعلى صُدورهم، فلا يتعايون في قضاء، ولا تبقى أرض إلاّ نودي فيها شهادة أن لا إله إلاّ الله، وحدهُ لا شريك له، وأنّ محمدًا رسول الله، وهو قوله: ﴿وَلَهُ أَسْلَمَ مَن فِي السَّمَاوَاتِ وَالْأَرْضِ طَوْعًا وَكَرْهًا وَإِلَيْهِ يُرْجَعُونَ﴾ ولا يقبل صاحب هذا الأمر الجِزية كما قبِلها رسول الله ﷺ، وهو قول الله: ﴿وَقَاتِلُوهُمْ حَتَّىٰ لَا تَكُونَ فِتْنَةٌ وَيَكُونَ الدِّينُ كُلُّهُ لِلَّهِ﴾.

قال أبو جعفر ﷺ: يُقاتلون والله حتّى يُوحِّد الله ولا يشرَك به شيئًا، وحتّى تخرُج العجوز الضعيفة من المشرِق تُريد المغرب، ولا ينهاها احدٌ، ويُخرِج الله من الأرض

wanting to rebel against him, so he will say to his companions: 'Go forth and overcome them with your military prowess.' So they will bring them to him as captives that he might sentence them, and then they will slaughter them. This will be the last group of dissenters ever to rise against the Qā'im of Muḥammad's family."' [8:39]

50. From Muḥammad b. Muslim, from one of the two [al-Bāqir or al-Ṣādiq]. He said, 'I asked him about God's verse: ﴿*Know that one-fifth of your battle gains belongs to God and the Messenger, to close relatives.*﴾' He replied, "They are the close relatives of the Messenger of God, peace be upon him and his family." So I asked him, "Are the orphans, the needy and the travelers from among them too?" He replied, "Yes."' [8:41]

51. From Ibn Sinān, from Abū 'Abd Allāh عليه السلام. He said, 'I heard him say, "Of the battle gains, he takes out one-fifth thereof and divides the rest among those who fought in it and was commanding it. As for the war booty and the spoils, then that is exclusively for the Messenger of God ﷺ."' [8:41]

52. From 'Abd Allāh b. Sinān, from Abū 'Abd Allāh عليه السلام who said, 'I heard that Najda, the Ḥarūrī wrote to Ibn 'Abbās asking him about the recipient of the one-fifth (*khums*) – to whom does it belong? So he wrote to him: "As for the *khums*, we claim that it belongs to us, although our community claims that it does not belong to us; so we have been patient."' [8:41]

53. From Zurāra, Muḥammad b. Muslim and Abū Baṣīr, that they asked him, 'What is the Imam's right over people's property?' He replied, 'War booty, battle gains, and *khums*, and all that falls within [the category of] war booty, battle gains, *khums*, and spoils – they are entitled to a fifth of it, for God says: ﴿*Know that one-fifth of your battle gains belongs to God and the Messenger, to close relatives and orphans, to the needy.*﴾ They have a share in everything in this world, and the one who gives them something [should remember that] that which they leave for him is greater than that which they take from him.' [8:41]

بَذرها، ويُنزِل من السماء قطرها، ويَخرُج الناس خَراجهم على رقابهم إلى المهديّ عليه السلام، ويوسّع الله على شيعتنا، ولولا ما يُدرِكهم من السعادة لبَغَوا، فبينا صاحب هذا الأمر قد حَكَم ببعض الأحكام وتكلَّم ببعض السُّنن، إذ خرجت خارِجة من المسجد يُريدون الخُروج عليه، فيقول لأصحابه: انطلقوا، فتلحقوا بهم في التمّارين، فيأتونه بهم أسرى، ليأمُر بهم فيُذبحون، وهي آخر خارجةٍ تخرُج على قائم آل محمّد صلى الله عليه وآله.

٥٠. محمّد بن مسلم، عن أحدهما عليه السلام، قال: سألتُه عن قول الله تعالى: ﴿وَاعْلَمُوا أَنَّمَا غَنِمْتُم مِّن شَيْءٍ فَأَنَّ لِلَّهِ خُمُسَهُ وَلِلرَّسُولِ وَلِذِي الْقُرْبَىٰ﴾، قال: هم أهل قرابة رسول الله عليه وآله السلام.

فسألتُه: مِنهُم اليتامى والمساكين وابن السبيل؟ قال: نعم.

٥١. عن ابن سنان، عن أبي عبدالله عليه السلام، قال: سمِعتُه يقول في الغنيمة: يُخرَج منها الخُمس، ويُقسَّم ما بقي فيمن قاتل عليه وولِيّ ذلك، فأمّا الفَيء والأنفال فهو خالصٌ لرسول الله صلى الله عليه وآله.

٥٢. عن عبدالله بن سِنان، عن أبي عبدالله عليه السلام، قال: سمِعتُه [يقول]: إنّ نَجدة الحَروري كتب إلى ابن عباس يسأله عن موضع الخُمس، لِمن هو؟ فكتب إليه: أمّا الخُمس فإنّا نزعُم أنّه لنا، ويزعُم قومنا أنه ليس لنا، فصبرنا.

٥٣. عن زُرارة ومحمّد بن مسلم وأبي بصير، أنّهم قالوا له: ما حقُّ الإمام في أموال الناس؟ قال: الفَيء والأنفال والخُمس، وكلّ ما دخل منه فَيء أو أنفال أو خُمس أو غنيمة، فإنّ لهم خُمسه، فانّ الله يقول: ﴿وَاعْلَمُوا أَنَّمَا غَنِمْتُم مِّن شَيْءٍ فَأَنَّ لِلَّهِ خُمُسَهُ وَلِلرَّسُولِ وَلِذِي

54. From Samāʿa, from Abū ʿAbd Allāh and Abū al-Ḥasan [al-Kāẓim], peace be upon them. He said, 'I asked one of them about the *khums*, so he said, "*Khums* only applies to [battle] gains."' [8:41]

55. From Muḥammad b. Muslim, from Abū Jaʿfar عليه السلام who said regarding God's verse: ﴾*Know that one-fifth of your battle gains belongs to God and the Messenger, to close relatives* [...]﴿, 'They are the close relatives of God's Prophet صلى الله عليه وآله.' [8:41]

56. From Muḥammad b. al-Fuḍayl, from Abū al-Ḥasan al-Riḍā عليه السلام. He said, 'I asked him about God's verse: ﴾*Know that one-fifth of your battle gains belongs to God and the Messenger, to close relatives* [...]﴿ He replied, "The one-fifth (*khums*) belongs to God and the Messenger, and it belongs to us."' [8:41]

57. From Sadīr, from Abū Jaʿfar عليه السلام. He said, 'He said: "Abū al-Faḍl, we have a right to the *khums* in God's Book, so whether they deny it and say, 'It is not from God' or claim that they do not know about it, it is the same thing."' [8:41]

58. From Ibn al-Ṭayyār, from Abū ʿAbd Allāh عليه السلام who said, 'One-fifth of the battle gains is taken out, then the remaining four fifths are divided up amongst those who fought and commanded [in it].' [8:41]

59. From Fayḍ b. Abī Shayba, from a man who cited Abū ʿAbd Allāh عليه السلام as having said, 'The worst state that people will face on the Day of Judgement will be when the rightful owner of the *khums* will stand up and say, "My Lord, [what about] my *khums*?" Our followers (*shīʿa*) will be safe from that, however.' [8:41]

﴿الْقُرْبَىٰ وَالْيَتَامَىٰ وَالْمَسَاكِينِ﴾ وكلّ شيء في الدنيا فإنّ لهم فيه نصيبًا، فمن وصلهم بشيءٍ، فمّا يدعون له أكثر ممّا يأخذون منه.

٥٤. عن سَماعة، عن أبي عبد الله وأبي الحسن عليهما السلام، قال: سألتُ أحدهما عن الخمس؟ فقال: ليس الخُمس إلاّ في الغنائم.

٥٥. عن محمّد بن مسلم، عن أبي جعفر عليه السلام، في قول الله تعالى: ﴿وَاعْلَمُوا أَنَّمَا غَنِمْتُم مِّن شَيْءٍ فَأَنَّ لِلَّهِ خُمُسَهُ وَلِلرَّسُولِ وَلِذِي الْقُرْبَىٰ﴾، قال: هم أهل قرابة نبيّ الله صلّى الله عليه وآله وسلّم.

٥٦. عن محمّد بن الفضيل، عن أبي الحسن الرضا عليه السلام، قال: سألته عن قول الله: ﴿وَاعْلَمُوا أَنَّمَا غَنِمْتُم مِّن شَيْءٍ فَأَنَّ لِلَّهِ خُمُسَهُ وَلِلرَّسُولِ وَلِذِي الْقُرْبَىٰ﴾ قال: الخُمس لله، وللرسول، وهو لنا.

٥٧. عن سدير، عن أبي جعفر عليه السلام، قال: قال: يا أبا الفضل، لنا حقّ في كتاب الله في الخُمس، فلو محَوه فقالوا: ليس من الله، أولم يَعلَمُوا به، لكان سَواء.

٥٨. عن ابن الطيّار، عن أبي عبد الله عليه السلام، قال: يُخرَج خُمس الغَنيمة، ثمّ يُقسَّم أربعة أخماسٍ، على مَن قاتل على ذلك ووليه.

٥٩. عن فيض بن أبي شيبة، عن رجلٍ، عن أبي عبد الله عليه السلام، قال: إنّ أشدّ ما يكون الناس حالاً يوم القيامة إذا قام صاحب الخُمس، فقال: يا ربّ خُمسي، وإنّ شيعتنا من ذلك لفي حِلّ.

60. From Isḥāq b. ʿAmmār who said, 'I heard him say, "A man cannot excuse himself from having bought something from the *khums* by saying, 'But my Lord, I bought it with my own money,' unless the rightful owners of the *khums* have allowed him to do so."' [8:41]

61. From Ibrāhīm b. Muḥammad who said, 'I wrote to the third Abū al-Ḥasan [al-Hādī] عليه السلام asking him about what is obligatory in times of loss. So he wrote back: "*Khums* comes after one's provisions." So I debated this with our associates, and they said, "Provisions come after the government has taken its taxes, and after individual expenditures."

So I wrote back to him, saying, "You had written that *khums* comes after provisions but our associates differ regarding the provisions." So he wrote, "*Khums* comes after the government has taken its taxes and after a man's provisions for himself and his dependents have been taken out."' [8:41]

62. From Isḥāq, from a man who cited Abū ʿAbd Allāh عليه السلام. He said, 'I asked him about the cream of the crop? So he replied, "It belonged to the Messenger of God ﷺ while the remaining four-fifths were reserved for the fighters and the commander. The one-fifth (*khums*) is divided among God's Messenger's allotment. We say that it belongs to us whereas the people say, 'It does not belong to you.' The share of the relatives is also ours, and the three remaining fifths are for the orphans, the needy and the travelers, which the Imam distributes between them. If after they have received equal amounts, dirham by dirham, the Imam sees any remainder, he puts it aside for the relatives." He said, "They refer it back to us."' [8:41]

63. From al-Minhāl b. ʿAmr, from ʿAlī b. al-Ḥusayn عليه السلام who said, 'It belongs to our orphans, our needy ones and our travelers.' [8:41]

64. From Zakariyyā b. Mālik al-Juʿfī from Abū ʿAbd Allāh عليه السلام. He said: 'I asked him about God's verse: ﴾*Know that one-fifth of your battle gains belongs to God and the Messenger, to close relatives and orphans, to the needy and travelers.*﴿ He replied, "As for God's share of the *khums*, it goes to His Messenger for him to spend in the way of God, and the *khums* belonging to the Messenger belongs to us and his relatives, and the *khums* of 'the close relative' is for his relatives, 'the orphans' are the orphans of his Ahl al-Bayt.

٦٠. عن إسحاق بن عمّار، قال: سَمِعتُه يقول: لا يُعذَر عبدٌ اشترى من الخُمس شيئًا أن يقول: يا ربّ اشتريته بمالي، حتّى يأذَنَ له أهل الخُمس.

٦١. عن إبراهيم بن محمّد، قال: كَتبتُ إلى أبي الحسن الثالث عليه السلام أسأله عمّا يجب في الضياع، فكتب: الخُمس بعد المؤنة. قال: فناظرتُ أصحابنا، فقالوا: المؤنة بعد ما يأخُذ السُّلطان، وبعد مُؤنة الرجل.

فكتبت إليه: أنّك قُلتَ: الخُمس بعد المؤنة، وإنّ أصحابنا اختلفوا في المؤنة؟ فكتب: الخُمس بعد ما يأخُذ السُّلطان، وبعد مُؤنة الرَّجُل وعِيالِه.

٦٢. عن إسحاق، عن رجُل، عن أبي عبد الله عليه السلام، قال: سألتُه عن سهم الصّفوة. فقال: كان لرسول الله صلى الله عليه وآله، وأربعة أخماس للمجاهدين والقُوّام، وخُمسٌ يُقسّم بين مقسم رسول الله صلى الله عليه وآله، ونحن نقول: هولنا، والناس يقولون: ليس لكم، وسهمٌ لذي القُربى وهو لنا، وثلاثة أسهامٍ لليتامى والمساكين وأبناء السبيل، يُقسّمه الإمام بينهم، فان أصابهم دِرهم درهم لكلّ فرقة منهم نظر الإمام بعد، فجعلها في ذي القُربى، قال: يرُدُّها إلينا.

٦٣. عن المِنهال بن عمرو، عن عليّ بن الحسين عليه السلام، قال: قال: لِيتامانا، ومساكيننا، وأبناء سبيلنا.

٦٤. زكريا بن مالك الجُعفي، عن أبي عبد الله عليه السلام، قال: سألتُه عن قول الله تعالى: ﴿وَاعْلَمُوا أَنَّمَا غَنِمْتُم مِّن شَيْءٍ فَأَنَّ لِلَّهِ خُمُسَهُ وَلِلرَّسُولِ وَلِذِي الْقُرْبَىٰ وَالْيَتَامَىٰ وَالْمَسَاكِينِ وَابْنِ

So he designated these four-fifths to be for them. As for the needy and the travelers – you know that since alms donations (*ṣadaqa*) can neither be consumed by us nor are they permissible for us to take, they are kept for the needy and the travelers."' [8:41]

65. From ʿĪsā b. ʿAbd Allāh al-ʿAlawī, on his father's authority, from Jaʿfar b. Muḥammad عليه السلام. He said, 'He said, "God – besides whom there is no god but He – when He forbade us alms donations, He revealed about the *khums* for us. Alms donations are prohibited for us whereas the *khums* is an obligation due unto us, and the generous gift is permissible for us [to accept]."' [8:41]

66. From al-Ḥalabī, from Abū ʿAbd Allāh عليه السلام about a man from among our companions who is under their banner and lives with them – does he receive the battle gains? He replied, 'He remits the one-fifth due to us, and it is good for him.' [8:41]

67. From Isḥāq b. ʿAmmār, from Abū ʿAbd Allāh عليه السلام who said, 'The two forces met in battle on the nineteenth of the month of Ramadan.' I asked, 'What is the [inner] meaning of His words: ﴿*the two forces met*﴾?' He replied, 'On that day, all that He wishes to advance and to delay comes together, as do His Will and His Decree.' [8:41]

68. From ʿAmr b. Saʿīd who said, 'A man from Medina was debating with me about the Night of Distinction when the two forces met, and this Medinan man was saying that it was the seventeenth night of Ramadan. I went to Abū ʿAbd Allāh عليه السلام and informed him of this. So he said to me, "The Medinan man denies it. What you mean is the day the Commander of the Faithful was struck, and he was struck on the nineteenth of Ramadan, which is also the night on which ʿIṣā b. Maryam عليه السلام was raised up."' [8:41]

السَّبِيلِ﴾. قال: أمّا خُمس الله فالرسول ﷺ يَضَعه في سبيل الله، ولنا خُمس الرسول ولأقاربه، وخُمس ذوي القُربى فهم أقرباؤه، واليتامى يتامى أهل بيته، فجعل هذه الأربعة الأسُهم فيهم، وأمّا المساكين وأبناء السبيل، فقد عَلِمت أنّا لا نأكل الصّدقة، ولا تحِلّ لنا، فهي للمساكين وأبناء السبيل.

٦٥. عن عيسى بن عبدالله العلوي، عن أبيه، عن جعفر بن محمّد عليه السلام، قال: إنّ الله لا إله إلّا هو، لمّا حرّم علينا الصّدقة، أنزل لنا الخُمس، والصّدقة علينا حرامٌ، والخُمس لنا فريضةٌ، والكَرامة أمرٌ لنا حَلال.

٦٦. عن الحلبي، عن أبي عبدالله عليه السلام، في الرجل من أصحابنا في لوائهم، فيكون معهم، فيصيب غنيمة؟ قال: يُؤدّي خُمسنا، ويطيب له.

٦٧. عن إسحاق بن عمّار، عن أبي عبدالله عليه السلام، قال: في تسعة عشر من شهر رمضان يلتقي الجمعان، قلت: ما معنى قوله: يلتَقي الجَمعان؟ قال: يجمع فيها ما يُريد من تقديمه وتأخيره وإرادته وقضائه.

٦٨. عن عمرو بن سعيد، قال: خاصمني رجلٌ من أهل المدينة في ليلة الفُرقان حين التقى الجمعان، فقال المدني: هي ليلة سَبعَ عَشرةَ من رمضان، قال: فدخلتُ على أبي عبدالله عليه السلام: فقلتُ له وأخبرته، فقال لي: جَحَد المدني، أنت تُريد مُصاب أمير المؤمنين عليه السلام، إنّه أُصيب ليلة تسع عشرة من رمضان، وهي الليلة التي رُفِع فيها عيسى بن مريم عليه السلام.

69. From Muḥammad b. Yaḥyā, from Abū ʿAbd Allāh عليه السلام regarding His words: ﴾*and the caravan was below you.*﴿ He said, 'Abū Sufyān and his associates.' [8:42]

70. From ʿAmr b. Abī al-Miqdām, on his father's authority, from ʿAlī b. al-Ḥusayn عليه السلام who said, 'When the troops were thirsty on the day of Badr, ʿAlī went out with a water-bag to fetch some water. He was at the edge of the well when a powerful wind came upon him then passed on. He remained there as he saw fit, then another wind came and passed, and another one after that, which almost shook him off the edge of the well. So he sat down until it had passed. When he returned to the Messenger of God ﷺ he informed him of that. So the Messenger of God said, 'The first wind encompassed Jibra'īl with one thousand angels; the second contained Mīkā'īl with one thousand angels, and the third had Isrāfīl with one thousand angels. They greeted you with peace, and they are our reinforcements. They are the ones whom upon seeing them, Iblīs has turned on his heels in retreat saying, ﴾*This is where I leave you: I see what you do not, and I fear God – God is severe in His punishment.*﴿' [8:48]

71. From Abū ʿAlī al-Maḥmūdī, on his father's authority who, without mentioning his source, cited him [i.e. an infallible] regarding this verse: ﴾*how they strike their faces and backs.*﴿ He said, 'Rather He meant their backsides. Indeed, God is noble and He alludes.' [8:50]

72. From Jābir, from Abū Jaʿfar عليه السلام. He said, 'I asked about this verse: ﴾*The worst creatures in the sight of God are those who reject Him and will not believe.*﴿ He said, "It was revealed about the Banū Umayya. They are the worst of God's creatures; according to the inner meaning of the Qur'an they are the ones who rejected and they are the ones who do not believe."' [8:55]

73. From Muḥammad b. ʿĪsā, from whoever cited it from Abū ʿAbd Allāh عليه السلام regarding God's statement: ﴾*Prepare whatever forces you* [*believers*] *can muster.*﴿ He said, 'Swords and shields.' [8:60]

٦٩. عن محمّد بن يحيي، عن أبي عبد الله عليه السلام، في قوله: ﴿وَالرَّكْبُ أَسْفَلَ مِنكُمْ﴾، قال: أبو سفيان وأصحابه.

٧٠. عن عمرو بن أبي المقدام، عن أبيه، عن عليّ بن الحسين عليه السلام، قال: لمّا عَطِش القوم يوم بَدرٍ، انطلق عليّ بالقِربة يستقي، وهو على القَليب، إذ جاءت ريحٌ شديدةٌ ثمّ مضَت، فلَبِث ما بدا له، ثمّ جاءت ريحٌ أُخرى ثمّ مضت، ثمّ جاءته أُخرى كادت أن تشغَله وهو على القَليب ثمّ جلس حتّى مضى، فلمّا رجع إلى رسول الله صلّى الله عليه وآله أخبره بذلك، فقال رسول الله صلّى الله عليه وآله: أمّا الريح الأولى ففيها جَبرئيل مع ألفٍ من الملائكة، والثانية فيها ميكائيل مع ألفٍ من الملائكة، والثالثة فيها إسرافيل مع ألفٍ من الملائكة، وقد سلّموا عليك وهم مَدَدٌ لنا، وهم الذين رآهم إبليس فنكَص على عقبيه يمشي القَهقَرى حتّى يقول: ﴿إِنِّي أَرَى مَا لَا تَرَوْنَ إِنِّي أَخَافُ اللَّهَ وَاللَّهُ شَدِيدُ الْعِقَابِ﴾.

٧١. أبو عليّ المحمودي، عن أبيه، رفعه، في قول الله: ﴿يَضْرِبُونَ وُجُوهَهُمْ وَأَدْبَارَهُمْ﴾، قال: إنّما أراد وأستاههم، إنّ الله كريم يكنّي.

٧٢. عن جابر، عن أبي جعفر عليه السلام، قال: سألتُهُ عن هذه الآية ﴿إِنَّ شَرَّ الدَّوَابِّ عِندَ اللَّهِ الَّذِينَ كَفَرُوا فَهُمْ لَا يُؤْمِنُونَ﴾، قال: نزلت في بني أميّة، هم شرّ خلق الله، هم الذين كفروا في بطن القرآن، وهم الذين لا يؤمنون.

74. From ʿAbd Allāh b. al-Mughīra who, without mentioning his source, cited the Messenger of God ﷺ as having said, ﴾*Prepare whatever forces you* [*believers*] *can muster*﴿ – he said, "Arrows." [8:60]

75. From Muḥammad al-Ḥalabī, from Abū ʿAbd Allāh عليه السلام regarding God's statement: ﴾*But if they incline towards peace, you* [*Prophet*] *must also incline towards it.*﴿ He was asked what peace was. He replied, 'To enter within your jurisdiction.' [8:61]

76. From ʿAmr b. Abī al-Miqdām, on his father's authority, on his grandfather's authority: 'Never have I experienced a day worse than the two days that ʿAlī experienced. The first one was the day in which the Messenger of God ﷺ was taken from this world. As for the second day, by God, I was sitting in Saqīfa Banī Sāʿida to the right of Abū Bakr whilst the people were pledging allegiance to him, when ʿUmar said to him, "You! You do not actually have anything in hand as long as ʿAlī has not pledged allegiance to you. Why do you not send for him so that he can come to you and pledge allegiance to you, for the people here are only laypeople."

So he sent Qunfudh to him, and told him to go and say to ʿAlī: 'Respond to God's Messenger's caliph.' So Qunfudh went, and it was not long before he came back, and said to Abū Bakr, "He said to tell you: 'The Messenger of God has not appointed anyone after him besides me.'"

He said, "Go back to him and say: 'You had better respond, for the people have all gathered to pledge allegiance to him, the *muhajirūn* and the *anṣār* all pledge allegiance as do the Quraysh, and you are a man from among the Muslims whose gain and loss is the same as theirs.'"

So Qunfudh went back to him, and it was not long before he returned saying, "He says to tell you: 'The Messenger of God ﷺ told me and made a bequest to me that once I have entered him in his grave, not to come out of my house until I have compiled God's Book, for it is still on palm leaves and camel hides.'"

ʿUmar said, "Let us all go to him." So Abū Bakr, ʿUmar, ʿUthmān, Khālid b. al-Walīd, al-Mughīra b. Shuʿba, Abū ʿUbayda b. al-Jarrāḥ, Sālim the protégé of Abū Ḥudhayfa, and Qunfudh all stood up, and I stood up with them. When we reached his door, Fāṭima, may God's blessings be upon her, saw them and she closed the door to them. She did not think that they would

٧٣. عن محمّد بن عيسى، عمّن ذكره، عن أبي عبدالله عليه السلام، في قول الله تعالى: ﴿وَأَعِدُّوا لَهُم مَا اسْتَطَعْتُم مِنْ قُوَّةٍ﴾، قال: سيفك وتُرس.

٧٤. عن عبدالله بن المُغيرة، رفعه، قال: قال رسول الله صلى الله عليه وآله ﴿وَأَعِدُّوا لَهُم مَا اسْتَطَعْتُم مِنْ قُوَّةٍ﴾، قال الرمي.

٧٥. عن محمّد الحلبي، عن أبي عبدالله عليه السلام، في قول الله: ﴿وَإِنْ جَنَحُوا لِلسَّلْمِ فَاجْنَحْ لَهَا﴾ فسُئِل ما السَّلم؟ قال: الدُّخول في أمرك.

٧٦. عن عمرو بن أبي المقدام، عن أبيه، عن جدّه: ما أتي عليّ يوم قطّ أعظم من يومين أتيا عليًّا، فأمّا اليوم الأوّل فيوم قُبِض رسول الله صلى الله عليه وآله، وأمّا اليوم الثاني فوالله إنّي لجالسٌ في سَقيفة بني ساعدة عن يمين أبي بكر، والنّاس يُبايعونه، إذ قال له عمر: يا هذا، ليس في يديك شيءٌ مهما لم يُبايعك عليّ، فابعث إليه حتّى يأتيك يُبايعك، فإنّما هؤلاء رَعاع، فبعث إليه قُنفُذ، فقال له: اذهب فقل لعليّ: أجب خليفة رسول الله صلى الله عليه وآله، فذهب قُنفُذ، فمّا لَبِث أن رَجَع فقال لأبي بكر: قال لك: ما خلّف رسول الله أحدًا غيري.

قال: ارجِع إليه فقُل: أجب، فإنّ الناس قد أجمعوا على بيعتهم إيّاه، وهؤلاء المهاجرون والأنصار يُبايعونه وقريش، وإنّما أنت رجلٌ من المسلمين، لك ما لهم وعليك ما عليهم، فذهب إليه قُنفُذ، فما لبِث أن رَجَع فقال: قال لك: إنّ رسول الله صلى الله عليه وآله قال لي وأوصاني أن إذا واريته في حُفرته لا أخرُج من بيتي حتّى أؤلّف كتاب الله، فإنّه في جرائد النخل وفي أكتاف الإبل.

enter upon her except with her permission. So 'Umar kicked the door down with his foot and broke it, it being made of rattan. Then they entered and dragged 'Alī ؑ out by the collar. So Fāṭima, peace be upon her, came out saying, "Abū Bakr, do you want to make me a widow? By God, if you do not leave him alone I will untie my hair, tear my clothes, go to my father's grave and cry out to my Lord."

Then she took al-Ḥasan and al-Ḥusayn, peace be upon them, and went out towards the grave of the Prophet ﷺ. So 'Alī ؑ said to Salmān, "Go and fetch Muḥammad's daughter, for I must ensure that both sides of Medina are protected. By God, if she unties her hair, tears her clothes, goes to her father's grave and cries out to her Lord, there will be nothing to stop Medina from collapsing to the ground [with its inhabitants]."

So Salmān – may God be pleased with him – fetched her. He said, "O daughter of Muḥammad, God sent your father as a mercy, so come back."

She replied, "Salmān, they want to kill 'Alī, and 'Alī has no patience. Let me go to my father's grave so that I may untie my hair, tear my clothes and cry out to my Lord."

So Salmān said, "I fear that Medina will collapse into the ground, and it is 'Alī who has sent me to you and commands you to go back to your house and abstain [from doing this]."

So she responded, "Very well then, I will go back and be patient, and I will listen to him and obey."'

He [the narrator] said, 'So they dragged him out of his house by the collar and made him walk past the Prophet's grave, peace be upon him and his family.' He said, 'I heard him say, ﴾*Son of my mother, these people over-powered me!*﴿ until the end of the verse.[4] Abū Bakr sat in Saqīfa Banī Sā'ida, and as 'Alī approached 'Umar said to him: "Pledge allegiance."

So 'Alī said to him, "And what if I do not?"

'Umar replied, "Then I will behead you, by God."

So 'Alī said to him, "In that case, by God, I will be God's murdered servant and the Prophet's brother."

So 'Umar retorted, "God's murdered servant – yes. But the Prophet's brother – no." And he said that three times.

---

4 ﴾*Son of my mother, these people over- powered me! They almost killed me! Do not give my enemies reason to rejoice! Do not include me with these evildoers!*﴿ (Q. 7:150)

قال عمر: قُوموا بنا إليه؛ فقام أبو بكر، وعمر، وعثمان وخالد بن الوليد، والمُغيرة بن شعبة، وأبو عبيدة بن الجرّاح، وسالم مولى أبي حُذيفة، وقُنفُذ، وقُمتُ معهم، فلمّا انتهينا إلى الباب فرأتهم فاطمة صلوات الله عليها، أغلقت الباب في وجُوههم، وهي لا تشُكُّ أن لا يُدخَل عليها إلاّ بإذنها، فضَرَب عُمر الباب برِجله فكَسَره، ثمّ دخلوا فأخرجوا عليّاً عليه السلام مُلبّياً، فخرجت فاطمة عليها السلام، فقالت: يا أبا بكر، أتُريد أن تُرَمّلني من زوجي، والله لئن لم تكُفَّ عنه لأنشُرَنَّ شعري، ولأشُقَّنَّ جيبي، ولآتينَّ قبر أبي، ولأصيحنَّ إلى ربّي، فاخذت بيد الحسن والحسين عليهما السلام، وخرجت تُريد قبر النبيّ صلى الله عليه وآله.

فقال عليّ عليه السلام لسلمان: أدرك ابنة محمّد، فإنّي أرى جنبتَي المدينة تكفيان، والله إن نَشَرت شعرها، وشقّت جَيبها، وأتت قبر أبيها، وصاحت إلى ربّها، لا يُناظر بالمدينة أن يُخسَف بها وبمن فيها. فأدركها سلمان عليه السلام، فقال: يا بنت محمّد، إنّ الله إنّما بعث أباك رحمة فارجعي. فقالت: يا سلمان، يُريدون قتل عليّ، ما على عليّ صبر، فدعني حتّى آتي قبر أبي، فأنشُر شَعري، وأشُقّ جيبي، وأصيح إلى ربّي.

فقال سلمان: إنّي أخاف أن يُخسَف بالمدينة، وعليٌّ بعثني إليك يأمُرك أن ترجِعي إلى بيتك وتَنصَرفي. فقالت: إذاً أرجع وأصبر وأسمع له وأُطيع.

قال: فأخرَجوه من منزله مُلبّياً، ومرّوا به على قبر النبيّ عليه وآله السلام، قال: فسمِعتُه يقول: ﴿يا ابْنَ أُمَّ إِنَّ الْقَوْمَ اسْتَضْعَفُونِي﴾ إلى آخر الآية، وجلس أبو بكر في سقيفة بني ساعدة، وقَدِم عليّ عليه السلام، فقال له عمر: بايع. فقال له عليّ عليه السلام: فإن أنا لم أفعل فمَه؟ فقال له عمر: إذاً أضرِبُ والله عُنُقك. فقال له عليّ عليه السلام: إذاً والله أكونُ عبد الله المقتول، وأخا

'Abbās b. 'Abd al-Muṭṭalib heard about all this and came running hurriedly, and I heard him say, "Be gentle with my nephew; I can make him pledge allegiance to you." Al-'Abbās came and took 'Alī's hand and stroked it upon Abū Bakr's hand. Then they left him there, angered, and I heard him say, lifting his head up to the sky, "O God! You know what the Prophet ﷺ had said to me: 'When there are twenty of you in total, fight them. This is Your statement in Your Book: ﴾*if there are twenty of you who are steadfast, they will overcome two hundred.*﴿' He [the narrator] said, 'I also heard him say, "O God! They have not even reached a total of twenty" until he had said that three times. Then he left.' [8:65]

77. From Furāt b. Aḥnaf[5], from one of his associates, from 'Alī عليه السلام that he said, 'Whenever a tribulation befalls people, my followers (*shī'a*) maintain the best state during it, and this is God's statement: ﴾*But God has lightened your burden for now, knowing that there is weakness in you.*﴿' [8:66]

78. From Ḥusayn b. Ṣāliḥ who said, 'I heard Abū 'Abd Allāh عليه السلام say, "'Alī – may God's blessings be upon him, used to say, 'Whoever flees from two men during the battle has indeed fled from the battle itself, and whoever flees from three men during the battle has not fled from the battle.'"' [8:66]

79. From Mu'āwiya b. 'Ammār, from Abū 'Abd Allāh عليه السلام. He said, 'I heard him say about this verse: ﴾*Prophet, tell those you have taken captive, 'If God knows of any good in your hearts, He will give you something better than what has been taken from you'*﴿ [i.e. as ransom]. He said, "It was revealed about al-'Abbās, 'Aqīl and Nawfal."[6] He also said, "The Messenger of God ﷺ forbade anyone from among the Banū Hāshim or Abū al-Bakhtarī to be killed on the day of Badr, so they were taken captive, and he dispatched 'Alī saying, 'Go and see who is here from the Banū Hāshim.'"

He said, "So 'Alī came across 'Aqīl b. Abī Ṭālib but paid no attention to him."

5 Furāt b. Aḥnaf al-'Abdī, a narrator of the fourth, fifth and sixth Imams who was accused of *ghuluww* and criticised heavily for fabricating *ḥadīth*s. See Ḥillī, *Khulāṣat al-aqwāl*, 387 (nr. 1555).

6 This is Nawfal b. al-Ḥārith b. 'Abd al-Muṭṭalib, a captive from the Battle of Badr.

رسول الله ﷺ. فقال عمر: أمّا عبد الله المقتول فنعم، وأمّا أخو رسول الله فلا — حتّى قالها ثلاثًا —.

فبلغ ذلك العبّاس بن عبد المطّلب، فأقبل مُسرِعًا يُهرول، فسَمِعتُه يقول: أرفِقوا بابن أخي، ولكم عليَّ أن يُبايعكم، فأقبل العبّاس، وأخذ بيد عليّ عليه السلام، فمسحها على يد أبي بكر، ثمّ خلّوه مُغضِبًا، فسمِعتُه يقول: اللّهمّ إنّك تعلم أنّ النبيّ ﷺ قد قال لي: «إن تمّوا عشرين فجاهِدهم» وهو قولك في كتابك: ﴿إِن يَكُن مِّنكُمْ عِشْرُونَ صَابِرُونَ يَغْلِبُوا مِائَتَيْنِ﴾، قال: وسَمِعتُه يقول: اللّهمّ وإنّهم لم يتِمّوا عشرين؛ حتّى قالها ثلاثًا، ثمّ انصَرف.

٧٧. عن فُرات بن أحنف، عن بعض أصحابه، عن عليّ عليه السلام، أنّه قال: ما نزل بالناس أزمة قطُّ إلّا كان شيعتي فيها أحسن حالاً، وهو قول الله: ﴿الْآنَ خَفَّفَ اللَّهُ عَنكُمْ وَعَلِمَ أَنَّ فِيكُمْ ضَعْفًا﴾.

٧٨. عن حسين بن صالح، قال: سمعتُ أبا عبد الله عليه السلام يقول: كان عليّ عليه السلام يقول: من فرّ من رجلين في القتال من الزّحف، فقد فرّ من الزّحف، ومن فرّ من ثلاثة رجال في القتال من الزّحف فلم يفِرّ.

٧٩. عن معاوية بن عمّار، عن أبي عبد الله عليه السلام، قال: سمِعتُه يقول في هذه الآية ﴿يَا أَيُّهَا النَّبِيُّ قُل لِّمَن فِي أَيْدِيكُم مِّنَ الْأَسْرَىٰ إِن يَعْلَمِ اللَّهُ فِي قُلُوبِكُمْ خَيْرًا يُؤْتِكُمْ خَيْرًا مِّمَّا أُخِذَ مِنكُمْ﴾، قال: نزلت في العبّاس وعقيل ونوفل. وقال: إنّ رسول الله ﷺ نهى

He said, "So he said to him, 'O son of my mother, 'Alī, by God, you have seen what situation I am in!'"

He said, "So he went back to the Messenger of God, peace be upon him and his family, and said to him, 'There is Abū al-Faḍl [i.e. al-'Abbās, the Prophet's uncle] held captive by so and so, 'Aqīl held by so and so, and Nawfal held by so and so [i.e. Nawfal b. al-Ḥārith].'

So the Messenger of God, peace be upon him and his family, stood up and went to 'Aqīl and said to him, 'Abū Yazīd, Abū Jahl has been killed.'

So he said, 'In that case, you will no longer fight in Tihāma [Mecca].'

He said, 'If you had already vanquished the people, [then you could release them]. Otherwise, keep them bound up in your control.'"

He said, "Then 'Abbās was brought and was told, 'Pay ransom for yourself and your two nephews.' So he replied, 'O Muḥammad, are you going to make me have to ask the Quraysh for my release?'

He replied, 'Pay out of what you had left behind with Umm Faḍl, when you said to her, "If anything happens to me, spend this on your son and yourself."'

He asked, 'My nephew! Who told you about this?'

He replied, 'Jibra'īl brought it to me from God.'

So he exclaimed, 'By the object of his oath, no one knows about this apart from her and myself. I bear witness that you are indeed God's Messenger.'"

He said, "The prisoners all went back as polytheists apart from al-'Abbās, 'Aqīl and Nawfal b. al-Ḥārith, and this verse was revealed about them: ﴾*Prophet, tell those you have taken captive* [...]﴿"' [8:70]

80. From 'Alī b. Asbāṭ who heard Abū al-Ḥasan al-Riḍā عليه السلام say that Abū 'Abd Allāh عليه السلام said, 'The Prophet ﷺ brought some money and said to al-'Abbās, "Spread out your cloak and take a portion of this money."'

He said, 'So he spread out his cloak and took a portion of that wealth.' He said, 'Then the Messenger of God ﷺ said, "This is what God has said: ﴾*Prophet, tell those you have taken captive, 'If God knows of any good in your hearts, He will give you something better than what has been taken from you'.*﴿"' [8:70]

يوم بدرٍ أن يُقتَل أحدٌ من بني هاشم أو أبو البَختَري، فأُسِروا، فأرسل عليًّا ﵇، فقال: انظُر من هاهنا من بني هاشم، قال: فمرّ عليٌّ على عقيل بن أبي طالب، فحاد عنه.

قال: فقال له: يا بن أمّ عليّ، أما والله لقد رأيتَ مكاني.

قال: فرجع إلى رسول الله ﷺ، فقال له: هذا أبو الفضل في يد فلان، وهذا عقيل في يد فلان، وهذا نوفَل في يد فلان، يعني نوفل بن الحارث.

فقام رسول الله ﷺ حتّى انتهى إلى عقيل، فقال له: يا أبا يزيد، قُتِل أبو جهل، فقال: إذًا لا تُنازعون في تِهامة، قال: إن كنتم أثخنتم القوم، وإلاّ فاركَبُوا أكتافهم.

قال: فجيء بالعبّاس، فقيل له: افِد نفسك، وافدِ ابنَي أخيك. فقال: يا محمّد، تركتني أسأل قريشًا في كفّي؟ قال: أعطِ ممّا خلّفت عند أمّ الفضل، وقلتَ لها: إن أصابني شيءٌ في وجهي فأنفقيه على ولدك ونفسك. قال: يا ابن أخي، من خبّرك بهذا؟ قال: أتاني به جَبرائيل فقال: ومَحلُوفه ما عَلِم بهذا إلاّ أنا وهي، أشهدُ أنّك رسول الله.

قال: فرَجَع الأُسارى كلُّهم مُشركين إلاّ العبّاس وعقيل ونَوفل بن الحارث، وفيهم نزلت هذه الآية ﴿قُل لِّمَن فِىٓ أَيۡدِيكُم مِّنَ ٱلۡأَسۡرَىٰٓ﴾ إلى آخرها.

٨٠. عن عليّ بن أسباط: أنّه سَمِع أبا الحسن الرضا ﵇ يقول: قال أبو عبد الله ﵇: أُتي النبيّ ﷺ بمالٍ فقال للعبّاس: ابسُط رِداءك فخُذ من هذا المال طَرفًا، قال: فبَسَط رداءه فأخذ طَرفًا من ذلك المال، قال: ثُمّ قال رسول الله ﷺ: هذا ممّا قال الله: ﴿يَٰٓأَيُّهَا ٱلنَّبِيُّ قُل لِّمَن فِىٓ أَيۡدِيكُم مِّنَ ٱلۡأَسۡرَىٰٓ إِن يَعۡلَمِ ٱللَّهُ فِى قُلُوبِكُمۡ خَيۡرٗا يُؤۡتِكُمۡ خَيۡرٗا مِّمَّآ أُخِذَ مِنكُمۡ﴾.

81. From Zurāra, Ḥumrān and Muḥammad b. Muslim, from Abū Ja'far and Abū 'Abd Allāh, peace be upon them. They said, 'We asked them about His verse: ﴾*As for those who believed but did not emigrate, you are not responsible for their protection until they have done so.*﴿ They said, 'Because the people of Mecca do not inherit from the people of Medina.' [8:72]

82. From 'Abd Allāh b. Sinān, from Abū 'Abd Allāh عليه السلام on his forefathers' authority who said, "Alī عليه السلام visited the Messenger of God صلى الله عليه وآله during his sickness when he had fainted with his head in Jibra'īl's lap when Jibra'īl was in the form of Diḥya al-Kalbī. When 'Alī عليه السلام entered, Jibra'īl said to him, "Take your cousin's head as you have greater right to it than me, for indeed God says in His Book: ﴾*but relatives still have prior claim over one another in God's Scripture.*﴿"

So 'Alī عليه السلام sat down and took God's Messenger's head and placed it on his lap. The head of God's Messenger صلى الله عليه وآله was still on his lap when the sun set, and the Messenger of God regained consciousness and lifted his head, looking at 'Alī and said, "'Alī, where is Jibra'īl?" He replied, "O Messenger of God, I only saw Diḥya al-Kalbī who handed me your head. He said, "Alī, take your cousin's head for you have greater right to it than me, for God says in His Book: ﴾*but relatives still have prior claim over one another in God's Scripture.*﴿' So I sat down and took your head, and you were still on my lap when the sun set."

The Messenger of God صلى الله عليه وآله then asked him, "Have you prayed the afternoon (*'aṣr*) prayer?" He replied, "No." He asked, "What prevented you from praying?" So he replied, "You had fainted, and your head was on my lap, and I could not bear to disturb you, O Messenger of God, and nor could I stand up and pray whilst putting your head down."

So the Messenger of God صلى الله عليه وآله said, "O God, he was only engaged in servitude to You and Your Messenger when he missed the afternoon prayer. O God, reverse the sun back for him that he may pray the afternoon prayer on time."'

He said, 'So the sun rose again until it became afternoon, bright and clear, and the people of Medina saw it. 'Alī stood up and prayed, and as soon as he had finished, the sun set and they prayed the evening (*maghrib*) prayer.' [8:75]

٨١. عن زُرارة وحُمران ومحمّد بن مسلم، عن أبي جعفر وأبي عبد الله عليهما السلام، قالوا: سألناهما عن قوله: ﴿وَالَّذِينَ آمَنُوا وَلَمْ يُهَاجِرُوا مَا لَكُمْ مِنْ وَلَايَتِهِمْ مِنْ شَيْءٍ حَتَّى يُهَاجِرُوا﴾، قالا: إنّ أهل مكّة لا يرِثون أهل المدينة.

٨٢. عن عبد الله بن سِنان، عن أبي عبد الله عليه السلام، عن أبيه، عن آبائه، قال: دخل عليّ عليه السلام على رسول الله صلى الله عليه وآله في مرضه، وقد أُغميَ عليه، ورأسه في حِجر جَبرئيل، وجَبرئيل في صورة دِحيَة الكلبي، فلمّا دخل عليّ عليه السلام قال له جَبرئيل: دُونك رأس ابن عمّك، فأنت أحقّ به منّي، لأنّ الله يقول في كتابه: ﴿وَأُولُوا الْأَرْحَامِ بَعْضُهُمْ أَوْلَى بِبَعْضٍ فِي كِتَابِ اللَّهِ﴾.

فجلس عليّ عليه السلام وأخذ رأس رسول الله صلى الله عليه وآله، فوضعه في حِجره، فلم يَزل رأس رسول الله في حِجره حتّى غابت الشمس، وإنّ رسول الله صلى الله عليه وآله أفاق، فرفع رأسه، ونظر إلى عليّ عليه السلام، فقال: يا عليّ، أين جَبرئيل؟ فقال: يا رسول الله، ما رأيت إلاّ دِحية الكلبي دفع إليّ رأسك، وقال: يا عليّ، دُونك رأس ابن عمّك، فأنتَ أحقّ به منّي، لأنّ الله يقول في كتابه: ﴿وَأُولُوا الْأَرْحَامِ بَعْضُهُمْ أَوْلَى بِبَعْضٍ فِي كِتَابِ اللَّهِ﴾ فجلستُ وأخذتُ رأسك، فلم يَزل في حِجري حتّى غابت الشمس.

فقال له رسول الله صلى الله عليه وآله: أفصلّيتَ العصر؟ فقال: لا، قال: فما منعك أن تُصلّي؟ فقال: قد أغمي عليك، وكان رأسك في حِجري، فكرِهتُ أن أشقّ عليك يا رسول الله، وكرِهت أن أقوم وأصلّي وأضع رأسك.

فقال رسول الله صلى الله عليه وآله: اللّهمّ إنّ عليّاً كان في طاعتك وطاعة رسولك حتّى فاتته صلاة العصر، اللّهمّ فرُدّ عليه الشمس حتّى يُصلّي العصر في وقتِها. قال: فطلعت

83. From Abū Baṣīr, from Abū Jaʿfar al-Bāqir عليه السلام who said, 'The maternal uncle and aunt can inherit if there is no one else besides them. God says: ﴾ *but relatives still have prior claim over one another in God's Scripture.* ﴿ If relations overlap, then the foremost relationship takes precedence when inheriting from relatives.' [8:75]

84. From Ibn Sinān, from Abū 'Abd Allāh عليه السلام who said, 'When 'Alī b. Abī Ṭālib عليه السلام and 'Uthmān b. 'Affān differed in the case of a man who dies with no immediate family to inherit from him, but he does have relatives who do not have a designated share stipulated through which they would inherit from him, 'Alī said, "His inheritance goes to his relatives, because God most High says: ﴾ *but relatives still have prior claim over one another in God's Scripture.* ﴿" 'Uthmān, however, said, "Put his inheritance in the public treasury of the Muslims, and none of his relatives inherit from him."' [8:75]

85. From Sulaymān b. Khālid, from Abū 'Abd Allāh عليه السلام who said, "Alī عليه السلام did not grant [inheritance] to protégés so long as there was an existing relative, whether he had a designated share or not. He used to say: ﴾ *but relatives still have prior claim over one another in God's Scripture: God has full knowledge of all things.* ﴿ He knew their position, so he did not place them with the relatives since He says: ﴾ *but relatives still have prior claim over one another in God's Scripture.* ﴿' [8:75]

الشمس، فصارت في وقت العصر بيضاء نقيّة، ونظر إليها أهل المدينة، وإنّ عليّاً عليه السلام قام وصلّى، فلمّا أنصرف غابت الشمس، وصلّوا المغرب.

٨٣. عن أبي بصير، عن أبي جعفر الباقر عليه السلام، قال: الخال والخالة يرثان إذا لم يكن معهم أحدٌ غيرهم، إنّ الله تبارك وتعالى يقول: ﴿وَأُوْلُوا الأَرْحَامِ بَعْضُهُمْ أَوْلَى بِبَعْضٍ فِي كِتَابِ اللهِ﴾ فإذا التقت القرابات، فالسابق أحقّ بالميراث من قرابته.

٨٤. عن ابن سنان، عن أبي عبدالله عليه السلام، قال: لمّا اختلف عليّ بن أبي طالب عليه السلام وعثمان بن عفّان في الرجل يموت وليس له عَصَبة يرِثونه، وله ذو قرابة لا يرِثونه ليس له سهم مفروضٌ، فقال عليّ عليه السلام: ميراثه لِذوي قرابته، لأنّ الله تعالى يقول: ﴿وَأُوْلُوا الأَرْحَامِ بَعْضُهُمْ أَوْلَى بِبَعْضٍ فِي كِتَابِ اللهِ﴾، وقال عثمان: اجْعل ميراثه في بيت مال المسلمين، ولا يَرِثه أحدٌ من قرابته.

٨٥. عن سُليمان بن خالد، عن أبي عبدالله عليه السلام، قال: كان عليّ عليه السلام لا يُعطي الموالي شيئًا مع ذي رَحِم، سُمّيت له فريضة أم لم تُسمّ له فريضة، وكان يقول: ﴿وَأُوْلُوا الأَرْحَامِ بَعْضُهُمْ أَوْلَى بِبَعْضٍ فِي كِتَابِ اللهِ إِنَّ اللهَ بِكُلِّ شَيْءٍ عَلِيمٌ﴾ قد علِم مكانهم، فلم يجعل لهم مع أولي الأرحام حيث قال: ﴿وَأُوْلُوا الأَرْحَامِ بَعْضُهُمْ أَوْلَى بِبَعْضٍ فِي كِتَابِ اللهِ﴾.

86. From Zurāra, from Abū Ja'far عليه السلام regarding God's verse: ﴾*but relatives still have prior claim over one another in God's Scripture.*﴿ 'Some of them have a greater claim to the inheritance over others because the closest to him [in kinship] has a greater claim.' Then Abū Ja'far said, 'They have a greater claim to the deceased. The closest ones to them are his mother, and his siblings from both parents. Is the mother not closer to the deceased than his brothers and sisters?' [8:75]

87. From Abū 'Amr al-Zubayrī, from Abū 'Abd Allāh عليه السلام. He said, 'I said to him: "Tell me about the transferal of the Imamate to the progeny of al-Ḥusayn rather than the progeny of al-Ḥasan – how does that work and what is the proof for it?" He replied, "When al-Ḥusayn was faced with God's authority that came to him, he was not allowed to pass it back to his brother's children nor leave it to them as a bequest. God says: ﴾*but relatives still have prior claim over one another in God's Scripture.*﴿ So his son was closer to him in kin than his brother's son, and they had a greater right over the Imamate. This verse precluded the progeny of al-Ḥasan from it, so the Imamate passed on to al-Ḥusayn. The verse ruled this in their favour, and it pertains to them until the Day of Judgement."' [8:75]

٨٦. عن زُرارة، عن أبي جعفر عليه السلام، في قول الله: ﴿وَأُوْلُوا الأَرْحَامِ بَعْضُهُمْ أَوْلَى بِبَعْضٍ فِي كِتَابِ اللهِ﴾ إنّ بعضهم أولى بالميراث من بعض، لأنّ أقربهم إليه رَحِمًا أولى به. ثمّ قال أبو جعفر عليه السلام: إنّه أولى بالميت وأقربهم إليه أمّه وأخوه وأُخته لأمّه وأبيه، أليس الأمّ أقرب إلى الميّت من إخوته وأخواته؟

٨٧. عن أبي عمرو الزبيري، عن أبي عبد الله عليه السلام، قال: قلتُ له: أخبرني عن خُروج الإمامة من ولد الحسن إلى ولد الحسين، كيف ذلك، وما الحجّة فيه؟ قال: لمّا حضر الحسين عليه السلام ما حضره من أمر الله، لم يجُز أن يرُدّها إلى ولد أخيه، ولا يوصي بها فيهم، لقول الله: ﴿وَأُوْلُوا الأَرْحَامِ بَعْضُهُمْ أَوْلَى بِبَعْضٍ فِي كِتَابِ اللهِ﴾ فكان ولده أقرب رحِمًا إليه من ولد أخيه، وكانوا أولى بالإمامة، فأخرجت هذه الآية ولد الحسن عليه السلام منها، فصارت الإمامة إلى ولد الحسين عليه السلام، وحكمت بها الآية لهم، فهي فيهم إلى يوم القيامة.

The Impunity

9. The Impunity[1]

1. From Abū Baṣīr, from Abū ʿAbd Allāh ﵇. He said, 'I heard him say, "One who recites the Chapter of the Impunity (*sūrat al-barāʾa*) and the Chapter of the Battle Gains (*sūrat al-anfāl*) every month shall never be infected by hypocrisy, and he will be one of the followers (*shīʿa*) of the Commander of the Faithful ﵇ in truth. On the Day of Judgement, he will already be enjoying the feasts of the Garden with his followers whilst others finish giving their account."'

2. From Dāwūd b. Sirḥān, from Abū ʿAbd Allāh ﵇ who said, 'The conquest [of Mecca] took place in the eighth year [after *hijra*], the *barāʾa* (declaration of impunity to the idolaters) in the ninth year, and the farewell pilgrimage in the tenth.' [9:1]

3. From Abū al-ʿAbbās, from one of the two [al-Bāqir or al-Ṣādiq] who said, 'The Chapter of the Battle Gains and the Chapter of the Impunity are one [chapter].'

4. From Ḥarīz, from Abū ʿAbd Allāh ﵇ who said, 'The Messenger of God ﷺ dispatched Abū Bakr to perform the Hajj with the declaration of impunity (*barāʾa*) so that he may read it to the people. Jibraʾīl subsequently came down and said, "No one should proclaim on your behalf apart from ʿAlī." So the Messenger of God ﷺ called ʿAlī and commanded him to take his camel al-ʿAḍbāʾ, catch up with Abū Bakr, seize the declaration of impunity from him and read it out to the people in Mecca.

   When this happened, Abū Bakr asked, "Is it out of displeasure?"

1 The Chapter of Impunity (*sūrat al-barāʾa*) is also known as the Chapter of Repentance (*sūrat al-tawba*).

بسم الله الرحمن الرحيم

من سورة براءة

١. عن أبي بصير، عن أبي عبدالله عليه السلام، قال: سَمِعته يقول: من قرأ سورة براءة والأنفال في كلّ شهرٍ لم يدخُله نِفاقٌ أبدًا، وكان من شيعة أمير المؤمنين عليه السلام حقًّا، وأكل يوم القيامة من موائد الجنّة مع شيعة عليّ عليه السلام حتّى يفرُغ الناس من الحساب.

٢. عن داود بن سِرحان، عن أبي عبدالله عليه السلام، قال: كان الفتح في سنة ثمان، وبراءة في سنة تسع، وحجّة الوداع في سنة عشر.

٣. عن أبي العباس، عن أحدهما عليهم السلام، قال: الأنفال وسورة براءة واحدة.

٤. عن حَريز، عن أبي عبدالله عليه السلام، قال: إنّ رسول الله صلى الله عليه وآله بعث أبا بكر مع براءة إلى الموسم ليقرأها على الناس، فنزل جَبرئيل عليه السلام، فقال: لا يُبلّغ عنك إلاّ عليّ عليه السلام، فدعا رسول الله صلى الله عليه وآله عليًّا عليه السلام، فأمره أن يركب ناقته العضباء، وأمره أن يلحَق أبا بكر، فيأخُذ منه براءة، ويقرأها على الناس بمكّة، فقال أبو بكر: أَسَخطَة؟ فقال: لا، إلاّ أنّه أُنزِل عليه أنّه لا يُبلِّغ إلاّ رجلٌ منك.

ʿAlī replied, "No, but this is what has been revealed to him: none but a man of your own should proclaim it."

When ʿAlī arrived at Mecca in the afternoon of the Day of Sacrifice, the day of the Great Pilgrimage, he stood up and said, "I am God's messenger to you all." Then he read it out to them: ﴾*An impunity by God and His Messenger from the treaty you [believers] made with the idolaters [is announced] – you [idolaters] may move freely about the land for four months*﴿ – twenty days from the month of Dhū al-Ḥijja, Muḥarram, Ṣafar and Rabīʿ I, and ten days of Rabīʿ II."

And he said, "No naked man or woman shall circumambulate the House, nor any idolater except one who has a treaty with God's Messenger, whose term is during these four months."' [9:1]

5. In Muḥammad b. Muslim's report, he [i.e. Abū Bakr] said, 'O ʿAlī, has anything been revealed about me since I left the Messenger of God?' He replied, 'No, but God has refused anyone save a man of his own to proclaim on Muḥammad's behalf.' So he performed the Hajj and proclaimed on the behalf of God and His Messenger at ʿArafa, Muzdalifa, by the pillars on the day of the Great Pilgrimage, and on all the days of *tashrīq*,[2] calling out: '﴾*An impunity by God and His Messenger from the treaty you [believers] made with the idolaters [is announced] – you [idolaters] may move freely about the land for four months*﴿, and no one shall circumambulate the House naked.' [9:1]

6. From Zurāra who said, 'I heard Abū Jaʿfar ؑ say, "Nay, I swear by God, the Messenger of God ﷺ did not dispatch Abū Bakr with the declaration of impunity. Does it make sense that he would have dispatched him with it only to then take it away from him? Rather he deployed him for the rites of Hajj and sent ʿAlī with it after Abū Bakr had been relieved of the Hajj duties. When he dispatched ʿAlī [with the Chapter of Impunity] he said to him: 'Indeed, none shall fulfil [any task] on my behalf apart from you and I.' [9:1]

7. From Abū Baṣīr, from Abū Jaʿfar ؑ who said, "ʿAlī addressed the people and drew his sword saying, "No one shall circumambulate the house naked,

2 The days of *tashrīq* are the 11–13th of Dhū al-Ḥijja. They immediately follow the stipulated days of Hajj and are a time when people are free to eat the meat they had sacrificed.

فلمّا قدم عليّ مكّة، وكان يوم النحر بعد الظهر، وهو يوم الحجّ الأكبر، قام ثمّ قال: إنّي رسولُ رسولِ الله إليكم: فقرأها عليهم: ﴿بَرَاءَةٌ مِنَ اللَّهِ وَرَسُولِهِ إِلَى الَّذِينَ عَاهَدْتُمْ مِنَ الْمُشْرِكِينَ ۝ فَسِيحُوا فِي الْأَرْضِ أَرْبَعَةَ أَشْهُرٍ﴾ عشرين من ذي الحجّة، والمحرّم، وصفر، وشهر ربيع الأوّل، وعشرًا من شهر ربيع الآخر.

وقال: لا يطوفُ بالبيت عُريان ولا عُريانة، ولا مُشرِك، إلاّ من كان له عهد عند رسول الله ﷺ فمدّته إلى هذه الأربعة الأشهر.

٥. وفي خبر محمّد بن مسلم، فقال: يا عليّ، هل نزل فيَّ شيء منذ فارقتَ رسول الله؟ قال: لا، ولكن أبى الله أن يُبلِّغ عن محمّد ﷺ إلاّ رجلٌ منه: فوافى الموسم، فبلغ عن الله وعن رسوله بعرفة والمزدلفة ويوم النحر عند الجمار، وفي أيّام التشريق كلّها ينادي: ﴿بَرَاءَةٌ مِنَ اللَّهِ وَرَسُولِهِ إِلَى الَّذِينَ عَاهَدْتُمْ مِنَ الْمُشْرِكِينَ ۝ فَسِيحُوا فِي الْأَرْضِ أَرْبَعَةَ أَشْهُرٍ﴾ ولا يطُوفنَّ بالبيت عُريان.

٦. عن زُرارة، قال: سمعتُ أبا جعفر عليه السلام يقول: لا واللهِ ما بعث رسول الله عليه السلام أبا بكر ببراءة، أهو كان يبعث بها معه، ثمّ يأخذها منه؟ ولكنّه استعمله على الموسم، وبعث بها عليًا عليه السلام بعد ما فَصَل أبو بكر عن الموسم، فقال لعليّ عليه السلام حين بعثه: إنّه لا يؤدّي عنّي إلاّ أنا وأنت.

٧. عن أبي بصير، عن أبي جعفر عليه السلام، قال: خطب عليّ عليه السلام الناس، واخترط سيفه، وقال: لا يَطوفنَّ بالبيت عُريان، ولا يَحُجنَّ بالبيت مُشرك، ومن كانت له مُدّةٌ فهو إلى مُدّته،

nor will an idolater or idolatress perform the pilgrimage to the House. Whoever has an agreed term will adhere to his term, and whoever does not have an agreed term then his term is four months:" – he was addressing them on the Day of Sacrifice – "they were twenty days from Dhū al-Ḥijja, Muḥarram, Ṣafar, Rabīʿ I and ten days of Rabīʿ II." He also said, "The day of Sacrifice is the day of the Great Pilgrimage."' [9:1]

8. In Abū al-Ṣabbāḥ's report on his authority, 'He proclaimed on behalf of God and His Messenger at ʿArafa, Muzdalifa and by the pillars throughout all the days of the Hajj season, calling out: ﴾*An impunity by God and His Messenger* [...]﴿, and no one shall circumambulate naked nor will the idolater approach the Sacred Mosque after this year of ours.' [9:1]

9. From Ḥanash[3], on ʿAlī's authority عليه السلام that the Prophet, peace be upon him and his family, when he dispatched ʿAlī with the declaration of impunity, he said, 'O Prophet of God, I am neither eloquent nor articulate.'

He said, 'It is imperative that either I take it or you.'

He replied, 'If it is imperative then, in that case, I will take it myself.'

He said, 'Set off, for indeed God will strengthen your tongue and guide your heart.'

Then he placed his hand upon his mouth and said, 'Go and read it out to the people.' Then he said, 'People will come to you to settle their disputes, so if two opposing parties come to you do not judge in favour of one without hearing the other one out; for it is better for you that you should know the whole truth.' [9:1]

10. From Zurāra, Ḥumrān and Muḥammad b. Muslim, from Abū Jaʿfar and Abū ʿAbd Allāh عليه السلام regarding His statement: ﴾*you* [*idolaters*] *may move freely about the land for four months.*﴿ He said, 'Twenty days of Dhū al-Ḥijja, Muḥarram, Ṣafar, Rabīʿ I and ten days of Rabīʿ II.' [9:2]

3 Ḥanash b. al-Muʿtabar, a companion of ʿAlī b. Abī Ṭālib. See Khūʾī, *Muʿjam*, 7:321 (nr. 4115).

ومن لم يكن له مُدّة فمدّته أربعة أشهر؛ وكان خطب يوم النحر، وكانت عشرون من ذي الحجّة، والمحرّم، وصفر، وشهر ربيع الأوّل، وعشر من شهر ربيع الآخر، وقال: يوم النحر يوم الحجّ الأكبر.

٨. وفي خبر أبي الصبّاح، عنه عليه السلام: فبلّغ عن الله وعن رسوله صلى الله عليه وآله بعرَفة والمُزدلِفة، وعند الجِمار، في أيّام الموسم كُلّها ينادي ﴿بَرَاءَةٌ مِنَ اللَّهِ وَرَسُولِهِ﴾ ولا يَطُوفنَّ بالبيت عُريان، ولا يقربَنَّ المسجد الحرام بعد عامنا هذا مُشرك.

٩. عن حَنَش، عن عليّ عليه السلام: أنّ النبي صلى الله عليه وآله حين بعثه براءة، وقال: يا نبيّ الله، إنّي لستُ بلَسِن ولا بخَطيب. قال: ما بُدّ أن أذهب بها، أو تذهب بها أنت. قال: فانطلِق، فإنّ الله يُثبّت لسانك ويهدي قلبك، ثمّ وضع يده على فمه، وقال: انطلق فاقرأها على الناس، وقال: إنّ الناس سيتقاضون إليك، فإذا أتاك الخصمان فلا تقضينّ لواحدٍ حتّى تسمع الآخر، فإنّه أجدر أن تعلمَ الحقّ.

١٠. عن زُرارة وحُمران ومحمّد بن مسلم، عن أبي جعفر وأبي عبد الله عليهما السلام، في قوله تعالى: ﴿فَسِيحُوا فِي الْأَرْضِ أَرْبَعَةَ أَشْهُرٍ﴾، قال عشرين من ذي الحجّة، والمحرّم، وصَفر، وشهر ربيع الأوّل، وعشر من شهر ربيع الآخر.

11. From Ja'far b. Aḥmad, from 'Alī b. Muḥammad b. Shujā' who said, 'Our associates narrated that Abū 'Abd Allāh ﷺ was once asked, "Why is no sin recorded down against the pilgrim for four months?" He replied, "God – exalted be His remembrance – commanded the idolaters saying: ﴾*you may move freely about the land for four months*﴿ without defining His threat [of chastisement] against that."' [9:2]

12. From Ḥakīm b. Jubayr,[4] from 'Alī b. al-Ḥusayn ﷺ who said, 'By God, 'Alī has such an appellation in the Qur'an that people do not know about.' He said, 'I asked, "May I be your ransom - what are you referring to?" So he said to me, ﴾*On the Day of the Great Pilgrimage* [*there will be*] *a proclamation from God and His Messenger to all people.*﴿ He continued, "So the Messenger of God ﷺ dispatched the Commander of the Faithful, and 'Alī was the herald who proclaimed. So he proclaimed God and His Messenger's announcement on the day of the Great Pilgrimage at all the stations. He called out that after this particular year, no one was to circumambulate naked and nor could an idolater approach the Sacred Mosque after this year."' [9:3]

13. From Ḥarīz, from Abū 'Abd Allāh ﷺ who said about the proclamation, 'This is a name in God's Book that no one knows save me.' [9:3]

14. From Ḥakīm b. Jubayr, from 'Alī b. al-Ḥusayn ﷺ who said regarding God's statement: ﴾*A proclamation from God and His Messenger*﴿: 'The proclamation is the Commander of the Faithful: 'Alī ﷺ.' [9:3]

15. From Jābir, from [Ja'far b. Muḥammad or] Abū Ja'far ﷺ who said regarding God's statement ﴾*On the Day of the Great Pilgrimage* [*there will be*] *a proclamation from God and His Messenger to all people*﴿: 'It is the emergence of the Qā'im and the proclamation of his invitation to himself.' [9:3]

---

4 'Ayyāshī narrates this tradition on the authority of Ḥakīm b. al-Ḥusayn, but this is a distortion of Ḥakīm b. Jubayr; see Ḥaskānī, *Shawāhid al-tanzīl*, 1:231 (no. 307); Kūfī, *Tafsīr Furāt*, 160; Mazzī, *Tahdhīb al-kamāl*, 7:165; Khū'ī, *Mu'jam*, 7:194 (no. 3900). Shaykh al-Ṭūsī includes Ḥakīm b. Jubayr among the companions of 'Alī b. al-Ḥusayn; see Ṭūsī, *Rijāl al-Ṭūsī*, 112 (no. 1105).

١١. جعفر بن أحمد، عن عليّ بن محمّد بن شجاع، قال: روى أصحابنا: قيل لأبي عبدالله عليه السلام: لِمَ صار الحاجّ لا يُكتَب عليه ذنبٌ أربعة أشهر؟ قال: إنّ الله جلّ ذكرُه أمر المشركين فقال: ﴿فَسِيحُوا فِي الأَرْضِ أَرْبَعَةَ أَشْهُرٍ﴾ ولم يكن يقصُر بِوفدِه عن ذلك.

١٢. عن حكيم بن جبير، عن عليّ بن الحسين عليه السلام، قال: والله إنّ لعليّ عليه السلام لاسماً في القرآن ما يعرِفه الناس. قال: قلتُ: وأيّ شيء تقول: جُعلتُ فداك؟

فقال لي: ﴿وَأَذَانٌ مِنَ اللهِ وَرَسُولِهِ إِلَى النَّاسِ يَوْمَ الْحَجِّ الأَكْبَرِ﴾ قال: فبعث رسول الله صلى الله عليه وآله أمير المؤمنين عليه السلام، فكان عليّ عليه السلام هو والله المؤذن، فأذّن بأذان الله ورسوله يوم الحجّ الأكبر في المواقف كلّها، فكان ما نادى به: أن لا يَطوف بعد هذا العام عُريان، ولا يقرب المسجد الحرام بعد هذا العام مُشرِك.

١٣. عن حريز، عن أبي عبدالله عليه السلام، قال في الأذان: هو اسمٌ في كتاب الله، لا يعلم ذلك أحدٌ غيري.

١٤. عن حكيم بن جُبير، عن عليّ بن الحسين عليه السلام، في قول الله: ﴿وَأَذَانٌ مِنَ اللهِ وَرَسُولِهِ﴾ قال: الأذان أمير المؤمنين عليّ عليه السلام.

١٥. عن جابر، عن أبي جعفر عليه السلام في قول الله تعالى: ﴿وَأَذَانٌ مِنَ اللهِ وَرَسُولِهِ إِلَى النَّاسِ يَوْمَ الْحَجِّ الأَكْبَرِ﴾، قال. خُروج القائم عليه السلام، وأذانُ دعوته إلى نفسه.

16. From ʿAbd al-Raḥmān, from Abū ʿAbd Allāh عليه السلام who said: 'The day of the Great Pilgrimage is the Day of Sacrifice, and the Minor Pilgrimage is the *ʿumra*.' [9:3]

17. In Ibn Sirḥān's report on his authority عليه السلام, he said, 'The Great Pilgrimage is the Day of ʿArafa, the gathering together[5] and the stoning of the pillars, at Mina whilst the Minor Pilgrimage is the *ʿumra*.' [9:3]

18. In Ibn Udhayna's report from Zurāra, on his authority he said, 'The Greater Pilgrimage is the staying at ʿArafa, at the gathering place and stoning the pillars at Mina, whilst the Minor Pilgrimage is the *ʿumra*.' [9:3]

19. In ʿAbd al-Raḥmān's report on his authority, he said, 'The day of the Great Pilgrimage is the Day of Sacrifice, and the day of the Minor Pilgrimage is the day of *ʿumra*.' [9:3]

20. In Fuḍayl b. ʿIyāḍ's narration on his authority عليه السلام. He said, 'I asked him about the Great Pilgrimage. He replied, "Ibn ʿAbbās used to say that it was [the Day of] ʿArafa.

The Commander of the Faithful عليه السلام said, 'The Great Pilgrimage is the Day of Sacrifice', evidencing it with God's statement: ﴾*you may move freely about the land for four months*﴿ which are twenty days of Dhū al-Ḥijja, Muḥarram, Ṣafar, Rabīʿ I and ten days of Rabīʿ II. Had the Great Pilgrimage been the Day of ʿArafa then it would have been four months and a day.'"' [9:2]

21. From Jaʿfar b. Muḥammad, from Abū Jaʿfar عليه السلام that 'God sent Muḥammad صلى الله عليه وآله with four swords: a sword with which he was to fight the Arab idolaters. God – exalted be His Countenance – said: ﴾*wherever you encounter the idolaters, kill them, seize them, besiege them, wait for them at every lookout post;*

5 The gathering together refers to the Sacred Place (*al-mashʿar al-ḥarām*), which is the closest of the two stations to Mecca. It is said to have been named thus because people would gather together here and seek the proximity of God altogether through worship, good-deeds and obedience. Another possibility is that it is called the place of gathering because Ādam is said to have reunited with Ḥawwāʾ here. See Yāqūt al-Ḥamawī, *Muʿjam al-buldān* (Beirut: Ḍār Ṣādir, 1993), 2:189.

١٦. عن عبد الرّحمن، عن أبي عبد الله عليه السلام، قال: يوم الحج الأكبر: يوم النحر، والحج الأصغر: العُمرة.

١٧. وفي رواية ابن سِرحان، عنه عليه السلام، قال: الحجّ الأكبر: يوم عَرفة وجَمع ورمي الجِمار بِمنى، والحجّ الأصغر: العُمرة.

١٨. وفي رواية ابن أُذينة، عن زُرارة، عنه عليه السلام، قال: الحجّ الأكبر: الوقوف بِعَرفة وبجَمع ورمي الجِمار بِمنى، والحجّ الأصغر: العُمرة.

١٩. وفي رواية عبد الرّحمن، عنه عليه السلام، قال: يوم الحجّ الأكبر: يوم النَّحر، ويوم الحجّ الأصغر: يوم العُمرة.

٢٠. وفي رواية فُضيل بن عِياض، عنه عليه السلام: قال: سألتُه عن الحجّ الأكبر، فإنّ ابن عباس كان يقول: عَرَفة.

[قال:] قال أمير المؤمنين عليه السلام: الحجّ الأكبر يوم النَّحر، ويحتجّ بقول الله: ﴿فَسِيحُوا فِي الأَرْضِ أَرْبَعَةَ أَشْهُرٍ﴾ عشرون من ذي الحجّة، والمحرّم، وصَفر، وشهر ربيع الأوّل، وعشر من شهر ربيع الآخر، ولوكان الحجّ الأكبر يوم عرَفة لكان أربعة أشهر ويومًا.

٢١. عن جعفر بن محمّد، عن أبي جعفر عليه السلام: أنّ الله بعث محمّدًا صلى الله عليه وآله بخمسة أسياف، فسيفٌ على مُشركي العرب، قال الله جلّ وجهه: ﴿فَاقْتُلُوا الْمُشْرِكِينَ حَيْثُ وَجَدْتُمُوهُمْ

but if they turn [to God] ﴿ – meaning if they believe ﴾ *then they are your brothers in faith.* ﴿(9:11) The only acceptable thing is for them to either be killed or to convert to Islam. Their children are not to be held captive [and nor do they receive battle gains].' [9:5]

22. From Zurāra, from Abū Jaʿfar عليه السلام who said regarding God's verse ﴾ *When the [four] forbidden months are over, wherever you encounter the idolaters, kill them* ﴿: 'This is the Day of Sacrifice until ten days past the start of the month of Rabīʿ II.' [9:5]

23. From Ḥanān b. Sadīr, from Abū ʿAbd Allāh عليه السلام. He said, 'I heard him say, "A group of people from Basra came to me and asked me about Ṭalḥa and Zubayr, so I said to them, 'They were two of the leaders at the forefront of disbelief. On the Day of Basra[6] when the troops were lined up, 'Alī – may God's blessings be upon him and his family – said to his companions, "Do not rush upon the enemy until I have absolved myself of what is between me and God and them."

Then he said, "O people of Basra. Have you found any tyranny in my rule?"

They replied, "No."

He asked, "How about any unfairness in my distribution?"

They replied, "No."

He asked, "How about any desire for this material world that I have grabbed for myself or my family instead of you that you need to avenge due to which you have broken your allegiance to me?"

They replied, 'No."

He asked, "Then have I executed legal punishments against you whilst failing to do so against others?"

They replied, "No."

He asked, "Then why is my allegiance being violated and not others'? I have done my utmost in this authority but have only found rebellion and mutiny therein." Then he turned to his companions and said, "God says in His Book: ﴾ *But if they break their oath after having made an agreement with*

6 A reference to the Battle of the Camel.

﴿وَخُذُوهُمْ وَاحْصُرُوهُمْ وَاقْعُدُوا لَهُمْ كُلَّ مَرْصَدٍ فَإِنْ تَابُوا﴾ يعني فإن آمنوا ﴿فَإِخْوَانُكُمْ فِي الدِّينِ﴾، لا يُقبَل منهم إلاّ القتل أو الدُّخول في الإسلام، ولا تُسبى لهم ذُرِّيّة، وما لهم فَيء.

٢٢. عن زُرارة، عن أبي جعفر ﷺ، فيقول الله: ﴿فَإِذَا انْسَلَخَ الْأَشْهُرُ الْحُرُمُ فَاقْتُلُوا الْمُشْرِكِينَ حَيْثُ وَجَدْتُمُوهُمْ﴾، قال: هي يوم النّحر إلى عشرٍ مَضين من شهر ربيع الآخر.

٢٣. عن حَنان بن سدير، عن أبي عبد الله ﷺ، قال: سَمِعتُه يقول: دَخَل عليَّ أُناس من أهل البصرة، فسألوني عن طلحة والزبير، فقلتُ لهم: كانا إمامين من أئمّة الكفر، إنّ عليّاً صلوات الله عليه يوم البصرة لمّا صفّ الخُيول قال لأصحابه: لا تَعجلوا على القوم حتّى أعذر فيما بيني وبين الله وبينهم، فقام إليهم، فقال: يا أهل البصرة، هل تجِدون عليّ جَوراً في الحكم؟ قالوا: لا، قال: فحيفاً في قَسم؟ قالوا: لا. قال: فرغبةً في دُنيا أصبتُها لي ولأهل بيتي دونكم، فنَقَمتم عليّ، فنكثتُم عليّ بيعتي؟ قالوا: لا. قال: فأقمتُ فيكم الحدود، وعطّلتُها عن غيركم؟ قالوا: لا.

قال: فما بال بيعتي تُنكَث، وبيعة غيري لا تُنكَث؟ إنّي ضَرَبتُ الأمر أنفهُ وعينهُ، فلم أجد إلاّ الكُفر أو السيف، ثُمّ ثنى إلى أصحابه، فقال: إنّ الله يقول في كتابه: ﴿وَإِنْ نَكَثُوا أَيْمَانَهُمْ مِنْ بَعْدِ عَهْدِهِمْ وَطَعَنُوا فِي دِينِكُمْ فَقَاتِلُوا أَئِمَّةَ الْكُفْرِ إِنَّهُمْ لَا

you, if they revile your religion, then fight the leaders of disbelief – oaths mean nothing to them – so that they may stop. ﴿"

Then the Commander of the Faithful عليه السلام continued, "By the One who split the seed, originated life and selected Muḥammad ﷺ for prophethood; indeed, you are the ones that this verse refers to," and they have not been fought since it has been revealed."'"' [9:12]

24. From Abū al-Ṭufayl who said, 'On the day of [the Battle of] the Camel, I heard 'Alī عليه السلام motivating people to fight them saying, "By God, the addressees of this verse whom this verse refers have never even thrown a *kināya* before this day. Fight the leaders of disbelief that they may stop, for oaths truly mean nothing to them."' So I asked Abū al-Ṭufayl, 'What is a *kināya*?' He replied, 'It is an arrow whose point is made of bone and which some Arabs term *kināya*.' [9:12]

25. From al-Ḥasan al-Baṣrī who said, "Alī b. Abī Ṭālib – may God's blessings be upon him – addressed us on this pulpit, and that was after he had dealt with the matter of Ṭalḥa, Zubayr and 'Ā'isha [at the Battle of the Camel]. He climbed the pulpit, praised and glorified God, invoked blessings on His Messenger ﷺ then said, "O people, by God I did not fight these people yesterday for anything other than a verse in God's Book from which I had abstained. God says: ﴾ *But if they break their oath after having made an agreement with you, if they revile your religion, then fight the leaders of disbelief – oaths mean nothing to them – so that they may stop.* ﴿ By God, the Messenger of God, peace be upon him and his family, had made an oath to me and said to me, 'O 'Alī, you will most definitely fight the rebellious faction, the faction violating [oaths] and the renegade faction.'"' [9:12]

26. From 'Ammār, from Abū 'Abd Allāh عليه السلام who said, 'Whoever reviles this religion of yours has indeed disbelieved. God says: ﴾ *if they revile your religion, then fight the leaders of disbelief – oaths mean nothing to them – so that they may stop.* ﴿' [9:12]

أَيۡمَـٰنَ لَهُـمۡ لَعَلَّهُـمۡ يَنتَهُونَ﴾ فقال أمير المؤمنين عليه السلام: والذي فلق الحبّة، وبرأ النّسمة، واصطفى محمّدا صلى الله عليه وآله بالنبوّة، إنّكم لأصحاب هذه الآية، وما قُوتلوا مُنذ نَزلت.

٢٤. عن أبي الطُّفيل، قال: سمِعتُ عليًّا صلّى الله عليه يوم الجمل، وهو يُحضِّض الناس على قتالهم، ويقول: والله ما رمى أهل هذه الآية بِكِنانة قبل اليوم ﴿فَقَـٰتِلُوٓاْ أَئِمَّـةَ ٱلۡكُفۡـرِ إِنَّهُـمۡ لَآ أَيۡمَـٰنَ لَهُـمۡ لَعَلَّهُـمۡ يَنتَهُونَ﴾.

فقلتُ لأبي الطفيل: ما الكِنانة؟ قال: السّهم يكون موضع الحديد فيه عظم، يُسمّيه بعض العرب الكِنانة.

٢٥. عن الحسن البصري، قال: خَطَبنا عليّ بن أبي طالب عليه السلام على هذا المِنبر، وذلك بعد ما فَرَغ من أمر طلحة والزبير وعائشة، صَعِد المِنبر فَحَمِد الله وأثنى عليه، وصلّى على رسوله صلى الله عليه وآله، ثمّ قال: أيُّها الناس، والله ما قاتلتُ هؤلاء بالأمس إلاّ بآية تركتها في كتاب الله، إنّ الله يقول: ﴿وَإِن نَّكَثُوٓاْ أَيۡمَـٰنَهُـم مِّنۢ بَعۡـدِ عَهۡدِهِـمۡ وَطَعَنُواْ فِي دِينِكُمۡ فَقَـٰتِلُوٓاْ أَئِمَّـةَ ٱلۡكُفۡـرِ إِنَّهُـمۡ لَآ أَيۡمَـٰنَ لَهُـمۡ لَعَلَّهُـمۡ يَنتَهُونَ﴾ أما والله لقد عَهِد إليّ رسول الله عليه وآله السلام، وقال لي: يا عليّ، لتُقاتلنّ الفِئة الباغية، والفِئة الناكِثة، والفئة المارِقة.

٢٦. عن عمّار، عن أبي عبدالله عليه السلام، قال: مَن طَعَن في دينكم هذا فقد كفر، قال الله: ﴿وَطَعَنُواْ فِي دِينِكُمۡ﴾ إلى قوله ﴿ينتهُون﴾.

27. From al-Shuʿbī who said, ʻAbū ʻAbd Allāh read: ﴾*But if they break their oath after having made an agreement with you*﴿ until the end of the verse, then said, "These people have not been fought yet, for when the Battle of the Camel took place ʻAlī عليه السلام recited it and said, ʻThe people to whom it refers have not been fought from the day it was revealed until today.'"' [9:12]

28. From Abū ʻUthmān, the protégé of Banū Quṣayy, who said, ʻI was watching ʻAlī this whole year and I never heard him express either adherence to or disassociation [from anyone], whilst I heard him say, "God has given me a pretext against Ṭalḥa and Zubayr who willingly pledged allegiance to me without any compulsion, then violated their allegiance without prior cause on my part. By God, the ones to whom this verse refers have not been fought since it was revealed, until I fought them, ﴾*But if they break their oath after having made an agreement with you, if they revile your religion, then fight the leaders of disbelief – oaths mean nothing to them – so that they may stop.*﴿"' [9:12]

29. From ʻAlī b. ʻUqba, on his father's authority who said, ʻMuʿallā and I went to Abū ʻAbd Allāh عليه السلام, so he said, "Rejoice for you are upon one of the two beautiful things: God will heal your feelings and remove rage from your hearts, and make you triumphant over your enemy, and this is as per God's statement: ﴾*He will heal the believers' feelings.*﴿ If you pass away before you see that happen, then you will have died upon God's religion which He has favoured for His Prophet, peace be upon him and his family, and for ʻAlī عليه السلام."' [9:14]

30. From Abū al-Agharr al-Tamīmī who said, ʻOn the day of the Battle of Ṣiffīn, I was standing when I noticed al-ʻAbbās b. Rabīʿa b. al-Ḥārith b. ʻAbd al-Muṭṭalib armed to the teeth. He had a helmet on his head and a wide Yemeni sword in his hand, mounted on a roan stallion of his. His eyes were like a viper's. While he was spurring his horse and getting ready for combat, someone known as ʻIrār b. Ad-ham called out from the Shām camp: "ʻAbbās! Come and fight a duel!"

He replied, "Dismount then; otherwise it will be impossible to engage."'

He said, ʻSo the Shāmī, who was enraged, dismounted saying: "If you come on horseback, then know that being mounted is our habit. And if you dismount, then we are a troop well accustomed to being on foot."'

٢٧. عن الشّعبي، قال: قرأ عبدالله ﴿وَإِن نَّكَثُوٓا۟ أَيْمَٰنَهُم مِّنۢ بَعْدِ عَهْدِهِمْ﴾ إلى آخر الآية: ثمّ قال: ما قوتل أهلها بعد، فلمّا كان يوم الجَمل قرأها عليّ عليه السلام، ثمّ قال: ما قُوتل أهلها منذ يوم نزلت حتّى كان اليوم.

٢٨. عن أبي عثمان مولي بني أفصى، قال: شهدتُ عليًّا صلّى الله عليه سنته كُلّها، فما سمعتُ منه ولايةً ولا براءةً، وقدسمعتُه يقول: عَذَرني الله من طلحة والزبير، بايَعاني طائعَين غير مُكرهَين، ثمّ نكَثا بَيعتي من غير حدثٍ أحدثتُه، والله ما قوتِل أهل هذه الآية منذُ نزلت حتّى قاتلتُهم ﴿وَإِن نَّكَثُوٓا۟ أَيْمَٰنَهُم مِّنۢ بَعْدِ عَهْدِهِمْ وَطَعَنُوا۟ فِى دِينِكُمْ﴾ الآية.

٢٩. عن عليّ بن عُقبة، عن أبيه، قال: دخلتُ أنا والمُعلّى على أبي عبدالله عليه السلام، فقال: أبشِروا، إنّكم على إحدى الحُسنين: [إن بقيتُم حتّى تَروا ما تمدّون إليه رِقابكم] شفى الله صُدوركم، وأذهب غيظ قُلوبكم، وأدالكم على عدوّكم، وهوقول الله: ﴿وَيَشْفِ صُدُورَ قَوْمٍ مُّؤْمِنِينَ﴾ وإن مضيتُم قبل أن تروا ذلك، مضيتم على دين الله الذي رضيه لنبيّه عليه وآله السّلام ولعليّ عليه السلام.

٣٠. عن أبي الأغرّ التميمي، قال: أنّي لواقفٌ يوم صِفّين، إذ نظرتُ إلى العبّاس بن ربيعة بن الحارث بن عبد المطّلب شاكٍ في السلاح، على رأسه مِغفَر، وبيده صفيحةٌ يمانيةٌ، وهو على فرسٍ له أدهم، وكأنّ عينيه عينا أفعى، فبينا هو يمغَثه، ويُليّن من عَريكته، إذ هَتَف به هاتِفٌ من أهل الشام، يقال له عِرار بن أدهم: يا عبّاس، هَلُمَّ إلى البِراز، قال: فالنُّزول إذًا، فإنّه إياس من القُفُول، قال: فنزل الشاميّ ووجد، وهو يقول:

He said, 'So 'Abbās flaunted his own might, saying: "This bold man will wrest your arrogance away from you, showing off greatness, using the blade of your own sword and your own tongue, and a deep gash like the most fascinating of words."'

He said, 'Then he tightened the strings of his armour and tucked them into his belt, then passed his horse on to a servant of his saying, "Take him. I can almost see the exquisite poetry [i.e. the wounds that I shall inflict on him]."

Then each one rushed towards his adversary, and I remembered the words of Abū Dhu'ayb: "So they dismounted while their horses stood still, both men veteran heroes at clashing duels."'

He said, 'They then combated with their swords for a long time since morning, neither one being able to vanquish the other due to their flawless armour, until al-'Abbās noticed a chink in the Shāmī's armour. So he lunged towards him with his hand and ripped it from his chest. Then he resumed his pursuit of him, for now, he could clearly see the tear in his armour. So al-'Abbās struck him with his sword and pierced his chest muscles.

The Shāmī fell dead to the ground on his cheek. [Al-'Abbās] then roamed around amidst the people and made them shout out 'God is great!' until the ground shook with them, and I heard a man say from behind me: ﴿*Fight them: God will punish them at your hands, He will disgrace them, He will help you to conquer them, He will heal the believers' feelings and remove the rage from their hearts. God turns to whoever He will in His mercy.*﴾'

I turned around, and there was the Commander of the Faithful 'Alī عليه السلام, and he said, "O Abū al-Agharr, who fought the duel with our enemy?"

I replied, "This one – the son of your chief, al-'Abbās b. Rabī'a."

He called out, "'Abbās!"

He replied, "At your service."

He asked, "Did I not forbid you, al-Ḥasan, al-Ḥusayn, and 'Abd Allāh b. Ja'far to go into the battlefield alone lest something happens to you?"

He replied, "That is right."

He asked, "Then what is left unclear about that?"

He replied, "May I be your ransom, O Commander of the Faithful. So even if I am challenged to a duel, I should not respond?"

He replied, "Yes. Obedience to your Imam is better than responding to your enemy. Mu'āwiya desires that not a single soul from among the Banū

إن تَرْكَبُوا فرُكُوبُ الخيلِ عادتنا أو تنزِلون فإنّا مَعشَرٌ نُزُل

قال: وثني عبّاس رِجله، وهو يقول:

وتَصُدّ عنك مَخيلةَ الرّجُل العِرّيض مُوضِحةٌ عن العَظْمِ

بحُسام سيفك أو لسِناك والكَلِمُ الأصيلُ كأرغَبِ الكَلِمِ

قال: ثمّ عصَبَ فضَلات دِرعه في حُجزتِه، ثمّ دفع فرَسه إلى غُلامٍ له يُقال له أسلم، كأنّي أنظُر إلى فلافِل شعره، ودَلَف كُلّ واحدٍ منهما إلى صاحبه.

قال: فذكرتُ قول أبي ذؤيب:

فتَنَازلا وتواقَفت خَيلاهُما وكِلاهما بَطَلُ اللِّقاءِ مُخدَّعُ

قال: ثُمّ تكافحا بسيفهما ملياً من نهارهما، لا يصل واحدٌ منهما إلى صاحبه، لكمال لأمّته، إلى أن لَحَظ العبّاس وهيًا في دِرع الشاميّ، فأهوى إليه بيده، فهتكه إلى ثندُوته، ثمّ عاود لمُجاولته، وقد أصحَرَ له، مُفتّق الدِّرع، فضربه العباس بالسيف، فانتظم به جوانح صدره، وخرّ الشامي صريعًا بخدّه، وانشَام [العباس] في النـاس، وكبّر النـاس تكبـيرةً ارتجّـت لهـا الأرض، فسَـمعتُ قـائلاً يقول من ورائي: ﴿قَاتِلُوهُمْ يُعَذِّبْهُمُ اللَّهُ بِأَيْدِيكُمْ وَيُخْزِهِمْ وَيَنصُرْكُمْ عَلَيْهِمْ وَيَشْفِ صُدُورَ قَوْمٍ مُّؤْمِنِينَ ۝ وَيُذْهِبْ غَيْظَ قُلُوبِهِمْ وَيَتُوبُ اللَّهُ عَلَىٰ مَن يَشَاءُ﴾، فالتفت فإذا هو أمير المؤمنين عليّ عليه السلام، فقال: يا أبا الأغرّ، مَن المُبارز لعدوّنا؟ قلتُ: هذا ابن شيخِكم العباس بن ربيعة.

Hāshim be left alive without killing them all to extinguish God's light, but God refuses for His light to be but brought to fullness, even if the disbelievers should abhor it. By God, the men on our side will overcome them, and others will humiliate them into oblivion until they are forced to beg for their lives and dig wells, should they come and combat you. So come back with me."

He said, 'The news reached Mu'āwiya, so he said, "By God, 'Irār's blood! Is there any man who will avenge 'Irār's blood?"'

He said, 'So two men from Lakhm volunteered saying, "We will."

So he said, "Go both of you, and whichever of you manages to kill al-'Abbās in a duel will receive such and such reward."

So they came to him and challenged him to a duel.

He said, "I have a commander whose orders I obey."'

He said, 'So he went to the Commander of the Faithful عليه السلام, and informed him of that.

He said, "Exchange your weapons for mine." So he did.'

He said, 'The Commander of the Faithful عليه السلام mounted al-'Abbās's horse and gave his horse to al-'Abbās, and rode out towards the two Shāmīs. They did not doubt that he was 'Abbās and said to him, "So your commander gave you permission then?"

He replied, "Yes," then recited: "﴾ *Those who have been attacked are permitted to take up arms because they have been wronged – God has the power to help them.* ﴿'"(22:39)

He said, 'The first one lunged towards him and it was as if he wrestled him down, then the second one made for him, and he did the same to him. Then he left, saying: "﴾ *A sacred month for a sacred month: violation of sanctity [calls for] fair retribution. So if anyone commits aggression against you, attack him as he attacked you.* ﴿(2:194)"

Then he said, "'Abbās, take your weapons and give me back mine."'

He said, 'The news reached Mu'āwiya, and he said, "May God disfigure that relentless man that he is still standing. Every time I attempt to surmount him, I fail."

So 'Amr b. al-'Āṣ said, "By God, the failures are the two men from Lakhm, not you."

"Be quiet, old man!" he retorted, "This is not your time [to speak]."

قال: يا عباس، قال: لبّيك. قال: ألم أنهك وحسنًا وحسينًا وعبدالله بن جعفر أن تخلّوا بمركزٍ، أو تُباشروا حدَثًا؟ قال: إنّ ذلك لكذلك، قال: فما عدا ممّا بدا؟ قال: أفأُدعى إلى البِراز يا أمير المؤمنين فلا أجيب، جعلني الله فِداك.

قال: نعم، طاعة إمامك أولى بك من إجابة عدوّك، ودّ مُعاوية أنّه ما بقي من بني هاشم نافخ ضرمةٍ إلاّ طُعِن في نَيطِه، إطفاءً لنور الله، ويأبى الله إلاّ أن يُتِمّ نُورَه ولو كرِه المُشركون، أما والله ليَملكنّهم منّا رجالٌ ورجالٌ، يسُومُونهم الخَسف. حتّى يتكفّفوا بأيديهم، ويحفُروا الآبار، إن عادوا لك فعُد لي.

قال: ونُمي الخبر إلى مُعاوية، فقال: الله دم عِرار، ألا رجل يطلُب بدم عِرار؟ قال: فانتدب له رجلان من لَخم، فقالا: نحن له، قال: اذهبا، فأيّكما قتل العباس بِرازًا فله كذا وكذا، فأتياه فدعواه إلى البِراز، فقال: إنّ لي سيّدًا أؤامره.

قال: فأتى أمير المؤمنين عليه السلام فأخبره، فقال: ناقلني سِلاحك بِسِلاحي، فناقله، قال: وركِب أمير المؤمنين عليه السلام على فَرَسِ العباس، ودفع فَرَسه إلى العباس، وبَرز إلى الشاميّين، فلم يشُكّا أنّه العباس، فقالا له: أذِن لك سيّدك؟ فحرِج أن يقول نعم، فقال: ﴿أُذِنَ لِلَّذِينَ يُقَاتَلُونَ بِأَنَّهُمْ ظُلِمُوا وَإِنَّ اللهَ عَلَى نَصْرِهِمْ لَقَدِيرٌ﴾.

قال: فبَرز إليه أحدهما، فكأنّما اختطفه، ثمّ برز إليه الثاني فألحقه بالأوّل، وانصرف وهو يقول: ﴿الشَّهْرُ الْحَرَامُ بِالشَّهْرِ الْحَرَامِ وَالْحُرُمَاتُ قِصَاصٌ فَمَنِ اعْتَدَى عَلَيْكُمْ فَاعْتَدُوا عَلَيْهِ بِمِثْلِ مَا اعْتَدَى عَلَيْكُمْ﴾، ثمّ قال: يا عباس، خُذ سِلاحك وهات سِلاحي.

He said, "And if God had not taken the two men from Lakhm to His mercy [i.e. if they had not been killed] – which I do not think possible! – by God, that would be detrimental to your position and a deal-breaker."

He replied, "True. And were it not for [the promise of the governorship of] Egypt, then it would have been our saving grace."

So he said, "By God, this is what has blinded you, and were it not for that [i.e. Egypt] then you would at least be perceptive."' [9:14–15]

31. From Abū al-ʿAbbās, from Abū ʿAbd Allāh عليه السلام who said, 'A man came to the Prophet ﷺ and said, "Take my oath, O Messenger of God."

He replied, "That you may kill your own father?"

So the man took his hand and said, "Take my oath, O Messenger of God."

He replied, "That you may kill your own father?"

The man replied, "Yes, so that I may kill my father."

So the Messenger of God, peace be upon him and his family, said, "To whom does one who takes a supporter besides God, His Messenger and the believers incline? We do not command you to kill your parents, but rather we command you to honour them both."' [9:14–15]

32. From Abān who said, 'I heard Abū ʿAbd Allāh عليه السلام say, "O young men, be God-conscious and do not go to the chieftains. Leave them be until they become followers of others. Do not take fellow men as your supporters besides God. By God, we are better for you than them," tapping his hand on his chest.' [9:16]

33. From Abū al-Ṣabbāḥ al-Kinānī who said, 'Abū Jaʿfar عليه السلام said, "Abū al-Ṣabbāḥ, beware of supporters, for every supporter besides us is an adversary."' [9:16]

قال: ونُمي الخبر إلى مُعاوية، فقال: فتح الله اللّجاج، إنّه لقَعُود، ما ركبْتُه قطّ إلاّ خُذِلت. فقال عمرو بن العاص: المَخذول والله اللّخميان لا أنت. قال: اسكُت أيّها الشيخ، فليس هذه من ساعاتك.

قال: فإن لم يكُن رَحِم الله اللّخميين، وما أراه يفعل! قال: ذلك والله أضيق لجُحرِك، وأخسر لصَفقتك. قال: أجل، ولولا مِصر لقد كانت المَنجاة منها. فقال: هي والله أعمَتك، ولولا ها لأُلفيت بصيرًا.

٣١. عن أبي العبّاس، عن أبي عبد الله عليه السلام، قال: أتى رجلٌ النبيّ صلى الله عليه وآله، فقال: بايعني يا رسول الله. فقال: على أن تَقتُل أباك. قال: فقبض الرجل يده، ثمّ قال: بايعني يا رسول الله. قال: على أن تقتُل أباك، فقال الرجل: نعم، على أن أقتُل أبي. فقال رسول الله صلى الله عليه وآله: الآن لم تتّخذ من دون الله ولا رسوله ولا المؤمنين وليجةً، إنّا لا نأمُرك إن تَقتُل والديك، ولكن نأمُرك أن تُكرِمهما.

٣٢. عن أبان، قال: سمعتُ أبا عبد الله عليه السلام يقول: يا معشر الأحداث، اتّقوا الله، ولا تأتوا الرؤساء، دعوهم حتّى يصيروا أذنابًا، لا تتّخذوا الرجال ولائجَ من دون الله، إنّا والله خيرٌ لكم منهم؛ ثمّ ضرب بيده إلى صدره.

٣٣. عن أبي الصّباح الكِناني، قال: قال أبو جعفر عليه السلام: يا أبا الصّباح، إيّاكم والولائج، فإنّ كلّ وليجةٍ دوننا فهي طاغوت، أو قال: نِدّ.

34. From Abū Baṣīr, from Abū ʿAbd Allāh ﵇ who said, 'The Commander of the Faithful, may God's blessings be upon him, was asked, "O Commander of the Faithful, inform us of the best of your virtues?"

He replied, "Very well. 'Abbās, 'Uthmān b. Abī Shayba and I were in the Sacred Mosque when 'Uthmān b. Abī Shayba said, 'The Messenger of God ﷺ has given me the treasure,' meaning the keys to the Kaʿba. And al-ʿAbbās said, 'And the Messenger of God ﷺ has given me the job of giving water [to pilgrims], which is [charge of] Zamzam, whilst he has not given you charge of anything, 'Alī.'"

He said, "So God revealed: ﴾*Do you consider giving water to pilgrims and tending the Sacred Mosque to be equal to the deeds of those who believe in God and the Last Day and who strive in God's path? They are not equal in God's eyes.*﴿"' [9:19]

35. From Abū Baṣīr, from one of the two [al-Bāqir or al-Ṣādiq], regarding God's verse: ﴾*Do you consider giving water to pilgrims and tending the Sacred Mosque* [...]﴿ He said, 'It was revealed about ʿAlī, Ḥamza, Jaʿfar, ʿAbbās and Shayba, when they were boasting about giving water to the pilgrims and being gatekeepers [of the Kaʿba], so God revealed: ﴾*Do you consider giving water to pilgrims and tending the Sacred Mosque to be equal to the deeds of those who believe in God and the Last Day and who strive in God's path? They are not equal in God's eyes. God does not guide such benighted people.*﴿ So ʿAlī, Ḥamza, and Jaʿfar, peace be upon them, were the ones who believed in God and the Last Day, and they are the ones who were striving in God's path. They are not equal in God's eyes.' [9:19]

36. From Jābir, from Abū Jaʿfar ﵇. He said, 'I asked him about this verse in God's words: ﴾*Believers, do not take your fathers and brothers as allies*﴿ until His words: ﴾*those who break away.*﴿ [He said,] "As for the phrase ﴾*do not take your fathers and brothers as allies if they prefer disbelief to faith*﴿, disbelief according to the inner meaning of this verse is the adherence to the authority of the first and the second, and this is disbelief. And His words: ﴾*to faith*﴿ – faith here is the adherence to the authority of ʿAlī b. Abī Ṭālib ﵇." He said, "﴾*those of you who do so are doing wrong.*﴿"' [9:23]

٣٤. عن أبي بصير، عن أبي عبد الله عليه السلام، قال: إنّ أمير المؤمنين صلوات الله عليه قيل له: يا أمير المؤمنين، أخبِرنا بأفضل مناقبك؟

قال: نعم، كنتُ أنا وعباس وعثمان بن أبي شيبة في المسجد الحرام، فقال عثمان بن أبي شيبة: أعطاني رسول الله عليه السلام الخِزانة، يعني مفاتيح الكعبة. وقال العباس: أعطاني رسول الله صلى الله عليه وآله السقاية، وهي زمزم، ولم يُعطِك شيئًا يا عليّ! قال: فأنزل الله: ﴿أَجَعَلْتُمْ سِقَايَةَ الْحَاجِّ وَعِمَارَةَ الْمَسْجِدِ الْحَرَامِ كَمَنْ آمَنَ بِاللهِ وَالْيَوْمِ الْآخِرِ وَجَاهَدَ فِي سَبِيلِ اللهِ لَا يَسْتَوُونَ عِنْدَ اللهِ﴾.

٣٥. عن أبي بصير، عن أحدهما عليه السلام، في قول الله تعالى: ﴿أَجَعَلْتُمْ سِقَايَةَ الْحَاجِّ وَعِمَارَةَ الْمَسْجِدِ الْحَرَامِ﴾، قال: نزلت في عليّ عليه السلام وحمزة وجعفر والعباس وشيبة، إنّهم فخَروا في السقاية والحِجابة، فأنزل الله: ﴿أَجَعَلْتُمْ سِقَايَةَ الْحَاجِّ﴾ إلى قوله: ﴿واليوم الآخر﴾ الآية، فكان عليّ وحمزة وجعفر عليهم السلام الذين آمنوا بالله واليوم الآخر، وجاهدوا في سبيل الله، لا يستوون عند الله.

٣٦. عن جابر، عن أبي جعفر عليه السلام، قال: سألتُه عن هذه الآية في قول الله: ﴿يَا أَيُّهَا الَّذِينَ آمَنُوا لَا تَتَّخِذُوا آبَاءَكُمْ وَإِخْوَانَكُمْ أَوْلِيَاءَ﴾ إلى قوله: ﴿الفاسقين﴾، فأمّا ﴿لَا تَتَّخِذُوا آبَاءَكُمْ وَإِخْوَانَكُمْ أَوْلِيَاءَ إِنِ اسْتَحَبُّوا الْكُفْرَ عَلَى الْإِيمَانِ﴾ فإنّ الكفر في الباطن في هذه الآية ولاية الأوّل والثاني، وهو كُفر، وقوله: ﴿عَلَى الْإِيمَانِ﴾ فالإيمان ولاية عليّ بن أبي طالب عليه السلام، قال: ﴿وَمَنْ يَتَوَلَّهُمْ مِنْكُمْ فَأُولَئِكَ هُمُ الظَّالِمُونَ﴾.

37. From Yūsuf b. al-Sukht who said, 'Al-Mutawakkil was suffering from a severe malady, so he pledged an oath to God that if He cured him he would donate much wealth to charity. He was then cured of his illness, so he asked his companions what to do. They informed him that his father had donated eight million dirhams and that he had been seen to donate five million dirhams, so he should give more than that. So Abū Yaḥyā b. Abī Manṣūr al-Munjim said, "What if you write to your cousin?" meaning Abū al-Ḥasan [i.e. Imam al-Hādī]. So he ordered for a letter to be written on his behalf that he may ask [about what he ought to do], and he wrote to him. So Abū al-Ḥasan wrote back: "Donate eighty dirhams." They replied, "That is wrong. Ask him where did he get that from?" He replied, "This is from God's Book. God said to His Messenger: ﴾*God has helped you* [*believers*] *on many battlefields.*﴿ And there were eighty such places were God helped His Messenger, peace be upon him and his family. So eighty dirhams in its place is a large amount of money."' [9:25]

38. From 'Ajalān, from Abū 'Abd Allāh عليه السلام who said regarding God's statement ﴾*even on the day of the Battle of Hunayn. You were well pleased with your large numbers, but they were of no use to you: the earth seemed to close in on you despite its spaciousness, and you turned tail and fled*﴿: '[This referred to] so-and-so's father.' [9:25]

39. From al-Ḥasan b. 'Alī b. Faḍḍāl[7] who said, 'Abū al-Ḥasan 'Alī al-Riḍā عليه السلام asked al-Ḥasan b. Aḥmad, "What do you people consider the *sakīna* (calm) as having been?" He replied, "I do not know – may I be your ransom – what is it?"

He replied, "It is a breeze from God whence a fragrance emanates. It has a form like the form of a human face and it accompanied the prophets. This is what came down to Ibrāhīm, the friend of the all-Beneficent when he built the Ka'ba. So it made him pick up such and such, and the foundation was built according to it."' [9:26]

7 Abū Muḥammad al-Ḥasan b. 'Alī b. Faḍḍāl al-Taylamī b. Rabī'a b. Bakr (d. 224/838–9), a pious ascetic and notable companion of the eighth Imam 'Alī b. Mūsā al-Riḍā. See Ḥillī, *Khulāṣat al-aqwāl*, 98–9 (nr. 223).

٣٧. يوسف بن السُّخت، قال: اشتكى المتوكّل شَكاةً شديدةً فنذر لله إن شفاهُ الله يتصدّق بمالٍ كثيرٍ، فعُوفي من عِلّته، فسأله أصحابه عن ذلك، فأعلمُوه أنّ أباه تصدّق بثمانية ألف ألف دِرهم، وإن أراه تصدّق بخمسة ألف ألف دِرهم، فاستكثَرَ ذلك. فقال أبو يحيى بن أبي منصور المُنجّم: لوكتبتَ إلى ابن عمّك – يعني أبا الحسن عليه السلام فأمر أن يُكتَب له فيسأله، فكتب إليه، فكتب أبو الحسن عليه السلام: تصدّق بثمانين درهمًا، فقالوا: هذا غلطٌ، سلُوه من أين قال هذا؟ فكتب عليه السلام، قال الله لرسوله: ﴿لَقَدْ نَصَرَكُمُ اللَّهُ فِي مَوَاطِنَ كَثِيرَةٍ﴾ والمواطن الّتي نصر الله رسوله عليه وآله السلام فيها ثمانون مَوطِنًا، فثمانون دِرهمًا من حِلّه مالٌ كثير.

٣٨. عن عجلان، عن أبي عبدالله عليه السلام، في قول الله تعالى: ﴿وَيَوْمَ حُنَيْنٍ إِذْ أَعْجَبَتْكُمْ كَثْرَتُكُمْ﴾ إلى ﴿ثُمَّ وَلَّيْتُمْ مُدْبِرِينَ﴾، فقال: أبو فلان.

٣٩. عن الحسن بن عليّ بن فضّال، قال: قال أبو الحسن عليّ الرضا عليه السلام للحسن بن أحمد: أيّ شيءٍ السّكينة عندكم؟ قال: لا أدري جُعِلت فِداك أيّ شيءٍ هو؟

فقال: ريحٌ من الله تخرُج طيِّبة، لها صورةٌ كصورةِ وجه الإنسان، فتكون مع الأنبياء، وهي التي نزلت على إبراهيم خليل الرّحمن حيثُ بنى الكعبة فجَعَلت تأخُذ كذا وكذا، فبنى الأساس عليها.

40. From ʿAbd al-Malik b. ʿUtba al-Hāshimī[8], from Abū ʿAbd Allāh عليه السلام on his father's authority. He narrated, 'He عليه السلام said, "Whoever kills people with his sword whilst calling them to himself when there is someone more knowledgeable than him among the Muslims, is a misleading charlatan." He said this about ʿUmar b. ʿUbayd when he asked him to pledge allegiance to [Muḥammad b.] ʿAbd Allāh b. al-Ḥasan.' [9:29]

41. From Zurāra, from Abū ʿAbd Allāh عليه السلام. He said, 'I asked him, "What is the maximum rate of poll tax (*jizya*) to be taken from the People of the Book, and is there a minimum amount payable by them that cannot be relinquished?"'

He said, 'So he replied, "No. That is up to the Imam. He can take whatever he wants from each person according to his wealth and what he can afford. Indeed, they are a community who have ransomed themselves instead of being subjugated or killed, so the poll tax (*jizya*) is taken from them according to what they can afford to pay towards it until they embrace Islam; for God says: ﴾*until they pay the tax and agree to submit.*﴿ How can they be made to submit when they are indifferent to what is taken from them? Not until they experience disgrace as a result of what has been taken away from them and suffer as a result will they then embrace Islam."' [9:29]

42. From Ḥafṣ b. Ghiyāth, from Jaʿfar b. Muḥammad, on his father's authority, peace be upon them both, who said, 'God sent Muḥammad ﷺ with five swords, of which one was against the *ahl al-dhimma*.[9] God said: ﴾*speak good words to all people.*﴿(2:83) This was revealed about the *ahl al-dhimma*, and was later abrogated by the verse: ﴾*Fight those of the People of the Book who do not [truly] believe in God and the Last Day, who do not forbid what God and His Messenger have forbidden, who do not obey the rule of justice, until they pay the tax and agree to submit.*﴿ So whoever from among them lives in Muslim lands, it is only acceptable for them to either pay the poll

8 ʿAbd al-Malik b. ʿUtba al-Hāshimī, a companion of the fifth and sixth Imams. He is often confused with his namesake ʿAbd al-Malik b. ʿUtba al-Nakhaʿī, the latter of whom is a reliable narrator. As for ʿAbd al-Malik b. ʿUtba al-Hāshimī, his reliability as a narrator is, according to most, undetermined. See Khūʾī, *Muʿjam*, 12:257 (nr. 7314).

9 The *ahl al-dhimma* were the non-Muslim subjects living freely in Muslim countries who in return for paying the capital poll tax (*jizya*) enjoyed the protection and safety of the Muslim state.

٤٠. عن عبد الملك بن عُتبة الهاشمي، عن أبي عبدالله، عن أبيه عليه السلام، قال: قال: من ضرب الناس بسيفه، ودعاهم إلى نفسه، وفي المسلمين من هو أعلم منه، فهو ضالّ متكلّف، قاله لعمر بن عبيد حيث سأله أن يُبايع [محمّد بن] عبدالله ابن الحسن.

٤١. عن زُرارة، عن أبي عبدالله عليه السلام، قال: قلتُ له: ما حدّ الجِزية على أهل الكتاب، وهل عليهم في ذلك شيء مُوظّف لا ينبغي أن يجاوزه إلى غيره.

قال: فقال: لا، ذاك إلى الإمام، يأخُذ منهم من كلّ إنسان ما شاء على قدر ماله وما يُطيق، إنّما هم قومٌ فَدَوا أنفسهم من أن يُستَعبدوا أو يُقتَلوا، فالجِزية تُؤخَذ منهم [على قدر] ما يطيقون له أن يأخُذَهم بها حتّى يسلموا، فإنّ الله يقول: ﴿حَتَّىٰ يُعْطُوا الْجِزْيَةَ عَن يَدٍ وَهُمْ صَاغِرُونَ﴾، وكيف يكون صاغرًا وهو لا يكترِث لما يُؤخَذ منه، لا حتّى يجِد ذُلاًّ لما أُخِذ منه، فيألم لذلك فيُسلِم.

٤٢. عن حَفص بن غياث، عن جعفر بن محمّد، عن أبيه عليه السلام، قال: إنّ الله بعث محمّدًا صلى الله عليه وآله بخمسة أسياف، فسيف على أهل الذِمّة، قال الله: ﴿وَقُولُوا لِلنَّاسِ حُسْنًا﴾ نزلت في أهل الذمّة، ثمّ نسختها أُخرى، قوله: ﴿قَاتِلُوا الَّذِينَ لَا يُؤْمِنُونَ بِاللَّهِ وَلَا بِالْيَوْمِ الْآخِرِ﴾ إلى ﴿وَهُمْ صَاغِرُونَ﴾ فمن كان منهم في دار الإسلام فلن يُقبَل منهم إلاّ أداء الجِزية أو القَتل، ويُؤخَذ مالُهم، وتُسبى ذراريهم، فإذا قبِلوا الجِزية حلّ لنا نِكاحهم لا ذَبائحهم، و [من كان منهم في دار الحرب، حلّ لنا سبيهم، ولم تحلّ لنا مُناكحتهم] لا يُقبل منهم إلاّ أداء الجِزية أو القَتل.

tax (*jizya*) or be killed, with their property confiscated and their children made captive. If however they agree to pay the poll tax (*jizya*), then we are allowed to marry them but not to consume what they have slaughtered. As for those of them in lands at war with Islam, we are allowed to capture them but not to marry them. The only option for them is to either pay the poll tax (*jizya*) or be killed.' [9:29]

43. From 'Aṭiyya al-'Awfī[10], from Abū Sa'īd al-Khudrī who said, 'The Messenger of God ﷺ said, "God's wrath was vehement against the Jews when they said that 'Uzayr was the son of God; and His wrath was vehement against the Christians when they said that the Messiah was the son of God; and His wrath is vehement against those who will spill my blood and hurt me with respect to my progeny."' [9:30]

44. From Yazīd b. 'Abd al-Malik[11], from Abū 'Abd Allāh ؑ who said, 'Nothing will ever express more anger for God's sake than the anger of the cactus and the lotus tree. The cactus used to be like the lemon tree and the lotus-tree like the watermelon, but when the Jews said "God's Hands are tied," they dropped their load of fruit. Then they shrank and started growing bumps. Then the bumps became larger. When the Christians said, "The Messiah is the son of God," they were alarmed, and these thorns started growing from them, and they shed their loads again and the spikes became their yield. The cactus lost all its fruit and will never again bear any until our Qā'im reappears.' He said, 'Whoever waters a cactus or lotus-tree, it is as if he has quenched a believer of his thirst.' [9:30]

45. From Abū Baṣīr, from Abū 'Abd Allāh ؑ regarding the verse of God, most High: ﴾ *They take their rabbis and their monks as lords besides God.* ﴿ He said, 'By God, it is not that they fasted for them or offered their prayers to them, but rather that they made permissible that which was prohibited, and forbade that which was allowed, so they followed them.' [9:31]

---

10 'Aṭiyya al-'Awfī, on whom there is scant information, was a companion of 'Alī b. Abī Ṭālib. See Khū'ī, *Mu'jam*, 12:164 (nr. 7721).

11 Yazīd b. 'Abd al-Malik, about whom there is scant information, was a companion of Imam Ja'far al-Ṣādiq. See Khū'ī, *Mu'jam*, 21:125 (nr. 13696).

٤٣. عن عطيّة العوفي، عن أبي سعيد الخُدري، قال: قال رسول الله ﷺ: اشتدّ غضب الله على اليهود حين قالوا: عُزير ابن الله، واشتدّ غضب الله على النصارى حين قالوا: المسيح ابن الله، واشتدّ غضب الله على من أراق دمي، وآذاني في عترتي.

٤٤. عن يزيد بن عبد الملك، عن أبي عبدالله عليه السلام، قال: إنّه لن يغضَب لله شيءٌ كغضب الطَّلح والسِّدر، إنّ الطَّلح كانت كالأُترجّ والسِّدر كالبطِّيخ، فلمّا قالت اليهود: يد الله مَغلولة، نقّصا حَملهما فصَغُر فصار له عَجَم، واشتدّ العَجَم، فلمّا أن قالت النصارى: المسيح ابن الله، أُذعِرَتا فخرج لهما هذا الشَّوك، ونقّصتا حَملهما، وصار الشوك إلى هذا الحَمل، وذهب حَمل الطَّلح، فلا يحمِل حتّى يقوم قائمنا أو تقوم الساعة، ثمّ قال: من سقى طلحةً أو سدرةً، فكأنّما سقى مؤمنًا من ظمأ.

٤٥. عن أبي بصير، عن أبي عبدالله عليه السلام، في قول الله تعالى: ﴿اتَّخَذُوا أَحْبَارَهُمْ وَرُهْبَانَهُمْ أَرْبَابًا مِنْ دُونِ اللهِ﴾. قال: أما والله ما صاموا لهم ولا صلّوا. ولكنّهم أحلّوا لهم حرامًا، وحرّموا عليهم حلالاً فاتّبعوهم.

46. In another report on his authority, he said, 'But they obeyed them in acts of disobedience to God.' [9:31]

47. From Jābir, from Abū 'Abd Allāh عليه السلام. He said, 'I asked him about God's verse: ﴾*They take their rabbis and their monks as lords besides God.*﴿ He replied, "In fact, it is not that they took them as their gods but rather that when they made the prohibited things permissible, they accepted it; and when they forbade the permissible things they accepted it. So these were their lords besides God."' [9:31]

48. Abū Baṣir also said, 'Abū 'Abd Allāh said, "They did not call them towards worshipping them, for if they had done so they would not have responded. However, they made the prohibited things permissible and forbade the permissible things, so in effect they were worshipping them without even realizing."' [9:31]

49. From Ḥudhayfa, 'He was asked about God's verse: ﴾*They take their rabbis and their monks as lords besides God*﴿, so he said, "They did not worship them, but when they used to permit them to do certain things they took them to be permissible, and when they forbade them certain things they took them to be forbidden."' [9:31]

50. From Abū al-Miqdām, from Abū Ja'far عليه السلام regarding God's statement: ﴾*to show that it is above all* [*other*] *religions, however much the idolaters may hate this*﴿, 'To be such that there will be no one left who has not testified to Muḥammad صلى الله عليه وآله.' [9:33]

51. And he said in another report on his authority. 'He said, ﴾*for God to show*﴿ during the *raj'a*.' [9:33]

٤٦. وقال في خبر آخر عنه: ولكنّهم أطاعوهم في معصية الله.

٤٧. عن جابر، عن أبي عبد الله عليه السلام، قال: سألتُهُ عن قول الله: ﴿اتَّخَذُوا أَحْبَارَهُمْ وَرُهْبَانَهُمْ أَرْبَابًا مِنْ دُونِ اللهِ﴾. قال: أما إنّهم لم يتّخذوهم آلهةً، إلاّ أنّهم أحلّوا لهم حرامًا فأخَذُوا به، وحرّموا عليهم حلالاً فأخذوا به، فكانوا أربابهم من دون الله.

٤٨. وقال أبو بصير، قال أبو عبد الله عليه السلام: ما دعوهم إلى عبادة أنفسهم، ولو دعُوهم إلى عبادة أنفسهم ما أجابوهم، ولكنَّهم أحلّوا لهم حرامًا، وحرّموا عليهم حلالاً، فكانوا يَعبدُونهم من حيث لا يَشعُرون.

٤٩. عن حُذيفة، سُئِل عن قول الله: ﴿اتَّخَذُوا أَحْبَارَهُمْ وَرُهْبَانَهُمْ أَرْبَابًا مِنْ دُونِ اللهِ﴾ فقال: لم يكُونوا يعبُدونهم، ولكن كانوا إذا أحلّوا لهم أشياء استحلّوها، وإذا حرّموا عليهم حرّموها.

٥٠. عن أبي المقدام، عن أبي جعفر عليه السلام، في قول الله: ﴿لِيُظْهِرَهُ عَلَى الدِّينِ كُلِّهِ وَلَوْ كَرِهَ الْمُشْرِكُونَ﴾ يكون أن لا يبقى أحدٌ إلاّ أقرّ بمحمّد صلى الله عليه وآله وسلم.

٥١. وقال في خبر آخر، عنه عليه السلام: قال: لِيظهره الله في الرَّجعَة.

52. From Samāʿa, from Abū ʿAbd Allāh ﷺ: ﴿*It is He who has sent His Messenger with guidance and the religion of truth, to show that it is above all* [*other*] *religions, however much the idolaters may hate this.*﴾ He said, 'When the Qāʾim emerges there will not be a single idolater who associates with God, the Great, nor a single disbeliever who will not despise his emergence.' [9:33]

53. From Saʿdān[12], from Abū Jaʿfar ﷺ regarding God's verse: ﴿*those who hoard gold and silver*﴾: 'This actually refers to that which exceeds two thousand dirhams in value.' [9:34]

54. From Muʿādh b. Kathīr, the clothes-vendor, who said, 'I heard Abū ʿAbd Allāh ﷺ say, "Our followers (*shīʿa*) are encouraged to spend whatever they possess in a goodly way, for when our Qāʾim reappears it will be prohibited for anyone who has hoards of treasure to keep it for himself so that he [the Imam] may come to him and seek assistance from him over his enemies. And this is the purport of God's statement: ﴿*tell those who hoard gold and silver instead of giving in God's cause that they will have a grievous punishment.*﴾"' [9:34]

55. From al-Ḥusayn b. ʿUlwān[13], from whoever mentioned it citing Abū ʿAbd Allāh ﷺ as having said: 'The believer can have as much as he possesses to spend on his family however he wants. But when the Qāʾim reappears he should take to him whatever he possesses [and make it available to him to use however he pleases]. Whatever is left over from that he will use to assist him in his mission, and he will have fulfilled the duty that is incumbent upon him.' [9:34]

---

12 Saʿdān b. Muslim, whose full name is Abū al-Ḥasan ʿAbd al-Raḥmān b. Muslim al-ʿĀmirī, was the client of Abū ʿAlāʾ Karaz b. Juʿayd and a companion of the fifth, sixth and seventh Imams. He is the author of one of the 400 pre-canonical books (*aṣl*) of Imāmī traditions. See Khūʾī, *Muʿjam*, 9:104–7 (nr. 5099).

13 Abū Muḥammad al-Ḥusayn b. ʿUlwān al-Kalbī, was a Sunnī narrator of Imam Jaʿfar al-Ṣādiq's traditions. See Ḥillī, *Khulāṣat al-aqwāl*, 338 (nr. 1337).

٥٢ . عن سماعة، عن أبي عبدالله عليه السلام: ﴿هُوَ الَّذِي أَرْسَلَ رَسُولَهُ بِالْهُدَى وَدِينِ الْحَقِّ لِيُظْهِرَهُ عَلَى الدِّينِ كُلِّهِ وَلَوْ كَرِهَ الْمُشْرِكُونَ﴾، قال: إذا خرج القائم عليه السلام، لم يبقَ مُشرِك بالله العظيم ولا كافر إلاّ كَرِه خُروجَه.

٥٣ . عن سَعدان، عن أبي جعفر عليه السلام، في قول الله: ﴿وَالَّذِينَ يَكْنِزُونَ الذَّهَبَ وَالْفِضَّةَ﴾ إنّما عنى بذلك ما جاوز ألفي دِرهَم.

٥٤ . عن مُعاذ بن كثير صاحب الأكسية، قال: سمعتُ أبا عبدالله عليه السلام يقول: مُوسَّع على شيعتنا أن يُنفِقُوا ممّا في أيديهم بالمعروف، فإذا قام قائمُنا عليه السلام حرّم على كُلّ ذي كنز كنزه، حتّى يأتيه فيستعين به على عَدُوّه، وذلك قول الله تعالى: ﴿وَالَّذِينَ يَكْنِزُونَ الذَّهَبَ وَالْفِضَّةَ وَلَا يُنفِقُونَهَا فِي سَبِيلِ اللَّهِ فَبَشِّرْهُم بِعَذَابٍ أَلِيمٍ﴾.

٥٥ . عن الحسين بن عُلوان، عمّن ذكره، عن أبي عبدالله عليه السلام، قال: المؤمن؟ إذا كان عنده من ذلك شيء يُنفِقه على عياله ما شاء، ثُمّ إذا قام القائم عليه السلام فيحمل إليه ما عنده، وما بقي من ذلك يستعين به على أمره، فقد أدّى ما يَجبُ عليه.

56. From Abū Khālid al-Wāsiṭī[14] who said, 'I came to Abū Ja'far on a day of doubt as to whether it was [the start of] Ramadan and when food had been laid out on a table and he was eating, whilst we wanted to ask him about that. So he said, "Have some food. If it is a day like today, then it cannot be ruled [as Ramadan] because you can see it [i.e. the moon], so do not fast."

Then he continued, "My father narrated to me, from 'Alī b. al-Ḥusayn, from the Commander of the Faithful that when the Messenger of God ﷺ had succumbed to his illness, he said, 'O people, the year consists of twelve months, of which four are sacred' – then counting on his hands he said, 'Rajab by itself; then Dhū al-Qa'da, Dhū al-Ḥijja and Muḥarram, three consecutive months; then this mandatory month of Ramadan – so fast upon seeing it and resume eating upon seeing it. If the moon is hidden, then complete the prescribed number of days, so Sha'bān will have thirty days, then fast on the thirty-first.'

Then counting on his fingers, he said, 'One, two, three.' Then he closed his thumb and said, 'O people, then this month and that month.'"

'Alī عليه السلام said, 'We fasted twenty-nine days with the Messenger of God ﷺ and did not complete it [i.e. to thirty days] and he considered it complete.'"' [9:36]

57. From Zurāra, from Abū Ja'far عليه السلام. He said, 'I was with him sitting behind the Station [of Ibrāhīm] while he was sat with his legs drawn up to his chest and wrapped in his cloak facing the Qibla. He said, "Looking at it is indeed an act of worship, and God has not created any place on earth more beloved to Him than it," pointing to the Ka'ba with his hand, "nor anything more honoured by Him than it since God has ordained the sanctity of the sacred months in His Book: ﴾*on the Day when He created the heavens and earth*﴿ – three consecutive months and the single month of Rajab for *'umra*." Abū 'Abd Allāh عليه السلام said, "Shawwāl, Dhū al-Qa'da, Dhū al-Ḥijja and Rajab."' [9:36]

14 Abū Khālid al-Wāsiṭī, on whom there is scant information. See Khū'ī, *Mu'jam*, 22:154–5 (nr. 14245).

٥٦ . عن أبي خالد الواسطي، قال: أتيتُ أبا جعفر عليه السلام يوم شكّ فيه من رمضان، فإذا مائدة موضوعة وهو يأكُل، ونحنُ نريد أن نسأله، فقال: ادنُوا الغَداء، إذا كان مثل هذا اليوم لم يَحكُم فيه سبب تَرَونه فلا تَصُوموا.

ثمّ قال: حدّثني أبي عليّ بن الحسين، عن أمير المؤمنين عليه السلام: أنّ رسول الله صلى الله عليه وآله وسلم لمّا ثَقُل في مرضه قال: يا أيّها الناس، إنّ السّنة اثنا عشر شهرًا، منها أربعة حُرُم، ثمّ قال بيده. رجبٌ مفرد، وذو القَعدة، وذو الحجّة، والمحرّم ثلاث متواليات، ألا وهذا الشهر المفروض رمضان، فَصُوموا لرُؤيته، وأفطروا لرُؤيته، فإذا خفي الشهر فأتمّوا العِدّة، شعبان ثلاثين، وصوموا الواحد والثلاثين.

وقال بيده: الواحد والاثنين والثلاثة، ثمّ ثنى إبهامه، ثمّ قال: أيّها الناس، شهر كذا، وشهر كذا.

وقال عليّ عليه السلام: صُمنا مع رسول الله صلى الله عليه وآله وسلم تسعًا وعشرين، ولم نَقضِه، ورآه تمامًا.

٥٧ . عن زُرارة، عن أبي جعفر عليه السلام، قال: كنتُ عنده قاعدًا خلف المقام، وهو مُحتّب، مستقبل القبلة، فقال: أمّا النظر إليها عبادة، وما خلق الله بُقعَةً في الأرض أحبّ إليه منها — ثمّ أهوى بيده إلى الكعبة — ولا أكرم عليه منها، لها حرّم الله الأشهر الحُرُم في كتابه يوم خلق السّماوات والأرض ثلاثة أشهر متوالية، وشهر مفرد للعُمرة، قال أبو عبد الله عليه السلام: شوّال، وذو القَعدة، وذو الحجّة، ورَجب.

58. From 'Abd Allāh b. Muḥammad al-Ḥajjāl[15] who said, 'I was with the second Abū al-Ḥasan [i.e. Imam 'Alī al-Riḍā ﷺ] and al-Ḥasan b. al-Jahm was there too. Al-Ḥasan said to him, "They dispute with us using God's words, Blessed and most High: ﴾*when the two of them were in the cave.*﴿" He said, "And what benefit is there for them in that? For, by God, He has indeed said: ﴾*and God sent His calm down upon* ***His Messenger***﴿[16] and did not mentioned him [i.e. Abū Bakr] in a positive light there."' He said, 'I said to him, "May I be your ransom, this is exactly as they read it." He said, "And that is exactly how I read it."' [9:40*]

59. Zurāra said, 'Abū Ja'far ﷺ said, '﴾*and God sent His calm down upon His Messenger*﴿ (48:26) – do you not see that the calm was sent down upon His Messenger – ﴾*and brought down the disbelievers' plan.*﴿' Then he said, "This is the statement made by 'Atīq, and Ḥalabī narrated on his authority."' [9:40]

60. From Zurāra, Ḥumrān and Muḥammad b. Muslim, from Abū Ja'far and Abū 'Abd Allāh ﷺ regarding His verse: ﴾*They would certainly have followed you* [*Prophet*] *if the benefit was within sight and the journey short but the distance seemed too great for them. They will swear by God, 'If we could, we certainly would go out* [*to battle*] *with you,' but they ruin themselves, for God knows that they are lying*﴿: 'They were able to, but God knew that they would only do it if the benefit were within sight and the journey short.' [9:42]

61. From al-Mughīra who said, 'I heard him say regarding God's verse ﴾*If they had really wanted to go out* [*to battle*] *with you, they would have made preparations*﴿: "By preparations, He means the intention. He is saying, 'If they had the intention to do so they would have gone out [to fight]."' [9:46]

---

15 Abū Muḥammad 'Abd Allāh b. Muḥammad al-Ḥajjāl al-Mazkhūf, considered very reliable by Ḥillī. See Ḥillī, *Khulāṣat al-aqwāl*, 193 (nr. 603).

16 The words ﴾*His Messenger*﴿ are substituted with ﴾*him*﴿ in the 'Uthmānic codex of the Qur'an. In this verse the object upon whom God's tranquility descended is indicated by the pronoun 'him,' which the majority of exegetes take as a reference to Abū Bakr, the first Caliph. However in two instances the Qur'an specifies Muḥammad as the one upon whom God's tranquility descends, namely Q. 48:26 and Q. 9:26.

٥٨. عن عبدالله بن محمّد الحجّال، قال: كنتُ عند أبي الحسن الثاني عليه السلام ومعي الحسن بن الجَهم، فقال له الحسن: إنّهم يحتجُّون علينا بقول الله تبارك وتعالى: ﴿ثَانِيَ اثْنَيْنِ إِذْ هُمَا فِي الْغَارِ﴾، قال: وما لهم في ذلك؟ فوالله لقد قال الله: ﴿فَأَنزَلَ اللَّهُ سَكِينَتَهُ عَلَيْهِ﴾ وما ذكره فيها بخير.

قال قلتُ له أنا: جُعِلتُ فداك، وهكذا تقرؤونها، قال: هكذا قرأتها.

٥٩. قال زُرارة: قال أبو جعفر عليه السلام: ﴿فأنزل الله سكينته على رسوله﴾ ألا ترى أنّ السكينة إنّما نزلت على رسوله؟ ﴿وَجَعَلَ كَلِمَةَ الَّذِينَ كَفَرُوا السُّفْلَى﴾ فقال: هو الكلام الّذي تكلّم به عَتيق. رواه الحلبي عنه.

٦٠. عن زُرارة وحُمران ومحمّد بن مسلم، عن أبي جعفر وأبي عبدالله عليهما السلام، في قول الله: ﴿لَوْ كَانَ عَرَضًا قَرِيبًا وَسَفَرًا قَاصِدًا لَّاتَّبَعُوكَ﴾ الآية، إنّهم يستطيعون، وقد كان في علم الله أنّه لو كان عرضًا قريبًا وسفرًا قاصدًا لَفعلوا.

٦١. عن المُغيرة، قال: سمِعتُه يقول في قول الله: ﴿وَلَوْ أَرَادُوا الْخُرُوجَ لَأَعَدُّوا لَهُ عُدَّةً﴾، قال: يعني بالعُدّة النّيّة، يقول: لو كان لهم نيّة لخرَجوا.

62. From Yūsuf b. Thābit[17], from Abū ʿAbd Allāh عليه السلام. He said, ʻWhen we went to visit him, he was told, "We love you because of your closeness to God's Messenger صلى الله عليه وآله and because of your right that God has made incumbent upon us. It is not because of any share in this world's life that we seek from you that we love you, only for God's sake and the abode of the Hereafter, and that each of us may secure his faith."

So Abū ʿAbd Allāh عليه السلام said, "You have spoken the truth, you have spoken the truth. And whoever loves us will accompany us on the Day of Judgement like this," holding up his two forefingers stuck together. Then he said, "By God, if a man was to fast during the day and pray the whole night, then meet God without having adhered to our authority, He will meet him displeased and disappointed with him." Then he said, "That is the purport of God's statement: ﴾*The only thing that prevents what they give from being accepted is the fact that they defy God and His Messenger, perform the prayer only lazily, and give only grudgingly. So [Prophet] do not let their possessions or their children impress you: through these God intends to punish them in this world and for their souls to depart while they disbelieve.*﴿"

Then he continued, "And such is faith – it cannot be spoiled by deeds; and the same with faithlessness, which cannot be remedied by mere good deeds."ʼ [9:54–55]

63. From Isḥāq b. Ghālib[18] who said, ʻAbū ʿAbd Allāh عليه السلام said, "Isḥāq, how many people do you think this verse applies to: ﴾*they are content if they are given a share, but angry if not*﴿?" He continued, "More than two-thirds of people are thus."ʼ [9:58]

64. From Samāʿa who said, ʻI asked him about the alms (*zakāt*) – who is allowed to take it? He replied, "It is for those whom God has mentioned in His Book: ﴾*for the poor, the needy, those who administer them, those whose hearts need winning over, to free slaves and help those in debt, for God's cause, and for travelers in need. This is ordained by God.*﴿ Alms may be permissible

17 Abū Umayya Yūsuf b. Thābit b. Abī Saʿīd, a reliable companion and narrator of Imam Jaʿfar al-Ṣādiq. See Ḥillī, *Khulāṣat al-aqwāl*, 296 (nr. 1101).

18 Isḥāq b. Ghālib al-Asadī who, along with his brother ʿAbd Allāh b. Ghālib, were two reliable narrators of Imam Jaʿfar al-Ṣādiq. See Ḥillī, *Khulāṣat al-aqwāl*, 59 (nr. 55).

٦٢. عن يوسف بن ثابت، عن أبي عبدالله عليه السلام، قال: قيل له لمّا دخلنا عليه: إنّا أحببناكم لقرابتكم من رسول الله صلى الله عليه وآله، ولما أوجب الله من حقكم، ما أحببناكم لدُنيا نصيبها منكم، إلاّ لوجه الله والدّار الآخرة، وليُصلِح امرؤ مِنّا دينه.

فقال: أبو عبدالله عليه السلام: صدَقتُم، صدَقتُم، ومن أحبَّنا جاء معنا يوم القيامة هكذا — ثمّ جمع بين السبّابتين — وقال: والله لو أنّ رجلاً صام النهار وقام الليل، ثمّ لقي الله بغير ولايتنا، لقيه غير راضٍ — أو ساخطًا عليه —. ثمّ قال: وذلك قول الله: ﴿وَمَا مَنَعَهُمْ أَنْ تُقْبَلَ مِنْهُمْ نَفَقَاتُهُمْ إِلاَّ أَنَّهُمْ كَفَرُوا بِاللهِ وَبِرَسُولِهِ﴾ إلى قوله ﴿وَهُمْ كَافِرُونَ﴾

ثمّ قال: وكذلك الإيمان لا يضُرّ معه عملٌ، وكذلك الكُفر لا ينفعُ معه عمل.

٦٣. إسحاق بن غالب، قال: قال أبو عبدالله عليه السلام: يا إسحاق، كم ترى أهل هذه الآية ﴿فَإِنْ أُعْطُوا مِنْهَا رَضُوا وَإِنْ لَمْ يُعْطَوْا مِنْهَا إِذَا هُمْ يَسْخَطُونَ﴾؟ قال: هم أكثر من ثُلثي الناس.

٦٤. عن سَماعة، قال: سألتُه عن الزكاة، لمن يَصلُح أن يأخُذها؟ فقال: هي للّذين قال الله في كتابه: ﴿لِلْفُقَرَاءِ وَالْمَسَاكِينِ وَالْعَامِلِينَ عَلَيْهَا وَالْمُؤَلَّفَةِ قُلُوبُهُمْ وَفِي الرِّقَابِ وَالْغَارِمِينَ وَفِي سَبِيلِ اللهِ وَابْنِ السَّبِيلِ فَرِيضَةً مِنَ اللهِ﴾ وقد تَحِلّ الزكاة لصاحب ثلاثمائة دِرهم، وتحرُم على صاحب خمسين دِرهمًا.

for one who has three hundred dirhams and yet prohibited for one who has fifty dirhams."'

I asked him, "How can that be?" He replied, "If the one who has three hundred dirhams has many dependents, and were he to share them out between them, it would not suffice them; then he should refrain from it [i.e. the alms] himself but should take it for his family. As for the man with fifty dirhams, alms are prohibited for him if he is single and has a skill that he can use to work. Through that he will earn enough to suffice him, God-willing." [9:60]

65. From Muḥammad b. Muslim, from Abū 'Abd Allāh عليه السلام who said regarding the poor and the needy, 'The poor man is the one who begs, whilst the needy one is even worse off than him who does not beg.' [9:60]

66. From Abū Baṣīr who said, 'I asked Abū 'Abd Allāh عليه السلام about: ﴾*Alms are meant only for the poor, the needy* [...]﴿ He said, "The poor man is the one who begs, the needy one is even worse off than him, and the wretched one worse off than them both."' [9:60]

67. From Aḥmad b. Muḥammad b. Abī Naṣr, from Abū al-Ḥasan [i.e. al-Riḍā] عليه السلام. He said, 'I asked him about a man who bequeaths a portion of his wealth but it is not known how much a portion is exactly. He replied, "Portions are eighths. This is why the Messenger of God صلى الله عليه وآله divided them into eight." Then he recited: ﴾*Alms are meant only for the poor* [...]﴿ Then he said, "A portion is one-eighth."' [9:60]

68. From Abū Maryam, from Abū 'Abd Allāh عليه السلام regarding God's statement: ﴾*Alms are meant only for the poor* [...]﴿ Then he said, 'Whether you designate it for all categories of them or whether you designate it for one group from among them, it has been fulfilled on your part.' [9:60]

69. From Zurāra, from Abū 'Abd Allāh. He said, 'I asked, "You know His verse: ﴾*Alms are meant only for the poor* [...]﴿ – are all of those people to be given even if one does not know them?"

He replied, "The Imam gives to all of them because they all attest to his obedience."'

فقلت له: وكيف يكون هذا؟ قال: إذا كان صاحب الثّلاثمائة دِرهم له عِيال كثير، فلو قسَّمها بينهم لم يَكفِهم، فليعفف عنها نفسه، وليأخُذها لعياله، وأمّا صاحب الخمسين فإنّها تحرم عليه إذا كان وحده، وهو محترفٌ يعمل بها، وهو يُصيب فيها ما يكفيه إن شاء الله.

٦٥. عن محمّد بن مسلم، عن أبي عبدالله عليه السلام، عن الفقير والمسكين، قال: الفقير الّذي يسأل، والمسكين أجهد منه الّذي لا يسأل.

٦٦. عن أبي بصير، قال: قلتُ لأبي عبدالله عليه السلام: ﴿إِنَّمَا الصَّدَقَاتُ لِلْفُقَرَاءِ وَالْمَسَاكِينِ﴾، قال: الفقير الذي يسأل، والمسكين أجهد منه، والبائس أجهدهما.

٦٧. عن أحمد بن محمّد بن أبي نصر، عن أبي الحسن عليه السلام، قال: سألتُه عن رجلٍ أوصى بسهمٍ من ماله، وليس يدري أيُّ شيء هو؟ قال: السِّهام ثمانية، وكذلك قسَّمها رسول الله عليه السلام، ثمّ تلا ﴿إِنَّمَا الصَّدَقَاتُ لِلْفُقَرَاءِ وَالْمَسَاكِينِ﴾ إلى آخر الآية، ثمّ قال: إنّما السَّهم واحدٌ من ثمانية.

٦٨. عن أبي مريم، عن أبي عبدالله عليه السلام، في قول الله: ﴿إِنَّمَا الصَّدَقَاتُ﴾ إلى آخر الآية، قال عليه السلام. إن جعلتها فيهم جميعًا، وإن جعلتها لواحدٍ أجزأ عنك.

٦٩. عن زُرارة، عن أبي عبدالله عليه السلام، قال: قلتُ: أرأيت قوله: ﴿إِنَّمَا الصَّدَقَاتُ﴾ إلى آخر الآية، كلّ هؤلاء يُعطى إن كان لا يعرف؟ قال: إنّ الإمام يعطي هؤلاء جميعًا، لأنّهم يُقِرّون له بالطاعة.

He said, 'I asked him, "And what if they do not know [him]?"

He replied, "Zurāra, if it were the case that only those who knew [us] would be given over those who did not know [us], then they would not find any beneficiaries for it; rather he would purposely give to those who did not know him in order to attract them to the faith, so that they may remain steadfast on it. These days, however, you and your companions should only give to those who know [us]."' [9:60]

70. From Muḥammad b. Muslim, from Abū Ja'far ﷺ who said regarding His words: ﴿*those who administer them*﴾: 'They are the couriers.' [9:60]

71. From Zurāra who said, 'I asked Abū Ja'far ﷺ about His words: ﴿*those whose hearts need winning over.*﴾ He replied, "They are people who have attested to God's oneness and have left the practices of those who worship anything besides God, Blessed and most High. They testify that there is no god but God and that Muḥammad is God's Messenger, but beyond that they still doubt in what Muḥammad ﷺ has brought. So God commanded their Prophet to win them over with wealth and donations so that it may improve their submission and make them steadfast on the faith they have entered into and attested to.

On the Day of Ḥunayn, the Messenger of God ﷺ brought their chieftains together with the chieftains of the Arabs from the tribe of Quraysh and the rest of Muḍarr. Among them were Abū Sufyān b. Ḥarb, 'Uyayna b. Ḥuṣayn al-Fazārī and the likes of them from among the people. So the *anṣār* were enraged, and all of them went to Sa'd b. 'Ubāda [their chief] and set off with him to go and meet the Messenger of God ﷺ at Ji'irrāna.

He said, 'O Messenger of God, do you permit me to speak?'

He replied, 'Yes.'

So he said, 'If this matter of the wealth that you have distributed among your people is something that God has commanded you to do, then we are satisfied. But if that is not the case then we are not happy.'"'

Zurāra said, 'I have heard Abū Ja'far ﷺ say, "The Messenger of God said, 'O assembly of *anṣār*! Are you all of the same opinion as Sa'd [your chief]?'

They replied, 'God is our chief, and His Messenger too.'

So he repeated it to them three times, and each time they said, 'God is our chief, and His Messenger too.'

قال: قلتُ له: فإن كانوا لا يعرِفون؟ فقال: يا زُرارة، لوكان يُعطي من يَعرف دون من لا يَعرف، لم يُوجد لها موضع، وإنّماكان يُعطي من لا يعرِف ليرغب في الدّين فيثْبُت عليه، وأمّا اليوم فلا تُعطها أنت وأصحابك إلاّ من يعرِف.

٧٠. عن محمّد بن مسلم، عن أبي جعفر عليه السلام، في قوله: ﴿وَالْعَامِلِينَ عَلَيْهَا﴾ قال: هم السُّعاة.

٧١. عن زُرارة، قال سألتُ أبا جعفر عليه السلام عن قوله ﴿وَالْمُؤَلَّفَةِ قُلُوبُهُمْ﴾. قال: هم قومٌ وحّدوا الله، وخَلَعوا عِبادة من يعبُد من دون الله تبارك وتعالى، وشَهدوا أن لا إله إلاّ الله، وأنّ محمّدًا رسول الله، وهم في ذلك شُكّاك من بعد ما جاء به محمّد صلى الله عليه وآله، فأمر الله عزّ وجلّ نبيّه صلى الله عليه وآله أن يتألّفهم بالمال والعَطاء لكي يَحسُن إسلامهم، ويَثْبُتوا على دينهم الذي قد دَخلوا فيه، وأقرّوا به.

وإنّ رسول الله صلى الله عليه وآله يوم حُنين تألّف رؤوسهم من رؤوس العرب من قريش وسائر مُضرّ، منهم أبو سفيان بن حرب، وعُيينة بن حُصين الفَزاري وأشباههم من الناس، فغَضِبَت الأنصارُ، فاجتمعوا إلى سعد بن عُبادة، فانطلق بهم إلى رسول الله صلى الله عليه وآله بالجِعرانة، فقال: يا رسول الله، أتأذن لي في الكلام؟ قال: نعم. فقال: إن كان هذا الأمر من هذه الأموال الّتي قسّمت بين قومك شيئًا أمرك الله به رضِينا، وان كان غير ذلك لم نَرضَ؟

قال زُرارة: فسمِعتُ أبا جعفر عليه السلام يقول: قال رسول الله صلى الله عليه وآله: يا معشر الأنصار، كلّكم على مثل قول سعد سيّدكم؟ قالوا: الله سيّدنا ورسوله. فأعادها عليهم ثلاث

Then after the third time they said, 'Yes, we hold the same opinion and statement as him.'"'

Zurāra said, 'I heard Abū Ja'far say, "So God diminished their light and made a share of the alms obligatory in the Qur'an for those whose hearts needed winning over."' [9:60]

72. From Zurāra, Ḥumrān and Muḥammad b. Muslim, from Abū Ja'far and Abū 'Abd Allāh عليهما السلام about ﴿*those whose hearts need winning over.*﴾ He said, 'They were people whom the Messenger of God won over and to whom he distributed some wealth.'

Zurāra said, 'Abū Ja'far عليه السلام said, "The next time, they came with double the number of people who had been captured, and many people embraced Islam."

He continued, "So the Messenger of God ﷺ stood up to address them saying, 'Is this better or that which you proposed? They have come with camel-loads with multitudes more than what I had given them, and so many people have embraced Islam. By the One who holds my soul in His Hand, I wished to have that which I could give as a ransom for every person having submitted to God, Lord of the worlds.'"'

There is a similar narration from Zurāra, from Abū Ja'far. [9:60]

73. Al-Ḥasan b. Mūsā mentioned another angle to this too, that he – without mentioning a source – quoted a man from among them who said, 'When the Prophet ﷺ distributed the spoils from Ḥunayn – [someone asked]: "What does God want to do with this particular share?" One of them said to him, "O enemy of God! How dare you say that about the Messenger of God?" Then he came to the Prophet ﷺ and informed him of what he had said. So he ﷺ replied, "My brother Mūsā was harassed much more than this, and he was patient."'

He said, 'He was giving away one hundred horses to each man from among those whose hearts needed winning over.' [9:60]

مرّات، كلّ ذلك يقولون: الله سيّدنا ورسوله. ثمّ قالوا بعد الثالثة: نحنُ على مثل قوله ورأيه.

قال زُرارة: سمِعتُ أبا جعفر عليه السلام يقول: فحطّ الله نُورهم، وفرض للمؤلَّفة قلوبهم سهمًا في القرآن.

٧٢. عن زُرارة وحُمران ومحمّد بن مسلم، عن أبي جعفر وأبي عبد الله عليهم السلام ﴿وَالْمُؤَلَّفَةِ قُلُوبُهُمْ﴾، قال: قوم تألّفهم رسول الله صلى الله عليه وآله، وقسّم فيهم الفَيء.

قال زُرارة: قال أبو جعفر عليه السلام: فلمّا كان في قابِلٍ، جاءوا بضِعف الّذي أخذوا، وأسلم ناسٌ كثير، قال: فقام رسول الله صلى الله عليه وآله خطيبًا، فقال: هذا خيرٌ أم الذي قُلتم؟ قد جاءوا من الإبل بكذا وكذا ضِعف ما أعطيتهم، وقد أسلم لله عالمٌ وناسٌ كثير، والذي نفسي بيده، لوددتُ أنّ عندي ما أُعطي كُلّ إنسانٍ دِيته على أن يُسلِم الله ربّ العالمين.

عن زُرارة، عن أبي جعفر عليه السلام، نحوه.

٧٣. قال الحسن بن موسى، ومن غير هذا الوجه أيضًا، رفعه، قال: قال رجلٌ منهم حين قسّم النبيّ صلى الله عليه وآله غنائم حُنين: إنّ هذه القِسمة ما يُريد الله بها؟ فقال له بعضهم: يا عدوّ الله، تقول هذا لرسول الله؟ ثمّ جاء إلى النبيّ صلى الله عليه وآله فأخبره مقالته، فقال صلى الله عليه وآله: قد أوذِي أخي موسى عليه السلام بأكثر من هذا فصبر. قال: وكان يعطي لكُلّ رجلٍ من المؤلَّفة قلوبهم مائة راحلة.

٧٤. عن سَماعة، عن أبي عبد الله - أو أبي الحسن عليه السلام - قال: ذكر أحدهما أنّ رجلاً دخل على رسول الله صلى الله عليه وآله يوم غنيمة حُنين، وكان يُعطي المؤلّفة قلوبهم، يُعطي الرجل منهم

74. From Samāʿa, from Abū ʿAbd Allāh عليه السلام or Abū al-Ḥasan عليه السلام. He said, 'One of them mentioned that a man went to visit the Messenger of God صلى الله عليه وآله on the day of the spoils of Ḥunayn while he was distributing wealth to those whose hearts needed winning over, giving each man one hundred horses and the like. The Messenger of God صلى الله عليه وآله was distributing in the manner he had been commanded. So that man came to him, and God had let his heart stray and become encrusted, so he said to him, "You have not been fair in your distribution." The Messenger of God صلى الله عليه وآله said to him, "Woe unto you for what you are saying! Have you not seen that I have distributed the ewes such that I have no ewes left myself? Have I not distributed the cows until I have no cow left? Have I not distributed the camels to the extent that not a single camel remains with me?" So some of his companions said, "O Messenger of God, let us behead this vile man!" So he said, "No. He considers himself among the people who read the Qur'an, therefore he must not be killed. Someone else will inevitably fight them."' [9:60]

75. From Zurāra who narrated the following: 'Ḥumrān and I went to visit Abū Jaʿfar عليه السلام and said, "Indeed we are upon this purifier." So he asked, "And what is this purifier?" We replied, "The religion. Whoever is in harmony with us, be they a descendent of ʿAlī or not, we endear ourselves to them; and whoever opposes us, we disassociate from them, be they a descendent of ʿAlī or not." He said, "God's Word is truer than your word – what about the one about whom God says: ﴿*but not so the truly helpless men, women, and children who have no means in their power nor any way to leave*﴾? (4:98) What about the ones who can only hope for God's mercy? What about those who have mixed up righteous deeds with bad deeds? What about the people of the heights? What about those whose hearts need to be won over?"' So Zurāra said, 'Both Abū Jaʿfar's voice and my own were raised to the extent that someone standing at the front door of the house would have been able to hear. After much talk between him and I, he said to me, "Zurāra, God would be right to admit you into the Garden."' [9:60]

مائة راحلة ونحوذلك، وقسّم رسول الله ﷺ حيث أُمِر، فأتاه ذلك الرجل، قد أزاغ الله قلبه، وران عليه، فقال له: ما عَدَلتَ حين قسّمت. فقال له رسول الله ﷺ: ويلك ما تقول، ألم تَرَ قسّمتُ الشّياه حتّى لم يبقَ معي شاةٌ؟ أولم أُقسّم البقر حتّى لم يبقَ معي بقرةٌ واحدةٌ؟ أولم أُقسّم الإبل حتّى لم يبقَ معي بعيرٌ واحدٌ؟

فقال بعض أصحابه له: اترُكنا – يا رسول الله – حتّى نضرِب عُنق هذا الخبيث، فقال: لا، هذا يخرج في قوم يقرءون القرآن لا يَجُوز تَراقِيهم، يلي قاتلهم غيري.

٧٥. عن زُرارة، قال: دخلتُ أنا وحُمران على أبي جعفر عليه السلام فقُلنا: إنّا بهذا المطهر، فقال: وما المطهر؟ قلنا: الدّين، فمن وافقنا من علويّ أو غيره تولّيناه، ومن خالفنا بَرِئنا منه من علويّ أو غيره.

قال: يا زُرارة، قول الله أصدق من قولك، فأين الذين قال الله تعالى: ﴿وَالْمُسْتَضْعَفِينَ مِنَ الرِّجَالِ وَالنِّسَاءِ وَالْوِلْدَانِ﴾ الذين ﴿لا يَسْتَطِيعُونَ حِيلَةً وَلا يَهْتَدُونَ سَبِيلاً﴾؟ أين المُرجَون لأمر الله؟ أين الذين خلَطُوا عملاً صالحًا وآخر سيّئًا؟ أين أصحاب الأعراف؟ أين المؤلَّفة قلوبهم؟

فقال زُرارة: ارتَفَع صوت أبي جعفر عليه السلام وصوتي حتّى كان يسمعه من على باب الدار، فلمّا كثُر الكلام بيني وبينه قال لي: يا زُرارة، حقًّا على الله أن يُدخِلك الجنّة.

76. From al-ʿĪṣ b. al-Qāsim[19], from Abū ʿAbd Allāh عليه السلام who said, 'Some individuals from the Banī Hāshim tribe came to the Messenger of God صلى الله عليه وآله and asked him to employ them in administering the alms for livestock and cattle, saying, "This share that God has designated for those who administer the alms and those whose hearts need winning over should belong to us, for we are more deserving of it."

So the Messenger of God said, "O sons of ʿAbd al-Muṭṭalib, alms are neither for you nor me, but I have been promised intercession." Then he [i.e. Abū ʿAbd Allāh] said, "I bear witness that He has indeed promised it" – for what do you think, O sons of ʿAbd al-Muṭṭalib, that when I take the chain of the gate of the Garden – do you think I would favour others over you?"' [9:60]

77. From Abū Isḥāq, from one of our associates, from al-Ṣādiq عليه السلام. He said, 'He asked about the slave who is unable to complete payment of his emancipation [contract] after having paid some of it.' He said, 'It can be paid from the alms, for God says in His Book: ﴿ *to free slaves.* ﴾' [9:60]

78. From Zurāra who said, 'I asked Abū ʿAbd Allāh عليه السلام, "What about a slave who fornicates?"

He replied, "He is to be lashed half of the prescribed punishment."'

He said, 'I then asked, "What if he repeats it?"

He replied, "He is to be beaten in the same way."'

He said, 'I then asked, "What if he does it again?"

He replied, "It is not increased from half of the prescribed [number of lashes]."'

He said, 'So I asked, "Does it ever become incumbent to stone him [to death] for anything that he may do?"

So he replied, "Yes, he is killed after the eighth time. So if he does it eight times."'

I asked, "Then what is the difference between him and the free man when the deed is one and the same?"

---

19 Abū al-Qāsim al-ʿĪṣ b. al-Qāsim b. Thābit, a reliable and praiseworthy companion of the sixth and seventh Imams. See Ḥillī, *Khulāṣat al-aqwāl*, 227 (nr. 761); Modarressi, *Tradition and Survival*, 293 (nr. 108).

٧٦ . عن العِيص بن القاسم، عن أبي عبدالله عليه السلام، قال: إنّ أُناسًا من بني هاشم أتوا رسول الله صلى الله عليه وآله، فسألوه أن يستعملهم على صَدَقة المواشي والنَّعَم، فقالوا: يكون لنا هذا السَّهم الذي جعله الله للعاملين عليها والمؤلَّفة قلوبهم، فنحن أولى به.

فقال رسول الله صلى الله عليه وآله: يا بني عبد المُطّلب، إنّ الصدقة لا تَحِلّ لي ولا لكم، ولكن وُعِدت الشّفاعة — ثمّ قال: أنا أشهد أنّه قد وُعِدها — فما ظنّكم — يا بني عبد المُطّلب — إذا أخذتُ بحَلَقة باب الجنّة، أتروني مُؤثِرًا عليكم غيركم؟

٧٧ . عن أبي إسحاق، عن بعض أصحابنا، عن الصادق عليه السلام. قال: سأل عن مُكاتب عجز عن مُكاتَبته، وقد أدّى بعضها؟ قال: يُؤدّي من مال الصدقة، إنّ الله يقول في كتابه: ﴿وَفِي الرِّقَابِ﴾.

٧٨ . عن زُرارة، قال: قلتُ لأبي عبدالله عليه السلام: عبدٌ زنى؟ قال: يُجلَد نصف الحدّ. قال: قلت: فإنّه عاد؟ فقال: يُضرَب مثل ذلك. قال: قلت: فإنّه عاد؟ قال: لا يُزاد على نِصف الحدّ.

قال: قلتُ: فهل يجب عليه الرَّجم في شيءٍ من فعلِه؟ فقال: نعم، يُقتَل في الثامنة، أن فعل ذلك ثمان مرّات.

فقلتُ: فما الفرق بينه وبين الحرّ، وإنّما فِعلُهما واحد؟ فقال: إنّ الله تعالى رحِمه أن يَجمَع عليه رِبق الرِّقّ وحَدّ الحُرّ، قال: ثمّ قال: وعلى إمام المسلمين أن يدفَع ثمنه إلى مولاه مِن سَهم الرِّقاب.

He replied, “God, most High, has mercy on him from having to bear both the shackles of slavery as well as the prescribed punishment of the free man.”

Then he said, “The leader of the Muslims must pay the price for his freedom to his master from the share of the alms kept for freeing slaves.” [9:60]

79. From al-Ṣabbāḥ b. Sayāba[20]. He said, ‘Any Muslim who dies leaving behind a debt that did not ensue from corruption or extravagance, it is incumbent for the leader [of is community] to settle it; and if he does not settle it, then he bears the sin for that. God says: ﴿*Alms are meant only for the poor, the needy, those who administer them, those whose hearts need winning over, to free slaves and help those in debt*﴾; so this is someone who is in debt, and he has a share due upon the imam. If he withholds it, then he bears its sin.’ [9:60]

80. From ‘Abd al-Raḥmān b. al-Ḥajjāj that Muḥammad b. Khālid asked Abū ‘Abd Allāh عليه السلام about alms. He said, ‘It is to be shared out among those whom God has designated. The share of those who are in debt is not to be given to those who make claims like those of pre-Islamic pagan times.’

I asked, ‘What is the claim of pre-Islamic times?’ He replied, ‘When a man would call out: “O tribe of so and so,” then cause bloodshed and murder among them. So that [blood money owed] is not counted as the share of those in debt [i.e. when blood money is exacted wrongfully through corrupt means] nor those who still owe their wives’ bridal gifts (*mahr*).’

He said, ‘I would not have known that, except that he said, “Nor those who are careless as to how they appropriate other people’s money.”’ [9:60]

81. From Muḥammad al-Qaṣrī[21], from Abū ‘Abd Allāh عليه السلام. He said, ‘I asked him about the alms, so he said, “It is to be shared out among those whom God has designated. The share of those who are in debt is not to be given to those who still owe their wives’ bridal gifts nor to those who make claims like those of pre-Islamic pagan times.”’

20 Al-Ṣabbāḥ b. Sayāba, brother of ‘Abd al-Raḥmān b. Sayāba, was a companion of Imam Ja‘far al-Ṣādiq who according to some is an unknown (*majhūl*) personality, whose reliability therefore cannot be verified. See Khū’ī, *Mu‘jam*, 10:98–100 (nr. 5886).

21 We did not find any individual by this name in either Ḥillī’s *Khulāṣāt al-aqwāl* or Khū’ī’s *Mu‘jam*.

٧٩. عن الصبّاح بن سَيابة، قال: أيُّما مسلم مات وترك دَينًا، لم يكن في فساد وعلى إسرافٍ، فعلى الإمام أن يقضيه، فإن لم يَقضِه فعليه إثم ذلك، إنّ الله تعالى يقول: ﴿إِنَّمَا الصَّدَقَاتُ لِلْفُقَرَاءِ وَالْمَسَاكِينِ وَالْعَامِلِينَ عَلَيْهَا وَالْمُؤَلَّفَةِ قُلُوبُهُمْ وَفِي الرِّقَابِ وَالْغَارِمِينَ﴾ فهو من الغارمين، وله سَهم عند الإمام، فإن حبسه فإثمه عليه.

٨٠. عن عبد الرّحمن بن الحجّاج أنَّ محمّد بن خالد سأل أبا عبدالله ﷺ عن الصّدقات، قال: اقسِمها فيمن قال الله، ولا يُعطى من سَهم الغارمين الذين ينادون نِداء الجاهلية.

قلتُ: وما نِداء الجاهلية؟ قال: الرجُل يقول: يا آل بني فلان، فيقع فيهم القتلُ والدّماء، فلا يُؤدّي ذلك مِن سَهم الغارمين، والذين يَغرَمون من مُهُور النساء. قال: ولا أعلمه إلاّ قال: ولا الذين لا يُبالون بما صَنَعوا في أموال الناس.

٨١. عن محمّد القَصري، عن أبي عبدالله ﷺ، قال: سألتُه عن الصّدقة؟ فقال: نعم، أقسِمها فيمن قال الله، ولا يُعطى من سهم الغارمين الذين يَغرَمون في مُهُور النِّساء، ولا الّذين يُنادُون بِنداء الجاهليّة.

قال: قلتُ: وما نداء الجاهليّة؟ قال: الرجل يقول: يا آل بني فلان، فيقع بينهم القتل، ولا يُؤَدّى ذلك من سَهم الغارِمين، ولا الّذين لا يُبالون ما صَنعوا بأموال الناس.

٨٢. عن الحسن بن راشد، قال: سألتُ العسكري ﷺ بالمدينة عن رجلٍ أوصى بمالٍ في سبيل الله، فقال: سبيلُ الله شِيعتُنا.

He said, 'I asked, "What is the claim of pre-Islamic times?" He replied, "When a man would call out: 'O tribe of so and so,' then cause bloodshed and murder among them. So that [blood money owed] is not to be settled from the share of those in debt; nor those who are careless as to how they appropriate other people's money."' [9:60]

82. From al-Ḥasan b. Rāshid who said, 'I asked al-ʿAskarī in Medina about a man who bequeathed some wealth in the way of God. So he replied, "The way of God refers to our followers (*shīʿa*)."' [9:60]

83. From al-Ḥasan b. Muḥammad who said, 'I said to Abū ʿAbd Allāh عليه السلام, "A man has made a bequest of wealth to me [to be used] in the path of God."' He said, 'So he said to me, "Spend it on Hajj."' He said, 'I said, "But he bequeathed it for the path [of God]." He said, "Spend it on Hajj, for I do not know of any of His paths to be better than Hajj."' [9:60]

84. From Ḥammād b. ʿUthmān, from Abū ʿAbd Allāh عليه السلام. He said, 'I wanted to entrust someone with some goods to be taken to Yemen for trade, so I came to Abū Jaʿfar عليه السلام and said, "I want to entrust so and so with some goods for trade." So he said to me, "Do you not know that he drinks alcohol?" I replied, "I have heard some of the believers say the same thing." So he said, "Believe them, for indeed God says: ﴾*he believes in God and trusts the believers.*﴿" He said, "It means that he [i.e. the Prophet] believes in God and believes the believers because he was kind and compassionate to the believers."' [9:61]

85. From Jābir al-Juʿfī who said, 'Abū Jaʿfar عليه السلام said, "This verse was revealed: ﴾*yet if you were to question them, they would be sure to say, 'We were just chatting, just amusing ourselves.' Say, 'Were you making jokes about God, His Revelations, and His Messenger? Do not try to justify yourselves; you have gone from belief to disbelief.' We may forgive some of you, but We will punish others.*﴿" He said, 'I asked Abū ʿAbd Allāh عليه السلام, "[What is] the exegesis of this verse?" He said, "Its exegesis – by God – no verse has ever been revealed except with an exegesis." Then he said, "It was revealed about the two enemies of God and ten others with them, making twelve in total. They plotted against the Messenger of God ﷺ at ʿAqaba and convened in secret amongst themselves to kill him. One of them said to the other, 'If he comes to realize,

٨٣. عن الحسن بن محمّد، قال: قلت لأبي عبد الله عليه السلام: إنّ رجلاً أوصى إليّ في السبيل، قال: فقال لي: اصرِف في الحجّ.

قال: قلتُ: إنّه أوصى في السبيل؟ قال اصرِفه في الحج، فإنّي لا أعلم سبيلاً من سُبُله أفضل من الحجّ.

٨٤. عن حمّاد بن عثمان، عن أبي عبد الله عليه السلام، قال: إنّي أردتُ أن أستبضع فلانًا بِضاعةً إلى اليمن، فأتيت إلى أبي جعفر عليه السلام، فقلتُ: إنّي أُريد أن أستبضع فلانًا؟ فقال لي: أما عَلِمتَ أنّه يشرَب الخَمر؟ فقلتُ: قد بلغني من المؤمنين أنّهم يقولون ذلك، فقال: صدِّقهم فإنّ الله يقول: ﴿يُؤْمِنُ بِاللهِ وَيُؤْمِنُ لِلْمُؤْمِنِينَ﴾، فقال: يعني يُصدِّق الله ويُصدِّق المؤمنين، لأنّه كان رؤوفًا رحيمًا بالمؤمنين.

٨٥. عن جابر الجُعفي، قال: قال أبو جعفر عليه السلام: نزلت هذه الآية: ﴿وَلَئِن سَأَلْتَهُمْ لَيَقُولُنَّ إِنَّمَا كُنَّا نَخُوضُ وَنَلْعَبُ﴾ إلى قوله ﴿نُعَذِّبْ طَائِفَةً﴾ قال: قلتُ لأبي جعفر عليه السلام: ما تفسير هذه الآية؟

قال: والله ما نزلت آية قطّ إلاّ ولها تفسير، ثمّ قال: نعم، نزلت في عَدُوَّي الله والعَشَرة معهما، إنّهم اجتمعوا اثنا عشر، فكَمَنوا لرسول الله صلى الله عليه وآله في العَقَبة، وائتَمَروا بينهم ليَقتُلوه، فقال بعضهم لبعض: إن فَطِن نقول إنّما كُنّا نَخُوض ونَلعَب، وإن لم يَفطَن لنَقتُلنَّه، فأنزل الله هذه الآية ﴿وَلَئِن سَأَلْتَهُمْ لَيَقُولُنَّ إِنَّمَا كُنَّا نَخُوضُ وَنَلْعَبُ﴾ فقال الله لنبيّه: ﴿قُلْ أَبِاللهِ وَآيَاتِهِ وَرَسُولِهِ﴾ يعني محمّدًا صلى الله عليه وآله ﴿كُنتُمْ تَسْتَهْزِئُونَ ۞ لَا تَعْتَذِرُوا

we will simply say that we were just chatting and amusing ourselves, and if he is none the wiser, we will certainly kill him.' So God revealed this verse: ﴾*yet if you were to question them, they would be sure to say, 'We were just chatting, just amusing ourselves.'*﴿ So God said to His Prophet: ﴾*Say, 'Were you making jokes about God, His Revelations, and His Messenger?* - meaning Muḥammad ﷺ – ﴾*do not try to justify yourselves; you have gone from belief to disbelief.' We may forgive some of you*﴿ referring to 'Alī if he were to forgive them two instead of cursing them both from the pulpits, and cursing others instead. That is the purport of His verse, most High: ﴾*We may forgive some of you but We will punish others.*﴿"' [9:65–66]

86. From Jābir, from Abū Ja'far ؑ [about]: ﴾*They have ignored God* [...]﴿ He said, 'They have disregarded God's obedience, ﴾*so He has ignored them,*﴿' He said, 'So he has disregarded them.' [9:67]

87. From Abū Ma'mar al-Sa'dī who said, "Alī ؑ said, "Regarding God's statement: ﴾*They have ignored God, so He has ignored them.*﴿ He means that they have ignored God in this worldly life and have not acted in obedience to Him, nor believed in Him and His Messenger, so He will ignore them in the Hereafter, i.e. He has not set aside a share of His reward for them, so they will be disregarded from all goodness."' [9:67]

88. From Ṣafwān al-Jammāl who said, 'I said to Abū 'Abd Allāh ؑ, "May my father and mother be your ransom – what if a Muslim woman comes to me who knows me for my good work and I know her for her devotion to Islam, her love for you and adherence to your authority, but she does not have a male custodian (*maḥram*)."

He said, "If such a Muslim woman comes to you, then take her along for the believing man is the *maḥram* of the believing woman," and he recited this verse: ﴾*The believers, both men and women, support each other.*﴿' [9:71]

89. From Thuwayr[22], from 'Alī b. al-Ḥusayn ؑ who said, 'When the people of the Garden enter into it, and the friend of God enters into his gardens and

22 Thuwayr b. Abī Fākhita [=Sa'īd b. 'Alāqa], whose reliability is uncertain. Ḥillī suspends judgment on him. See Ḥillī, *Khulāṣat al-aqwāl*, 87 (nr. 182).

قَدْ كَفَرْتُم بَعْدَ إِيمَانِكُمْ إِن نَّعْفُ عَن طَائِفَةٍ مِّنكُمْ﴾ يعني عليًّا ﵇ إن يعفُ عنهما في أن يلعنهما على المنابر، ويلعن غيرهما، فذلك قوله تعالى: ﴿إِن نَّعْفُ عَن طَائِفَةٍ مِّنكُمْ نُعَذِّبْ طَائِفَةً﴾.

٨٦. عن جابر، عن أبي جعفر ﵇ ﴿نَسُوا اللَّهَ﴾، قال: قال: تَركوا طاعة الله ﴿فَنَسِيَهُمْ﴾ قال فتَرَكهم.

٨٧. عن أبي مَعمَر السَّعدي، قال: قال عليّ ﵇: في قول الله: ﴿نَسُوا اللَّهَ فَنَسِيَهُمْ﴾ فإنّما يعني أنّهم نَسُوا اللهَ في دار الدنيا، فلم يعمَلُوا له بالطاعة، ولم يُؤمنوا به وبرسوله، فنسيَهم في الآخرة، أي لم يجعَل لهم في ثوابه نصيبًا، فصاروا مَنسيّين من الخير.

٨٨. عن صفوان الجمّال، قال: قلتُ لأبي عبدالله ﵇: بأبي أنتَ وأمي، تأتيني المرأة المسلمة قد عَرَفتني بعملي، وعرَفتها بإسلامها وحُبّها إيّاكم وولايتها لكم، وليس لها محْرَم.

قال: فإذا جاءتك المرأة المسلمة فاحمِلها، فإنّ المؤمن محْرَم المؤمنة، وتلا هذه الآية ﴿وَالْمُؤْمِنُونَ وَالْمُؤْمِنَاتُ بَعْضُهُمْ أَوْلِيَاءُ بَعْضٍ﴾.

٨٩. عن ثُوير، عن عليّ بن الحسين ﵇، قال: إذا صار أهل الجنّة في الجنُّة، ودخل وليّ الله إلى جنّاته ومساكنه، واتّكأ كُلّ مؤمنٍ منهم على أريكته، حَفَّته خُدّامه، وتَهَدّلت عليه الثِّمار، وتفجّرت حوله العُيون، وجرَت من تحته الأنهار، وبُسِطت له الزّرابيّ، وصُفِّفت له النّمارق، وأتته الخُدّام بما شاءت شَهوتُه من قبل أن يسألهم ذلك. قال: ويخرُج عليهم

his houses, and when every believer from among them reclines on his comfortable couch, with his servants at his disposal, fruits hanging down within reach, springs gushing forth around him, rivers flowing underfoot, carpets spread out beneath him, cushions scattered for his comfort, and servants bringing him all that his heart desires before he can even beckon them...' He continued, 'Wide-eyed maidens will come out to them from the gardens, and they will stay there for as long as God wills. Then the Almighty will look down upon them and say to them, "My friends, obedient ones, dwellers of My Garden in My vicinity, shall I tell you about something even better than the state that you are in right now?"

So they will say, "Our Lord! What can be better than what we are enjoying right now, of whatever our souls desire, whatever bounties our eyes can enjoy looking at in the vicinity of the Kind One?"

He said, 'Then He will repeat the question, and they will say, "Yes, our Lord. Grant us better than what we are enjoying right now."

So He, Blessed and most High, will say to them, "My pleasure with you and My love for you is better than and supersedes the state you are in right now."'

He said, 'So they will say, "Yes, our Lord, Your pleasure with us and Your love for us is better and more pleasurable for our souls."

Then ʿAlī b. al-Ḥusayn عليه السلام recited this verse: ﴾*God has promised the believers, both men and women, Gardens graced with flowing streams where they will remain; good, peaceful homes in Gardens of lasting bliss; and - greatest of all - God's good pleasure. That is the supreme triumph.*﴿' [9:72]

90. From Jābir b. Arqam[23] who said, 'Whilst we were seated in one of our sessions with my brother Zayd b. Arqam narrating to us, a man approached on horseback who looked as though he were a traveler. He greeted us with peace, then stood and said, "Is there a Zayd b. Arqam among you?"

So Zayd said, "I am Zayd b. Arqam. What do you want?"

The man said, "Do you know where I have come from?"

He said, "No."

23 We were unable to find any individual by this name in either Ḥillī's *Khulāṣat al-aqwāl* or Khūʾī's *Muʿjam*.

الحُور العِين من الجِنان، فيمكُثون بذلك ما شاء الله، ثمّ إنّ الجبار يُشرِف عليهم فيقول لهم: أوليائي وأهل طاعتي، وسُكّان جنّتي في جِواري، ألا هل أُنبّئكم بخيرٍ ممّا أنتم فيه؟

فيقولون: ربّنا وأيّ شيءٍ خيرٌ ممّا نحن فيه، نحن فيما اشتهت أنفُسنا، ولَذّت أعيُننا من النِّعم في جِوار الكريم. قال: فيَعُود عليهم بالقول، فيقولون: ربَّنا نعم، فأتنا بخيرٍ ممّا نحن فيه.

فيقول لهم تبارك وتعالى: رضاي عنكم ومحبّتي لكم خيرٌ وأعظم ممّا أنتم فيه. قال: فيقولون: نعم يا ربّنا، رضاك عنّا ومحبّتك لنا خيرٌ لنا وأطيب لأنفسنا.

ثمّ قرأ عليّ بن الحسين عليه السلام هذه الآية ﴿وَعَدَ اللَّهُ الْمُؤْمِنِينَ وَالْمُؤْمِنَاتِ جَنَّاتٍ تَجْرِي مِنْ تَحْتِهَا الْأَنْهَارُ خَالِدِينَ فِيهَا وَمَسَاكِنَ طَيِّبَةً فِي جَنَّاتِ عَدْنٍ وَرِضْوَانٌ مِنَ اللَّهِ أَكْبَرُ ذَٰلِكَ هُوَ الْفَوْزُ الْعَظِيمُ﴾.

٩٠. عن جابر بن أرقم، قال: بينا نحنُ في مجلسٍ لنا وأخي زيد بن أرقم يُحدّثنا، إذ أقبل رجلٌ على فرسه، عليه هيئة السفر، فسلّم علينا ثمّ وقف، فقال: أفيكم زيد بن أرقم؟ فقال زيد: أنا زيد بن أرقم، فما تُريد؟ فقال الرجل: أتدري من أين جئتُ؟ قال: لا، قال: من فُسطاط مصر، لأسألك عن حديثٍ بلغني عنك تذكُره عن رسول الله صلى الله عليه وآله. فقال له زيد: وما هو؟ قال: حديث غدير خُمّ في ولاية عليّ بن أبي طالب عليه السلام.

فقال: يا بن أخي، إنّ قبل غدير خُمّ ما أُحدّثك به، إنّ جَبرئيل الرّوح الأمين عليه السلام نزل على رسول الله صلى الله عليه وآله بولاية عليّ بن أبي طالب عليه السلام، فدعا قومًا أنا فيهم، فاستشارهم في ذلك، ليقوم به في الموسم، فلم نَدرِ ما نقول له، وبكى صلى الله عليه وآله فقال له جَبرئيل: مالك يا محمّد، أجَزِعتَ من أمر الله؟ فقال: كلاّ يا جَبرئيل، ولكن قد عَلِم ربّي ما لَقِيت من قُريش، إذ لم

He said, "From Fusṭāṭ in Egypt, to ask you about a narration (*ḥadīth*) that I have heard on your authority that you quote from the Messenger of God ﷺ."

So Zayd said to him, "Which one is it?"

He replied, "The narration of Ghadīr Khumm about the sacred authority of ʿAlī b. Abī Ṭālib عليه السلام."

So he said, "Son of my brother, let me narrate to you from before Ghadīr Khumm – that Jibra'īl, the trustworthy spirit, may God's blessings be upon him, descended upon God's Messenger ﷺ with the sacred authority of ʿAlī b. Abī Ṭālib عليه السلام. He called a group of people, and I was among them, to consult with them about it in order to implement it at the right time, but we did not know what to say to him. He ﷺ wept, and Jibra'īl asked him, 'What is wrong, Muḥammad? Are you upset with God's command?'

He replied, 'Absolutely not, Jibra'īl, but my Lord knows what I faced from the Quraysh when they did not attest to my prophethood until He commanded me to fight them and had to send down an army from the heavens to help me. So how will they ever attest to ʿAlī after me?'

So Jibra'īl left him and this verse descended unto him: ﴾*So* [*Prophet*] *are you going to abandon some part of what is revealed to you, and let your heart be oppressed by it?*﴿ (11:12) Then, when we stopped at al-Juḥfa on the way back [from Hajj], and pitched our canopies, Jibra'īl brought down this verse: ﴾*Messenger, proclaim everything that has been sent down to you from your Lord – if you do not, then you will not have communicated His message – and God will protect you from people.*﴿ (5:67)

So while we were there, we heard the Messenger of God ﷺ calling out: "O people! Answer the one who calls to God. I am God's Messenger." We came to him hurriedly in the intense heat and there he was, pulling part of his garment over his head and part of it under his feet to protect himself from the heat. He requested for the area under some large trees to be swept; so any thorns and stones were swept away from under them.

Then a man said, "He has only called for this place to be cleared just as he is getting ready to leave this world so that he can bring a calamity down on you today."

When they had finished clearing, the Messenger of God ﷺ requested for the saddles of our horses, and the pillions and saddlebags of our camels to be brought, and we piled them on top of each other. Then we threw

يُقِرّوا بالرّسالة حتّى أمرني بجِهادهم، وأهبط إليّ جنودًا من السّماء فنصروني، فكيف يُقِرّوا لعليّ من بعدي. فانصرف عنه جَبرئيل، ثمّ نزل عليه: ﴿فَلَعَلَّكَ تَارِكُۢ بَعۡضَ مَا يُوحَىٰٓ إِلَيۡكَ وَضَآئِقُۢ بِهِۦ صَدۡرُكَ﴾.

فلمّا نزلنا الجُحفة راجعين وضَرَبنا أخبيتنا، نَزَل جَبرئيل عليه السلام بهذه الآية: ﴿يَٰٓأَيُّهَا ٱلرَّسُولُ بَلِّغۡ مَآ أُنزِلَ إِلَيۡكَ مِن رَّبِّكَۖ وَإِن لَّمۡ تَفۡعَلۡ فَمَا بَلَّغۡتَ رِسَالَتَهُۥۚ وَٱللَّهُ يَعۡصِمُكَ مِنَ ٱلنَّاسِ﴾ فبينا نحن كذلك إذ سمِعنا رسول الله صلى الله عليه وآله وهو يُنادي: «أيّها الناس، أجيبوا داعي الله، أنا رسول الله». فأتيناه مُسرعين في شدّة الحرّ، فإذا هو واضعٌ بعض ثوبه على رأسه وبعضه على قدميه من الحَرّ، وأمر بقَمّ ما تحت الدّوح، فقُمّ ما كان ثمّة من الشوك والحجارة، فقال رجل: ما دعاه إلى قمّ هذا المكان، وهو يُريد أن يَرحَل من ساعته، ليأتينّكم اليوم بداهية!

فلمّا فرغوا من القَمّ، أمر رسول الله صلى الله عليه وآله أن يُوتى بأحلاس دوابّنا وأثاث إبلنا وحقائبها، فوضعنا بعضها على بعض، ثمّ ألقينا عليها ثوبًا، ثمّ صَعِد عليها رسول الله صلى الله عليه وآله فحَمِد الله أثنى عليه، ثمّ قال: «أيّها الناس، إنّه نزل عليّ عشيّة عَرَفة أمرٌ ضِقت به ذرعًا مخافةَ تكذيبِ أهل الإفك، حتّى جاءني في هذا الموضع وَعيدٌ من ربّي إن لم أفعل، ألا وإنّي غير هائبٍ لقومٍ، ولا مُحابٍ لقرابتي.

أيّها الناس، مَن أولى بكم من أنفسكم؟»

قالوا: الله ورسوله.

a cloth over them, and the Messenger of God ﷺ climbed on top of it. He praised God and glorified Him, then said, "O people, on the eve of 'Arafa a command was revealed to me that I found very difficult to bear for fear of being disbelieved by the liars, until a warning came to me from my Lord in this very place if I do not act upon it. Indeed, [know that] I am neither scared of people nor biased in favour of my own relatives.

O people, who has more authority over you than your own selves?"

They replied, "God and His Messenger."

He said, "O God, bear witness, and you too Jibra'īl bear witness." He said these three times, then he took 'Alī b. Abī Ṭālib عليه السلام by the hand and hoisted him up to himself. Then he said, "O God, for whomsoever I am master 'Alī is his master. O God, support whoever supports him, oppose whoever opposes him, help whoever helps him and disgrace whoever disgraces him."

He said this three times, then asked, "Did you all hear?"

So they replied, "O God, of course."

He asked, "So do you attest to it?"

They replied, "O God, yes."

Then he said, "O God, bear witness and you too, Jibra'īl, bear witness." Then he descended, and we went back to our horses.

Next to my canopy was the canopy of a few individuals from the Quraysh – three of them. Ḥudhayfa b. al-Yamān was with me, and we heard one of the three say, "By God, Muḥammad is a fool if he thinks that the authority will last with 'Alī after him."

Others said, "You make him out to be a fool, but do you not know that he is actually mad, and almost had a fit near Ibn Abī Kabsha's wife?"

The third said, "He can be whatever he wants; fool or madman but by God, what he says is never going to happen."

So Ḥudhayfa became enraged at their words, lifted the side of the tent and stuck his head inside it saying to them, "How can you say that when the Messenger of God, peace be upon him and his family, is right here among you, and God's revelation is descending upon you? By God, I am going to inform him about your words tomorrow."

They said to him, "O Abū 'Abd Allāh, you were nearby and happened to hear what we said – keep this secret for every neighbour has a trust to keep."

قال: «اللّهمّ اشهد، وأنت يا جَبرئيل فاشهَد» حتّى قالها ثلاثًا، ثمّ أخذ بيد عليّ بن أبي طالب ﷺ فرفعه إليه، ثمّ قال: «اللّهمّ مَن كنتُ مولاه فعليٌّ مولاه، اللّهمّ والِ مَن والاهُ، وعادِ من عاداهُ، وانصُر من نَصَره، واخذُل مَن خَذله» . قالها ثلاثًا، ثمّ قال: «هل سمِعتُم؟» فقالوا: اللّهمّ بلى. قال: «فأقرَرتُم؟» قالوا: اللّهمّ نَعَم. ثمّ قال: «اللّهمّ اشهَد وأنت يا جَبرئيل فاشهد» .

ثمّ نزل فانصرفنا إلى رِحالنا، وكان إلى جانب خِبائي خِباء نفر من قُرَيش وهم ثلاثة، ومعي حُذيفة بن اليمان، فسمِعنا أحد الثلاثة وهو يقول: والله إنّ محمّدًا لأَحمق، إن كان يرى أنّ الأمر يستقيم لعليّ من بعده! وقال آخرون: أتجعله أحمق، ألم تعلم أنّه مجنون، قد كاد أن يُصرَع عند امرأة ابن أبي كَبشة؟ وقال الثالث: دعوه إن شاء أن يكون أحمق، وإن شاء أن يكون مجنونًا، والله ما يكون ما يقول أبدًا! فغَضِب حُذيفة من مقالتهم، فرفع جانب الخِباء، فأدخل رأسه إليهم، وقال: فعَلتُموها ورسول الله عليه وآله السلام بين أظهركم، ووحي الله ينزِل عليكم، والله لأُخبرنّه بُكرةً بِمقالتكم.

فقالوا له: يا أبا عبد الله، وإنّك لها هنا وقد سَمِعت ما قُلنا! اكتُم علينا، فإنّ لكُلّ جِوار أمانة. فقال لهم: ما هذا من جِوار الأمانة، ولا من مجالسها، ما نَصَحتُ اللهَ ورسوله إن أنا طويتُ عنه هذا الحديث.

فقالوا له: يا أبا عبد الله، فاصنع ما شِئتَ، فوالله لنحلِفنّ إنّا لم نَقل، وإنّك قد كذبتَ علينا، أفَتَراه يُصدِّقك ويُكذِّبنا ونحنُ ثَلاثة؟

So he replied to them, "This is neither a neighbourly trust and nor do I want to be complicit in it, and unless I convey this talk to him I will not have been true to God and His Messenger."

So they said to him, "Do what you want then, Abū ʿAbd Allāh, for by God, we will swear oaths that we never said any such thing and that you are falsely accusing us. Do you think he will believe you and disbelieve us when there are three of us?"

So he said to them, "I do not care as long as I have fulfilled my sincere obligation to God and His Messenger, so you can say whatever you want to say."

Then he went off until he came to the Messenger of God ﷺ whilst ʿAlī عليه السلام was next to him, sitting with the sheath of his sword across his crossed legs. So he informed him of the people's words and the Messenger of God ﷺ sent for them.

They came to him and he asked them, "What did you say?"

They replied, "By God, we have not said anything. If you have heard anything about us then we are being falsely accused."

So Jibraʾīl brought down this verse: ﴾ *They swear by God that they did not, but they certainly did speak words of defiance and became defiant after having submitted; they tried to do something, though they did not achieve it* [...] ﴿

Upon hearing this ʿAlī عليه السلام said, "Let them say whatever they want, for by God, my heart is still between my ribs and my sword hanging from my neck. And if they attempt anything then certainly so will I."

So Jibraʾīl said to the Prophet ﷺ, "Be patient with what is yet to come."

So the Prophet ﷺ informed ʿAlī عليه السلام of what Jibraʾīl had just told him.

He replied, "Then I will be patient over what has been decreed."'"

Abū ʿAbd Allāh عليه السلام said, 'An old man from among the chiefs said, "If we were to behave with our people the way that he speaks, we would be worse than donkeys."' He said, 'Another young man next to him then said, "If you were right, then we would be worse off than donkeys."' [9:74]

91. From Jaʿfar b. Muḥammad al-Khuzāʿī, on his father's authority who said, 'I heard Abū ʿAbd Allāh عليه السلام say, "When the Messenger of God ﷺ said what he said at Ghadīr Khumm, and people had gone into their tents, Miqdād was passing by a group of them who were saying, 'By God, if we were with the Caesar we would be clad in silk and embroidery and brocade and fine woven cloths, but we have been with him in the coarsest of times, eating coarse

فقال لهم: أمّا أنا فلا أبالي إذا أدّيتُ النصيحة إلى الله وإلى رسوله، فقولوا ما شِئتُم أن تقولوا.

ثمّ مضى حتّى أتى رسول الله ﷺ، وعليّ عليه السلام إلى جانبه مُحتبٍ بحمائل سيفه، فأخبره بمقالة القوم، فبعث إليهم رسول الله ﷺ فأتوه، فقال لهم: ماذا قُلتم؟ فقالوا: والله ما قلنا شيئًا، فإن كنتَ أُبلغت عنّا شيئًا فمكذوبٌ علينا. فهَبَط جَبرئيل بهذه الآية: ﴿يَحۡلِفُونَ بِٱللَّهِ مَا قَالُواْ وَلَقَدۡ قَالُواْ كَلِمَةَ ٱلۡكُفۡرِ وَكَفَرُواْ بَعۡدَ إِسۡلَٰمِهِمۡ وَهَمُّواْ بِمَا لَمۡ يَنَالُواْ﴾، وقال عليّ عليه السلام عند ذلك: لقولوا ما شاءوا، والله إنّ قلبي بين أضلاعي، وإنّ سيفي لفي عُنقي، ولئن همّوا لأَهُمّنّ.

فقال جَبرائيل للنّبيّ ﷺ: اصبِر للأمر الّذي هو كائن، فأخبر النّبيّ ﷺ عليًّا عليه السلام بما أخبره به جَبرئيل. فقال: إذًا أصبِر للمقادير.

قال أبو عبد الله عليه السلام: وقال رجلٌ من الملأ شيخ: لئن كنّا بين أقوامنا كما يقول هذا، لنحن شرٌّ من الحَمير. قال: وقال آخر شابّ إلى جنبه: لئن كنتَ صادقًا لنحن شرٌّ من الحَمير.

٩١. عن جعفر بن محمّد الخُزاعي، عن أبيه، قال: سمِعتُ أبا عبد الله عليه السلام يقول: لمّا قال النّبيّ ﷺ ما قال في غدير خُمّ، وصاروا بالأخبية، مرّ المقداد بجماعةٍ منهم، وهم يقولون: والله إن كنّا وقيصر لكنّا في الخَزّ والوشي والدِّيباج والنساجات، وإنّا معه في الأخشنين؛ نأكل الخَشِن، ونلبس الخَشِن، حتّى إذا دنا موته، وفنيت أيّامه، وحضر اجله، أراد أن يُولّيها عليًّا من بعده، أما والله ليَعلمنّ. قال: فمضى المِقداد وأخبر النّبيّ ﷺ به، فقال: الصّلاة جامعة،

food, and wearing coarse clothing until now when his death is approaching, his days are coming to an end and his time is up, and he wants to appoint 'Alī after him! By God, wait till he comes to know!'"

He said, "So Miqdād went and told the Prophet ﷺ about that, so he said, 'The prayer will be prayed in congregation.'"

He said, 'So they said, "Miqdād is falsely accusing us, so let us stand up and swear oaths against him."'

So they came and sat directly in front of him saying, 'May our fathers and mothers be your ransom, O Messenger of God ﷺ – No, by the One who sent you with the truth and by the One who honoured you with prophethood, we did not say what you have heard; no, by the One who chose you over all people.'"

He said, "So the Prophet ﷺ said, '﴾*In the Name of God, the all-Beneficent, all-Merciful. They swear by God that they did not, but they certainly did speak words of defiance and became defiant after having submitted; they tried to do something, though they did not achieve it,*﴿ – *with you on the eve of 'Aqaba, Muḥammad.* ﴾*being spiteful was their only response to God and His Messenger enriching them out of His bounty.*﴿ One of them used to sell heads [of cattle], another their trotters, and another used to twist hair-twines so God enriched them through his Prophet, then they set their sharp tongues and iron [i.e. swords] upon him.'"' [9:74]

92. Abān b. Taghlib said on his عليه السلام authority, 'When the Messenger of God appointed 'Alī on the day of Ghadīr Khumm, he said, "For whomsoever I am master, 'Alī is his master." Thereupon two men from among the Quraysh put their heads together to plot saying, "By God, we will never submit to what he has said."

So the Prophet, peace be upon him and his family, was informed about that, so he asked them what they had been saying. But they lied and swore by God that they had not said anything. So Jibra'īl descended to the Messenger of God, peace be upon him and his family, with the verse: ﴾*They swear by God that they did not* [...]﴿" Abū 'Abd Allāh عليه السلام said, "They both turned away but did not repent."' [9:74]

93. From al-'Abbās b. Hilāl, from Abū al-Ḥasan al-Riḍā عليه السلام who said, 'God, most High, said to Muḥammad ﷺ: ﴾*God will not forgive them even if you*

قال: فقالوا: قد رمانا المِقداد، فقوموا نحلف عليه، قال:فجاءوا حتّى جَثَوا بين يديه، فقالوا: بآبائنا وأمّهاتنا يا رسول الله، لا والّذي بعثك بالحقِ نبيًّا، والذي أكرمك بالنّبوة، ما قُلنا ما بَلَغك، لا والّذي اصطفاك على البشر.

قال: فقال النّبيّ ﷺ: بِسمِ الله الرّحمن الرّجيم ﴿يَحْلِفُونَ بِاللهِ مَا قَالُوا وَلَقَدْ قَالُوا كَلِمَةَ الْكُفْرِ وَكَفَرُوا بَعْدَ إِسْلَامِهِمْ وَهَمُّوا بِمَا لَمْ يَنَالُوا﴾ بك يا محمّد ليلة العقبة ﴿وَمَا نَقَمُوا إِلاَّ أَنْ أَغْنَاهُمُ اللهُ وَرَسُولُهُ مِن فَضْلِهِ﴾ كان أحدهم يبيع الرؤوس، وآخر يبيع الكِراع ويفتِل القرامِل. فأغناهم الله برسوله ﷺ، ثمّ جعلوا حدّهم وحديدهم عليه.

٩٢. قال أبان بن تغلِب، عنه ؏: لمّا نصَب رسول الله ﷺ عليًّا ؏ يوم غدير خُمّ، فقال: «من كنتُ مولاه فعليٌّ مولاه» ضمّ رجلان من قُريش رؤوسهما، وقالا: والله لا نُسلّم له ما قال أبدًا، فأخبر النّبيّ ﷺ فسألهما عمّا قالا، فكذّبا وحلّفا بالله ما قالا شيئًا، فنزل جَبرئيل ؏ على رسول الله ﷺ ﴿يَحْلِفُونَ بِاللهِ مَا قَالُوا﴾ الآية، قال أبو عبدالله ؏: لقد تولّيا وما تابا.

٩٣. عن العباس بن هِلال، عن أبي الحسن الرضا ؏، قال: إنّ الله تعالى قال لمحمّد ﷺ: ﴿إِنْ تَسْتَغْفِرْ لَهُمْ سَبْعِينَ مَرَّةً فَلَنْ يَغْفِرَ اللهُ لَهُمْ﴾ فاستغفر لهم مائة مرّة ليغفر لهم، فأنزل الله: ﴿سَوَاءٌ عَلَيْهِمْ أَسْتَغْفَرْتَ لَهُمْ أَمْ لَمْ تَسْتَغْفِرْ لَهُمْ

ask seventy times.﴿. So he sought forgiveness for them one hundred times that He may forgive them, so God revealed: ﴾*It makes no difference* [*Prophet*] *whether you ask forgiveness for them or not: God will not forgive them*﴿ (63:6) and He said: ﴾*Do not hold prayers for any of them if they die, and do not stand by their graves*﴿, so he neither sought forgiveness for them after that, nor stood by any of their graves.' [9:80, 84]

94. From Abū al-Jārūd, from Abū 'Abd Allāh عليه السلام who said regarding God's words: ﴾*those who criticize the believers who give freely*﴿, 'Alī, the Commander of the Faithful, volunteered to go and fill every bucket with dates that he would pick himself. He gathered the dates and brought them to the Prophet, peace be upon him and his family, and 'Abd al-Raḥmān b. 'Awf was standing at the door. He criticized him, as in he scorned him, so this verse was revealed: ﴾*It is they who criticize the believers who give freely and those who can only give a little with great effort: they scoff at such people, but it is God who scoffs at them - a painful punishment awaits them. It makes no difference* [*Prophet*] *whether you ask forgiveness for them or not: God will not forgive them even if you ask seventy times* [...]﴿' [9:79–80]

95. From Zurāra who said, 'I heard Abū Ja'far عليه السلام say, "The Prophet ﷺ said to 'Abd Allāh b. Ubayy's[24] son, "When you are bereaved of your father then come and inform me." No sooner had he died than he came to him and informed him, so the Messenger of God, peace be upon him and his family, took off his sandals to stand for prayer. So 'Umar said to him, "Has God not said: ﴾*Do not hold prayers for any of them if they die, and do not stand by their graves*﴿?" So he replied him, "Woe unto you, I am only saying: 'O God, fill his grave with fire, his corpse with fire and burn him in the Fire on the Day of Judgement.'"' [9:84]

96. From Ḥanān b. Sadīr, on his father's authority, from Abū Ja'far عليه السلام, 'A man from among the hypocrites died, so the Messenger of God sent a message to his son: "When you are ready to leave [for the burial] inform me." When his request arrived, they sent for the Prophet, peace be upon him and his family, so he ﷺ went up to them and held the son by the hand during the funeral,

24 'Abd Allāh b. 'Ubayy b. Abī Salūl was one of the chief hypocrites of Medina.

﴿لَنْ يَغْفِرَ اللَّهُ لَهُمْ﴾، وقال: ﴿وَلا تُصَلِّ عَلَى أَحَدٍ مِنْهُمْ مَاتَ أَبَدًا وَلا تَقُمْ عَلَى قَبْرِهِ﴾ فلم يستغفر لهم بعد ذلك، ولم يَقُم على قبر أحدٍ منهم.

٩٤. عن أبي الجارود، عن أبي عبد الله عليه السلام، في قول الله: ﴿الَّذِينَ يَلْمِزُونَ الْمُطَّوِّعِينَ مِنَ الْمُؤْمِنِينَ فِي الصَّدَقَاتِ﴾.

قال: ذهب عليّ أمير المؤمنين عليه السلام، فآجر نفسه على أن يستقي كُلّ دلوٍ بتمرةٍ يختارها، فجمع تمرًا فأتى به النبيّ صلى الله عليه وآله، وعبد الرحمن بن عوف على الباب، فلَمَزَه – أي وقع فيه – فأُنزلت هذه الآية: ﴿الَّذِينَ يَلْمِزُونَ الْمُطَّوِّعِينَ مِنَ الْمُؤْمِنِينَ فِي الصَّدَقَاتِ﴾ إلى قوله: ﴿اسْتَغْفِرْ لَهُمْ أَوْ لا تَسْتَغْفِرْ لَهُمْ إِنْ تَسْتَغْفِرْ لَهُمْ سَبْعِينَ مَرَّةً فَلَنْ يَغْفِرَ اللَّهُ لَهُمْ﴾.

٩٥. عن زُرارة، قال: سمِعتُ أبا جعفر عليه السلام يقول: إنّ النبيّ صلى الله عليه وآله قال لابن عبد الله بن أُبيّ: إذا فرغت من أبيك فأعلمني، وكان قد تُوفّي، فأتاه فأعلمه، فأخذ رسول الله عليه وآله السلام نعليه للقيام، فقال له عمر: أليس قد قال الله: ﴿وَلا تُصَلِّ عَلَى أَحَدٍ مِنْهُمْ مَاتَ أَبَدًا وَلا تَقُمْ عَلَى قَبْرِهِ﴾؟ فقال له: ويحك – أو ويلك – إنّما أقول: اللّهمّ املأ قبره نارًا، وأملأ جوفه نارًا، وأصلِه يوم القيامة نارًا.

٩٦. حنان بن سدير، عن أبيه، عن أبي جعفر عليه السلام، تُوفّي رجلٌ من المنافقين، فأرسل رسول الله صلى الله عليه وآله إلى ابنه: إذا أردتم أن تُخرِجوه فأعلموني: فلمّا خضر أمرُه أرسلوا إلى النبيّ عليه وآله السلام، فأقبل نحوهم، حتّى أخذ بيد ابنه في الجنازة فمضى، قال: فتصدّى له عمر، ثمّ

then walked.' He said, 'So 'Umar turned to him and said, "O Messenger of God, has your Lord not prohibited you from praying over any of them who dies and from standing by their grave?" So the Prophet ﷺ did not respond to him.' He continued, 'Just as they were about to put him into the grave, 'Umar again said to the Messenger of God ﷺ, "Has your Lord not prohibited you from praying over any of them who dies and from standing by their grave ﴿*because they disbelieved in God and His Messenger and died as disbelievers*﴾?" So thereupon the Messenger of God ﷺ said to 'Umar, "Can you not see that we have neither prayed funeral prayers over him nor stood by his grave." Then he said, "His son is indeed one of the believers, and it is his right over us that we must fulfill." So 'Umar said to him, "I seek refuge in God from God's displeasure and your displeasure, O Messenger of God."' [9:84]

97. From Muḥammad b. al-Muhājir[25], from his mother Umm Salama who said, 'I went to Abū ʿAbd Allāh عليه السلام and said to him, "May God make you prosper – a woman from the Murji'ites accompanied me [on Hajj]. When we entered al-Rabadha, the people (i.e. the Sunnis) all entered the state of *iḥrām* and she did too along with them, but I delayed my *iḥrām* until al-ʿAqīq. So she said, 'You Shīʿa! You oppose the [majority of] people in everything: the people enter the state of *iḥrām* in al-Rabadha and you enter into it at al-ʿAqīq. Similarly you differ from the people in the funeral prayer: they say "*Allāhu akbar*" four times whereas you do it five times'; and she was calling upon God as a witness that the funeral prayer has four *takbīr*." So Abū ʿAbd Allāh عليه السلام said, "When the Messenger of God ﷺ used to pray over the deceased person, he would say '*Allāhu akbar*,' then recite the *shahāda* [declaration of God's oneness and Muḥammad's prophethood], then say '*Allāhu akbar*' and invoke blessings and supplications on the Prophet ﷺ, then say '*Allāhu akbar*' and seek forgiveness for the believers, then say '*Allāhu akbar*' and supplicate for the deceased person, then finally say '*Allāhu akbar*' and finish. So when God prohibited him from praying over the hypocrites, he would instead recite '*Allāhu akbar*' and the *shahāda*, then say '*Allāhu akbar*' and the invocation of blessings on the Prophet, then '*Allāhu akbar*' and the

25 Muḥammad b. Muhājir [*sic.*] b. ʿAbīd al-Azdī, about whom there is scant information, is regarded by Ḥillī to have been a reliable narrator. See Ḥillī, *Khulāsat al-aqwāl*, 250 (nr. 846).

قال: يا رسول الله، أما نهاك ربّك عن هذا أن تُصلّي على أحدٍ منهم مات أبدًا، أو تقوم على قبره؟! فلم يُجِبه النبيّ صلى الله عليه وآله وسلم.

قال: فلمّا كان قبل أن ينتُهوا به إلى القبر، قال عمر أيضًا لرسول الله صلى الله عليه وآله وسلم: أما نهاك الله عن أن تصلّي على أحدٍ منهم مات أبدًا، أو تقوم على قبره؟! ذلك بأنّهم كفروا بالله وبرسوله وماتوا وهم كافرون.

فقال النبيّ صلى الله عليه وآله وسلم لعمر عند ذلك: ما رأيتنا صلّينا له على جنازةٍ، ولا قُمنا له على قبر، ثمّ قال: إنّ ابنه رجلٌ من المؤمنين، وكان يحقُّ علينا أداء حقّه.

فقال له عمر: أعوذُ بالله من سخَط الله وسخطِك يا رسول الله.

٩٧. عن محمّد بن المُهاجر، عن أمّه أمّ سلمة، قالت: دخلتُ على أبي عبدالله عليه السلام فقلتُ له: أصلحك الله، صَحبتني امرأةٌ من المُرجِئة، فلمّا أتينا الرَّبَذة أحرم الناس، فأحرَمت معهم، وأخّرتُ إحرامي إلى العقيق، فقالت: يا معشر الشيعة، تُخالفون الناس في كُلّ شيء، يُحرِم الناس من الرَّبَذة وتُحرِمون من العقيق، وكذلك تُخالفون الناس في الصلاة على الميّت، يُكبّر الناس أربعًا، وتُكبّرون خمسًا، وهي تشهد بالله أنّ التكبير على الميّت أربع.

فقال أبو عبدالله عليه السلام. كان رسول الله صلى الله عليه وآله وسلم إذا صلّى على الميّت كبّر فتشهّد، ثمّ كبّر فصلّى على النبيّ صلى الله عليه وآله وسلم ودعا، ثمّ كبّر واستغفر للمؤمنين، ثمّ كبّر فدعا للميّت، ثمّ كبّر وانصرف، فلمّا نهاه الله عن الصلاة على المنافقين كبّر وتشهّد، ثمّ كبّر وصلّى على النبيّ، ثمّ كبّر فدعا للمؤمنين، ثمّ كبّر فانصرف، ولم يدعُ للميّت.

supplication for the believers, then '*Allāhu akbar*' at the end without supplicating for the deceased person."' [9:84]

98. From Jābir, from Abū Ja'far ﷺ who said regarding His verse: ﴾*they prefer to be with those who stay behind*﴿, 'With the women.' [9:87]

99. From 'Abd Allāh al-Ḥalabī. He said, 'I asked him about His verse: ﴾*they prefer to be with those who stay behind.*﴿ So he said, "[With] the women. They would say, 'Our houses are exposed,' whilst their houses would be towards the end of the other houses where people would go to detach themselves. So God called their bluff saying: ﴾*They only desired to run away*﴿ (33:13) for they were tall and safe houses in reality."' [9:87]

100. From 'Abd al-Raḥmān b. Ḥarb[26] who said, 'When the people went forth with the Commander of the Faithful ﷺ on the way back from Ṣiffīn, we went forth with him, and he took a different route to the one that we had taken on the way there. When we reached al-Nukhayla and could see the houses of Kufa in the distance, there was an old man sitting under the shade of a house with signs of illness on his face. So the Commander of the Faithful approached him, and we went along with him. He greeted him with peace, and so did we. He replied so courteously that we assumed that he had recognized him. So the Commander of the Faithful said to him, "Why is it that I see your face looking feeble and pale? How did that happen? Is it from sickness?"

He replied, "Yes."

Then he asked, "You probably find it unbearable?"

So he said, "I do not like it to affect me so much."

He said, "Consider it a goodness that has befallen you." He continued, "Rejoice in God's mercy and His forgiveness of your sins. Who are you, O servant of God?"

So he replied, "I am Ṣāliḥ b. Sulaym."

He asked, "From who [i.e. which family]?"

26 We could not find any individual by this name in either of Ḥillī's *Khulāṣat al-aqwāl* or Khū'ī's *Mu'jam*.

٩٨. عن جابر، عن أبي جعفر ﵇، في قوله: ﴿رَضُوا بِأَنْ يَكُونُوا مَعَ الْخَوَالِفِ﴾، قال: مع النساء.

٩٩. عن عبدالله الحلبي، قال: سألتُه عن قوله: ﴿رَضُوا بِأَنْ يَكُونُوا مَعَ الْخَوَالِفِ﴾، فقال: النساء، إنّهم قالوا: إنّ بيوتنا عورة، وكانت بُيوتُهم في أطراف البيوت، حيث يتفرّد النّاس، فأكذبهم الله قال: ﴿وَمَا هِيَ بِعَوْرَةٍ إِنْ يُرِيدُونَ إِلاَّ فِرَارًا﴾ وهي رفيعةُ السُّمك حَصِينة.

١٠٠. عن عبد الرّحمن بن حَرب، قال: لمّا أقبل الناس مع أمير المؤمنين ﵇ من صِفّين أقبلنا معه، فأخذ طريقاً غير طريقنا الذي أقبلنا فيه، حتّى إذا جُزنا النُّخيلة ورأينا أبيات الكوفة، إذا شيخٌ جالِسٌ في ظِلّ بيتٍ وعلى وجهه أثر المرض، فأقبل إليه أمير المؤمنين ﵇، ونحن معه، حتّى سلّم عليه وسلّمنا معه، فردّ ردّاً حَسَنًا، فظننّا أنّه قد عرَفه.

فقال له أمير المؤمنين ﵇: مالي أرى وجهك مُنكسِرًا مصفارًّا؟ فمّم ذاك، أمِن مرض؟ فقال: نعم.

فقال: لعلّك كرِهته؟ فقال: ما أُحِبّ أنّه يَعتريني. قال: [أليس] احتسابًا للخير فيما أصابك به؟ [قال: بلى].

قال: فابشر برحمة الله وغُفران ذَنبك، فَمَن أنت يا عبدالله؟

فقال: أنا صالح ابن سليم.

He said, "I am originally from Salāmān b. Ṭayyi', but my affiliation and conversion was through Banī Sulaym b. Manṣūr."

So the Commander of the Faithful عليه السلام said, "What beautiful names you, your father, your grandfathers, and forefathers have! Have you been present in these conquests of ours?"

He replied, "No. Despite wanting to, the agitation of this fever has prevented me from them."

So the Commander of the Faithful recited: ﴾*there is no blame attached to the weak, the sick, and those who have no means to spend, provided they are true to God and His Messenger – there is no reason to reproach those who do good: God is most forgiving and merciful*﴿ – "What is the people's opinion about all that is going on between us and the people of Shām?"

He replied, "There are those who are secretly pleased and malicious about what is going on between you and them, and they are the most deceptive of people towards you."

So he عليه السلام responded to him, "You are right."

He continued, "And there are those who are dejected and enraged because of all that, and they are the sincerest advisors towards you."

So he عليه السلام said to him, "You are right. May God make your ailment a cause of reduction in your mistakes, for although there is no reward to be gained from illness, it does not leave the servant with any sin without reducing it. Indeed, reward lies in speaking with the tongue and acting with our arms and legs, for God will admit throngs of people into the Garden as a result of their sincere intention and upright conscience."' [9:91]

101. From al-Ḥalabī from Zurāra, Ḥumrān and Muḥammad b. Muslim, from Abū Ja'far and Abū 'Abd Allāh, peace be upon them both, who said, 'God holds people to task with only that which He has given them and with which He has acquainted them. Then He sent a messenger to them. Then He sent down a scripture and gave them instructions and prohibitions therein. He commanded the Messenger of God ﷺ to pray, but he fell asleep. So He said, "I am the One who makes you sleep, and I am the One who wakes you up. Perform the prayer when you wake up so that they may know what to do if the same thing happens to them. It is not as they think, that one is ruined if one falls asleep. Similarly with the fasting person: I am the One who makes him fall ill, and I am the One who restores him to health. He should repay

فقال: ممّن؟ قال: أمّا الأصل فمِن سلاَمان بن طَيِّئ، وأمّا الجِوار والدّعوة فمن بني سُليم بن منصور.

فقال أمير المؤمنين عليه السلام: ما أحسن اسمك، واسم أبيك، واسم أجدادك، واسم من اعتزيتَ إليه؛ فهل شَهِدت معنا غَزاتنا هذه؟ فقال: لا، ولقد أردتُها، ولكن ما ترى من لَحَب الحُمّى خَذَلني عنها.

فقال أمير المؤمنين عليه السلام: ﴿لَيْسَ عَلَى الضُّعَفَاءِ وَلا عَلَى الْمَرْضَى وَلا عَلَى الَّذِينَ لا يَجِدُونَ﴾ إلى آخر الآية، ما قول الناس فيما بيننا وبين أهل الشام؟ قال: منهم المسرور والمحبور فيما كان بينك وبينهم، وأولئك أغشّ الناس لك. فقال له: صَدَقت، قال: ومنهم الكاسف الأسِف لما كان من ذلك، وأولئك نُصحاء الناس لك.

فقال له: صدقت، جعل الله ما كان من شكواك حَطًّا لسيّئاتك، فإنّ المرض لا أجر فيه، ولكن لا يَدَع على العبد ذَنبًا إلا حطّه، وإنّما الأجر في القول باللسان والعمل باليد والرِّجل، فإنّ الله ليُدخِل بصِدق النيّة والسريرة الصالحة [عالمًا] جمًّا من عباده الجنّة.

١٠١. عن الحلبي، عن زُرارة وحُمران ومحمّد بن مسلم، عن أبي جعفر وأبي عبد الله عليهما السلام، قال: إنّ الله احتجّ على العباد بالّذي آتاهم وعرّفهم، ثمّ أرسل إليهم رسولاً، ثمّ أنزل عليهم كتابًا فأمر فيه ونهى، وأمر رسول الله صلى الله عليه وآله بالصلاة فنام عنها، فقال: أنا أنمتُك، وأنا أيقظتُك، فإذا قمتَ فصلِّ، ليعلموا إذا أصابهم ذلك كيف يصنعون، وليس كما يقولون: إذا نام عنها هَلَك، وكذلك الصيام، أنا أمرضتُك وأنا أُصِحُّك، فإذا شَفيتُك فأقْضِه.

[the fast] whenever I cure him." This is the case if you look at all situations – you should not find anyone to be constrained, and you should only find that [to be true] when God has proof against him, and He does as He wills.'

He continued, 'So do not say that they can do as they please and refuse to do what does not please them.' He said, 'God causes whoever He wills to stray and guides whoever He wills. He has only charged His servants to be observant of their efforts. Every single thing that He has commanded people to do and that they take on, their capacity for it is increased. And they are exempted from all that they are prevented from doing, but people have no goodness in them.'

Then he recited this verse: ﴾*there is no blame attached to the weak, the sick, and those who have no means to spend*﴿ – he said, 'He has exempted them from that which the good-doers have to do, and God is all-Forgiving, all-Merciful. ﴾*And there is no blame attached to those who came to you [Prophet] for riding animals and to whom you said, 'I cannot find a mount for you': they turned away with their eyes overflowing with tears of grief that they had nothing they could contribute.*﴿' He said, 'He exempted them since they could not find anything to contribute. ﴾*The ones open to blame are those who asked you for exemption despite their wealth and who preferred to be with those who stay behind. God has sealed their hearts: they do not understand.'*﴿ He said, 'He has imposed it on them because they can afford it. ﴾*The ones open to blame are those who asked you for exemption despite their wealth and who preferred to be with those who stay behind*﴿ – He makes them open to reproach because they can afford it, and not ﴾*those who came to you [Prophet] for riding animals and to whom you said, 'I cannot find a mount for you': they turned away with their eyes overflowing with tears of grief that they had nothing they could contribute.*﴿'

He said, "Abd Allāh b. Budayl b. Warqā' al-Khuzā'ī[27] was one of them.' [9:91–93]

102. From 'Abd al-Raḥmān b. Kathīr who said, 'Abū 'Abd Allāh ﷺ said, 'O 'Abd al-Raḥmān, by God, our followers (*shī'a*) are not prone to committing sins

27 The sources cite 'Abd Allāh b. Yazīd as the narrator but this is a transcription error. See 'Abd Allāh b. Budayl's biographical entry in Ibn al-Athīr, *Usd al-ghāba fī ma'rifat al-ṣaḥāba* (Beirut: Dār Ibn Ḥazm, 2012), 642 (no. 2835).

وكذلك إذا نظرتَ في جميع الأمور لم تجد أحدًا في ضيقٍ، ولم تجد أحدًا إلاّ ولله عليه الحُجّة، وله فيه المشيّة، قال: فلا يقولون إنّه ما شاءوا صنعوا، وما شاءوا لم يصنعوا.

وقال: إنّ الله يُضِلّ من يشاء، ويهدى من يشاء، وما أُمِر العباد إلاّ بدون سَعَتهم، وكلّ شيءٍ أُمِر الناس فأخذوا به فهم يَسعون له، وما [لا] يسَعون له فهو موضوعٌ عنهم، ولكن النّاس لا خير فيهم، ثمّ تلا هذه الآية: ﴿لَيْسَ عَلَى الضُّعَفَاءِ وَلَا عَلَى الْمَرْضَىٰ وَلَا عَلَى الَّذِينَ لَا يَجِدُونَ مَا يُنفِقُونَ حَرَجٌ﴾، قال: وضع عنهم ﴿مَا عَلَى الْمُحْسِنِينَ مِن سَبِيلٍ وَاللَّهُ غَفُورٌ رَّحِيمٌ ۞ وَلَا عَلَى الَّذِينَ إِذَا مَا أَتَوْكَ لِتَحْمِلَهُمْ قُلْتَ لَا أَجِدُ مَا أَحْمِلُكُمْ عَلَيْهِ تَوَلَّوا وَّأَعْيُنُهُمْ تَفِيضُ مِنَ الدَّمْعِ حَزَنًا أَلَّا يَجِدُوا مَا يُنفِقُونَ﴾ قال: وضع عنهم إذ لا يجِدون ما يُنفقون.

وقال: ﴿إِنَّمَا السَّبِيلُ عَلَى الَّذِينَ يَسْتَأْذِنُونَكَ وَهُمْ أَغْنِيَاءُ﴾ إلى قوله: ﴿لَا يَعْلَمُونَ﴾، قال: وُضع عليهم لأنّهم يُطيقون، ﴿إِنَّمَا السَّبِيلُ عَلَى الَّذِينَ يَسْتَأْذِنُونَكَ وَهُمْ أَغْنِيَاءُ رَضُوا بِأَن يَكُونُوا مَعَ الْخَوَالِفِ﴾ فجعل السبيل عليهم لأنّهم يُطيقون ﴿وَلَا عَلَى الَّذِينَ إِذَا مَا أَتَوْكَ لِتَحْمِلَهُمْ﴾ الآية، قال: عبدالله بن بُديل بن ورقاء الخُزاعي أحدهم.

١٠٢. عن عبد الرّحمن بن كثير، قال: قال أبو عبدالله عليه السلام: يا عبد الرّحمن، شيعتنا والله لا تختم الذنوب والخطايا، هم صفوةُ الله الّذين اختارهم لدينه، وهو قول الله: ﴿مَا عَلَى الْمُحْسِنِينَ مِن سَبِيلٍ﴾.

and mistakes; they are God's chosen ones whom He has selected for His religion, and this is the purport of God's statement: ﴾*there is no reason to reproach those who do good.*﴿' [9:91]

103. From Dāwūd b. al-Ḥuṣayn, from Abū ʿAbd Allāh عليه السلام. He said, 'I asked him about His verse: ﴾*But there are also some desert Arabs who believe in God and the Last Day and consider their contributions as bringing them nearer to God*﴿ – will He reward them for it?' He replied, 'Yes.' [9:99]

104. In another narration on his authority, 'Will they be rewarded for it?' He replied, 'Yes.' [9:99]

105. From Abū ʿAmr al-Zubayrī, from Abū ʿAbd Allāh عليه السلام who said, 'God, Mighty and Exalted, races the believers just as one races horses on the day of a horse-racing competition.'

I asked, 'Tell me about how God commissions the believers to compete in faith.' He replied, 'God's verse: ﴾*So race for your Lord's forgiveness and a Garden as wide as the heavens and earth, prepared for those who believe in God and His messengers.*﴿ (57:21) And He has said: ﴾*And those in front – ahead indeed! For these will be the ones brought nearest to God*﴿ (56:10–11) and ﴾*God will be well pleased with the first emigrants and helpers and those who followed them in good deeds, and they will be well pleased with Him.*﴿ So He begins with the first emigrants (*muhājirūn*) based on their precedence, then secondly the helpers (*anṣār*), then third, those who followed them in good deeds. He places each group according to their levels and positions in proximity to Him.' [9:100]

106. From Muḥammad b. Khālid b. al-Ḥajjāj al-Karkhī, from one of his associates, which he referred to Khaythama, who said, 'Abū Jaʿfar عليه السلام said about God's verse: ﴾*who have done some righteous deeds and some bad ones: God may well accept their repentance*﴿, "The ﴾*may well*﴿ here from God is obligatory, and it has actually been revealed about our Shīʿa who commit sins."' [9:102]

١٠٣. داود بن الحُصين، عن أبي عبد الله عليه السلام، قال: سألتُه عن قوله: ﴿وَمِنَ الأَعْرَابِ مَنْ يُؤْمِنُ بِاللهِ وَالْيَوْمِ الآخِرِ وَيَتَّخِذُ مَا يُنفِقُ قُرُبَاتٍ عِندَ اللهِ﴾ أيُثيبهم عليه؟ قال: نعم.

١٠٤. وفي رواية أُخرى عنه: يُثابون عليه: قال: نعم.

١٠٥. عن أبي عمر والزبيري، عن أبي عبد الله عليه السلام، قال: إنّ الله عزّ وجلّ سَبّقَ بين المؤمنين كما سُبّقَ بين الخيل يوم الرِّهان.

قلتُ: أخبرني عمّا نَدب الله المؤمن من الاستباق إلى الإيمان. قال عليه السلام: قول الله عزّ وجلّ: ﴿سَابِقُوا إِلَى مَغْفِرَةٍ مِنْ رَبِّكُمْ وَجَنَّةٍ عَرْضُهَا كَعَرْضِ السَّمَاءِ وَالأَرْضِ أُعِدَّتْ لِلَّذِينَ آمَنُوا بِاللهِ وَرُسُلِهِ﴾ وقال: ﴿وَالسَّابِقُونَ السَّابِقُونَ ۞ أُوْلَئِكَ الْمُقَرَّبُونَ﴾، وقال: ﴿وَالسَّابِقُونَ الأَوَّلُونَ مِنَ الْمُهَاجِرِينَ وَالأَنصَارِ وَالَّذِينَ اتَّبَعُوهُم بِإِحْسَانٍ رَضِيَ اللهُ عَنْهُمْ وَرَضُوا عَنْهُ﴾ فبدأ بالمُهاجرين الأوّلين على درجة سبقهم، ثمّ ثنّى بالأنصار، ثمّ ثلّث بالتابعين لهم بإحسان، فوضع كُلّ قومٍ على قدر درجاتهم ومنازلهم عنده.

١٠٦. عن محمّد بن خالد بن الحجّاج الكرخي، عن بعض أصحابه، رفع إلى خيثمة، قال: قال أبو جعفر عليه السلام في قول الله: ﴿خَلَطُوا عَمَلاً صَالِحًا وَآخَرَ سَيِّئًا عَسَى اللهُ أَنْ يَتُوبَ عَلَيْهِمْ﴾ والعسى من الله واجبٌ، وإنّما نزلت في شعيتنا المُذنبين.

107. From Aḥmad b. Muḥammad b. Abī Naṣr who without mentioning his source cited the Shaykh [Mūsā al-Kāẓim] as having said regarding God's verse: ﴾*who have done some righteous deeds and some bad ones.*﴿ He said, '[It refers to] the group of people who committed sins such as killing Ḥamza and Ja'far al-Ṭayyār, and repented thereafter.'

Then he said, 'But whoever kills a believer is not granted the opportunity to repent. It is only that God does not want to thwart His servants' expectations of Him, so He gives them hope in it.' Either he or someone else said, 'The ﴾*may well*﴿ from God is binding.' [9:102]

108. From al-Ḥalabī, from Zurāra, Ḥumrān, and Muḥammad b. Muslim, from one of the two [al-Bāqir or al-Ṣādiq] that he said, 'The phrase ﴾*one who confesses to his wrongdoing*﴿ refers to people who have confessed to their wrongdoings, having done some righteous deeds and some bad ones.' [9:102]

109. From Abū Bakr al-Ḥaḍrāmī who said, 'Muḥammad b. Sa'īd said, "Ask Abū 'Abd Allāh عليه السلام [on my behalf] and convey my statement to him. Tell him: 'I adhere to your authority and disassociate myself from your enemies. I believe in the Divine decree, and is my opinion on it the same as yours?'"

He said, 'So I conveyed his statement to Abū 'Abd Allāh عليه السلام and he shook his hand saying, ﴾*they have done some righteous deeds and some bad ones: God may well accept their repentance.*﴿' He said, 'Then he said, "I do not know him to have been among the adherents of the Commander of the Faithful."

I said, "He claims that Hishām's authority is not endorsed by God." So he replied, "Woe unto him! What is wrong with him? Does he not know that God made a government for Ādam and a separate government for Iblīs?"' [9:102]

110. From Zurāra, from Abū Ja'far عليه السلام who said regarding God's verse: ﴾*And there are others who have confessed their wrongdoing, who have done some righteous deeds and some bad ones*﴿, 'They are sinning people who make mischief despite their faith – sins that the believers would consider shameful and abhorrent; and those are the ones whose repentance God may well accept.' [9:102]

١٠٧. عن أحمد بن محمّد بن أبي نصر، رفعه إلى الشيخ، في قوله تعالى: ﴿خَلَطُوا عَمَلًا صَالِحًا وَآخَرَ سَيِّئًا﴾، قال: قومٌ اجترَحوا ذُنوبًا مثل قتل حمزة وجعفر الطيّار، ثمّ تابوا.

ثمّ قال: ومن قتل مؤمنًا لم يُوفّق للتوبة، إلاّ أنّ الله لا يقطعُ طَمَع العِباد فيه، ورَجاءهم منه. وقال هو أو غيره: إنّ عسى من الله واجبٌ.

١٠٨. عن الحلبي، عن زُرارة وحُمران ومحمّد بن مسلم، عن أحدهما عليه السلام، قال: المُعترِف بذنبه قومٌ اعترفوا بِذُنوبهم، خَلطوا عملاً صالحًا وآخر سيئًا.

١٠٩. عن أبي بكر الحضرمي، قال: قال محمّد بن سعيد: اسأل ابا عبد الله عليه السلام، فاعرِض عليه كلامي، وقل له: إنّي أتولاّكم، وأبرأ من عدوّكم، وأقول بالقَدر، وقولي فيه قولك؟

قال: فعرضتُ كلامه على أبي عبد الله عليه السلام، فحرّك يده، ثمّ قال: ﴿خَلَطُوا عَمَلًا صَالِحًا وَآخَرَ سَيِّئًا عَسَى اللَّهُ أَنْ يَتُوبَ عَلَيْهِمْ﴾، قال: ثمّ قال: ما أعرفه من موالي أمير المؤمنين عليه السلام.

قلت: يزعُم أنّ سلطان هِشام ليس من الله. فقال: ويله ما له؛ أما عَلِم أنّ الله جعل لآدم دولة، ولإبليس دولة؟

١١٠. عن زُرارة، عن أبي جعفر عليه السلام، في قول الله تعالى: ﴿وَآخَرُونَ اعْتَرَفُوا بِذُنُوبِهِمْ خَلَطُوا عَمَلًا صَالِحًا وَآخَرَ سَيِّئًا عَسَى اللَّهُ أَنْ يَتُوبَ عَلَيْهِمْ﴾.

قال: أولئك قوم مُذنبون يُحدِثون في إيمانهم من الذّنوب الّتي يعيبها المؤمنون ويكرهها، فأولئك عسى الله أن يتوب عليهم.

111. From Zurāra, from Abū Jaʿfar عليه السلام. He said, 'We said to him, "Whoever is in harmony with us, be they a descendent from 'Alī or not, we endear ourselves to them; and whoever opposes us, we disassociate from them, be they a descendent of 'Alī or not." He said, "Zurāra, God's Word is truer than your word – what about the ones who have done some righteous deeds and some bad ones?"' [9:102]

112. From 'Alī b. Ḥassān al-Wāsiṭī[28], from one of our associates, from Abū 'Abd Allāh عليه السلام. He said, 'I asked him about God's verse: ﴾*In order to cleanse and purify them* [*Prophet*], *accept a gift out of their property*﴿ – Does this apply to the Imam after the Messenger of God صلى الله عليه وآله as well? He replied, "Yes."' [9:103]

113. From Zurāra, from Abū 'Abd Allāh عليه السلام. He said, 'I asked him about the verse: ﴾*In order to cleanse and purify them* [*Prophet*], *accept a gift out of their property*﴿ – is this the same as ﴾*pay the prescribed alms*﴿?' He said, 'He said, "Alms (*ṣadaqa*) is from crops and cattle, whereas the prescribed alms (*zakāt*) is from gold, silver, and the alms of fasting."' [9:103]

114. From Jābir al-Juʿfī, from Abū Jaʿfar عليه السلام who said, 'The Commander of the Faithful عليه السلام said, "I was donating a dinar to charity one day, when the Messenger of God صلى الله عليه وآله told me, 'Do you know that no sooner does the believer's charity leave his hand than it breaks the jaws of seventy devils, and no sooner does it land in the beggar's hand than it lands in the Hand of the Lord Himself, Blessed and most High? Does He not say: ﴾*Do they not know that it is God Himself who accepts repentance from His servants and receives what is given freely for His sake? He is always ready to accept repentance, most merciful.*﴿?'"' [9:104]

115. From Muʿallā b. Khunays[29] who said, 'Abū 'Abd Allāh عليه السلام went out on a night when it was drizzling, heading for the Banī Sāʿida shelter. So I followed him

---

28 Abū al-Ḥasan 'Alī b. Ḥassān al-Wāsiṭī al-Qaṣīr, who lived to over a hundred years of age, was a very reliable and trustworthy companion of Imam Jaʿfar al-Ṣādiq. See Ḥillī, *Khulāṣat al-aqwāl*, 182 (nr. 541).

29 Abū 'Abd Allāh Muʿallā b. Khunays (d. 133/750), the protégé of Imam Jaʿfar al-Ṣādiq, is considered by Najāshī and Ibn al-Ghaḍā'irī to have been extremely weak and someone to whom the heterodox *ghulāt* inclined heavily. However, there are differing opinions

١١١ . عن زُرارة، عن أبي جعفر عليه السلام، قال: قلتُ له: مَن وافقنا من علويّ أو غيره تولّيناه، ومن خالفَنا بَرِئنا منه من علويّ أو غيره. قال: يا زُرارة، قول الله أصدق من قولك: أين الذين خلطوا عملاً صالحًا وآخر سيئًا.

١١٢ . عن عليّ بن حسان الواسطي، عن بعض أصحابنا، عن أبي عبد الله عليه السلام، قال: سألتُه عن قول الله تعالى: ﴿خُذْ مِنْ أَمْوَالِهِمْ صَدَقَةً تُطَهِّرُهُمْ وَتُزَكِّيهِم بِهَا﴾ جاريةٌ هي في الإمام بعد رسول الله صلى الله عليه وآله؟ قال: نعم.

١١٣ . عن زُرارة، عن أبي عبد الله عليه السلام، قال: قلتُ له: قوله: ﴿خُذْ مِنْ أَمْوَالِهِمْ صَدَقَةً تُطَهِّرُهُمْ وَتُزَكِّيهِم بِهَا﴾ أهو قوله: ﴿وَآتُوا الزَّكَاةَ﴾؟ قال: قال: الصّدقات في النبات والحيوان، والزكاة في الذّهب والفضّة، وزكاة الصوم.

١١٤ . عن جابر الجُعفي، عن أبي جعفر عليه السلام، قال: قال أمير المؤمنين عليه السلام: تصدّقتُ يومًا بدينار، فقال لي رسول الله صلى الله عليه وآله: أما علِمت أنّ صدقة المؤمن لا تخرُج من يده حتّى يُفكّ بها عن لَحيي سبعين شيطانًا، وما تقع في يد السائل حتّى تقع في يد الربّ تبارك وتعالى؟ ألم يقُل هذه الآية: ﴿أَلَمْ يَعْلَمُوا أَنَّ اللَّهَ هُوَ يَقْبَلُ التَّوْبَةَ عَنْ عِبَادِهِ وَيَأْخُذُ الصَّدَقَاتِ﴾؟ إلى آخر الآية.

١١٥ . عن مُعلّى بن خُنيس، قال: خرج أبو عبد الله عليه السلام في ليلةٍ قد رشّت وهو يُريد ظُلّة بني ساعِدة؟ فأتبعتُه فإذا هو قد سَقَط منه شيءٌ، فقال: «بسم الله، اللّهمّ أرْدُده علينا» فأتيته

and found that he had dropped something, and was saying, "In the Name of God. O God, return it to us." I approached him and greeted him with peace.

He asked, "Mu'allā?"

I replied, "Yes – may I be your ransom."

He said, "Feel around [on the ground] with your hand please, and hand me whatever you find there."

I found many scattered loaves of bread, and began passing him a loaf or two at a time. He also had a sack that he was struggling to carry, so I said, "May I be your ransom – let me carry it for you. He said, "I should be the one to carry it, not you, but you can walk with me."

So we came to the Banī Sā'ida shelter and found some people asleep there. He began to slip a loaf or two under their coverings until he had given to the last of them. Then we left, and I said to him, "Are these people aware of this?"

He replied, "No. If they came to know, it would be incumbent upon us to give them salt as well. God has not created anything without an owner who treasures it, apart from charity. That is kept by the Lord Himself, Blessed and most High. When my father used to donate anything, he would place it in the beggar's hand, then take it back momentarily, kiss it, smell it, then return it back to the beggar's hand. And that is because it lands in God's Hand before it even lands in the beggar's hand. And I too wanted to kiss it because it had touched God's Hand as well as my father's. Charity given in the nighttime extinguishes the Lord's wrath, wipes away great sins, and facilitates the Reckoning [on the Day of Judgement]; whilst charity given in the daytime causes an increase in one's wealth and lifespan."' [9:104]

116. From Muḥammad b. Muslim, from Abū 'Abd Allāh عليه السلام who said, 'Every single thing has an angel in charge of it except for charity, for that lands directly into God's Hand.' [9:104]

---

concerning him due to the fact that there are traditions in which he is both praised and blamed. According to Shaykh al-Ṭūsī, he was not only praised by Imam al-Ṣādiq but was also one of his most loyal supporters. He was killed by the Abbasid governor of Medina, Dāwūd b. 'Alī. See Ḥillī, *Khulāṣat al-aqwāl*, 408–9 (nr. 1652); Modarressi, *Tradition and Survival*, 326 (nr. 142).

وسلّمتُ عليه، فقال: مُعلّى؟ قلتُ: نعم، جُعِلتُ فداك. قال: التمس بيدك، فما وجدتَ من شيء فادفعه إليّ؛ فإذا أنا بخبزٍ كثير منتشر فجعلتُ أدفع إليه الرّغيف والرّغيفين، وإذا معه جِرابٌ أعجزُ عن حملِه. فقلتُ: جُعِلت فداك، أحمِلُه؟ فقال: أنا أولى به منك، ولكن امضِ معي.

فأتينا ظُلّة بني ساعِدة، فإذا نحنُ بقوم نيام فَجَعَل يدُسُّ الرّغيف والرّغيفين، حتّى أتى على آخره، حتّى إذا انصرفنا قلتُ له: يعرِف هؤلاء هذا الأمر؟ قال: لا، لو عرَفوا كان الواجب علينا أن نُواسهم بالدُّقّة — وهو الملح — إنّ الله لم يخلُق شيئًا إلاّ وله خازِن يخزُنه إلاّ الصّدقة، فإنّ الرّبّ تبارك وتعالى يليها بنفسه، وكان أبي إذا تصدّق بشيءٍ وضعَه في يد السائل، ثمّ ارتجعَه منه فقبّله وشمّه، ثمّ ردّه في يد السائل، وذلك أنّها تقع في يد الله قبل أن تقع في يد السائل، فأحببتُ أن أقبّلها إذ وليها الله ووليها أبي، إنّ صدقة الليل تُطفئ غَضَب الرّبّ، وتمحو الذنب العظيم، وتُهوّن الحِساب، وصدقة النهار تُمي المال وتزيد في العمر.

١١٦. عن محمّد بن مسلم، عن أبي عبد الله عليه السلام. قال: ما من شيءٍ إلاّ وكّل به مَلَك إلاّ الصدقة، فإنّها تقع في يد الله تعالى.

117. From Abū Bakr, from al-Sakūnī, from Ja'far b. Muḥammad on his father's authority, on his forefathers' authority who said, 'The Messenger of God ﷺ said, "There are two actions that I do not like for anyone to assist me in: my minor ablution (*wuḍū'*) for it is for my own prayer, and my charity from my own hand into the beggar's hand, for it lands directly into the Hand of the all-Beneficent."' [9:104]

118. From Muḥammad b. Muslim, from one of the two [al-Bāqir or al-Ṣādiq] who said, 'When 'Alī b. al-Ḥusayn, may God's blessings be upon him, used to give to a beggar, he would kiss the beggar's hand. He was once asked, "Why do you do that?" He replied, "Because it lands in God's Hand before even His servant's." He also said, "Every single thing has an angel in charge of it except for charity for that lands directly in God's Hand." Al-Faḍl said, "I think he even kissed the bread and the dirham."' [9:104]

119. From Mālik b. 'Aṭiyya[30], from Abū 'Abd Allāh عليه السلام who said, "Alī b. al-Ḥusayn عليه السلام said, "I have been guaranteed by my Lord that charity does not land in the servant's hand before it lands in His Hand first; and this is as per His words: ﴾*it is God Himself who accepts repentance from His servants and receives what is given freely for His sake.*﴿' [9:104]

120. From Muḥammad b. Muslim, from one of the two [al-Bāqir or al-Ṣādiq]. He said, 'He was asked about the deeds and whether they are exposed to the Messenger of God? So he replied, "Without a doubt." He was asked, "Have you considered God's verse: ﴾*Say* [*Prophet*], *'Take action! God will see your actions – as will His Messenger and the believers*﴿?" He said, "God has witnesses on His earth."' [9:105]

121. From Zurāra who said, 'I asked Abū Ja'far عليه السلام about God's verse: ﴾*Take action! God will see your actions – as will His Messenger and the believers.*﴿ He said, "Do you want to see 'Alī – he is the one in your soul."' [9:105]

30 Abū al-Ḥusayn Mālik b. 'Aṭiyya al-Aḥmasī al-Bajalī, a reliable companion and narrator of Imam Ja'far al-Ṣādiq. See Ḥillī, *Khulāṣat al-aqwāl*, 277 (nr. 1009); Modarressi, *Tradition and Survival*, 316–7 (nr. 133).

١١٧. عن أبي بكر، عن السّكوني، عن جعفر بن محمّد، عن أبيه، عن آبائه عليهم السلام، قال: قال رسول الله صلى الله عليه وآله وسلم: خَلّتان لا أحِبّ أن يُشاركني فيهما أحد: وضوئي فإنّه من صلاتي، وصدَقتي من يدي إلى يد سائلٍ، فإنّها تقع في يد الرّحمن.

١١٨. عن محمّد بن مسلم، عن أحدهما عليهما السلام، قال: كان عليّ بن الحسين صلوات الله عليه إذا أعطى السائل قبّل يد السائل، فقيل له: لِمَ تفعل ذلك؟ قال: لأنّها تقع في يد الله قبل يد العبد. وقال: ليس من شيءٍ إلاّ وُكِّلَ به مَلَك إلاّ الصدقة، فإنّها تقع في يد الله، قال الفضل: أظنّه يُقبّل الخبز أو الدِّرهَم.

١١٩. عن مالك بن عطيّة، عن أبي عبد الله عليه السلام، قال: قال عليّ بن الحسين صلوات الله عليه: ضَمِنتُ على ربّي أنّ الصدقة لا تقع في يد العبد حتّى تقع في يد الربّ. وهو قوله تعالى: ﴿هُوَ يَقْبَلُ التَّوْبَةَ عَنْ عِبَادِهِ وَيَأْخُذُ الصَّدَقَاتِ﴾.

١٢٠. عن محمّد بن مسلم، عن أحدهما عليهما السلام، قال: سُئِل عن الأعمال، هل تُعرَض على رسول الله صلى الله عليه وآله وسلم؟ فقال: ما فيه شكّ.

قيل له: أرأيت قول الله: ﴿وَقُلِ اعْمَلُوا فَسَيَرَى اللَّهُ عَمَلَكُمْ وَرَسُولُهُ وَالْمُؤْمِنُونَ﴾؟ قال: لله شُهداء في أرضه.

١٢١. عن زُرارة، قال: سألتُ أبا جعفر عليه السلام عن قول الله: ﴿وَقُلِ اعْمَلُوا فَسَيَرَى اللَّهُ عَمَلَكُمْ وَرَسُولُهُ وَالْمُؤْمِنُونَ﴾؟ قال: تُريد أن تروا عليّ، هو الذي في نفسك.

122. From Yaḥyā b. Musāwir, from Abū ʿAbd Allāh عليه السلام. I said, 'Narrate a *ḥadīth* to me about ʿAlī.'

He said, 'Would you like the detailed version or the summary?'

I said, 'The summary.'

So he said, "ʿAlī is the gate of guidance. Whoever goes ahead of him is a disbeliever and whoever lags behind him is a disbeliever.'

I said, 'Tell me more.'

He said, 'On the Day of Judgement, a pulpit will be raised up on the right of the Throne with a staircase of twenty-four steps. Then ʿAlī will come with the flag in his hand, which he will hoist up and then climb up onto it [i.e. the pulpit], and all people will be presented before him. Whoever acknowledges him will enter the Garden and whoever rejects him will enter the Fire.'

I said to him, 'Find it for me in God's Book.'

He replied, 'Very well. It is what this verse speaks about. He, Blessed and most High, says: ﴿*God will see your actions – as will His Messenger and the believers*﴾, and by God, this is ʿAlī b. Abī Ṭālib.' [9:105]

123. From Abū Baṣīr, from Abū ʿAbd Allāh عليه السلام that Abū al-Khaṭṭāb used to say, 'His community's actions are displayed to the Messenger of God صلى الله عليه وآله every Thursday.' So Abū ʿAbd Allāh عليه السلام said, 'That is not how it is, rather the community's actions are displayed to the Messenger of God صلى الله عليه وآله every morning, both the good people's as well as the bad, so be careful; and this is as per God's statement: ﴿*God will see your actions – as will His Messenger and the believers.*﴾' [9:105]

124. From Muḥammad b. al-Fuḍayl, from Abū al-Ḥasan عليه السلام. He said, 'I asked him about the verse of God, Blessed and most High: ﴿*God will see your actions – as will His Messenger and the believers.*﴾ He replied, "His community's actions are displayed to the Messenger of God, peace be upon him and his family, every morning, both the good people's as well as the bad, so be careful."' [9:105]

125. [From Zurāra], from Burayd al-ʿIjlī who said, 'I asked Abū ʿAbd Allāh عليه السلام about God's words: ﴿*Take action! God will see your actions – as will His Messenger and the believers*﴾, so he said, "Not a single believer or disbeliever dies and is put in his grave without his actions being displayed to the Messenger

١٢٢. عن يحيى بن مُساور قلتُ: حدّثني في عليّ ﵇ حديثًا فقال: اشرَحه لك أم اجمَعُه؟ قلتُ: بل أجمَعهُ، فقال: عليٌّ باب هدى، من تقدّمه كان كافرًا، ومن تخلّف عنه كان كافرًا.

قلتُ: زِدني. قال: إذا كان يوم القيامة نُصِب مِنبرٌ عن يمين العرش له أربع وعشرون مَرقاة، فيأتي عليّ ﵇ وبيده اللواء حتّى يَركَبه ويُعرَض الخَلق عليه، فمن عَرَفه دخل الجنّة، ومن أنكره دخل النار.

قلتُ له: تُوجدنيه من كتاب الله؟ قال: نعم، ما تقول هذه الآية؟ يقول تبارك وتعالى: ﴿فَسَيَرَى اللهُ عَمَلَكُمْ وَرَسُولُهُ وَالْمُؤْمِنُونَ﴾ هو والله عليّ بن أبي طالب ﵇.

١٢٣. عن أبي بصير، عن أبي عبدالله ﵇: أنّ أبا الخطّاب كان يقول: إنّ رسول الله ﷺ تُعرَض عليه أعمال أُمّته كلّ خميس. فقال أبو عبدالله ﵇: ليس هو هكذا، ولكن رسول الله ﷺ تُعرَض عليه أعمال أمّته كلّ صباح أبرارها وفُجّارها فاحذَروا، وهو قول الله تبارك وتعالى: ﴿فَسَيَرَى اللهُ عَمَلَكُمْ وَرَسُولُهُ وَالْمُؤْمِنُونَ﴾.

١٢٤. عن محمّد بن الفضيل، عن أبي الحسن ﵇، قال: سألتُه عن قول الله تبارك وتعالى: ﴿فَسَيَرَى اللهُ عَمَلَكُمْ وَرَسُولُهُ وَالْمُؤْمِنُونَ﴾. قال: تُعرَض على رسول الله عليه وآله السلام أعمال أمّته كُلّ صَباح أبرارها وفُجّارها فاحذَروا.

١٢٥. عن بُريد العجلي، قال: قلتُ لأبي جعفر ﵇: في قول الله تعالى: ﴿اعْمَلُوا فَسَيَرَى اللهُ عَمَلَكُمْ وَرَسُولُهُ وَالْمُؤْمِنُونَ﴾. فقال: ما مِن مؤمنٍ يموت، ولا كافرٍ يُوضَع في قبره

of God ﷺ and ʿAlī عليه السلام, so carry on [working hard] until the last one whose obedience God has made obligatory for His servants."' [9:105]

126. Abū ʿAbd Allāh عليه السلام said, ﴾*and the believers*﴿ – they are the Imams.' [9:105]

127. From Muḥammad b. Muslim, from Abū ʿAbd Allāh عليه السلام who said regarding: ﴾*Take action! God will see your actions – as will His Messenger and the believers*﴿, 'God has a witness on His earth, and people's actions are displayed to the Messenger of God, peace be upon him and his family.' [9:105]

128. From Muḥammad b. Ḥassān al-Kūfī, from Muḥammad b. Jaʿfar, on his father Jaʿfar's عليه السلام authority, on his father's authority who said, 'On the Day of Judgement, a pulpit will be raised up to the right of the Throne with a staircase of twenty-four steps. Then ʿAlī will come with the flag in his hand, which he will hoist up and then climb up onto it [i.e. the pulpit], and all people will be presented before him. Whoever acknowledges him will enter Paradise and whoever rejects him will enter the Fire. The explanation of that is in God's Book: ﴾*Take action! God will see your actions – as will His Messenger and the believers.*﴿ He said, 'By God, this is the Commander of the Faithful ʿAlī b. Abī Ṭālib, may God's blessings be upon him.' [9:105]

129. From Hishām b. Sālim, from Abū ʿAbd Allāh عليه السلام who said regarding the verse: ﴾*And there are others who are waiting for God's decree*﴿, 'These are a group of people from the polytheists who shed the blood of Muslims then embraced Islam thereafter; so they are waiting for God's decree.' [9:106]

130. From Zurāra, Ḥumrān and Muḥammad b. Muslim, from Abū Jaʿfar and Abū ʿAbd Allāh عليه السلام who said, 'The ones waiting for God's decree are a group of people who fought [the Muslims] in the battles of Badr, Uḥud, and Ḥunayn; they sided with the polytheists then embraced Islam later on. So He may either chastise them or pardon them.' [9:106]

حتّى يُعرَض عمله على رسول الله ﷺ وعليّ ﵇، فهلمّ جرّا إلى آخر من فرض الله طاعته على العباد.

١٢٦. وقال أبو عبد الله ﵇: ﴿وَالْمُؤْمِنُونَ﴾ هم الأئمّة.

١٢٧. عن محمّد بن مسلم، عن أبي عبد الله ﵇، في قوله تعالى: ﴿اعْمَلُوا فَسَيَرَى اللَّهُ عَمَلَكُمْ وَرَسُولُهُ وَالْمُؤْمِنُونَ﴾، قال: إنّ لله شاهدًا في أرضه، وإنّ أعمال العباد تُعرَض على رسول الله عليه وآله السلام.

١٢٨. عن محمّد بن حسّان الكوفي، عن محمّد بن جعفر، عن أبيه جعفر، عن أبيه ﵇، قال: إذا كان يوم القيامة نُصِب مِنبَر عن يمين العرش له أربع وعشرون مَرقاة، ويجيءُ عليّ بن أبي طالب ﵇ وبيده لواء الحمد، فيرتقيه ويركبه، وتُعرَض الخلائق عليه، فمن عَرَفه دخل الجنّة، ومن أنكره دخل النار، وتفسير ذلك في كتاب الله ﴿وَقُلِ اعْمَلُوا فَسَيَرَى اللَّهُ عَمَلَكُمْ وَرَسُولُهُ وَالْمُؤْمِنُونَ﴾، قال: هو والله أمير المؤمنين عليّ بن أبي طالب ﵇.

١٢٩. هِشام بن سالم، عن أبي عبد الله ﵇، في قول الله تعالى: ﴿وَآخَرُونَ مُرْجَوْنَ لِأَمْرِ اللَّهِ﴾ قال: هُم قومٌ من المشركين أصابوا دمًا من المسلمين ثمّ أسلموا، فهم المُرجَون لأمرِ الله.

١٣٠. عن زُرارة وحمران ومحمّد بن مسلم، عن أبي جعفر وأبي عبد الله ﵇، قالا: المُرجَون هم قومٌ قاتلوا يوم بدر، وأُحد ويوم حُنين، وسَلَوا عن المشركين، ثمّ أسلموا بعد تأخّر، فإمّا يُعذّبهم وإمّا يتُوب عليهم.

131. From Zurāra, from Abū Jaʿfar عليه السلام who said regarding God's verse: ﴾*And there are others who are waiting for God's decree*﴿, 'They are a group of polytheists who killed the likes of Ḥamza, Jaʿfar, and other believers. Then they embraced Islam afterwards and professed God's Oneness and abandoned polytheism. They did not believe seriously enough to be considered believers and be mandatorily admitted into the Garden, but nor did they disbelieve to the extent that they should necessarily enter the Fire. So they remain in that state awaiting God's decree.' [9:106]

132. Ḥumrān said, 'I asked Abū ʿAbd Allāh عليه السلام about the truly helpless people. He said, "They are neither believers nor disbelievers, and they await the decree of God."' [9:106]

133. From Ibn al-Ṭayyār who said, 'Abū ʿAbd Allāh عليه السلام said, "People fall into six categories – three of them are classed according to belief, disbelief, and misguidance, for whom God's promise holds true in that He has promised them either the Garden or the Hellfire. [Altogether] they are the believers, the disbelievers, the truly helpless ones, the ones awaiting God's decree, those who have confessed their sins but have mixed righteous deeds with wrongdoings, and the people of the heights."'

134. From Zurāra, from Abū Jaʿfar عليه السلام who said, '﴾*those who are waiting for God's decree*﴿ were some polytheists who killed the likes of Ḥamza, Jaʿfar, and people of their like. Then they entered into Islam, professed God's Oneness and left polytheism. They did not truly recognise faith with their hearts so as to be [classified as] believers whereupon the Garden would be mandatory for them, but nor were they persistent in their rebellion that they be disbelievers and necessarily enter the Fire. So they remain in that state – He may either chastise them or pardon them.'

Abū ʿAbd Allāh عليه السلام said, 'He will consider them with His judgement.' He said, 'I asked him, "May I be your ransom – how are they sustained?" He replied, "However God may wish."'

Abū Ibrāhīm [i.e. Imam Mūsā al-Kāẓim] said, 'These are people whom He has stalled until He will consider them with His judgement.' [9:106]

١٣١. عن زُرارة، عن أبي جعفر ﷺ، في قول الله تعالى: ﴿وَآخَرُونَ مُرْجَوْنَ لِأَمْرِ اللهِ﴾. قال: هم قومٌ مُشرِكون، فقتَلوا مثل حمزة وجعفر وأشباههما من المؤمنين، ثمّ أنّهم دخلوا في الإسلام فوحّدوا الله وتركوا الشِّرك، ولم يؤمنوا فيكونوا من المؤمنين فتَجِب لهم الجنّة، ولم يكفُروا فتَجِب لهم النّار، فهم على تلك الحال مُرجَون لأمر الله.

١٣٢. قال حُمران: سألتُ أبا عبدالله ﷺ عن المُستضعفين. قال: هم ليسوا بالمؤمنين ولا بالكفّار، وهم المُرجَون لأمر الله.

١٣٣. عن ابن الطيّار قال: قال أبو عبدالله ﷺ: الناس على ستّ فرق، يؤتُون إلى ثلاث فِرق: الإيمان، والكُفر، والضلال، وهم أهل الوَعد من الذين وَعد الله الجنّة والنّار، وهم المؤمنون، والكافرون، والمُستضعفون، والمُرْجَون لأمر الله إمّا يُعذِّبهم وإمّا يَتُوب عليهم، والمُعترِفون بذنوبهم خَلَطوا عملاً صالحًا وآخر سيّئًا، وأهل الأعراف.

١٣٤. عن زُرارة، عن أبي جعفر ﷺ، قال: المُرجَون لأمر الله: قومٌ كانوا مشركين، فقَتَلوا مثل حمزة وجعفر وأشباههما، ثمّ دخلوا بعد في الإسلام، فوحّدوا اللهَ وتَركوا الشِّرك، ولم يعرِفوا الإيمان بِقلوبهم فيكونوا من المؤمنين فيجب لهم الجنّة، ولم يكونوا على جُحودهم فيكفُروا فتجِب لهم النّار، فهم على تلك الحال إمّا يُعذِّبهم وإمّا يتُوب عليهم.

قال أبو عبدالله ﷺ: يرى فيهم رأيه.

قال: قلتُ: جُعِلتُ فداك، مِن أين يُرزَقون؟ قال: من حيثُ شاء الله.

وقال أبو إبراهيم ﷺ: هؤلاء قومٌ وقّفهم حتّى يرى فيهم رأيه.

135. From al-Ḥārith, from Abū ʿAbd Allāh ﷺ. He said, 'I asked him whether there was a state between belief and disbelief? So he replied, "Yes, various states. If he rebels in any of them, then God will throw him face down into the Fire; whereas there are others among them who await the decree of God, and others who are truly helpless, others who have mixed up righteous deeds with wrongdoings, and yet others about whom God says: ﴾*men on the heights.*﴿"' [9:106]

136. From Dāwūd b. Farqad who said, 'I said to Abū ʿAbd Allāh ﷺ, "Al-Marqūm cited the virtues of ʿAlī to them, so they said, 'We do not know if that is true or not." He responded, "Give respite." He said, ﴾*there are others who are waiting for God's decree either to punish them or to show them mercy. God is all knowing and wise.*﴿' [9:106]

137. From al-Ḥalabī, from Abū ʿAbd Allāh ﷺ. He said, 'I asked him about the mosque ﴾*founded from its first day on consciousness of God.*﴿ He replied, "[It is] the Mosque of Qubā."' [9:108]

138. From Zurāra, Ḥumrān and Muḥammad b. Muslim, from Abū Jaʿfar and Abū ʿAbd Allāh ﷺ who said regarding His verse: ﴾*a mosque founded from its first day on consciousness of God*﴿, '[It is] the Mosque of Qubā. As for His words: ﴾*You should rather pray in it*﴿ it means rather than in the mosque [founded on] hypocrisy, which was on the way when he went to the Mosque of Qubā. He would stand and spray it with water infused with fragrant berry leaves. Then he would lift his clothing away from his legs and walk flush towards the side of the path hurriedly, and disliked his clothing from getting wet.'

So I asked him, 'Did the Prophet ﷺ used to pray in the Mosque of Qubā?' He replied, 'Yes. He was staying at Saʿd b. Khaythama al-Anṣārī's house.'

Then I asked him, 'Did the Prophet's Mosque have a roof?' So he replied, 'No. Some of the companions would ask him, "Will you not roof our mosque, O Messenger of God?" He replied, "It is a shack like Mūsā's shack."' [9:108]

١٣٥ . عن الحارِث، عن أبي عبد الله عليه السلام، قال: سألتُه بين الإيمان والكفر منزلة؟ فقال: نعم، ومنازل لو يجحد شيئًا منها أكبّه الله في النّار، بينهما آخرون مُرجَون لأمر الله، وبينهما المُستضعفون، وبينهما آخرون خَلَطوا عملاً صالحًا وآخر سيّئًا، وبينهما قوله: ﴿وَعَلَى الأَعْرَافِ رِجَالٌ﴾.

١٣٦ . عن داود بن فَرقد، قال: قلتُ لأبي عبد الله عليه السلام: المُرجَون [قوم] ذُكِر لهم فضل عليّ عليه السلام فقالوا: ما ندري لعلّه كذلك، وما ندري لعلّه ليس كذلك. قال: أرجِه قال: ﴿وَآخَرُونَ مُرْجَوْنَ لأَمْرِ الله﴾ الآية.

١٣٧ . عن الحلبي، عن أبي عبد الله عليه السلام، قال: سألتُه عن ﴿المسجِد الّذي أُسِّسَ عَلى التّقوى من أوّل يومٍ﴾ فقال: مسجد قُبا.

١٣٨ . عن زُرارة وحُمران ومحمّد بن مسلم، عن أبي جعفر وأبي عبد الله عليهما السلام، عن قوله تعالى: ﴿لَمَسْجِدٌ أُسِّسَ عَلَى التَّقْوَى مِنْ أَوَّلِ يَوْمٍ﴾ قال: مسجد قُبا.

وأمّا قوله: ﴿أَحَقُّ أَنْ تَقُومَ فِيهِ﴾ قال: يعني من مسجد النِّفاق، وكان على طريقه إذا أتى مسجد قُبا، فكان ينضح بالماء والسِّدر، ويرفع ثِيابه عن ساقيه، ويمشي على حَجَرٍ في ناحية الطريق، ويُسرِع المشي، ويكره أن يُصيب ثيابه منه شيءٌ.

فسألتُه هل كان النبيّ صلى الله عليه وآله يصلّي في مسجد قُبا؟ قال: نعم، كان منزله على سعد بن خَيثمة الأنصاري.

139. From al-Ḥalabī, from Abū ʿAbd Allāh عليه السلام who said, ʻI asked him about God's verse: ﴿*in this mosque there are men who desire to grow in purity.*﴾ He said, "They were those who love to purify themselves by cleansing themselves before the ablution (*wuḍūʾ*) by washing themselves with water after using the lavatory." He said, "This verse was revealed about the people of [the mosque of] Qubā."' [9:108]

140. In a narration of Ibn Sinān's, on his authority he said, ʻI asked him, "What kind of purification is that?" He replied, "Cleansing oneself before *wuḍūʾ* when any of them used the lavatory, so God commended them for their desire to purify themselves."' [9:108]

141. From Zurāra who said, ʻI did not like to ask Abū Jaʿfar عليه السلام directly about the *rajʿa*, so I broached the subject through a subtle question by which I would get my answer. So I said, "May I be your ransom – tell me about someone who is killed: can he [be said to] have died?" He replied, "No. [Natural] death is death, and killing is murder."

He said, ʻSo I asked him, "Can anyone be killed and be said to have died?" So he said, "Zurāra, God's words are truer than yours, for He has distinguished between them in the Qurʾan saying: ﴿*Whether you are killed for God's cause or die*﴾ (3:157) and ﴿*Whether you die or are killed, it is to God that you will be gathered.*﴾ (3:158) It is not as you are saying, Zurāra. Death is death, and killing is murder. And God has said: ﴿*God has purchased the persons and possessions of the believers in return for the Garden – they fight in God's way: they kill and are killed – this is a true promise given by Him in the Torah, the Gospel, and the Qurʾān. Who could be more faithful to his promise than God? So be happy with the bargain you have made: that is the supreme triumph.*﴾'

He said, ʻSo I said to him, "But God says: ﴿*Every soul will taste death*﴾ (3:185) – so are you saying that the one who is killed does not taste death?"'

He said, ʻHe replied, "The one who is killed by the sword is not like the one who dies in his sleep. The one who is killed must be returned to life so that he may taste death."' [9:111]

فسألتُه هل كان لمسجد رسول الله ﷺ سقف؟ فقال: لا، وقد كان بعض أصحابه قال: ألا تسقف مسجدنا يا رسول الله؟ قال: عَريشٌ كعَريش موسى.

١٣٩. عن الحلبي، عن أبي عبدالله عليه السلام، قال: سألتُه عن قول الله تعالى: ﴿فِيهِ رِجَالٌ يُحِبُّونَ أَنْ يَتَطَهَّرُوا﴾. قال: الّذين يُحبّون أن يتطهّروا نظف الوضوء، وهو الاستنجاء بالماء. وقال: قال عليه السلام: نزلت هذه الآية في أهل قُبا.

١٤٠. وفي رواية ابن سِنان، عنه عليه السلام، قال: قلتُ له: ما ذلك الطُّهر؟ قال: نظف الوضوء، إذا خرج أحدهم من الغائط، فمدحهم الله بِتطهُّرهم.

١٤١. عن زُرارة، قال: كرِهتُ أن أسأل أبا جعفر عليه السلام في الرجعة، فاحتلتُ مسألة لطيفة أبلُغُ فيها حاجتي. فقلتُ: جُعِلت فداك، أخبِرني عمّن قُتِل مات؟ قال: لا، الموتُ موتٌ، والقتلُ قتلٌ.

قال: فقلتُ له: ما أحدٌ يُقتَل إلّا مات. قال: فقال: يا زُرارة، قول الله أصدق من قولك، قد فرّق بينهما في القرآن، قال: ﴿أَفَإِنْ مَاتَ أَوْ قُتِلَ﴾، وقال ﴿وَلَئِنْ مُتُّمْ أَوْ قُتِلْتُمْ لَإِلَى اللَّهِ تُحْشَرُونَ﴾، ليس كما قلتَ يا زُرارة، الموت موت، والقتل قتل، وقد قال الله: ﴿إِنَّ اللَّهَ اشْتَرَى مِنَ الْمُؤْمِنِينَ أَنْفُسَهُمْ وَأَمْوَالَهُمْ بِأَنَّ لَهُمُ الْجَنَّةَ﴾ الآية.

قال: فقلتُ له: إنّ الله يقول: ﴿كُلُّ نَفْسٍ ذَائِقَةُ الْمَوْتِ﴾ أفرأيت من قُتِل لَم يذُق الموت؟

قال: فقال: ليس من قُتِل بالسيف كمن مات على فِراشه، إنّ من قُتِل لا بُدَّ من أن يرجع إلى الدنيا حتّى يذُوق الموت.

142. From Abū Baṣīr, from Abū Jaʿfar ﵇. He said, 'I asked him about God's verse: ﴾*God has purchased the persons and possessions of the believers in return for the Garden – they fight in God's way: they kill and are killed – this is a true promise given by Him in the Torah, the Gospel, and the Qur'ān. Who could be more faithful to his promise than God? So be happy with the bargain you have made: that is the supreme triumph.*﴿' He replied, "It refers to the covenant."' He said, 'Then I read to him: ﴾*al-tā'ibūn al-ʿābidūn... those who turn to God in repentance; who worship and praise Him...*﴿ So Abū Jaʿfar said, "No, read it as ﴾*al-tā'ibīn al-ʿābidīn*﴿ He also said, "When you see these people, then you will understand that these are the ones whose souls and possessions have been purchased from them, i.e. during the *rajʿa*."' [9:111]

143. From Muḥammad b. al-Ḥasan, from al-Ḥusayn b. Khurrazād, from al-Barqī regarding this particular narration, after which he said, 'Every single believer experiences both a death and a killing. Whoever dies is resurrected that he may be killed, and whoever is killed is resurrected that he may experience death.' [9:111]

144. From Ṣabbāḥ b. Sayāba regarding God's verse: ﴾*God has purchased the persons and possessions of the believers.*﴿ He said, 'He said, "Then He goes on to describe them saying: ﴾*those who turn to God in repentance; who worship and praise Him; who bow down and prostrate themselves; who order what is good and forbid what is wrong and who observe God's limits. Give glad news to such believers.*﴿" He continued, "They are the Imams, peace be upon them."' [9:111]

145. From ʿAbd Allāh b. Maymūn al-Qaddāḥ[31], from Abū ʿAbd Allāh ﵇ who said, 'When ʿAlī would set out into the battlefield he would call out with these supplications: "O God, You have shown me one of Your paths wherein you have placed Your pleasure and have urged Your friends towards it. You have designated it to be the noblest of Your paths in Your regard, the worthiest reward and the most beloved course to You. Then You purchased

31 ʿAbd Allāh b. Maymūn al-Aswad al-Qaddāḥ, client of the Banū Makhzūm, was a reliable transmitter of Imam Jaʿfar al-Ṣādiq's traditions. See Ḥillī, *Khulāṣat al-aqwāl*, 197 (nr. 614); Modarressi, *Tradition and Survival*, 145–50 (nr. 12).

١٤٢. عن أبي بصير، عن أبي جعفر ﷺ، قال: سألتُه عن قول الله: ﴿إِنَّ اللَّهَ اشْتَرَىٰ مِنَ الْمُؤْمِنِينَ أَنفُسَهُمْ وَأَمْوَالَهُم بِأَنَّ لَهُمُ الْجَنَّةَ﴾ الآية، قال: يعني في الميثاق.

قال: ثمّ قرأتُ عليه: ﴿التَّائِبُونَ الْعَابِدُونَ﴾، فقال أبو جعفر ﷺ: لا، ولكن اقرأها (التَّائِبِينَ الْعَابِدِينَ) إلى آخر الآية: وقال: إذا رأيت هؤلاء فعند ذلك هؤلاء اشترى منهم أنفسهم وأموالهم، يعني في الرَّجعة.

١٤٣. محمّد بن الحسن، عن الحسين بن خُرّزاد، عن البرقي — في هذا الحديث — ثمّ قال: ما من مؤمنٍ إلاّ وله مِيتَة وقَتلة، مَن مات بُعِث حتّى يُقتَل، ومن قُتِل يُبعَث حتّى يموت.

١٤٤. صبّاح بن سَيابة، في قول الله: ﴿إِنَّ اللَّهَ اشْتَرَىٰ مِنَ الْمُؤْمِنِينَ أَنفُسَهُمْ وَأَمْوَالَهُم﴾، قال: ثمّ قال: ثمّ وصفهم فقال: ﴿التَّائِبُونَ الْعَابِدُونَ الْحَامِدُونَ﴾ الآية، قال: هم الأئمّة عليهم السلام.

١٤٥. عن عبدالله بن ميمون القدّاح، عن أبي عبدالله ﷺ، قال: كان عليّ ﷺ إذا أراد القِتال قال هذه الدعوات: «اللّهمّ إنّك أعلَمتَ سبيلاً من سُبلك، جَعلتَ فيه رِضاك، وندَبتَ إليه أولياءك، وجَعلتَه أشرفَ سُبلك عندك ثوابًا، وأكرَمها إليك مآبًا، وأحبَّها إليك مَسلكًا، ثمّ اشتريتَ فيه من المؤمنين أنفسهم وأموالهم بأنّ لهم الجنّة، يُقاتلون في سبيل الله فَيقتُلون ويُقتَلون، وَعدًا عليه حقًّا، فاجعلني مِمّن اشتريتَ فيه منك نفسهُ، ثمّ وفيَ لك ببيعته الّتي بايعك عليها غير ناكثٍ، ولا ناقضٍ عهدًا، ولا مُبدّلاً تبديلاً، مختصر.

from the believers thereupon their souls and possessions in return for the Garden, that they may fight in God's way, to either kill or be killed – this is a true promise. So make me one whose soul you have purchased, and who then fulfills to You his pledge that he has made with You, never turning back on it, breaking it or altering it in any way." [9:111]

146. From ʿAbd al-Raḥīm, from Abū Jaʿfar عليه السلام. He said, 'He recited the verse: ﴾*God has purchased the persons and possessions of the believers in return for the Garden*﴿ and then said, "Do you know what it means?" So I replied, "That the believers should fight, then kill and be killed."' He continued, "No, it is that whoever from among the believers dies, he will be returned to life that he may be killed, and whoever is killed will be returned that he may experience death. This is the Divine decree so do not spurn it."' [9:111]

147. From Yūnus b. ʿAbd al-Raḥmān, from Abū ʿAbd Allāh عليه السلام that he said, 'If someone arrests a thief then pardons him [then that is up to him], but when it [i.e. the case] is taken to the imam, he can amputate him. A grant of pardon can only be given before he is referred to the imam? This is what God's words: ﴾*who observe God's limits*﴿ mean. So if the case goes as far as the imam to penalize, then no one has the right to let him go.' [9:111]

148. From Ibrāhīm b. Abī al-Bilād, from some of his associates who said, 'Abū ʿAbd Allāh عليه السلام asked, "What is the opinion of the majority on God's verse: ﴾*Ibrāhīm only asked forgiveness for his father because he had made a promise to him*﴿?" I said, "They say that Ibrāhīm had promised his father that he would seek forgiveness for him."

He said, "That is not the case. Ibrāhīm made him promise that he would submit [to God] then sought forgiveness for him, but when he realized that he was an enemy of God, he renounced him."' [9:114]

149. From Zurāra, from Abū Jaʿfar عليه السلام. He said, 'I asked about His verse: ﴾*Ibrāhīm was tender-hearted and forbearing.*﴿ He replied, "The tender-hearted is one who supplicates a lot."' [9:114]

150. From Abū Isḥāq al-Hamadānī, from a man who said, 'A man was praying next to me and he sought forgiveness for his parents who had died in the

١٤٦. عن عبد الرّحيم، عن أبي جعفر عليه السلام، قال: قرأ هذه الآية ﴿إِنَّ اللهَ اشْتَرَى مِنَ الْمُؤْمِنِينَ أَنفُسَهُمْ وَأَمْوَالَهُم بِأَنَّ لَهُمُ الْجَنَّةَ﴾ فقال: هل تدري ما يعني؟ فقلتُ: يُقاتل المؤمنون فيقتُلون ويُقتَلون.

قال: لا ولكن مَن مات من المؤمنين رُدَّ حتّى يُقتَل، ومَن قُتِل رُدّ حتّى يمُوت، وتلك القدرة فلا تُنكِرها.

١٤٧. عن يُونس بن عبد الرّحمن، عن أبي عبد الله عليه السلام، أنّه قال: من أخذ سارقًا فعفا عنه [فذلك له]، فإذا رُفِع إلى الإمام قَطعه، وإنّما الهِبَة قبل أن يُرفع إلى الإمام، وذلك قول الله: ﴿وَالْحَافِظُونَ لِحُدُودِ اللهِ﴾ فإذا انتهى الحدّ إلى الإمام، فليس لأحدٍ أن يَترُكه.

١٤٨. عن إبراهيم بن أبي البلاد، عن بعض أصحابه، قال: قال أبو عبد الله عليه السلام: ما يقول الناس في قول الله تعالى: ﴿وَمَا كَانَ اسْتِغْفَارُ إِبْرَاهِيمَ لِأَبِيهِ إِلَّا عَن مَّوْعِدَةٍ وَعَدَهَا إِيَّاهُ﴾؟.

قلت: يقولون: إنّ إبراهيم عليه السلام وعد أباه ليستغفر له. قال: ليس هو هكذا، إنّ إبراهيم عليه السلام وعده أن يُسلِم فاستَغفَر له، فلمّا تبيّن له أنّه عدُوٌّ لله تبرّأ منه.

١٤٩. عن زُرارة، عن أبي جعفر عليه السلام، قال: قلتُ: قوله: ﴿إِنَّ إِبْرَاهِيمَ لَأَوَّاهٌ حَلِيمٌ﴾؟ قال: الأوّاه: الدّعّاء.

١٥٠. عن أبي إسحاق الهمداني، عن رجل، قال: صلّى رجلٌ إلى جنبي، فاستغفر لأبويه، وكانا ماتا في الجاهليّة. فقلتُ: تستغفر لأبويك، وقد ماتا في الجاهليّة؟ فقال: قد استغفر

state of pre-Islamic paganism. So I said to him, "You are seeking forgiveness for your parents whilst they died in the state of paganism?" So he replied, "Ibrāhīm too sought forgiveness for his father." I did not know how to respond to him, so I mentioned it to the Prophet ﷺ; then God revealed: ﴿*Ibrāhīm only asked forgiveness for his father because he had made a promise to him, but once he realized that his father was an enemy of God, he washed his hands of him.*﴾ He said, "When he died, he realized that he was an enemy of God, so he stopped seeking forgiveness for him."' [9:114]

151. From 'Alī b. Abī Ḥamza who said, 'I said to Abū al-Ḥasan عليه السلام [al-Kāẓim], "Your father had informed us of his descendant after him, so why do you not also tell us?" So he took my hand and shook it, then said: ﴿*God would not allow to stray those He has already guided* [*to the faith*] *before making entirely clear to them what they should avoid.*﴾' He said, 'Then I dropped my head drowsily, so he said to me, "No, do not accustom your eyes to much sleep for they are the most ungrateful part of the body."' [9:115]

152. From 'Abd al-A'lā who said, 'I asked Abū 'Abd Allāh عليه السلام about God's verse: ﴿*God would not allow to stray those He has already guided* [*to the faith*] *before making entirely clear to them what they should avoid.*﴾ He said, "Until He makes known to them what pleases Him and what displeases Him." Then he said, "However we would censure a believer for committing something in ignorance that God Himself does not excuse from [lay] people. Stopping in the face of ambiguity is better than rushing headlong into destruction, and desisting from narrating a report that you have not memorised is better for you than transmitting a report you have not accounted for. Every truth has a reality above it and every correct course a light. Take whatever corresponds with God's Book, and whatever contradicts it cast it aside. Many people in this world, however, will not cast it aside."' [9:115]

153. From 'Alī b. Abī Ḥamza, from Abū 'Abd Allāh عليه السلام. He said, 'I asked him about God's verse: ﴿*And to the three men who stayed behind.*﴾ He said, "Ka'b, Murāra b. al-Rabī' and Hilāl b. Umayya."' [9:118]

إبراهيم لأبيه، فلم أدرِ ما أرُدّ عليه، فذكرت ذلك للنبيّ ﷺ، فأنزل الله: ﴿وَمَا كَانَ اسْتِغْفَارُ إِبْرَاهِيمَ لِأَبِيهِ إِلَّا عَنْ مَوْعِدَةٍ وَعَدَهَا إِيَّاهُ فَلَمَّا تَبَيَّنَ لَهُ أَنَّهُ عَدُوٌّ لِلَّهِ تَبَرَّأَ مِنْهُ﴾ قال: لمّا مات تبيّن أنّه عدوٌّ لله، فلم يستغفر له.

١٥١. عن عليّ بن أبي حمزة، قال: قلتُ لأبي الحسن عليه السلام: إنّ أباك أخبرنا بالخَلف من بعده، فلو أخبرتنا به؟ قال: فأخذ بيدي فهزّها، ثمّ قال: ﴿وَمَا كَانَ اللَّهُ لِيُضِلَّ قَوْمًا بَعْدَ إِذْ هَدَاهُمْ حَتَّى يُبَيِّنَ لَهُمْ مَا يَتَّقُونَ﴾ قال: فخفقتُ، فقال لي: مَه، لا تُعوّدِ عينيك كَثرة النوم، فإنّها أقلّ شيءٍ في الجَسَد شُكرًا.

١٥٢. عن عبد الأعلى، قال: سألتُ أبا عبد الله عليه السلام عن قول الله: ﴿وَمَا كَانَ اللَّهُ لِيُضِلَّ قَوْمًا بَعْدَ إِذْ هَدَاهُمْ حَتَّى يُبَيِّنَ لَهُمْ مَا يَتَّقُونَ﴾ قال: حتّى يُعرّفهم ما يُرضيه وما يُسخِطه.

ثمّ قال: أمّا إنّا أنكرنا لمؤمن بما لا يَعذِر اللهُ الناس بجَهالته، والوقوف عند الشُّبهة خيرٌ من الاقتحام في الهَلَكة، وترك رواية حديثٍ لم تَحفَظ خيرٌ لك من رواية حديثٍ لم تُحصه، إنّ على كُلّ حقٍّ حقيقة، وعلى كُلّ صوابٍ نُورًا، فما وافق كتاب الله فخُذوه، وما خالف كتاب الله فَدعُوه، ولن يَدَعَهُ كثيرٌ من أهل هذا العالَم.

١٥٣. عن عليّ بن أبي حمزة، عن أبي عبد الله عليه السلام، قال: سألتُه عن قول الله: ﴿وَعَلَى الثَّلَاثَةِ الَّذِينَ خُلِّفُوا﴾ قال: كعب، ومُرارة بن الرّبيع، وهلال ابن أميّة.

154. From Fayḍ b. al-Mukhtār who said, 'Abū 'Abd Allāh عليه السلام asked, "How do you read this verse from the Chapter of the Impunity: ﴾*And to the three men who were left behind*﴿?' He said, 'I said, "They were left behind." He said, "If they were left behind, then that would mean that they were in a prior state of obedience."'

Al-Ḥusayn b. al-Mukhtār added to this on his authority, 'And if they had been left behind then there would be no blame against them. Rather they opposed 'Uthmān and his two companions. However, by God, no sooner did they hear the sound of hooves and the clanging of weapons than they exclaimed: 'We are coming.' So God let fear encompass them until they came to their senses.' [9:118]

155. Ṣafwān said, 'Abū 'Abd Allāh عليه السلام said, "Abū Lubāba was one of them, meaning one of ﴾*the three men who were left behind*﴿"' [9:118]

156. From Sallām, from Abū Ja'far عليه السلام regarding His verse: ﴾*He turned to them in mercy in order for them to return* [*to Him*].﴿ He said, 'He acquitted them, but they did not repent.' [9:118]

157. From Abū Ḥamza al-Thumālī who said, 'Abū Ja'far عليه السلام said, "O Abū Ḥamza, only those who truly know God worship him. As for those who do not know God, it is as if they worship other than Him; that is how they stray."

I said, "May God make you prosper – what is true knowledge of God?"

He replied, "It is to believe God and believe Muḥammad, the Messenger of God صلى الله عليه وآله about the adherence to 'Alī and taking him as the Imam, as well as the Imams of guidance after him, and to disassociate from their enemies unto God. This is true knowledge of God."'

He said, 'I asked, "May God make you prosper – what one thing can I do to perfect the reality of my faith?"

He replied, "Take God's friends as allies and His enemies as enemies. Then you will indeed stand with those who are true as God has commanded you to be."'

He said, 'I asked, "So who are God's friends and who are His enemies?"

He replied, "God's friends are Muḥammad, the Messenger of God, 'Alī, al-Ḥasan, al-Ḥusayn, 'Alī b. al-Ḥusayn, then the authority passed on to us, then to my son Ja'far," pointing to Ja'far, who was sitting there, "Whoever

١٥٤. عن فَيض بن المُختار، قال: قال أبو عبدالله عليه السلام: كيف تقرأ هذه الآية في التوبة: ﴿وَعَلَى الثَّلَاثَةِ الَّذِينَ خُلِّفُوا﴾؟ قال: قلت: ﴿خُلِّفُوا﴾.

قال: لو خُلِّفُوا لكانوا في حال طاعة — وزاد الحسين بن المُختار عنه: لو كانوا خُلّفوا ما كان عليهم من سبيل — ولكنّهم خالفوا، عثمان وصاحباه، أما والله ما سمِعوا صَوت حافرٍ ولا قَعقَعة حَجَر إلاّ قالوا أُتينا، فسلّط الله عليهم الخَوف حتّى أصبحوا.

١٥٥. قال صفوان: قال أبو عبدالله عليه السلام: كان أبو لُبابة أحدهم، يعني في آية ﴿وَعَلَى الثَّلَاثَةِ الَّذِينَ خُلِّفُوا﴾.

١٥٦. عن سلاّم، عن أبي جعفر عليه السلام، في قوله: ﴿ثُمَّ تَابَ عَلَيْهِمْ لِيَتُوبُوا﴾، قال: أقالهم فوالله ما تابوا.

١٥٧. عن أبي حمزة الثُّمالي، قال: قال أبو جعفر عليه السلام: يا أبا حمزة، إنّما يعبُد الله من عرف الله، فأمّا من لا يَعرِف الله كأنّما يَعبُد غيره هكذا ضالاً.

قلتُ: أصلحك الله، وما معرفة الله؟ قال: يُصدّق الله ويُصدّق محمّدًا رسول الله صلى الله عليه وآله في مُوالاة عليّ عليه السلام والائتمام به وبأئمّة الهُدى من بعده، والبراءة إلى الله من عدوّهِم، وكذلك عِرفان الله.

قال: قلتُ: أصلحك الله، أيّ شيءٍ إذا عَمِلته أنا استكملت حقيقة الإيمان؟ قال عليه السلام: تُوالي أولياء الله، وتُعادي أعداء الله، وتكون مع الصادقين كما أمرك الله.

adheres to these has indeed adhered to God and stands with those who are true as God has commanded him to do."

I asked, "May God make you prosper – and who are God's enemies?"

He said, "The four idols."'

He said, 'I asked, "Who are they?"

He replied, "Abū al-Faṣīl, Ruma', Na'thal, and Mu'āwiya,[32] and those who follow their creed. So whoever takes them as enemies are indeed enemies of God's enemies."' [9:119]

158. Al-Mu'allā b. Khunays narrated that Abū 'Abd Allāh ﷺ said regarding His verse: ' ﴿*stand with those who are true*﴾ in their obedience.' [9:119]

159. From Hishām b. 'Ajalān who said, 'I said to Abū 'Abd Allāh ﷺ, "I want to ask you about something that I would not need to ask anyone else after you. I want to ask you about the extent of faith that people cannot afford to be ignorant of."

So he replied, "To bear witness that there is no deity but God, and that Muḥammad is God's messenger; to attest to what he brought from God, to establish the prayer, pay the alms, go for Hajj, fast in the month of Ramadan, adhere to us and disassociate from our enemies, and that you be with the veracious ones."' [9:119]

160. From Ya'qūb b. Shu'ayb, from Abū 'Abd Allāh ﷺ who said, 'I asked him, "If something were to happen to the Imam, what should the people do?" He replied, "They should be as God has commanded: ﴿*out of each community, a group should go out to gain understanding of the religion, so that they can teach their people when they return and so that they can guard themselves against evil.*﴾"'

He said, 'I asked, "What will their state [i.e. the people waiting] be?" He replied, "They will be absolved."' [9:122]

---

32 The first of these three names refer to Abū Bakr, 'Umar and 'Uthmān respectively. Abū Bakr was sometimes referred to as Abū al-Faṣīl; both *bakr* and *faṣīl* share similar meanings: namely a young weaned camel. Others have claimed that Abū Bakr's agnomen before his conversion to Islam was Abū al-Faṣīl, and that the agnomen Abū Bakr was assigned to him after his conversion. As for Ruma', it is simply an anagram of the name 'Umar. Na'thal is said to have been the name of a rash and short-tempered man, and since 'Uthmān shared these attributes he was covertly referred to by this name.

قال: قلتُ: ومَن أولياء الله، ومن أعداء الله؟ فقال: أولياء الله محمّد رسول الله وعليّ والحسن والحسين وعليّ بن الحسين، ثمّ انتهى الأمر إلينا، ثمّ ابني جعفر – وأومأ إلى جعفر وهو جالس – فمن والى هؤلاء فقد والى أولياء الله، وكان مع الصادقين كما أمره الله.

قلت: ومَن أعداء الله، أصلحك الله؟ قال: الأوثان الأربعة، قال: قلتُ: من هم؟ قال: أبو الفصيل ورمع ونعثل ومعاوية، ومن دان بدينهم، فمن عادى هؤلاء فقد عادى أعداء الله.

١٥٨. وروى المُعلّى بن خُنيس، عن أبي عبد الله عليه السلام، في قوله: ﴿وَكُونُوا مَعَ الصَّادِقِينَ﴾ بِطاعتهم.

١٥٩. عن هِشام بن عجلان، قال: قلتُ لأبي عبد الله عليه السلام: أسألُكَ عن شيءٍ لا أسأل عنه أحدًا بعدك، أسألك عن الإيمان الذي لا يَسَع الناس جهلُه؟

فقال: شهادة أن لا إله إلاّ الله، وأن محمّدًا رسول الله، والإقرار بما جاء من عند الله، وإقام الصلاة، وإيتاء الزكاة، وحجّ البيت، وصوم شهر رمضان، والولاية لنا، والبراءة من عدوّنا، وتكون مع الصِدّيقين.

161. Also on his authority in another narration, 'What is your opinion about a community whose Imam has died – what should they do?' So he said to me, 'Have you not read God's Book: ﴾ *out of each community, a group should go out to gain understanding of the religion, so that they can teach their people when they return and so that they can guard themselves against evil.* ﴿' I said, 'May I be your ransom – what about the people who are waiting for the group who have gone to gain an understanding of religion to return?'

He said, 'So he said to me, "May God have mercy on you – did you know that there were two hundred and fifty years[33] between Muḥammad and 'Isā عليه السلام. So the people who died on the creed of 'Isā whilst waiting for Muḥammad's creed will be rewarded twice by God."' [9:122]

162. From Aḥmad b. Muḥammad, from Abū al-Ḥasan al-Riḍā عليه السلام. He said, 'He wrote to me saying, "Our followers (*shīʿa*) are those who follow us and do not oppose us. When we are in a state of fear, so are they. And when we feel secure, they do too." God has said: ﴾ *ask those who have knowledge* [*of the Reminder*] *if you do not know* ﴿ (16:43; 21:7) and ﴾ *out of each community, a group should go out to gain understanding of the religion, so that they can teach their people when they return and so that they can guard themselves against evil.* ﴿ You have been obligated to question and to refer to us, but we are not obliged to respond."' [9:122]

163. From 'Abd al-A'lā who said, 'I said to Abū 'Abd Allāh عليه السلام, "What [do we do] when we hear about the Imam's passing away?"

He replied, "You must hasten out."

I asked, "All of us together?"

He replied, "God says: ﴾ *Out of each community, a group should go out to gain understanding of the religion, so that they can teach their people when they return and so that they can guard themselves against evil.* ﴿"

I asked, "What if we leave and some of us die on the way?"'

He said, 'So he replied: ﴾ *and if anyone leaves home as a migrant towards God and His Messenger and is then overtaken by death, his reward from God is sure.* ﴿ (4:100)

33 The number of years which elapsed between 'Īsā and Muḥammad is clearly false in this tradition.

١٦٠. عن يعقوب بن شُعيب، عن أبي عبد الله عليه السلام، قال: قلتُ له: إذا حَدَثَ للإمام حَدثٌ، كيف يصنع الناس؟ قال: يكونوا كما قال الله: ﴿فَلَوْلَا نَفَرَ مِن كُلِّ فِرْقَةٍ مِّنْهُمْ طَائِفَةٌ لِّيَتَفَقَّهُوا فِي الدِّينِ﴾ إلى قوله: ﴿يَحْذَرُونَ﴾.

قال: قلتُ: فما حالهم؟ قال: هم في عُذر.

١٦١. وعنه أيضًا، في رواية أُخرى: ما تقول في قوم: هلك إمامهم، كيف يصنعون؟ قال: فقال لي: أما تقرأ كتاب الله ﴿فَلَوْلَا نَفَرَ مِن كُلِّ فِرْقَةٍ﴾ إلى قوله: ﴿يَحْذَرُونَ﴾؟

قلتُ: جُعِلتُ فداك، فما حال المُنتظِرين حتّى يرجع المُتفقّهون؟ قال: فقال لي: رحمك الله، أما علِمتَ أنّه كان بين محمّد وعيسى صلّى الله عليهما خمسون ومائتا سنة؟ فمات قوم على دين عيسى، انتِظارًا لدين محمّد صلى الله عليه وآله وسلم، فأتاهُم الله أجرهم مرّتين.

١٦٢. عن أحمد بن محمّد، عن أبي الحسن الرضا عليه السلام، قال: كتب إليّ: إنّما شيعتنا من تابعنا ولم يخالفنا، فإذا خفنا خاف، وإذا أمِنّا أمِن، قال الله: ﴿فَاسْأَلُوا أَهْلَ الذِّكْرِ إِن كُنتُمْ لَا تَعْلَمُونَ﴾، ﴿فَلَوْلَا نَفَرَ مِن كُلِّ فِرْقَةٍ مِّنْهُمْ طَائِفَةٌ﴾ الآية، فقد فُرِضت عليكم المسألة والردّ إلينا، ولم يُفرَض علينا الجواب.

١٦٣. عن عبد الأعلى، قال: قلتُ لأبي عبد الله عليه السلام: [إنْ] بلَغنا وفاة الإمام، [كيف نصنع]؟ قال: عليكم النّفر. قلتُ: جميعًا؟ قال: إنّ الله يقول: ﴿فَلَوْلَا نَفَرَ مِن كُلِّ فِرْقَةٍ مِّنْهُمْ طَائِفَةٌ لِّيَتَفَقَّهُوا فِي الدِّينِ﴾ الآية.

I said, "What if we were to go to Medina and find the rightful owner of this authority under house arrest, and have no access to him?"

He replied, "This authority can only be established by a manifest directive, whereby when you enter Medina and ask: To who did so and so bequeath [the authority] after him? They would say: To so and so."' [9:122]

164. From Abū Baṣīr who said, 'I heard Abū Jaʿfar ﷺ say, "Gain understanding of the religion, for one who does not do so from among you is like a desert Bedouin. God says in His Book: ﴾*they should go out to gain understanding of the religion, so that they can teach their people when they return and so that they can guard themselves against evil.*﴿"' [9:122]

165. From ʿImrān b. ʿAbd Allāh al-Qummī[34], from Jaʿfar b. Muḥammad ﷺ who said regarding God's verse: ﴾*Fight the disbelievers near you*﴿, 'The Daylamīs.'[35] [9:123]

166. From Zurāra b. Aʿyan, from Abū Jaʿfar ﷺ who said regarding: ﴾*But, as for the perverse at heart, each new Sūra adds further to their perversity*﴿, '[It adds] further doubt to their existing doubt.' [9:125]

167. From Thaʿlaba, from Abū ʿAbd Allāh ﷺ who said, 'God, Blessed and most High said: ﴾*A Messenger has come to you from among yourselves*﴿ This is about us. He said: ﴾*Your suffering distresses him*﴿ – this is also about us. He said: ﴾*he is deeply concerned for you*﴿ – also about us. And: ﴾*full of kindness and mercy towards the believers.*﴿ He said, 'This fourth phrase is shared between us and the believers, but the previous three phrases are exclusively about us.' [9:128]

---

34 ʿImrān b. ʿAbd Allāh al-Qummī, about whom there is considerable difference of opinion, was a narrator of Imam al-Ṣādiq's traditions. He is praised in traditions which he himself narrates from the Imam and cannot thus be relied on as a witness to his own reliability. Ḥillī suspends judgment on him, but the fact is that his reliability is unknown (*majhūl*) and undetermined. See Ḥillī, *Khulāṣat al-aqwāl*, 218–9 (nr. 721).

35 The Daylamites resided in what is modern-day Gilan and were a people who resisted all efforts made at converting them to Islam.

قلتُ: نفرنا، فمات بعضُنا في الطريق؟ قال: فقال: ﴿وَمَن يَخْرُجْ مِنْ بَيْتِهِ مُهَاجِرًا إِلَى اللَّهِ﴾ إلى قوله: ﴿أَجْرُهُ عَلَى اللَّهِ﴾.

قلتُ: فقَدِمنا المدينة، فوجدنا صاحب هذا الأمر مُغلقًا عليه بابه، مُرخى عليه سِتره؟ قال: إنّ هذا الأمر لا يكون إلاّ بأمرٍ بيّن، هو الذي إذا دخلتَ المدينة قلت: إلى من أوصى فلان؟ قالوا: إلى فلان.

١٦٤. عن أبي بصير، قال: سمِعتُ أبا جعفر ﷺ يقول: تفقَّهوا فإنَّ من لم يَتفقَّه منكم فإنّه أعرابيّ، إنّ الله يقول في كتابه: ﴿لِيَتَفَقَّهُوا فِي الدِّينِ﴾ إلى قوله: ﴿يَحْذَرُونَ﴾.

١٦٥. عن عِمران بن عبدالله القمّي، عن جعفر بن محمّد ﷺ، في قول الله تبارك وتعالى: ﴿قَاتِلُوا الَّذِينَ يَلُونَكُم مِّنَ الْكُفَّارِ﴾ قال: الدَّيلم.

١٦٦. عن زُرارة بن أعين، عن أبي جعفر ﷺ ﴿وَأَمَّا الَّذِينَ فِي قُلُوبِهِم مَّرَضٌ فَزَادَتْهُمْ رِجْسًا إِلَى رِجْسِهِمْ﴾ يقول: شكًّا إلى شكّهم.

١٦٧. عن ثعلبة، عن أبي عبدالله ﷺ، قال: قال الله تبارك وتعالى: ﴿لَقَدْ جَاءَكُمْ رَسُولٌ مِّنْ أَنفُسِكُمْ﴾ قال: فينا، ﴿عَزِيزٌ عَلَيْهِ مَا عَنِتُّمْ﴾ قال: فينا، ﴿حَرِيصٌ عَلَيْكُم﴾ قال: فينا، ﴿بِالْمُؤْمِنِينَ رَءُوفٌ رَّحِيمٌ﴾ قال: شركَنا المؤمنون في هذه الرابعة، وثلاثة لنا.

168. From ʿAbd Allāh b. Sulaymān, from Abū Jaʿfar ﷺ. He said, 'He recited this verse: ﴾*A Messenger has come to you from among yourselves*﴿, saying, "From among ourselves." Then: ﴾*Your suffering distresses him*﴿ – saying, "Our suffering." ﴾*he is deeply concerned for you*﴿ – "[concerned] for us." ﴾*full of kindness and mercy towards the believers.*﴿ – "Full of mercy and kindness towards our followers (*shīʿa*). So three of the four phrases apply to us, and the last one applies to our followers (*shīʿa*)."' [9:128]

١٦٨. عن عبد الله بن سليمان، عن أبي جعفر عليه السلام، قال: تلا هذه الآية ﴿لَقَدْ جَاءَكُمْ رَسُولٌ مِنْ أَنفُسِكُمْ﴾ قال: مِن أنفسنا. قال: ﴿عَزِيزٌ عَلَيْهِ مَا عَنِتُّمْ﴾ قال: ما عَنِتْنَا، قال: ﴿حَرِيصٌ عَلَيْكُمْ﴾ قال: علينا، ﴿بِالْمُؤْمِنِينَ رَءُوفٌ رَحِيمٌ﴾ قال: بشيعتنا رؤوفٌ رحيمٌ، فلنا ثلاثة أرباعها، ولشيعتنا رُبعها.

Yūnus

10. Yūnus

1. From Abān b. ʿUthmān, from Muḥammad who said, ʿAbū Jaʿfar ﷺ said, "Recite."

I asked, "What shall I recite from?"

He said, "[Recite] from the Seventh Chapter."'

He said, "So I began to look for it."

Then he said, "Recite the Chapter of Jonah."

So I recited it until I reached: ﴿*Those who did well will have the best reward and more besides. Neither darkness nor shame will cover their faces*﴾(10:26). He said, "That is enough. God's Messenger ﷺ said, 'It amazes me how my hair does not turn white whenever I recite the Qurʾan.'" [10:26]

2. From Fuḍayl al-Rassān[1], from Abū ʿAbd Allāh ﷺ who said, 'Whoever recites the Chapter of Jonah (*sūra Yūnus*) once every two or three months need not fear about being categorised among the ignorant ones. On the Day of Judgement, he will be among those who are in the proximity of God.'

3. From Yūnus, from whoever mentioned it regarding God's verse ﴿*and give glad news to those who believe, that they are on a sure footing with their Lord*﴾: '[This refers to] authority (*walāya*).' [10:2]

4. From Yūnus b. ʿAbd al-Raḥmān, from Abū ʿAbd Allāh ﷺ who said regarding His verse ﴿*and give glad news to those who believe, that they are on a sure footing with their Lord*﴾: '[This refers to] authority (*walāya*).' [10:2]

---

1 Fuḍayl b. al-Zubayr al-Rassān, a companion of the fifth and sixth Imams. See Khūʾī, *Muʿjam*, 14:346–7 (nr. 9430).

بسم الله الرحمن الرحيم

من سورة يونس

١. عن أبان بن عثمان، عن محمّد، قال: قال أبو جعفر عليه السلام: اقرأ.

قلتُ: من أيّ شيء أقرأ؟ قال: اقرأ من السورة السابعة، قال: فجعلتُ ألتمسها، فقال: اقرأ سورة يونس، فقرأتُ حتّى انتهيتُ إلى ﴿لِلَّذِينَ أَحْسَنُوا الْحُسْنَىٰ وَزِيَادَةٌ ۖ وَلَا يَرْهَقُ وُجُوهَهُمْ قَتَرٌ وَلَا ذِلَّةٌ﴾ ثمّ قال: حسبُك، قال رسول الله صلّى الله عليه وآله: «إني لأعجب كيف لا أشيبُ إذا قرأت القرآن».

٢. عن فُضيل الرسّان، عن أبي عبد الله عليه السلام، قال: من قرأ سورة يونس في كل شهرين أو ثلاثة، لم يَخَف أن يكون من الجاهلين، وكان يوم القيامة من المقرّبين.

٣. عن يونس، عمّن ذكره، في قول الله: ﴿وَبَشِّرِ الَّذِينَ آمَنُوا﴾ إلى آخر الآية، قال عليه السلام: الولاية.

٤. عن يونس بن عبد الرحمن، عن أبي عبد الله عليه السلام، في قوله: ﴿وَبَشِّرِ الَّذِينَ آمَنُوا أَنَّ لَهُمْ قَدَمَ صِدْقٍ عِنْدَ رَبِّهِمْ﴾، قال: الولاية.

5. From Ibrāhīm b. ʿUmar, from whoever mentioned it from Abū ʿAbd Allāh عليه السلام who said regarding God's verse ﴾ *and give glad news to those who believe, that they are on a sure footing with their Lord* ﴿ : 'This is the Messenger of God صلى الله عليه وآله.' [10:2]

6. From Abū Jaʿfar, from a man from Abū ʿAbd Allāh عليه السلام who said, ﴾ *Your Lord is God who created the heavens and earth in six Days* ﴿ – so six days are missing from the year.' [10:3]

7. From al-Ṣabbāḥ b. Sayāba, from Abū Jaʿfar عليه السلام who said, 'God created the months to be twelve, equaling three hundred and sixty days in total. Then He subtracted six of those days within which He created the heavens and the earth, so some months were shorter than others.' [10:3]

8. From Jābir, from Abū Jaʿfar عليه السلام who said, 'The Commander of the Faithful عليه السلام said, "God – exalted be His mention and sanctified His Names – created the earth before the sky, then He established Himself on the Throne to govern everything."' [10:3]

9. From Zayd al-Shaḥḥām, from Abū ʿAbd Allāh عليه السلام. He said, 'I asked him about the glorification, so he replied, "It is one of the Names of God and the imploration of the people of the Garden."' [10:3]

10. From al-Thumālī, from Abū Jaʿfar عليه السلام regarding God's verse ﴾ *When Our clear revelations are recited to them, those who do not expect to meet with Us say, 'Bring [us] a different Qur'an, or change it.' [Prophet], say, 'It is not for me to change it of my own accord; I only follow what is revealed to me* ﴿ : 'They said, "Change ʿAlī's position for Abū Bakr or ʿUmar so that we may follow them instead."' [10:15]

٥. عن إبراهيم بن عمر، عمّن ذكره، عن أبي عبد الله عليه السلام، في قول الله تعالى: ﴿وَبَشِّرِ الَّذِينَ آمَنُوا أَنَّ لَهُمْ قَدَمَ صِدْقٍ عِنْدَ رَبِّهِمْ﴾، قال هو رسول الله صلى الله عليه وآله.

٦. عن أبي جعفر، عن رجلٍ، عن أبي عبد الله عليه السلام، قال: إنّ الله خلق السّماوات والأرض في ستّة أيّام، فالسَّنة تنقُص ستَّة أيّام.

٧. عن الصبّاح بن سيّابة، عن أبي جعفر عليه السلام، قال: إنّ الله خلق الشهور اثنا عشر شهرًا، وهي ثلاثمائة وستّون يومًا، فحجر منها ستّة أيّام، خلق فيها السماوات والأرض، فمن ثمّ تقاصرت الشهور.

٨. عن جابر، عن أبي جعفر عليه السلام، قال: قال أمير المؤمنين صلى الله عليه وآله: إنّ الله جلّ ذكره وتقدّست أسماؤه خَلَق الأرض قبل السماء، ثمّ استوى على العرش لتدبير الأمور.

٩. عن زيد الشحّام، عن أبي عبد الله عليه السلام، قال: سألتُه عن التسبيح، فقال: هو اسم من أسماء الله، ودعوى أهل الجنّة.

١٠. عن الثمالي، عن أبي جعفر عليه السلام، فيقول الله تعالى: ﴿وَإِذَا تُتْلَى عَلَيْهِمْ آيَاتُنَا بَيِّنَاتٍ قَالَ الَّذِينَ لا يَرْجُونَ لِقَاءَنَا ائْتِ بِقُرْآنٍ غَيْرِ هَذَا أَوْ بَدِّلْهُ قُلْ مَا يَكُونُ لِي أَنْ أُبَدِّلَهُ مِنْ تِلْقَاءِ نَفْسِي إِنْ أَتَّبِعُ إِلاَّ مَا يُوحَى إِلَيَّ﴾ قالوا: لو بُدِّل مكان عليّ أبو بكر أو عمر اتَّبعناه.

11. From Abū al-Safātij, from Abū ʿAbd Allāh عليه السلام regarding God's verse: ﴾*Bring* [*us*] *a different Qurʾan, or change it*﴿, 'It means the Commander of the Faithful عليه السلام.' [10:15]

12. From Manṣūr b. Ḥāzim, from Abū ʿAbd Allāh عليه السلام who said, 'The Messenger of God صلى الله عليه وآله continuously used to say ﴾*I fear the torment of an awesome Day, if I were to disobey my Lord*﴿ until the Chapter of the Victory (*sūrat al-fatḥ*) was revealed, after which he never again repeated those words.' [10:15]

13. From Manṣūr b. Yūnus, from Abū ʿAbd Allāh عليه السلام: 'Three things backfire against their perpetrators: treachery, rebellion and deception. God says: ﴾*Your outrageous behaviour only works against yourselves.*﴿' [10:23]

14. From al-Fuḍayl b. Yasār who said, 'I said to Abū Jaʿfar عليه السلام, "May I be your ransom – we talk about the family of Jaʿfar having a flag [of governorship] and the family of so-and-so having a flag, so does that have any significance?"

So he replied, "As for the family of Jaʿfar having a flag, no. The flag of Banū so-and-so, however, they have a lagging kingdom, where what once seemed far-off is now slowly approaching; and they are only delaying what is imminent. Their government is full of hardship not ease, and they have no markers of goodness in their authority at all. They are gripped by deep anxieties, all of which are manifest. And even though they may consider themselves safe from God's plot and secure from His chastisement, they will soon come to know that they are as bad as the disbelievers. There will only be a single blast to smite them after which not even a street-caller will remain to listen to them or join them.

This is the purport of God's words: ﴾*But when the earth has taken on its finest appearance, and adorns itself, and its people think they have power over it, then the fate We commanded comes to it, by night or by day, and We reduce it to stubble, as if it had not flourished just the day before. This is the way We explain the revelations for those who reflect.*﴿ Usually, tyrannical rulers have some remnants left after them, but not the family of so-and-so: they will have no remnant."

He said, 'May I be your ransom – they will not have any remnants?'

١١. عن أبي السفاتج، عن أبي عبدالله عليه السلام، فيقول الله: ﴿آتِ بِقُرآنٍ غَيرِ هَذا أَو بَدِّلهُ﴾ يعني أمير المؤمنين عليه السلام.

١٢. عن منصور بن حازم، عن أبي عبدالله عليه السلام، قال: لم يَزَل رسول الله صلى الله عليه وآله يقول: ﴿إِنّي أَخافُ إِن عَصَيتُ رَبّي عَذابَ يَومٍ عَظيمٍ﴾ حتّى نزلت سورة الفتح، فلم يَعُد إلى ذلك الكلام.

١٣. عن منصور بن يونس، عن أبي عبدالله عليه السلام، قال: ثلاث يَرجِعن على صاحبهنّ: النَّكث، والبَغي، والمكر، قال الله: ﴿يا أَيُّهَا النّاسُ إِنَّما بَغيُكُم عَلى أَنفُسِكُم﴾.

١٤. عن الفُضيل بن يسار، قال: قلتُ لأبي جعفر عليه السلام: جُعِلت فِداك، إنّا نتحدّث أن لآل جعفر راية، ولآل فلان راية، فهل في ذلك شيء؟

فقال: أمّا لآل جعفر فلا، وأمّا راية بني فلان، فإنّ لهم ملكًا مبطئًا، يُقرّبون فيه البعيد، ويُبعّدون فيه القريب، وسُلطانهم عسرٌ ليس فيه يُسر، لا يعرِفون في سُلطانهم من أعلام الخير شيئًا، تصيبهم فيه فَزَعات، كلّ ذلك يتجلّى عنهم، حتّى إذا أمِنوا مَكر الله وأمِنوا عذابه، وظنّوا أنّهم قد استقرّوا، صِيح فيهم صَيحةٌ، لم يكن لهم فيها منادٍ يَسمعهم ولا يَجمعهم، وذلك قول الله: ﴿حَتّى إِذا أَخَذَتِ الأَرضُ زُخرُفَها﴾ إلى قوله ﴿لِقَومٍ يَتَفَكَّرونَ﴾ ألا إنّهُ ليس أحدٌ من الظّلمة إلاّ ولهم بُقيا إلاّ آل فلان، فإنّهم لا بُقيا لهم.

قال: جُعِلت فداك، أليس لهم بُقيا؟ قال: بلى، ولكنّهم يُصيبون منّا دمًا، فيظلمهم نحن وشيعتنا، ومن يظلمه نحن وشيعتنا فلا بُقيا له.

He replied, "No. They will instead be killed off and obliterated by us, and whomever we and our followers (*shīʿa*) obliterate have no remnants left."' [10:24]

15. From al-Fuḍayl b. Yasār who said, 'I heard Abū Jaʿfar ﷷ say, "The Messenger of God ﷺ said, 'Any servant of God whose eyes overflow with tears, God will prohibit the Fire from touching his body; and no sooner does an eye well up with tears from the awe of God than neither darkness nor shame will ever cover that face."' [10:27]

16. From Muḥammad b. Marwān[2], from a man from Abū Jaʿfar ﷷ who said, 'Every single thing has a [proportionate] weight and reward except for tears, for a single tear drop can extinguish seas of Fire; and when one's eyes overflow with tears, God, Mighty and Exalted, will prohibit the Fire from touching even the rest of his body. If the tears flow onto his cheeks, his face will never be covered with darkness nor shame. And if a servant were to cry for an entire community, God would have mercy on it.' [10:27]

17. From Abū Baṣīr, from Abū ʿAbd Allāh ﷷ who said regarding God's verse: ﴾*as though their faces were covered with veils cut from the darkness of the night*﴿: 'Have you not seen how at night, it is darker inside the house than outside? Similarly, their faces will be intensely dark.' [10:27]

18. From ʿAmr b. al-Qāsim[3] who said, 'I heard Abū ʿAbd Allāh ﷷ while mentioning the companions of the Prophet ﷺ reciting: ﴾*Is someone who shows the way to the Truth more worthy to be followed, or someone who cannot find the way unless he himself is shown? What is the matter with you? How do you judge?*﴿ So we asked, 'May God grant you the best – who is it referring to?' He replied, "We have heard that it is ʿAlī [b. Abī Ṭālib]."' [10:35]

2 Muḥammad b. Marwān al-Ḥannāṭ of Medina was a reliable but infrequent narrator of Imam al-Bāqir's traditions. See Ḥillī, *Khulāṣat al-aqwāl*, 262 (nr. 920).

3 There are at least three individuals by this name in Khūʾī's *Muʿjam*: ʿAmr b. al-Qāsim, ʿAmr b. al-Qāsim al-Majāshiʿī and ʿAmr b. al-Qāsim al-Najāshī – all of whom were companions of Imam Jaʿfar al-Ṣādiq. See Khūʾī, *Muʿjam*, 14:133 (nr. 8980, 8981, 8982).

١٥. عن الفُضيل بن يسار، قال سمعتُ أبا جعفر عليه السلام يقول: قال رسول الله صلى الله عليه وآله: ما من عبدٍ اغرورقت عيناه بمائها إلاّ حرّم الله ذلك الجسد على النار، وما فاضت عينٌ من خَشية الله إلاّ لم يرهَق ذلك الوجه قترٌ ولا ذِلّةٌ.

١٦. عن محمّد بن مروان، عن رجال، عن أبي جعفر عليه السلام، قال: ما من شيءٍ إلاّ وله وزر أو ثوابٌ إلاّ الدموع، فإنّ القطرة تُطفئ البحار من النار، فإذا اغرورقَت عيناه بمائها حرّم الله عزّ وجلّ سائر جسده على النار، وإن سالت الدموع على خدّيه لم يَرهَق وجهه قَترٌ ولا ذِلّة، ولو أنّ عبدًا بكى في أمّة لرَحِمها الله.

١٧. عن أبي بصير، عن أبي عبدالله عليه السلام، في قول الله: ﴿كَأَنَّمَا أُغۡشِيَتۡ وُجُوهُهُمۡ قِطَعٗا مِّنَ ٱلَّيۡلِ مُظۡلِمًا﴾، قال: أما ترى البيت إذا كان الليل كان أشدّ سوادًا من خارج؟ فكذلك وجوههم تزداد سوادًا.

١٨. عن عمرو بن القاسم، قال: سَمِعتُ أبا عبدالله عليه السلام وذكر أصحاب النبيّ صلى الله عليه وآله، ثمّ قرأ ﴿أَفَمَن يَهۡدِيٓ إِلَى ٱلۡحَقِّ أَحَقُّ أَن يُتَّبَعَ﴾ إلى قوله ﴿تَحۡكُمُونَ﴾ فقلنا: مَن هو، أصلحك الله؟ فقال: بلغنا أنّ ذلك عليّ عليه السلام.

19. From Masʿada b. Ṣadaqa, from Abū ʿAbd Allāh عليه السلام. He said, 'He was asked about significant events in the future that have not yet taken place, so he said, "It is not yet time to disclose them, as per God's words: ﴾*But they are denying what they cannot comprehend – its prophecy has yet to be fulfilled for them.*﴿"' [10:39]

20. From Ḥumrān who said, 'I asked Abū Jaʿfar عليه السلام about significant events such as the return (*al-rajʿa*) and the like, so he said, "Now is not the time to disclose such matters. God says: ﴾*But they are denying what they cannot comprehend – its prophecy has yet to be fulfilled for them.*﴿"' [10:39]

21. From Abū al-Safātij who said, 'Abū ʿAbd Allāh عليه السلام said, "There are two verses in the Qur'an wherein God restrains people from speaking about that which they do not know; God's verse: ﴾*Was a pledge not taken from them, written in the Scripture, to say nothing but the truth about God?*﴿(7:169) and His verse: ﴾*But they are denying what they cannot comprehend – its prophecy has yet to be fulfilled for them.*﴿" [10:39]

22. From Isḥāq b. ʿAbd al-ʿAzīz [=Abū al-Safātij] who said, 'I heard Abū ʿAbd Allāh عليه السلام say, "God has specifically addressed this community with two verses from His Book: (1) that they should not speak about that which they do not know (2) nor reject what they have no knowledge thereof." Then he recited: ﴾*Was a pledge not taken from them, written in the Scripture, to say nothing but the truth about God?*﴿ and His verse: ﴾*But they are denying what they cannot comprehend – its prophecy has yet to be fulfilled for them. In the same way, those before them refused to believe – see what was the end of those evildoers!*﴿ [10:39]

23. From Jābir, from Abū Jaʿfar عليه السلام. He said, 'I asked him about the interpretation of this verse: ﴾*Every community is sent a messenger, and when their messenger comes, they will be judged justly; they will not be wronged.*﴿' He said, 'Its inward meaning is that every generation from this community has a messenger from the family of Muḥammad, who comes to the specific generation for whom he is [designated as] a messenger; they are the vicegerents (*awliyā'*) and they are the messengers.

١٩. عن مَسعدة بن صدقة، عن أبي عبدالله عليه السلام، قال: سُئِل عليه السلام عن الأمور العظام الّتي تكون ممّا لم يكُن، فقال: لم يئْنِ أوان كشفِها بعد، وذلك قوله: ﴿بَلْ كَذَّبُوا بِمَا لَمْ يُحِيطُوا بِعِلْمِهِ وَلَمَّا يَأْتِهِمْ تَأْوِيلُهُ﴾.

٢٠. عن حُمران، قال: سألتُ أبا جعفر عليه السلام عن الأمور العظام من الرجعة وغيرها؟ فقال: إنّ هذا الذي تسألوني عنه لم يأتِ أوانُه، قال الله تعالى: ﴿بَلْ كَذَّبُوا بِمَا لَمْ يُحِيطُوا بِعِلْمِهِ وَلَمَّا يَأْتِهِمْ تَأْوِيلُهُ﴾.

٢١. عن أبي السفاتج، قال: قال أبو عبدالله عليه السلام: آيتان في كتاب الله حصر الله الناس ألاّ يقولوا مالا يعلمون، قول الله: ﴿أَلَمْ يُؤْخَذْ عَلَيْهِمْ مِيثَاقُ الْكِتَابِ أَنْ لَا يَقُولُوا عَلَى اللَّهِ إِلَّا الْحَقَّ﴾، وقوله: ﴿بَلْ كَذَّبُوا بِمَا لَمْ يُحِيطُوا بِعِلْمِهِ وَلَمَّا يَأْتِهِمْ تَأْوِيلُهُ﴾.

٢٢. عن إسحاق بن عبد العزيز، قال: سَمِعت أبا عبدالله عليه السلام يقول: إنّ الله خصّ هذه الأمّة بآيتين من كتابه: ألاّ يقولوا ما لا يعلمون، وألاّ يرُدّوا ما لا يعلمون، ثمّ قرأ: ﴿أَلَمْ يُؤْخَذْ عَلَيْهِمْ مِيثَاقُ الْكِتَابِ﴾ الآية، وقوله ﴿بَلْ كَذَّبُوا بِمَا لَمْ يُحِيطُوا بِعِلْمِهِ وَلَمَّا يَأْتِهِمْ تَأْوِيلُهُ﴾ إلى قوله ﴿الظَّالِمِينَ﴾.

٢٣. عن جابر، عن أبي جعفر عليه السلام، قال: سألتُه عن تفسير هذه الآية ﴿وَلِكُلِّ أُمَّةٍ رَسُولٌ فَإِذَا جَاءَ رَسُولُهُمْ قُضِيَ بَيْنَهُمْ بِالْقِسْطِ وَهُمْ لَا يُظْلَمُونَ﴾.

As for His words: ﴾ *and when their messenger comes, he will judge equitably between them* ﴿ – it means that the messengers judge equitably and never wrong anyone as God said.' [10:47]

24. From Ḥumrān who said, 'I asked Abū 'Abd Allāh عليه السلام about God's verse: ﴾ *There is an appointed term for every community, and when it is reached they can neither delay nor hasten it, even for a moment.* ﴿ He said, 'This is what is dictated to the Angel of Death on the Night of Decree." [10:49]

25. From Yaḥyā b. Sa'īd, from Abū 'Abd Allāh عليه السلام on his father's authority regarding God's verse: ﴾ *They ask you [Prophet], 'Is it true?' Say, 'Yes, by my Lord, it is true.* ﴿ He said, 'The people of Mecca ask you, O Muḥammad, about 'Alī b. Abī Ṭālib – is he really the Imam? Say, ﴾ *Yes, by my Lord, it is true.* ﴿' [10:53]

26. From Ḥammād b. 'Īsā, from whoever narrated it from Abū 'Abd Allāh عليه السلام. He said, 'He was asked about God's verse: ﴾ *When they see the punishment, they will repent in secret.* ﴿ He said, 'He was asked, "What use will a secret repentance be if they are already being punished?" He replied, "To avoid the malicious gloating of their enemies."' [10:54]

27. From al-Sakūnī, from Abū 'Abd Allāh عليه السلام on his father's authority عليه السلام who said, 'A man complained to the Prophet ﷺ of a pain in his chest [heart] so he said, 'Seek a cure with the Qur'an; for God says: ﴾ *a healing for what is in [your] hearts.* ﴿' [10:57]

قال: تفسيرها في الباطن أنّ لكلّ قرنٍ من هذه الأمّة رسولاً من آل محمّد ﷺ يخرُج إلى القرن الذي هو إليهم رسول، وهم الأولياء، وهم الرُّسل.

وأمّا قوله: ﴿فَإِذَا جَاءَ رَسُولُهُمْ قُضِيَ بَيْنَهُم بِالْقِسْطِ﴾، قال: معناه أنّ الرسل يقضُون بالقِسط ﴿وَهُمْ لَا يُظْلَمُونَ﴾ كما قال الله.

٢٤. عن حُمران، قال: سألتُ أبا عبدالله عليه السلام عن قول الله ﴿إِذَا جَاءَ أَجَلُهُمْ فَلَا يَسْتَأْخِرُونَ سَاعَةً وَلَا يَسْتَقْدِمُونَ﴾. قال: هو الّذي سُمّي لملك الموت ﷺ في ليلة القَدر.

٢٥. عن يحيى بن سعيد، عن أبي عبدالله عليه السلام عن أبيه، في قول الله: ﴿وَيَسْتَنبِئُونَكَ أَحَقٌّ هُوَ﴾ قال: يستنبئك — يا محمّد — أهل مكّة عن عليّ بن أبي طالب عليه السلام إمامٌ هو؟ ﴿قُلْ إِي وَرَبِّي إِنَّهُ لَحَقٌّ﴾.

٢٦. عن حمّاد بن عيسى، عمّن رواه، عن أبي عبدالله عليه السلام، قال: سُئِل عليه السلام عن قول الله تعالى: ﴿وَأَسَرُّوا النَّدَامَةَ لَمَّا رَأَوُا الْعَذَابَ﴾، قال: قيل له: وما ينفعهم إسرارُ النّدامة وهم في العذاب؟ قال: كَرِهوا شماتة الأعداء.

٢٧. عن السّكوني، عن أبي عبدالله عليه السلام، عن أبيه عليه السلام، قال: شكا رجلٌ إلى النّبيّ ﷺ وجعًا في صدره، فقال: استشفِ بالقرآن، لأنّ الله يقول: ﴿وَشِفَاءٌ لِّمَا فِي الصُّدُورِ﴾.

28. From al-Aṣbagh b. Nubāta, from the Commander of the Faithful عليه السلام who said regarding God's verse: ﴾*Say* [*Prophet*]*, 'In God's grace and mercy let them rejoice: these are better than all they accumulate*﴿, 'Let our followers (*shīʿa*) rejoice; this is better than the gold and silver that our enemies have been given.' [10:58]

29. From Abū Ḥamza, from Abū Jaʿfar عليه السلام. He said, 'I asked about: ﴾*Say* [*Prophet*]*, 'In God's grace and mercy let them rejoice: these are better than all they accumulate.*﴿' So he replied, "Attesting to the prophethood of Muḥammad, peace be upon him and his family, and taking the Commander of the Faithful عليه السلام as an Imam is better than all that these people can accumulate in their worldly existence." [10:58]

30. From 'Abd al-Raḥmān b. Sālim al-Ashall[4], from one of the jurists who said, 'The Commander of the Faithful said, ﴾*But for those who are on God's side there is no fear, nor shall they grieve.*﴿ Then he said, "Do you know who the ones on God's side are?"

They retorted, "Who are they, O the Commander of the Faithful?"

He replied, "They are us and our followers. So whoever follows us even after our passing then it is a pleasure for us, a joy indeed! And a joy for them too, though their joy will be greater than ours."

He was asked, "Why would their joy exceed the joy we experience now? Are we not on the same footing as them?"

He replied, "No, because they will have to bear burdens that you have not been made to bear, and they will master what you have not mastered." [10:62]

31. From Burayd al-ʿIjlī, from Abū Jaʿfar عليه السلام who said, 'We found written in ʿAlī b. al-Ḥusayn's book: ﴾*But for those who are on God's side there is no fear, nor shall they grieve.*﴿' He said, "When they fulfill what God has made obligatory, adopt the practices of God's Messenger, remain aloof from God's prohibitions and abstain from the fleeting embellishments of this world, desiring

4 'Abd al-Raḥmān b. Sālim b. 'Abd al-Raḥmān al-Ashall, a frequent narrator of the fifth and sixth Imams and from Abū Baṣīr, is deemed weak and unreliable in his narrations. See Ḥillī, *Khulāṣat al-aqwāl*, 375 (nr. 1394).

٢٨. عن الأصبغ بن نباتة، عن أمير المؤمنين عليه السلام، في قول الله تعالى: ﴿قُلْ بِفَضْلِ اللَّهِ وَبِرَحْمَتِهِ فَبِذَٰلِكَ فَلْيَفْرَحُوا﴾. قال: فليفرَح شيعتُنا هو خيرٌ ممّا أُعطي عدوّنا من الذهب والفضّة.

٢٩. عن أبي حمزة، عن أبي جعفر عليه السلام، قال: قلتُ: ﴿قُلْ بِفَضْلِ اللَّهِ وَبِرَحْمَتِهِ فَبِذَٰلِكَ فَلْيَفْرَحُوا هُوَ خَيْرٌ مِّمَّا يَجْمَعُونَ﴾؟ فقال: الإقرار بنبوّة محمّد عليه وآله السلام، والائتمام بأمير المؤمنين عليه السلام هو خيرٌ ممّا يجمع هؤلاء في دنياهم.

٣٠. عن عبد الرّحمن بن سالم الأشلّ، عن بعض الفُقهاء، قال: قال أمير المؤمنين عليه السلام: ﴿أَلَا إِنَّ أَوْلِيَاءَ اللَّهِ لَا خَوْفٌ عَلَيْهِمْ وَلَا هُمْ يَحْزَنُونَ﴾، ثمّ قال: تدرون من أولياء الله؟ قالوا: من هم يا أمير المؤمنين؟ فقال: هم نحن وأتباعنا، فمن تبعنا من بعدنا، طُوبى لنا، وطوبى لهم أفضل من طُوبى لنا.

قيل يا أمير المؤمنين: ما شأن طوبى لهم أفضل من طوبى لنا؟ ألسنا نحنُ وهم على أمرٍ؟ قال: لا، إنّهم حُمِلوا ما لم تُحَمَّلوا عليه، وأطاقوا ما لم تُطيقوا.

٣١. عن بُريد العجلي، عن أبي جعفر عليه السلام، قال: وجدنا في كتاب عليّ ابن الحسين عليه السلام: ﴿أَلَا إِنَّ أَوْلِيَاءَ اللَّهِ لَا خَوْفٌ عَلَيْهِمْ وَلَا هُمْ يَحْزَنُونَ﴾ إذا أدّوا فرائض الله، وأخذوا بسُنَن رسول الله صلى الله عليه وآله، وتورّعوا عن محارم الله، وزَهَدوا في عاجل زَهرَة الدنيا، ورَغِبوا فيما عند الله، واكتسبوا الطيّب من رِزق الله، لا يُريدون به التفاخُر والتكاثُر، أنفقوا فيما

only what is with God while earning a wholesome livelihood from God's sustenance, wanting to neither compete for excess nor vainglory and spending on the dues incumbent upon them – then those are people whom God blesses in whatever they earn, and who are rewarded for whatever they send forth for their life hereafter." [10:62]

32. From ʿAbd al-Raḥīm who said, 'Abū Jaʿfar عليه السلام said, "Indeed, when the Angel of Death descends upon any of you and your soul reaches right here [pointing to his throat], he will say to him, "I am going to give you all that you are hoping for, and keep you safe from all that you fear." Then he will open a door to his house in the Garden, and he will be told, "Behold your dwelling place in the Garden! See – there's the Messenger of God, there are ʿAlī, al-Ḥasan, and al-Ḥusayn, peace be upon them, your comrades." This is God's statement: ﴾ *For those who believe and are conscious of God, for them there is good news in this life and in the Hereafter.* ﴿" [10:63–64]

33. From ʿUqba b. Khālid[5] who said, 'Muʿallā and I went in to visit Abū ʿAbd Allāh عليه السلام, so he said, "ʿUqba, on the Day of Resurrection, God will accept naught from His servants except this creed which you adhere to; and the only thing keeping you from actually seeing that which will delight your eyes is for your soul to reach here," pointing to his jugular vein.

Then he leant back, and Muʿallā squeezed my arm and urged me to ask him further. So I said, "O son of God's Messenger! So when his soul does reach this point, what will he see exactly?"

So he said, "He will see..." and I persisted asking some ten or twelve times, "What will he see?"

Finally he said, "ʿUqba!"

I replied, "At your service!"

He continued, "Will you not give up until you know?"

I replied, "Yes, O son of God's Messenger. My creed is my life, and if I were to lose my creed, I might as well be dead, so how must it be for you, O son of God's Messenger."

5 ʿUqba b. Khālid, about whom there is scant information. See Ḥillī, *Khulāṣat al-aqwāl*, 221 (nr. 732); Modarressi, *Tradition and Survival*, 388–9 (nr. 212).

يَلزَمهم من حُقُوقٍ واجبةٍ، فأولئك الذين بارك الله لهم فيما اكتسبوا، ويُثابون على ما قدّموا لآخرتهم.

٣٢. عن عبد الرّحيم، قال: قال أبو جعفر عليه السلام: إنّما أحدكم حين تبلُغ نفسُه هاهنا، فينزِل عليه مَلَك الموت، فيقول له: أمّا ماكنت ترجو فقد أُعطيته، وأمّا ماكنتَ تخافه فقد أمِنتَ منه؛ ويُفتح له باب إلى منزله من الجنّة، ويقال له: انظُر إلى مسكنك من الجنّة، وانظُر هذا رسول الله وعليّ والحسن والحسين عليهم السلام رُفقاؤك، وهو قول الله: ﴿الَّذِينَ آمَنُوا وَكَانُوا يَتَّقُونَ ۝ لَهُمُ الْبُشْرَى فِي الْحَيَاةِ الدُّنْيَا وَفِي الْآخِرَةِ﴾.

٣٣. عن عُقبة بن خالد، قال: دخلتُ أنا والمُعلّى على أبي عبد الله عليه السلام، فقال: يا عُقبة، لا يَقبَل الله من العباد يوم القيامة إلاّ هذا الدّين الّذي أنتُم عليه، وما بين أحدكم وبين أن يرى ما تقرّ به عينيه إلا أن يبلُغ نفسه إلى هذه، وأومأ بيده إلى الوريد ثمّ اتّكأ.

وغمزني المُعلّى أن سَله، فقلتُ: يا بن رسول الله، إذا بلغت نفسه إلى هذه، فأيّ شيءٍ يرى؟ فقال: يرى، فقلت له بضع عشر مرّة: أيّ شيء يرى؟

فقال في آخرها: يا عُقبة. فقلت: لبّيك وسَعديك، فقال: أبيتَ إلاّ أن تعلم؟ فقلتُ: نعم يا بن رسول الله، إنّما ديني مع دمي، فإذا ذهب ديني كان ذلك، فكيف بك يا بن رسول الله كُلّ ساعة؟ وبكيتُ فرقّ لي، فقال: يراهما والله. فقلت: بأبي وأمّي، مَن هما؟ فقال: رسول الله صلى الله عليه وآله وعليّ عليه السلام، يا عُقبة، لن تموت نفس مؤمنةٌ أبدًا حتّى تراهما.

Then I began weeping, so he had pity on me, and said, "By God, he will see the two of them."

I asked, "I would give up my father and mother for you – who are these two?"

So he said, "The Messenger of God ﷺ and 'Alī عليه السلام. 'Uqba, no believing soul shall die without seeing them both."

I asked, "And when the believer sees them both, does he return to life in this world?"

He replied, "No. It will flash before him. When he sees them both, it will flash before him."

I asked him, "May I be your ransom – will they say anything to him?"

So he replied, "Yes they will both come to see the believer. The Messenger of God ﷺ will sit by his head and 'Alī عليه السلام at his feet and the Messenger of God ﷺ will come very close to his face and say, 'O friend of God, rejoice at the fact that I am God's Messenger. I am better for you than everything that you are leaving behind in the world.' Then the Messenger of God, peace be upon him and his family, will get up and 'Alī عليه السلام will stand and move in closer to his face saying, 'O friend of God, rejoice at the fact that I am 'Alī b. Abī Ṭālib whom you used to love. Indeed, I will be of benefit to you.'

Then he said, "This is actually in God's Book."

I said, "May I be your ransom – where in God's Book?"

He replied, "In the Chapter of Jonah (*sūra Yūnus*): ﴾*For those who believe and are conscious of God, for them there is good news in this life and in the Hereafter – there is no changing the promises of God – that is truly the supreme triumph.*﴿' [10:63–64]

34. From Abū Ḥamza al-Thumālī who said, 'I asked Abū Ja'far عليه السلام, "What will happen to a person at the time of death?"

He replied, "By God, Abū Ḥamza, the only thing keeping any of you from seeing his status with God and his relationship with us, which will delight his eyes, is for his soul to reach here" – pointing to his throat. "Shall I give you glad tidings, Abū Ḥamza?"

I replied, "Of course! May I be your ransom."

So he said, "When that is the case, the Messenger of God ﷺ will come to him along with 'Alī عليه السلام. He will sit by his head and when it happens [i.e. death] the Messenger of God ﷺ will say to him, 'Do you not recognise me?

قلتُ: فإذا نظر إليهما المؤمن، أيرجع إلى الدنيا؟ قال: لا يمضي أمامه، إذا نظر إليهما مضى أمامه.

فقلتُ له: يقولان له شيئًا، جُعلتُ فداك؟ فقال: نعم، يدخلان جميعًا على المؤمن، فيجلس رسول الله ﷺ عند رأسه، وعليّ عليه السلام عند رجليه، فيكبّ عليه رسول الله ﷺ فيقول: يا وليّ الله، أبشِر بأنّي رسول الله، إنّي خيرٌ لك ممّا تركتَ من الدنيا؛ ثمّ ينهض رسول الله عليه وآله السلام فيقوم عليّ عليه السلام حتى يُكبّ عليه، فيقول: يا وليّ الله، أبشر أنا عليّ بن أبي طالب الّذي كنتَ تُحبّني، أما لأنفعنّك. ثمّ قال: أما إنّ هذا في كتاب الله.

قلتُ: جُعلتُ فداك، أين في كتاب الله؟ قال: في يونس: ﴿الَّذِينَ آمَنُوا وَكَانُوا يَتَّقُونَ ۝ لَهُمُ الْبُشْرَىٰ فِي الْحَيَاةِ الدُّنْيَا وَفِي الْآخِرَةِ﴾ إلى قوله: ﴿الْعَظِيمُ﴾.

٣٤. عن أبي حمزة الثُّمالي، قال: قلتُ لأبي جعفر عليه السلام: ما يُصنَع بأحد عند الموت؟ قال: أما والله يا أبا حمزة، ما بين أحدكم وبين أن يرى مكانه من الله ومكانه منّا إلاّ أن تبلُغ نفسه هاهنا ــ ثمّ أهوى بيده إلى نحره ــ ألا أبشّرك يا أبا حمزة، فقلتُ: بلى، جُعلت فداك؟

فقال: إذا كان ذلك أتاه رسول الله ﷺ وعليّ عليه السلام معه، فقعدا عند رأسه، فقال له إذا كان ذلك رسول الله ﷺ: أما تعرِفني؟ أنا رسول الله، هلمّ إلينا، فما أمامك خيرٌ لك ممّا خلّفت، أمّا ما كنتَ تخاف فقد أمِنته، وأمّا ما كنتَ ترجو فقد هجَمت عليه، أيّتها الروح اخرُجي إلى روح الله ورِضوانه، ويقول له عليّ عليه السلام مثل قول رسول الله ﷺ، ثمّ قال: يا أبا حمزة، ألا أخبِرك بذلك من كتاب الله؟ قوله تعالى: ﴿الَّذِينَ آمَنُوا وَكَانُوا يَتَّقُونَ﴾ الآية.

I am God's Messenger. Come to us. What lies ahead of you is better than all that you are leaving behind. You are now safe from all that you feared, and you are about to be immersed into all that you had anticipated. O soul, come out to God's Spirit and His good pleasure.' Then 'Alī عليه السلام will say the same as what the Messenger of God ﷺ had said.'

Then he said, 'Abū Ḥamza, shall I tell you where that is in God's Book?' His words: ﴾*For those who believe and are conscious of God, for them there is good news in this life and in the Hereafter – there is no changing the promises of God – that is truly the supreme triumph.*﴿' [10:63–64]

35. From Zurāra and Ḥumrān, from Abū Ja'far عليه السلام and Abū 'Abd Allāh عليه السلام who said, 'God originated all creatures and sent to them His Messenger, Muḥammad ﷺ, while they were still shadows. Some of them believed in him and some rejected him. Then He sent him to the final phase of creation; so those who had believed in him previously as shadows believed in him, and those who had rejected him then rejected him now.' Then he said: ﴾*But they would not believe in anything they had already rejected.*﴿' [10:74]

36. From Abū Baṣīr, from Abū 'Abd Allāh عليه السلام who said with respect to His verse: ﴾*Then, after him, We sent messengers to their peoples bringing them clear signs. But they would not believe in anything they had already rejected*﴿, 'God sent messengers to His creatures when they were still in the loins of men and in the wombs of women. So whoever believed in them at that time believed in them after that too; and whoever rejected them at that time, rejected them after that.' [10:74]

37. From 'Abd Allāh b. Muḥammad al-Ju'fī, from Abū 'Abd Allāh عليه السلام who said, 'God originated all creation, creating those whom He loved from that which He loved, which was the clay of the Garden. And He created those whom He despised from that which He despised, namely the clay of Hellfire. Then he sent them to the shadows.'

So I asked, 'What are the shadows?'

He replied, 'Do you not see your shadow in the sunlight, how it is something yet nothing at the same time? So He sent prophets to them, calling them to attest to God. Some attested and others refused. Then the prophets called them towards adherence to our authority, and by God, those whom

٣٥. عن زُرارة وحُمران، عن أبي جعفر وأبي عبد الله عليه السلام، قالا: إنّ الله خلق الخَلق وهم أظِلّة، فأرسل رسوله محمّدًا صلى الله عليه وآله وسلم، فمنهم من آمن به، ومنهم من كذّبه، ثمّ بعثه في الخَلق الآخر، فآمن به من كان آمن به في الأظلّة، وجَحَده من جَحَد به يومئذٍ، فقال: ﴿فَمَا كَانُوا لِيُؤْمِنُوا بِمَا كَذَّبُوا بِهِ مِنْ قَبْلُ﴾.

٣٦. عن أبي بصير، عن أبي عبد الله عليه السلام، في قوله: ﴿ثُمَّ بَعَثْنَا مِنْ بَعْدِهِ رُسُلًا إِلَى قَوْمِهِمْ﴾ إلى ﴿بِمَا كَذَّبُوا بِهِ مِنْ قَبْلُ﴾، قال: بعث الله الرُّسل إلى الخلق وهم في أصلاب الرجال وأرحام النساء، فمن صدّق حينئذٍ صدّق بعد ذلك، ومن كذّب حينئذٍ كذّب بعد ذلك.

٣٧. عن عبد الله بن محمّد الجُعفي، عن أبي عبد الله عليه السلام، قال: إنّ الله خلق الخَلق،فخلق من أحبّ ممّا أحبّ، وكان ما أحب أن خلقه من طينةٍ من الجنّة، وخَلق من أبغض ممّا أبغض، وكان ما أبغض أن خلقَه من طِينة النار، ثمّ بعثهم في الظِّلال.

فقلت: وأيّ شيءٍ الظِّلال؟ فقال: أما ترى ظِلُّك في الشمس شيء وليس بشيء، ثمّ بعث فيهم النّبيّين يدعونهم إلى الإقرار بالله، فأقرّ بعضهم وأنكر بعض، ثمّ دعوهم إلى ولايتنا فأقرّ بها والله من أحبّ الله، وأنكرها من أبغض الله، وهو قوله: ﴿فَمَا كَانُوا لِيُؤْمِنُوا بِمَا كَذَّبُوا بِهِ مِنْ قَبْلُ﴾ ثمّ قال أبو جعفر عليه السلام: كان التكذيب ثمّ.

God loved attested to it, and those whom He despised rejected it. This is [the purport of] His words: ﴾*But they would not believe in anything they had already rejected.*﴿'

Then Abū Jaʿfar عليه السلام said, 'The rejection had already occurred from before.' [10:74]

38. From Zurāra, Ḥumrān and Muḥammad b. Muslim, from Abū Jaʿfar and Abū ʿAbd Allāh, peace be upon them both, who said regarding His verse: ﴾*Lord! Do not make us an object of persecution for the oppressors*﴿: 'Do not allow them to dominate us, thereby using us as objects of their persecution.' [10:85]

39. From Abū Rāfiʿ who said, 'The Messenger of God ﷺ addressed the people, saying, "O people, God commanded Mūsā and Hārūn to house their people in Egypt and not to spend the night in a state of ritual impurity in their mosque, nor go near their women therein, with the exception of Hārūn and his progeny. Similarly, ʿAlī is to me as Hārūn and his progeny were to Mūsā. No one, therefore, is allowed to go near their women in my mosque nor spend the night in a state of impurity therein, apart from ʿAlī and his progeny. Those who violate that will end up right there,' pointing towards Shām.'" [10:87]

40. From Hishām b. Sālim, from Abū ʿAbd Allāh عليه السلام who said, 'Between the time of God's saying: ﴾*Your prayers are answered*﴿ and the time of Pharaoh's downfall there was a span of forty years.' [10:89]

41. From Ibn Abī ʿUmayr, from one of our associates who, without mentioning his source, cited an infallible عليه السلام as having said, 'When Mūsā went into the sea, Pharaoh and his army followed him, but Pharaoh's horse was too frightened to go into the sea. So Jibraʾīl appeared mounted on a mare, and when Pharaoh's horse saw the mare it followed it into the sea along with its fellow horses, and they all drowned.' [10:90]

42. From Muḥammad b. Saʿīd al-Azdī that Mūsā b. Muḥammad b. al-Riḍā عليه السلام informed him that Yaḥyā b. Aktham wrote to him, asking him about some issues saying: "Tell me about God's verse: ﴾*So if you* [*Prophet*] *are in doubt*

٣٨. عن زُرارة وحُمران ومحمّد بن مسلم، عن أبي جعفر وأبي عبدالله عليهما السلام، في قوله تعالى: ﴿رَبَّنَا لا تَجْعَلْنَا فِتْنَةً لِلْقَوْمِ الظَّالِمِينَ﴾، قالا: لا تُسلِّطهم علينا فَتفتِنَهم بنا.

٣٩. عن أبي رافع، قال: إنّ رسول الله صلى الله عليه وآله خطب الناس فقال: أيّها الناس، إنّ الله أمر موسى وهارون عليهما السلام أن يَبنِيا لقومهما بمصر بيوتًا، وأمرهما أن لا يبيت في مسجدهما جُنُب، ولا يَقرَب فيه النساء إلاّ هارون وذرّيته، وإنّ عليًّا منّي بمنزلة هارون وذرّيته من موسى، فلا يحلّ لأحد أن يقرَب النساء في مسجدي، ولا يبِيت فيه جُنُبًا إلاّ عليّ وذُرّيته، فمَن ساءه ذلك فهاهنا، وأشار بيده نحو الشام.

٤٠. عن هشام بن سالم، عن أبي عبدالله عليه السلام، قال: كان بين قوله تعالى: ﴿قَالَ قَدْ أُجِيبَت دَعْوَتُكُمَا﴾ وبين أن أخذ فرعون أربعون سنة.

٤١. عن ابن أبي عمير، عن بعض أصحابنا، يرفعه، قال: لمّا صار موسى في البحر أتبعه فرعون وجنُوده، قال: فتهيّب فَرَس فِرعون أن يدخُل البحر فتمثّل له جَبرئيل عليه السلام على رَمَكة، فلمّا رأى فَرَس فِرعون الرَّمَكة أتبعها، ودخل البحر هو وأصحابه فغرِقوا.

٤٢. عن محمّد بن سعيد الأزدي: إنّ موسي بن محمد بن الرضا عليه السلام أخبره أنّ يحيى بن أكثم كتب إليه يسأله عن مسائل: أخبرني عن قول الله تبارك وتعالى: ﴿فَإِن كُنتَ فِي شَكٍّ مِّمَّا أَنزَلْنَا إِلَيْكَ فَاسْأَلِ الَّذِينَ يَقْرَءُونَ الْكِتَابَ مِن قَبْلِكَ﴾ مَن المُخاطب بالآية،

about what We have revealed to you, ask those who have been reading the scriptures before you﴿ – who is the addressee of the verse? If it is being addressed to the Prophet, then he would surely not have doubted in what God revealed. If it addresses someone else, then how can it be that the Book was revealed to someone other than him?"

Mūsā said, 'I asked my brother about that. He said, "As for His verse: ﴾*So if you* [*Prophet*] *are in doubt about what We have revealed to you, ask those who have been reading the scriptures before you*﴿ – the addressee is the Messenger of God ﷺ. However it was not that he doubted in what God had revealed to him. The ignorant pagans were saying: 'Why did He not send us one of the angels as a prophet. He should have distinguished him as a prophet by making him needless of food, drink and transacting in the markets.' So God revealed to his Prophet: ﴾*ask those who have been reading the scriptures before you*﴿ in the presence of these ignorant pagans, as if to say: 'Has God ever sent a messenger before you who did not eat, drink and transact in the markets, so that you could take him as a role model?' He only said: ﴾*So if you* [*Prophet*] *are in doubt*﴿ so that they would follow him and not because he was actually [in doubt].

Similarly, He says elsewhere: ﴾*Say, 'Come, let us gather our sons and your sons, our women and your women, ourselves and yourselves, and let us pray earnestly and invoke God's rejection on those of us who are lying.*﴿(3:61) Had he merely said, "Come let us pray earnestly and invoke God's rejection on you," they would never have come for the contest. He knew that your Prophet had conveyed His Message and was definitely not one of the liars, and so did the Prophet ﷺ know that he was truthful in everything he said; but he wanted to be equitable in his own self [by proposing that]."' [10:94]

43. From 'Abd al-Ṣamad b. Bashīr, from Abū 'Abd Allāh ؑ who said regarding God's verse: ﴾*So if you* [*Prophet*] *are in doubt about what We have revealed to you, ask those who have been reading the scriptures before you*﴿: 'When the Prophet ﷺ was taken on the Night Journey and he had finished conversing with his Lord, he returned to the Oft-visited House (*bayt al-ma'mūr*), which is a house directly above the Ka'ba in the fourth heaven. God gathered all the prophets, messengers and angels together and requested Jibra'īl to sound the call for prayer (*adhān*) and announce its commencement (*iqāma*).

فإن كان المُخاطَب بها النبيّ ﷺ أليس قد شكّ فيما أنزل الله، وإن كان المُخاطَب بها غيره فعلى غيره إذاً أنزل الكتاب؟

قال موسى: فسألتُ أخي عليّ بن محمّد عليه السلام عن ذلك، قال: فأمّا قوله: ﴿فَإِنْ كُنْتَ فِي شَكٍّ مِمَّا أَنْزَلْنَا إِلَيْكَ فَاسْأَلِ الَّذِينَ يَقْرَءُونَ الْكِتَابَ مِنْ قَبْلِكَ﴾ فإنّ المُخاطَب بذاك رسول الله ﷺ، ولم يكُ في شكّ ممّا أنزل الله، ولكن قالت الجَهَلة: كيف لم يَبعث إلينا نبيًّا من الملائكة؟ إنّه لم يُفرِّق بين نبيّه وبين غيره في الاستغناء عن المأكل والمشرب والمشي في الأسواق. فأوحى الله إلى نبيّه ﴿فَاسْأَلِ الَّذِينَ يَقْرَءُونَ الْكِتَابَ مِنْ قَبْلِكَ﴾ بمَحضَر الجهلة: هل بعث الله رسولاً قبلك إلاّ وهو يأكُل الطّعام ويشرب ويمشي في الأسواق؟ ولك بهم أسوة، وإنّما قال: ﴿فَإِنْ كُنْتَ فِي شَكٍّ﴾ ولم يكن، ولكن ليتبعهم، كما قال له ﷺ، ﴿فَقُلْ تَعَالَوْا نَدْعُ أَبْنَاءَنَا وَأَبْنَاءَكُمْ وَنِسَاءَنَا وَنِسَاءَكُمْ وَأَنْفُسَنَا وَأَنْفُسَكُمْ ثُمَّ نَبْتَهِلْ فَنَجْعَلْ لَعْنَتَ اللَّهِ عَلَى الْكَاذِبِينَ﴾ ولو قال: تعالَوا نَبتهِل فنجعل لعنة الله عليكم، لم يكونوا يَجيئون للمُباهلة، وقد عرَف أنّ نبيّه مؤدٍّ عنه رسالته، وما هو من الكاذِبين، وكذلك عرَف النّبيّ ﷺ أنّه صادقٌ فيما يقول: ولكن أحبّ أن يُنصِف من نفسه.

٤٣. عن عبد الصمد بن بشير، عن أبي عبد الله عليه السلام، في قول الله تعالى: ﴿فَإِنْ كُنْتَ فِي شَكٍّ مِمَّا أَنْزَلْنَا إِلَيْكَ فَاسْأَلِ الَّذِينَ يَقْرَءُونَ الْكِتَابَ مِنْ قَبْلِكَ﴾.

قال: لمّا أُسري بالنبيّ ﷺ ففرَغ من مناجاة ربه، رُدّ إلى البيت المعمُور - وهو بيت في السماء الرابعة بحِذاء الكعبة - فجمع الله النبيّين والرُّسل والملائكة، وأمر جبرئيل فأذّن

Then he [i.e. the Prophet] stepped forwardand led them all in prayer. When he had completed it, he turned towards him and said: ﴾*So ask those who have been reading the scriptures before you. The Truth has come to you from your Lord, so be in no doubt and do not deny God's signs.*﴿' [10:94]

44. From Abū 'Ubayda al-Ḥadhdhā', from Abū Ja'far ﷷ. He said, 'I heard him say, "We found written in one of the Commander of the Faithful's books that he said, 'The Messenger of God ﷺ narrated to me that Jibra'īl narrated to him that Yūnus b. Muttā ﷷ was sent to his people when he was thirty years old. He was a short-tempered man, of little patience and affability with his people. Unable to shoulder the weights of the great burdens and banners of prophethood, he buckled under them just as a trunk buckles under the weight of its load of fruit. He stayed and preached among them for thirty-three years, calling them to have faith in God, to believe in him and to follow him, but no one from his community believed in him nor followed him save two people. The first one was called Ruwaybil and the second Tanūkhā.

Ruwaybil hailed from a household that valued knowledge, prophethood and wisdom, and was an old friend of Yūnus b. Muttā's from before God had sent him as a prophet. Tanūkhā was a meek, abstemious man completely devoted to worship but devoid of knowledge and wisdom. Ruwaybil owned some sheep, which he herded and lived off, whereas Tanūkhā was a wood-gatherer who would carry the firewood on his head for a living. Ruwaybil's position with respect to Yūnus was different to Tanūkhā's position in his eyes, due to Ruwaybil's knowledge and wisdom, and because of his old friendship with him.

So when Yūnus found that his people were neither responding to him nor believing in him, he became exasperated and felt himself losing patience with them. He, therefore, complained to his Lord saying, "My Lord, You sent me to my people when I was thirty years old. I have stayed with them for the last thirty-three years, calling them to have faith in you and to believe in my message, threatening them with Your punishment and vengeance. But they have belied me and have not believed me. They rejected my prophethood, and made a mockery of my message and have even threatened me to the extent that I fear for my life. So send Your punishment down unto them for they are indeed people who will not believe."'

وأقام، فتقدّم فصلّى بهم، فلمّا فرَغ التفت إليه فقال: ﴿فَاسْأَلِ الَّذِينَ يَقْرَءُونَ الْكِتَابَ مِنْ قَبْلِكَ﴾ إلى قوله ﴿مِنَ الْمُمْتَرِينَ﴾.

٤٤. عن أبي عبيدة الحذّاء، عن أبي جعفر عليه السلام، قال: سمِعتُه يقول: وجدنا في بعض كتب أمير المؤمنين عليه السلام، قال: حدّثني رسول الله صلى الله عليه وآله أنّ جَبرئيل عليه السلام حدّثه: أنّ يونس بن متّى عليه السلام بعثه الله إلى قومه وهو ابن ثلاثين سنة، وكان رجلاً تَعتَريه الحدّة، وكان قليل الصبر على قومه والمُداراة لهم، عاجزًا عمّا حُمِّل من ثِقل حِمل أوقار النبوّة وأعلامها، وأنّه تفسَّخ تحتها كما يتفسَّخ الجَذَع تحت حِمله، وأنّه أقام فيهم يدعوهم إلى الإيمان بالله والتصديق به واتّباعه ثلاثًا وثلاثين سنة، فلم يؤمن به ولم يتَّبعه من قومه إلاّ رجلان، اسم أحدهما روبيل، واسم الآخر تنوخا.

وكان روبيل من أهل بيت العلم والنبوة والحكمة، وكان قديم الصُّحبة ليونس بن متّى من قبل أن يبعثه الله بالنبوّة، وكان تنوخا رجلاً مستضعفًا عابدًا زاهدًا منهمكًا في العبادة وليس له علمٌ ولا حُكم، وكان روبيل صاحب غنمٍ يرعاها ويتقوّت منها، وكان تنوخا رجلاً حطّابًا يحتطِب على رأسه، ويأكل من كَسبه، وكان لـ لروبيل منزلةٌ من يونس عليه السلام غير منزلة تنوخا، لعلم روبيل وحكمته وقديم صُحبته.

فلمّا رأى يونس عليه السلام أنّ قومه لا يُجيبونه ولا يُؤمنون ضَجر، وعرَف من نفسه قلّة الصبر، فشكا ذلك إلى ربّه، وكان فيما شكا أن قال: «يا ربّ، إنّك بعثتَني إلى قومي ولي ثلاثون سنة، فلَبِثتُ فيهم أدعوهم إلى الإيمان بك والتصديق برسالاتك، وأخوّفُهم عذابك

He continued, 'So God informed Yūnus that, "There are pregnant women, foetuses, children, old men, weak women, helpless and disabled people among them, and I am the all-Wise, the Just. My compassion precedes My wrath, and I would never chastise the youth for the sins of the elders of your community. Yūnus, they are My servants after all, My creatures, beings belonging to me that subsist in My lands and on My sustenance. I love to give them time and be gentle with them and to await their repentance. I have only sent you to your people that you may be a protector over them, showing compassion to them liberally and munificently, and giving them time by virtue of the gentleness of prophethood. So have patience with them with the clemency that comes with the message. Let your comportment among them be as a knowledgeable doctor who administers medicine to his patients. You have instead breached their trust; you have not treated their hearts gently nor dealt with them with the diplomacy befitting messengers. Then you ask Me to punish them due to your own low opinion of them, resulting from your lack of patience with them. My servant Nūḥ endured much more than you from his people and was more affable and affectionately patient in My consideration. He had more of an excuse [than you] so I displayed My wrath when he became angry with Me, and I answered him when he called Me."

So Yūnus replied, "My Lord, I only became angry with them on Your account, and only invoked Your wrath on them when they disobeyed You. So by Your Honour, I will never be affectionate towards them nor treat them kindly nor regard them with good counsel and favour after their rebellion, their disbelief in me and their rejection of my prophethood. So send Your punishment down on them for they are certainly never going to believe."

So God said, "Yūnus, there are more than a hundred thousand of My creatures who inhabit My lands and who give birth to My servants. I love to let them take their time to come towards that which I already know about them and you. My decree and My plan are different to your knowledge and your estimation of things. You are a messenger whereas I am the Wise Lord, and My knowledge about them, Yūnus, is hidden in the non-manifest whose limits are unbeknownst, whereas your knowledge about them is superficial with no inward aspect. Yūnus, I will respond to your request of Me to send punishment down onto them, but know that this will neither increase in your lot with Me nor enhance your position in My regard. The punishment

ونِقمتك ثلاثًا وثلاثين سنة، فكذّبوني ولم يؤمنوا بي، وجحدوا نبوّتي، واستخفّوا برسالاتي، وقد تواعدوني، وخِفتُ أن يَقتلوني، فأنزِل عليهم عذابك، فإنّهم قومٌ لا يؤمنون» .

قال: فأوحى الله إلى يونس ﷺ: أنّ فيهم الحَمل والجَنين والطِّفل، والشيخ الكبير، والمرأة الضعيفة، والمستضعف المهين، وأنا الحَكَم العَدل، سبقت رحمتي غضبي، لا أُعذِّب الصِّغار بذُنوب الكِبار من قومك، وهم — يا يونس — عبادي وخلقي وبريَّتي في بلادي، وفي عَيلتي، أُحِبّ أن أتأنّاهم وأرفُق بِهم، وأنتظِر توبتَهم، وإنّما بعثتُك إلى قومك لتكون حفيظًا عليهم، تعطِف عليهم بسِجال الرّحمة الماسّة منهم، وتتأنّاهم برأفة النُّبوّة، وتصبر معهم بأحلام الرسل وتكون لهم كهيئة الطبيب المداوي العالِم بمُداواة الدّواء،فخَرِقت بهم، ولم تستمِل قلوبهم بالرِّفق، ولم تَسُسهم بسِياسة المُرسلين، ثمّ سألتَني مع سُوء نظرِك العذاب لهم عند قِلّة الصبر منك، وعبدي نوح كان أصبر منك على قومه، وأحسن صُحبَةً، وأشدّ تأنّيًا في الصبر عندي، وأبلغ في العُذر، فغَضِبت له حين غَضِب لي، وأجَبتُه حين دعاني.

فقال يونس ﷺ: يا ربّ، إنّما غَضِبتُ عليهم فيك، وإنّما دعوتُ عليهم حين عَصَوك، فوَعِزّتك لا أتَعطّف عليهم برأفةٍ أبدًا، ولا أنُظر إليهم بنصيحة شفيقٍ بعد كُفرهم وتكذيبهم إيّاي، وجَحدهم نبوّتي، فأنزِل عليهم عذابك فإنّهم لا يُؤمنون أبدًا.

فقال الله تعالى: يا يونس، إنّهم مائة ألف أو يزيدون من خَلقي، يعمُرون بلادي، ويَلِدون عبادي، ومحبّتي أن أتأنّاهم للّذي سبق من عِلمي فيهم وفيك، وتقديري وتدبيري غير عِلمك وتقديرك، وأنت المُرسَل وأنا الربّ الحكيم، وعلمي فيهم يا يونس باطنٌ في الغيب عندي لا يُعلَم ما مُنتهاه، وعلمُك فيهم ظاهرٌ لا باطن له.

will befall them on Wednesday in the middle of the month of Shawwāl after sunrise, so inform them of that."

This gladdened Yūnus and did not upset him, as he had no clue what his own consequence would be. So Yūnus set off to Tanūkhā, the worshipper, and informed him about what God had revealed to him about the descent of punishment on the appointed day. He said to him, "Go and inform them of what God has revealed to me about the descent of the punishment."

So Tanūkhā said, "Just leave them immersed in their disobedience until God punishes them."

So Yūnus said to him, "Let us go and meet Ruwaybil first and consult him, for he is a knowledgeable and wise man descended from a household of prophethood."

So they set off to meet Ruwaybil, and Yūnus informed him about what God had revealed to him about the descent of the punishment on his people on a Wednesday in the middle of Shawwāl after sunrise.

So he said to him, "What do you think about coming with us so we can tell them about that?"

So Ruwaybil said to him, "Go back to your Lord as a wise prophet and a noble messenger, and request him to avert the punishment away from them, for surely He has no need to punish them; for He is One who loves to be kind to His servants. Furthermore, this will not harm your position or stance with Him. Moreover, your people might just believe one day, even after all the rejection and rebellion that you have experienced from them. So be patient with them and give them time."

So Tanūkhā said to him, "Woe betide you, Ruwaybil, for what you are advising and telling Yūnus to do even after their disbelief in God, their rejection of His prophet, their belying him, their expelling him from his home, and their threats to stone him to death."

So Ruwaybil said to Tanūkhā, "Be quiet for you are a mere worshipper who does not know anything." Then he approached Yūnus and said, "Yūnus, when God descends His punishment on your people, do you know whether it is going to destroy them all or whether some will be destroyed and others left alone?"

Yūnus replied, "It will destroy them all since that is what I asked Him for. I felt no compassion for them at the time, so I had better go back to God and ask Him to avert it from them."

يا يونس، قد أجبْتُك إلى ما سألتَ من إنزَال العذاب عليهم، وما ذلك يا يونس بأوفر لحظّك عندي، ولا أجمل لشأنك، وسيأتيهم العذاب في شوّال يوم الأربعاء وسط الشهر بعد طُلوع الشمس، فأعلِمْهم ذلك.

قال: فسَرّ ذلك يونس، ولم يَسُؤه، ولم يدرِ ما عاقبته، وانطلقَ يونس عليه السلام إلى تنوخا العابد، فأخبره بما أوحى الله تعالى إليه من نزول العذاب على قومه في ذلك اليوم، وقال له: أنْطلق حتّى أُعلمهم بما أوحى الله إليّ من نزول العذاب.

فقال تنوخا: فدعهُم في غَمرَتهم ومَعصِيتهم حتّى يُعذِّبهم الله.

فقال له يونس عليه السلام: بل نلقى روبيل فنشاوره، فإنّه رجلٌ عالمٌ حكيمٌ من أهل بيت النبوّة؛ فانطلقا إلى روبيل، فأخبره يونس عليه السلام بما أوحى الله إليه من نزول العذاب على قومه في شوّال يوم الأربعاء في وسط الشهر بعد طُلوع الشمس، فقال له: ما ترى؟ انطلق بنا حتّى أُعلمهم ذلك.

فقال له روبيل: ارجِع إلى ربّك رجعة نبيٍّ حكيمٍ ورسولٍ كريمٍ، واسأله أن يَصرِف عنهم العذاب، فإنّه غنيّ عن عذابهم، وهو يُحبّ الرِفق بعباده وما ذلك بأضرّ لك عنده، ولا أسوأ لمنزلتك لديه، ولعلّ قومك بعد ما سَمِعت ورأيت من كُفرهم وجُحودهم يُؤمنون يومًا، فصابرهم وتأنّهم.

فقال له تنوخا: ويحك يا روبيل! ما أشرت على يونس وأمرته به بعد كُفرهم بالله وجَحدهم لنبيّه، وتكذيبهم إيّاه، وإخراجهم إيّاه من مساكنه، وما همّوا به من رجمه.

So Ruwaybil said to him, "Yūnus, do you know that if God does indeed send down punishment upon them and they sense it coming they may repent to Him and seek His forgiveness, upon which He will have mercy on them for He is indeed the most Compassionate of all. He will avert the punishment from them even after you have told them about God descending His punishment upon them on Wednesday. In that case, you will be considered a liar by them."

Tanūkhā then said to him, "Woe betide you, Ruwaybil! How dare you say such a grave thing? The emissary and prophet himself is telling you what God has revealed to him about the punishment that is to descend and you are disputing God's Word and doubting Him as well as His messenger's statement? Go away for your deeds are null and void!"

So Ruwaybil said to Tanūkhā, "Your opinion is invalid." Then he went to Yūnus and said, "When God's revelation and His command about them descends just as news of the descent of His punishment on them came down to you – and His Word is true – have you considered the consequences of what might happen if all your people are destroyed and their village ruined? Will God not efface your name from prophethood and nullify your bearing of His message, and you will simply be another weak human being? More than one hundred thousand people will perish because of you."

Yūnus refused to take his advice, however, and left with Tanūkhā, and they withdrew themselves away to a place not too far. Then Yūnus returned to his people to inform them what God had revealed to him: that He was going to punish them on Wednesday in the middle of the month of Shawwāl after sunrise; but they rejected his words, belied him and forcefully drove him out of their village.

So Yūnus, accompanied by Tanūkhā, left the village and retreated to a place not too far from there, and sat waiting for the punishment.

Meanwhile, Ruwaybil stayed with his people in their village until the month of Shawwāl set in, when he shouted out from the top of the mountain to his people: "I am Ruwaybil. I feel for you and I care about you. This month of Shawwāl has now set in, and Yūnus, your prophet and the messenger sent to you from your Lord has informed you of God's revelation to him about the descent of punishment upon you after sunrise on Wednesday in the middle of Shawwāl. God will never break his promise to his prophets, so think about what you are going to do."

فقال روبيل لتنوخا: اسكُت فإنّك رجلٌ عابدٌ لا علم لك؛ ثمّ أقبلَ على يونس ﷺ، فقال: أرأيتَ يا يونس، إذا أنزل الله العذاب على قومك، أينزلُه فيُهلكهم جميعًا، أو يُهلِك بعضًا ويُبقي بعضًا؟ فقال له يونس ﷺ: بل يُهلِكهم الله جميعًا، وكذلك سألته، ما دخلتني لهم رحمة تَعطّفٍ فأُراجع الله فيهم وأسأله أن يصرِفه عنهم.

فقال له روبيل: أتدري يا يونس، لعلّ الله إذا أنزل عليهم العذاب فأحسّوا به، أن يتوبوا إليه، وَيستغفروه فيرحمهم، فإنّه أرحم الراحمين، ويكشف عنهم العذاب من بعد ما أخبرتهم عن الله أنّه ينزل عليهم العذاب يوم الأربعاء، فتكون بذلك عندهم كذّابًا.

فقال له تنوخا: ويحك يا روبيل، لقد قلتَ عظيمًا، يُخبِرك النبيّ المُرسل أنّ الله أوحى إليه بأنّ العذاب ينزِل عليهم، فتَرُدّ قول الله، وتشُكّ فيه وفي قول رسوله؟! اذهب فقد حَبِط عمَلُك.

فقال روبيل لتنوخا: لقد فشِل رأيك، ثمّ أقبل على يونس ﷺ فقال: إذا نزل الوحيُ والأمر من الله فيهم على ما أُنزِل عليك فيهم من إنزال العذاب عليهم، وقوله الحقّ، أرأيت إذا كان ذلك فهلَكَ قومك كلّهم وخَرِبت قريتُهم، أليس يمحو الله اسمَك من النبوّة، وتبطُل رسالتُك، وتكون كبعض ضُعفاء الناس، ويهلِكُ على يديك مائة ألف أو يزيدون من الناس؟

فأبى يونس أن يقبل وصيّته، فانطلق ومعه تنوخا من القرية، وتنحّيا عنهم غير بعيد، ورجع يونس إلى قومه، فأخبرهم أنّ الله أوحى إليه أنّه مُنزِلُ العذاب عليكم يوم الأربعاء في شوّال في وسط الشهر بعد طُلوع الشمس، فردّوا عليه قوله، وكذّبوه وأخرجوه من

His words alarmed them and the reality of the descent of this punishment penetrated into their hearts, so they urgently rushed to Ruwaybil and said to him, "What is it that you are trying to indicate to us, Ruwaybil? You are indeed a knowledgeable and wise man whom we have always known to be kind and compassionate to us. We did indeed hear what you were saying about Yūnus regarding us. So tell us what you think now and show us what to do."

So Ruwaybil said to them, "I will tell you what I think and will show you what to do – you must wait and plan for when the sun rises on Wednesday in the middle of the month. You must separate the children from their mothers and take them to the foot of the mountain down in the valleys. Let the mothers stand on the flat plateau of the mountain. Separate all the cattle from their young too. All this must be done before sunrise. When you see a yellow wind emerging from the east, both young and old from among you should wail and cry loudly, screaming and crying and beseeching God, repenting to Him and seeking His forgiveness. Lift your heads up to the sky and say, 'Our Lord, we have indeed wronged ourselves and rejected Your prophet. We repent to You of our sins. If You do not forgive us and have mercy on us, then we will surely be punished losers. So accept our repentance and have mercy on us, O most compassionate of all.' Do not stop crying, wailing and beseeching God and repenting to Him until God averts the punishment away from you before the sun comes out fully."

His whole community unanimously agreed to do as Ruwaybil had advised them.

So when the Wednesday on which they were expecting the punishment came, Ruwaybil retreated to a place away from the village from where he would still be able to hear their wails and see the punishment if it descended. So when dawn broke on Wednesday, Yūnus's people did as they had been told to do by Ruwaybil. When the sun rose, a dark, gusty, yellow wind rose up, howling, whistling and roaring. When they saw it approaching they all began to wail and scream and cry, beseeching God in repentance and seeking His forgiveness. The children cried with loud voices for their mothers, the lambs bleated insistently searching for their mothers' udders, and the cattle mooed looking for pasture. Meanwhile, Yūnus and Tanūkhā could hear their moans and screams, and invoked God's curse on them, praying for the punishment on them to be intensified; whilst Ruwaybil could hear

قريتهم إخراجًا عنيفًا. فخرج يونس ﵇ ومعه تنوخا من القرية، وتنحّيا عنهم غير بعيد، وأقاما ينتظِران العذاب.

وأقام روبيل مع قومه في قريتهم، حتّى إذا دخل عليهم شوّال صرَخ روبيل بأعلى صوته في رأس الجبل إلى القوم: أنا روبيل، شفيقٌ عليكم، رحيمٌ بكم، هذا شوّال قد دخل عليكم، وقد أخبرَكم يونس نبيّكم ورسول ربّكم أنّ الله أوحى إليه أنَّ العذاب ينزِل عليكم في شوّال في وسط الشهر يوم الأربعاء بعد طُلُوع الشمس، ولن يُخلِف الله وعدَه رُسُلَه، فانظروا ما أنتم صانعون، فأفزعهم كلامه، ووقع في قُلوبهم تحقيق نُزُول العذاب، فأجفلوا نحو روبيل، وقالوا له: ماذا أنت مُشيرٌ به علينا يا روبيل؟ فإنّك رجلٌ عالمٌ حكيمٌ، لم نَزل نعرِفك بالرقّة علينا، والرّحمة لنا، وقد بلَغنا ما أشرت به على يونس فينا، فمُرنا بأمرِك، وأشِر علينا برأيك.

فقال لهم روبيل: فإنّي أرى لكم وأُشِير عليكم أن تَنظُروا وتعمِدوا إذا طَلَع الفجر يوم الأربعاء في وسط الشهر أن تعزلوا الأطفال عن الأمّهات في أسفل الجبل في طريق الأودية، وتوقِفوا النساء في سَفح الجبل، ويكون هذا كلّه قبل طلوع الشمس، فإذا رأيتُم ريحًا صفراء أقبلت من المشرِق، فعجّوا عجيجًا، الكبير منكم والصغير بالصُّراخ والبُكاء، والتضرُّع إلى الله، والتوبة إليه، والاستِغفار له، وارفَعُوا رؤوسكم إلى السماء، وقولوا: «ربّنا ظلمنا أنفسنا، وكذّبنا نبيّك، وتُبنا إليك من ذُنوبنا، وإن لا تغفِر لنا وترحَمنا لنكونَنَّ من الخاسرين المُعذَّبين، فاقبل توبتنا وارحمنا يا أرحم الراحمين». ثمّ لا تملّوا من البُكاء والصُّراخ والتضرُّع إلى الله والتوبة إليه حتّى تُوارى الشمس بالحِجاب، أو يكشِف الله عنكم العذاب قبل ذلك. فأجمع رأي القوم جميعًا على أن يفعلوا ما أشار به عليهم روبيل.

their screams and wailing from where he was and he could see what was coming, and supplicated God to remove the punishment from them.

When the sun was high in the sky, the doors of the heavens were wide open, and the Lord's wrath had subsided, the most Compassionate One had mercy on them and responded to their pleas. He accepted their repentance and dismissed their offences. God revealed to Isrāfīl saying, "Go down to Yūnus's people, for they are wailing and crying, beseeching Me. They have repented to Me and sought My forgiveness, so I have turned to them mercifully, for I am God, the Oft-pardoning and the all-Merciful. I rush to accept My servant's repentance when he is remorseful. My messenger and servant, Yūnus, had asked Me to send punishment down on his people so I did send it down upon them, for I am God, the Truest One to His promise; I did indeed send it down upon them. However, when Yūnus asked Me to send punishment down on them, he did not specify that I should destroy them. So go down and avert from them My punishment that has befallen them."

So Isrāfīl said, "My Lord, Your punishment is already touching their backs and may almost ruin them. From what I can see, it has already descended in their midst, so where can I avert it to?"

So God said, "No! I have commanded My angels to halt it and to prevent it to descend upon them until My resolve and command to do so is issued to them. So go down, Isrāfīl, and avert it from them. Move it away to the mountains, onto the waterfalls and gushing streams on the side of the tall, overbearing and high mountains that tower over all the others, so crush them and soften them thereby until they can be moulded into hard iron."

So Isrāfīl went down to them, spread his wings over them and drove the punishment away from them until he struck it against the mountains that God had told him to move it away to.'

Abū Ja'far عليه السلام continued, 'These are the mountains that lie near Mosul today, and they have been turned into iron until the Day of Judgement. When Yūnus's people saw that the punishment had moved away from them, they climbed down from the mountaintops to their homes and embraced their women and children, and their possessions. They praised God for having averted it from them.

Yūnus and Tanūkhā woke up on Thursday morning in the same place where they were staying, with no doubt in their minds that the punishment had indeed befallen them and destroyed them all when the sound of their

فلمّا كان يوم الأربعاء الذي توقَّعوا العذاب، تنحّى روبيل عن القرية، حيث يسمع صُراخهم، ويرى العذاب إذا نزل، فلمّا طلع الفجر يوم الأربعاء، فعل قوم يونس ما أمرهم روبيل به، فلمّا بزغت الشمس أقبلت ريحٌ صفراء مُظلمةٌ مُسرعةٌ لها صريرٌ وحفيفٌ وهديرٌ، فلمّا رأوها عجّوا جميعًا بالصُّراخ والبُكاء والتضرُّع إلى الله، وتابوا إليه واستغفروه، وصرخت الأطفال بأصواتها تطلُب أمّهاتها، وعجّت سِخال البهائم تطلُب الثدي، وعجّت الأنعام تطلُب الرَّعي، فلم يزالوا بذلك ويونس وتنوخا يسمعان ضجيجهم وصُراخهم، ويدعوان الله عليهم بتغليظ العذاب عليهم، وروبيل في موضعه يسمع صُراخهم وعجيجهم، ويرى ما نزل، وهو يدعو الله بكَشف العذاب عنهم.

فلمّا أن زالت الشمس، وفُتِحت أبواب السماء، وسكن غَضَب الربّ تعالى، رَحِمهم الرحمن، فاستجاب دعاءهم، وقَبِل توبتهم، وأقالهم عثرتهم، فأوحى الله إلى إسرافيل عليه السلام: أن اهبِط إلى قوم يونس، فإنّهم قد عجّوا إليّ بالبُكاء والتضرُّع، وتابوا إليّ واستغفروني، فرَحِمتُهم وتُبتُ عليهم، وأنا الله التوّاب الرحيم، أُسرِع إلى قبول توبة عبدي التائب من الذّنوب، وقد كان عبدي يونس ورسولي سألني نزول العذاب على قومه، وقد أنزلته عليهم، وأنا الله أحقّ من وفى بعهده، وقد أنزلته عليهم، ولم يكُن اشترط يونس حين سألني أن أُنزل عليهم العذاب أن أُهلكهم، فأهبِط إليهم، فأصرِف عنهم ما قد نزل بهم من عذابي.

فقال إسرافيل: يا ربّ، إنّ عذابك قد بلغ أكتافهم، وكاد أن يَهلِكهم، وما أراه إلاّ وقد نزل بساحتهم، فإلى أين أصرفه؟

voices had subsided. So they made their way towards the village on Thursday at sunrise to see what had become of the people. When they neared the people, however, and were met by the sight of the woodcutters, the donkey-drivers and the shepherds herding their sheep, and saw the villagers safe and sound, Yūnus said to Tanūkhā, "Tanūkhā, the revelation proved me wrong, and my promise to my community has turned out to be false! No, by My Lord's Honour! I can never again face them after the revelation has proved me wrong."

So Yūnus turned on his heels and ran away towards the sea of Ayla, angry on account of his Lord, disguised and fleeing from there before any of his people could see him and call him a liar. That is why God says: ﴾*And remember the man with the whale, when he went off angrily, thinking We could not restrict him, but then he cried out in the deep darkness, 'There is no God but You, glory be to You, I was wrong.'*﴿ (21:87)

Tanūkhā returned to the village and met Ruwaybil. He said to him, "Tanūkhā, so which suggestion turned out to be the correct and worthier one of being followed? Mine or yours?"

So Tanūkhā replied, "Your suggestion was correct of course, and you were indeed pointing out the opinion of intelligent and wise people."

Tanūkhā continued, "I used to consider myself better than you for my abstemiousness and by virtue of my worship, until your superiority became evident due to the virtue of your knowledge and the wisdom that God, your Lord, has bestowed upon you; along with the fact that God-consciousness is better than abstemiousness and worship without knowledge."

So they remained friends and continued to live with their people, while Yūnus had turned his face away from them in anger on account of his Lord. That is what God informs us about in His Book saying: ﴾*and when they believed, We relieved them of the punishment of disgrace in the life of this world, and let them enjoy life for a time*﴿ and it is all part of his story.'

Abū 'Ubayda said, 'I asked Abū Ja'far عليه السلام, "How long had Yūnus been away from his people until he returned to them as a prophet and a messenger and they finally believed in him and attested to him?"

He replied, "Four lots of seven, of which it took him seven to get to the sea, and seven to come back again to his people."

So I asked him, "So these four lots of seven – are they months, days or hours?"

فقال الله: كلاّ إنّي قد أمرتُ ملائكتي أن يصرفوه، ولا ينزلوه عليهم حتّى يأتيهم أمري فيهم وعزيمتي، فاهبِط — يا إسرافيل — عليهم وأصرِفه عنهم، وأصرِف به إلى الجبال بِنَاحية مفائض العيون ومجاري السُّيول في الجبال العاتية المستطيلة على الجبال، فأذِلّها به وليّنها حتّى تصير ملتئمة حديدًا جامدًا.

فهَبط إسرافيل عليهم، فنشر أجنحته، فاستاق بها ذلك العذاب، حتّى ضَرَب بها تلك الجبال الّتي أوحى الله إليه أن يصرِفه إليها — قال أبو جعفر عليه السلام: وهي الجبال الّتي بناحية الموصل اليوم — فصارت حديدًا إلى يوم القيامة، فلمّا رأى قوم يونس أنّ العذاب قد صُرِف عنهم، هبطوا إلى منازلهم من رُؤوس الجبال، وضمّوا إليهم نساءهم وأولادهم وأموالهم، وحَمِدوا الله على ما صَرَف عنهم.

وأصبح يونس وتنوخا يوم الخميس في موضعهما الذي كانا فيه، لا يشُكّان أنّ العذاب قد نَزَل بهم وأهلكهم جميعًا، لمّا خفيت أصواتهم عنهما، فأقبلا ناحية القرية يوم الخميس مع طُلُوع الشمس يَنظُران إلى ما صار إليه القوم، فلمّا دَنَوا من القوم واستقبلهم الحطّابون والحمّارة والرُّعاة بأغنامهم. ونَظَروا إلى أهل القرية مُطمئنّين، قال يونس لتنوخا: يا تنوخا، كذّبني الوحي، وكذّبت وعدي لقومي، لا وعزّة ربّي لا يَرَون لي وجهًا أبدًا بعد ما كذّبني الوحي.

فانطلق يونس هاربًا على وجهه، مغاضبًا لربّه، ناحية بحر أيلة متنكّرًا. فرارًا من أن يَراه أحدٌ من قومه، فيقول له: يا كذّاب، فلذلك قال الله: ﴿وَذَا النُّونِ إِذ ذَّهَبَ مُغَاضِبًا فَظَنَّ أَن لَّن نَّقْدِرَ عَلَيْهِ﴾ الآية.

He replied, "Abū 'Ubayda, the punishment descended on them on Wednesday in the middle of Shawwāl and was averted on the same day, at which Yūnus became angry and left. So seven days passed from Thursday until he reached the sea; then seven days in the belly of the whale, seven days under the gourd tree exposed to the elements, and seven days making his way back to his people. So a total of twenty-eights days passed between his having left and his return. Then he came to them and they believed in him, attested to his prophethood and followed him. That is why God has said: ﴾*If only a single town had believed and benefited from its belief! Only Yūnus's people did so, and when they believed, We relieved them of the punishment of disgrace* [...]﴿' [10:98]

ورَجَع تنوخا إلى القرية، فلقي روبيل، فقال له: يا تنوخا، أيّ الرأيين كان أصوب وأحقّ أن يُتَّبع، رأيي أو رأيك؟ فقال له تنوخا بل رأيك كان أصوب، ولقد كنتَ أشرتَ برأي الحكماء والعلماء.

وقال له تنوخا؛ أما إنّي لم أزل أرى أنّي أفضل منك لزُهدي وفضل عبادتي، حتّى استَبان فضلك بفضل عِلمك، وما أعطاك الله ربّك من الحكمة مع التقوى أفضل من الزُّهد والعِبادة بلا علم؛ فاصطحبا فلم يزالا مُقيمين مع قومهما، ومضى يونس عليه السلام على وجهه مُغاضبًا لربّه، فكان من قِصّته ما أخبر الله به في كتابه إلى قوله: ﴿فَـَٔامَنُوا فَمَتَّعۡنَاهُمۡ إِلَىٰ حِينٖ﴾.

قال أبو عبيدة: قلتُ لأبي جعفر عليه السلام: كم كان غاب يونس عن قومه حتّى رجع إليهم بالنبوّة والرّسالة فآمنوا به وصدّقوه؟ قال: أربعة أسابيع، سبعًا منها في ذِهابه إلى البحر، وسبعًا منها في رُجوعه إلى قومه.

فقلتُ له: وما هذا الأسابيع، شُهور، أو أيّام، أو ساعات؟ فقال: يا أبا عبيدة، إنّ العذاب أتاهم يوم الأربعاء في النصف من شوّال، وصُرِف عنهم من يومهم ذلك، فانطلق يونس مغاضبًا، فمضى يوم الخميس سبعة أيّام في مسيره إلى البحر، وسبعة أيّام في بطن الحوت، وسبعة أيّام تحت الشجرة بالعَراء، وسبعة أيّام في رُجُوعه إلى قومه، فكان ذهابه ورجوعه مسير ثمانية وعشرين يومًا، ثمّ أتاهم فآمنوا به وصدّقوه واتّبعوه، فلذلك قال الله: ﴿فَلَوۡلَا كَانَتۡ قَرۡيَةٌ ءَامَنَتۡ فَنَفَعَهَآ إِيمَٰنُهَآ إِلَّا قَوۡمَ يُونُسَ لَمَّآ ءَامَنُواْ كَشَفۡنَا عَنۡهُمۡ عَذَابَ ٱلۡخِزۡيِ﴾.

45. From Abū Baṣīr, from Abū ʿAbd Allāh عليه السلام who said, 'When the punishment loomed over Yūnus's people, they beseeched God so He averted it from them.' I asked, 'How can that be?' He replied, 'He already knew that He would avert it from them." [10:98]

46. From al-Thumālī, from Abū Jaʿfar عليه السلام who said, 'When Yūnus's people harassed him, he invoked God's curse upon them, so they woke up on the first day with pale faces and on the second day with blackened faces.'

He continued, 'God had threatened to punish them, so the punishment came to them which they tried to avert with their spears. Then they separated the women from their children and the cows from their calves; they wore fur and wool, tied ropes around their necks, poured dirt on their heads, and all pleaded in unison with their Lord. They said, "We believe in Yūnus's God."

He continued, 'So God averted the punishment away from them to the Āmid mountain range. Yūnus woke up assuming that they had been destroyed but found them to be alive and well, so he became angry and left ﴾*in a rage*﴿ as God has stated, until he boarded a boat in which were two men.

The boat was capsizing so the captain said, "There must be a wanted man on my boat."

So Yūnus said, "Yes, it is I." So he stood up to throw himself overboard, but he saw a fish with its mouth wide open. Terrified of it, he held on to the two men. So they said to him, "There is only one of you and two of us."

So he requested them to draw lots, which they did, and the lots were not in his favour. The custom at the time was that is lots were drawn three times [with the same result], there was no mistake about it. So he threw himself overboard, and the fish swallowed him up, swimming around the seven seas until it ended up in the ever-filled sea, which was the same one being used to chastise Qārūn. Qārūn heard an echoing sound and asked the angel about it, so he informed him that it was Yūnus and that God had imprisoned him in the belly of the fish.

So Qārūn asked him, "Would you permit me to speak to him?"

So he gave him permission, and he asked him about Mūsā.

So he told him that he had died, at which he wept.

Then he asked him about Hārūn, and again he informed him of his death, so the latter wept and became very grieved.

٤٥. عن أبي بصير، عن أبي عبد الله عليه السلام، قال: لمّا أظلّ قوم يونس العذاب، دَعَوا الله فصَرفه عنهم. قلت: كيف ذلك؟ قال: كان في العِلم أنّه يُصرَف عنهم.

٤٦. عن الثّمالي، عن أبي جعفر عليه السلام، قال: إنّ يونس عليه السلام لمّا آذاه قومه دعا الله عليهم، فأصبحوا أوّل يوم ووجوههم صُفر، وأصبحوا اليوم الثاني ووجوههم سُود، قال: وكان الله واعدهم أن يأتيهم العذاب، فأتاهم العذاب حتّى نالوه برِماحهم، ففرّقوا بين النساء وأولادهنّ، والبقر وأولادها، ولَبَسوا المُسُوح والصُّوف، ووضعوا الحِبال في أعناقهم، والرّماد على رؤوسهم، وضجُّوا ضجّةً واحدةً إلى ربّهم؛ وقالوا: آمنّا بإله يونس.

قال: فصرَفَ الله عنهم العذاب إلى جبال آمِد، قال: وأصبح يونس عليه السلام وهو يظُنّ أنّهم هَلَكوا، فوجدهم في عافِية، فغَضِب وخَرَج، كما قال الله تعالى: ﴿مُغاضِباً﴾ حتّى رَكِب سفينةً فيها رجلان، فاضطربت السفينة، فقال الملاّح: يا قوم، في سفينتي مطلوبٌ، فقال يونس عليه السلام: أنا هو: وقام ليُلقي نفسه، فأبصر السمكة وقد فتحت فاها فهابَها، وتعلّق به الرّجلان، وقالا له: أنت وحدك ونحن رجلان، فساهمهم فوقعت السِّهام عليه، فجَرت السُّنّة بأنّ السّهام إذا كانت ثلاث مرّات أنّها لا تُخطئ، فألقى نفسه فالتقمَه الحوت، فطاف به البحار السبعة، حتّى صار إلى البحر المسجُور، وبه يُعذّب قارون، فسمِع قارون دويًّا، فسأل المَلَك عن ذلك فأخبره أنّه يونس عليه السلام، وأنّ الله قد حَبَسه في بطن الحوت، فقال له قارون: أتأذَن لي أن أكلّمه، فأذِن له، فسأله عن موسى عليه السلام فأخبره أنّه مات وبَكى، ثمّ سأله عن هارون عليه السلام فأخبره أنه مات، فبكا وجَزِع جزعًا شديدًا،

Then he asked about his sister Kaltham who had been betrothed to him, so he informed him of her death too. So he exclaimed, "How intense my grief over the family of 'Imrān!"

He said, 'So God revealed to the angel in charge of him to absolve him of his punishment for the remainder of his days on earth because of his affection for his relatives.' [10:98]

47. From Ma'mar who said, 'Abū al-Ḥasan al-Riḍā عليه السلام said, "When the command of God came to Yūnus and he informed his people about it and the punishment loomed over them, they separated themselves from their children, and separated the cattle from their young, then beseeched and pleaded to God. God removed the punishment from them, after which Yūnus left them in his rage, and the fish subsequently swallowed him up and swam around in the sea for seven days."

I asked him, "How long did he stay in the belly of the fish?"

He replied, "Three days, then the fish spat him out. His skin and hair had dissolved, so God made a gourd tree grow which shaded him [from the sun]. When he became stronger, it began to wither, so he said, "My Lord, the tree that shaded me is withering away!"

So God revealed to him, saying, "Yūnus, you are upset about a tree that shaded you but were not upset about punishment befalling more than one hundred thousand people?"' [10:98]

48. From 'Alī b. 'Uqba, on his father's authority who said, 'I heard Abū 'Abd Allāh عليه السلام say, "Entrust this matter of yours [i.e. the Imamate] to God and not to the people, for what is dedicated to God is truly God's and what is done for people does not reach God. Do not dispute with the people about your creed, for dispute makes the heart fall sick. God said to His Prophet: 'Muḥammad, ﴾*You cannot guide everyone you love to the truth; it is God who guides whoever He wills*﴿(28:56) and: ﴾*So can you [Prophet] compel people to believe?*﴿ Leave the people, for the people have learned but from other people, whereas you have learned from none other than God's Messenger ﷺ and 'Alī عليه السلام. I have heard my father عليه السلام say, 'When God decrees for a servant to enter under the banner of this authority, then it materialises for him faster than a bird can fly to its nest.'" [10:99]

وسأله عن أُختِه كلثَم ــ وكانت مُسمّاة له ــ فأخبره أنّها ماتت، فبَكى وجَزِع جزَعًا شديدًا، قال: فأوحى الله إلى المَلَك الموكّل به: أن ارفَع عنه العذاب بَقيّة الدنيا، لرِقّته على قَرابته.

٤٧. عن مَعمَر قال: قال أبو الحسن الرضا عليه السلام إنّ يونس عليه السلام لمّا أمره الله بما أمره، فأعلم قومه، فأظلّهم العذاب، ففرّقوا بينهم وبين أولادهم وبين البهائم وأولادها، ثمّ عجّوا إلى الله وضجّوا، فكفَّ الله العذاب عنهم، فذهب يونس مُغاضِبًا، فالتقمه الحُوت، فطاف به سبعةً في البحر.

فقلتُ له: كم بقي في بطن الحُوت؟ قال: ثلاثة أيّام، ثمّ لفظه الحُوت، وقد ذهب جِلده وشعره، فأنبت الله عليه شجرةً من يقطين فأضلّته، فلمّا قوي أخذت في اليُبس، فقال: يا ربّ شجرة أظلّتني يبُست، فأوحى الله إليه: يا يونس، تجزَع لشجرةٍ أظلّتك، ولا تجزَع لمائة ألف أو يزيدون من العذاب؟

٤٨. عن عليّ بن عُقبة، عن أبيه، قال: سمِعتُ أبا عبد الله عليه السلام يقول: اجعلوا أمركم هذا لله، ولا تجعلوه للنّاس، فإنّه ما كان لله فهو لله، وما كان للنّاس فلا يصعَدُ إلى الله، ولا تُخاصموا الناس بدينكم، فإنّ الخُصومة ممرضةٌ للقلب، إنّ الله قال لنبيّه صلى الله عليه وآله: يا محمّد ﴿إِنَّكَ لَا تَهْدِي مَنْ أَحْبَبْتَ وَلَكِنَّ اللَّهَ يَهْدِي مَنْ يَشَاءُ﴾ وقال ﴿أَفَأَنْتَ تُكْرِهُ النَّاسَ حَتَّى يَكُونُوا مُؤْمِنِينَ﴾ ذرُوا النّاس، فإنّ الناس أخذوا من الناس، وإنّكم أخذتم من رسول الله وعليّ عليه السلام، ولا سَواء، إنّي سمِعتُ أبي عليه السلام هو يقول: إنّ الله إذا كتَب إلى عبدٍ أن يدخُل في هذا الأمر، كان أسرع إليه من الطير إلى وَكرِه.

49. From 'Abd Allāh b. Yaḥyā al-Kāhilī, from Abū 'Abd Allāh عليه السلام. He said, 'I heard him say, "When the Messenger of God – peace be upon him and his family – was taken on the Night Journey, Jibra'īl عليه السلام brought al-Burāq to him which he mounted and went to the Holy Sanctuary (*al-bayt al-muqaddas*). There he met with [his brothers from among] the previous prophets. Then he returned, and when he awoke he told his companions, 'I went to the Holy Sanctuary last night and met my brothers from among the prophets.'

So they said, 'O Messenger of God, how can you have gone to the Holy Sanctuary last night?'

So he replied, 'Jibra'īl عليه السلام brought me al-Burāq which I rode. The evidence of it is that I passed by one of Abū Sufyān's caravans at the oasis of so-and-so, and they were looking for a camel of theirs that they had lost.'

He continued, "So people began saying to each other, 'He could have ridden extremely fast. However, you people who have just come from Shām and know it well, ask him about its marketplaces, its gates and its traders [to test him thereby].'"

He said, "So they quizzed him, saying, 'O Messenger of God, what is Shām like? What are its marketplaces like?'

The Messenger of God صلى الله عليه وآله was such that whenever he was asked about something that he did not know, he became anxious and it would show on his face."

He continued, "He was barely in that state when Jibra'īl عليه السلام came to him saying, 'O Messenger of God, behold Shām that has been raised up here for you.'

The Messenger of God – peace be upon him and his family – looked up and there he was in Shām with its gates and its traders. So he asked, 'Where is the man who asked about Shām?'

They, in turn, asked him, 'Where is so-and-so's house?' and 'Where is such and such a place?'

He answered every single thing that they asked him about, but very few of them believed. This is the purport of God's words: ﴿*But what use are signs and warnings to people who will not believe?*﴾ We seek refuge in God from disbelieving in God and His Messenger. We believe in God and His Messenger, we believe in God and His Messenger."' [10:101]

٤٩. عن عبد الله بن يحيى الكاهلي، عن أبي عبد الله عليه السلام، قال: سمِعتُه يقول: لمّا أُسرِي برسول الله عليه وآله السلام آتاه جَبرئيل عليه السلام بالبُراق فركِبها، فأتى بيت المَقدِس، فلقي مَن لقي من إخوانه من الأنبياء، ثمّ رجَع فأصبح يُحدِّث أصحابه: إنّي أتيتُ بيت المقدِس اللّيلة، ولقيتُ إخواني من الأنبياء، فقالوا: يا رسول الله، وكيف أتيتَ بيت المقدِس اللّيلة؟ فقال: جاءني جَبرئيل عليه السلام بالبُراق فركِبتُها، وآية ذلك أنّي مررتُ بعِيرٍ لأبي سُفيان على ماء بني فلان، وقد أضلّوا جَملاً لهم، وهو في طَلَبه.

قال: فقال القوم بعضُهم لبعضٍ: إنّما جاء راكِبًا سريعًا، ولكنّكم قد أتيتُم الشام وعرفتموها، فسلُوه عن أسواقها وأبوابها وتُجّارها، قال: فسألوه، فقالوا: يا رسول الله، كيف الشام وكيف أسواقها؟ وكان رسول الله عليه السلام إذا سُئِل عن الشيء لا يَعرِفه شقّ عليه حتّى يرى ذلك في وجهه.

قال: فبينا هو كذلك إذ أتاه جَبرائيل عليه السلام، فقال: يا رسول الله، هذه الشام قد رُفِعت لك؛ فالتفت رسول الله عليه السلام فإذا هو بالشام، وأبوابها، وتُجّارها، فقال: أين السائل عن الشام؟ فقالوا: أين بيت فلان ومكان فلان؟ فأجابهم في كُلّ ما سألوه عنه.

قال: فلم يؤمِن منهم إلاّ قليل، وهو قول الله: ﴿وَمَا تُغْنِي الآيَاتُ وَالنُّذُرُ عَنْ قَوْمٍ لا يُؤْمِنُونَ﴾ فنعوذُ بالله أن لا نؤمن بالله ورسوله، آمنّا بالله وبرسوله صلى الله عليه وآله وسلم.

50. From Muḥammad b. al-Fuḍayl, from Abū al-Ḥasan al-Riḍā عليه السلام. He said, 'I asked him something about the relief [when the Mahdī reappears], so he replied, "Don't you know that waiting for that relief is relief in itself? God says: ﴾*'Wait then, I am waiting too.'*﴿ [10:102]

51. From Maṣqala al-Ṭaḥḥān[6], from Abū 'Abd Allāh عليه السلام who said, 'What stops you from bearing witness that whosoever dies from amongst you having adhered to this authority is indeed deserving of the Garden? God Himself says: ﴾*We take it upon Ourself to save the believers.*﴿' [10:103]

6 Maṣqala al-Ṭaḥḥān, about whom there is scant information, is listed by Barqī as a companion of Imam Ja'far al-Ṣādiq. See Khū'ī, *Mu'jam*, 19:194 (nr. 12419).

٥٠. عن محمّد بن الفُضيل، عن أبي الحسن الرضا عليه السلام، قال: سألتُه عن شيءٍ في الفَرَج، فقال: أوَ ليس تعلم أنّ انتظار الفَرج من الفَرج، إنّ الله يقول: ﴿فَانْتَظِرُوا إِنِّي مَعَكُمْ مِنَ الْمُنْتَظِرِينَ﴾.

٥١. عن مَصقَلة الطّحّان، عن أبي عبد الله عليه السلام، قال: ما يمنعكم أن تَشهَدوا على من مات منكم على هذا الأمر أنّه من أهل الجنّة، إنّ الله يقول: ﴿كَذَٰلِكَ حَقًّا عَلَيْنَا نُنْجِ الْمُؤْمِنِينَ﴾.

Hūd

11. Hūd

1. From Ibn Sinān from Jābir, from Abū Jaʿfar ﵇ who said, 'Whoever recites the Chapter of Hūd every Friday, God will resurrect him on the Day of Judgement in the company of the believers and the prophets. He will be given an easy account and there will be no record of him having committed any sins.'

2. From Sadīr, from Abū Jaʿfar ﵇ who said, 'Jābir b. ʿAbd Allāh informed me that the polytheists used to pass by the Messenger of God ﷺ and that one of them would push his head and his back forward like this, and then cover his head up with his cloak so that the Messenger of God ﷺ could not see who it was. So God revealed: ﴾*See how they* [*the disbelievers*] *wrap themselves up, to hide their feelings from Him. But even when they cover themselves with their clothes, He knows what they conceal and what they reveal.*﴿' [11:5]

3. From Muḥammad b. Fuḍayl from Jābir, from Abū Jaʿfar ﵇ who said, 'A Bedouin came to the Messenger of God ﷺ and said, "O Messenger of God, I have sons, daughters, brothers, sisters, grandchildren, nieces and nephews to support, and our livelihood is meagre. Please, O Messenger of God, could you supplicate to God to grant us ample livelihood?"

   He continued, 'And he was crying, so the Muslims were sympathetic towards him, so the Messenger of God ﷺ said: ﴾*There is not a creature that moves on earth whose provision is not His concern. He knows where it lives and its* [*final*] *resting place: it is all* [*there*] *in a clear record.*﴿ Whoever takes responsibility for feeding these mouths whom God has promised to feed, God will pour provision down unto him like a downpour of rain, however little or much it may be." Then the Messenger of God ﷺ supplicated for him, and the Muslims all said Amen.'

بسم الله الرحمن الرحيم

من سورة هود

١. عن ابن سِنان، عن جابر، عن أبي جعفر عليه السلام، قال: مَن قرأ سورة هود في كلّ جمعة بَعثَه الله يوم القيامة في زُمرة المؤمنين والنبيّين، وحُوسِب حسابًا يسيرًا، ولم يُعرَف [له] خطيئة عَمِلها يوم القيامة.

٢. عن سَدير، عن أبي جعفر عليه السلام، قال: أخبرني جابر بن عبدالله أنّ المشركين كانوا إذا مرّوا برسول الله صلى الله عليه وآله، طأطأ أحدهم رأسه وظهره هكذا، وغطّى رأسه بثوبه، حتّى لا يراه رسول الله صلى الله عليه وآله، فأنزل الله: ﴿أَلَا إِنَّهُمْ يَثْنُونَ صُدُورَهُمْ﴾ إلى ﴿وَمَا يُعْلِنُونَ﴾.

٣. عن محمّد بن فُضيل، عن جابر، عن أبي جعفر عليه السلام، قال: أتى رسول الله صلى الله عليه وآله رجلٌ من أهل البادية، فقال: يا رسول الله، إنّ لي بنين وبنات، إخوة وأخوات، وبني بنين وبني بنات، وبني إخوة وبني أخوات، والمعيشة علينا خفيفة، فإن رأيتَ يا رسول الله أن تدعو الله أن يُوسّع علينا، قال: وبكى، فرقّ له المسلمون، فقال رسول الله صلى الله عليه وآله: ﴿وَمَا مِنْ دَابَّةٍ فِي الْأَرْضِ إِلَّا عَلَى اللَّهِ رِزْقُهَا وَيَعْلَمُ مُسْتَقَرَّهَا وَمُسْتَوْدَعَهَا كُلٌّ فِي كِتَابٍ مُبِينٍ﴾ من كَفَل بهذه الأفواه المضمونة على الله رزقها صبّ الله عليه الرزق صبًّا

He continued, 'Abū Ja'far عليه السلام said, "Someone who met the man again at the time of 'Umar and asked him about his situation narrated to me that he replied, "I am among the best to have been granted a permissible livelihood and the wealthiest."' [11:6]

4. From 'Abd Allāh b. Sinān, from Abū 'Abd Allāh عليه السلام who said, 'God created good on Sunday, and He would never create evil before good. On Sunday and Monday, He created the land masses, and on Tuesday their means of subsistence. On Wednesday, He created the heavens, and on Thursday and Friday their means of subsistence. This is as per His statement: ﴾*It is He who created the heavens and the earth in six Days*﴿, and this is why the Jews are abstinent on Saturday [the Sabbath].' [11:7]

5. From Muḥammad b. Muslim, from Abū Ja'far عليه السلام who said, 'God, Blessed and most High, is as He describes Himself; and ﴾*His rule extends over the waters too.*﴿ The water is in the air, and the air does not move.' [11:7]

6. Muḥammad b. 'Imrān al-'Ijlī[1] said, 'I asked Abū 'Abd Allāh عليه السلام, "Where was the location of the place where the water was in God's statement: ﴾*His rule extends over the waters too*﴿?" He replied, "It was a white abyss, meaning a pearl."' [11:7]

7. From Abān b. [Abī] Musāfir,[2] from Abū 'Abd Allāh عليه السلام who said regarding God's verse ﴾*If We defer their punishment for a determined time*﴿ – meaning as much as the number [of people] at Badr – ﴾*they are sure to say, 'What is holding it back?' But on the Day it comes upon them, nothing will divert it from them.*﴿ He said, 'The punishment.' [11:8]

---

1 Muḥammad b. 'Imrān al-'Ijlī, on whom there is scant information. See Khū'ī, *Mu'jam*, 18:87–8 (nr. 11510).

2 Abān b. Abī Musāfir, a companion of Imam Ja'far al-Ṣādiq. See Khū'ī, *Mu'jam*, 1:130 (nr. 23).

كالماء المُنهَمر، إن قليل فقليلاً، وإن كثير فكثيرًا، قال: ثمّ دعا رسول الله ﷺ وأمّن له المسلمون.

قال: قال أبو جعفر عليه السلام: فحدّثني من رأى الرجل في زمن عُمر، فسأله عن حاله، فقال: مِن أحسن مَن خوّله حلالاً، وأكثرهم مالاً.

٤. عن عبد الله بن سِنان، عن أبي عبد الله عليه السلام، قال: إنّ الله خلق الخير يوم الأحد، وما كان ليخلُق الشرّ قبل الخير، وخلق يوم الأحد والاثنين الأرضين، وخلق يوم الثُلاثاء أقواتها، وخلق يوم الأربعاء السماوات، وخلق يوم الخميس أقواتها والجُمعة، وذلك في قوله تعالى: ﴿خَلَقَ السَّمَاوَاتِ وَالأَرْضَ فِي سِتَّةِ أَيَّامٍ﴾ فلذلك أمسكت اليهود يوم السبت.

٥. عن محمّد بن مسلم، عن أبي جعفر عليه السلام، قال: كان الله تبارك وتعالى كما وَصَف نفسه ﴿وَكَانَ عَرْشُهُ عَلَى الْمَاءِ﴾ والماء على الهواء، والهواء لا يجري.

٦. قال محمّد بن عِمران العِجلي: قلتُ لأبي عبد الله: أيّ شيءٍ كان موضع البيت حيث كان الماء في قول الله: ﴿وَكَانَ عَرْشُهُ عَلَى الْمَاءِ﴾؟ قال: كانت مَهاة بيضاء، يعني دُرَّة.

٧. عن أبان بن أبي مُسافر، عن أبي عبد الله عليه السلام، في قول الله: ﴿وَلَئِنْ أَخَّرْنَا عَنْهُمُ الْعَذَابَ إِلَى أُمَّةٍ مَعْدُودَةٍ﴾ يعني عِدّة كعِدّة بدرٍ ﴿لَيَقُولُنَّ مَا يَحْبِسُهُ أَلَا يَوْمَ يَأْتِيهِمْ لَيْسَ مَصْرُوفًا عَنْهُمْ﴾، قال: العذاب.

8. From ʿAbd al-Aʿlā al-Ḥalabī who said, 'Abū Jaʿfar ﷺ said, "The companions of the Qā'im will be some three hundred and a few men. By God, they are the determined number that God mentions in His Book: ﴾*If We defer their punishment for a determined time.*﴿' He continued, 'They will gather together for him all at the same time as the gathering of the autumn rain clouds.' [11:8]

9. From al-Ḥusayn from al-Kharrāz, from Abū ʿAbd Allāh ﷺ regarding the verse: ﴾*If We defer their punishment for a determined time,*﴿ he said, 'This is referring to the Qā'im and his companions.' [11:8]

10. From Jābir b. Arqam, from his brother Zayd b. Arqam who said, 'Jibra'īl, the trustworthy spirit, descended upon God's Messenger ﷺ with the authority of ʿAlī b. Abī Ṭālib ﷺ on the eve of *ʿarafa*, at which time the Messenger of God ﷺ became anxious out of fear of being rejected by the skeptics and hypocrites. So he called a group of people, I being one of them, to consult them about that, so that he could implement it at the right time. However, we did not know what to say to him; so he ﷺ wept and Jibra'īl asked him, 'What is wrong, Muḥammad? Are you upset with God's command?' So he said, 'Absolutely not, Jibra'īl, but my Lord knows what I faced from the Quraysh when they did not attest to my prophethood until finally, He commanded me to fight them, and had to send down an army from the heavens to help me. So how will they ever attest to ʿAlī after me?' So Jibra'īl left him and this verse descended unto him: ﴾*So* [*Prophet*] *are you going to abandon some part of what is revealed to you, and let your heart be oppressed by it?*﴿' [11:12]

11. From ʿAmmār b. Suwayd[3] who said, 'I heard Abū ʿAbd Allāh ﷺ say regarding this verse: ﴾*So* [*Prophet*] *are you going to abandon some part of what is revealed to you, and let your heart be oppressed by it, because they say, 'Why is no treasure sent down to him? Why has no angel come with him?*﴿ He said, 'When the Messenger of God ﷺ stopped at Qudayd,[4] he said to ʿAlī ﷺ, "I

3 ʿAmmār b. Suwayd, a companion of Imam Jaʿfar al-Ṣādiq. See Khū'ī, *Muʿjam*, 13:271 (nr. 8648).

4 Qudayd, a region near Mecca.

٨. عن عبد الأعلى الحلبي، قال: قال أبو جعفر عليه السلام: أصحاب القائم عليه السلام الثلاثمائة والبِضعة عشر رَجُلاً، هم والله الأُمَّة المعدودة الّتي قال الله في كتابه: ﴿وَلَئِنْ أَخَّرْنَا عَنْهُمُ الْعَذَابَ إِلَىٰ أُمَّةٍ مَّعْدُودَةٍ﴾ قال: يُجمَعُون له في ساعةٍ واحدةٍ قَزَعًا كقَزَعِ الخريف.

٩. عن الحسين، عن الخزّاز، عن أبي عبدالله عليه السلام: ﴿وَلَئِنْ أَخَّرْنَا عَنْهُمُ الْعَذَابَ إِلَىٰ أُمَّةٍ مَّعْدُودَةٍ﴾، قال عليه السلام: هو القائم وأصحابه.

١٠. عن جابر بن أرقم، عن أخيه زيد بن أرقم، قال: إنَّ جبَرئيل الرُّوح الأمين نزل على رسول الله صلى الله عليه وآله بولاية عليّ بن أبي طالب عليه السلام عَشيّة عَرفة، فضاق بذلك رسول الله صلى الله عليه وآله مخافة تكذيب أهل الإفك والنِّفاق، فدعا قومًا أنا فيهم، فاستشارهم في ذلك ليقوم به في الموسم، فلم ندرِ ما نقول له، وبكى صلى الله عليه وآله، فقال له جبَرئيل: ما لك يا محمَّد، أجزِعت من أمر الله؟ فقال: كلاّ يا جبَرئيل، ولكن قد علِم ربّي ما لقيتُ من قُريش، إذ لم يُقِرّوا لي بالرسالة حتّى أمرني بجهادهم، وأهبط إليّ جُنودًا من السماء فنصروني، فكيف يُقِرُّون لعليٍّ من بعدي! فانصرف عنه جبَرئيل، فنزل عليه: ﴿فَلَعَلَّكَ تَارِكٌ بَعْضَ مَا يُوحَىٰ إِلَيْكَ وَضَائِقٌ بِهِ صَدْرُكَ﴾.

١١. عن عمّار بن سويد، قال: سَمِعتُ أبا عبدالله عليه السلام يقول في هذه الآية ﴿فَلَعَلَّكَ تَارِكٌ بَعْضَ مَا يُوحَىٰ إِلَيْكَ وَضَائِقٌ بِهِ صَدْرُكَ﴾ إلى قوله: ﴿أَوْ جَاءَ مَعَهُ مَلَكٌ﴾.

قال: إنَّ رسول الله صلى الله عليه وآله لمّا نزل قُديدًا

asked my Lord to make a strong bond of patronage between you and me, so He did. I asked my Lord to make us brothers, and He did. Then I asked my Lord to make you my successor, and He has done so." So two men from the Quraysh said, "By God, we would much rather have a bunch of dates in a cool, wet water-skin than what Muḥammad has asked his Lord for. He could have asked for an angel to assist him against his enemies or treasure that he can use in his time of need. By God, and no sooner did he supplicate to Him for the wrong thing than He gave it to him."

So God revealed unto him: ﴾*So* [*Prophet*] *are you going to abandon some part of what is revealed to you, and let your heart be oppressed by it, because they say, 'Why is no treasure sent down to him? Why has no angel come with him?' You are only there to warn; it is God who is in charge of everything.*﴿ The Messenger of God – peace be upon him and his family – supplicated for the Commander of the Faithful at the end of his prayer in a loud voice that people could hear, saying, "O God, grant 'Alī the love that is in the believers' hearts, and place fear and awe of him in the hypocrites' hearts."

So God revealed: ﴾*But the Lord of Mercy will give love to those who believe and do righteous deeds: We have made it easy, in your own language* [*Prophet*], *so that you may bring glad news to the righteous and warnings to a stubborn people*﴿(19:96–97) meaning the Banū Umayya. So Ruma'[5] said, "By God, I would much rather prefer a bunch of dates in a cool, wet water-skin than what Muḥammad wants from his Lord. He could have asked for an angel to assist him against his enemies or treasure that he can fall back on to support him in his time of need."

So God revealed ten verses from the Chapter of Hūd, beginning with: ﴾*So* [*Prophet*] *are you going to abandon some part of what is revealed to you... if they say, 'He has invented it himself,*﴿ – referring to 'Alī's authority; ﴾*say, 'Then produce ten invented sūrahs like it ... if they do not answer you*﴿ regarding 'Alī's authority; ﴾*then you will all know that it is sent down containing knowledge from God, and that there is no god but Him. Then will you submit to Him?*﴿ in his appointment of 'Alī; ﴾*If any desire* [*only*] *the life of this world with all its finery*﴿ – referring to [Abū Bakr] and ['Umar b. al-Khaṭṭāb] – ﴾*We shall repay them in full in this life for their deeds... their work here will be fruitless and their deeds futile. Can they be compared to those who have clear*

5 An anagram of the name 'Umar.

قال لعليّ عليه السلام: إنّي سألتُ ربّي أن يوالي بيني وبينك ففعل، وسألتُ ربّي أن يُؤاخي بيني وبينك ففعل، وسألتُ ربّ أن يجعلك وصيّي ففعل، فقال رجلان من قريش: والله لصاعٌ من تمرٍ في شَنٍّ بالٍ أحبّ إلينا ممّا سأل محمد ربّه، فهلاّ سأله مُلكًا يعضُدُه على عدوّه، أوكنزًا يستعين به على فاقته؟ّوالله ما دعاه إلى باطلٍ إلاّ أجابه له، فأنزل الله عليه ﴿فَلَعَلَّكَ تَارِكٌ بَعْضَ مَا يُوحَى إِلَيْكَ﴾ إلى آخر الآية.

قال: ودعا رسول الله صلى الله عليه وآله وسلم لأمير المؤمنين عليه السلام في آخر صلاته رافعًا بها صوته يُسمِع الناس، يقول: «اللّهُمّ هَب لعليّ المودَّة في صدور المؤمنين، والهيبة والعظمة في صُدُور المنافقين» فأنزل الله: ﴿إِنَّ الَّذِينَ آمَنُوا وَعَمِلُوا الصَّالِحَاتِ سَيَجْعَلُ لَهُمُ الرَّحْمَنُ وُدًّا ۞ فَإِنَّمَا يَسَّرْنَاهُ بِلِسَانِكَ لِتُبَشِّرَ بِهِ الْمُتَّقِينَ وَتُنْذِرَ بِهِ قَوْمًا لُدًّا﴾ بني أُميّة.

فقال رمع: والله لصاعٌ من تمرٍ في شَنٍّ بالٍ أحبُّ إليَّ ممّا سأل محمد ربّه، أفلا سأله مُلكًا يَعضُده، أوكنزًا يستظهر به على فاقته؟ فأنزل الله فيه عشر آيات من هود أوّلها: ﴿فَلَعَلَّكَ تَارِكٌ بَعْضَ مَا يُوحَى إِلَيْكَ﴾ إلى: ﴿أَمْ يَقُولُونَ افْتَرَاهُ﴾ ولاية عليّ عليه السلام ﴿قُلْ فَأْتُوا بِعَشْرِ سُوَرٍ مِثْلِهِ مُفْتَرَيَاتٍ﴾ إلى: ﴿فَإِنْ لَمْ يَسْتَجِيبُوا لَكُمْ﴾ في ولاية عليّ ﴿فَاعْلَمُوا أَنَّمَا أُنْزِلَ بِعِلْمِ اللَّهِ وَأَنْ لَا إِلَهَ إِلَّا هُوَ فَهَلْ أَنْتُمْ مُسْلِمُونَ﴾ لعليّ ولايته ﴿مَنْ كَانَ يُرِيدُ الْحَيَاةَ الدُّنْيَا وَزِينَتَهَا﴾ يعني فلانًا وفلانًا ﴿نُوَفِّ إِلَيْهِمْ أَعْمَالَهُمْ فِيهَا﴾، ﴿أَفَمَنْ كَانَ عَلَى بَيِّنَةٍ مِنْ رَبِّهِ﴾ رسول الله صلى الله عليه وآله وسلم ﴿وَيَتْلُوهُ شَاهِدٌ مِنْهُ﴾ أمير المؤمنين عليه السلام ﴿وَمِنْ قَبْلِهِ كِتَابُ مُوسَى إِمَامًا وَرَحْمَةً﴾، قال: كانت ولاية عليّ عليه السلام في كتاب موسى ﴿أُولَئِكَ يُؤْمِنُونَ بِهِ وَمَنْ يَكْفُرْ بِهِ مِنَ

proof from their Lord﴿ – i.e. the Messenger of God ﷺ – ﴾*recited by a witness from Him*﴿ – i.e. the Commander of the Faithful عليه السلام – ﴾*and before it the Book of Mūsā, as a guide and mercy*﴿ – He said, 'The authority of 'Alī is mentioned in Mūsā's Book – ﴾*These people believe in it, whereas those groups that deny its truth are promised the Fire. So have no doubt about it*﴿ – i.e. 'Alī's authority – ﴾*it is the Truth from your Lord though most people do not believe so… and the witnesses will say*﴿ – they are the Imams, peace be upon them – ﴾*'These are the ones that lied about their Lord'… can these two groups be alike? How can you not take heed?*﴿(11:18–24)' [11:12–17]

12. From Burayd b. Mu'āwiya al-'Ijlī, from Abū Ja'far عليه السلام who said, 'The one who has clear proof from his Lord is the Messenger of God ﷺ, and the one who recited it after him as a witness from himself is the Commander of the Faithful عليه السلام and then his successors one after the other.' [11:17]

13. From Jābir, from 'Abd Allāh b. Yaḥyā who said, 'I heard 'Alī عليه السلام say, "There is not a single man from among the Quraysh who has not had a verse or two revealed about him in God's Book."

A man from the community asked him, "So what has been revealed about you, the Commander of the Faithful?" He replied, "Have you not read the verse in [the chapter of] Hud: ﴾*Can they be compared to those who have clear proof from their Lord, recited by a witness from Him*﴿ – Muḥammad ﷺ is the one with a clear proof from His Lord, and I am the witness."' [11:17]

14. From Abū 'Ubayda who said, 'I asked Abū Ja'far عليه السلام about God's verse: ﴾*Who could do more wrong than someone who invents lies about God? Such people will be brought before their Lord, and the witnesses will say, 'These are the ones that lied about their Lord.' God's rejection is the due of those who do such wrong, who hinder others from God's path, trying to make it crooked* […]﴿ So he replied, "These are four kings from the Quraysh, who will follow one another." [11:18–19]

15. From Abū Usāma who said, 'I said to Abū 'Abd Allāh عليه السلام, "There is a man among us called Kulayb who no sooner does he hear of anything that has been issued by you than he says: 'I submit.' So we have named him Kulayb of Submission." He replied, "Then be extra kind to him." Then he said, "Do

الأَحْزَابِ فَالنَّارُ مَوْعِدُهُ فَلاَ تَكُ فِي مِرْيَةٍ مِنْهُ﴾ في ولاية عليّ ﴿إِنَّهُ الْحَقُّ مِنْ رَبِّكَ﴾ إلى قوله: ﴿وَيَقُولُ الأَشْهَادُ﴾ هُمُ الأئمّة عليهم السلام ﴿هَؤُلاَءِ الَّذِينَ كَذَبُوا عَلَى رَبِّهِمْ﴾ إلى قوله: ﴿هَلْ يَسْتَوِيَانِ مَثَلاً أَفَلاَ تَذَكَّرُونَ﴾.

١٢. عن بُريد بن معاوية العِجلي، عن أبي جعفر عليه السلام، قال: الذي على بيّنه من ربّه رسول الله صلى الله عليه وآله، والذي تلاه من بعده الشاهد منه أمير المؤمنين عليه السلام، ثمّ أوصياؤه واحد بعد واحد.

١٣. عن جابر، عن عبدالله بن يحيى، قال: سَمِعتُ عليّاً عليه السلام وهو يقول: ما من رجلٍ من قريش إلاّ وقد أُنزِلت فيه آيةٌ أو آيتان من كتاب الله.

فقال له رجل من القوم: فما نزل فيك يا أمير المؤمنين؟ فقال عليه السلام: أما تقرأ الآية الّتي في هود ﴿أَفَمَنْ كَانَ عَلَى بَيِّنَةٍ مِنْ رَبِّهِ وَيَتْلُوهُ شَاهِدٌ مِنْهُ﴾ محمّد صلى الله عليه وآله على بيّنةٍ من ربّه، وأنا الشاهد.

١٤. عن أبي عبيدة، قال: سالتُ أبا جعفر عليه السلام عن قول الله تعالى: ﴿وَمَنْ أَظْلَمُ مِمَّنِ افْتَرَى عَلَى اللهِ كَذِباً أُولَئِكَ يُعْرَضُونَ عَلَى رَبِّهِمْ﴾ إلى قوله: ﴿وَيَبْغُونَهَا عِوَجاً﴾، فقال: هم أربعة مُلوك من قريش، يتبع بعضهم بعضاً.

١٥. عن أبي أُسامة، قال: قلتُ لأبي عبدالله عليه السلام: إنّ عندنا رجلاً يسمّى كُليباً، لا يجيء عنكم شيء إلاّ قال: أنا أُسلّم، فسمّيناه كليب تسليم؟ قال: فترحّم عليه، ثمّ قال: أتدرون

you know what submission actually is?" We remained quiet, so he said, "By God, it is to humble oneself. God says: ﴾*But those who believed, did good deeds, and humbled themselves before their Lord* [...]﴿"' [11:23]

16. From Ibn Abī Naṣr al-Biẓanṭī[6], from Abū al-Ḥasan al-Riḍā عليه السلام who said, 'God said regarding Nūḥ's community: ﴾*My advice will be of no use to you if God wishes to leave you to your delusions.*﴿ He said, "The decision is up to God whether He guides or leaves them to stray."' [11:34]

17. From Abū al-Ṭufayl, from Abū Ja'far, on his father's authority, peace be upon them both, who said regarding God's verse: ﴾*My advice will be no use to you if God wishes to leave you to your delusions*﴿, 'It was revealed about al-'Abbās.' [11:34]

18. From Ismā'īl [b. Jābir] al-Ju'fī, from Abū Ja'far عليه السلام who said, 'Nūḥ's legal code was simply that God is worshipped exclusively and sincerely with no rivals; and it was the innate nature that people have been predisposed to. So He made the covenant with Nūḥ and the other prophets to worship God and to not associate anything with Him. He commanded him to pray, to enjoin the good, forbid the evil, and observe the prohibited and permissible. He did not impose laws of prescribed punishments on him nor laws of inheritance, and this was his code of law. So he remained with them for nine hundred and fifty years, propagating to them in private as well as in public. When they refused and rebelled, he said, ﴾*My Lord, I am defeated so help me!*﴿(54:10) So God revealed: ﴾*None of your people will believe, other than those who have already done so, so do not be distressed by what they do.*﴿ This is why Nūḥ said: ﴾*if you leave them they will lead Your servants astray and beget only sinners and disbelievers.*﴿(71:27) Then God revealed to him: ﴾*Build the Ark* [...]﴿' [11:36]

19. From al-Mufaḍḍal b. 'Umar who said, 'I was with Abū 'Abd Allāh عليه السلام in Kufa when he went to visit Abū al-'Abbās. When we reached a pile of rubbish, he looked to his left and said, "Mufaḍḍal, my uncle Zayd, may God have mercy on him, was crucified right here." Then he went on until he came to the arch

6 A reference to Aḥmad b. Muḥammad b. Abī Naṣr al-Bizanṭī.

ما التسليم؟ فسكتنا، فقال: هو والله الإخبات، قول الله: ﴿إِنَّ الَّذِينَ آمَنُوا وَعَمِلُوا الصَّالِحَاتِ وَأَخْبَتُوا إِلَى رَبِّهِمْ﴾.

١٦. عن ابن أبي نَصر البَزَنطي، عن أبي الحسن الرضا عليه السلام، قال: قال الله في قوم نوح، ﴿وَلَا يَنْفَعُكُمْ نُصْحِي إِنْ أَرَدْتُ أَنْ أَنْصَحَ لَكُمْ إِنْ كَانَ اللَّهُ يُرِيدُ أَنْ يُغْوِيَكُمْ﴾، قال: الأمر إلى الله يهدي ويُضِلّ.

١٧. عن أبي الطُّفيل، عن أبي جعفر، عن أبيه عليهما السلام، في قول الله: ﴿وَلَا يَنْفَعُكُمْ نُصْحِي إِنْ أَرَدْتُ أَنْ أَنْصَحَ لَكُمْ﴾، قال: نَزَلت في العباس.

١٨. عن إسماعيل الجُعفي، عن أبي جعفر عليه السلام، قال: كانت شريعة نُوح أن يُعبَد الله بالتوحيد والإخلاص وخَلع الأنداد، وهي الفِطرة الّتي فَطَر الناس عليها، وأخذ مِيثاقه على نُوح والنّبيّين أن يعبدوا الله ولا يُشركوا به شيئًا، وأمره بالصلاة والأمر والنهي، والحرام والحلال، ولم يفرِض عليه أحكام حُدود ولا فَرض مواريث، فهذه شريعته، فلَبِث فيهم ألف سنة إلاّ خمسين عامًا يدعوهم سرًّا وعلانيةً، فلمّا أبَوا وعتَوا قال: ربّ إنّي مغلوبٌ فانتصر، فأوحى الله إليه ﴿أَنَّهُ لَنْ يُؤْمِنَ مِنْ قَوْمِكَ إِلَّا مَنْ قَدْ آمَنَ فَلَا تَبْتَئِسْ بِمَا كَانُوا يَفْعَلُونَ﴾. فلذلك قال نوح: ﴿وَلَا يَلِدُوا إِلَّا فَاجِرًا كَفَّارًا﴾ وأوحى الله إليه ﴿أَنِ اصْنَعِ الْفُلْكَ﴾.

of olive trees at the end of the saddlers' [market]. He dismounted and said to me, "Get down for this is the original place of the very first Mosque of Kufa that Ādam had founded, and I would hate for us to enter it on horseback."

So I asked him, "Who moved it from its original place?" He replied, "The first to do that was the flood at the time of Nūḥ, then some of the companions of the Caesar and Nuʿmān b. Mundhir changed it after that. Then Ziyād b. Abī Sufyān."

So I said to him, "May I be your ransom – did Kufa and its mosque exist at the time of Nūḥ?" He replied, "Yes, Mufaḍḍal. Nūḥ and his people lived in a village towards the side of the Euphrates that lies to the west of Kufa."

He continued, "Nūḥ was a carpenter, so God chose him and sent him as a messenger. Nūḥ was the first to build a boat that could float on the surface of the water; and he remained among his people for nine hundred and fifty years, calling them to guidance, but they would pass him by and mock him. When he experienced that from them he cursed them, saying: ﴿*Lord, do not leave any of the disbelievers on the earth – if you leave them they will lead Your servants astray and beget only sinners and disbelievers.*﴾(71:27) He continued, "So God revealed: O Nūḥ, ﴿*Build the Ark*﴾ wide and hurry in completing it ﴿*under Our [watchful] Eyes and with Our inspiration.*﴾(23:27) So Nūḥ worked on the Ark in the Mosque of Kufa with his hands, bringing the wood from afar until he had completed it."

Mufaḍḍal said, 'Then Abū ʿAbd Allāh's narration stopped there as it was noon, so he got up and prayed the *ẓuhr* prayer and then the *ʿaṣr*. Then he went out of the mosque and turned to his left, pointing with his hand to one of the two safe houses, being the location of Ibn Ḥakīm's house. This is where the Euphrates is today. Then he said to me, "Mufaḍḍal, this is the place where the idols of Nūḥ's community – Yaghūth, Yaʿūq, and Nasr – were stood up."

Then he went ahead and mounted his horse.

So I asked him, "May I be your ransom – how long did it take Nūḥ to complete his building of the Ark?"

He replied, "Two cycles of time."

I asked, "How long are two cycles exactly?"

He replied, "Eighty years."

I said, "The majority [i.e. the Sunnis] say that it took him five hundred years."

١٩. عن المُفَضّل بن عمر، قال: كنتُ مع أبي عبد الله ﷺ، بالكوفة أيّام قَدِم على أبي العباس، فلمّا انتهينا إلى الكُناسة فنظر عن يساره، ثمّ قال: يا مُفضّل ها هنا صُلِب عمّي زيد رحمه الله، ثمّ مضى حتّى أتى طاق الزيّاتين، وهو آخر السرّاجين، فنزل فقال لي: انزِل، فإنّ هذا الموضع كان مسجد الكوفة الأوّل الذي خطّه آدم ﷺ، وأنا أكره أن أدخُله راكبًا.

فقلت له: فمن غيّره عن خُطّته؟ فقال: أمّا أوّل ذلك فالطُّوفان في زمن نوح، ثمّ غيّره بعد أصحاب كِسرى والنُّعمان بن المُنذر، ثمّ غيّره زياد بن أبي سفيان.

فقلتُ له: جُعِلتُ فِداك، وكانت الكوفة ومسجدها في زمن نوح ﷺ؟ فقال: نعم يا مفضلّ، وكان منزل نوح وقومه في قرية على مَتن الفُرات ممّا يلي غربيّ الكوفة.

قال: وكان نوح ﷺ رجلاً نجّارًا، فانتبأه وانتبجه، ونوح أوّل من عَمِل سفينةً تجري على ظَهر الماء، وإنّ نوحًا لبث في قومه ألف سنة إلاّ خمسين عامًا، يدعوهم إلى الهُدى، فيمرّون به ويَسخَرون منه، فلمّا رأى ذلك منهم دعا عليهم، فقال: ﴿رَبِّ لَا تَذَرْ عَلَى الْأَرْضِ مِنَ الْكَافِرِينَ دَيَّارًا﴾ إلى قوله: ﴿إِلَّا فَاجِرًا كَفَّارًا﴾، قال: فأوحى الله إليه: يا نوح ﴿أَنِ اصْنَعِ الْفُلْكَ﴾ وأوسعها وعجّل عملها ﴿بِأَعْيُنِنَا وَوَحْيِنَا﴾ فعَمِل نوح سفينته في مسجد الكوفة بيده، يأتي بالخشب من بُعد حتّى فَرَغَ منها.

قال مفضّل: ثمّ انقطع حديث أبي عبد الله ﷺ عند ذلك، عند زوال الشمس، فقام فصلّى الظهر ثمّ العصر، ثمّ أنصرف من المسجد، فالتفت عن يساره، وأشار بيده إلى موضع دار الداريين، وهو في موضع دار ابن حكيم، وذلك فُرات اليوم، فقال لي: يا مُفضّل، ها هنا نصِبت أصنام قوم نوح، يغوث ويعوق ونسر، ثمّ مضى حتّى رَكِب دابّته.

He said, "Never. How can that be when God says: ﴿*and with Our inspiration.*﴾' [11:37–49]

20. From 'Īsā b. 'Abd Allāh al-'Alawī, on his father's authority who said, 'The Ark measured forty in length by forty in height, and had a deck on it. It also had two portholes: one letting sunlight in during the day and one letting in moonlight at night; and [by these] they used to be able to identify the timings for the prayers. He had Ādam's bones with him in the Ark, and when he disembarked from it he made a grave for him under the minaret of the Mosque of Mina.' [11:37]

21. From al-Mufaḍḍal who said, 'I asked Abū 'Abd Allāh عليه السلام, "You know God's verse: ﴿*When Our command came, and water gushed up out of the earth*﴾ – What is this furnace? Where was it located and how was it?"

He replied, "The furnace was just as I have previously described to you."

I asked, "So the water first started to gush out from that furnace?"

He replied, "Yes. God wanted Nūḥ's community to witness the phenomenon. Then after that, God sent downpours of rain that caused a flood. The Euphrates flooded too as did all its springs. God drowned them and saved Nūḥ and those who were with him aboard the Ark."

Then I asked him, "How long did Nūḥ and his fellow companions stay aboard the Ark until the water receded and they disembarked?"

He replied, "They stayed on it for seven days and seven nights. It circumambulated the House then settled on the Jūdī, which is the Euphrates [near] Kufa."

Then I asked him, "The old Mosque of Kufa?"

He replied, "Yes, the one which was the place where several prophets prayed, and where the Messenger of God ﷺ had prayed when Jibra'īl journeyed with him on al-Burāq. When he brought him to Dār al-Salām [the Abode of Peace] first, which is behind Kufa, on the way to the Holy Sanctuary [in Jerusalem], he said to him, 'Muḥammad, this is the mosque of your father Ādam, and the place of prayer of many prophets. So dismount and pray in it.'

The Messenger of God ﷺ dismounted and prayed, then set off again towards the Holy Sanctuary, where he prayed too. Then Jibra'īl ascended with him to the heavens."' [11:40]

فقلتُ له: جُعِلتُ فِداك، في كم عَمِل نوح ﷺ سفينته حتّى فَرَغ منها؟ قال: في الدَّورين. فقلتُ: وكم الدَّوران؟ قال: ثمانون سنة. قلت: فإنّ العامّة تقول عَمِلها في خمسمائة عام؟ قال: فقال: كلاّ، كيف والله يقول: ﴿وَوَحۡيِنَا﴾؟

٢٠. عن عيسى بن عبدالله العَلوى عن أبيه، قال: كانت السفينة طُولها أربعين في أربعين سَمكها، وكانت مُطبقة بطبقٍ، وكان معه خَرَزَتان، تُضيءُ إحداهما بالنهار ضوء الشمس، وتُضيءُ إحداهما بالليل ضوء القمر، وكانوا يعرِفون وقت الصلاة، وكان عِظام آدم معه في السفينة، فلمّا خَرَج من السفينة صيّر قبره تحت المَنارة التي بمسجد مِنى.

٢١. عن المُفضّل، قال: قلتُ لأبي عبدالله ﷺ: أرأيتَ قول الله: ﴿حَتَّىٰٓ إِذَا جَآءَ أَمۡرُنَا وَفَارَ ٱلتَّنُّورُ﴾ ما هذا التنّور، وأين كان موضعه؟ وكيف كان؟ فقال: كان التنور حيث وصفت لك.

فقلتُ: فكان بَدْء خُروج الماء من ذلك التنّور؟ فقال: نعم، إنّ الله أحبَّ أن يُري قوم نوحٍ الآية، ثمّ إنّ الله بعد أرسل عليهم مَطرًا يَفيض فَيضًا، وفاض الفُرات فيضًا أيضًا، والعيون كُلُّهنّ عليها، فغرّقهم الله وأنجى نوحًا ﷺ ومن معه في السفينة.

فقلتُ له: فكم لَبِث نوح ومَن معه في السفينة حتّى نَضَب الماء، وخرجوا منها؟ فقال: لَبِثوا فيها سبعة أيّام ولياليها، وطافت بالبيت ثمّ استوت على الجُودي، وهو فُرات الكُوفة.

22. From al-Ḥasan b. ʿAlī, from one of his associates, from Abū ʿAbd Allāh عليه السلام who said, 'Nūḥ's wife came to him while he was working on the Ark, and said to him, "There is water coming out of the furnace!" So he rushed to it quickly and covered it with the lid, sealing it shut with its seal. So the water stopped, but as soon as Nūḥ had completed the Ark he came to the seal and broke it, opened the lid and the water gushed forth.' [11:40]

23. From Abū ʿUbayda al-Ḥadhdhāʾ, from Abū Jaʿfar عليه السلام who said, 'The Mosque of Kufa is where the water gushed forth from, where the Ark was constructed; it is the centre of Babylon and the gathering place of the prophets.' [11:40]

24. From Salmān al-Fārisī, from the Commander of the Faithful عليه السلام in a narration of his about the virtues of the Mosque of Kufa, that Nūḥ constructed his Ark therein, and that is whence the water gushed forth as well as the place where Nūḥ's house and mosque were located; and that the water gushed forth from the right-hand corner of the Mosque of Kufa. [11:40]

25. From al-Aʿmash[7] who, without mentioning his source, cited ʿAlī عليه السلام regarding His verse: ﴾ *When Our command came, and water gushed out of the 'furnace.'* ﴿ He said, 'By God, it was not a bread oven!' Then he pointed to the sun with his hand saying, '[It refers to] its rising.' [11:40]

7 Abū Muḥammad Sulaymān b. Mihrān al-Aʿmash, a notable companion of Imam Jaʿfar al-Ṣādiq who is known for his trustworthiness and reliability as a narrator but is surprisingly not mentioned by Ḥillī in his *Khulāṣat al-aqwāl*. See Khūʾī, *Muʿjam*, 9:294–5 (nr. 5518).

فقلتُ له: إنّ مسجد الكوفة قديم؟ فقال: نعم. وهو مُصلّى الأنبياء، ولقد صلّى فيه رسول الله ﷺ حيث انطلق به جَبرئيل عليه السلام على البُراق، فلمّا انتهى به إلى دار السلام، وهو ظهر الكوفة، وهو يُريد بيت المقدِس، قال له: يا محمّد، هذا مسجد أبيك آدم عليه السلام ومُصلّى الأنبياء، فأنزِل فصلِّ فيه، فنزل رسول الله ﷺ وصلّى، ثمّ انطلق به إلى بيت المقدِس، فصلّى، ثمّ إنّ جَبرئيل عَرَج به إلى السماء.

٢٢. عن الحسن بن عليّ، عن بعض أصحابه، عن أبي عبدالله عليه السلام، قال: جاءت امرأةُ نوح إليه وهو يعمل السفينة، فقالت له: إنّ التنّور قد خَرج منه ماء، فقام إليه مُسرعًا حتّى جعل الطّبق عليه فختمه بخاتَمه، فقام الماء، فلمّا فَرَغ نوح من السفينة جاء إلى خاتَمه ففضّه، وكشف الطبق، ففار الماء.

٢٣. أبو عبيدة الحذّاء، عن أبي جعفر عليه السلام، قال: مسجد كُوفان فيه فار التنّور، ونُجِرت السفينة، وهو سُرّة بابل ومَجمَع الأنبياء.

٢٤. عن سلمان الفارسي، عن أمير المؤمنين عليه السلام – في حديث له في فضل مسجد الكوفة –: فيه نَجَر نوح سفينته، وفيه فار التنّور، وبه كان بيت نوح ومسجده، وفي زاويته اليمنى فار التنّور، يعني مسجد الكوفة.

٢٥. عن الأعمش، رفعه إلى عليّ عليه السلام، في قوله: ﴿حَتَّىٰٓ إِذَا جَآءَ أَمۡرُنَا وَفَارَ ٱلتَّنُّورُ﴾، قال: أما والله ما هو تنّور الخُبز، ثمّ أومأ بيده إلى الشمس، فقال: طُلوعها.

26. From Ismāʿīl b. Jābir al-Juʿfī, from Abū ʿAbd Allāh ﷺ who said, 'It took him one hundred years to build it, then He commanded him to carry aboard it two of each species of animal (permissible to consume) from the eight animals in pairs that came out of the Garden with Ādam in order that there be provision for Nūḥ's progeny on the earth after him, just as Ādam's progeny had subsisted; for the earth and everything on it would be flooded except for what Nūḥ carried with him in his Ark.'

He continued, 'So Nūḥ carried the eight animals in pairs, which God mentions: ﴾*He gave you eight animals, in [four] pairs: a pair of sheep and a pair of goats ... and a pair of camels and a pair of cattle ...*﴿(6:143–144) So there were two pairs of sheep: one pair to be raised and looked after by humans, and another pair of wild sheep that would live in the mountains, which He made permissible for them to hunt. Similarly, there were two pairs of goat: one pair raised by humans and one pair of deer [known as the second pair]; and two pairs of cattle: one raised by humans and the other being wild buffalo; and two pairs of camels: one Bactrian and one desert. [There was] also every species of bird: wild and domestic. Then the earth flooded.' [11:40]

27. From Ibrāhīm, from Abū ʿAbd Allāh ﷺ that Nūḥ carried dogs on the Ark too but did not carry anyone born out of wedlock. [11:40]

28. From ʿAbd Allāh [or ʿUbayd Allāh] al-Ḥalabī, on his ﷺ authority. He said, 'The person born out of wedlock must not be allowed to give testimony nor lead people in prayer. Nūḥ did not carry such a person on board his Ark, while he carried dogs and pigs therein.' [11:40]

29. From Ḥumrān, from Abū Jaʿfar ﷺ regarding God's verse: ﴾*though only a few believed with him.*﴿ He said, 'There were eight of them.' [11:40]

٢٦. عن إسماعيل بن جابر الجُعفي، عن أبي عبدالله عليه السلام، قال: صنعها في مائة سنة، ثمّ أمره أن يحمِل فيها من كُلّ زوجين اثنين، الأزواج الثّمانية الحلال الّتي خرج بها آدم عليه السلام من الجنّة، لتكون معيشةً لعَقِب نوح عليه السلام في الأرض، كما عاش عَقِب آدم عليه السلام، فإنّ الأرض تَغرَق وما فيها إلاّ ما كان معه في السفينة.

قال: فحمل نوح في السفينة من الأزواج الثمانية الّتي قال الله: ﴿وَأَنزَلَ لَكُمْ مِنَ الأَنْعَامِ ثَمَانِيَةَ أَزْوَاجٍ﴾ ﴿مِنَ الضَّأْنِ اثْنَيْنِ وَمِنَ الْمَعْزِ اثْنَيْنِ... وَمِنَ الإِبِلِ اثْنَيْنِ وَمِنَ الْبَقَرِ اثْنَيْنِ﴾ فكان زوجين من الضأن: زوج يُربّيها الناس ويقومون بأمرها، وزوج من الضأن التي تكون في الجبال الوحشيّة أحلّ لهم صيدها، ومن المعز اثنين: يكون زوج يُربّيه الناس، وزوج من الظّباء، سَميّ الزوج الثاني، ومن البقر اثنين، زوج يُربّيه الناس، وزوج هو البقر الوحشيّ، ومن الإبل زوجين: وهي البَخَاتي، والعِراب، وكُلّ طيرٍ وحشيّ أو إنسي، ثمّ غَرِقت الأرض.

٢٧. عن إبراهيم، عن أبي عبدالله عليه السلام: إنّ نوحًا عليه السلام حَمَل الكلب في السَّفينة، ولم يحمِل وَلَد الزِّنا.

٢٨. عن عبيد الله الحلبي، عنه عليه السلام، قال: ينبغي لوَلَد الزِّنا أن لا تَجُوز له شهادة، ولا يَؤمّ بالناس، لم يَحمِله نوح عليه السلام في السفينة، وقد حَمَل فيها الكَلب والخِنزير.

٢٩. عن حُمران، عن أبي جعفر عليه السلام، في قول الله: ﴿وَمَا آمَنَ مَعَهُ إِلاَّ قَلِيلٌ﴾، قال: كانوا ثمانية.

30. From Muḥammad b. Muslim, from Abū Jaʿfar عليه السلام. He said: ﴾*and Nūḥ called out to his son*﴿ – he said, ‘It is a shortened vernacular word ‘*abnih*’ with an ‘a’ vowel, meaning ‘his wife’s son.’ [11:42]

31. From Mūsā, from al-ʿAlā b. Sayāba from Abū ʿAbd Allāh عليه السلام regarding God’s verse: ﴾*and Nūḥ called out to his son*﴿ – he said, ‘It was not his own son but rather his wife’s son, which they would have shortened to the word *ibanha* [instead of *ibnihā*]. Then Nūḥ said, ﴾*My Lord, I take refuge with You from asking for things I know nothing about. If You do not forgive me, and have mercy on me, I shall be one of the losers.*﴿’ [11:42–47]

32. From Zurāra, from Abū Jaʿfar عليه السلام who said regarding Nūḥ’s statement: ﴾*‘Come aboard with us, my son’*﴿, ‘It is not his son.’ He said, ‘I asked, “But didn’t Nūḥ say: ‘My son’?” He replied, “Nūḥ only said that because he did not know any better.”’ [11:42]

33. From Ibrāhīm b. Abī al-ʿAlā[8], on someone else’s authority, from one of the two [al-Bāqir or al-Ṣādiq] who said, ‘When God said: ﴾*‘Earth, swallow up your water, and sky, hold back’*﴿, the earth said, “I have only been commanded to swallow up my own water, not the water from the sky.”’ He said, ‘So the earth swallowed up its own water, and the water from the sky remained and became a sea around the earth.’ [11:44]

34. From ʿAbd al-Raḥmān b. al-Ḥajjāj, from Abū ʿAbd Allāh عليه السلام who said regarding His statement: ﴾*‘Earth, swallow up your water’*﴿, ‘It was revealed in an Indian language, meaning “drink up”.’ [11:44]

35. In a narration from ʿAbbād [b. Ṣuhayb], on his عليه السلام authority, ‘ ﴾*‘Earth, swallow up your water’*﴿ – was in Ethiopian.’ [11:44]

8 We were unable to find an individual by this name in either Ḥillī’s *Khulāṣat al-aqwāl* or Khūʾī’s *Muʿjam*.

٣٠. عن محمّد بن مسلم، عن أبي جعفر ﷺ، قال: ﴿وَنَادَىٰ نُوحٌ ابْنَهُ﴾، قال: إنّما في لغة طيّئ (أبنهُ) بنصب الألف، يعني ابن امرأته.

٣١. عن موسى، عن العَلاَء بن سَيابة، عن أبي عبدالله ﷺ في قول الله: ﴿وَنَادَىٰ نُوحٌ ابْنَهُ﴾، قال: ليس بابنه، إنّما هو ابن امرأته، وهو لغة طيّئ يقولون لابن امرأته (أبنه)، قال نوح: ﴿رَبِّ إِنِّي أَعُوذُ بِكَ﴾ إلى ﴿الْخَاسِرِينَ﴾.

٣٢. عن زُرارة، عن أبي جعفر ﷺ، في قول نوح ﷺ: ﴿يَا بُنَيَّ ارْكَب مَّعَنَا﴾، قال: ليس بابنه. قال: قلتُ: إنّ نوحًا ﷺ قال: يا بُنيّ؟ قال: فإنّ نوحًا قال ذلك وهو لا يعلم.

٣٣. عن إبراهيم بن أبي العلاء، عن غير واحد، عن أحدهما عليهما السلام، قال: لمّا قال الله: ﴿يَا أَرْضُ ابْلَعِي مَاءَكِ وَيَا سَمَاءُ أَقْلِعِي﴾ قالت الأرض: إنّما أُمرتُ أن أبلع مائي أنا فقط، ولم أُؤمَر أن أبلَع ماء السماء، قال: فبلعت الأرض ماءها، وبقي ماء السماء، فصُيّر بحرًا حول الدنيا.

٣٤. عن عبد الرّحمن بن الحجّاج، عن أبي عبدالله ﷺ، في قوله: ﴿يَا أَرْضُ ابْلَعِي مَاءَكِ﴾، قال: نزلت بِلُغة الهند: اشرَبي.

٣٥. وفي رواية عبّاد، عنه ﷺ: ﴿يَا أَرْضُ ابْلَعِي مَاءَكِ﴾ حَبَشية.

36. From al-Ḥasan b. Ṣāliḥ[9], from Abū ʿAbd Allāh ﷺ. He said, 'I heard Abū Jaʿfar ﷺ talking to ʿAṭāʾ saying, "The length of Nūḥ's Ark measured one hundred and twenty cubits, its width was eight hundred cubits and its height eighty cubits. It circumambulated the House seven times, sailed between Ṣafā and Marwa seven times, then settled on the Jūdī."' [11:44]

37. From al-Mufaḍḍal b. ʿUmar, from Abū ʿAbd Allāh ﷺ: 'It settled on the Jūdī, which is the Euphrates of Kufa.' [11:44]

38. From Abū Baṣīr, from Abū al-Ḥasan ﷺ. He narrated, 'He said, "Abū Muḥammad, God inspired the mountains that I will settle Nūḥ's Ark upon one of you during the storm. So they all tried to tower and exalt themselves over each other, but a particular mountain in Mosul called al-Jūdī humbled itself, so in the storm the Ark encircled all the mountains until it finally settled on the Jūdī, and stayed there. Nūḥ called out: '*Bārāt qanī, bārāt qanī*'."

He said, 'I asked him, "May I be your ransom – what do these words mean?" He replied, "O God, settle it right! O God, settle it right."' [11:44]

39. From Abū Baṣīr, from Abū al-Ḥasan Mūsā ﷺ who said, 'Nūḥ remained on the Ark for a long time, as much as God willed; and it was controlled [by God] so Nūḥ let it take its course. God then inspired the mountains that I am going to settle the Ark of My servant Nūḥ upon one of you. So they tried to tower and exalt themselves over each other, except for the Jūdi, which is a mountain in Mosul. So the bow of the Ark struck against it, and at that moment Nūḥ exclaimed, ﴿*Rabbi atqin*﴾ which in Arabic means 'My Lord, settle it right.'' [11:44]

9 Abū ʿAbd Allāh al-Ḥasan b. Ṣāliḥ b. Ḥayy al-Hamdānī al-Thawrī (d. 168/784), a companion of Imam Muḥammad al-Bāqir and eponymous founder of the Ṣāliḥiyya sect of the Zaydī school of thought. See Ḥillī, *Muʿjam*, 337 (nr. 1330); Modarressi, *Tradition and Survival*, 256–7 (nr. 84).

٣٦. عن الحسن بن صالح، عن أبي عبد الله ﷺ، قال: سَمِعتُ أبا جعفر ﷺ يُحدّث عطاء، قال: كان طُول سفينة نوح ألف ذِراع ومائتي ذِراع، وعرضها ثمانمائة ذِراع، وطُولها في السماء ثمانون ذراعًا، وطافت بالبيت سبعًا، وسَعَت بين الصَّفا والمَروة سبعة أشواط، ثمّ استوت على الجُوديّ.

٣٧. عن المُفضّل بن عمر، عن أبي عبد الله ﷺ، قال: استوت على الجُوديّ، هو فُرات الكوفة.

٣٨. عن أبي بصير، عن أبي الحسن ﷺ، قال: قال: يا أبا محمّد، إنّ الله أوحى إلى الجبال: أنّي مُهرِق سفينة نوح على جبلٍ منكُنّ في طُّوفان؛ فتطاولت وشَمَخت، وتَواضَع جبلٌ عندكم بالمَوصِل، يقال له الجُوديّ، فمرّت السفينة تدور في الطُّوفان على الجبال كُلّها حتّى انتهت إلى الجوديّ، فوقعت عليه، فقال نوح ﷺ، بارات قني بارات قني.

قال: قلتُ له: جُعلت فِداك، أيّ شيء هذا الكلام؟ فقال: اللّهمّ اصلِح، اللّهُمّ أصلِح.

٣٩. عن أبي بصير، عن أبي الحسن موسى ﷺ، قال: كان نوح ﷺ في السفينة، فلَبِث فيها ما شاء الله، وَكانت مأمورةً،فخلّى سبيلها نوح، فأوحى الله إلى الجبال أنّي واضعٌ سفينة عبدي نوح على جبلٍ منكم؛ فتطاولت الجبال وشَمَخت غير الجُوديّ، وهو جبل بالمَوصِل، فضرب جُؤجُؤ السفينة الجبلَ، فقال نوح ﷺ عند ذلك: ربّ أتقِن، وهو بالعربية: ربّ أصلِح.

40. Kathīr al-Nawwā' narrated from Abū Ja'far عليه السلام who said, 'Nūḥ heard the Ark grinding against the Jūdī, so he became scared. He stuck his head out of the porthole that it had and raised his hand pointing up with his finger, saying "*rub'amān atqin*" which means, 'My Lord, fix it.'' [11:44]

41. From 'Abd al-Ḥamīd b. Abī al-Daylam[10], from Abū 'Abd Allāh عليه السلام who said, 'When Nūḥ boarded the Ark, it was said: ﴾*'Gone are those evildoing people!'*﴿' [11:44]

42. From al-Ḥasan b. 'Alī al-Washshā' who said, 'I heard al-Riḍā عليه السلام say, "Abū 'Abd Allāh عليه السلام said, 'God said to Nūḥ: ﴾*he was not one of your family*﴿ because he opposed him, and He designated those who followed him to be part of his family.'"

He said, 'And he asked me how they read this verse about Nūḥ.' I replied, 'The people read it in two ways: either *innahu 'amalun ghayru ṣāliḥin* [it is not a righteous act] or *innahu 'amila ghayra ṣālihin* [what he did was not right].' So he said, 'They are wrong. He was indeed his son, but God disassociated him from him when he opposed him in his faith.' [11:46]

43. From Abū Ma'mar al-Sa'dī who said, "Alī b. Abī Ṭālib عليه السلام said regarding His verse ﴾*My Lord is on a straight path*﴿: "It means that He is on what is right – He recompenses goodness with good and evil with bad, and He pardons and forgives whomever He wills – glorified and exalted is He."' [11:56]

44. From Mufaḍḍal b. 'Umar, from Abū 'Abd Allāh عليه السلام who said, "Alī b. al-Ḥusayn, may God's blessings be upon him, was sitting in the Sacred Mosque when a man from Kufa said to him, "Did 'Alī عليه السلام actually say that our brothers have oppressed us?" So 'Alī b. al-Ḥusayn عليه السلام said to him, 'O Abū 'Abd Allāh, have you not read God's book: ﴾*To the people of 'Ād, We sent their brother, Hūd*﴿ and God destroyed the people of 'Ād but saved Hūd, and: ﴾*To the Thamūd, We sent their brother, Ṣāliḥ*﴿, where He destroyed Thamūd and saved Ṣāliḥ.' [11:50, 61]

---

10 'Abd al-Ḥamīd b. Abī al-Daylam, on whom there is scant information, is considered by Ibn al-Ghaḍā'irī to have been a weak narrator. See Ḥillī, *Khulāṣat al-aqwāl*, 384–5 (nr. 1546).

٤٠. وروى كثير النوّاء، عن أبي جعفر عليه السلام يقول: سَمِع نوح عليه السلام صَرير السَّفينة على الجُودي فخاف عليها، فأخرج رأسه من كُوّةٍ كانت فيها، فرفع يده، وأشار بإصبعه، وهو يقول: ربعمان أتقِن، تأويلها، رَبّ أحسن.

٤١. عن عبد الحميد بن أبي الدَّيلم، عن أبي عبدالله عليه السلام، قال: لمّا ركِب نوح عليه السلام في السَّفينة قيل: بُعدًا للقوم الظالمين.

٤٢. عن الحسن بن عليّ الوشّاء، قال: سَمِعتُ الرضا عليه السلام يقول: قال أبو عبدالله عليه السلام: إنّ الله قال لنوح عليه السلام: ﴿إِنَّهُۥ لَيۡسَ مِنۡ أَهۡلِكَ﴾ لأنّه كان مُخالِفًا له، وجَعَل من اتَّبعه من أهله.

قال: وسألني كيف يقرؤون هذه الآية في نوح؟ قلت: يقرؤها الناس على وجهين: ﴿إِنَّهُۥ عَمَلٌ غَيۡرُ صَٰلِحٖ﴾ و (إِنَّهُ عَمِلَ غَيْرَ صَالِحٍ)، فقال كَذَبوا هو ابنه، ولكنّ الله نفاه عنه حين خالفه في دينه.

٤٣. عن أبي مَعْمَر السَّعدي، قال: قال عليّ بن أبي طالب عليه السلام، في قوله: ﴿إِنَّ رَبِّي عَلَىٰ صِرَٰطٖ مُّسۡتَقِيمٖ﴾ يعني أنّه على حَقّ، يَجزي بالإحسان إحسانًا، وبالسيّء سيّئًا، ويعفو عمّن يشاء ويغفِرُ سبحانه وتعالى.

٤٤. عن مُفضَّل بن عمر، عن أبي عبدالله عليه السلام، قال: إنّ عليّ بن الحسين صلوات الله عليه كان في المسجد الحرام جالسًا، فقال له رجلٌ من أهل الكوفة: قال عليٌّ عليه السلام: إنّ إخواننا بَغَوا علينا؟ فقال له عليّ بن الحسين عليه السلام: يا عبدالله، أما تقرأ كتاب الله ﴿وَإِلَىٰ عَادٍ

45. From Abū Ḥamza al-Thumālī, from Abū Jaʿfar ﷺ who said, 'When God, Blessed and most High, decided to punish Lūṭ's people and decreed it thus, He wished to turn Ibrāhīm's attention away from their punishment by granting him a knowledgeable son who would console him for the destruction of Lūṭ's people.' He continued, 'So God sent messengers to Ibrāhīm to give him the glad tidings of Ismāʿīl.'

He continued, 'So they went to visit him at night, and he was startled fearing that they were thieves. When the messengers saw him startled and frightened, ﴾*They said, 'Peace.' He answered, 'Peace ... We are afraid of you'*﴿(15:52) ﴾*But they said, 'Do not be afraid... 'We bring you good news of a son who will have great knowledge.*﴿'(15:53) Abū Jaʿfar said, 'The son with great knowledge was Ismāʿīl, the son of Hājar.

So Ibrāhīm said to the messengers: ﴾*He said, 'How can you give me such news when old age has come to me? What sort of news is this?' They said, 'We have told you the truth, so do not despair.'*﴿"(15:54–55)

Ibrāhīm asked the messengers, "And what is your business after these glad tidings?' ﴾*They replied, 'We have been sent to a people who are guilty*﴿(15:58) ﴾*We have been sent against the people of Lūṭ... they are a shameless people*﴿(21:74) to warn them of their Lord's punishment."'

Abū Jaʿfar ﷺ said: ﴾*Ibrāhīm said, 'But Lūṭ lives among them.' They answered, 'We know who lives there better than you do. We shall save him and his household, except for his wife: she will be one of those who stay behind.'*﴿(29:32) When God had punished them, He sent messengers to Ibrāhīm giving him glad tidings of Isḥāq and consoling him for the destruction of the people of Lūṭ – as per His statement: ﴾*To Ibrāhīm Our messengers brought good news. They said, 'Peace.' He answered, 'Peace, and without delay he brought in a roasted calf*﴿ – fresh, juicy and well-roasted – ﴾*When he saw that their hands did not reach towards the meal, he found this strange and became afraid of them. But they said, 'Do not be afraid. We have been sent against the people of Lūṭ.' His wife was standing*﴿ – Abū Jaʿfar said, 'It means that Sāra was standing when they gave her the good news of Isḥāq' – ﴾*and after him, of Yaʿqūb, so she laughed*﴿ – i.e. she was surprised at their words.'

In a narration of Abū ʿAbd Allāh's regarding ﴾*so she laughed*﴿, he said: 'She menstruated and was surprised at their words: ﴾*She said, 'Alas for me! How am I to bear a child when I am an old woman, and my husband here is an old man? That would be a strange thing!' They said, 'Are you astonished at*

﴿أَخَاهُمْ هُودًا﴾ فأهلك الله عادًا، وانجى هودًا ﴿وَإِلَى ثَمُودَ أَخَاهُمْ صَالِحًا﴾ فأهلك الله ثمودًا، وأنجى صالحًا.

٤٥. عن أبي حمزة الثمالي، عن أبي جعفر عليه السلام، قال: إنّ الله تبارك وتعالى لمّا قضى عذاب قوم لوط وقدّره، أحبَّ أن يعوّض إبراهيم عليه السلام من عذاب قوم لوط بُغلام عليم، ليُسلّي به مُصابه بهلاك قوم لُوط، قال: فبعث الله رسلاً إلى إبراهيم عليه السلام يُبشّرونه بإسماعيل، قال: فَدخلوا عليه ليلاً، ففَزِع منهم، وخاف أن يكونوا سُرّاقًا، فلمّا رأته الرُّسل فَزِعًا مَذعُورًا ﴿فَقَالُوا سَلَامًا قَالَ إِنَّا مِنكُمْ وَجِلُونَ ۝ قَالُوا لَا تَوْجَلْ إِنَّا نُبَشِّرُكَ بِغُلَامٍ عَلِيمٍ﴾. قال أبو جعفر عليه السلام: والغلام العليم هو إسماعيل بن هاجَر.

فقال إبراهيم عليه السلام للرسل: ﴿أَبَشَّرْتُمُونِي عَلَىٰ أَن مَّسَّنِيَ الْكِبَرُ فَبِمَ تُبَشِّرُونَ ۝ قَالُوا بَشَّرْنَاكَ بِالْحَقِّ فَلَا تَكُن مِّنَ الْقَانِطِينَ﴾

قال إبراهيم عليه السلام للرسل: ﴿فَمَا خَطْبُكُمْ﴾ بعد البِشارة؟ ﴿قَالُوا إِنَّا أُرْسِلْنَا إِلَىٰ قَوْمٍ مُّجْرِمِينَ﴾ قوم لوطٍ، إنّهم كانوا قومًا فاسقين لُننذرهم عذاب ربّ العالمين.

قال أبو جعفر عليه السلام: قال إبراهيم عليه السلام: ﴿قَالَ إِنَّ فِيهَا لُوطًا قَالُوا نَحْنُ أَعْلَمُ بِمَن فِيهَا لَنُنَجِّيَنَّهُ وَأَهْلَهُ إِلَّا امْرَأَتَهُ﴾، ﴿قَدَّرْنَا إِنَّهَا لَمِنَ الْغَابِرِينَ﴾. فلمّا عذّبهم الله أرسل الله إلى إبراهيم رُسلاً يُبشّرونه بإسحاق، ويُعزّونه بهلاك قوم لوط، وذلك قوله: ﴿وَلَقَدْ جَاءَتْ رُسُلُنَا إِبْرَاهِيمَ بِالْبُشْرَىٰ قَالُوا سَلَامًا قَالَ سَلَامٌ﴾ قوم منكرون ﴿فَمَا لَبِثَ أَن جَاءَ بِعِجْلٍ حَنِيذٍ﴾ يعني زكيًا مشويًّا نَضيجًا ﴿فَلَمَّا رَأَىٰ أَيْدِيَهُمْ لَا تَصِلُ إِلَيْهِ نَكِرَهُمْ وَأَوْجَسَ مِنْهُمْ خِيفَةً قَالُوا لَا تَخَفْ إِنَّا أُرْسِلْنَا إِلَىٰ قَوْمِ لُوطٍ ۝

what God ordains? The grace of God and His blessings be upon you, people of this house! For He is worthy of all praise and glory.' ﴾

After Ibrāhīm had been given the good news of Isḥāq and he was no longer afraid, he began to plead with his Lord about Lūṭ's people, asking Him to remove the affliction away from them, but God said, ﴿ *Ibrāhīm, cease your pleading: what your Lord has ordained has come about.* ﴾ My punishment is definitely and irrevocably befalling them this morning after sunrise.' [11:71–76]

46. From Abū Yazīd al-Ḥammār, from Abū 'Abd Allāh ﷺ who said, 'God sent down four angels to destroy the people of Lūṭ: Jibra'īl, Mīkā'īl, Isrāfīl, and Karrūbīl. They called in on Ibrāhīm wearing turbans and greeted him with peace, though he did not recognize them, but he could see that they were handsome. He said, "None shall serve them, but I myself," as he loved hosting guests. So he roasted a fat calf for them until it was well-cooked, then placed it before them. When he placed it in front of them, ﴿ *he saw that their hands did not reach towards it; he found this strange and became afraid of them.* ﴾ When Jibra'īl saw that he removed the turban away from his face, and Ibrāhīm recognized him and said, "Is that you?" He replied, "Yes."

Then his wife, Sāra came in so ﴿ *we gave her good news of Isḥāq and, after him, of Ya'qūb.* ﴾

She said, "What has God said exactly?"

So they replied her with what was in the Book.

Then Ibrāhīm asked, "What have you come for?"

They replied, "For the destruction of Lūṭ's people."

So he said to them, "What if there are one hundred believers among them, will you still destroy them?"

So Jibra'īl said to him, "No."

He asked, "What about fifty?"

He replied, "No."

He replied, "What if there are thirty of them?"

He replied, "No."

He asked, "What if there are twenty?"

He replied, "No."

He asked, "And if they are ten of them?"

He replied, "No."

وَامْرَأَتُهُ قَائِمَةٌ﴾ قال أبو جعفر عليه السلام: إنّما عنى سارة قائمة، فبشّروها بإسحاق ومن وراء إسحاق يعقوب ﴿فَضَحِكَتْ﴾ يعني فعجبت من قولهم — وفي رواية أبي عبدالله عليه السلام ﴿فَضَحِكَتْ﴾ قال: حاضت — و ﴿قَالَتْ يَا وَيْلَتَى أَأَلِدُ وَأَنَا عَجُوزٌ وَهَـٰذَا بَعْلِي شَيْخًا إِنَّ هَـٰذَا لَشَيْءٌ عَجِيبٌ﴾ إلى قوله: ﴿حَمِيدٌ مَجِيدٌ﴾.

فلمّا جاءت إبراهيم عليه السلام البشارة بإسحاق، فذهب عنه الرّوع، وأقبل يناجي ربّه في قوم لوط، ويسأله كشف البلاء عنهم، فقال الله: ﴿يَا إِبْرَاهِيمُ أَعْرِضْ عَنْ هَـٰذَا إِنَّهُ قَدْ جَاءَ أَمْرُ رَبِّكَ وَإِنَّهُمْ آتِيهِمْ﴾ عذابي بعد طُلوع الشمس من يومك محتومًا ﴿غَيْرُ مَرْدُودٍ﴾.

٤٦. عن أبي يزيد الحمّار، عن أبي عبدالله عليه السلام، قال: إنّ الله بعث أربعة أملاك بإهلاك قوم لوط: جَبرَئيل، ومِيكائيل، وإسرافيل، وكرّوبيل، فمرّوا بإبراهيم عليه السلام وهم مُتعمّمون، فسلّموا عليه فلم يَعرِفهم، ورأى هيئةً حسنةً، فقال: لا خدِم هؤلاء إلاّ أنا بنفسي، وكان صاحب أضياف، فشوى لهم عِجلاً سَمينًا حتّى أنضجه، ثمّ قرّبه إليهم، فلمّا وضعه بين أيديهم ورأى أيديهم لا تصِلُ إليه نَكِرَهم وأوجس منهم خِيفة، فلمّا رأى ذلك جَبَرَئيل عليه السلام حَسَر العِمامة عن وجهه، فعرفه إبراهيم فقال له: أنت هو؟ قال: نعم.

ومرّت امرأته سارة، فبشّرها بإسحاق، ومن وراء إسحاق يعقوب، قالت ما قال الله، وأجابوها بما في الكتاب.

فقال إبراهيم عليه السلام: فيما جئتم؟ قالوا: في هلاك قوم لوط.

فقال لهم: إن كان فيها مائة من المؤمنين أتُهلِكونهم؟ فقال له جَبَرَئيل عليه السلام: لا.

قال: فإن كانوا خمسين؟ قال: لا.

He asked, "What about five?"

He replied, "No."

He asked, "So what if there is only one?"

He replied, "No."

He said, "But Lūṭ lives among them."

﴾*They answered, 'We know who lives there better than you do. We shall save him and his household, except for his wife: she will be one of those who stay behind.'*﴿(29:32) Then they left.'

Al-Ḥasan b. 'Alī [i.e. Ibn Faḍḍāl] said, 'This discussion of his can only have been in an attempt to stall them, as per God's statement: ﴾*he pleaded with Us for Lūṭ's people.*﴿' [11:69–74]

47. There is a similar narration from 'Abd Allāh b. Abī al-Hilāl[11], from Abū 'Abd Allāh عليه السلام with the following addition:

He said to them, "Eat."

They replied, "We will not eat until you tell us what its value is."

So he said, "When you eat, say, 'In the Name of God,' and when you finish, say, 'Praise be to God.'

He said, 'So Jibra'īl turned to his companions – and there were four of them all together with Jibra'īl heading them – and said, "God is right to take this man as His Friend." [11:70]

48. From 'Abd Allāh b. Sinān who said, 'I asked Abū 'Abd Allāh عليه السلام about: ﴾*he brought in a roasted calf.*﴿ He said, "Well-roasted and juicy."' [11:69]

49. From [al-]Faḍl b. Abī Qurra who said, 'I heard Abū 'Abd Allāh عليه السلام say, "God revealed to Ibrāhīm that you will have a son. So he informed Sāra, and she said, 'How can I give birth when I am an old woman?' So God revealed to him: "She will indeed give birth, and her offspring will suffer for four hundred years because she answered back at Me."'

He said, "When the suffering of the Children of Israel was prolonged, they cried and pleaded to God for forty mornings, so God revealed to Mūsā

11 There are several entries for the name 'Abd Allāh b. Hilāl in Khū'ī's *Mu'jam al-rijāl*, but none as far as we know for 'Abd Allāh b. Abī Hilāl.

قال: فإن كانوا ثلاثين؟ قال: لا.

قال: فإن كانوا عشرين؟ قال: لا.

قال: فإن كانوا عشرًا؟ قال: لا.

قال: فإن كانوا خمسة؟ قال: لا.

قال فإن كان واحدًا؟ قال: لا.

قال: إنّ فيها لوطًا؟

قالوا: ﴿نَحۡنُ أَعۡلَمُ بِمَن فِيهَا لَنُنَجِّيَنَّهُۥ وَأَهۡلَهُۥٓ إِلَّا ٱمۡرَأَتَهُۥ كَانَتۡ مِنَ ٱلۡغَٰبِرِينَ﴾.

قال: وقال الحسن بن علي: لا أعلم هذا القول إلاّ وهو يَستَبقيهم، وهو قول الله تعالى: ﴿يُجَٰدِلُنَا فِي قَوۡمِ لُوطٍ﴾.

٤٧. عن عبدالله بن أبي هلال، عن أبي عبدالله عليه السلام، مثله، وزاد فيه: فقال كُلوا، فقالوا: لا نأكُل حتى تُخبِرنا ما ثمنُه؟ فقال: إذا أكَلتُم فقولوا: بسم الله، وإذا فرَغتم فقولوا: الحمد لله، قال: فالتفت جبَرئيل إلى أصحابه — وكانوا أربعة رئيسهم جبَرئيل — فقال: حقّ لله أن يتّخذ هذا خليلاً.

٤٨. عن عبدالله بن سِنان، قال: سألتُ أبا عبدالله عليه السلام: ﴿جَآءَ بِعِجۡلٍ حَنِيذٖ﴾؟ قال: مشويًا نضيجًا.

٤٩. عن فضل بن أبي قُرّة، قال: سَمِعتُ أبا عبدالله عليه السلام يقول: أوحى الله إلى إبراهيم عليه السلام أنّه سيُولد لك، فقال لسارة، فقالت: أألد وأنا عجوز؟ فأوحى الله إليه: أنّها ستَلد، ويعذّب

and Hārūn to deliver them from Pharaoh, and He absolved them of one hundred and seventy years [of that suffering]."

He said, 'Abū 'Abd Allāh عليه السلام continued, "Similarly, if you do that then God will give us relief too. If you do not, then the situation will ride its course until the end."' [11:72]

50. From Abū 'Ubayda, from Abū Ja'far عليه السلام who said, "Alī b. Abī Ṭālib once came across a community whom he greeted with peace, so they replied, "And may the peace, mercy, blessings, forgiveness and pleasure of God be upon you." So the Commander of the Faithful said to them, "Do not greet us with more than that which the messengers greeted our father Ibrāhīm when they said: ﴾ *'May the grace of God and His blessings be upon you, people of this house! For He is worthy of all praise and glory.* ﴿"

Al-Ḥasan b. Muḥammad narrated something similar, except that he said, "What the angels said to our father." [11:73]

51. From 'Abd al-Raḥmān, from Abū 'Abd Allāh عليه السلام who said regarding God's verse ﴾ *Ibrāhīm was forbearing, tender-hearted, and devout* ﴿: 'He supplicated persistently.'

There is a similar narration from Zurāra, Ḥumrān and Muḥammad b. Muslim, from Abū Ja'far عليه السلام and Abū 'Abd Allāh عليه السلام. [11:75]

52. From Abū Baṣīr, from one of the two [al-Bāqir and al-Ṣādiq] who said, 'Ibrāhīm pleaded for Lūṭ's people, saying: ﴾ *'But Lūṭ lives among them.' They answered, 'We know who lives there better than you do.'* ﴿ So Ibrāhīm insisted, and Jibra'īl said: ﴾ *'Ibrāhīm, cease your pleading: what your Lord has ordained has come about; punishment is coming to them, which cannot be turned back.'* ﴿' [11:76]

أولادها أربعمائة سنة بردّها الكلام عليّ، قال: فلمّا طال على بني إسرائيل العذاب ضجّوا وبكوا إلى الله أربعين صباحًا، فأوحى الله إلى موسى وهارون عليهما السلام أن يخلّصهم من فِرعون، فحطّ عنهم سبعين ومائة سنة.

قال: وقال أبو عبدالله عليه السلام: وهكذا أنتم، لو فعلتم لفرّج الله عنّا، فأمّا إذا لم تكونوا، فإنّ الأمر ينتهي إلى مُنتهاه.

٥٠. عن أبي عبيدة، عن أبي جعفر عليه السلام، قال: إنّ عليّ بن أبي طالب عليه السلام مرّ بقومٍ فسلّم عليهم، فقالوا: وعليكم السلام ورحمة الله وبركاته ومغفرته ورضوانه. فقال لهم أمير المؤمنين عليه السلام: لا تجاوزوا بنا ما قالت الأنبياء لأبينا إبراهيم عليه السلام، إنّما قالوا: ﴿رَحْمَتُ اللهِ وَبَرَكَاتُهُ عَلَيْكُمْ أَهْلَ الْبَيْتِ إِنَّهُ حَمِيدٌ مَجِيدٌ﴾.

وروى الحسن بن محمّد مثله، غير أنّه قال: ما قالت الملائكة لأبينا عليه السلام.

٥١. عن عبد الرّحمن، عن أبي عبدالله عليه السلام، في قول الله تعالى: ﴿إِنَّ إِبْرَاهِيمَ لَحَلِيمٌ أَوَّاهٌ مُنِيبٌ﴾، قال: دعّاء.

عن زُرارة وحُمران ومحمّد بن مسلم، عن أبي جعفر، وأبي عبدالله عليهما السلام، مثله.

٥٢. عن أبي بصير، عن أحدهما عليهما السلام، قال: إنَّ إبراهيم عليه السلام جادل عن قوم لوط، وقال: ﴿إِنَّ فِيهَا لُوطًا قَالُوا نَحْنُ أَعْلَمُ بِمَنْ فِيهَا﴾ فزاد إبراهيم عليه السلام، فقال جبرئيل: ﴿يَا إِبْرَاهِيمُ أَعْرِضْ عَنْ هَذَا إِنَّهُ قَدْ جَاءَ أَمْرُ رَبِّكَ وَإِنَّهُمْ آتِيهِمْ عَذَابٌ غَيْرُ مَرْدُودٍ﴾.

53. From Abū Yazīd al-Ḥammār, from Abū ʿAbd Allāh ﷺ who said, 'God, most High, sent down four angels for the destruction of Lūṭ's people: Jibraʾīl, Mīkāʾīl, Isrāfīl, and Karrūbīl. They came to Lūṭ when he was out in the fields near the village. They greeted him with peace and wore turbans. When he saw them, he saw that they were handsome clad in white clothes and white turbans. So he offered for them to come to his house. They replied, "Yes." So he went ahead of them and they walked behind him, and he regretted leading them to his house, saying to himself, "What have I done by bringing them before my people, knowing what they are like?" So he turned to them and warned, "You are about to come across the worst of God's creatures."

God said to Jibraʾīl, "Do not be so quick to judge them until this has been witnessed from them three times." Jibraʾīl said, "This was the first."

Then they walked for an hour, until he turned to them saying, "You are about to come across the worst of God's creatures," at which Jibraʾīl said, "That is the second time."

Then they walked on, and when they came to the city gates, he turned to them again and said, "You are about to come across the worst of God's creatures," so Jibraʾīl said, "That is the third time."

Then he entered the city, and they entered with him until they reached his house. When his wife saw them and noticed how handsome they were, she climbed to the roof and shouted out, but they did not hear her. So she let out a smoke signal, and when they saw the smoke they hurried there and came up to the door. The woman descended and said to them, "With him are some people – I have never seen anyone more handsome than them."

So they tried to come to the door to enter in, and when Lūṭ saw them he stood up to them and said: ﴾*'Have some fear of God and do not disgrace me with my guests. Is there not a single right-minded man among you?'*﴿ He said: ﴾*'here are my daughters. They are more wholesome for you',*﴿ calling them towards that which was permissible. ﴾*They said, 'You know very well that we have no right to your daughters. You know very well what we want.'*﴿ He said to them: ﴾*'If only I had the strength to stop you or could rely on strong support!'*﴿

He said, 'So Jibraʾīl said, "If only he knew what strength he has."

He said, 'So they outnumbered him and forced entry into the house, so Jibraʾīl shouted out to him, "Let them enter, Lūṭ!"

٥٣. عن أبي يزيد الحمّار، عن أبي عبدالله عليه السلام، قال: إنّ الله تعالى بعث أربعة أملاك في هلاك قوم لوط: جَبرئيل، ومِيكائيل، وإسرافيل، وكرّوبيل، فأتوا لوطًا وهو في زراعةٍ قُرب القَرية، فسلّموا عليه وهم متعمّمون، فلمّا رآهم رأى لهم هيئةً حَسَنةً، عليهم ثياب بيض، وعمائهم بيض، فقال لهم: المنزل؟ فقالوا: نعم، فتقدَّمهم ومَشَوا خلفه، فنَدِم على عَرضِه المنزل عليهم، فقال: أيّ شيءٍ صنعتُ، آتي بهم قومي وأنا أعرفهم؟! فالتفت إليهم، فقال: إنّكم لتأتون شِرارًا من خلق الله.

وقال الله تعالى لجبرَئيل عليه السلام: لا تعجَل عليهم، حتّى يشهَدَ عليهم ثلاث مرّات، فقال جَبرَئيل عليه السلام: هذه واحدة. ثمّ مضى ساعةً، ثمّ التفت إليهم، فقال: إنّكم لتأتون شرارًا من خلق الله. فقال جَبرَئيل عليه السلام: هذه اثنتين، ثمّ مشى، فلمّا بلغ باب المدينة التفت إليهم، فقال: إنّكم لتأتون شِرارًا من خَلق الله. فقال جَبرَئيل عليه السلام: هذه الثالثة.

ثمّ دخل ودخلوا معه، حتّى دخل منزله، فلمّا رأتهم امرأته رأت هيئةً حَسَنَةً، فصَعِدت فوق السطح، فصَعِقت فلم يسمعوا، فدخّنت، فلمّا رأوا الدُّخان أقبلوا يُهرَعُون حتّى جاءوا إلى الباب، فنزلت المرأة، فقالت: عنده قوم ما رأيتُ قومًا قطّ أحسن هيئةً منهم؛ فجاءوا إلى الباب ليدخلوها، فلمّا رآهم لوط عليه السلام قام إليهم، فقال لهم: يا قوم ﴿فَاتَّقُوا اللَّهَ وَلَا تُخْزُونِ فِي ضَيْفِي أَلَيْسَ مِنْكُمْ رَجُلٌ رَشِيدٌ﴾؟ وقال: ﴿هَؤُلَاءِ بَنَاتِي هُنَّ أَطْهَرُ لَكُمْ﴾ فدعاهم إلى الحَلال فقالوا: ﴿مَا لَنَا فِي بَنَاتِكَ مِنْ حَقٍّ وَإِنَّكَ لَتَعْلَمُ مَا نُرِيدُ﴾ قال لهم: ﴿لَوْ أَنَّ لِي بِكُمْ قُوَّةً أَوْ آوِي إِلَى رُكْنٍ شَدِيدٍ﴾ قال: فقال جَبرَئيل عليه السلام: لو يعلم أيّ قوّةٍ له.

When they entered, Jibra'īl motioned towards them with his finger, and they lost their eyesight, as per God's words: ﴾*so We sealed their eyes*﴿(54:37)

Then Jibra'īl called out to him: ﴾*'Lūṭ, we are your Lord's messengers. They will not reach you. Leave with your household in the dead of night'*﴿ And Jibra'īl also said to him, 'We have been sent to destroy them.'

So he said, 'Then do it fast, Jibra'īl!' So he replied: ﴾*Their appointed time is the morning: is the morning not near?*﴿

Then he commanded him to leave with those who were with him except for his wife. Then Jibra'īl uprooted it, i.e. the town, with his wings, from under seven layers of the earth. Then he raised it high up so that the dwellers of the heavens could hear the dogs barking and the cockerels screeching, and then turned it upside down, and stones of baked clay rained down on it and the surrounding areas.' [11:77–81]

54. From Abū Baṣīr, from one of the two [al-Bāqir or al-Ṣādiq] who said, 'When Jibra'īl came to Lūṭ to destroy his people, and they [the angels] had gone into his house and were rushed upon by his people, he [Lūṭ] placed his hand on the door and pleaded with them, saying ﴾*'Have some fear of God and do not disgrace me with my guests.'*﴿

They said, "Have we not managed to have our way with everyone else?"

So he suggested his own daughters to them in marriage, but they said: ﴾*'We have no right to your daughters. You know very well what we want.'*﴿

So he retorted: ﴾*'Is there not a single right-minded man among you?'*﴿

They refused, so he said: ﴾*'If only I had the strength to stop you or could rely on strong support!'*﴿'

He continued, 'Jibra'īl looked at them and said, "If only he were aware of his own strength!" So he [Lūṭ] called him in, and he came. They opened the door and came inside too, whereupon Jibra'īl motioned with his hand and they were turned blind, reaching out to touch the walls with their hands, promising God that they would not spare anyone from Lūṭ's family when their sight was restored.'

He continued, 'So when Jibra'īl said: ﴾*'Lūṭ, we are your Lord's messengers...*﴿, Lūṭ said to him, "Jibra'īl do it fast!"

He said, "Yes."

He again said, "Jibra'īl, hurry!"

قال: فكاثروه حتّى دخلوا البيت فصاح به جَبرَئيل عليه السلام، فقال: يا لوط دَعهم يَدخُلون، فلمّا دَخَلُوا أهوى جَبرَئيل بإصبعه نحوهم، فذهبت أعينهم، وهو قول الله: ﴿فَطَمَسْنَا أَعْيُنَهُمْ﴾.

ثمّ ناداه جَبرَئيل: ﴿إِنَّا رُسُلُ رَبِّكَ لَن يَصِلُوا إِلَيْكَ فَأَسْرِ بِأَهْلِكَ بِقِطْعٍ مِّنَ اللَّيْلِ﴾، وقال له جَبرَئيل عليه السلام: إنّا بُعِثنا في إهلاكهم. فقال: يا جَبرَئيل، عجّل، فقال: ﴿إِنَّ مَوْعِدَهُمُ الصُّبْحُ أَلَيْسَ الصُّبْحُ بِقَرِيبٍ﴾ فأمره فتحمّل ومن معه إلاّ امرأته، ثمّ اقتلعها — يعني المدينة — جَبرَئيلُ عليه السلام بجَناحه من سبع أرضين، ثمّ رفعها حتّى سَمِع أهل السماء الدنيا نِباح الكلاب وصُراخ الدُّيوك، ثمّ قَلَبها وأمطر عليها وعلى من حول المدينة حِجارةً من سِجّيل.

٥٤. عن أبي بصير، عن أحدهما عليهما السلام، قال: إنّ جَبرَئيل عليه السلام لمّا أتى لوطاً عليه السلام في هلاك قومه ودخلوا عليه وجاءه قومه يُهرَعون إليه، قام فوَضَع يده على الباب، ثمّ ناشدهم، فقال: ﴿وَاتَّقُوا اللهَ وَلَا تُخْزُونِ فِي ضَيْفِي﴾ ﴿قَالُوا أَوَلَمْ نَنْهَكَ عَنِ الْعَالَمِينَ﴾، ثمّ عَرَض عليهم بَناته بنكاح، فقالوا: ﴿مَا لَنَا فِي بَنَاتِكَ مِنْ حَقٍّ وَإِنَّكَ لَتَعْلَمُ مَا نُرِيدُ﴾، قال: فما منكم رجلٌ رشيد؟ قال: فأبَوا، فقال: ﴿لَوْ أَنَّ لِي بِكُمْ قُوَّةً أَوْ آوِي إِلَى رُكْنٍ شَدِيدٍ﴾ قال: وجَبرَئيل ينظُر إليهم، فقال: لو يعلم أيّ قوّةٍ له!

ثمّ دعاه وأتاه، ففتحوا الباب ودخلوا، فأشار جَبرَئيل عليه السلام بيده، فرجعوا عُميان يَلمسون الجُدار بأيديهم، يُعاهدون الله لئن أصبحنا لا نستبقي أحداً من آل لوط.

He replied: ﴾*Their appointed time is the morning: is the morning not near?*﴿

Then Jibra'īl said, 'Lūṭ, leave the town with your children until you reach such and such a place.'

He replied, 'Jibra'īl, my mules are too weak.'

He said, 'Then set out right away.'

So he set out and left.

When it was morning Jibra'īl descended upon it [the town], slid his wings under it and turned it upside down on top of them. Then Jibra'īl threw stones of baked clay down upon them. Lūṭ's wife heard the terrible rumbling and perished as a result of it.'

55. Regarding ﴾*'here are my daughters. They are more wholesome for you',*﴿ he said, 'Abū 'Abd Allāh said, 'He presented his daughters to them in marriage.' [11:77–81]

56. From Ṣāliḥ b. Sa'd[12], from Abū 'Abd Allāh ﷺ who said regarding God's verse: ﴾*'If only I had the strength to stop you or could rely on strong support!'*﴿: 'The strength and strong support of the Qā'im will be his three hundred and thirteen companions.' [11:80]

57. From al-Ḥusayn b. 'Alī b. Yaqṭīn[13] who said, 'I asked Abū al-Ḥasan [al-Riḍā] about a man entering his wife from behind.' He replied, 'A verse in the Qur'an makes it permissible, where Lūṭ says: ﴾*'here are my daughters. They are more wholesome for you',*﴿ knowing full well that they were not interested in their genitals.' [11:78]

58. From Abū Ḥamza, from Abū Ja'far ﷺ who said, 'The Messenger of God ﷺ asked Jibra'īl about how the people of Lūṭ were destroyed. So he replied, "O Muḥammad, the people of Lūṭ were the inhabitants of a village who did not clean themselves after defecating, nor purify themselves after intercourse.

---

12 Ṣāliḥ b. Sa'd al-Ju'fī al-Kūfī, about whom there is scant information. See Khū'ī, *Mu'jam*, 10:71 (nr. 5817).

13 Al-Ḥusayn b. 'Alī b. Yaqṭīn, a reliable companion of Imam 'Alī b. Mūsā al-Riḍā. See Ḥillī, *Khulāṣat al-aqwāl*, 114 (nr. 277).

قال: فلمّا قال جبرئيل عليه السلام: ﴿إِنَّا رُسُلُ رَبِّكَ﴾ قال له لوط: يا جبرئيل، عجّل قال: نعم، ثمّ قال: جبَرئيل، عجّل. قال: الصبحُ موعدهم، أليس الصبح بقريب؟ ثمّ قال جبَرئيل: يا لوط، اخرُج منها أنت وولدك حتّى تبلُغ موضع كذا وكذا.

قال: يا جبَرئيل، إنّ حُمُراتي حُمرات ضِعاف. قال: ارتحل فاخرُج منها. فارتحل حتّى إذا كان السَّحر نزل إليها جبَرئيل عليه السلام، فأدخل جَناحه تحتها، حتّى إذا استقلّت قلبها عليهم، ورمى جبَرئيل عليه السلام المدينة بحِجارة من سِجّيل، وسَمِعت امرأة لوط الهَدّة فهَلكت منها.

٥٥. قال: ﴿هَٰؤُلَاءِ بَنَاتِي هُنَّ أَطْهَرُ لَكُمْ﴾، قال أبو عبد الله عليه السلام: عَرَض عليهم التَّزويج.

٥٦. عن صالح بن سعد، عن أبي عبد الله عليه السلام، في قول الله ﴿لَوْ أَنَّ لِي بِكُمْ قُوَّةً أَوْ آوِي إِلَىٰ رُكْنٍ شَدِيدٍ﴾، قال: قوّة القائم، والرُّكن الشديد الثَلاثمائة وثلاثة عشر أصحابه.

٥٧. عن الحسين بن عليّ بن يقطين، قال: سألتُ أبا الحسن عليه السلام عن إتيان الرجل المرأة من خلفها، قال: أحلّتها آية في كتاب الله قول لوط عليه السلام: ﴿هَٰؤُلَاءِ بَنَاتِي هُنَّ أَطْهَرُ لَكُمْ﴾ وقد علم أنّهم ليس الفَرج يُريدون.

٥٨. عن أبي حمزة، عن أبي جعفر عليه السلام، قال: إنّ رسول الله صلى الله عليه وآله سأل جبَرئيل عليه السلام: كيف كان مَهلِك قوم لوط؟

They were miserly and greedy for food. Lūṭ remained with them for thirty years, and had been sent to them [from outside]; he had neither family nor clan among them. He called them to believe in God and to follow him. He used to prohibit them from indecencies and urged them to obey God, but they neither responded to him nor followed him.

When God decided to punish them, He first sent messengers to them to warn them as a proof and a warning. However, when they rebelled against His command God sent angels down to them to remove any believers that lived in their village, and they only found one household devoted [to God]. So they took them out from there and said to Lūṭ, 'Leave with your family tonight in the dead of night, and none of you should turn back; go to where you have been commanded.'

He said, "In the middle of the night, Lūṭ set off with his daughters, and his wife turned back and went running to her people to tell them that Lūṭ had left with his daughters.

I was called from the direction of the Throne when dawn broke: 'O Jibra'īl, the command of God will be fulfilled in punishing Lūṭ's people today, so descend upon their village and its surroundings. Uproot it from under seven layers of earth, then raise it up to the sky. Hold it there until the All-Conqueror's command comes to you, then turn it upside down. Leave Lūṭ's house standing as a clear sign and a lesson for passers-by.'

So I descended upon the wrongdoing people of the village and grabbed whatever was to the east of it with my right wing and whatever was to the west of it with my left wing. Then I uprooted it, O Muḥammad, from under seven layers of earth, except for Lūṭ's house, as a sign for passers-by. Then I took it up to the sky, nestled in my wings, where I held it such that the dwellers of the sky could hear the screeching of its cockerels and the barking of its dogs. No sooner did the sun rise than I was commanded from the direction of the Throne: 'O Jibra'īl, turn the village upside down over the guilty people.' So I turned it upside down on top of them until its bottom was at the top, and God rained stones of baked clay down upon them, layer upon layer, marked by your Lord. This is not that remote from the wrongdoing people of your community, Muḥammad."'

He continued, 'So the Messenger of God, peace be upon him and his family, said to him, "Jibra'īl, where was this village of theirs situated with respect to other countries?"

فقال: يا محمّد، إنَّ قوم لوط كانوا أهل قرية لا يتنظّفون من الغائط، ولا يتطهَّرون من الجَنابة، بُخلاء، أشحّاء على الطعام، وإنّ لوطًا ﷺ لَبِث فيهم ثلاثين سنة، وإنَّما كان نازلاً عليهم، ولم يكن منهم، ولا عشيرة له فيهم ولا قوم، وإنّه دعاهم إلى الإيمان بالله واتّباعه، وكان ينهاهم عن الفواحش، ويحُثّهم على طاعة الله، فلم يجيبوه ولم يتّبعوه.

وإنَّ الله لمّا همَّ بعذابهم، بعث إليهم رُسُلاً مُنذرين عُذرًا ونُذرًا، فلمّا عَتَوا عن أمره، بعث الله إليه ملائكةً ليُخرجوا من كان في قريتهم من المؤمنين، فما وجدوا فيها غير بيتٍ من المسلمين، فأخرجوهم منها، وقالوا للوط ﷺ: ﴿فَأَسْرِ بِأَهْلِكَ﴾ من هذه الليلة ﴿بِقِطْعٍ مِنَ اللَّيْلِ... وَلاَ يَلْتَفِتْ مِنكُمْ أَحَدٌ وَامْضُوا حَيْثُ تُؤْمَرُونَ﴾، قال: فلمّا انتصف الليل سار لوط ﷺ ببناته، وتولّت امرأته مُدبِرةً، فانطلقت إلى قومها تسعى بلوط، وتُخبِرهم أنّ لوطًا قد سار ببناته.

وإنّي نُوديتُ من تِلقاء العرش لمّا طَلَع الفجر: يا جَبرئيل، حقَّ القولُ مِنَ الله بحَتم عذاب قوم لوط اليوم، فاهبِط إلى قرية قوم لوط وما حَوَت، فاقلَعها من تحت سبع أرضين، ثمّ اعرُج بها إلى السماء، فأوقفها حتّى يأتيك أمر الجبّار في قلبها، ودَع منها آيةً بيّنةً منزل لوط عِبرةً للسيّارة.

فهَبَطتُ على أهل القرية الظالمين، فضربتُ بجَناحيَ الأيمن على ما حوى عليه شرقُها، وضربتُ بجَناحيَ الأيسر على ما حوى غربُها، فاقتلعتُها — يا محمّد — من تحت سبع أرضين إلاّ منزل لوط آية للسيّارة، ثمّ عَرَجتُ بها في جوافي جَناحي إلى السماء حتّى أوقفتها حيث يَسمَع أهل السماء زُقاء دُيوكها ونِباح كِلابها، فلمّا أن طَلَعت الشمسُ نُوديتُ من تِلقاء

He replied, "The location of their village at that time was by a lakeside, which is the lake of al-Ṭabariyya today, towards Shām."

So the Messenger of God ﷺ said to him, "Jibra'īl, when you turned it upside down on top of them, did you see which place it was that the village and its people landed?" So he replied, "Muḥammad, it landed somewhere between Shām and Egypt, and became hills in the sea."' [11:77–83]

59. From ʿAlī b. Abī Ḥamza, from Abū ʿAbd Allāh عليه السلام regarding God's verse ﴾*'We are your Lord's messengers. They will not reach you. Leave with your household in the dead of dark night.'*﴿ He said, 'Abū ʿAbd Allāh عليه السلام said, 'This is how the Commander of the Faithful عليه السلام recited it.' [11:81]

60. From Maymūn al-Labbān[14] who said, 'I was with Abū ʿAbd Allāh عليه السلام when someone was reading verses from the Chapter of Hūd in his presence. When he reached: ﴾*And we rained down stones of baked clay on it, layer upon layer, marked from your Lord. It is not far from the evildoers,*﴿ he said, "Whoever dies having persisted in sodomy will only die after God pelts him with those stones, which will cause his death without anyone seeing him."' [11:82]

14 This may be a transcription error for Maymūn Albān.

العرش: يا جَبرئيل، اقلِب القرية على القوم المُجرمين، فقلبتُها عليهم حتى صار أسفلها أعلاها، وأمطر الله عليهم حِجارةً من سِجّيلٍ مَنضودٍ مُسوَّمةً عند ربّك، وما هي — يا محمّد — من الظّالمين من أُمّتك ببعيد.

قال: فقال له رسول الله ﷺ: يا جَبرئيل، وأين كانت قريتهم من البلاد؟ قال: كان موضع قريتهم إذ ذلك في موضع البحيرة — بحيرة الطّبرية اليوم — في نواحي الشام.

فقال له رسول الله ﷺ: يا جَبرئيل، أرأيت حيث قلبتَها عليهم، في أيّ موضع من الأرض وقعت القرية وأهلها؟ فقال: يا محمّد، وقعت فيما بين الشام إلى مصر، فصارت، تلالاً في البحر.

٥٩. عن علي بن أبي حمزة، عن أبي عبدالله عليه السلام، في قول الله: ﴿ إِنَّا رُسُلُ رَبِّكَ لَن يَصِلُوٓا إِلَيۡكَ فَأَسۡرِ بِأَهۡلِكَ بِقِطۡعٖ مِّنَ ٱلَّيۡلِ ﴾ مظلمًا، قال: قال أبو عبدالله عليه السلام: وهكذا قراءة أمير المؤمنين عليه السلام.

٦٠. عن ميمون اللبّان، قال: كنتُ عند أبي عبدالله عليه السلام، فقرأ عنده آيات من هود، فلمّا بَلَغ ﴿ وَأَمۡطَرۡنَا عَلَيۡهِمۡ حِجَارَةٗ مِّن سِجِّيلٖ مَّنضُودٖ مُّسَوَّمَةً عِندَ رَبِّكَۖ وَمَا هِيَ مِنَ ٱلظَّٰلِمِينَ بِبَعِيدٖ ﴾ فقال: من مات مُصِرًّا على اللّواط، لم يَمُت حتّى يَرميه اللهُ بحَجرٍ من تلك الحِجارة، تكون فيه منيّته ولا يراه أحدٌ.

61. From al-Sakūnī, from Abū Jaʿfar, on his father's authority who said, 'The Prophet, peace be upon him and his family, said, "When Lūṭ's people did what they did, the earth wept to its Lord so much that its tears reached the sky, and the sky cried so much that its tears reached the Throne. So God revealed to the sky to rain stones down upon them, and to the earth to swallow them up."' [11:82]

62. From Aḥmad b. Muḥammad b. ʿĪsā[15], from one of our associates, from Abū ʿAbd Allāh عليه السلام regarding God's verse: ﴾*I see you are prospering*﴿, he said, 'Their prices were low.' [11:84]

63. From Muḥammad b. al-Fuḍayl, from al-Riḍā عليه السلام. He said, 'I asked him about waiting for relief [i.e. the reappearance of the Twelfth Imam]. So he replied, "Do you not know that waiting for relief is a source of relief in itself?" Then he said, "God, Blessed and most High, says: ﴾*So be on watch, I too will be watching along with you.'*﴿' [11:93]

64. From Abū Baṣīr, from Abū ʿAbd Allāh عليه السلام that he read it as: *fa minhā Qāʾiman wa-haṣīdan* in the accusative case – ﴾*some of them are still standing; some have been mown down*﴿, then he said, 'Abū Muḥammad, they can only have been mown down by iron.' [11:100*]

65. In another narration: ﴾*Some of them are still standing; some have been mown down*﴿ – 'Can they have been mown down by anything other than iron?' [11:100]

66. From Muḥammad b. Muslim, from one of the two [al-Bāqir or al-Ṣādiq] who said with regard to God's verse: ﴾*That is a Day in which all people will be gathered together, a Day for all to see*﴿: 'That is the Day of Resurrection, the promised Day.' [11:103]

67. From Masʿada b. Ṣadaqa who said, 'Abū ʿAbd Allāh عليه السلام related to us the accounts of the inhabitants of the Garden and the inmates of the Fire when

15 Aḥmad b. Muḥammad b. ʿĪsā, if mentioned without the *nisba* al-Ashʿarī, is an unknown (*majhūl*) individual according to Khūʾī. See Khūʾī, *Muʿjam*, 3:84 (nr. 899).

٦١. عن السّكوني، عن جعفر، عن أبيه عليهما السلام: قال النبي ﷺ: لمّا عَمِل قوم لوطٍ ما عَمِلوا، بكت الأرض إلى ربّها حتّى بلغت دموعها إلى السماء، وبكت السماء حتّى بَلَغت دموعها العَرش، فأوحى الله إلى السماء: أن احصبيهم، وأوحى إلى الأرض أن اخسفي بهم.

٦٢. عن أحمد بن محمّد بن عيسى، عن بعض أصحابنا، عن أبي عبد الله عليه السلام، في قول الله تعالى: ﴿إِنِّي أَرَاكُم بِخَيْرٍ﴾، قال: كان سِعرهم رخيصًا.

٦٣. عن محمّد بن الفُضيل، عن الرضا عليه السلام، قال: سألتُه عن انتظار الفَرَج، فقال: أو ليس تعلم أنّ انتظار الفَرج من الفَرج؟ ثمّ قال: إنّ الله تبارك وتعالى يقول: ﴿وَارْتَقِبُوا إِنِّي مَعَكُمْ رَقِيبٌ﴾.

٦٤. عن أبي بصير، عن أبي عبد الله عليه السلام، أنّه قرأ ﴿فَمِنْهَا قَائِمًا وَحَصِيدًا﴾ بالنصب، ثمّ قال: يا أبا محمّد، لا يكون حصيدًا إلاّ بالحديد.

٦٥. وفي رواية أُخرى: ﴿فَمِنها قَائِمٌ وَحَصِيدٌ﴾ أيكون الحصيد إلاّ بالحديد.

٦٦. عن محمّد بن مسلم، عن أحدهما عليهما السلام، قال: في قول الله: ﴿ذَٰلِكَ يَوْمٌ مَّجْمُوعٌ لَّهُ النَّاسُ وَذَٰلِكَ يَوْمٌ مَّشْهُودٌ﴾ فذلك يوم القيامة، وهو اليوم الموعود.

٦٧. عن مَسعدة بن صَدَقة، قال: قصّ أبو عبد الله عليه السلام قَصصَ أهل المِيثاق من أهل الجنّة وأهل النار؛ فقال في صفات أهل الجنّة: فمنهم من لقي الله شهيدًا لرُسله، ثمّ مرّ في

they made the Covenant. So in his description of the inhabitants of the Garden he said, "There will be some among them who will meet God, having borne witness to his messengers."' Then he continued describing them until he reached God's statement about His exception with respect to both groups.[16]

Someone unacquainted with the meanings of the Qur'an may say, "This exception made by God refers specifically to the people of the Garden and the Fire, and that the people of either group can all be taken out of their respective places such that there be no one left therein." However they are wrong. What He means by this exception is that for as long as humans (i.e. Ādam's offspring) and the Jinns live on this earth under the shade of the skies, He lets the believers stray away until He lets them go out into the jurisdiction of the devils, which is the Fire.

That is what God intends about the people of the Garden and the Fire, to remain thus in this world for as long as the heavens and the earth endure. God, Blessed and most High, is never going to take the dwellers of the Garden out from there, nor the inmates of the Fire out from there either. How could He when He has already said in His Book: ﴿*to remain therein forever*﴾ (18:3) without exception?

That is exactly what Abū Ja'far said, "Whoever enters under the authority of Muḥammad's family will enter the Garden, and whoever enters under the authority of their enemy will enter the Fire. This is what God intends by His exception about entrance into the Garden and the Fire, and exit from them respectively." [11:107–108]

68. From Zurāra who said, 'I asked Abū Ja'far عليه السلام about God's verse: ﴿*As for those who have been blessed, they will be in the Garden, there to remain as long as the heavens and earth endure, unless your Lord wills otherwise – an unceasing gift.*﴾ He said, "These two verses are talking about blessed and wretched people who have not been decreed to abide therein for eternity. If He wills, He can take them out from there. And Zurāra, do not assume that I claim that."' [11:108]

16 Referring to Q. 11:106–107: ﴿*The wretched ones will be in the Fire, sighing and groaning, there to remain for as long as the heavens and earth endure, unless your Lord wills otherwise: your Lord carries out whatever He wills.*﴾

صِفتهم حتّى بَلَغ من قوله: ثمّ جاء الإستثناء من الله في الفريقين جميعًا، فقال الجاهل بعلم التفسير: إنَّ هذا الإستثناء من الله إنّما هو لمن دخل الجنّة والنّار، وذلك أنَّ الفريقين جميعًا يخرُجان منهما فيبقيان وليس فيهما أحدٌ وكَذَبوا، لكن عنى بالإستثناء أنّ ولد آدم كلّهم وولد الجانّ معهم على الأرض والسماوات تُظِلّهم، فهو ينقُل المؤمنين حتّى يُخرجهم إلى ولاية الشياطين وهي النار.

فذلك الذي عنى الله في أهل الجنّة وأهل النار ﴿مَا دَامَتِ السَّمَاوَاتُ وَالأَرْضُ﴾ يقول: في الدنيا، والله تبارك وتعالى ليس بمخرج أهل الجنّة منها أبدًا، ولا كُلّ أهل النار منها أبدًا، وكيف يكون ذلك وقد قال الله في كتابه: ﴿مَاكِثِينَ فِيهِ أَبَدًا﴾

لس فيها إستثناء؟

وكذلك قال أبو جعفر ﵇: من دخل في ولاية آل محمّد دخل الجنّة، ومن دخل في ولاية عدوّهم دخل النار، وهذا الذي عنى الله من الإستثناء في الخُروج من الجنّة والنار والدُّخول.

٦٨. عن زُرارة، قال: سألتُ أبا جعفر ﵇ عن قول الله تعالى: ﴿وَأَمَّا الَّذِينَ سُعِدُوا فَفِي الْجَنَّةِ﴾ إلى آخر الآيتين. قال: هاتان الآيتان في غير أهل الخُلود من أهل الشّقاوة والسّعادة، إن شاء الله يجعلهم خارجين، ولا تزعُم يا زُرارة أنّي أزعُم ذلك.

69. From Ḥumrān who said, 'I asked Abū Jaʿfar, "May I be your ransom – regarding God's statement: ﴾*there to remain for as long as the heavens and earth endure*﴿ about the people of the Fire. What about the same statement of His regarding the people of the Garden and ﴾*that they will remain therein for as long as the heavens and the earth endure unless your Lord wills otherwise*﴿?" He replied, "Yes. If He wills, He can make a lower world for them and relegate them to it and do whatever He wills."

I asked him about God's verse: ﴾*there to remain for as long as the heavens and earth endure, unless your Lord wills otherwise.*﴿ So he replied, "This refers to those who may come out of the Fire."' [11:107–108]

70. From Abū Baṣīr, from Abū Jaʿfar عليه السلام regarding His statement: ﴾*and some of them will be wretched and some happy.*﴿ He said, 'When mentioning the inmates of the Fire, He makes an exception, but does not do so for the inhabitants of the Garden: ﴾*As for those who have been blessed, they will be in Paradise, there to remain as long as the heavens and earth endure, unless your Lord wills otherwise – an unceasing gift.*﴿ [11:105–108]

71. In Ḥammād's narration, from Ḥarīz from Abū ʿAbd Allāh عليه السلام: '"*aṭā'an ghayra majdhūdh* – (*an unceasing gift*) is spelled with the letter *dhāl*.' [11:108]

72. From some of our associates – one of them said, 'He was asked about God's verse: ﴾*Do not rely on those who do evil, lest the Fire may touch you.*﴿ He said, "This refers to any one of our Shīʿa (followers) who holds the same opinion as these tyrants."' [11:113]

73. From ʿUthmān b. ʿĪsā, from a man from Abū ʿAbd Allāh عليه السلام regarding: ﴾*Do not rely on those who do evil, lest the Fire may touch you.*﴿ He said, 'It is basically that He has not decreed for it to be an eternity [in the Fire], but that Fire may touch you so do not rely on them.' [11:113]

٦٩. عن حُمران، قال: سألتُ أبا جعفر عليه السلام: جُعِلتُ فِداك، قول الله: ﴿خَـالِدِينَ فِيهَا مَـا دَامَتِ السَّمَـاوَاتُ وَالأَرْضُ إِلاَّ مَـا شَـاءَ رَبُّكَ﴾ لأهل النّار، أفرأيت قوله لأهل الجنّة: ﴿خَـالِدِينَ فِيهَا مَـا دَامَتِ السَّمَـاوَاتُ وَالأَرْضُ إِلاَّ مَـا شَـاءَ رَبُّكَ﴾.

قال: نعم، إن شاء جعل لهم دُنيًا فردّهم، وما شاء.

وسألتُه عن قول الله: ﴿خَـالِدِينَ فِيهَا مَـا دَامَتِ السَّمَـاوَاتُ وَالأَرْضُ إِلاَّ مَـا شَـاءَ رَبُّكَ﴾، فقال: هذه هي في الّذين يخرُجون من النار.

٧٠. عن أبي بصير، عن أبي جعفر عليه السلام في قوله: ﴿فَمِنْهُمْ شَقِيٌّ وَسَعِيدٌ﴾. قال: في ذِكر أهل النّار استثنى، وليس في ذِكر أهل الجنّة استثناء ﴿وَأَمَّا الَّذِينَ سُعِدُوا فَفِي الْجَنَّةِ خَالِدِينَ فِيهَا مَـا دَامَتِ السَّمَـاوَاتُ وَالأَرْضُ إِلاَّ مَـا شَـاءَ رَبُّكَ عَطَاءً غَيْرَ مَجْذُوذٍ﴾.

٧١. وفي رواية حمّاد، عن حَريز، عن أبي عبد الله عليه السلام ﴿عَطَاءً غَيْرَ مَجْذُوذٍ﴾ بالذال.

٧٢. عن بعض أصحابنا، فقال أحدهم: إنّه سُئل عن قول الله: ﴿وَلاَ تَرْكَنُوا إِلَى الَّذِينَ ظَلَمُوا فَتَمَسَّكُمُ النَّارُ﴾، قال: هو الرجل من شيعتنا يقول بقول هؤلاء الجبّارين.

٧٣. عن عثمان بن عيسى، عن رجلٍ، عن أبي عبد الله عليه السلام: ﴿وَلاَ تَرْكَنُوا إِلَى الَّذِينَ ظَلَمُوا فَتَمَسَّكُمُ النَّارُ إِلَى الَّذِينَ ظَلَمُوا فَتَمَسَّكُمُ النَّارُ﴾، قال: أما إنّه لم يجعلها خُلودًا، ولكن تَمَسّكم النار، فلا تَركَنوا إليهم.

74. From Ḥarīz, from Abū ʿAbd Allāh عليه السلام who said: ‘﴾ *Keep up the prayer at both ends of the day* ﴿ – its ends are at sunset (*maghrib*) and morning, ﴾ *and during parts of the night,* ﴿ which is the *ʿishāʾ* prayer at the end.’ [11:114]

75. From Abū Ḥamza al-Thumālī who said, ‘I heard one of the two [al-Bāqir or al-Ṣādiq] say, “ʿAlī عليه السلام approached the people and asked, ‘Which verse from God’s Book do you think holds the most weight?’

So some of them said: ﴾ *God does not forgive the joining of partners with Him: anything less than that He forgives to whoever He wills.* ﴿(4:48)

He said, ‘That is a good one, but that is not the one.’

So one of them said, ﴾ *My servants who have harmed yourselves by your own excess, do not despair of God’s mercy* [...] ﴿(39:53)

He عليه السلام said, ‘That is a good one, but it is not the one.’

So someone said: ﴾ *Those who remember God and implore forgiveness for their sins if they do something shameful or wrong themselves.* ﴿(3:135)

He said, ‘That is a good one, but it is not the one.’

He said, “Then the people shied away in fear, so he said, ‘What is wrong with you, O Muslims?’

They replied, ‘By God, there is nothing wrong with us.’”’

He said, ‘I heard the Messenger of God ﷺ say, “The weightiest verse in God’s Book is ﴾ *Keep up the prayer at both ends of the day, and during parts of the night* [...] ﴿ and he read the whole verse.

He said, “O ʿAlī, by the One who sent me as a harbinger and a warner, no sooner does any of you stand up to do his ablution than sins start to fall off his body. When he goes to meet God, facing Him with his heart, he does not finish the prayer with a single sin left on him, just as his mother gave birth to him. If he was to commit a sin between two prayers, then that state is restored again until he has completed all five prayers.”

Then he said, “O ʿAlī, the status of the prayer for my community is like a river that flows on each of your doorsteps. Can you imagine if any of you were to have any dirt on his body and he bathed in that river five times a day, would there be any dirt left on his body? By God, that is what the five prayers are for my community.”’ [11:114]

٧٤. عن حَرِيز، عن أبي عبد الله عليه السلام، قال: ﴿وَأَقِمِ الصَّلَاةَ طَرَفَيِ النَّهَارِ﴾ وطَرَفاه: المَغرب والغَداة ﴿وَزُلَفًا مِنَ اللَّيْلِ﴾ وهي صلاة العِشاء الآخرة.

٧٥. عن أبي حمزة الثُّمالي، قال: سَمِعتُ أحدهما عليهما السلام يقول: إنّ عليًّا عليه السلام أقبل على الناس فقال: أيّ آية في كتاب الله أرجى عندكم؟

فقال بعضهم: ﴿إِنَّ اللهَ لَا يَغْفِرُ أَنْ يُشْرَكَ بِهِ وَيَغْفِرُ مَا دُونَ ذَٰلِكَ لِمَنْ يَشَاءُ﴾، قال حَسَنة، وليست إيّاها.

فقال بعضهم: ﴿يَا عِبَادِيَ الَّذِينَ أَسْرَفُوا عَلَىٰ أَنْفُسِهِمْ لَا تَقْنَطُوا مِنْ رَحْمَةِ اللهِ﴾، قال: حَسَنة، وليست إيّاها.

وقال بعضهم: ﴿وَالَّذِينَ إِذَا فَعَلُوا فَاحِشَةً أَوْ ظَلَمُوا أَنْفُسَهُمْ ذَكَرُوا اللهَ فَاسْتَغْفَرُوا لِذُنُوبِهِمْ﴾، قال: حسنة، وليست إيّاها.

قال: ثمّ أحجم الناس، فقال: ما لكم يا معشر المسلمين؟ قالوا: لا والله ما عندنا شيء. قال: سَمِعتُ رسول الله صلى الله عليه وآله يقول: «أرجى آيةٍ في كتاب الله ﴿وأَقِمِ الصَّلَاةَ طَرَفَيِ النَّهَارِ وَزُلَفًا مِنَ اللَّيْلِ﴾» وقرأ الآية كُلّها. وقال: «يا علي، والّذي بعثني بالحقّ بشيرًا ونذيرًا، إنّ أحدكم ليقوم إلى وضوئه فتتسَاقطُ عن جَوارحه الذُنوب، فإذا استقبل الله بوجهه وقلبه، لم يَنفتل عن صلاته وعليه من ذُنوبه شيء، كما ولدته أُمُّه، فإن أصاب شيئًا بين الصلاتين، كان له مثل ذلك»، حتّى عدّ الصلوات الخمس.

76. From Ibrāhīm al-Karakhī[17] who said, 'I was with Abū 'Abd Allāh عليه السلام when a client of his came in, so he asked him, "O so-and-so, when did you arrive?"

He remained silent.

So Abū 'Abd Allāh said, "You have come from here and there. Consider what your day has consisted of for you have with you an angel charged with recording everything that you do. So do not disregard a sin, however small it be, for it will torment you one day. And neither should you underestimate a good deed, for there is nothing more effective at attracting [good] and repelling [evil] than the good deed. It repels even the gravest and oldest of sins and does away with it. God says in His Book: ﴾*good deeds efface misdeeds.*﴿"

He continued, "The night prayer effaces the sins of the day."

He also said, "It effaces whatever wrong you have done."' [11:114]

77. From Ibrāhīm b. 'Umar who, without mentioning his source, cited Abū 'Abd Allāh عليه السلام as having said with regard to God's verse: ﴾*Keep up the prayer at both ends of the day, and during parts of the night, for good deeds efface misdeeds*﴿, 'The prayer performed by the believer in the middle of the night drives away whatever sin he committed during the day.' [11:114]

78. From Samā'a b. Mihrān who said, 'A man from the mountains asked Abū 'Abd Allāh about money that he receives from the sultan which he gives away in charity, using it to maintain relations with his kin and to go on pilgrimage so that he might be forgiven for what he has earned [as an unlawful livelihood], saying: ﴾*good deeds efface misdeeds.*﴿ So Abū 'Abd Allāh said, "Two wrongs do not make a right, but a right can certainly redress a wrong." Then Abū 'Abd Allāh عليه السلام said, "If the lawful and unlawful earnings have been mixed up together to an extent that it is impossible to distinguish the lawful from the unlawful [earnings], then there is no problem."' [11:114]

---

17 Ibrāhīm b. Abī Ziyād al-Karakhī, a prominent companion of Imam Ja'far al-Ṣādiq and Imam Mūsā al-Kāẓim. See Khū'ī, *Mu'jam*, 1:177–8 (nr. 83).

ثمّ قال: «يا عليّ، إنّما منزلة الصلوات الخمس لأُمّتي كنهرٍ جارٍ على باب أحدكم، فما ظنّ أحدكم لو كان في جسده دَرَن ثمّ اغتسل في ذلك النهر خمس مرّات في اليوم، أكان يبقى في جسده دَرَن؟ فكذلك والله الصلوات الخمس لأُمّتي».

٧٦. عن إبراهيم الكرخي، قال: كنتُ عند أبي عبد الله عليه السلام فدخل عليه مولىً له، فقال: يا فلان، متى جئت؟ فسكت، فقال أبو عبد الله عليه السلام: جئت من هاهنا ومن هاهنا، انظُر بما تقطع به يومك، فإنَّ معك مَلَكًا مُوكّلاً يَحفَظ عليك ما تعمل، فلا تحتقر سيّئةً وإن كانت صغيرةً، فإنّها ستسوؤك يومًا، ولا تحتقر حسنةً فإنّه ليس شيء أشدّ طلبًا ولا أسرع دَرَكًا من الحسنة، إنّها لتُدرِك الذنب العظيم القديم فتذهب به، وقد قال الله في كتابه: ﴿إِنَّ الْحَسَنَاتِ يُذْهِبْنَ السَّيِّئَاتِ﴾

قال: قال: صلاة الليل تذهب بذُنُوب النهار، وقال: تذهب بما جرَحتُم.

٧٧. عن إبراهيم بن عمر، يرفعه إلى أبي عبد الله عليه السلام، في قول الله تعالى: ﴿وَأَقِمِ الصَّلَاةَ طَرَفَيِ النَّهَارِ﴾ إلى: ﴿السَّيِّئَاتِ﴾، فقال: صلاة المؤمن بالليل تذهب بما عَمِل من ذَنَب النهار.

٧٨. عن سَماعة بن مِهران، قال: سأل أبا عبد الله عليه السلام رجلٌ من أهل الجِبال عن رجلٍ أصاب مالاً من أعمال السلطان، فهو يتصدَّق منه، ويَصِل قرابته، ويحُجّ ليُغفَر له ما اكتسب، وهو يقول: ﴿إِنَّ الْحَسَنَاتِ يُذْهِبْنَ السَّيِّئَاتِ﴾.

79. Also on his authority, in a report by al-Mufaḍḍal b. Mazīd[18] that he said, 'See that whatever fortune comes your way you share it with your brothers, for God says: ﴾*good deeds efface misdeeds.*﴿' Al-Mufaḍḍal said, 'I was my brother's deputy over the treasury.' He continued, 'And I had asked him, "May I be your ransom – you see the position I hold with these people – what is your opinion of that?" He said, "If only he had not appointed you [to that position]."' [11:114]

80. From al-Mufaḍḍal b. Mazīd, a secretary of the chancellery, who said, 'Abū 'Abd Allāh عليه السلام came to visit me whilst I had been commanded to take out certain monetary dues for the Banū Hāshim. I did not know that he was right behind me when I was recording, so I was startled by him. He asked me about what had been commanded for them. So I handed him the book.

He said, "I do not see anything for Ismā'īl here." So I said, "This is what has been issued to us."

Then I asked him, "May I be your ransom – what do you think of my position here among these people?" He replied, "See that whatever fortune comes your way, you share it with your brothers, for God says: ﴾*good deeds efface misdeeds.*﴿"' [11:114]

81. From Ibrāhīm al-Karakhī who said, 'I was with Abū 'Abd Allāh عليه السلام when a man from Medina came in to see him, so Abū 'Abd Allāh عليه السلام asked him, "Where have you come from?" Then he said to him, "When you amble here and there, neither working to earn a livelihood nor striving to secure your Hereafter, then consider carefully how your day and night is divided up. Know that with you is a noble angel charged with recording whatever you do. He has access to your secrets that you hide from people, so feel embarrassed [before committing anything]. Do not disregard any misdeed for it will surely torment you one day, nor underestimate any good deed, however small you consider it to be and however insignificant it might seem in your eyes, for it will definitely bring you joy one day. Know that there is nothing more harmful in the end that you will be quick to regret than sin. [Know also] that there is nothing that attracts goodness and repels evil faster than

18 Al-Mufaḍḍal b. Mazīd, about whom there is very little information, was the brother of Shu'ayb al-Kātib. See Ḥillī, *Khulāṣat al-aqwāl*, 274 (nr. 999).

فقال أبو عبدالله عليه السلام: إنَّ الخطيئة لا تُكفِّرُ الخَطيئة، ولكنّ الحَسَنة تُكفّر الخَطيئة، ثمّ قال أبو عبدالله عليه السلام: إن كان خَلَط الحرام حلالاً، فاختلط جميعًا، فلم يعرِف الحلال من الحرام، فلا بأس.

٧٩. وعنه، في رواية المُفضَّل بن مزيد، أنّه قال: انظُر ما أصبت به فَعُد به على إخوانك، فإنَّ الله تعالى يقول: ﴿إِنَّ الْحَسَنَاتِ يُذْهِبْنَ السَّيِّئَاتِ﴾.

قال المُفضّل: كنتَ خليفة أخي على الديوان. قال: وقد قلتُ: جُعِلت فِداك، قد ترى مكاني من هؤلاء القوم وما ترى؟ قال: لو لم يكن كتب.

٨٠. عن المفضّل بن مزيد الكاتب، قال: دخل عليَّ أبو عبدالله عليه السلام، وقد أُمِرتُ أن أُخرج لبني هاشم جوائز، فلم أعلم إلاّ وهو على رأسي وأنا مستخلٍ، فوفَوثبتُ إليه، فسألني عمّا أُمر لهم، فناولته الكتّاب، فقال: ما أرى لإسماعيل هاهنا شيئًا؟ فقلت: هذا الذي خرج إلينا.

ثمّ قلت له: جُعلت فِداك، قد ترى مكاني من هؤلاء القوم؟ فقال لي: انظُر ما أصبت به، فعُد على أصحابك، فإنَّ الله تعالى يقول: ﴿إِنَّ الْحَسَنَاتِ يُذْهِبْنَ السَّيِّئَاتِ﴾.

٨١. عن إبراهيم الكرخي، قال: كنتُ عند أبي عبدالله عليه السلام، إذ دخل عليه رجلٌ من أهل المدينة، فقال له أبو عبدالله عليه السلام: من أين جئت؟ ثمّ قال له: جئتَ من هاهنا وهاهنا لغير معاشٍ تطلُبه ولا لعمل آخرة، انظر بماذا تقطع يومك وليلتك، واعلم أنّ معك ملكًا كريمًا موكّلاً بك، يَحْفَظ عليك ما تفعل، ويطّلع على سِرّك الذي تُخفيه من الناس، فاستحي

the good deed itself. Indeed, it repels even the old, grave sin that has been forgotten about by its perpetrator – so it revives him by taking it away from him and effacing it after he has committed it. This is God's statement: ﴾*good deeds efface misdeeds – this is a reminder for those who are aware.*﴿"' [11:114]

82. He read from Ibn Khidāsh from Abū 'Abd Allāh عليه السلام, who said: ﴾*Good deeds efface misdeeds.*﴿ He said, 'The night prayer expiates the sins that were committed during the day.' [11:114]

83. From 'Abd Allāh b. Sinān who said, 'Abū 'Abd Allāh عليه السلام was asked about God's verse: ﴾*If your Lord had pleased, He would have made all people a single community, but they continue to have their differences – except those on whom your Lord has mercy.*﴿ He replied, "They were a single community, then God sent prophets in order to have proof against them."' [11:118]

84. From 'Abd Allāh b. Ghālib, on his father's authority, from a man who said, 'I asked 'Alī b. al-Ḥusayn عليه السلام about God's verse: ﴾*But they continue to have their differences.*﴿ He said, "By that He meant those from among the community who oppose us, and that they all differ with each other in their religion. As for His statement: ﴾*Except those on whom your Lord has mercy – for He created them to be this way*﴿, those are our adherents from among the believers, and He has created them thus from the good clay. Have you not heard Ibrāhīm's supplication: ﴾*My Lord, make this land secure and provide with produce those of its people who believe in God and the Last Day.*﴿(2:126) He said, "We are the ones he meant, his adherents, his followers, and the followers of his vicegerent."

He continued: [God said]: ﴾*As for those who disbelieve, I will grant them enjoyment for a short while and then subject them to the torment of the Fire.*﴿ By that He is referring to those of his community who rebelled against His vicegerent and did not follow him. By God, that is exactly the case with this community."' [11:118–119]

ولا تحقِرنّ سيّئةً، فإنّها ستسوؤك يومًا، ولا تحقِرنّ حسنةً وإن صَغُرت عندك، وقَلّت في عينك، فإنّها ستَسُرّك يومًا.

واعلم أنّه ليس شيءٌ أضرّ عاقبةً ولا أسرع ندامةً من الخطيئة، وأنّه ليس شيءٌ أشدّ طلبًا ولا أسرع دَركًا للخطيئة من الحَسَنة، أما أنّها لتُدرِك الذنب العظيم القديم المنسيّ عند عامله، فتجذبه وتُسقِطه وتذهب به بعد إثباته، وذلك قول الله: ﴿إِنَّ الْحَسَنَاتِ يُذْهِبْنَ السَّيِّئَاتِ ذَلِكَ ذِكْرَى لِلذَّاكِرِينَ﴾.

٨٢. وقرأ عن ابن خِداش، عن أبي عبد الله ﷺ، قال: ﴿إِنَّ الْحَسَنَاتِ يُذْهِبْنَ السَّيِّئَاتِ﴾، قال: صلاة الليل تكفّر ما كان من ذُنوب النهار.

٨٣. عن عبد الله بن سِنان، قال: سُئل أبو عبد الله ﷺ عن قول الله: ﴿وَلَوْ شَاءَ رَبُّكَ لَجَعَلَ النَّاسَ أُمَّةً وَاحِدَةً﴾ إلى: ﴿مَنْ رَحِمَ رَبُّكَ﴾، قال: كانوا أُمّةً واحدةً، فبعث الله النبيّين ليتّخذ عليهم الحُجّة.

٨٤. عن عبد الله بن غالب، عن أبيه، عن رجل، قال: سألتُ عليّ بن الحسين ﷺ عن قول الله: ﴿وَلَا يَزَالُونَ مُخْتَلِفِينَ﴾، قال: عنى بذلك من خالفَنا مِن هذه الأمّة، وكُلّهم يخالف بعضهم بعضًا في دينهم، وأمّا قوله: ﴿إِلَّا مَنْ رَحِمَ رَبُّكَ وَلِذَلِكَ خَلَقَهُمْ﴾ فأُولئك أولياؤنا من المؤمنين، ولذلك خلقهم من الطِّينة الطَّيبة، أما تسمع لقول إبراهيم ﷺ: ﴿رَبِّ اجْعَلْ هَذَا بَلَدًا آمِنًا وَارْزُقْ أَهْلَهُ مِنَ الثَّمَرَاتِ مَنْ آمَنَ مِنْهُمْ بِاللَّهِ﴾، قال: إيّانا عنى وأولياءه وشيعته وشيعة وصيّه.

85. From Yaʿqūb b. Shuʿayb, from Abū ʿAbd Allāh ﷺ. He said, 'I asked him about God's verse: ﴾*I created jinn and mankind only to worship Me.*﴿(51:56) He said, "[It means] He created them to worship."

I said, "So what about His saying: ﴾*but they continue to have their differences – except those on whom your Lord has mercy – for He created them to be this way*﴿?' So he replied, "This one was revealed after that one."' [11:118–119]

86. From Saʿīd b. al-Musayyab, from ʿAlī b. al-Ḥusayn ﷺ regarding God's verse: ﴾*But they continue to have their differences – except those on whom your Lord has mercy – for He created them to be this way*﴿: 'So those are our adherents from among the believers, and He created them to be this way from the good clay. Have you not heard Ibrāhīm's supplication: ﴾*My Lord, make this land secure and provide with produce those of its people who believe in God and the Last Day*﴿(2:126)? We are the ones he meant by that, as well as his adherents, his followers, and the followers of his vicegerent. ﴾*As for those who disbelieve, I will grant them enjoyment for a short while and then subject them to the torment of the Fire.*﴿ By God, by that He is referring to those of his community who rebelled against his vicegerent and did not follow him. By God, that is exactly the case with this community.' [11:118–119]

قال: ﴿وَمَن كَفَرَ فَأُمَتِّعُهُ قَلِيلاً ثُمَّ أَضْطَرُّهُ إِلَى عَذَابِ النَّارِ﴾، قال: عنى بذلك من جحد وصيّه ولم يتّبعه من أمّته، وكذلك والله حال هذه الأمّة.

٨٥. عن يعقوب بن شعيب، عن أبي عبدالله ﷺ، قال: سألتُهُ عن قول الله عزّ وجلّ: ﴿وَمَا خَلَقْتُ الْجِنَّ وَالإِنْسَ إِلاَّ لِيَعْبُدُونِ﴾، قال: خلقهم للعبادة.

قال: قلت: وقوله: ﴿وَلاَ يَزَالُونَ مُخْتَلِفِينَ ۞ إِلاَّ مَنْ رَحِمَ رَبُّكَ وَلِذَلِكَ خَلَقَهُمْ﴾؟ فقال: نزلت هذه الآية بعد تلك.

٨٦. عن سعيد بن المسيّب، عن عليّ بن الحسين ﷺ، في قوله: ﴿وَلاَ يَزَالُونَ مُخْتَلِفِينَ ۞ إِلاَّ مَنْ رَحِمَ رَبُّكَ وَلِذَلِكَ خَلَقَهُمْ﴾ فأُولئك هم أولياؤنا من المؤمنين ولذلك خلقهم من الطيّنة الطّيبة، أما تسمع لقول إبراهيم ﷺ: ﴿رَبِّ اجْعَلْ هَذَا بَلَداً آمِناً وَارْزُقْ أَهْلَهُ مِنَ الثَّمَرَاتِ مَنْ آمَنَ مِنْهُم بِاللهِ﴾؟ إيّانا عنى بذلك وأولياءه وشيعته وشيعة وصيّة ﴿وَمَن كَفَرَ فَأُمَتِّعُهُ قَلِيلاً ثُمَّ أَضْطَرُّهُ إِلَى عَذَابِ النَّارِ﴾، عنى بذلك والله من جحد وصيّه ولم يتّبعه من أُمّته، وكذلك والله حال هذه الأُمّة.

Yūsuf

12. Yūsuf

1. From Abū Baṣīr, from Abū ʿAbd Allāh ﵇. He said, 'I heard him say, "Whoever reads the Chapter of Yūsuf (*sūra Yūsuf*) every day or every night, God will resurrect him on the Day of Judgement as handsome as Yūsuf, and he will not be gripped by the terror that will grip other people on that day. His neighbours will be God's righteous servants."

Then he said, "Yūsuf was indeed one of God's righteous servants, and was protected from being a fornicator or an indecent man in this world."'

2. From Masʿada b. Ṣadaqa who said, 'Jaʿfar b. Muḥammad ﵇ said, "My father ﵇ said, 'By God, I play with any one of my children, sit him on my lap, show him more affection, as well as express my appreciation for him, even though another child of mine may be more entitled to it. I only do this out of fear that the rest of them may behave with him as Yūsuf's brothers did with him. God revealed the Chapter of Yūsuf only as parables lest one of us displays envy towards another, as Yūsuf's brothers were envious of him when they bullied him. He made it a proof for those who adhere to us and incline to us with affection, and fight against our enemies who declare war and animosity against us.'"'

بسم الله الرحمن الرحيم

من سورة يوسف

١. عن أبي بصير، عن أبي عبد الله عليه السلام، قال: سَمِعتُه يقول: من قرأ سورة يوسف عليه السلام في كلّ يوم، أو في كلّ ليلةٍ، بعثه الله يوم القيامة وجماله كجمال يوسف عليه السلام، ولا يُصيبه يوم القيامة ما يُصيب الناس من الفَزَع، وكان جيرانه من عِباد الله الصالحين.

ثمّ قال: إنّ يوسف عليه السلام كان من عباد الله الصالين، وأومن في الدنيا أن يكون زانيًا أو فحّاشًا.

٢. عن مَسعدة بن صَدَقة، قال: قال جعفر بن محمّد عليهما السلام: قال والدي عليه السلام: والله إنّي لأصانع بعض ولدي، وُاجلسه على فَخِذي، وأُكثِر له المحبَّة، وأُكثِر له الشُّكر، وإنّ الحقّ لغيره من ولدي، ولكن مخافة عليه منه ومن غيره، لئلاّ يصنعوا به ما فعل بيوسف إخوته، وما أنزل الله سورة يوسف إلاّ أمثالاً، لكيلا يَحسُد بعضنا بعضًا كما حَسَد يوسف إخوته وبَغَوا عليه، فجعلها حُجّةً على من تَولاّنا، ودان بحبّنا، وجَحَد أعداءنا: من نَصَب لنا الحرب والعَداوة.

3. From Zurāra, from Abū Jaʿfar عليه السلام who said, 'Prophets are of five types: there are those who hear a sound like a ringing noise and know what that means; then there are those who are informed in their dreams such as Yūsuf and Ibrāhīm; then there are those who witness with their own eyes; then there are some who get inspiration straight into their hearts; and finally there are those who receive it straight into their ears.'

4. From Abū Khadīja[1], from a man from Abū ʿAbd Allāh عليه السلام who said, 'Yaʿqūb suffered the loss of Yūsuf only as a result of a fat sheep that he was slaughtering whilst a man from among his companions belonging to a needy community had nothing to break his fast with, and he ignored him and did not feed him. Therefore he was afflicted with Yūsuf's loss. After that, every morning a caller would announce on his behalf: "Whoever is not fasting, come and attend Yaʿqūb's lunch." And every evening, "Whoever has been fasting, come and attend Yaʿqūb's dinner."'

5. From Abū Ḥamza al-Thumālī who said, 'I prayed the dawn prayer with ʿAlī b. al-Ḥusayn عليه السلام in Medina on Friday, and he called in a client of his called Wushayka and said to her, "No beggar should be turned away from my door today without you giving him something, for it is Friday."

So I said, "But not everyone who begs is deserving – may I be your ransom."

Then he said, "Thābit, I would fear for someone deserving to ask from us and we do not feed him and turn him away instead, and consequently that which afflicted Yaʿqūb and his family would afflict us, the Ahl al-Bayt. Feed them all, feed them all!"

Then he continued, "Yaʿqūb used to slaughter a sheep every day, and from it he would give in charity as well as feed himself and his family. Once a believing, fasting, righteous man with a lofty position with God who was a stranger passing through the town came to Yaʿqūb's door begging on the eve of Friday at the time of breaking his fast. He called at the door: "Please spare some of your leftovers to feed this hungry foreign traveler." He called thus several times at the door while they could hear him, but they ignored his rights and did not believe his words. When he despaired of being fed by

1 Most likely referring to Sālim b. Mukarram al-Jammāl.

٣. عن زُرارة، عن أبي جعفر عليه السلام، قال: الأنبياء على خمسة أنواع، منهم من يسمع الصوت مثل صوت السِّلسلة، فيعلم ما عُني به، ومنهم من ينبّأ في مَنامه مثل يوسف وإبراهيم، ومنهم من يُعاين، ومنهم من يُنكَت في قلبه، ويُوقَر في أُذنه.

٤. عن أبي خَديجة، عن رجل، عن أبي عبد الله عليه السلام، قال: إنّما ابتُلي يعقوب بيوسف أنّه ذَبَح كَبشًا سَمينًا، ورجل من أصحابه يُدعى بقوم محتاجٌ لم يجد ما يُفطِر عليه، فأغفله ولم يُطعِمه، فابتُلي بيوسف، وكان بعد ذلك كلّ صباح مناديه ينادي: من لم يكن صائمًا فليشهد غَداء يعقوب، فإذا كان المساء نادى: من كان صائمًا فليشهد عَشاء يعقوب.

٥. عن أبي حمزة الثُّمالي، قال: صلّيت مع عليّ بن الحسين صلوات الله عليه الفَجر بالمدينة في يوم الجمعة، فدعا مولاة له يقال لها وشيكة، فقال: لا يَقِفنَّ على بابي اليوم السائل إلاّ أعطيتموه، فإنّ اليوم الجمعة. فقلتُ: ليس كلّ من يسأل مُحق، جُعلت فِداك؟ فقال: يا ثابت، أخاف أن يكون بعض من يسألنا مُحقًّا فلا نُطعمه ونَرُدّه، فينزل بنا أهل البيت ما نزل بيعقوب وآله، أطعِموهم، أطعِموهم.

ثمّ قال: إنّ يعقوب عليه السلام كان كلّ يوم يذبح كبشًا يتصدّق منه، ويأكُل هو وعياله، وإنّ سائلاً مؤمنًا صوّامًا قوّامًا، له عند الله منزلةٌ، مجتازًا غريبًا، اعترّ بباب يعقوب عليه السلام عَشيّة جمعة عند أوان إفطار، فهتف ببابه: أطعِموا السائل المجتاز الغريب الجائع من فَضل طعامكم؛ يهتف بذلك على بابه مِرارًا وهم يسمعونه، جَهلوا حقَّه، ولم يُصَدِّقوا قوله، فلمّا أيس منهم أن يُطعَم وتغشّاه الليلُ، استرجع واستعبر، وشكا جُوعه إلى الله، وبات طاويًا،

them and night had fallen, he said, ﴾*We belong to God and to Him we are returning*﴿ and his eyes welled up. He complained to God of his hunger and fell asleep famished. He woke up fasting and hungry, still persevering and praising God, whilst Ya'qūb and his family had slept with satiated stomachs and awoken with food left over."

He continued, "So God revealed to Ya'qūb the following morning, 'You have humiliated My servant in such a way that you have beckoned My anger towards you, and forced Me to discipline you and descend My consequences and affliction upon you and your offspring, O Ya'qūb. Do you not know that the most beloved and dearest of My prophets to Me are the ones who have compassion on My destitute servants? Those who draw them near to Me, who feed them, and who are a safe haven and source of refuge for them. Ya'qūb, why did you not have compassion on Dhimyāl, My servant, who strives hard to worship Me, who is content with the simple things in this worldly life? Yesterday evening, when he humbled himself at your door at the fast-breaking time, calling out to you: "Please feed this foreign travelling man," you did not feed him anything. And he said: ﴾*We belong to God and to Him we are returning*﴿ and cried, complaining to Me about it, and slept on an empty stomach, still praising Me with patience and awoke fasting whilst you, Ya'qūb, and your offspring slept on full stomachs and awoke with food still left over in your house.

Do you not know, Ya'qūb, that I am quicker at disciplining and afflicting My friends than I am My enemies, and that is only because of My kind regard for My friends and My gradual baiting of My enemies. By My honour, I will descend an affliction upon you and will make you and your offspring an object of My tribulation, and I will certainly discipline you with My punishment. So prepare for My affliction, accept My decree and bear the tribulations patiently."'

Abū Ḥamza said, 'Then I asked 'Alī b. al-Ḥusayn عليه السلام, "When did Yūsuf see the dream?"

He replied, "On that same night when Ya'qūb and his children slept well-satiated and Dhimyāl slept hungry and distressed. The next morning, he awoke and related it to Ya'qūb, who became worried when he heard about the dream related to him by Yūsuf, especially given what God had just revealed to him about preparing for affliction. So he said to Yūsuf, 'Do not relate this dream of yours to your brothers for I fear that they may plot

وأصبح صائمًا جائعًا صابرًا حامدًا لله تعالى، وبات يعقوب وآله شِباعًا بِطانًا، وأصبحوا وعندهم فَضلةٌ من طعامهم.

قال: فأوحى الله إلى يعقوب في صبيحة تلك الليلة: لقد ذللت عبدي ذِلّة استجررت بها غضبي، واستوجبت بها أدبي، ونزول عُقوبتي وبلواي عليك وعلى ولدك يا يعقوب، أما علمت أنّ أحبّ أنبيائي إليّ وأكرمهم عليّ من رَحِم مساكين عبادي، وقرّبهم إليه وأطعمهم، وكان لهم مأوى وملجأً؟

يا يعقوب، أما رَحِمت ذميال عبدي، المجتهد في عبادتي، القانع باليسير من ظاهر الدنيا عَشاءَ أمس لمّا اعترّ ببابك عند أوان إفطاره؟ يهتِف بكم: أطعموا السائل الغريب المجتاز؛ فلم تُطعِموه شيئًا، واسترجع واستعبر وشكا ما به إليّ، وبات طاويًا حامدًا صابرًا، وأصبح لي صائمًا، وبتّ يا يعقوب وولدك ليلكم شِباعًا، وأصبحتم وعندكم فَضلةٌ من طَعامكم.

أوَ ما عَلِمت يا يعقوب أنّي بالعقوبة والبلوى إلى أوليائي أسرع منّي بها إلى أعدائي، وذلك منّي حُسن نظر لأوليائي، واستدراج منّي لأعدائي، أما وعزّتي لأُنزلنّ بك بلواي، ولأجعلنّك وولدك غرضًا لِمُصابي، ولأُؤدّبنّك بعقوبتي، فاستعدّوا لبلائي، وارضُوا بقضائي، واصبروا للمصائب.

قال أبو حمزة: فقلت لعليّ بن الحسين عليهما السلام: متى رأى يوسف عليه السلام الرُّؤيا؟ فقال: في تلك الليّلة التي بات فيها يعقوب وولده شباعًا، وبات فيها ذميال جائعًا، رآها فأصبح فقصّها على يعقوب عليه السلام من الغد، فاغتمّ يعقوب لمّا سَمِع من يوسف الرُّؤيا مع ما

against you.’ However, Yūsuf did not conceal his dream and instead related it to his brothers.”

‘Alī b. al-Ḥusayn عليه السلام then said, “So the first affliction to descend upon Ya‘qūb and his family was the jealousy towards Yūsuf when they heard him talk about the dream that he had had.” He continued, “Ya‘qūb’s affection for Yūsuf grew as he feared that God’s revelation to him about preparing for affliction was specifically about Yūsuf, and so his affection for him intensified, and he feared that the affliction would descend upon Yūsuf out of all his children.

So when Yūsuf’s brothers saw how kindly Ya‘qūb was treating Yūsuf and how much he favoured him over them, they found this unbearable and began to be affected. They started to discuss amongst themselves saying, ‘Yūsuf and his brother are dearer to our father than us while we are a hardy group. Kill Yūsuf or banish him to another land, and your father’s attention will be free to turn to you. After that, you can be righteous’ – meaning after that you can repent.

Thereupon they said: ﴾ *‘Why do you not trust us with Yūsuf? Send him with us tomorrow and he will enjoy himself and play.’* ﴿ Ya‘qūb replied: ﴾ *‘The thought of you taking him away with you worries me: I am afraid a wolf may eat him when you are not paying attention.’* ﴿ He was anxious that God’s affliction upon Ya‘qūb would touch Yūsuf, and Ya‘qūb was prepared for the affliction to be specifically directed at Yūsuf.”

He continued, “God’s power, decree and the execution of His command prevailed with Ya‘qūb, Yūsuf and his brothers. Since Ya‘qūb عليه السلام was neither able to avert the tribulation from himself, nor from Yūsuf and his brothers, he let him go with them, albeit reluctantly, expecting God’s tribulation to affect Yūsuf specifically because of the place he occupied in his heart and due to his intense love for him.

So when they were leaving the house with him he followed them hastily and grabbed him out of their hands, drew him close to himself and embraced him, weeping. Then he reluctantly passed him on to them and they set off hurriedly, fearing that he would take him away from them and not let him come with them. When they were alone with him, they took him to a thicket of trees and said, ‘Let us kill him and leave him under this tree so that the wolves can eat him tonight.’

أوحى الله إليه: أن استعِدّ للبلاء؛ فقال ليوسف: لا تَقصُص رُؤياك هذه على إخوتك، فإنّي أخافُ أن يَكيدُوك، فلم يكتُم يوسف رُؤياه، وقصّها على إخوته.

فقال عليّ بن الحسين عليهما السلام: فكان أوّل بلوى نزلت بيعقوب وآله الحسد ليوسف عليه السلام لمّا سَمِعوا منه الرّؤيا الّتي رآها؛ قال: واشتدَّت رِقّة يعقوب على يوسف، وخاف أن يكون ما أوحى الله إليه من الاستعداد للبلاء إنّما ذلك في يوسف عليه السلام، فاشتدَّت رِقّته عليه، وخاف أن ينزِل به بلاء في يوسف عليه السلام من بين ولده.

فلمّا أن رأوا إخوة يوسف ما يَصنَع يعقوب بيوسف من إكرامه وإيثاره إيّاه عليهم اشتدّ ذلك عليهم، وابتدأ البلاء فيهم، فتآمرُوا فيما بينهم، وقالوا: إنَّ يوسف وأخاه أحبُّ إلى أبينا منّا ونحن عُصبة، اقتُلوا يوسف أو ألقوه أرضًا يخلُ لكم وجه أبيكم وتكونوا من بعده قومًا صالحين، أي تتوبون، فعند ذلك قالوا: ﴿يَا أَبَانَا مَا لَكَ لَا تَأْمَنَّا عَلَىٰ يُوسُفَ ... أَرْسِلْهُ مَعَنَا غَدًا يَرْتَعْ وَيَلْعَبْ﴾، قال يعقوب: ﴿إِنِّي لَيَحْزُنُنِي أَنْ تَذْهَبُوا بِهِ وَأَخَافُ أَنْ يَأْكُلَهُ الذِّئْبُ وَأَنْتُمْ عَنْهُ غَافِلُونَ﴾ حَذرًا منه عليه، وأن تكون البَلوى مِن الله على يعقوب في يوسف، وكان يعقوب عليه السلام مستعدًا للبَلوى في يوسف خاصّة، قال: فَغَلبت قُدرة الله وقضاؤه ونافذُ أمره في يعقوب ويوسف وإخوته، فلم يقدِر يعقوبُ عليه السلام على دفع البلاء عن نفسه، ولا عن يوسف وإخوته، فدفعه إليهم، وهو لذلك كارهٌ، متوقّع للبلاء من الله في يوسف خاصّة، لموقعه من قلبه وحُبّه له.

فلمّا خرَجُوا به من منزله لَحِقهم مسرعًا، فانتزعه من أيديهم، فضمّه إليه واعتنقه وبكى، ثمّ دفعه إليهم وهو كاره، فانطلقوا به مسرعين مخافة أن يأخُذه منهم ثمّ لا يدفعه إليهم،

So the oldest of them said: ﴾ *'Do not kill Yūsuf, but, if you must, throw him into the hidden depths of a well where some caravan may pick him up.'* ﴿

So they took him off to the well and threw him into its depths, thinking that he would probably drown. He called out to them from the bottom of the well, 'O sons of Rūmīn, greet Ya'qūb with peace from me.' So when they heard his voice, they said to each other, 'Let us not disperse away from here until we know for certain that he has died.'"

He continued, "They stayed with him for a while, and then they gave up; ﴾ *and at nightfall they returned to their father weeping. They said, 'We went off racing one another, leaving Yūsuf behind with our things, and a wolf ate him.* ﴿ When he heard their words he said: ﴾ *We belong to God and to Him we are returning.* ﴿ His eyes welled up and he remembered what God had revealed to him about being prepared for affliction. So he remained patient and yielded to the affliction, saying to them: ﴾ *Your souls have prompted you to do wrong! But patience is graceful* [...] ﴿ God would never have allowed wolves to eat Yūsuf's flesh without seeing his dream realized."'

Abū Ḥamza then said, 'At this point 'Alī b. al-Ḥusayn stopped talking.' [12:1–18]

6. From Misma' Abū Sayyār, from Abū 'Abd Allāh عليه السلام who said, 'When Yūsuf was thrown into the well, Jibra'īl descended upon him and said to him, "What are you doing here, young man? Who has thrown you into this well?"

So he replied, "My brothers were jealous of me because of my closeness to my father, so they threw me into this well."

So Jibra'īl said to him, "Would you like to come out of this well?" He replied, "That is up to the God of Ibrāhīm, Isḥāq, and Ya'qūb."

So Jibra'īl said to him, "Well, the God of Ibrāhīm, Isḥāq and Ya'qūb says for you to say: 'O God, I ask You – for all praise belongs to You – there is no god but You, the Bestower and the Originator of the heavens and the earth, Lord of Might and Honour – to send blessings on Muḥammad and the family of Muḥammad, and to give me release and a way out from this predicament of mine, and to provide for me whence I do not even expect.'

So Yūsuf said it, and God gave him release from the well that very day, a way out from the plot of the woman, and bestowed the kingdom of Egypt to him whence he did not even expect."'

فلمّا أمعنوا به مالوا به إلى غَيضة أشجارٍ، فقالوا: نَذبَحه ونُلقيه تحت هذه الشجرة فتأكُله الذئاب الليلة، فقال كبيرهم: لا تقتُلوا يوسف، ولكن ألقُوهُ في غَيابةِ الجُبّ يلتَقِطه بَعضُ السَّيارةِ إن كنتم فاعلينَ، فانطلقوا به إلى الجُبّ، فألقوه في غَيابة الجُبّ وهم يَظُنّون أنّه يغرَق فيه، فلمّا صار إلى قَعر الجُبّ ناداهم: يا ولد رومين، أقرئوا يعقوب منّي السلام، فلمّا سَمِعوا كلامه قال بعضهم لبعض: لا تَفَرّقوا من هاهنا حتّى تعلموا أنّه قد مات.

قال: فلم يَزالُوا بحضرته حتّى أيسوا، فرجعوا إلى أبيهم عشاءً يبكون، قالوا: يا أبانا، إنا ذهبنا نستبق، وتركنا يوسف عند متاعِنا فأَكَلُه الذِئبُ، فلمّا سَمِع مقالتهم استرجع واستعبر، وذكر ما أوحى الله إليه من الاستعداد للبلاء، فصبر وأذعن للبلوى، وقال لهم: بل سوّلت لكم أنفسكم أمرًا فصبرٌ جَميل، وماكان الله ليُطِعم لحم يوسف الذئب من قبل أن أرى تأويل رؤياه الصادقة.

قال أبو حمزة: ثمّ انقطع ما قال عليّ بن الحسين عليهما السلام عند هذا الوضع.

٦. عن مِسمَع أبي سيّار، عن أبي عبدالله ﵇، قال: لمّا أُلقي يوسف ﵇ في الجُبّ نزل عليه جَبَرئيل ﵇، فقال له: يا غلام، ما تصنع هاهنا، مَن طَرَحك في هذا الجُبّ؟ فقال: إخوتي، لمنزلتي من أبي حَسدوني، ولذلك في هذا الجبّ طَرَحُوني.

فقال له جَبرئيل ﵇: أتُحِبّ أن تخرُج من هذا الجُبّ؟ فقال: ذلك إلى إله إبراهيم وإسحاق ويعقوب.

فقال له جَبرئيل ﵇: إنّ إله إبراهيم وإسحاق ويعقوب يقول لك: قل «اللّهمّ إنّي أسألك بأنّ لك الحمد لا إله إلاّ أنت المنّان بديع السماوات والأرض، ذو الجلال

7. In another narration on his authority, 'And to provide for me whence I expect and whence I do not even expect.' [12:15]

8. From Zayd al-Shaḥḥām, from Abū 'Abd Allāh عليه السلام regarding God's verse: ﴿*You will tell them of all this* [*at a time*] *when they do not realize* [*who you are*]*!*﴾ He said, 'He was seven years old [at the time].' [12:15]

9. From Jābir b. 'Abd Allāh al-Anṣārī, regarding God's verse: ﴿*I dreamed of eleven stars and the sun and the moon: I saw them all bow down before me.*﴾ He said, 'As far as the names of the stars go, they were: al-Ṭāriq, Ḥūbān, al-Rayān, Dhū al-Kanafān, Wābis, Waththāb, 'Umrawān, Faylaq, Faṣīḥ, al-Ṣarḥ, and al-Budū'; and the glow and the light, meaning the sun and the moon. All these stars are contained in the sky.' [12:4]

10. From Abū Jamīla, from a man, from Abū 'Abd Allāh عليه السلام who said, 'When Yūsuf's shirt was brought to Ya'qūb, he said, "O God, at least he was a kind wolf who did not rip the shirt." He said, 'It had splashes of blood on it.' [12:18]

والإكرام، أن تُصلّي على محمّد وآل محمّدٍ، وأن تجعل لي من أمري فَرَجًا ومَخرَجًا، وتَرزُقَني من حيث لا أحتسب» .

فقالها يوسف،فَجَعَل الله له من الجُبّ يومئذٍ فَرَجًا، ومن كَيد المرأة مَخرَجًا، وآتاه مُلك مِصر من حيث لم يَحتَسب .

٧. وفي رواية أُخرى عنه: وترزقني من حيث أحتسب، ومن حيث لا أحتسب .

٨. عن زيد الشحّام، عن أبي عبد الله ﵇، في قول الله تعالى: ﴿لَتُنَبِّئَنَّهُم بِأَمْرِهِمْ هَٰذَا وَهُمْ لَا يَشْعُرُونَ﴾، قال: كان ابن سبع سنين .

٩. عن جابر بن عبد الله الأنصاري، في قول الله تعالى: ﴿إِنِّي رَأَيْتُ أَحَدَ عَشَرَ كَوْكَبًا وَالشَّمْسَ وَالْقَمَرَ رَأَيْتُهُمْ لِي سَاجِدِينَ﴾ .

قال في تسمية النّجُوم، هو الطارق، وحوبان، والريان، وذو الكنفان، ووابس، ووثاب، وعمروان، وفيلق، وفصيح، والصرح، والبدوع، والضياء، والنور - يعني الشمس والقمر - وكُلّ هذه النجوم محيطةٌ بالسماء .

١٠. عن أبي جميلة، عن رجل، عن أبي عبد الله ﵇، قال: لمّا أُوتي بقميص يوسف إلى يعقوب، فقال: اللّهمّ لقد كان ذِئبًا رَفيقًا حين لم يَشُقّ القميص، قال: وكان به نَضحٌ من دم .

11. From Abū Ḥamza who said, 'Then at this point 'Alī b. al-Ḥusayn stopped talking. The next morning, I went to him and said, "May I be your ransom – yesterday you were narrating the account of Ya'qūb and his children to me and then you stopped. So what was the story of Yūsuf after that?"

So he replied, "When they awoke the next morning they said, 'Let us go and see how Yūsuf is, and whether he is dead or alive. When they reached the well, they found a caravan next to the well which had sent someone to draw water who had let his bucket down. When he drew his bucket back up, there was a boy hanging on to his bucket. So he said to his companions, 'Good news! Here is a boy!' So when they took him out, Yūsuf's brothers came to him and said, 'This is our slave-boy who fell into this well yesterday, and we have come today to take him out of there.' And they snatched him away from their hands, took him to one side, and said to him, 'Either you confirm to them that you are indeed our slave-boy and we can sell you to some people in this caravan or we will kill you.' So Yūsuf said to them, 'Do whatever you want but do not kill me.'

So they took him to the caravan and said, 'Would any of you like to buy this slave-boy from us?' A man bought him off them for twenty dirhams and they did not show much interest in him. The man who bought him travelled with him until he arrived in Egypt, and in turn sold him to the king of Egypt. That is the purport of God's words: ﴾*The Egyptian who bought him said to his wife, 'Look after him well! He may be useful to us, or we may adopt him as a son.'*﴿' [12:21]

12. From al-Ḥasan, from a man from Abū 'Abd Allāh عليه السلام with respect to His verse: ﴾*and they sold him for a small price, for a few pieces of silver*﴿. He said, 'They were twenty dirhams.' [12:20]

١١. عن أبي حمزة، قال: ثمّ انقطع ما قال عليّ بن الحسين عليهما السلام عند هذا الموضع، فلمّا كان من غدٍ غدوت إليه، فقلتُ له: جُعلتُ فِداك، إنّك حدّثتني أمسِ حديثَ يعقوب وولده، ثمّ قطعتَه، فما كان من قِصَّة يوسف بعد ذلك؟

فقال: إنَّهم لمّا أصبحوا قالوا: انطلقوا بنا حتّى ننظُر ما حال يوسف، مات أم هو حيّ؟ فلمّا انتهوا إلى الجُبّ وجدوا بحضرة الجُبّ السيارة قد أرسلوا واردهم فأدلى دَلوه، فلمّا جَذَب دَلوه إذا هم بغُلام مُتعلّق بدَلوه، فقال لأصحابه: يا بُشرى هذا غلام، فلمّا أخرجه أقبل إليه إخوة يوسف، فقالوا: هذا عبدنا سَقَط منّا أمسِ في هذا الجُبّ، وجئنا اليوم لنُخرِجه. فانتزعوه من أيديهم، وتنحّوا به ناحية، ثمّ قالوا له: إمّا أن تُقِرّ لنا بأنّك عبدٌ لنا، فنبيعك من بعض أهل هذه السيارة أو نقتُلك. فقال لهم يوسف ﷺ: لا تقتُلوني واصنعوا ما شئتم.

فأقبلوا به إلى السيّارة، فقالوا: هل منكم أحدٌ يشتري منّا هذا العبد؟ فاشتراه رجلٌ منهم بعشرين دِرهمًا وكانوا فيه من الزاهدين، وسار به الذي اشتراه حتّى أُدخل مصر، فباعه الذي اشتراه من البَدو من ملك مِصر، وذلك قول الله: ﴿وَقَالَ الَّذِي اشْتَرَاهُ مِنْ مِصْرَ لِامْرَأَتِهِ أَكْرِمِي مَثْوَاهُ عَسَى أَنْ يَنْفَعَنَا أَوْ نَتَّخِذَهُ وَلَدًا﴾.

١٢. عن الحسن، عن رجل، عن أبي عبدالله ﷺ، في قوله: ﴿وَشَرَوْهُ بِثَمَنٍ بَخْسٍ دَرَاهِمَ مَعْدُودَةٍ﴾، قال: كانت عشرين دِرهمًا.

13. There is a similar narration from Abū al-Ḥasan al-Riḍā عليه السلام with the following addition: 'The word *bakhs* meaning 'worthless,' and this is the value of a hunting dog – when it is killed, the blood money owed is twenty dirhams.' [12:20]

14. From 'Abd Allāh b. Sulaymān, from Ja'far b. Muḥammad عليه السلام who said, 'Yūsuf was treated honourably by his parents, then he became a slave sold for the cheapest and most paltry price. Then God allowed him to attain such a position that he became a king.' [12:20–22]

15. From Ibn Ḥuṣayn, from Abū Ja'far عليه السلام who said regarding God's verse: ﴾*and they sold him for a small price, for a few pieces of silver*﴿, 'They were eighteen dirhams.' [12:20]

16. With the same chain of narration from al-Riḍā عليه السلام who said, 'They were twenty dirhams, which is the value of a hunting dog when it is killed. The word *bakhs* means 'worthless.'' [12:20]

17. Abū Ḥamza said, 'I asked 'Alī b. al-Ḥusayn, "How old was Yūsuf the day that he was thrown into the well?" He replied, "Seven years old."

I asked, "How far was the distance between Ya'qūb's house and Egypt at that time?" He replied, "A distance of eighteen days."

He continued, "Yūsuf was one of the most handsome people of his time, and when he came of age the king's wife tried to seduce him, so he said to her, 'God forbid! We are the people of a household who do not fornicate.' So she bolted the doors upon them both and said, 'Do not fear!' throwing herself onto him. He slipped away from her and raced to the door and opened it, but she got to him and pulled his shirt from behind to remove it from him. However, Yūsuf slipped away from her with his clothes on."' [12:21–23]

١٣. عن أبي الحسن الرضا ﵇، مثله وزاد فيه: البَخس: النَّقص، وهي قيمة كلب الصيد إذا قُتِل كانت دِيته عشرين دِرهمًا.

١٤. عن عبدالله بن سليمان، عن جعفر بن محمّد عليهما السلام، قال: قد كان يوسف بين أبويه مُكرّما، ثمّ صار عبدًا حتّى بيع بأخسّ وأوكس الثَّمن، ثمّ لم يمنع الله أن بَلَغ به حتّى صار مَلِكًا.

١٥. عن ابن حُصين، عن أبي جعفر ﵇، في قول الله: ﴿وَشَرَوْهُ بِثَمَنٍ بَخْسٍ دَرَاهِمَ مَعْدُودَةٍ﴾، قال: كانت الدراهم ثمانية عشر دِرهمًا.

١٦. وبهذا الإسناد، عن الرضا ﵇، قال: كانت الدراهم عشرين درهمًا، وهي قيمة كلب الصيد إذا قُتِل، والبَخس: النَّقص.

١٧. قال أبو حمزة: قلت لعليّ بن الحسين عليهما السلام: ابن كم كان يوسف ﵇ يوم أُلقي في الجبّ؟ فقال: ابن سبع سنين.

قلت: فكم كان بين منزل يعقوب يومئذٍ وبين مصر؟ قال: مسيرة ثمانية عشر يومًا. قال: وكان يوسف ﵇ من أجمل أهل زمانه، فلمّا راهق راودته امرأة المَلِك عن نفسه، فقال لها: معاذ الله إنّا من أهل بيت لا يَزنُون، فغلَّقت الأبواب عليها وعليه، وقالت: لا تَخَف، وألقت نفسها عليه، فأفْلتَ منها هاربًا إلى الباب، ففتحه ولحقته فجذبت قميصه من خلفه، فأخرجته منه، وأفلتَ يوسف ﵇ منها في ثيابه.

18. From one of our associates, from Abū ʿAbd Allāh ﷺ who said, 'When she made advances for him, and he would have succumbed to her, she said, "Stay where you are." He asked, "Why?" So she said, "So that I can cover my idol's face lest he sees us." So he remembered God at that moment, knowing that God was watching him and rushed to escape from her.' [12:24]

19. From Muḥammad b. Qays, from Abū ʿAbd Allāh ﷺ. He said, 'I heard him say, "When Yūsuf undid his trousers, he saw an apparition of Yaʿqūb standing there biting his hand [in deep chagrin] saying to him, 'O Yūsuf!'" He said, "So he [Yūsuf] escaped."

Then Abū ʿAbd Allāh ﷺ said, "By God, I have never seen my father's shame nor has my father ever seen my grandfather's shame, and nor did my grandfather ever see his father's shame." He continued, "So [he saw] him biting his hand, and he jumped and the water came out of the big toe of his foot."' [12:24]

20. From one of our associates, from Abū Jaʿfar ﷺ who asked, 'What do the people [i.e. the Sunnis] say about God's verse: ﴾*if he had not seen the evidence of his Lord*﴿?' I replied, 'They say that he saw Yaʿqūb biting his hand.'

So he said, 'No, it is not as they say.' I said, 'Then what is it that he saw?' He replied, 'When she made for him and he made for her, she stood up to go to an idol of hers in the house and threw a cloth over it. So Yūsuf asked her, "What are you doing?" She said, "I am throwing a cloth over it for I would be ashamed for him to see us." So Yūsuf said, "You are ashamed in front of your idol who can neither hear nor see, and I do not feel ashamed in front of my Lord?"' [12:24]

21. He went back to the narration by Abū Ḥamza: "So Yūsuf slipped away from her fully-clothed, ﴾*and at the door they met her husband. She said, 'What, other than prison or painful punishment, should be the reward of someone who tried to dishonour your wife?'*﴿ He said, "So the king went to attack Yūsuf and to punish him, but Yūsuf said to him, 'By the God of Yaʿqūb, I did not intend any harm to your wife, but she was the one who tried to seduce me. Ask this child here who tried to seduce whom.'

١٨. عن بعض أصحابنا، عن أبي عبد الله ﵇، قال: لمّا همّت به وهمّ بها، قالت له: كما أنت. قال: ولم؟ قالت: حتّى أُغطّي وجه الصّنم لا يرانا، فذكر الله عند ذلك، وقد علِم أنّ الله يراه، ففرّ منها.

١٩. عن محمّد بن قيس، عن أبي عبد الله ﵇: قال: سَمِعتُه يقول: إنّ يوسف لمّا حلّ سراويله رأى مثال يعقوب عاضًّا على إصبعه وهو يقول له: يا يوسف، قال: فَهَرب.

ثمّ قال أبو عبد الله ﵇: لكنّي والله ما رأيتُ عَورة أبي قطّ، ولا رأى أبي عَورة جَدّي قطّ، ولا رأى جَدّي عَورة أبيه قطّ، قال: وهو عاض على إصبعه، فوثب فخرج الماء من إبهام رِجله.

٢٠. عن بعض أصحابنا، عن أبي جعفر ﵇، قال: أيّ شيء يقول الناس في قول الله جلّ وعزّ: ﴿لَوْلاَ أَنْ رَأَى بُرْهَـانَ رَبِّـهِ﴾؟ قلتُ: يقولون رأى يعقوب عاضًّا على إصبعه.

فقال: لا، ليس كما يقولون. فقلت: فأيّ شيء رأى؟ قال: لمّا همّت به وهمّ بها، قامت إلى صَنَم معها في البيت، فألقت عليه ثوبًا، فقال لها يوسف، ما صنعتِ؟ قالت: طَرَحتُ عليه ثوبًا، أستحيي أن يَرانا. قال: فقال يوسف ﵇: فأنتِ تستحين من صَنَمك وهو لا يَسمَع ولا يُبصِر، ولا أستحيي أنا من ربّي؟!

٢١. عاد إلى حديث أبي حمزة: وأفلتَ يوسف منها في ثيابه ﴿وَأَلْفَيَا سَيِّدَهَـا لَدَى الْبَابِ قَـالَتْ مَـا جَـزَاءُ مَنْ أَرَادَ بِأَهْلِكَ سُوءًا إِلاَّ أَنْ يُسْجَنَ أَوْ عَـذَابٌ أَلِيـمٌ﴾ قال: فهمّ

There was a child from her family staying with her as a guest so God made him speak by Divine decree. So he said to the king, 'Look at the shirt, your Highness. If it is torn from the front then he is the one who tried to seduce her. But if it is torn from behind, then she is the one who tried to seduce him and he is telling the truth whilst she is a liar.'

So when the king heard the infant's speech and what he had just uttered, he was gripped by an intense fear. He called for the shirt and inspected it, and when he saw it rent from behind, he said to her: ﴾*'This is another instance of women's treachery: your treachery is truly great.'*﴿ And He said to Yūsuf: ﴾*'Yūsuf, overlook this',*﴿ lest anyone hears about it, and keep it a secret.

But Yūsuf did not keep it a secret and announced it in the city, such that the women of the city were saying: ﴾*'The governor's wife is trying to seduce her slave!'*﴿ She heard about this, so she sent for them and prepared a banquet for them. Then she served them citrus fruits and gave each of them a knife. She said to Yūsuf, 'Come out to them.' So when they saw him, they were stunned by his beauty and cut their hands in the process, and said what they said, at which she said to them, 'This is the one you blamed me for being in love with?'

He ['Alī b. al-Ḥusayn] continued, "The women left her house, and each one of them sent secret proposals to Yūsuf asking him to visit them, but he refused them all saying: ﴾*'My Lord!* [...] *If You do not protect me from their treachery, I shall yield to them and do wrong.'*﴿

When talk of Yūsuf, the governor's wife and the women spread in Egypt, the king, despite having heard the infant's words, decided to imprison Yūsuf. So he locked him up in prison, and two young men entered the prison at the same time as him. God tells us their stories alongside Yūsuf's story in His Book."

Abū Ḥamza said, 'Then 'Alī b. al-Ḥusayn's narrative cut off there.' [12:24–34]

المَلِك بيوسف ليُعذّبه، فقال له يوسف عليه السلام: وإله يعقوب ما أردتُ بأهلك سُوءًا، هي راودتني عن نفسي، فسل هذا الصبي، أيّنا راود صاحبه عن نفسه؟

قال: وكان عندها صبيّ من أهلها زائرٌ لها، فأنطق الله الصّبيّ بفَصل القضاء، فقال للمَلِك: اُنظُر أيُّها المَلِك إلى القميص، فإن كان مقدودًا من قُدّامه فهو راودها وإن كان مَقدُودًا من خلفه فهي الّتي راودته عن نفسه، وصدق وهي من الكاذبين.

فلمّا سَمِع المَلِك كلام الصبيّ، وما اقتصّ، أفزعه ذلك فَزَعًا شديدًا، فدعا بالقميص فنظر إليه، فلمّا رأى القميص مقدودًا من خلفه قال لها: إنّه من كيدِكُنّ، إنّ كيدكُنّ عظيم، وقال ليوسف عليه السلام: أعرِض عن هذا، فلا يسمعه منك أحدٌ واكتُمه.

فلم يَكتُمه يوسف، وأذاعه في المدينة، حتّى قال نسوة منهنّ: امرأةُ العَزيز تراوِدُ فتاها عن نفسِهِ؛ فبلغها ذلك، فأرسلت إليهنّ، وهيّأت لهنّ طعامًا ومجلسًا، ثمّ أتتهنّ بأُترجّ، وآتت كُلّ واحدةٍ منهنّ سِكّينًا، وقالت ليوسف عليه السلام: اخرُج عليهنّ، فلمّا رأينه أكبَرنه وقَطّعن أيديهُنّ، وقلن ما قلن. فقالت لهنّ: فهذا الذي لُمتنّني في حُبّه؟

قال: فخرج النسوة من عندها، فأرسلت كُلّ واحدةٍ منهنّ إلى يوسف عليه السلام سِرًّا من صواحبها تسأله الزيارة، فأبى عليهنّ، وقال: ربِّ إلاّ تصرِف عنّي كَيدَهُنّ أصبُ إليهنّ وأكُن من الجاهلين.

فلمّا ذاع أمر يوسف عليه السلام وأمر امرأة العزيز والنسوة في مِصر، بدا للملك بعد ما سَمِع من قول الصبيّ ما سَمِع ليَسجُننّ يوسف، فحبسه في السجن، ودخل مع يوسف عليه السلام في

22. From Muḥammad b. Marwān, from a man, from Abū ʿAbd Allāh عليه السلام who said, 'Yūsuf was courting a beautiful woman during his time, but she refused him saying, "How can a slave of the king court me?"'

He said, 'So he asked her father for her hand, but her father said to him, "The decision is up to her."'

He said, 'So he asked his Lord for her and wept. So God revealed to him, "I will make you marry her." Then he sent her a message saying that he wanted to visit them, so she sent one back asking him to come. When he went inside, the whole house lit up by his light, and she said, ﴾*'He must be a precious angel!'*﴿ Then he asked for some water, so she got up to raise the bowl of water to let him drink from it. As he went to drink from the cup in her hand, he met her mouth there instead. So he said to her, "Wait. Not so fast."'

He said, 'Then he married her.' [12:30–31]

23. From al-ʿAbbās b. Hilāl who said, 'I heard Abū al-Ḥasan al-Riḍā عليه السلام say, "The prison guard said to Prophet Yūsuf, 'I love you.' So Yūsuf said to him, 'Please do not say that, for my aunt loved me and made me out to be a thief; my father loved me and as a result, my brothers were jealous of me and sold me; and the governor's wife loved me and I ended up incarcerated as a result.'" [12:33]

24. From Ibn Sinān, from Abū ʿAbd Allāh عليه السلام who said, 'Jibra'īl came to Yūsuf in prison and said, "After every obligatory prayer, say: 'O God, give me release and a way out, and provide for me whence I expect as well as whence I do not expect.'"'

السِّجن فَتَيان، فكان من قِصّتهما وقصَّة يوسف عليه السلام ما قصّه الله في كتابه، قال أبو حمزة، ثمّ انقطع حديث عليّ بن الحسين عليهما السلام عند ذلك.

٢٢. عن محمّد بن مَروان، عن رجل، عن أبي عبد الله عليه السلام، قال: إنّ يوسف خَطَب امرأةً جميلةً كانت في زمانه، فردّت عليه: إنّ عبد الملك إيّاي يطلُب، قال: فطلبها إلى أبيها، فقال له أبوها: إنّ الأمر أمرها، قال: فطلبها إلى ربّه وبكى، فأوحى الله إليه: أنّي قد زوّجتكها.

ثمّ أرسل إليه: أنّي أُريد أن أزوركم، فأرسلت إليه: أن تَعَالَ؛ فلمّا دَخَلَ عليها أضاء البيت لنُوره، فقالت: ما هذا إلاّ مَلكٌ كريمٌ؛ فاستسقى فقامت إلى الطاس لتسقيه فجعل يتناول الطاس من يدها فتناوله فاها فجعل يقول لها: انتظري ولا تعجلي، قال: فتزوّجها.

٢٣. عن العباس بن هلال، قال: سَمِعت أبا الحسن الرضا عليه السلام يقول: إنَّ يوسف النبيّ عليه السلام قال له السجّان: إنّي لأُحبّك. فقال له يوسف: لا تقُل هكذا، فإنَّ عمّتي أحبَّتني فسرّقتني، وإنّ أبي أحبّني فحسدني إخوتي فباعوني، وإنّ امرأة العزيز أحبّتني فسُجنتُ.

٢٤. عن ابن سِنان، عن أبي عبد الله عليه السلام، قال: جاء جَبرئيل عليه السلام إلى يوسف في السِّجن، فقال: قُل في دُبر كلّ صلاة فريضة: «اللّهُمّ اجعَل ليّ فَرَجًا ومَخرَجاَ وارزُقني من حيث لا أحتسب».

25. From Ṭirbāl[2], from Abū ʿAbd Allāh ﷺ who said, 'When the king ordered for Yūsuf to be imprisoned, God inspired him with the interpretation of dreams, and he used to interpret the dreams of his inmates for them. Two young men were imprisoned on the day that he was incarcerated. After sleeping the night, they awoke in the morning and said to him, "We had some dreams, so please interpret them for us."

He asked, "What did you see?" One of them said: ﴾*'I dreamed that I was carrying bread on my head and that the birds were eating it.'*﴿ The other said, "I saw that I was serving the king some wine."

He interpreted their dreams for them just as is written in the Book. Then he said to the one that he knew would be saved, "Mention me to your master."

He said, 'What Yūsuf did not do was turn exclusively to God in that state of his, and supplicate Him instead.' God says: ﴾*but Shayṭān made him forget to do this, and so Yūsuf remained in prison for a number of years.*﴿'

He continued, 'So God revealed to Yūsuf at that moment, "Yūsuf, who showed you the dream that you saw?" He replied, "You, my Lord."

He asked, "Who was the one who made you beloved to your father?" He replied, "You, my Lord."

He then asked, "Who sent the caravan to you?" He said, "You, my Lord."

He asked, "Who taught you the supplication that you used to be liberated from the well?" He said, "You, my Lord."

He asked, "Who made the infant speak in your defense?" He replied, "You, my Lord."

He asked, "Who averted the plots of the governor's wife and the women away from you?" He replied, "You, my Lord."

He asked, "And who inspired you with the interpretation of dreams?" He said, "You, my Lord."

He said, "Then how could you seek help from other people and not Me to take you out of this prison? How could you ask for help and place your hope in a mere servant of mine to mention you to another mere creature of Mine who himself is in My control? You did not turn to Me instead? Now

---

2 Most likely referring to Ṭirbāl b. Rajāʾ about whom there is very little information. See Khūʾī, *Muʿjam*, 10:175 (nr. 6011).

٢٥. عن طِرِبال، عن أبي عبدالله عليه السلام، قال: لمّا أمر الملك بحَبس يوسف عليه السلام في السجن، ألهمه الله عِلم تأويل الرُّؤيا، فكان يُعبّر لأهل السِّجن رُؤياهم، وإنّ فتيين أُدخلا معه السِّجن يوم حَبسه، فلمّا باتا أصبحا فقالا له: إنّا رأينا رُؤيا فعبِّرها لنا.

فقال: وما رأيتما؟ فقال أحدهما: إنّي أراني أحمِل فوق رَأسي خُبزًا تأكُلُ الطَّير منه. وقال الآخر: إنّي رأيت أنّي أسقي المَلِك خَمرًا. ففسَّر لهما رُؤياهما على ما في الكتاب، ثمَّ قال للّذي ظنَّ أنّه ناجٍ منهما: اذكُرني عند ربّك. قال: ولم يَفزَع يوسف عليه السلام في حاله إلى الله فيدعوه، فلذلك قال الله: ﴿فَأَنسَاهُ الشَّيطَانُ ذِكرَ رَبِّهِ فَلَبِثَ فِي السِّجنِ بِضعَ سِنِينَ﴾.

قال: فأوحى الله إلى يوسف عليه السلام في ساعته تلك: يا يوسف، من أراك الرّؤيا الّتي رأيتها؟ فقال: أنت يا ربّي. قال: فمن حبّبك إلى أبيك؟ قال: أنت يا ربّي. قال: فمن وَجَّه السيّارة إليك؟ فقال: أنت يا ربّي. قال: فمن جعل لك من كَيد المرأة مَخرجًا؟ قال: أنت يا ربّي؟ قال: فمن أنطق لسان الصبيّ بعُذرك؟ قال: أنت يا ربّي. قال: فمن صرف عنك كيد امرأة العزيز والنِّسوة؟ قال: أنت يا ربي. قال: فمن ألهمك تأويل الرؤيا؟ قال: أنت يا ربّي.

قال: فكيف استَغَثت بغيري، ولم تَستَغِث بي، وتسألني أن أُخرجك من السِّجن، واستَغثت وأمّلت عبدًا من عبادي ليَذكُرك إلى مخلوقٍ من خَلقي في قبضتي، ولم تَفزَع إليّ؟ البَث في السجن بذنبك بِضع سنين بإرسالك عبدًا إلى عبد.

قال ابن أبي عمير، قال ابن أبي حمزة: فمكث في السجن عشرين سنة.

stay in the prison for a few more years for your sin of having sent a message with a mere servant to another servant."'

Ibn Abī 'Umayr said, 'Ibn Abī Ḥamza said, "He remained in the prison for twenty years." [12:36–42]

26. From Samāʿa regarding God's verse: ﴾ *'Mention me to your master.'* ﴿ He said, 'This refers to the governor.' [12:42]

27. From Ibn Abī Yaʿfūr, from Abū ʿAbd Allāh عليه السلام regarding the verse: ﴾ *the other said, 'I dreamed that I was carrying bread on my head* [...] ﴿ He said, '[It means] I was carrying a corpse on my head upon which there was bread that the birds were eating from.' [12:36]

28. From Yaʿqūb b. Shuʿayb, from Abū ʿAbd Allāh عليه السلام who said, 'God said to Yūsuf: "Am I not the one who made you beloved to your father and distinguished you above others in your beauty? Am I not the one who drove the caravan to you, rescued you and took you out of the well? Am I not the one who averted the women's plot away from you? Then how dare you hold high expectations of a mere creature and call on him instead of Me? Now stay in the prison for a few years as a result of what you said."' [12:42]

29. From ʿAbd Allāh b. ʿAbd al-Raḥmān[3], from whoever narrated it on his authority, that he said, 'When he said to the young man: "Mention me to your master," Jibra'īl came to him and struck the ground with his foot until the seventh layer of the earth was split open, and said to him, "Look inside – what do you see?" He said, "I see a small rock with a crack in it."

He asked, "Now what do you see?" He said, "I can see a small worm."

He asked, "Who sustains it?" He replied, "God."

He said, "Well, your Lord says: 'I did not forget this worm in that rock in the depth of the seventh layer of the earth. Did you think that I would forget

---

3 Possibly referring to ʿAbd Allāh b. ʿAbd al-Raḥmān al-Aṣamm al-Mismaʿī, a renowned liar from Basra accused of exaggerating the status of the Imams. He is condemned in the harshest terms as a weak narrator who fabricated traditions. See Ḥillī, *Khulāṣat al-aqwāl*, 372 (nr. 1475).

٢٦. سَماعة، عن قول الله: ﴿اذْكُرْنِي عِنْدَ رَبِّكَ﴾، قال: هو العزيز.

٢٧. ابن أبي يَعفور، عن أبي عبد الله عليه السلام: ﴿وَقَالَ الآخَرُ إِنِّي أَرَانِي أَحْمِلُ فَوْقَ رَأْسِي خُبْزًا﴾، قال: أحمِل فوق رأسي جَفنَةً فيها خُبزٌ تأكُلُ الطيرُ منها.

٢٨. عن يعقوب بن شعيب، عن أبي عبد الله عليه السلام، قال: قال الله تعالى ليوسف عليه السلام: ألستُ الذي حبَّبتُك إلى أبيك، وفضَّلتك على الناس بالحُسن؟ أولستُ الّذي سُقتُ إليك السيّارة، وأنقذتُك، وأخرجتُك من الجُبّ؟ أولستُ الّذي صرفتُ عنك كَيد النِّسوة؟ فما حملك على أن ترفع رغبتك، وتدعو مخلوقًا دُوني؟ فالبَث لما قلتَ في السِّجن بِضع سنين.

٢٩. عن عبد الله بن عبد الرّحمن، عمَّن ذكره، عنه عليه السلام، قال: لمّا قال للفتى: اذكُرني عند ربّك، أتاه جبرَئيل عليه السلام، فضرب برجله، حتّى كَشَط له عن الأرض السابعة، فقال له: يا يوسف، انظُر ماذا ترى؟ قال: أرى حَجَرًا صغيرًا ففَلَق الحَجَر، فقال: ماذا ترى؟ قال: أرى دُودةً صغيرةً، قال: فمن رازِقُها؟ قال الله.

قال: فإنَّ ربّك يقول: لم أنسَ هذه الدودة في ذلك الحَجر، في قَعر الأرض السابعة، أظننتَ أنّي أنساك حتّى تقول للفتى، اُذكُرني عند ربّك؟ لتَلبَثَنَّ في السِّجن بمقالتك هذه بضع سنين.

قال: فبكى يوسف عليه السلام عند ذلك حتّى بكى لبُكائه الحِيطان، قال: فتأذّى به أهل السِّجن، فصالحهم على أن يبكيَ يومًا ويسكُت يومًا، فكان في اليوم الذي يسكُت أسوأ حالاً.

you that you said to the young man: ﴾*'Mention me to your master.'*﴿ You will remain in this prison for a few years as a result of these words of yours!'

He said, 'So Yūsuf cried so much upon hearing this that even the fish cried with him.'

He said, 'The inmates of the prison were irritated by him, so they convinced him to cry every other day instead. On the days that he would be silent, he would be in an even worse state.' [12:42]

30. From Hishām b. Sālim, from Abū 'Abd Allāh عليه السلام who said, 'No one has ever cried the way these three have cried: Ādam, Yūsuf and Dāwūd.' So I asked, 'To what extent did they cry?'

He replied, 'Ādam cried when he was expelled from the Garden. His head was at one of the gates of the heavens and he cried so much that the inhabitants of the heavens were getting upset by it, so they complained to God, and he was made to go down from that place. Dāwūd cried so much that the grass overgrew as a result of his tears, and he would heave out a sigh so piercing that it would burn up whatever had grown as a result of his tears. As for Yūsuf, he used to cry so much for his father, Ya'qūb, when he was in the prison that the inmates were getting irritated and convinced him to cry every other day instead.' [12:42]

31. From Shu'ayb al-'Aqarqūfī, from Abū 'Abd Allāh عليه السلام who said, 'Jibra'īl came to Yūsuf and said, "Yūsuf, the Lord of the universe sends greetings of peace unto you and says, 'Who made you the most handsome of all His creatures?'

He said, 'So he cried and placed his cheek on the earth, then said, 'You, my Lord.'"

He said, 'Then he said to him, "He is asking you: Who made you more beloved to your father than your brothers?"'

He said, 'He cried and placed his cheek on the ground and said, "You, my Lord."'

He said, 'He is asking you: Who took you out of the well after you were thrown in there and were convinced you were going to perish?'

He said, 'So he cried and placed his cheek on the ground again and said: "You, my Lord."'

He said, 'Your Lord has decreed a consequence for you and your turning to others for help instead of Him, so stay in the prison for a few years.'

٣٠. عن هِشام بن سالم، عن أبي عبد الله ، قال: ما بكى أحدٌ بُكاء ثلاثة: آدم، ويوسف، وداود. فقلت: ما بلغ من بُكائهم؟

قال: أمّا آدم فبكى حين أُخرج من الجنَّة، وكان رأسه في باب من أبواب السماء، فبكى حتّى تأذّى به أهل السماء، فشَكَوا ذلك إلى الله فحَطّ من قامته، وأمّا داود فإنّه بكى حتّى هاج العُشبُ من دُمُوعه، وإنّه كان ليزفِر الزفرة فيُحرِق ما نبت من دُمُوعه، وأمّا يوسف فإنّه كان يبكي على أبيه يعقوب وهو في السجن، فتأذّى به أهل السجن، فصالحهم على أن يبكي يومًا، ويسكُت يومًا.

٣١. عن شُعيب العَقَرقُوفي، عن أبي عبد الله ، قال: إنَّ يوسف أتاه جَبرَئيل ، فقال: يا يوسف، إنَّ ربَّ العالمين يقرؤك السلام، ويقول لك: من جَعَلك أحسن خَلقه؟ قال: فصاح ووضع خدّه على الأرض، ثمّ قال: أنت يا ربّ.

قال: ثمّ قال له: ويقول لك: من حبَّبك إلى أبيك دون إخوتك؟ قال: فصاح ووضع خدَّه على الأرض، ثمّ قال: أنت يا ربّ.

قال: ويقول لك: من أخرجك من الجُبّ بعد أن طُرِحتَ فيها وأيقنتَ بالهَلَكة؟ قال: فصاح ووضع خدّه على الأرض ثمّ قال: أنت يا ربّ.

قال: فإنَّ ربّك قد جعل لك عقوبةً في استغاثتك بغيره، فالبَث في السِّجن بِضع سنين.

He continued, 'So when some time had passed, He allowed him to supplicate to Him for relief, so he placed his cheek on the ground and said: "O God, if my sins have disfigured my face in Your eyes, then I turn to You with the faces of my righteous forefathers, Ibrāhīm, Ismā'īl, Isḥāq, and Ya'qūb."

He said, 'So God released him from it.'

He said, 'I asked him, "May I be your ransom – should we use this supplication too?"

He replied, "Supplicate with a similar one: 'O God, if my sins have disfigured my face in Your eyes, then I turn to You with the face of Your prophet, the Prophet of Compassion, and 'Alī, Fāṭima, al-Ḥasan and al-Ḥusayn, and the Imams, peace be upon them all.'" [12:42]

32. From Ya'qūb b. Yazīd[4] who, without mentioning his source, cited from Abū 'Abd Allāh عليه السلام regarding God's verse: ﴾*so Yūsuf remained in prison for a number of years*﴿ that he said, 'For seven years.' [12:42]

33. From Abū Baṣīr, from Abū 'Abd Allāh عليه السلام who said, 'Fāṭima saw in her sleep as if al-Ḥasan and al-Ḥusayn were being slaughtered or killed, and it upset her.'

He said, 'So she told the Messenger of God ﷺ about it, and he said, "O [true] dream!" and it took form in front of him. He asked it, "Were you the one to show Fāṭima this affliction?" It replied, "No." So he summoned, "O confused dream, were you the one to show Fāṭima this affliction?" It replied, "Yes, O Messenger of God." He asked, "What did you do that for?" It said, "I wanted to upset her."

So he said to Fāṭima, "Hear that? It is nothing."' [12:44]

34. From Abān, from Muḥammad b. Muslim, from the two [Imams] who said, 'The Messenger of God ﷺ said, "Were I to have been in Yūsuf's position when the king sent for him to ask him about his dream, I would not have told him until I had stipulated that he would release me from prison. I am

4 Abū Yūsuf Ya'qūb b. Yazīd b. Ḥammād al-Anbārī al-Sulamī, a member of the Caliph al-Muntaṣir's chancellery. Both he and his father Ya'qūb b. Yaqṭīn were reliable and trustworthy narrators of Imam al-Riḍā's traditions. See Ḥillī, *Khulāṣat al-aqwāl*, 298 (nr. 1107).

قال: فلمّا انقضت المُدّة أذِن له في دُعا الفَرَج، ووضع خدّه على الأرض، ثمّ قال: «اللّهم إن كانت ذُنُوبي قد أخلقت وجهي عندك، فإنّي أتوجهَ إليك بوجه آبائي الصالحين، إبراهيم وإسماعيل وإسحاق ويعقوب» قال: ففرّج الله عنه.

قال: فقلت له: جُعلت فِداك، أندعو نحن بهذا الدعاء؟ فقال: ادعُ بمثله «اللّهُمّ إن كانت ذُنُوبي قد أخلقت وجهي عندك، فإنّي أتوجّه إليك بوجه نبيّك نبيّ الرحمة صلّى الله عليه وسلم، وعليّ وفاطمة والحسن والحسين والأئمّة عليهم السلام».

٣٢. عن يعقوب بن يزيد، رفعه، عن أبي عبدالله عليه السلام، في قول الله تعالى: ﴿فَلَبِثَ فِي السِّجْنِ بِضْعَ سِنِينَ﴾، قال: سبع سنين.

٣٣. عن أبي بصير، عن أبي عبدالله عليه السلام، قال: رأت فاطمة عليها السلام في النوم كأنّ الحسن والحسين عليهما السلام ذُبِحا أو قُتِلا، فأحزَنها ذلك، فأخبرت به رسول الله صلى الله عليه وآله وسلم، فقال: يا رُؤيا، فتمثّلت بين يديه، قال: أنتِ أريتِ فاطمة هذا البلاء؟ قالت: لا. فقال: يا أضغاث، أنتِ أريتِ فاطمة هذا البلاء؟ قالت: نعم يا رسول الله.

قال: فما أردتِ بذلك؟ قالت: أرَدتُ أن أُحزِنها، فقال لفاطمة عليها السلام: اسمعي ليس هذا بشيء.

٣٤. عن أبان، عن محمّد بن مسلم، عنهما عليهما السلام، قال: قالا: إنّ رسول الله صلى الله عليه وآله وسلم قال: لو كنتُ بمنزلة يوسف حين أرسل إليه المَلِك يسأله عن رُؤياه، ما حدّثته حتّى اشترط عليه أن يُخرِجني من السِّجن، وعجبتُ صبره عن شأن امرأة المَلِك حتّى أظهر الله عُذره.

surprised at his remaining patient with the matter of the king's wife until God manifested the proof in his defense."' [12:45]

35. From Ibn Abī Ya'fūr who said, 'I heard Abū 'Abd Allāh ﷺ recite: *'sab'a sanābila khuḍrin' (seven green ears of corn)* [instead of *sab'a sunbulātin khuḍrin*].' [12:46]

36. From Ḥafṣ b. Ghiyāth, from Abū 'Abd Allāh ﷺ who said, 'The years of inflation [that preceded] when Yūsuf was in charge affected the people like never before.'

He said, 'Some merchants came to him and said, "Sell to us."

He replied, "You may buy."

They said, "We will take this much for such and such a price."

So he said, "Take [what you need]" and ordered for it to be weighed for them, and they carried it away until they came to the city. There, another group of merchants met them and asked them, "How much did you get it for?"

They replied, "This much for this price," but they inflated the price.

Those people then went to Yūsuf and said, "Sell some to us."

He said, "You may buy. How much would you like?"

They replied, "Sell it to us as you did previously for that particular price."

He replied, "It was not as they said, but take it anyway."

Then they left until they entered the city, and some others met them and asked, "How much did you get it for?"

They replied, "This much for this price," again inflating the price. And people found it too expensive, and said, "Take us there so we can buy it ourselves."

They went to Yūsuf and said, "Sell it to us."

He replied, "You may buy."

They said, "Sell it to us for the same price you sold it before."

He asked, "And how much did I sell it for?"

They replied, "This much for that particular [inflated] price."

So he said, "That is not the case, but take it anyway."

They took it and returned to the city, and told people about it. They said to each other, "Let us go and do the same thing and lie to lower the price just as we lied to inflate it." So they went to Yūsuf and said to him, "Sell to us."

٣٥. عن ابن أبي يعفور، قال: سَمِعتُ أبا عبدالله ﷺ يقرأ ﴿سَبع سنابل خُضـر﴾.

٣٦. عن حَفْص بن غِياث، عن أبي عبدالله ﷺ، قال: كان سنين يوسف الغَلاء الذي أصاب الناس، ولم يتمنّ الغَلاء لأحدٍ قطّ، قال: فأتاه التُّجّار فقالوا: بِعنا، فقال: اشتروا، فقالوا: نأخُذ كذا بكذا، فقال: خُذوا، وأمر فكالوهم فحَمَلوا، ومضوا حتّى دخلوا المدينة، فلَقيهم قوم تجّار، فقالوا لهم: كيف أخذتم؟ قالوا: كذا بكذا، وأضعفوا الثمن.

قال: فقدموا أُولئك على يوسف ﷺ، فقالوا بِعنا، فقال: اشتروا، كيف تأخُذون؟ قالوا: بِعنا كما بعتَ كذا بكذا، فقال: ما هو كما تقولون، ولكن خُذوا، فأخذوا.

ثمّ مَضَوا حتى دَخَلُوا المدينة، فلَقِيهم آخرون، فقالوا: كيف أخذتم؟ فقالوا: كذا بكذا، وأضعفوا الثمن، قال: فعظّم الناس ذلك الغَلاء، وقالوا: اذهبوا بنا حتّى نشتري، قال: فذهبوا إلى يوسف ﷺ فقالوا: بِعنا، فقال: اشتروا، فقالوا: بِعنا كما بعتَ، فقال: وكيف بعتُ؟ قالوا: كذا بكذا، فقال: ما هو كذلك، ولكن خُذوا.

قال: فأخذوا ورجعوا إلى المدينة، فأخبروا الناس، فقالوا فيما بينهم: تَعَالَوا حتّى نكذِب في الرُّخص كما كَذَبنا في الغَلاء، قال: فذهبوا إلى يوسف ﷺ، فقالوا له: بِعنا، فقال: اشتروا، فقالوا: بِعنا كما بِعتَ، قال: وكيف بعتُ؟ قالوا: كذا بكذا، بالحطّ من السعر الأوّل، فقال: ما هو هكذا ولكن خُذوا.

قال: فأخذوا وذهبوا إلى المدينة، فلَقِيهم الناس، فسألوهم بكم اشتريتم؟ فقالوا: كذا بكذا، بنصف الحطّ الأوّل.

He replied, "You may buy."

They said, "Sell it to us for the price that you sold it previously."

He asked, "And how much was that?"

They said, "This much for that price," lowering the figure.

So he said, "That is not what it is, but take it anyway."

So they went off to the city. Some people met them there and asked them, "How much did you buy it for?"

They replied, "This much for this price," halving the original price. So those people said, "Let us go and buy some ourselves."

They went to Yūsuf and said, "Sell to us."

So he said, "Go ahead and buy."

They said, "Sell it to us for what you sold it previously."

So he asked, "And how did I sell it previously?"

They replied, "This much for that price," halving the original price.

He said, "It is not as they are claiming, but take it anyway."

So they continued lying to each other thus until the price returned to its original value as God had willed.' [12:55–57]

37. From Muḥammad b. ʿAlī al-Ṣayrafī[5], from a man, from Abū ʿAbd Allāh عليه السلام who recited it as: *ʿāmun fīhi yugāthu al-nāsu wa-fīhi yaʿṣirūn* (﴾ *after that will come a year when the people will have abundant rain and will press grapes* ﴿) with a 'u' vowel on the 'y' [of *yugāthu*] meaning "they will be rained upon." Then he said, 'Have you not heard His words: ﴾ *Did We not send water pouring down from the clouds* ﴿(78:14)?' [12:49]

38. From ʿAlī b. Maʿmar[6], on his father's authority from Abū ʿAbd Allāh عليه السلام who said with regard to God's verse: ﴾ *after that will come a year when the people will have abundant rain and will press grapes* ﴿, 'It is with a 'u' vowel.' Then he said: ﴾ *Did We not send water pouring down from the clouds* ﴿?'[12:49]

5 Muḥammad b. ʿAlī al-Ṣayrafī, about whom there is scant information. See Khūʾī, *Muʿjam*, 18:53 (nr. 11412).

6 ʿAlī b. Maʿmar, about whom not much is known. See Khūʾī, *Muʿjam*, 13:197 (nr. 8537)

فقال الآخرون: اذهبوا بنا حتّى نشتري، فذهبوا إلى يوسف عليه السلام، فقالوا: بِعنا، فقال: اشتروا، فقالوا: بِعنا كما بِعتَ، فقال: وكيف بِعتُ؟ فقالوا: كذا بكذا، بأحطّ من النصف، فقال: ما هو كما تقولون، ولكن خُذوا، فلم يزالوا يتكاذبون حتّى رجَع السِّعر إلى الأمر الأوّل، كما أراد الله.

٣٧. عن محمد بن عليّ الصيرفي، عن رجل، عن أبي عبدالله عليه السلام ﴿عَامٌ فِيهِ يُغَاثُ النَّاسُ وَفِيهِ يَعْصِرُونَ﴾ بضم الياء: يُمطَرُون، ثمّ قال: أما سَمِعتَ قوله: ﴿وَأَنزَلْنَا مِنَ الْمُعْصِرَاتِ مَاءً ثَجَّاجًا﴾؟

٣٨. عن عليّ بن مَعْمَر، عن أبيه، عن أبي عبدالله عليه السلام، في قول الله: ﴿عَامٌ فِيهِ يُغَاثُ النَّاسُ وَفِيهِ يُعْصَرُونَ﴾ مضمومة، ثمّ قال: ﴿وَأَنزَلْنَا مِنَ الْمُعْصِرَاتِ مَاءً ثَجَّاجًا﴾.

39. From Samāʿa who said, 'I asked him about God's verse: ﴾*Go back to your master and ask him about what happened to those women who cut their hands.*﴿ He said, "It refers to the governor."' [12:50]

40. From al-Ḥasan b. Mūsā who said, 'Our associates narrated on al-Riḍā's authority saying, "A man asked him, 'May God make you prosper – how did you manage to secure this from Ma'mūn when he denied you the same thing previously?'

So Abū al-Ḥasan said to him, 'O man, which of these two is better: the prophet or the vicegerent?'

He replied, 'The Prophet ﷺ of course.'

He asked, 'Then which of the two is better: a Muslim or a polytheist?'

He replied, 'A Muslim, of course.'

He said, 'Well, the governor of Egypt was a polytheist whereas Yūsuf was a prophet. Ma'mūn is a Muslim whilst I am the vicegerent [of the Prophet]. Yūsuf had asked the governor to let him govern saying: ﴾*'Put me in charge of the nation's storehouses: I shall manage them prudently and knowledgeably',*﴿ whereas Ma'mūn forced me up to where I am now."'

He said, 'He said in His verse: ﴾*prudent and knowledgeable.*﴿'

He said, 'He was ﴾*prudent*﴿ with what was in his keep and ﴾*knowledgeable*﴿ of every language.' [12:55]

41. Sulaymān said that Sufyān reported, 'I asked Abū ʿAbd Allāh عليه السلام, "Is a man not allowed to promote himself?" He replied, "Yes, if he is compelled to. Have you not heard Yūsuf's words: ﴾*'Put me in charge of the nation's storehouses: I shall manage them prudently and knowledgeably',*﴿ and the righteous servant's words: ﴾*I am your sincere and honest adviser.*﴿(7:68)' [12:55]

42. From al-Thumālī, from Abū Jaʿfar عليه السلام who said, 'Yūsuf governed Egypt and its lands, which he did not relinquish to go anywhere else.' [12:56]

٣٩. عن سَماعة، قال: سألتُهُ عن قول الله: ﴿ارْجِعْ إِلَىٰ رَبِّكَ فَاسْأَلْهُ مَا بَالُ النِّسْوَةِ﴾، قال: يعني العَزيز.

٤٠. عن الحسن بن موسى، قال: روى أصحابنا عن الرضا عليه السلام، قال: قال له رجل: أصلحك الله، كيف صِرتَ إلى ما صِرتَ إليه من المأمون؟ وكأنّه أنكر ذلك عليه.

فقال له أبو الحسن عليه السلام: يا هذا، أيُّهما أفضل: النّبيّ أو الوصيّ؟ فقال: لا بل النّبيّ صلى الله عليه وآله. قال: فأيُّهما أفضل مسلم أو مشرك؟ قال: لا بل مسلم. قال: فإنّ العزيز عَزيز مِصر كان مشركًا، وكان يوسف عليه السلام نبيًّا، وإنّ المأمون مسلم، وأنا وصيّ؟ ويوسف عليه السلام سأل العزيز أن يولّيه حتّى قال: استعملني على خزائن الأرض إنّي حفيظٌ عليمٌ، والمأمون أجبرني على ما أنا فيه.

قال: وقال في قوله: ﴿حَفِيظٌ عَلِيمٌ﴾ قال: حافظٌ لِمَا في يدي، ﴿عَلِيمٌ﴾ عالم بكلّ لسان.

٤١. قال سليمان: قال سفيان: قلتُ لأبي عبد الله عليه السلام: ما يجوز أن يُزكّي الرجل نفسه؟ قال: نعم، إذا اضطرّ إليه، أما سَمِعت قول يوسف: ﴿اجْعَلْنِي عَلَىٰ خَزَائِنِ الْأَرْضِ إِنِّي حَفِيظٌ عَلِيمٌ﴾، وقول العبد الصالح: ﴿وَأَنَا لَكُمْ نَاصِحٌ أَمِينٌ﴾؟

٤٢. عن الثُّمالي، عن أبي جعفر عليه السلام، قال: مَلَك يوسف عليه السلام مِصر وبراريها، لم يُجاوزها إلى غيرها.

43. From Abū Baṣīr who said, 'I heard Abū Ja'far عليه السلام narrate, "When Ya'qūb was missing Yūsuf, he grieved and wept so much that his eyes turned blind out of sorrow. He felt an extreme yearning for him and his whole disposition changed."

He continued, "He used to import wheat from Egypt for his family twice a year, for winter and summer. He sent several of his sons to Egypt with a few simple goods to barter in exchange. When they went into Yūsuf's presence – and this was after the king of Egypt had placed him in charge – Yūsuf recognized them, but his brothers did not recognize him in his royal garb and his prestige. He said to them, 'Bring your goods to barter.' Then he said to his servants, 'Weigh up the grain for them quickly and give it to them. When you finish, place these goods of theirs back in their saddle-bags without telling them.'

So they did that. Then Yūsuf asked them, 'I have heard that you had two other paternal brothers. Where are they?'

They replied, 'The eldest of the two was eaten by a wolf, and we have left the youngest behind with our father who is possessive and protective over him.'

He said, 'Well I would love for you to bring him with you when you next come to import, ﴾ *You will have no more corn from me if you do not bring him to me, and you will not be permitted to approach me.' They said, 'We shall do all we can to persuade his father to send him with us, indeed we shall.'* ﴿'

When they returned to their father they opened their bags and found their goods in them. They said, 'We need no more [goods to barter]: look, our goods have been returned to us, and more than a camel-load of corn was weighed up for us, so ﴾ *send our brother back with us and we shall be given another measure. We shall guard him carefully.' He said, 'Am I to entrust him to you as I did his brother before?'* ﴿

However, when they needed to import more after six months, Ya'qūb sent them back with a few simple goods [to trade] and Bin Yāmīl, for whom he made them swear a pledge by God that they would bring him back to him. Otherwise they would all be culpable. So they set off with their goods until they entered in Yūsuf's presence. He asked them, 'Have you brought Bin Yāmīl with you?'

They replied, 'Yes, he is with the caravan.'

He said, 'Bring him to me then.' So they brought him into the palace.

٤٣. عن أبي بصير، قال: سَمِعتُ أبا جعفر عليه السلام يُحدّث قال: لمّا فقد يعقوب يوسف اشتدّ حُزنه عليه وبُكاؤه حتّى ابيضّت عيناه من الحزن، واحتاج حاجةً شديدةً وتغيّرت حاله.

قال: وكان يمتارُ القَمْحَ من مِصر لعياله في السنة مرّتين للشتاء والصيف، وإنّه بعث عِدّةً من ولده ببضاعة يسيرة إلى مِصر مع رِفْقَةٍ خَرَجت، فلمّا دَخَلُوا على يوسف عليه السلام، وذلك بعدما ولاّه العزيز مِصَر، فعَرَفهم يوسف عليه السلام ولم يعرفه إخوته لهيبة المُلك وعزّه، فقال لهم: هلمُّوا بِضاعتكم قبل الرِّفاق، وقال لِفتيانه: عجِّلوا لهؤلاء الكَيْل وأوفوهم، فإذا فَرَغتم فاجعلوا بضاعتهم هذه في رحالهم ولا تُعلِموهم بذلك، ففعلوا.

ثمّ قال لهم يوسف عليه السلام: قد بلغني أنّه كان لكم أخَوان لأبيكم، فما فعلا؟ قالوا: أمّا الكبير منهما فإنّ الذئب أكله، وأمّا الصغير فخلّفناه عند أبيه، وهو به ضَنينٌ وعليه شَفيقٌ، قال: فإنّي أُحبّ أن تأتوني به معكم إذا جئتم لتمتارون، فإن لم تأْتُوني به، فلا كَيل لكم عندي ولا تَقْرَبون. قالوا: سَنُراوِد عَنه أباه، وإنّا لفاعِلون.

فلمّا رَجَعوا إلى أبيهم فتحوا مَتاعهم، فوجدوا بِضاعتهم فيه، قالوا: يا أبانا، ما نبغي؟ هذه بضاعتنا قد رُدّت إلينا، وكِيل لنا كَيْلٌ قد زاد حِمل بعير، فأرسِل معنا أخانا نَكْتَلْ وإنّا لَهُ لَحافِظُون. قالَ: هَل آمَنكُم عليه إلاّ كَما أمِنْتُكُم عَلى أخيه من قَبْلُ!

فلمّا احتاجوا إلى المِيرة بعد ستّة أشهر بعثهم يعقوب عليه السلام، وبعث معهم بِضاعةً يسيرةً، وبعث معهم ابن يامين، وأخذ عليهم بذلك موثِقًا من الله لتأتُنَّني به إلاّ أن يُحاط بكم أجمعين، فانطلقوا مع الرِّفاق حتّى دَخَلوا على يوسف عليه السلام، فقال لهم: معكم ابن يامين؟ قالوا: نعم، هو في الرَّحل، قال لهم: فأتوني [به]، فأتوه به، وهو في دار المُلك، قد

He said, 'Let him come in alone,' so they let him come to him by himself. Yūsuf hugged him and cried and said to him, 'I am your brother, Yūsuf, so do not worry about what you see me doing. Keep what I have told you to yourself, and neither be sad nor afraid.' Then he sent him back out to them and commanded his servants to take their trading goods, and to quickly give them their measure of corn; and when they had finished, to place the measuring cup in the saddle-bag belonging to Bin Yāmīl. So they did just that.

The group set off with their goods and left. Yūsuf and his servants followed them and called out: ﴾*'People of the caravan! You are thieves!' and they turned and said, 'What have you lost?' They replied, 'The king's drinking-cup is missing,' and, 'Whoever returns it will get a camel-load [of grain],' and, 'I give you my word.' They said, 'By God! You must know that we did not come to make mischief in your land: we are no thieves.' They asked them, 'And if we find that you are lying, what penalty shall we apply to you?' and they answered, 'The penalty will be [the enslavement of] the person in whose bag the cup is found: this is how we punish wrongdoers.' [Yūsuf] began by searching their bags, then his brother's, and he pulled it out from his brother's bag... [His brothers] said, 'If he is a thief then his brother was a thief before him.'*﴿

So Yūsuf said to them, 'Get out of our land.' ﴾*They said, 'Mighty governor, he has an elderly father,*﴿ who took a pledge from us that we would return him back to him, ﴾so *take one of us in his place. We can see that you are a very good man,*﴿ if you would do that. ﴾*He replied, 'God forbid that we should take anyone other than the person on whom we found our property...'*﴿

The oldest of them said, 'I will not leave this land until my father gives me leave or God decides for me.' So Yūsuf's brothers left until they came to Ya'qūb. He asked them, 'Where is Bin Yāmīl?'

They replied, 'Bin Yāmīl stole the king's measuring cup, so the king arrested him for his theft and has kept him there with him. You can ask in the town where we have been, and the people we travelled with, and they will tell you about it.' So he said: ﴾*We belong to God and to Him we are returning.*﴿ He cried and became extremely grieved to such an extent that he became hunchbacked."'

From Abū Ḥamza, from Abū Baṣīr, on his authority that he said Bin Yāmīn instead of Bin Yāmīl. [12:59–79]

خلا وحده فأدخلوه عليه، فضمَّه يوسف عليه السلام إليه وبكى، وقال له: أنا أخوك يوسف، فلا تبتئس بما تراني أعمل، واكتُم ما أخبرتُك به ولا تحْزَن ولا تخَف، ثمّ أخرجه إليهم، وأمر فِتْيَته أن يأخُذوا بِضاعتهم، ويُعَجّلوا لهم الكَيْل، فإذا فرَغوا جعلوا المِكيال في رَحْل ابن يامِيل، ففعلوا به ذلك. وارتحل القومُ مع الرّفقة فمَضوا، فلَحِقهم يوسف عليه السلام وفتيته، فنادوا فيهم: أيَّتُها العِيرُ، إنّكم سارِقُون. ﴿قَالُوا وَأَقْبَلُوا عَلَيْهِم مَّاذَا تَفْقِدُونَ ۝ قَالُوا نَفْقِدُ صُوَاعَ الْمَلِكِ وَلِمَن جَاءَ بِهِ حِمْلُ بَعِيرٍ وَأَنَا بِهِ زَعِيمٌ ۝ قَالُوا تَاللَّهِ لَقَدْ عَلِمْتُم مَّا جِئْنَا لِنُفْسِدَ فِي الْأَرْضِ وَمَا كُنَّا سَارِقِينَ ۝ قَالُوا فَمَا جَزَاؤُهُ إِن كُنتُمْ كَاذِبِينَ ۝ قَالُوا جَزَاؤُهُ مَن وُجِدَ فِي رَحْلِهِ فَهُوَ جَزَاؤُهُ﴾ قال ﴿فَبَدَأَ بِأَوْعِيَتِهِمْ قَبْلَ وِعَاءِ أَخِيهِ ثُمَّ اسْتَخْرَجَهَا مِن وِعَاءِ أَخِيهِ﴾، قالوا: ﴿إِن يَسْرِقْ فَقَدْ سَرَقَ أَخٌ لَّهُ مِن قَبْلُ﴾.

فقال لهم يوسف: ارتحلوا عن بلادنا. قالوا: يا أيُّها العزيز، إنَّ له أبًا شيخًا كبيرًا، وقد أخذ علينا موثِقًا من الله لنَرُدّ به إليه، فخُذ أحدنا مكانه، إنّا نراك من المُحسنين إن فعلت.

قال: مَعاذ الله أن نأخُذ إلاّ من وَجَدنا مَتاعنا عنده.

فقال كبيرهم: إنّي لستُ أبرح الأرض حتّى يأذَن لي أبي أو يحكُمَ اللهُ لي، ومضى إخوة يوسف حتّى دَخَلوا على يعقوب عليه السلام، فقال لهم: فأين ابن يامِيل؟

قالوا: ابن يامِيل سَرَق مِكيال المَلِك، فأخذه المَلِك بسرقته، فحُبِس عنده، فسل أهل القرية والعِير حتّى يخْبِروك بذلك، فاسترجع واستعبر، واشتدّ حُزنه حتّى تقَوّس ظَهْرُهُ.

44. From Abān al-Aḥmar, from Abū ʿAbd Allāh عليه السلام who said, 'When Yūsuf's brothers went to him having brought their brother along with them, he spread out a banquet for them; then he said, "Let each one of you partake of the food with his maternal brother."

So they all sat down and his brother was left standing, so he asked him, "Why are you not sitting down with your brothers?"

He replied, "I do not have a maternal brother among them."

He said, "Did you not have a maternal brother whom they claim was eaten by a wolf?"

He replied, "Yes."

He said, "So sit and eat with me instead."'

He continued, 'So Yūsuf's brothers stopped eating saying, "We have only ever wanted one thing, and God is not only refusing it to us but raising the son of Yāmīn over us."

When they had finished packing their bags, he commanded for the drinking cup to be placed in his brother's saddle-bag. After they had left, a caller shouted out: ﴾*'People of the caravan! You are thieves!'*﴿

He said, ﴾*'so they turned and said, 'What have you lost?' They replied, 'The king's drinking-cup is missing,' and, 'Whoever returns it will get a camel-load [of grain],' and, 'I give you my word.' They said, 'By God! You must know that we did not come to make mischief in your land: we are no thieves.' They asked them, 'And if we find that you are lying, what penalty shall we apply to you?' and they answered, 'The penalty will be [the enslavement of] the person in whose bag the cup is found;*﴿ – they meant that the custom was such that he would be arrested. ﴾*[Yūsuf] began by searching their bags, then his brother's, and he pulled it out from his brother's bag... [His brothers] said, 'If he is a thief then his brother was a thief before him.*﴿"

Al-Ḥasan b. ʿAlī al-Washshāʾ said, 'I heard al-Riḍā عليه السلام say, "They were referring to the girdle."' 'When he had finished eating, he said, "How much have you grieved over your brother?" He replied, "I have had ten sons, and I have named each one of them with a derivative of his name."

So he said to him, "I do not see that you could have been that upset if you were able to enjoy women after his death."

He said, "Mighty king, I have a righteous old father who said to me, 'My son, get married so that you may beget children who will fill the earth with the testimony that there is no god but God.'"

أبو حمزة، عن أبي بصير، عنه ﷺ، ذَكَرَ فيه ابن يامين، ولم يذكُرُ ابن ياميل.

٤٤. عن أبان الأحمر، عن أبي عبد الله ﷺ، قال: لمّا دخل إخوة يوسف عليه، وقد جاءوا بأخيهم معهم، وضَعَ لهم الموائد، ثمّ قال: يمتاز كلّ واحدٍ منكم مع أخيه لأمّه على الخِوان، فجلسوا، وبقي أخوه قائمًا، فقال له: ما لك لا تجلِس مع إخوتك؟ قال: ليس لي منهم أخ من أُمّي. قال: فلك أخٌ من أُمّك زَعَم هؤلاء أنّ الذئب أكله؟ قال: نعم. قال: فاقْعُد وكُل معي.

قال: فترك إخوته الأكل، وقالوا: إنّا نُريد أمرًا، ويأبى الله إلاّ أن يرفع ولد يامين علينا.

قال: ثمَّ حين فرَغوا من جهازهم، أمر أن يُوضَع الصاع في رَحْل أخيه، فَلَمّا فَصَلوا نادى منادٍ: ﴿أَيَّتُهَا الْعِيرُ إِنَّكُمْ لَسَارِقُونَ﴾ قال: فرجعوا فقالوا: ﴿مَاذَا تَفْقِدُونَ ۝ قَالُوا نَفْقِدُ صُوَاعَ الْمَلِكِ﴾ إلى قوله: ﴿جَزَاؤُهُ مَنْ وُجِدَ فِي رَحْلِهِ فَهُوَ جَزَاؤُهُ﴾ يَعْنُون السُّنَّة التي تجري فيهم أن يحْبِسه ﴿فَبَدَأَ بِأَوْعِيَتِهِمْ قَبْلَ وِعَاءِ أَخِيهِ ثُمَّ اسْتَخْرَجَهَا مِنْ وِعَاءِ أَخِيهِ﴾ فقالوا: ﴿إِنْ يَسْرِقْ فَقَدْ سَرَقَ أَخٌ لَهُ مِنْ قَبْلُ﴾.

قال الحسن بن عليّ الوشّاء: فسَمِعت الرِّضا ﷺ يقول: يَعْنُون المِنْطَقة، فلمّا فَرَغ من غدائه قال: ما بَلَغ من حُزنك على أخيك؟ قال: ولد لي عشرة أولاد، فكُلّهم شَقَقتُ لهم اسمًا من اسمه. قال: فقال له: ما أراك حَزِنت عليه حيث اتّخذت النساء من بعده. قال: أيّها العزيز، إنّ لي أبًا شيخًا كبيرًا صالحًا، فقال: يا بُنيّ تزوّج، لعلّك تُصيب ولدًا يُثقِل الأرض بشهادة أن لا إله إلاّ الله.

قال أبو محمّد عبد الله بن محمّد: هذا من رواية الرِّضا ﷺ.

Abū Muḥammad ʿAbd Allāh b. Muḥammad said that this was part of al-Riḍā's narration. [12:69–80]

45. From ʿAlī b. Mahziyār, from one of our associates, on his father's authority from Abū ʿAbd Allāh عليه السلام who said, 'He had prepared some food for them. When they entered, he said to them, "Each person should sit at the same table as his maternal brothers." So they sat down and Bin Yāmīn remained standing, so Yūsuf asked him, "Why do you not sit down?"

He replied, "You requested for maternal brothers to sit together at one table, but I do not have a maternal brother."

So Yūsuf asked, "Did you not used to have a maternal brother?"

He replied, "Yes, I did."

Yūsuf asked, "What happened to him?"

He said, "These people claim that a wolf ate him."

He said, "To what extent have you grieved over him?"

He said, "I have had eleven children, and have derived each of their names from his name."

So Yūsuf said to him, "But I see that you have embraced women and hugged children after his death."

Bin Yāmīn said to him, "I have a righteous father who said to me, 'Get married so that God may bring forth offspring from your loins who will fill the earth with glorification.'"

So he said to him, "Come and sit with me at my table."

So Yūsuf's brothers said, "God favoured Yūsuf and his brother, and now even the king has seated him at his own table."' [12:69–80]

46. From Jābir b. Yazīd, from Abū Jaʿfar عليه السلام. He said, 'I asked him, "May I be your ransom – why is the Commander of the Faithful called the Commander of the Faithful (*amīr al-muʾminīn*)?" He replied, "Because he brings them knowledge to feed them thereof. Have you not heard God's words: ﴾*we shall bring corn to feed our household*﴿?"' [12:65]

47. From Abū Baṣīr who said, 'I heard Abū Jaʿfar عليه السلام say, "There is no goodness in one who does not have *taqiyya* [dissimulation of his faith], for Yūsuf said, ﴾*'People of the caravan! You are thieves!'*﴿ when they had not really thieved." [12:70]

٤٥. عن عليّ بن مَهْزيار، عن بعض أصحابنا، عن أبيه، عن أبي عبدالله عليه السلام، قال: وقد كان هيّأ لهم طعامًا، فلمّا دخلوا إليه، قال: ليجلِس كُلّ بني أُمٍّ على مائدة، قال: فجَلَسُوا وبقي ابن يامين قائمًا، فقال له يوسف عليه السلام: مالك لا تجلِس؟ قال له: إنّك قلت: ليجلِس كُلّ بني أُمٍّ على مائدة، وليس لي منهم ابن أُمّ.

فقال يوسف عليه السلام: أماكان لك ابن أمّ؟ قال له ابن يامين: بلى. قال يوسف عليه السلام: فما فعل؟ قال: زَعَم هؤلاء أنّ الذئب أكله، قال: فما بلغ من حُزنك عليه؟ قال: ولد لي أحد عشر ابنًا كلّهم اشتقّ له اسمًا من اسمه.

فقال له يوسف عليه السلام: أراك قد عانقت النساء، وشممت الولد من بعده؟ قال له ابن يامين: إنّ لي أبًا صالحًا، وإنّه قال: تزوّج لعلّ الله أن يُخرج منك ذُريّة تثقِل الأرض بالتسبيح، فقال له: تَعال فاجلِس معي على مائدتي، فقال إخوة يوسف: لقد فضّل اللهُ يوسف وأخاه، حتّى إنّ المَلِك قد أجلسه معه على مائدته.

٤٦. عن جابر بن يزيد، عن أبي جعفر عليه السلام، قال: قلتُ جُعلت فِداك، لِمَ سُمّي أمير المؤمنين أمير المؤمنين؟ قال: لأنّه يميرهم العِلم، أما سَمِعت كلام الله: ﴿وَنَمِيرُ أَهْلَنَا﴾.

٤٧. عن أبي بصير، قال: سَمِعتُ أبا جعفر عليه السلام يقول: لا خير فيمن لا تقيَّة له، ولقد قال يوسف عليه السلام ﴿أَيَّتُهَا الْعِيرُ إِنَّكُمْ لَسَارِقُونَ﴾ وما سرقوا.

48. In a narration of Abū Baṣīr's from Abū 'Abd Allāh عليه السلام who said, '*Taqiyya* is part of God's religion, for Yūsuf had said: ﴿*'People of the caravan! You are thieves!'*﴾ when they had neither stolen anything and nor was he lying.' [12:70]

49. In another narration from Abū Baṣīr, from Abū Ja'far عليه السلام. He said, 'He was asked while I was with him, "Sālim b. Abī Ḥafṣa narrates on your authority that you say things from seventy different angles in order to have a scapegoat."

He replied, "What does Sālim want from me? Does he want me to bring angels down? By God, none of the prophets ever brought them down. Ibrāhīm had said, ﴿*I am sick*﴾(37:89) and by God he was not really sick, but he was not lying either. Ibrāhīm also said: ﴿*No, it was done by the biggest of them*﴾(21:80), but neither had the biggest of them done it and nor was he lying. Yūsuf too said: ﴿*'People of the caravan! You are thieves!'*﴾ By God, they had neither stolen anything and nor was he lying."' [12:70]

50. From a man from among our associates, from Abū 'Abd Allāh عليه السلام. He said, 'I asked him about God's words pertaining to Yūsuf: ﴿*'People of the caravan! You are thieves!'*﴾

He said, "They had stolen Yūsuf from his father. Do you not see how he replied them when they said: ﴿*'What have you lost?' They replied, 'The king's drinking-cup is missing',*﴾ and they did not directly say: 'You stole the king's drinking-cup.' What they meant was: You stole Yūsuf from his father."' [12:70]

51. From Abū Ḥamza al-Thumālī, from Abū Ja'far عليه السلام. He said, 'I heard him say, "The 'king's drinking-cup' referred to the vessel that he would drink from."' [12:72]

٤٨. وفي رواية أبي بصير، عن أبي عبدالله عليه السلام، قال: التقيّة من دين الله، ولقد قال يوسف عليه السلام: ﴿أَيَّتُهَا الْعِيرُ إِنَّكُمْ لَسَارِقُونَ﴾ ووالله ماكانوا سَرَقوا شيئًا، وماكَذَب.

٤٩. وفي رواية أُخرى، عن أبي بصير، عن أبي جعفر عليه السلام، قال: قيل له وأنا عنده: إنَّ سالم بن أبي حَفْصة يروي عنك أنَّك تكلّم على سبعين وجهًا لك منها المخرج؟

فقال: مايُريد سالم منّي، أيُريد أن أجيء بالملائكة! فوالله ما جاء بهم النبيُّون، ولقد قال إبراهيم عليه السلام ﴿إِنِّي سَقِيمٌ﴾ ووالله ماكان سقيمًا، وماكَذَب ولقد قال إبراهيم عليه السلام ﴿بَلْ فَعَلَهُ كَبِيرُهُمْ﴾ وما فعله كبيرهم، وماكَذَب، ولقد قال يوسف عليه السلام: ﴿أَيَّتُهَا الْعِيرُ إِنَّكُمْ لَسَارِقُونَ﴾ والله ماكانوا سَرَقوا، وماكَذَب.

٥٠. عن رجلٍ من أصحابنا، عن أبي عبدالله عليه السلام، قال: سألتُهُ عن قول الله في يوسف عليه السلام: ﴿أَيَّتُهَا الْعِيرُ إِنَّكُمْ لَسَارِقُونَ﴾.

قال: إنّهم سَرَقوا يوسف عليه السلام من أبيه، ألا ترى أنَّه قال لهم حين قالوا لهم: ماذا تفقِدون؟ قالوا: نَفْقِدُ صُواعَ المَلِكِ، ولم يقولوا: سَرَقتم صُواع الملك، إنَّما عنى سَرَقتم يوسف من أبيه.

٥١. عن أبي حمزة الثُّمالي، عن أبي جعفر عليه السلام، قال: سَمِعته يقول: صُواع المَلِك: الطاس الذي يشرب فيه.

52. From Muḥammad b. Abī Ḥamza, from whoever mentioned it from Abū ʿAbd Allāh عليه السلام regarding His words: ﴾ *the king's drinking-cup.* ﴿ He said, 'It was a goblet made of gold.' He also said, 'Yūsuf's cup was such that when he used it to measure, it would say in a beautiful voice: ﴾ *May God curse the swindlers – do not swindle with it.* ﴿' [12:72]

53. From Ismāʿīl b. Hammām who said, 'Al-Riḍā عليه السلام said with regard to God's verse: ﴾ *'If he is a thief then his brother was a thief before him,' but Yūsuf kept his secrets and did not reveal anything to them.'* ﴿

He said, 'Prophet Isḥāq had a girdle that he had inherited from the prophets and ancestors, and it was kept by Yūsuf's paternal aunt [i.e. Yaʿqūb's sister]. Yūsuf was at her house, and she used to love him very much. Yūsuf's father sent for him saying, "Send him back to me, and then I will return him to you." So she sent a message back saying, "Let him stay the night with me so I can get my fill of him, then I will send him back to you tomorrow." When she woke up, she took the girdle and tied it around his waist; then dressed him in a shirt and sent him to him. She then claimed, "The girdle has been stolen!" and it was found on him. The custom of that time was that if someone stole something he himself would be sent to the rightful owner, who would keep him [as ransom]. So she took him and he stayed with her.' [12:77]

54. From al-Ḥasan b. ʿAlī al-Washshā' who said, 'I heard al-Riḍā عليه السلام say, "The law at the time of the Children of Israel was that if anyone stole something he himself would be its ransom. Yūsuf was staying with his paternal aunt when he was little, and she loved him very much. Isḥāq had a girdle that he had made Yaʿqūb wear, and that was kept at his sister's house. Yaʿqūb requested for Yūsuf to be taken back from his aunt, but she was upset by that and said to him, "Leave him with me until I send him to you myself." Then she agreed to send him, but she took the girdle and tied it around his waist under his clothes.

٥٢. عن محمّد بن أبي حمزة، عمّن ذكره، عن أبي عبد الله ﷺ، في قوله: ﴿صُوَاعَ ٱلْمَلِكِ﴾، قال: كان قَدَحًا من ذَهَب، وقال: كان صُواع يوسف إذا كِيل به قال: لَعنَ الله الخَوّان، لا تَخُونوا به، بصوتٍ حَسَن.

٥٣. عن إسماعيل بن همّام، قال: قال الرضا ﷺ: في قول الله: ﴿إِن يَسْرِقْ فَقَدْ سَرَقَ أَخٌ لَّهُۥ مِن قَبْلُ فَأَسَرَّهَا يُوسُفُ فِى نَفْسِهِۦ وَلَمْ يُبْدِهَا لَهُمْ﴾.

قال: كانت لإسحاق النبيّ ﷺ مِنْطَقَة يَتَوارثُها الأنبياء والأكابر، فكانت عند عمّة يوسف، وكان يوسف ﷺ عندها، وكانت تُحِبُّه، فبعث إليها أبوه: أن ابعثيه إليّ وأرُدّه إليك، فبعثتْ إليه: أن دَعْهُ عندي الليلة أشُمّه ثمّ أرْسله إليك غُدوةً؛ فلمّا أصبحَتْ أخذت المِنْطَقة، فَرَبطتها في حَقْوه، وألبسته قميصًا، وبعثت به إليه، وقالت: سُرِقت المِنطقة. فَوُجِدتْ عليه، وكان إذا سَرَق أحدٌ في ذلك الزمان، دُفِع إلى صاحب السَّرقة، فأخذته فكان عندها.

٥٤. عن الحسن بن عليّ الوشّاء، قال: سَمِعتُ الرضا ﷺ يقول: كانت الحكومة في بني إسرائيل إذا سرق أحدٌ شيئاً استُرِقَّ به، وكان يوسف ﷺ عندعمّته وهو صغير وكانت تُحِبّه، وكانت لإسحاق ﷺ مِنْطقة ألبسها يعقوب، وكانت عند أُخته، وإنّ يعقوب طلب يوسف أن يأخُذه من عمّته، فاغتمّت لذلك، وقالت له: دعه حتّى أُرسله إليك، فأرسلته وأخذت المِنطَقة فشدّتها في وَسَطه تحت الثياب.

When Yūsuf came to his father, she came and asked, "Did you steal the girdle?" So she searched him and found it on his waist. That is why Yūsuf's brothers said what they did when the cup had been placed in their brother's bag, and Yūsuf asked them, 'What is the penalty for one in whose saddle-bag it is found?' They said, 'Its penalty is for the customary law to be applied to him.' So he started with their bags before his brother's bag, then pulled it out from his brother's bag. That is why Yūsuf's brothers said: ﴾*'If he is a thief then his brother was a thief before him.'*﴿ They meant the girdle, ﴾*but Yūsuf kept his secrets and did not reveal anything to them.*﴿"

There is a similar narration from al-Ḥasan b. 'Alī al-Washshā' from al-Riḍā.' [12:77–79]

55. From al-Ḥusayn b. Abī al-'Alā' [Khālid], from Abū 'Abd Allāh عليه السلام. He said, 'He mentioned Ya'qūb's sons and said, "When they got angry, their anger was so intense that their skins would drip with bile, and they were saying, ﴾*'Take one of us in his place'*﴿ as his ransom. However, he took the one whose bag the cup was found in."' [12:78]

56. From Hishām b. Sālim, from Abū 'Abd Allāh عليه السلام who said, 'When Yūsuf's brothers were despairing of their brother's release, Yahūdā – who was the eldest of them – said: ﴾*'I will not leave this land until my father gives me leave or God decides for me – He is the best decider.'*﴿ He said, 'He then went back to Yūsuf to talk to him regarding his brother, so he discussed with him until the debate between them got heated and Yahūdā became angry. Whenever he got angry the hair on his shoulders would stand up and they would bleed.'

He continued, 'One of Yūsuf's young sons was in front of him playing with a golden pomegranate. So Yūsuf took it from the child and rolled it towards Yahūdā. The child crawled towards Yahūdā to go and get it back from him and touched Yahūdā, who calmed down. Then he resumed his discussion with Yūsuf about his brother until again the discussion became heated and Yahūdā got angry, his hair stood on end and blood started flowing out. So Yūsuf took the pomegranate from the child and rolled it towards Yahūdā. The child crawled towards Yahūdā and Yahūdā calmed down, then said, 'There is an offspring of Ya'qūb here in this house with us.'

At that point, Yūsuf said to them: ﴾*'Do you now realize what you did to Yūsuf and his brother when you were ignorant?'*﴿'

فلمّا أتى يوسف ﷺ أباه، جاءت فقالت: سُرِقت المِنطَقة؟ فَفَتّشته فوجدتها في وسطه، ولذلك قال إخوة يوسق حيث جعل الصاع في وِعاء أخيه، فقال لهم يوسف: ما جزاء من وجدنا في رَحْله؟ قالوا: جزاؤه بإجراء السُّنَّة الَّتي تجري فيهم، فبدأ بأوعيتهم قبل وِعاء أخيه، ثمّ استخرجها من وِعاء أخيه، فلذلك قال إخوة يوسف: إن يسرق فقد سرق أخٌ له من قبل، يعنون المِنطقة، فأسرّها يوسف ﷺ في نفسه، ولم يُبدِها لهم.

عن الحسن بن علي الوشّاء، عن الرضا ﷺ، وذكر مثله.

٥٥. عن الحسين بن أبي العلاء، عن أبي عبد الله ﷺ، قال: ذكر بني يعقوب، فقال: كانوا إذا غَضِبوا، اشتدّ غضبهم حتّى تقطُر جُلوُدهم دمًا أصفر، وهم يقولون: خُذ أحدنا مكانه، يعني جزاءه، فأخذ الذي وُجِد الصاع عنده.

٥٦. عن هِشام بن سالم، عن أبي عبد الله ﷺ قال: لمّا استيأس إخوة يوسف من أخيهم قال لهم يهودا، وكان أكبرهم: لن أبرح الأرض حتّى يأذَن لي أبي، أو يحكُم الله لي، وهو خير الحاكمين. قال: ورجع إلى يوسف يُكلِمه في أخيه، فكلّمه حتّى ارتفع الكلام بينهما، حتّى غَضِب يهودا، وكان إذا غَضِب قامت شعرة في كَتِفه، وخرج منه الدم.

قال: وكان بين يدي يوسف ﷺ ابن له صغير معه رُمّانة من ذهب، وكان الصبيّ يلعب بها. قال: فأخذها يوسف ﷺ من الصبى، فدحرجها نحو يهودا، قال، وحبا الصبيّ نحو يهودا ليأخُذها، فمسّ يهودا فسكن يهودا، ثمّ عاد إلى يوسف فكلّمه في أخيه، حتّى ارتفع الكلام بينهما، حتّى غضب يهودا، وقامت الشعرة، وسال منها الدم، فأخذ

57. In Hishām b. Sālim's narration on his authority he said, 'When Yūsuf arrested his brother, his other brothers ganged up on him and said to him, ﴾*'Take one of us in his place',*﴿ with their skins dripping with bile, continuously saying: ﴾*'Take one of us in his place.'*﴿ When he refused and they had left, Yahūdā said to them, "You know very well what you did to Yūsuf, and ﴾*'I will not leave this land until my father gives me leave or God decides for me – He is the best decider.'*﴿

He said, 'They returned to their father whilst Yahūdā stayed behind.' He continued, 'He went in to see Yūsuf and discussed with him about his brother until the discussion between them became heated, and he became angry. He had hair on his shoulders, which would stand on end whenever he became angry and which would bleed continuously until touched by one of Ya'qūb's children.

He continued, Yūsuf had a son of his there with him playing with a golden pomegranate. So when Yūsuf saw him getting angry and his hair standing on end and bleeding, he took the pomegranate from the child's hands and rolled it towards Yahūdā. The child followed it to take it back, and his hand touched Yahūdā, and his anger vanished.

He continued, 'So Yahūdā was puzzled. Then the child went back to Yūsuf with the pomegranate. Then the discussion between them resumed and became heated once more, until he got angry again and his hair stood on end and started to bleed. When Yūsuf saw that, he rolled the pomegranate towards Yahūdā, and the child followed it to go and get it back. His hand again touched Yahūdā, and his anger subsided. So Yahūdā said, "One of Ya'qūb's offspring is present in this house," and this happened three times.' [12:78–89]

يوسف ﵇ الرُّمانة من الصبيّ، فدحرجها نحو يهودا، وحبا الصبيّ نحو يهودا، فسكن يهودا، فقال يهودا: إنّ في البيت معنا لبعض ولد يعقوب! قال: فعند ذلك قام لهم يوسف ﵇: هل عِلِمتُم ما فعَلتُم بيُوسُفَ وأخيهِ إذْ أنتُمْ جاهلُون؟

٥٧. وفي رواية هِشام بن سالم، عنه ﵇: قال: لمّا أخذ يوسف ﵇ أخاه، اجتمع عليه إخوته، فقالوا له: خُذ أحدنا مكانه، وجُلُودهم تقطُر أصفر، وهم يقولون: خُذ أحدنا مكانه، قال: لمّا أن أبي عليهم وأُخرِجوا من عنده، قال لهم يهودا: قد عَلِمتم ما فعلتم بيوسف، فلن أبرح الأرض حتّى يأذَن لي أبي، أو يحكُم الله لي، وهو خير الحاكمين.

قال: فرجعوا إلى ابيهم، وتخلَّف يهودا، قال: فدخل على يوسف ﵇، فكلَّمه في أخيه، حتّى ارتفع الكلام بينه وبينه وغَضِب، وكان على كَتِفه شعرة إذا غَضِب قامت الشعرة، فلا تزال تقذِف بالدم حتّى يَمَسَّه بعض ولد يعقوب.

قال: فكان بين يدي يوسف ابن له صغير، في يده رُمّانة من ذهب يلعب بها، فلمّا رآه يوسق قد غَضِب وقامت الشعرة تقذِف بالدم، أخذ الرُّمانة من يدي الصبيّ، ثمّ دحرجها نحو يهودا، وأتبعها الصبيّ ليأخذها، فوقعت يده على يهودا، قال: فذهب غَضَبه.

قال: فارتاب يهودا، ورجع الصبيّ بالرّمانة إلى يوسف ﵇، ثمّ ارتفع الكلام بينهما حتّى غَضِب، وقامت الشعرة فجعلت تقذِف بالدّم، فلمّا رآه يوسف دَحرَج الرُّمانة نحو يهودا، وأتبعها الصبي ليأخُذها، فوقعت يده على يهودا، فسكن غضبه، قال: فقال يهودا: إنّ في البيت لمن ولد يعقوب! حتّى صَنَع ذلك ثلاث مرّات.

58. From Jābir who said, 'I asked Abū Ja'far عليه السلام, "May God have mercy on you – what is 'graceful patience'?"

He replied, "That is the kind of patience that is not accompanied by any complaint to people. Ibrāhīm once sent Ya'qūb with an errand to a monk from among the monks, a fellow worshipper. When he saw Ya'qūb, he mistook him for Ibrāhīm and leapt on him and embraced him. Then he said, 'Welcome, O friend of the all-Beneficent.' Ya'qūb replied, 'I am not Ibrāhīm. I am Ya'qūb, son of Isḥāq, son of Ibrāhīm.'

So the monk asked him, 'So what has happened to you that I see such old age in you?' He replied, 'Grief and sorrow and weakness.' No sooner had he gone out of the side door than God revealed to him, 'Ya'qūb, you complained to My servants about Me?' So he fell prostrate at the threshold of the door saying, 'My Lord, I will never do that again.' So God revealed to him, 'I have forgiven you for it, but do not ever do such a thing again.' So he never again complained of a single thing that afflicted him from the tribulations of this world, such that he even said one day: ﴿*'I only plead my grief and sorrow before God. I have knowledge from God that you do not have.'*﴾'" [12:86]

59. From Hishām b. Sālim, from Abū 'Abd Allāh عليه السلام. He said, 'One of our associates asked him, "To what extent had Ya'qūb's grief over Yūsuf reached?" He said, "The grief of seventy mothers bereaved of their children."' [12:86]

60. With the same chain of transmission, on his authority, he was asked, "How could Ya'qūb grieve so much over Yūsuf when Jibra'īl had told him that he had not died and that he would return to him in the future?" So he replied, "He forgot that." [12:86]

61. From Muḥammad b. Sahl al-Baḥrānī[7] from one of our associates, from Abū 'Abd Allāh عليه السلام who said, 'There are five people who cried profusely: Ādam, Ya'qūb, Yūsuf, Fāṭima (the daughter of Muḥammad), and 'Alī b. al-Ḥusayn, peace be upon them all. As for Ya'qūb, he cried so much over Yūsuf that he lost his eyesight, and he was told: ﴿*'You will ruin your health if you do not stop thinking of Yūsuf, or even die.'*﴾' [12:85]

7 Muḥammad b. Sahl al-Baḥrānī, about whom there is scant information. See Khū'ī, *Mu'jam*, 17:180 (nr. 10954).

٥٨. عن جابر، قال: قلتُ لأبي جعفر عليه السلام: رحمك الله، ما الصبر الجميل.

فقال: ذاك صبرٌ ليس فيه شكوى إلى الناس، إنّ إبراهيم عليه السلام بعث يعقوب إلى راهبٍ من الرُّهبان، عابد من العُبّاد في حاجة، فلمّا رآه الراهب حَسِبه إبراهيم فوَثَب إليه فاعتنقه، ثمّ قال: مرحبًا بخليل الرّحمن، قال يعقوب عليه السلام: إنّي لستُ بإبراهيم، ولكنّي يعقوب بن إسحاق بن إبراهيم.

فقال له الراهب: فما بلغ بك ما أرى من الكِبَر؟ قال: الهمّ والحُزن والسَّقم، فما جاوز صِير الباب حتّى أوحى الله إليه: أن يا يعقوب شكوتني إلى العباد! فخرّ ساجدًا عند عتبة الباب يقول: ربّ لا أعود، فأوحى الله إليه: أنّي قد غَفَرتُها لك، فلا تَعُودنّ إلى مثلها، فما شكا ممّا أصابه من نوائب الدنيا، إلاّ أنّه قال يومًا: ﴿إِنَّمَا أَشْكُو بَثِّي وَحُزْنِي إِلَى اللهِ وَأَعْلَمُ مِنَ اللهِ مَا لاَ تَعْلَمُونَ﴾.

٥٩. عن هشام بن سالم، عن أبي عبدالله عليه السلام، قال: قال له بعض أصحابنا: ما بلغ من حُزن يعقوب على يوسف؟ قال: حُزن سبعين ثَكلى حَرّى.

٦٠. وبهذا الإسناد، عنه عليه السلام، قال: قيل له: كيف يَحْزَن يعقوب على يوسف، وقد أخبره جَبْرَئيل أنّه لم يَمُتَ، وأنّه سيرجِع إليه؟ فقال: إنّه نسي ذلك.

٦١. عن محمّد بن سهل البحراني، عن بعض أصحابنا، عن أبي عبدالله عليه السلام، قال: البكّاؤون خمسة: آدم، ويعقوب، ويوسف، وفاطمة بنت محمّد، وعليّ بن الحسين عليهم

62. From Ismāʿīl b. Jābir, from Abū ʿAbd Allāh ﷺ who said, 'Yaʿqūb once went to a king in their region to ask him for something. The king asked him, "Are you Ibrāhīm?" He replied, "No." He said, "Then are you Isḥāq, son of Ibrāhīm?" He said, "No." He asked, "Then who are you?" He replied, "I am Yaʿqūb, son of Isḥāq."

He said, "Then what has happened to you that I do not see youth in you?" He replied, "Grief over my son, Yūsuf." He said, "Yaʿqūb, this grief has indeed overtaken you." He said, "Us prophets are the fastest to be struck by tribulation, then other people after that in order of exemplariness." So he fulfilled his need.

No sooner had he gone through the inner door than Jibraʾīl came down to him and said, "Yaʿqūb, your Lord greets you with peace and says to you: 'You complained to people about Me?' So he rubbed his face in the dirt, and said, "My Lord, I made a mistake and I will never do it again."

Then Jibraʾīl returned to him and said, 'Yaʿqūb, raise your head up for your Lord greets you with peace and says: 'I have pardoned you, so never again complain about Me to My creatures.' And he was never again seen speaking such words, and even when his sons came to him he turned his face away towards the wall and said: ﴾*'I only plead my grief and sorrow before God. I have knowledge from God that you do not have.'*﴿' [12:86]

63. In another narration on his authority, Yaʿqūb came to Nimrūd asking for something, and when he entered in and resembled Ibrāhīm the most, he asked him, "Are you Ibrāhīm, the friend of the all-Beneficent?" He replied, "No." [the rest of the narration continued]. [12:86]

السلام، وأمّا يعقوب فبكى على يوسف حتّى ذهب بصرُه، وحتّى قيلَ له: ﴿تَاللَّهِ تَفْتَأُ تَذْكُرُ يُوسُفَ حَتَّىٰ تَكُونَ حَرَضًا أَوْ تَكُونَ مِنَ الْهَالِكِينَ﴾ .

٦٢. عن إسماعيل بن جابر، عن أبي عبدالله عليه السلام، قال: إنّ يعقوب عليه السلام أتى مَلِكًا بناحيتهم يسأله الحاجة، فقال له المَلِك: أنت إبراهيم؟ قال: لا. قال: فأنت إسحاق بن إبراهيم؟ قال: لا. قال: فمن أنت؟ قال: أنا يعقوب بن إسحاق.

قال: فما بلغ عنك ما أرى مع حَدَاثة السنّ؟ قال: الحُزن على ابني يوسف. قال: لقد بَلَغ الحُزن يا يعقوب كُلّ مبلغ. فقال: إنّا معشر الأنبياء أسرع شيءٍ البلاء إلينا، ثمّ الأمثل فالأمثل من الناس، فقضى حاجته.

فلمّا جاوز صِير بابه هبط عليه جَبْرَئيل عليه السلام، فقال له: يا يعقوب، ربّك يُقرِئك السلام، ويقول لك: شكوتني إلى الناس، فعفّر وجهه في التُّراب، وقال: يا ربّ زلّة أقلنيها، فلا أعود بعد هذا أبدًا.

ثمّ عاد إليه جَبْرَئيل، فقال: يا يعقوب، ارفع رأسك، ربّك يُقرئك السلام، ويقول لك: قد أَقَلْتُك، فلا تَعُد تشكوني إلى خَلْقي، فما رُؤيَ ناطقًا بكلمةٍ ممّا كان فيه حتّى أتاه بنوه، فصرف وجهه إلى الحائط، فقال: ﴿إِنَّمَا أَشْكُو بَثِّي وَحُزْنِي إِلَى اللَّهِ وَأَعْلَمُ مِنَ اللَّهِ مَا لَا تَعْلَمُونَ﴾ .

٦٣. وفي حديث آخر عنه عليه السلام: جاء يعقوب عليه السلام إلى نُمرود في حاجةٍ، فلمّا دخل عليه — وكان أشبه الناس بإبراهيم — قال له: أنت إبراهيم خليل الرّحمن؟ قال: لا «الحديث».

64. From al-Fuḍayl b. Yasār who said, 'I heard Abū 'Abd Allāh ﵇ say: "[The verse] ﴿*'I only plead my grief and sorrow before God'*﴾ is in the accusative case." [12:86]

65. From Ḥanān b. Sadīr [on his father's authority] who said, 'I said to Abū Ja'far ﵇, "Tell me about the time when Ya'qūb said: ﴿*'go and seek news of Yūsuf and his brother'*﴾ – did he know that he was alive despite having been separated from him for twenty years and after having lost his eyesight?" He replied, "Yes, he knew that he was alive."

He asked, "How did he know?" He replied, "He supplicated at dawn for the angel of death to come down to him, so Tirbāl, who is the angel of death, said to him, 'What do you need, Ya'qūb?' He replied, 'Tell me about the souls that you seize – do you take them all together or separately?' He replied, 'No separately, one by one.' He asked, 'Have you come across Yūsuf's soul yet?' He replied, 'No.' He said, "At that moment, he knew that he was still alive, and said to his sons: ﴿*'go and seek news of Yūsuf and his brother'.*﴾"'

In another report: "'Izrā'īl, who is the angel of death, and so on." [12:87]

66. From Abū Baṣīr, from Abū Ja'far ﵇ going back to the first *ḥadīth*, he said, 'He [i.e. Ya'qūb] became extremely grieved to such an extent that he became hunchbacked, and the world too detached itself from Ya'qūb and his sons until they faced extreme poverty and their provisions of food ran out. At that point, Ya'qūb said to his sons: ﴿*My sons, go and seek news of Yūsuf and his brother and do not despair of God's mercy – only disbelievers despair of God's mercy.*﴾

So a group of them went forth with a few simple goods to trade, and he sent a letter with them addressed to the governor of Egypt to elicit his empathy towards himself and his sons. He told his sons to hand the letter over to him before the goods.

He wrote:

'In the Name of God, the all-Beneficent, the all-Compassionate. To the governor of Egypt – the Manifestation of Equity and the Bestower of good measure on Ya'qūb, son of Ishāq, son of Ibrāhīm. He was the friend of God and the contemporary of Nimrūd, who had gathered firewood and fire to burn him therein but God made it cold and safe for him and saved him from it.

٦٤. الفُضيل بن يَسار، قال: سَمِعتُ أبا عبدالله عليه السلام يقول: ﴿إِنَّمَا أَشْكُو بَثِّي وَحُزْنِي إِلَى اللَّهِ﴾ منصوبة.

٦٥. عن حَنان بن سَدير، عن أبيه، قال: قلت لأبي جعفر عليه السلام: أخبرني عن يعقوب عليه السلام حين قال: ﴿اذْهَبُوا فَتَحَسَّسُوا مِن يُوسُفَ وَأَخِيهِ﴾ أكان عَلِم أنّه حيّ وقد فارقه منذ عشرين سنة، وذهبت عيناه من الحُزن؟ قال: نعم، عَلِم أنّه حيّ.

قال: وكيف عَلِم؟ قال: إنّه دعا في السَّحَر أن يهبطَ عليه مَلَك الموت، فهبَطَ عليه تربال، وهو مَلَك الموت، فقال له تربال، ما حاجتُك يا يعقوب؟ قال: أخبرني عن الأرواح، تَقْبِضها مجتمعةً أو مُتفرّقةً؟ قال: بل متفرّقة رُوحًا روحًا. قال: فمرّ بك روح يوسف؟ قال: لا. قال: فعند ذلك عَلِم أنّه حيّ فقال لولده: ﴿اذْهَبُوا فَتَحَسَّسُوا مِن يُوسُفَ وَأَخِيهِ﴾.

وفي خبر آخر: عزرائيل، وهو مَلَك الموت، وذكر نحوه عنه.

٦٦. عن أبي بصير، عن أبي جعفر عليه السلام عاد إلى الحديث الأوّل، قال: واشتدّ حُزنه — يعني يعقوب عليه السلام — حتّى تقوّس ظهره، وأدبرت الدنيا عن يعقوب وولده حتّى احتاجوا حاجةً شديدةً، وفنيت ميرتهم، فعند ذلك قال يعقوب عليه السلام لولده: ﴿اذْهَبُوا فَتَحَسَّسُوا مِن يُوسُفَ وَأَخِيهِ وَلَا تَيْأَسُوا مِن رَّوْحِ اللَّهِ إِنَّهُ لَا يَيْأَسُ مِن رَّوْحِ اللَّهِ إِلَّا الْقَوْمُ الْكَافِرُونَ﴾.

فخرج منهم نَفَرٌ، وبعث معهم بِضاعةٍ يسيرةٍ، وكتب معهم كتابًا إلى عزيز مِصر يتعطّفه على نفسه وولده، وأوصى ولده أن يبدءوا بدفع كتابه قبل البِضاعة، فكتب:

I write to inform you, O mighty governor, that we are the people of a long-established and venerable household, who have been constantly experiencing the fast descent of tribulation from God, that He may test us thereby in both ease and hardship. Afflictions have been continuously striking me for the past twenty years; the first of which was that I had a son whom I called Yūsuf, who was my greatest joy out of all my children. He was the delight of my heart and the apple of my eye. His brothers of another mother requested me to send him with them to have fun and play. So I sent him with them in the morning, and in the evening they came to me crying and brought his shirt to me with fake blood on it, claiming that a wolf had eaten him. My grief at his loss was intense, and I have wept so much over my separation from him that my eyes have turned white.

He had a brother born of his mother's sister, whom I also liked very much and was very fond of, and who kept me company. Whenever I missed Yūsuf, I would hug him close to my chest and some of the pain I felt therein would subside. His brothers mentioned to me, O mighty governor, that you commanded them to bring him to you, and that if they did not do so you would deny them the provision of wheat from Egypt. So I sent him with them so that they could bring back some wheat for us, but they came back to me without him saying that he had stolen the king's measuring-cup. We are a household who do not steal, but you have arrested him and distressed me as a result. My separation from him is upsetting me so much that my back has bent over. This has only added to the successive and continuous afflictions that I have been suffering from. So please be kind to me as to clear his way and release him from his arrest. Grant us a measure of wheat and give us a good price for it, and quickly send Ya'qūb's family back to him.'

When Ya'qūb's sons had left him and were headed towards Egypt with his letter, Jibra'īl came down to Ya'qūb and said, 'Ya'qūb, your Lord says to you: "Who afflicted you with these tribulations that you wrote about to the governor of Egypt?"

Ya'qūb replied, 'You are the One who afflicted me, and You are the One who punishes me and disciplines me.'

God said: "So can anyone other than Me avert them from you?"

Ya'qūb replied, 'O God, no.'

بسم الله الرحمن الرحيم

إلى عزيز مِصر، ومُظهِر العَدل، ومُوفي الكَيل، من يعقوب بن إسحاق بن إبراهيم خليل الله صاحب نُمرود الذي جَمَع لإبراهيمَ الخَليل الحَطب والنار ليُحرِقه بها فجعلها الله عليه بردًا وسلامًا، وأنجاه منها.

أُخبرك — أيّها العزيز— أنّا أهل بيتٍ قديم، لم يَزَل البلاء إلينا سريعًا من الله، ليَبْلُونا بذلك عند السرّاء والضرّاء، وأنّ مصائب تتابعت عليّ منذ عشرين سنة، أوّلها أنّه كان لي ابن سمّيته يوسف، وكان سُروري من بين ولدي، وقُرّة عيني، وثَمرة فُؤادي، وأنّ إخوته من غير أُمّه سألوني أن أبعثه معهم يرتع ويلعب، فبعثته معهم بُكرةً، وأنّهم جاءوني عِشاءً يبكُون، وجاءوني على قميصه بدمٍ كَذِب، فزعموا أنّ الذئب أكله، فاشتدّ لفقده حُزني، وكَثُر على فِراقه بُكائي، حتّى أبيضّت عيناي من الحُزن.

وإنّه كان له أخٌ من خالته، وكُنت به مُعجبًا، وعليه رَفيقًا، وكان لي أنيسًا، وكنت إذا ذكرت يوسف ضَمَمتُه إلى صدري، فيسكُن بعض ما أجِدُ في صدري، وإنّ إخوته ذكروا لي أنّك — أيّها العزيز- سألتهم عنه، وأمرتهم أن يأتُوك به، وإن لم يأتُوك به مَنَعتَهم المِيرة لنا من القَمْح من مِصر، فبعثته معهم ليمتَارُوا لنا قَمْحًا فرجَعُوا إليّ وليس هو معهم، وذَكَروا أنّه سَرَق مِكيال المَلِك، ونحن أهل بيت لا نسرق، وقد حَبَسْتَه وفَجَعْتَني به، وقد اشتدّ لفِراقه حُزني حتّى تَقوّس لذلك ظهري، وعَظُمَت به مُصيبتي مع مصائب مُتتابعات عليّ، فمُنّ عليّ بتخلية سبيله وإطلاقه من مَحْبِسه، وطيّب لنا القَمح، وأسمح لنا في السِّعر، وعجّل بسَراح آل يعقوب.

He said: "Then did you not feel ashamed in front of Me to complain of your afflictions to someone other than Me, when you had neither asked Me for help nor complained to Me about it?"

Ya'qūb said, "I seek Your forgiveness my God, and I turn to You in repentance. I plead my grief and sorrow before You."

So God, Blessed and most High, said, "I have completed My discipline of you and your erring sons, Ya'qūb. If you had only complained to Me of your troubles during their descent upon you and sought My forgiveness and turned to Me penitent for your sin, I would have averted them away from you straight after My decreeing them for you. Shayṭān, however, made you forget to remember Me, and you ended up despairing of My Mercy, whilst I am God, the all-Generous and Kind. I love my remorseful servants who seek My forgiveness and desire only from Me that which is with Me. Ya'qūb, I will return Yūsuf and his brother to you. I will also return whatever loss of wealth [and flesh and blood] you have incurred. I will return your eyesight back to you and straighten your back. So let your soul be at ease and your eyes gladdened, for what I have done to you has only been My way of disciplining you – so accept My discipline."'

He continued, 'So Ya'qūb's sons headed towards Egypt with his letter, until they entered into Yūsuf's presence at the royal palace. ﴾*They said, 'Mighty governor, misfortune has afflicted us and our family. We have brought only a little merchandise, but give us full measure. Be charitable to us'*﴿ and give us back our brother Bin Yāmīn. This is a letter for you from our father, Ya'qūb, requesting his release, and for you to give him back to us."

فلمّا مضى ولد يعقوب من عنده نحو مِصر بكتابه، نزل جَبْرئيل على يعقوب ﵇، فقال له: يا يعقوب، إنَّ ربَّك يقول لك: مَن ابتلاك بمصائبك الّتي كتبت بها على عزيز مِصر؟ قال يعقوب ﵇: أنت بَلَوتني بها عُقوبةً منك وأدبًا لي. قال الله: فهل كان يقدِر على صَرْفها عنك أحدٌ غيري؟ قال يعقوب ﵇: اللّهم لا. قال: أفما استحييت منّي حين شَكَوت مصائبك إلى غيري، ولم تَسْتَغِثْ بي وتشكو ما بك إليّ؟

فقال يعقوب: أَسْتَغْفِرُك يا إلهي وأتوبُ إليك، وأشكو بثّي وحُزني إليك. فقال الله تبارك وتعالى: قد بَلَغتُ بك يا يعقوب وبولدك الخاطئين الغاية في أدبي، ولوكنتَ يا يعقوب شَكَوت مصائبك إليّ عند نُزُولها بك واستغفرتَ وتُبتَ إليّ من ذنبك، لَصَرفتُها عنك بعد تقديري إيّاها عليك، ولكنَّ الشيطان أنساك ذكري فصِرت إلى القُنُوط من رحمتي، وأنا الله الجَواد الكَريم أُحِبّ عبادي المستغفرين التّائبين الراغبين إليّ فيما عندي.

يا يعقوب، أنا رادٌّ إليك يوسف وأخاه، ومُعيدٌ إليك ما ذهب من مالك ولحمك ودمك، ورادٌّ إليك بصرك، ومُقوّم لك ظهرك، وطِب نفسًا، وقَرّ عينًا، وإنّ الذي فعلتُه بك كان أدبًا منّي لك، فاقبل أدبي.

قال: ومضى ولد يعقوب بكتابه نحو مِصر، حتّى دَخَلُوا على يوسف ﵇ في دار المملكة، فقالُوا: أيُّها العَزيزُ، مَسَّنا وَأهلَنَا الضُّرّ وجِئنا بِبضاعة مُزْجاةٍ فَأَوْفِ لنَا الكَيل وتصَدّق علينا بأخِينا ابن يامين، وهذا كتابُ أبينا يعقوب إليك في أمره، يسألك تخْلية سَبيله، فامُنن به عليه.

He continued, 'So Yūsuf took Ya'qūb's letter, kissed it, placed it on his eyes and cried and wept so much that his tears wet the shirt that he was wearing. Then he went up to them and said: ﴾*'Do you now realize what you did to Yūsuf*﴿ to begin with, ﴾*and his brother*﴿ afterwards? ﴾*And they cried, 'Could it be that you are Yūsuf?' He said, 'I am Yūsuf. This is my brother. God has been gracious to us... They said, 'By God! God really did favour you over all of us.'*﴿ Please do not expose us nor punish us; forgive us. ﴾*'He said, 'You will hear no reproaches today. May God forgive you.'*﴿

There is a similar account in another narration on Abū Baṣīr's authority, from Abū Ja'far. [12:88–92]

67. From 'Amr b. 'Uthmān[8], from one of our associates who said, 'When Yūsuf's brothers said: ﴾*'Mighty governor, misfortune has afflicted us and our family',*﴿ Yūsuf said, "The family of Ya'qūb has no patience over misfortune." Then he said, ﴾*Do you now realize what you did to Yūsuf and his brother when you were ignorant?*﴿' [12:88–89]

68. From Aḥmad b. Muḥammad, from Abū al-Ḥasan al-Riḍā عليه السلام. He said, 'I asked him about His verse: ﴾*'We have brought only a little merchandise.'*﴿ He said, "Frankincense."'

Also in this narration: ﴾*'We have brought only a little merchandise.'*﴿ He said, 'It was frankincense. Their town was known for its frankincense, and this was the merchandise.' [12:88]

69. From Ibn Abī 'Umayr, from one of our associates who, without mentioning his source, cited, 'Prophet Ya'qūb wrote to Yūsuf saying: "From Ya'qūb, son of Isḥāq, God's sacrifice, son of Ibrāhīm, God's friend; to the governor of Egypt.

We are the people of a household who are quick to be afflicted with continuous tribulations. My grandfather Ibrāhīm was tried and thrown into the fire. Then my father Isḥāq was tried with the sacrifice. I used to have a son who was the apple of my eye , and he used to delight me. Then I was afflicted in that a wolf ate him, and I lost my sight due to grief in weeping over him.

---

8 'Amr b. 'Uthmān, who always narrates from other companions of the Imams and never from the Imams directly. See Khū'ī, *Mu'jam*, 14:49 (nr. 8781).

قال: فأخذ يوسف كتاب يعقوب فقبّله، ووَضَعه على عينيه، وبكى وانتحب حتّى بَلّت دُمُوعُه القميص الّذي عليه، ثمّ أقبل عليهم فقال: هلْ عَلِمْتُمْ ما فَعَلْتُم بِيوسُفَ من قبلُ وَأخِيهِ من بعد؟ قالوا: إنّك لأنت يُوسُفَ! قال: أنا يُوسُف، وهَذا أَخي، قد مَنَّ اللهُ علينا. قالوا: تَاللهِ لَقد آثرك اللهُ علينا، فلا تَفْضَحْنا ولا تُعاقِبْنا اليومَ واغْفِرْ لنا. قال: لا تَثْرِيبَ عليكُمُ اليَوم يغفر اللهُ لكُمْ.

وفي رواية أُخرى، عن أبي بصير، عن أبي جعفر ﷺ، نحوه.

٦٧. عن عمرو بن عثمان، عن بعض أصحابنا، قال: لمّا قال إخوة يوسف، يا أيّها العزيز، مَسَّنا وأهلُنا الضُّرّ، قال: قال يوسف: لا صبر على ضُرّ آل يعقوب، فقال عند ذلك: ﴿هَلْ عَلِمْتُم مَا فَعَلْتُم بِيُوسُفَ وَأَخِيهِ﴾ إلى آخر الآية.

٦٨. عن أحمد بن محمّد، عن أبي الحسن الرضا ﷺ، قال: سألتُه عن قوله: ﴿وَجِئْنَا بِبِضَاعَةٍ مُزْجَاةٍ﴾. قال: المُقْل.

وفي هذه الرواية ﴿وَجِئْنَا بِبِضَاعَةٍ مُزْجَاةٍ﴾، قال: كانت المُقْل، وكانت بلادهم بلاد المُقْل، وهي البِضاعة.

٦٩. عن ابن أبي عُمير، عن بعض أصحابنا، رفعه، قال: كتب يعقوب النبي ﷺ إلى يوسف، من يعقوب بن إسحاق ذبيح الله بن إبراهيم خليل الله إلى عزيز مِصر.

أمّا بعد، فإنّا أهل بيت لم يَزَل البلاء سريعًا إلينا، ابتُلي جَدّي إبراهيم فأُلقي في النار، ثمّ ابتُلي أبي إسحاق بالذّبح، فكان لي ابن، وكان قُرّة عيني وكُنتُ أُسَرُّ به، فابتُليتُ بأن أكَلَه

He had a brother who I was also fond of after him but you have arrested him for stealing, whereas we are the people of a household who have never stolen anything, and who have never been known to steal. If you can be so considerate as to give him back to me, then please do so."

He said, 'When Yūsuf was given the letter he opened it and read it. Then he gasped, stood up and entered into his chamber. He read it there, wept, then washed his face and came out to his brothers. Then he went back again, read it, cried and wept. Then he got up once more, went back into his chamber, read it and wept. Then he washed his face and came back out to his brothers and said: ﴾*Do you now realize what you did to Yūsuf and his brother when you were ignorant?*﴿ Then he gave them his shirt, which had been Ibrāhīm's shirt. Yaʿqūb was in Ramla at the time. So when they left Egypt with the shirt, Yaʿqūb said: ﴾*'You may think I am senile but I can smell Yūsuf.' But [people] said, 'By God! You are still lost in that old illusion of yours!'*﴿' [12:89–94]

70. From al-Mufaḍḍal b. ʿUmar, from Abū ʿAbd Allāh عليه السلام who said, 'Not a single man from the progeny of Fāṭima dies or departs from this world without first attesting to the Imamate of the Imam, just as the sons of Yaʿqūb attested to Yūsuf when they said: ﴾*'By God! God really did favour you over all of us...'*﴿' [12:91]

71. From Murāzim's brother, from Abū ʿAbd Allāh عليه السلام who said with respect to His verse: ﴾*Later, when the caravan departed, their father said, 'You may think I am senile but I can smell Yūsuf'*﴿, 'Yaʿqūb could smell the scent of Ibrāhīm's shirt when the caravan was leaving Egypt whilst he was still in Palestine.' [12:94]

72. From Mufaḍḍal al-Juʿfī, from Abū ʿAbd Allāh عليه السلام. He said, 'I heard him say, "Do you know what Yūsuf's shirt was?" He said, 'I said, "No." He said, "When they ignited the fire to burn Ibrāhīm, Jibraʾīl brought him clothes from Paradise which he wore, and as a result no heat or cold could harm him. When Ibrāhīm was on his deathbed, he made it into an amulet and hung it around Isḥāq's neck, and Isḥāq hung it around Yaʿqūb. When Yūsuf was born to Yaʿqūb, he hung it on him. It was on his upper arm until the events came to pass. When Yūsuf took the shirt out of the amulet, Yaʿqūb smelled its scent,

الذئب، فَذَهب بَصَري حُزنًا عليه من البُكاء، وكان له أخٌ، وكنت أُسَرّ إليه بعده، فأخَذْتَه في سَرَق، وإنّا أهل بيتٍ لم نَسْرِق قطّ، ولا يُعْرَف لنا السَّرق، فإن رأيت أن تَمُنَّ عليَّ به فعلت.

قال: فلمّا أُوتي يوسف عليه السلام بالكتاب فَتحه وقرأه فصاح، ثمّ قام فدخل منزله، فقرأ وبكى، ثمّ غسل وجهه، ثمّ خرج إلى إخوته، ثمّ عاد فقرأه فصاح وبكى، ثمّ قام فدخل منزله، فقرأه وبكى، ثمّ غسل وجهه، وعاد إلى إخوته، فقال: هل عَلِمتم ما فعلتُم بيوسف وأخيه إذ أنتم جاهلون؟ وأعطاهم قميصه، وهو قميص إبراهيم عليه السلام، وكان يعقوب عليه السلام بالرَّملة، فلمّا فَصَلُوا بالقَميص من مِصر، قال يعقوب: إنّي لأجِدُ رِيحَ يُوسُفَ لَولاَ أن تُفَنِّدونَ. قالوا: تَاللهِ إنّكَ لَفي ضَلالِكَ القديم.

٧٠. عن المَفضّل بن عمر، عن أبي عبدالله عليه السلام، قال: ليس رجلٌ من ولد فاطمة عليها السلام يموت ولا يَخرُج من الدنيا حتى يُقِرّ للإمام بإمامته، كما أقرّ ولد يعقوب ليوسف عليه السلام حين قالوا: تَاللهِ لَقَدْ آثَرَكَ اللهُ عَلَيْنَا.

٧١. عن أخي مُرازِم، عن أبي عبدالله عليه السلام، في قوله: ﴿وَلَمَّا فَصَلَتِ الْعِيرُ﴾، قال: وَجَد يعقوب ريح قَميص إبراهيم حين فَصَلت العِير من مِصر وهو بفِلَسْطِين.

٧٢. عن مُفضّل الجُعفي، عن أبي عبدالله عليه السلام، قال: سَمِعتُه يقول: أتدري ما كان قَميص يوسف؟ قال: قلت: لا. قال: إنّ إبراهيم عليه السلام لمّا أوقدوا النّار أتاه جَبْرَئيل عليه السلام من ثِياب الجنّة فألبسه إيّاه، فلم يَضُرّه معه حرٌّ ولا بردٌ. فلمّا حَضَر إبراهيم عليه السلام الموت جَعَله في تَميمةٍ

as per His verse: ﴾*'You may think I am senile but I can smell Yūsuf.'*﴿ This is that same shirt which had descended from Paradise." I asked, "May I be your ransom – who did the shirt pass on to after that?" He replied, "To his family." Then he said, "Every prophet has inherited either knowledge or something else, and it ended up with Muḥammad ﷺ."' [12:93–94]

73. From Ibrāhīm b. Abī al-Bilād, from whoever mentioned it to him from Abū 'Abd Allāh عليه السلام who said, 'The shirt was the same one that was brought down for Ibrāhīm from Paradise in a casket of silver or iron. When he wore it, it was loose and wide. When they left Egypt with the shirt, Ya'qūb was in Ramla, and Ya'qūb said: ﴾*'I can smell Yūsuf.'*﴿ He meant the smell of Paradise as soon as they left with the shirt because it had been in Paradise.' [12:94]

74. From Muḥammad b. Ismā'īl b. Bazī'[9] who, without mentioning his source, cited with his chain of transmission saying, 'Ya'qūb could smell the scent of Yūsuf's shirt from a distance of ten nights' journeying away; Ya'qūb was in Jerusalem whereas Yūsuf was in Egypt. This was the shirt that had descended from Paradise for Ibrāhīm, who had passed it down to Isḥāq, and Isḥāq in turn to Ya'qūb. Ya'qūb had then given it to Yūsuf عليه السلام.' [12:93–94]

75. From Nashīṭ b. Ṣāliḥ al-'Ijlī[10] who said, 'I asked Abū 'Abd Allāh عليه السلام, "Were the brothers of Yūsuf – may God's blessings be upon him – prophets?" He replied, "No, and neither were they good and pious people, for then how could they say to their father, Ya'qūb: ﴾*'By God! You are still lost in that old illusion of yours!'*﴿"' [12:95]

---

9 Abū Ja'far Muḥammad b. Ismā'īl b. Bazī', a client of the Abbasid Caliph Abū Ja'far al-Manṣūr. He is regarded as one the leading personalities of the Imāmī school and a reliable narrator of the Imams' traditions. He was a prominent companion of the eighth and ninth Imams. See Khū'ī, *Mu'jam*, 16:103–10 (nr. 10272).

10 Nashīṭ b. Ṣāliḥ b. Lafāfa al-'Ijlī, a companion of the sixth and seventh Imams. See Khū'ī, *Mu'jam*, 20:145–6 (nr. 13033).

وعلّقه على إسحاق عليه السلام، وعلّق إسحاق على يعقوب عليه السلام، فلمّا ولد ليعقوب يوسف عليه السلام علّقه عليه، وكان في عَضُده حتّى كان من أمره ما كان، فلمّا أَخْرَج يوسف عليه السلام القَميص من التَّميمية وَجَد يعقوب عليه السلام ريحه، وهو قوله: ﴿إِنِّي لَأَجِدُ رِيحَ يُوسُفَ لَوْلَا أَن تُفَنِّدُونِ﴾ فهو ذلك القميص الذي أُنزِل من الجنَّة.

قلت: جُعِلت فِداك، فإلى مَن صار ذلك القميص؟ فقال لي: إلى أهله. ثمّ قال: كُلّ نبيّ ورث عِلماً أو غيره فقد انتهى إلى محمّد صلّى الله عليه وآله.

٧٣. عن إبراهيم بن أبي البلاد، عمّن ذكره، عن أبي عبد الله عليه السلام، قال: كان القميص الذي أُنزل به على إبراهيم عليه السلام من الجنَّة في قَصَبةٍ من فِضّة أو حديد، وكان إذا لُبِس كان واسعاً كبيراً، فلمّا فَصَلُوا بالقَميص ويعقوب عليه السلام بالرَّملة، قال يعقوب عليه السلام: إنّي لأجدُ ريح يوسف، عنى ريح الجنّة حتّى فصلوا بالقَميص، لأنّه كان في الجنّة.

٧٤. عن محمّد بن إسماعيل بن بَزيع، رفعه، بإسنادٍ له، قال عليه السلام: إنّ يعقوب عليه السلام وَجَد ريح قَميص يوسف من مَسيرة عَشرة ليالٍ، وكان يعقوب ببيت المَقْدِس ويوسف بمِصْر، وهو القَميص الذي نَزَل على إبراهيم عليه السلام من الجنَّة، فدفعه إبراهيم إلى إسحاق عليه السلام، وإسحاق إلى يعقوب عليه السلام، ودفعه يعقوب إلى يوسف عليهم السلام.

٧٥. عن نَشيط بن صالح العِجلي، قال: قلتُ لأبي عبد الله عليه السلام: أكان إخوة يوسف عليه السلام أنبياء؟ قال: لا، ولا بَرَرة أتقياء، وكيف وهم يقولون لأبيهم يعقوب عليه السلام: تالله إنّك لفي ضَلالك القَديم؟!

76. From Sulaymān b. ʿAbd Allāh al-Ṭalḥī who said, ʿI asked Abū ʿAbd Allāh ﷺ, "What was the state of Yaʿqūb's sons – are they [considered] as having left [the state of] belief?" He replied, "Yes." I asked him, "So what do you say about Ādam?" He replied, "Leave aside Ādam."ʾ [12:95]

77. From one of our associates, from Abū ʿAbd Allāh ﷺ who said, "As a result of what Yaʿqūb's sons did to Yūsuf they sinned, so how can they have been prophets?" [12:95]

78. From Nashīṭ, from a man from Abū ʿAbd Allāh ﷺ. He said, ʿI asked him, "Were Yaʿqūb's sons prophets?" He replied, "No, and neither were they good and pious people. How could that be the case while they could say to Yaʿqūb: ﴾*ʿBy God! You are still lost in that old illusion of yours!ʾ*﴿"ʾ [12:95]

79. From Muqarran, from Abū ʿAbd Allāh ﷺ who said, ʿThe governor of Egypt wrote to Yaʿqūb saying: "This son of yours, Yūsuf, I bought for a paltry price of a few dirhams and made him my slave; and this son of yours, Bin Yāmīn, I arrested for having stolen and have made him my slave."ʾ

He continued, ʿYaʿqūb had never faced a greater blow than that letter, so he said to the messenger, "Wait right here while I respond to him:" ʿI comprehend the contents of your letter that you adopted my son, Yūsuf, for a paltry price and took him on as a slave and that you arrested my son, Bin Yāmīn, and kept him as a slave for having stolen. However, we are the people of a household who do not steal, but rather we come from a household that is tested. Our father Ibrāhīm was tested in the fire, and God protected him. Our father Isḥāq was tested with the threat of slaughter, and God protected him. And I have been tested with the loss of my eyesight and the loss of my son, and God may well restore them both back to me.ʾʾ He said, ʿSo when the messenger had departed from him, he raised his hands to the sky and said,

"O Best Companion, O Generous Provider, O Goodness itself, grant me energy and relief from Yourself." So Jibraʾīl descended unto him and said to Yaʿqūb, "Shall I teach you supplications through which God will restore your eyesight and return your son back to you?" So he replied, "Of course." So he said, "Say: ʿO He Whom no one knows what He is like, nor where He is, nor the extent of His Power, except for Himself. O He who keeps the

٧٦. عن سليمان بن عبد الله الطَّلحي، قال: قلتُ لأبي عبد الله عليه السلام: ما حال بني يعقوب، هل خَرَجُوا من الإيمان؟ فقال: نعم. قلتُ له: فما تقول في آدم؟ قال: دَع آدم.

٧٧. عن بعض أصحابنا، عن أبي عبد الله عليه السلام، قال: إنَّ بني يعقوب بعد ما صَنَعُوا بيوسف عليه السلام أذنبوا، فكانوا أنبياء؟!

٧٨. عن نَشيط، عن رجل، عن أبي عبد الله عليه السلام، قال: سألتُه أكان ولد يعقوب أنبياء؟ قال: لا ولا بَرَرة أتقياء، كيف يكونون كذلك وهم يقولون ليعقوب عليه السلام: تالله إنّك لفي ضَلالك القديم؟!

٧٩. عن مُقرّن، عن أبي عبد الله عليه السلام، قال: كتب عزيز مِصر إلى يعقوب عليه السلام: أمّا بعد، فهذا ابنك يوسف، اشتريته بثمن بَخْس دَراهِم معدودة، واتّخذته عبداً، وهذا ابنك ابن يامين أخذته، قد سَرَق واتّخذته عبداً.

قال: فما وَرَد على يعقوب عليه السلام شيءٌ أشدّ عليه من ذلك الكتاب، فقال للرسول: مكانك حتّى أُجيبه، فكتب إليه يعقوب عليه السلام: أمّا بعد، فقد فَهِمتُ كتابك أنّك أخذت ابني بثَمنٍ بَخْسٍ واتَّخذته عبداً، وأنّك اتّخذت ابني ابن يامين وقد سَرَق فاتّخذته عبداً، فإنّا أهل بيتٍ لا نَسرِق، ولكنّا أهل بيت نُبتلى، وقد ابتُلِيَ أبونا إبراهيم بالنار، فوَقاه الله، وابتُلِيَ أبونا إسحاق بالذَّبح فوَقاه، وإنّي قد ابتُليتُ بذَهاب بَصَري وذَهاب ابني، وعسى الله أن يأتيني بهم جميعاً.

atmosphere fixed in the sky and the earth on the water, and who has chosen the best Names for Himself. Grant me energy and relief from Yourself.'"

No sooner had the light of dawn broken than he was brought the shirt, which he threw onto his face; and God restored his eyesight and returned his son to him.' [12:96]

80. From Abū Baṣīr, from Abū Jaʿfar عليه السلام who returned to the original *ḥadīth*, which we split up. ﴾*But he said, 'You will hear no reproaches today. May God forgive you: He is the Most Merciful of the merciful. Take my shirt*﴿ which has been wetted by my tears ﴾*and lay it over my father's face: he will recover his sight*﴿ if he but smells my scent. ﴾*Then bring your whole family back to me.'*﴿ He sent them back to Yaʿqūb that same day, giving them whatever provisions they needed. So when their caravan departed from Egypt, Yaʿqūb smelt Yūsuf's scent and said to those of his sons who were present with him: ﴾*'You may think I am senile but I can smell Yūsuf.'*﴿

He said, 'His sons drew nearer, eager to run back with the shirt, happy and gladdened by the royal state that they had seen Yūsuf enjoy that God had given him as well as by the honour that they had experienced under Yūsuf's authority. Their journey from Egypt to Yaʿqūb's town took nine days; and when the forerunner arrived, he threw the shirt onto Yaʿqūb's face and he recovered his sight. He asked them, "What happened to Bin Yāmīl?" They replied, "We left him behind safe and sound with his brother."

So Yaʿqūb praised God upon hearing that and fell prostrate to his Lord in gratitude. With his eyesight restored and his back straightened, he said to his sons, "Let us all go together to Yūsuf on this very day." So they travelled to Yūsuf along with Yaʿqūb, and Yūsuf's maternal aunt, Yāmīl, joyfully hastening to him, and they reached Egypt in nine days.' [12:92–100]

قال: فلمّا ولّى الرسول عنه، رَفَع يده إلى السماء، ثمّ قال: يا حَسَنَ الصُّحبة، يا كريمَ المعُونة، يا خيراً كلّه، ائتني برَوْح وفَرَج من عندك.

قال: فَهَبط عليه جبْرئيل ﷺ، فقال ليعقوب: ألا أعَلّمك دعواتٍ يرُدّ الله عليك بها بصرك، ويرُدّ عليك ابنك؟ فقال: بلى. فقال: قُل: يا مَن لا يعلمُ أحدٌ كيف هو وحيث هو وقُدرته إلّا هو، يا من سدّ الهواء بالسماء، وكَبسَ الأرض على الماء، واختار لنفسه أحسن الأسماء، ائتني برَوْح منك، وفَرَجٍ من عندك. فما انفجرعَمُود الصُّبح حتّى أُتي بالقميص، فطُرِح على وجهه، فرَدَّ الله عليه بَصَره، ورَدّ عليه ولده.

٨٠. عن أبي بصير، عن أبي جعفر ﷺ، عاد إلى الحديث الأوّل الذي قَطعناه ــ قال: لا تَثْرِيبَ عليكم اليوم يغفِرُ الله لكم اذهبوا بقَميصي هذا الّذي بلّته دُمُوع عيني، فألْقُوهُ على وَجْهِ أبي يَرْتَدَّ بَصيرًا، لو قد شَمّ ريحي، وأْتُوني بِأَهْلِكُمْ أَجْمَعِينَ، ورَدّهم إلى يعقوب ﷺ في ذلك اليوم، وجَهَّزهم بجميع ما يَحتاجون إليه، فلمّا فَصَلت عِيرهم من مِصر، وَجَد يعقوب ﷺ ريح يوسف، فقال لمَن بحَضْرته من ولده: إنّي لأجدُ ريحَ يوسف لولا أن تُفَنِّدون.

قال: وأقبل ولده يَحُثّون السَّير بالقَميص فَرَحًا وسُرورًا بما رَأوا من حال يوسف ﷺ والمُلْك الذي أعطاه الله، والعِزّ الذي صاروا إليه في سُلطان يوسُف، وكان مَسيرهم من مِصر إلى بَلَد يعقوب تسعة أيّام، فلمّا أن جاء البشير ألقى القميص على وجهه، فارتدّ بصيرًا، وقال لهم: ما فعل ابن ياميل؟ قالوا: أخلفناه عند أخيه صالحًا.

81. From Muḥammad b. Abī ʿUmayr, from one of our associates, from Abū ʿAbd Allāh عليه السلام who said with respect to His saying: ﴾*'I shall ask my Lord to forgive you all'*,﴿ 'He deferred praying for them until dawn, when he said: "O Lord, their sin is between them and me." So God revealed: "I have indeed forgiven them."' [12:98]

82. From Muḥammad b. Muslim, from Abū ʿAbd Allāh عليه السلام who said regarding His saying: ﴾*'I shall ask my Lord to forgive you all'*,﴿ 'He deferred praying for them until dawn on the eve of Friday.' [12:98]

83. From Muḥammad b. Saʿīd al-Azdī, the companion of Mūsā b. Muḥammad b. al-Riḍā عليه السلام, from Mūsā, who said to his brother, 'Yaḥyā b. Aktham wrote to him asking him a few questions. He said, "Tell me about God's verse: ﴾*He took his parents up to* [*his*] *throne. They all bowed down before him*﴿ – did Yaʿqūb and his sons bow down to Yūsuf?"' He said, 'So I asked my brother about that, and he said, "Yaʿqūb and his sons' bowing down before Yūsuf was by way of gratitude to God, for reuniting them. Do you not see that he says in gratitude at that moment: ﴾*My Lord! You have given me authority; You have taught me something about the interpretation of dreams; Creator of the heavens and the earth, You are my protector in this world and in the Hereafter. Let me die in true devotion to You. Join me with the righteous'*﴿?"' [12:100–101]

قال: فحَمِد الله يعقوب عند ذلك، وسَجَد لربّه سجدة الشُّكر، ورَجَع إليه بَصَرُه، وتقوّم له ظَهْرُه، وقال لولده: تَحَمّلوا إلى يوسف في يومكم هذا بأجمعكم. فساروا إلى يوسف ومعهم يعقوب عليه السلام وخالة يوسف ياميل، فأَحَثّوا السّير فرحًا وسرور، فساروا تسعة أيّام إلى مِصر.

٨١. عن محمّد بن أبي عُمير، عن بعض أصحابنا، عن أبي عبد الله عليه السلام، في قوله: ﴿سَوْفَ أَسْتَغْفِرُ لَكُمْ رَبِّيٓ﴾، قال: أخّرَهم إلى السَّحر، قال: يا ربّ إنّما ذنبهم فيما بيني وبينهم، فأوحى الله: أنّي قد غَفَرتُ لهم.

٨٢. عن محمّد بن مسلم، عن أبي عبد الله عليه السلام، في قوله: ﴿أَسْتَغْفِرُ لَكُمْ رَبِّيٓ﴾، قال: أخرّها إلى السَّحر ليلة الجُمعة.

٨٣. عن محمّد بن سعيد الأزدي صاحب موسى بن محمّد بن الرضا، عن موسى قال لأخيه: إنّ يحيى بن أكثم كتب إليه يسأله عن مسائل، فقال: أخبرني عن قول الله: ﴿وَرَفَعَ أَبَوَيْهِ عَلَى ٱلْعَرْشِ وَخَرُّوا۟ لَهُۥ سُجَّدًا﴾ أسجد يعقوب وولده ليوسف؟

قال: فسألت أخي عن ذلك، فقال: أمّا سُجود يعقوب وولده ليوسف فشُكرًا لله، لاجتماع شَملهم، ألا ترى أنّه يقول في شُكر ذلك الوقت: ﴿رَبِّ قَدْ ءَاتَيْتَنِى مِنَ ٱلْمُلْكِ وَعَلَّمْتَنِى مِن تَأْوِيلِ ٱلْأَحَادِيثِ﴾؟ الآية.

84. He returned to the original narration from Abū Baṣīr, from Abū Jaʿfar عليه السلام who said, 'They travelled to Egypt in nine days, and when they entered into Yūsuf's presence in the royal palace, he hugged and kissed his father and cried. Then he took him and his maternal aunt up onto the royal throne. Then he went into his chamber, anointed himself and applied kohl to his eyes, wore his stately royal garb and came back out to them. When they saw him they all fell prostrate before him, by way of respect for him and gratitude to God. At that point, he said: ﴾*'Father, this is the fulfilment of that dream I had long ago. My Lord has made it come true and has been gracious to me – He released me from prison and He brought you here from the desert – after Shayṭān sowed discord between me and my brothers.'*﴿ He said, 'And in those twenty years Yūsuf had never anointed himself, beautified his eyes, perfumed himself, laughed out loud, or enjoyed women, until God had finally reunited him with Yaʿqūb and his brothers.' [12:100]

85. From al-Ḥasan b. Asbāṭ[11] who said, 'I asked Abū al-Ḥasan عليه السلام, "With how many of his sons did Yaʿqūb go to visit Yūsuf?" He replied, "With eleven of them." He was asked, "[They were] the tribes (*al-asbāṭ*)?" He replied, "Yes." Then I asked him about Yūsuf and his brother, and whether he was his brother from the same mother or his maternal aunt." So he replied, "He was his maternal aunt's son."' [12:99]

86. From Ibn Abī 'Umayr, from one of our associates from Abū 'Abd Allāh عليه السلام regarding God's verse: ﴾*He took his parents up to* [*his*] *throne*﴿. He said, 'The throne was the seat of authority.' And regarding: ﴾*They all bowed down before him*﴿ he said, 'Their prostration was by way of worship to God.' [12:100]

87. From Muḥammad b. Bihrūz, from Jaʿfar b. Muḥammad عليه السلام who said, 'When they met, Yaʿqūb said to Yūsuf, "Tell me what happened to you, my son." So Yūsuf said to him, "I was taken away, then tied up at the top of the well and told to remove my shirt. I said to them, 'I beg you for the sake of my honest father, Yaʿqūb, not to expose my shame and not to wrest my shirt away from me.' So one of them threatened me with a knife." Yaʿqūb fainted and when

11 Al-Ḥasan b. Asbāṭ, about whom there is scant information. See Khūʾī, *Muʿjam*, 5:273 (nr. 2728).

٨٤. عاد إلى الحديث الأوّل عن أبي بصير، عن أبي جعفر ﷺ، قال: فساروا تسعة أيّام إلى مِصر، فلمّا دَخلوا على يوسف في دار المُلك، اعتنق أباه فقبَّله وبكى، ورَفعَه ورفع خالته على سَرير المُلك، ثمّ دخل منزله فادّهن واكْتَحل، ولَبِس ثِياب العِزّ والمُلك، ثمّ خَرَج إليهم، فلمّا رأوه سَجَدوا جميعًا له، إعظامًا له وشُكرًا لله، فعند ذلك قال: ﴿يَا أَبَتِ هَـٰذَا تَأْوِيلُ رُؤْيَايَ مِن قَبْلُ﴾ إلى قوله: ﴿بَيْنِي وَبَيْنَ إِخْوَتِي﴾.

قال: ولم يَكُن يوسف ﷺ في تلك العشرين سنة يَدّهن ولا يَكْتَحل ولا يتطيّب ولا يَضْحَك ولا يمسّ النساء حتّى جَمَعَ الله ليعقوب ﷺ شَمْله، وجمع بينه وبين يعقوب وإخوته.

٨٥. عن الحسن بن أسباط، قال: سألتُ أبا الحسن ﷺ في كم دَخَل يعقوب من ولده على يوسف؟ قال: في أحد عشر ابنًا له. فقيل له: أسباط؟ قال: نعم.

وسألتُه عن يوسف وأخيه، أكان أخاه لأُمّه أم ابن خالته؟ فقال: ابن خالته.

٨٦. عن ابن أبي عمير، عن بعض أصحابنا، عن أبي عبد الله ﷺ، في قول الله تعالى: ﴿وَرَفَعَ أَبَوَيْهِ عَلَى الْعَرْشِ﴾، قال: العَرْش: السَّرير.

وفي قوله: ﴿وَخَرُّوا لَهُ سُجَّدًا﴾، قال: كان سُجُودهم ذلك عِبادةً لله.

٨٧. عن محمّد بن بِهروز، عن جعفر بن محمّد ﷺ، قال: إنّ يعقوب قال ليوسف ﷺ حيث التقيا: أخبرني يا بُنيّ كيف صُنِع بك؟

فقال له يوسف ﷺ: انطُلِق بي، فأُقعدت على رأس الجُبّ فقيل لي: انزَع القَميص، فقلت لهم: إنّي أسألكم بوجه أبي الصدّيق يعقوب لا تُبدوا عَورتي، ولا تَسْلِبوني قَميصي،

he regained consciousness, he said to him, "Tell me what was done to you." Yūsuf replied him, "My father, I implore you to refrain from asking me, so he stopped." [12:100]

88. From Muḥammad b. Muslim who said, 'I asked Abū Ja'far ﷺ, "How long did Ya'qūb live with Yūsuf in Egypt after God had reunited Ya'qūb's family and showed them the realization of Yūsuf's true dream?" He replied, "He lived for two years." I asked, "So who was God's proof on the earth at that time – Ya'qūb or Yūsuf?" He replied, "Ya'qūb was the proof, though the kingdom belonged to Yūsuf. When Ya'qūb died, Yūsuf carried Ya'qūb's bones in a casket to the land of Shām and buried him in Jerusalem. Then Yūsuf, son of Ya'qūb, was the proof." [12:100–101]

89. From Isḥāq b. Yasār, from Abū 'Abd Allāh ﷺ that he said, 'God revealed to Yūsuf while he was in prison, "O son of Ya'qūb, what has made you end up here with the criminals?" He replied, "My crime." He said, "So he confessed his crime and was released, having confessed it in an intimate gathering therein like a man would confess before his family." Then he said to him, "Now beseech with this supplication: 'O He Who is greater than every great person, O He Who has neither partner nor minister, O Creator of the sun and the illuminating moon, O Fortress of the desperate and endangered, O Overthrower of every obstinate oppressor, O Enricher of the destitute pauper, O Mender of broken bones, O One Who can release the shackled prisoner – I beseech You for the sake of Muḥammad and the family of Muḥammad to give me relief and a way out from my situation, and to provide for me whence I expect and whence I do not expect.'"' When he woke up the next morning the king called him and released him. That is the purport of His verse: ﴾*'He has been gracious to me and He released me from prison.'*﴿" [12:100]

قال: فأخرج عليّ فلانٌ السِّكّين، فغُشي على يعقوب ﷺ، فلمّا أفاق قال له يعقوب ﷺ: حدِّثني كيف صُنع بك؟ فقال له يوسف ﷺ: إنّي أُطالبُ يا أبتاه لمّا كَفَفْتَ، فكَفّ.

٨٨. عن محمّد بن مسلم، قال: قلتُ لأبي جعفر ﷺ: كم عاش يعقوب ﷺ مع يوسف بمصر بعد ما جَمَع الله ليعقوب شَمْله، وأراه تأويل رُؤيا يوسف ﷺ الصادقة؟ قال: عاش حَولين.

قلتُ: فَمَن كان يومئذٍ الحُجَّة لله في الأرض، يعقوب أم يوسف؟ فقال: كان يعقوب ﷺ الحُجَّة، وكان المُلك ليوسف ﷺ، فلمّا مات يعقوب حَمَل يوسف عظام يعقوب في تابوت إلى أرض الشام، فدفنه في بيت المَقْدِس، ثمّ كان يوسف ابن يعقوب الحُجّة.

٨٩. عن إسحاق بن يَسَار، عن أبي عبد الله ﷺ، أنّه قال: إنّ الله بعث إلى يوسف ﷺ وهو في السِّجن: يا ابن يعقوب، ما أسكنك مع الخطّائين؟ قال: جُرمي. قال: فاعترف بجُرمه فأخرج، فاعترف بمَجْلِسه منها مَجْلِس الرجُل من أهله، فقال له: ادعُ بهذا الدُّعاء: يا كبير، يا من لا شريك له ولا وزير، يا خالق الشمس والقمر المُنير، يا عِصمة المُضْطرّ الضَّرير، قاصِمَ كُلِّ جبّارٍ مُبير، يا مُغني البائِس الفقير، يا جابرَ العَظْم الكسير، يا مُطلِق المُكبّل الأسير، أسألُك بحَقّ محمّدٍ وآل محمّد أن تجعلَ لي من أمري فَرَجًا ومَخْرَجًا، وتَرْزُقني من حيث أحتسب ومن حيث لا أحتسب.

قال: فلمّا أصبح دعاه المَلِك فخَلّى سَبيله، وذلك قوله: ﴿وَقَدْ أَحْسَنَ بِيٓ إِذْ أَخْرَجَنِي مِنَ ٱلسِّجْنِ﴾.

90. From ʿAbbās b. Yazīd[12] who said, 'I heard Abū ʿAbd Allāh ﷺ say, "When the Messenger of God was sitting with the people of his household one day, he said, 'Yūsuf wanted reassurance for his soul.' He said, "So he was asked: 'Through what, O Messenger of God?' He replied, 'When the governor of Egypt released him from Egypt he wore two new garments [or two clean garments] and went out into the barren plain. He prayed two units of prayer, and upon completion he raised his hands to the sky and said: ﴾*My Lord! You have given me authority; You have taught me something about the interpretation of dreams; Creator of the heavens and the earth, You are my protector in this world and in the Hereafter.*﴿' He said, 'So Jibra'īl descended unto him and said, "Yūsuf, what do you need?" He said, "My Lord, ﴾*let me die in true devotion to You. Join me with the righteous.*﴿"' Then Abū ʿAbd Allāh ﷺ said, "He feared temptations."'' [12:101]

91. From Zurāra who said, 'I asked Abū Jaʿfar ﷺ about God's verse: ﴾*Most of them will only believe in God while also joining others with Him.*﴿ He said, "This includes when someone says: 'By your life.'"' [12:106]

92. From Yaʿqūb b. Shuʿayb who said, 'I asked Abū ʿAbd Allāh ﷺ about: ﴾*Most of them will only believe in God while also joining others with Him.*﴿ He replied, "They used to say: we will foretell such and such a prophecy. This includes the fact that they would give donations to priests and then believe whatever they would tell them."' [12:106]

93. From Muḥammad b. al-Fuḍayl, from al-Riḍā ﷺ who said, 'Associating others with God is unsurpassed even by faithlessness.' [12:106]

12 ʿAbbās b. Yazīd al-Kharazī, on whom there is scant information. He is considered a reliable narrator of traditions. See Khū'ī, *Muʿjam*, 10:273 (nr. 6221).

٩٠. عباس بن يزيد، قال: سَمِعتُ أبا عبدالله عليه السلام يقول: بَينا رسول الله صلى الله عليه وآله جالسٌ في أهل بيته، إذ قال: أحبَّ يوسف أن يستوثق لنفسه، قال: فقيل: بماذا، يا رسول الله؟

قال: لما عَجِّل له عزيز مِصر عن مِصر لَبِس ثوبين جديدين — أو قال: نظيفين — وخَرَج إلى فَلاةٍ من الأرض، فصلّى رَكَعات، فلمّا فَرَغ رفع يده إلى السماء، فقال: رَبَّ قَد آتَيتَني مِنَ المُلك، وَعَلَّمتَني من تَأويلِ الأحاديثِ، فاطِرَ السَّماواتِ والأرضِ، أَنتَ وَليّ في الدُّنيا والآخِرَة.

قال: فهبَطَ إليه جبرَئيل عليه السلام، فقال له: يا يوسف، ما حاجتك؟ فقال: رَبِّ تَوفَّني مُسلِمًا وألحِقني بالصّالِحينَ. فقال أبو عبدالله عليه السلام: خَشي الفِتَن.

٩١. عن زُرارة، قال: سألتُ أبا جعفر عليه السلام عن قول الله: ﴿وَمَا يُؤْمِنُ أَكْثَرُهُم بِاللَّهِ إِلَّا وَهُم مُّشْرِكُونَ﴾، قال: من ذلك قول الرجل: لا وَحَياتك.

٩٢. عن يعقوب بن شُعيب، قال: سألتُ أبا عبدالله عليه السلام: ﴿وَمَا يُؤْمِنُ أَكْثَرُهُم بِاللَّهِ إِلَّا وَهُم مُّشْرِكُونَ﴾؟

قال: كانوا يقولون: نُمطَر بنوء كذا، وبنوء كذا لا نُمطَر؛ ومنهم أنّهم كانوا يأتون الكُهّان فيُصَدّقُونهم بما يَقُولون.

٩٣. عن محمّد بن الفُضيل، عن الرضا عليه السلام، قال: شِركٌ لا يُبلَغ به الكُفر.

94. From Zurāra, from Abū Ja'far عليه السلام who said, 'Associating anyone in God's obedience is when a man says: 'By God and by so and so'; and 'Were it not for God, I would have appointed so and so' even if the latter be a wrongdoer.' [12:106]

95. From Abū Baṣīr, from Abū Isḥāq who said, 'It is when a man says: 'Were it not for God and for you, such and such would not have happened to me,' and: 'Were it not for God and for you, such and such would not have been averted from me,' and other such things.' [12:106]

96. From Zurāra, from Abū Ja'far عليه السلام who said, 'It is association of others in God's obedience and not polytheism as regards His worship. To commit acts of disobedience that God has obligated to be punishable by the Fire is to associate [others] in His obedience. They obey Shayṭān and associate him with God's obedience. That is not the same as polytheism where they worship others besides God.' [12:106]

97. From Mālik b. 'Aṭiyya, from Abū 'Abd Allāh عليه السلام who said with respect to His verse: ﴾*Most of them will only believe in God while also joining others with Him*﴿, 'This is when a man says: "Were it not for so and so, I would have died," and "Were it not for so and so, this affliction would have struck me," and "Were it not for so and so, I would have lost my family." Do you not see that he has joined someone else with God in His kingdom to provide for him and look after him?' He said, 'I asked, "And what if he says: "Were it not for God's granting me so and so's help, I would have died"?' He replied, "Yes, that is fine." [12:106]

98. From Zurāra, Ḥumrān and Muḥammad b. Muslim, from Abū Ja'far and Abū 'Abd Allāh عليه السلام. They said, 'We asked the two of them about it [i.e. polytheism]. They replied, "Accrediting others for [God's] blessings." [12:106]

99. From Zurāra, from Abū Ja'far عليه السلام who said, 'It is association of others in God's obedience and not polytheism that applies in the case of committing acts of disobedience – so that is the association of others in God's obedience. They obey Shayṭān therein and associate him with God's obedience. This is not the polytheism where they worship other than God.' [12:106]

٩٤. عن زُرارة، عن أبي جعفر عليه السلام، قال: شِركُ طاعةٍ؟ قول الرجل: لا والله وفلان، ولولا الله لوكلت فلان، والمعصية منه.

٩٥. وأبو بصير، عن أبي إسحاق، قال: هو قول الرجل: لولا الله وأنت ما فُعِل بي كذا وكذا، ولولا الله وأنت ما صُرِف عنّي كذا وكذا، وأشباه ذلك.

٩٦. عن زُرارة، عن أبي جعفر عليه السلام، قال: شِرك طاعة وليس بشِرك عبادة، والمعاصي التي ترتكبون ممّا أوجب الله عليها النار شِرك طاعة، أطاعوا الشيطان وأشركوا بالله في طاعته، ولم يكُن بشِرك عِبادة، فيَعْبُدون مع الله غيره.

٩٧. عن مالك بن عطيّة، عن أبي عبدالله عليه السلام، في قوله: ﴿وَمَا يُؤْمِنُ أَكْثَرُهُم بِاللَّهِ إِلَّا وَهُم مُّشْرِكُونَ﴾، قال: هو قول الرجل: لولا فلان لهلكت، ولولا فلان لأصبت كذا وكذا، ولولا فلا لضاع عيالي؛ ألا ترى أنّه قد جَعَل لله شريكًا في مُلكه يَرْزُقه ويدفع عنه.

قال: قلتُ: فيقول: لولا أنّ الله مَنّ عليّ بفلان لَهَلَكت؟ قال: نعم، لا بأس بهذا.

٩٨. عن زُرارة وحُمران ومحمد بن مسلم، عن أبي جعفر وأبي عبدالله عليهما السلام، قالوا: سألناهما، فقالا: شِرك النِّعم.

٩٩. عن زُرارة، عن أبي جعفر عليه السلام، قال: شِرك طاعة وليس شِرك عبادة في المعاصي التي يرتكبون، فهي شِرك طاعة، أطاعوا فيها الشيطان فأشركوا بالله في طاعة غيره، وليس بإشراك عِبادة أن يَعْبُدوا غير الله.

100. From Ismāʿīl al-Juʿfī who said, 'Abū Jaʿfar ﵇ said regarding: ﴾*'This is my way: based on clear evidence, I, and all who follow me, call [people] to God glory be to God! – I do not join others with Him.'*﴿ 'He said, "[It refers] specifically to Alī b. Abī Ṭālib ﵇, and if that is not the case then may the intercession of Muḥammad, peace be upon him and his family, not touch me."' [12:108]

101. From 'Alī b. Asbāṭ, from the second Abū al-Ḥasan [i.e. Imam 'Alī al-Riḍā]. He said, 'I said to him, "May I be your ransom – they are debating about your young age [at the time of Imamate]." He said, "What they are saying is not worth anything. God, most High says: ﴾*'This is my way: based on clear evidence, I, and all who follow me, call [people] to God glory be to God! – I do not join others with Him.'*﴿ By God, it was only 'Alī who was following him at the time and he was only seven years old. When my father passed away, I was seven years old. So what they are saying cannot possibly hold water."

He continued, "There are also signs about it [i.e. the Imamate] and other people who preceded. Both paths lead to the same conclusion, and it is only the outer aspect that differs. This is the peak of conviction. God says in His Book: ﴾*By your Lord, they will not be true believers until they let you decide between them in all matters of dispute, and find no resistance in their souls to your decisions, accepting them totally.*﴿(4:65)"' [12:108]

102. From Sallām b. al-Mustanīr, from Abū Jaʿfar ﵇ with respect to His verse: ﴾*Say, 'This is my way: based on clear evidence, I, and all who follow me, call [people] to God glory be to God! – I do not join others with Him.'*﴿ He said, '[It refers to] 'Alī.' Then he added, 'The Messenger of God, 'Alī, and the vicegerents succeeding them both.' [12:108]

103. From Abū Baṣīr, from Abū Jaʿfar and Abū 'Abd Allāh, peace be upon them both, who said regarding His verse, Exalted be He: ﴾*When the messengers lost all hope and realized that they had been dismissed as liars*﴿, 'The messengers thought that the devils were appearing before them pretending to be angels.' [12:110]

١٠٠. عن إسماعيل الجُعفي، قال: قال أبو جعفر عليه السلام: ﴿قُلْ هَٰذِهِ سَبِيلِي أَدْعُو إِلَى اللَّهِ عَلَىٰ بَصِيرَةٍ أَنَا وَمَنِ اتَّبَعَنِي﴾.

قال: فقال: عليّ بن أبي طالب عليه السلام خاصّة، وإلاّ فلا أصابني شفاعة محمّد صلى الله عليه وآله.

١٠١. عن عليّ بن أسباط، عن أبي الحسن الثاني عليه السلام، قال: قلت: جُعِلت فِداك، إنّهم يقولون في الحَداثَة.

قال: وأي شيء يقولون؟ إنّ الله تعالى يقول: ﴿قُلْ هَٰذِهِ سَبِيلِي أَدْعُو إِلَى اللَّهِ عَلَىٰ بَصِيرَةٍ أَنَا وَمَنِ اتَّبَعَنِي﴾ فوالله ما كان اتّبعه إلاّ عليّ وهو ابن سبع سنين، وما مضى أبي إلاّ وأنا ابن سبع سنين، فما عسى أن يقولوا؟

قال: ثمّ كانت أمارات فيها وقبلها أقوام، الطريقان في العاقبة سَواء، الظاهر مختلف، هو رأس اليقين، إنّ الله يقول في كتابه: ﴿فَلَا وَرَبِّكَ لَا يُؤْمِنُونَ حَتَّىٰ يُحَكِّمُوكَ﴾ إلى قوله: ﴿وَيُسَلِّمُوا تَسْلِيمًا﴾.

١٠٢. عن سَلاّم بن المُستنير، عن أبي جعفر عليه السلام، قوله: ﴿قُلْ هَٰذِهِ سَبِيلِي﴾ إلى: ﴿أَنَا وَمَنِ اتَّبَعَنِي﴾: قال: عليّ عليه السلام، وزاد قال: رسول الله صلى الله عليه وآله وعليّ والأوصياء من بعدهما.

١٠٣. عن أبي بصير، عن أبي عبد الله عليه السلام، في قوله تعالى: ﴿حَتَّىٰ إِذَا اسْتَيْأَسَ الرُّسُلُ وَظَنُّوا أَنَّهُمْ قَدْ كُذِبُوا﴾ مُخفَّفة، قال: ظنّت الرُّسل أنّ الشياطين تُمثّل لهم على صُورة الملائكة.

104. From Ibn Shu'ayb, from Abū 'Abd Allāh ﷵ who said, 'God left them to their own devices for less than the blink of an eye.' [12:110]

105. From Ya'qūb, from Abū 'Abd Allāh ﷵ who said, 'It is actually the worldly people who are showed up to be liars, whereas these [messengers] were only among those whom God leaves to their own devices that He may show them grace.' [12:110]

106. From Muḥammad b. Hārūn[13], from Abū 'Abd Allāh ﷵ who said, 'The Messenger of God only realised that Jibra'īl was sent down by God due to Divine succour.' [12:109]

107. From Zurāra who said, 'I asked Abū 'Abd Allāh ﷵ, "How was it that the Messenger of God was not anxious about what was coming down to him from God, in that it might have been contaminated by Shayṭān?" He replied, "When God appoints a servant as His messenger, then he descends tranquility and composure down unto him, such that whatever was being revealed to him from God was as clear as if he was seeing it with his own eyes."' [12:111]

13 There are multiple individuals with this name in the books of Shī'ī *rijāl*.

١٠٤. عن ابن شُعيب، عن أبي عبد الله عليه السلام، قال: وَكَلهُم الله إلى أنفسهم أقلّ من طَرفة عَينٍ.

١٠٥. عن يعقوب، عن أبي عبد الله عليه السلام، قال: أمّا أهل الدنيا فقد أظهروا الكَذِب، وما كانوا إلاّ من الذين وَكلهم الله إلى أنفسهم ليمُنّ عليهم.

١٠٦. عن محمّد بن هارون، عن أبي عبد الله عليه السلام، قال: ما عَلِم رسول الله صلى الله عليه وآله وسلم أنّ جبرَئيل من عند الله إلاّ بالتّوفيق.

١٠٧. عن زُرارة، قال: قلتُ لأبي عبد الله عليه السلام: كيف لم يَخَفْ رسول الله صلى الله عليه وآله وسلم فيما يأتيه من قبل الله أن يكون ذلك ممّا يَنْزَغ به الشيطان.

قال: فقال: إنّ الله إذا اتّخذ عبدًا رسولاً أنزل عليه السّكينة والوَقار، فكان الذي يأتيه من قبل الله مِثل الذي يَراه بعَينه.

www.ingramcontent.com/pod-product-compliance
Ingram Content Group UK Ltd.
Pitfield, Milton Keynes, MK11 3LW, UK
UKHW020721160326
11284UKWH00040B/3007

9 781838 03208